ZAGATSURVEY.

NEW YORK CITY SHOPPING

**Editors: Catherine Bigwood,
Randi Gollin and Troy Segal**

Published and distributed by
ZAGAT SURVEY, LLC
4 Columbus Circle
New York, New York 10019
Tel: 212 977 6000
E-mail: nycshopping@zagat.com
Web site: www.zagat.com

Acknowledgments

We thank Joyce Bautista, Donna Bulseco, Amy Chozick, Jacques Dehornois, Laurie Dwek, Ed Dwyer, Kimberly Forrest, David Goldman, Dana Gordon, Sohrab Habibion, Amanda Hallowell, Nancy Hawley, Evie Joselow, Martin Kaufmann, Althea Keough, Ann Lewinson, Diane Maglio, Nikki Moustaki, Frank Oteri, Dori Perrucci, Melissa Sones, William Stout, Matt Sullivan, Edina Sultanik and Carole Therie.

This guide would not have been possible without the hard work of our staff, especially Betsy Andrews, Reni Chin, Anna Chlumsky, Liz Daleske, Griff Foxley, Schuyler Frazier, Brooke Gosin, Katherine Harris, Gail Horwood, Natalie Lebert, Mike Liao, Dave Makulec, Lorraine Mead, Laura Mitchell, Rob Poole, Robert Seixas and Sharon Yates.

The reviews published in this guide are based on public opinion surveys, with numerical ratings reflecting the average scores given by all survey participants who voted on each establishment and text based on direct quotes from, or fair paraphrasings of, participants' comments. Phone numbers, addresses and other factual information were correct to the best of our knowledge when published in this guide; any subsequent changes may not be reflected.

© 2003 Zagat Survey, LLC
ISBN 1-57006-420-2
Printed in the United States of America

Contents

About This Survey 5
What's New 6
Key to Ratings/Symbols 8
Most Popular 9
TOP RATINGS
   Merchandise 10
   Location 16
   Presentation 19
   Service 20
   Good Values 21
DIRECTORY
   Names, Addresses, Subway Stops, Phone Numbers,
     Web Sites, Ratings and Reviews 23
INDEXES
   Store Type 278
     Auction Houses 278
     Chain Stores 279
     Branches for Top Chains 280
     Department/Large Specialty Stores 283
     Discounters/Outlets 283
     Museum Shops 283
     Theme Stores 283
   Locations 284
   Maps
     East Village/Lower East Side/NoHo 309
     Flatiron/Union Square 310
     Midtown 311
     SoHo/NoLita 312
     TriBeCa/Financial Dist./Seaport 314
     Upper East Side 315
     Upper West Side 316
     West Vlg./Greenwich Vlg./Meatpacking District 317
     Brooklyn 318
   Merchandise 319
   Fashion/Beauty
     Accessories 319
     Activewear 319
     Bridal 319
     Clothing: Designer 320
     Clothing: Men's 321
     Clothing: Men's/Women's 323
     Clothing: Women's 324
     Clothing/Shoes: Children's 327
     Clothing/Shoes: Tween/Teen 328
     Consignment/Thrift/Vintage 328
     Cosmetics/Toiletries 329
     Eyewear 329
     Furs 330
     Handbags 330
     Hosiery/Lingerie 330
     Jeans 331
     Jewelry 331
     Maternity 333

Shoes: Men's/Women's 333
Sneakers 334
Watches. 334
Home/Garden
Bathroom Fixtures/Tiles. 335
Bed/Bath 335
Cabinetry. 336
Children's Bedding/Layette 336
Cookware 336
Fine China/Crystal. 336
Furniture/Home Furnishings 337
Garden. 338
Hardware. 339
Lighting 339
Major Appliances 339
Silver 339
Lifestyle
Art Supplies 339
Baby Gear 339
Cameras/Video Equipment 340
CDs/Videos/Records/DVDs. 340
Cigar/Smoke Shops 340
Drugstores (Specialty) 340
Electronics. 340
Fabrics/Notions. 341
Gadgets. 341
Gifts/Novelties 341
Instruments/Sheet Music 341
Knitting/Needlepoint 342
Luggage. 342
Pet Supplies 342
Sex Shops. 342
Sporting Goods 342
Stationery 343
Toys 343
Special Features 344
Avant-Garde 344
Browsing Appeal 344
Celebrity Clientele 346
Comfortable Loos. 347
Custom-Made Goods 347
Final Sale. 348
Frequent-Buyer Programs 350
High-Design 350
Hip/Hot Places. 351
House Charge 353
Insider Secrets 353
Legendary 354
New Age/Health-Oriented 355
Noteworthy Newcomers 355
Offbeat. 356
Only in New York 356
Registry: Baby. 356
Registry: Bridal/Gift 357
Repairs/Alterations on Premises 358
Special Delivery Services. 361
Status Goods 362
Tween/Teen Appeal 364

About This Survey

For 24 years, Zagat Survey has reported on the shared experiences of diners, travelers and, of late, golf, movie and nightlife enthusiasts. Now, we're proud to bring you the ultimate guide to shopping in New York City.

By surveying thousands of people, we hope to have achieved a uniquely current and accurate guide, one that will lead shoppers to new finds as well as reliably smart, self-assured decisions.

For our first effort, we excluded certain categories like antiques and art dealers, along with service providers such as salons and spas, in order to concentrate on the retail products most sought after by our voters. Thus, this edition covers well over 2,000 establishments ranging from fashion to furniture. To ensure this guide is up-to-the-moment, we've also included some places that have yet to be rated.

The stores covered herein were rated separately on the quality of their Merchandise, Presentation and Service by 7,176 surveyors, who shop an average of 2.72 times a week (adding up to more than a million trips a year). Of those reviewers, fully 72% are women and only 28% men. The breakdown by age is 34% in their 20s; 30% 30s; 16% 40s; 14% 50s; and 6% 60s and above. As with all our guides, we have synopsized our surveyors' opinions, with their comments in quotation marks. We sincerely thank each of our participants; this book is really "theirs."

To assist you, we have also prepared a number of lists. See Most Popular (page 9), Top Ratings (pages 10–20), Good Values (page 21) and 81 handy indexes.

We are especially grateful to our key local editors: Donna Bulseco, a fashion editor who has worked at *WWD* and *W*, Joyce Bautista, senior editor for *Real Simple* magazine, and Althea Keough, style editor for *BabyTalk* magazine.

As companions to this book, we also publish guides to *New York City Restaurants*, *Marketplace* (a food and entertaining resource) and *Nightlife*, along with guides and maps to 70 other markets around the world. Most of these are accessible on mobile devices and at **zagat.com**, where you can vote and shop as well. If you register and vote in any of our upcoming Surveys, you'll receive a free copy of the resulting guide.

Since this *Survey* is a first-time effort, we would appreciate your comments, and even criticisms, so that we can improve. Contact us at nycshopping@zagat.com. We look forward to hearing from you.

New York, NY
March 3, 2003

Nina and Tim Zagat

What's New

No question about it – New Yorkers love to shop as much as they adore dining out. So it seemed logical for *Zagat Survey* to do for stores what we do for restaurants and offer this guide to NYC shopping. The retail scene here has always been known for its legendary purveyors like Bergdorf Goodman, Brooks Brothers, FAO Schwarz, Harry Winston, Loehmann's, Macy's, Paragon Sporting Goods, Ralph Lauren, Steinway and Sons, Tiffany & Co. – and of course, Bloomingdale's, the quintessential NYC store according to our surveyors. But the city is also known for its never-ending stream of newcomers. All in all, the diversity, depth and quality of our stores support New York City's claim to be "The Shopping Capital of the World." This guide covers over 2,000 of them, from the best-known to the barely discovered.

Retail Rebound: While the post-9/11 economic climate admittedly has been tepid, shopping has returned to near-normal levels, thanks to New Yorkers' insatiable appetite for the new and the exciting. And retailers are responding by making major commitments to the city. Witness the splashy openings of stores like Adidas, Agent Provocateur, Baker, buybuy Baby, Jil Sander and Vitra. Two behemoths birthed equally impressive offshoots: ABC Carpet & Home debuted in Dumbo, and Crate & Barrel cloned itself in NoHo. Shoppers' hunger has been further whetted by savvy, innovative promotions such as the "beauty event nights" – complete with cocktails, canapés and gift certificates – hosted by Bergdorf Goodman, Henri Bendel and Macy's on their cosmetics floors. Small wonder, with all these attractions, that 65% of our surveyors typically shop for pleasure.

New Neighborhoods: It began with intrepid restaurateurs turning neighborhoods that had been no-man's-lands into must-go destinations. But it didn't take long for savvy shopkeepers to follow the foodies. For example, after the eateries Pastis, Markt and Rhône settled in the Meatpacking District, they were joined by the mini-department store Jeffrey, and now a whole host of high-profile clothiers, such as Alexander McQueen, Dernier Cri, Rubin Chapelle and Stella McCartney, have further tamed the once-wild West 14th Street area. Other enclaves, including NoLita, TriBeCa and Brooklyn's Atlantic Avenue and Park Slope, have also cemented their positions of late. And SoHo, the Downtown pioneer of it all, is now experiencing a virtual renaissance of retailing, inspiring 34% of our surveyors to say it offers the best shopping in town.

Surf 'N' Shop: But shopping is not only a social scene – nowadays, it can be done 24/7 from the privacy of one's own home. So, where applicable, we've included the Web addresses of the increasing number of retailers who cater to those who like to buy online. Indeed, our surveyors make an astonishing 20% of their purchases that way.

Blizzard of Boutiques: Although the city's known for its legendary department stores, 69% of our *Survey* respondents prefer the intimacy of smaller shops. This past year alone has seen a boutique boom from big-name designers such as Issey Miyake, Jean Paul Gaultier, Marni – plus a new jewelry-only branch of Chanel – along with some newly hot names, such as Charles Tyrwhitt, Constança Basto and Gas Bijoux.

Such a Deal: For most people today, it turns out that the thrill of the score is integral to the joy of shopping. In fact, 76% of our voters deem themselves bargain-hunters and only 31% admit to paying full retail. As further evidence of bargain hunting, 72% of our shoppers report that they live for seasonal sales, sample sales and close-outs. But they don't have to wait, since plenty of stores, like Century 21, the *Survey*'s Top Discount clothing destination, offer good values just about every day, and we've included a list of them on page 21.

Service Smarts: The stores in this guide were rated on Merchandise, Presentation and Service. While surveyors were appreciative of the wares available to them, they found service to be the weak link in the shopping experience. Overall, the average Merchandise score was 22, whereas Service received 18. Given this four-point discrepancy, retailers should give more attention to hiring and training their sales personnel – if they want to keep their business vital. Good help is not limited to luxury providers or to any particular field, as our Top Service list indicates.

There's More in Store: Louis Vuitton's new flagship should be flying over 57th Street and Fifth Avenue by summer, while Kate's Paperie is unwrapping a branch down the block. Both Samsung and Williams-Sonoma are slated to be tenants in Columbus Circle's heralded AOL Time Warner Center. Bloomingdale's has plans for a space in SoHo, and eveningwear-and-bridal designer Reem Acra is making her debut on the Upper East Side. What does this tell us? Our retailers still have faith in this city.

New York, NY
March 3, 2003

Catherine Bigwood
Randi Gollin
Troy Segal

vote at zagat.com

Key to Ratings/Symbols

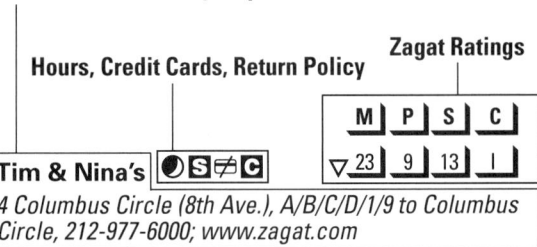

Name, Address, Subway Stop, Phone Numbers & Web Site

Hours, Credit Cards, Return Policy

Zagat Ratings

M	P	S	C
▽ 23	9	13	I

Tim & Nina's

4 Columbus Circle (8th Ave.), A/B/C/D/1/9 to Columbus Circle, 212-977-6000; www.zagat.com

◪ Packed with "enough merchandise to fill a walk-in closet", this flea-size "world-class canine clothing boutique" at Columbus Circle attracts an international mix of "stylish spaniels" and "bargain hounds"; P.S. "delish doggie biscuits" are "doled out" with purchase.

Review, with surveyors' comments in quotes

Stores with the highest overall ratings and greatest popularity and importance are printed in CAPITAL LETTERS.

Before reviews a symbol indicates whether responses were uniform ◼ or mixed ◪.

Hours: ◐ usually open after 7 PM
   S open on Sunday

Credit Cards: ⌀ no credit cards accepted

Return Policy: C store credit only

Locations: NYC addresses for the 10 top-rated chains are listed in the Branches for Top Chains index on page 280. For chains with more than 10 locations in NYC, the flagship address is listed with their reviews.

Maps: Maps show locations for stores with the highest overall ratings and greatest popularity and importance.

Ratings: Merchandise, Presentation and Service are rated on a scale of **0** to **30**. The Cost (C) column reflects our surveyors' estimate of the price range of merchandise.

M	Merchandise	P	Presentation	S	Service	C	Cost
23		9		13		I	

0–9   poor to fair   **20–25**   very good to excellent
10–15 fair to good   **26–30**   extraordinary to perfection
16–19 good to very good   ▽ low response/less reliable

The price range is indicated by the following symbols:

| I | Inexpensive | E | Expensive |
| M | Moderate | VE | Very Expensive |

8   subscribe to zagat.com

Most Popular

Each of our reviewers has been asked to name his or her five favorite stores. The 50 places most frequently named, in order of their popularity, are:

1. Bloomingdale's
2. Century 21
3. Saks Fifth Avenue
4. Bed, Bath & Beyond
5. Barneys
6. Macy's
7. Banana Republic
8. Bergdorf Goodman
9. Anthropologie
10. Costco Wholesale
11. Met. Museum of Art
12. ABC Carpet & Home
13. H&M
14. Henri Bendel
15. Kate's Paperie
16. Loehmann's
17. Ann Taylor
18. Ann Taylor Loft
19. Tiffany & Co.
20. Gap
21. T.J. Maxx
22. B&H Photo-Video
23. Crate & Barrel
24. Lord & Taylor
25. J&R Computer World
26. Daffy's
27. Sephora
28. MoMA Design Store
29. Scoop
30. J. Crew
31. Zabar's
32. Filene's Basement
33. Kate Spade
34. Takashimaya
35. Kiehl's
36. Pearl Paint
37. FAO Schwarz
38. Old Navy
39. Brooks Brothers
40. Gracious Home
41. Virgin Megastore*
42. Paragon
43. Intermix
44. Syms
45. Kmart
46. Express
47. J&R Music World
48. Nine West
49. Tower Records
50. Club Monaco

While the above list contains many obvious big names, it's interesting that a number of the stores, such as ABC Carpet & Home, B&H Photo-Video, Bergdorf Goodman, Gracious Home, Kiehl's and Kate's Paperie, are of the "born in NY" variety, proof that New Yorkers love – and support – individuality in their shopping choices. What's more, if you turn to page 21 you'll see that shopping here can also be a world-class bargain.

---

* Tied with store directly above it

vote at zagat.com

Top Ratings

Department stores received separate ratings for their various categories.

Top Fashion/Beauty

- **29** Harry Winston
- Graff
- Van Cleef & Arpels
- Cartier
- Creed
- Turnbull & Asser
- **28** Loro Piana
- Piaget
- Reinstein Ross*
- Mikimoto
- Stuart Moore
- Manolo Blahnik
- Hermès
- Bulgari
- A La Vieille Russie
- Buccellati
- Asprey
- Cellini
- Eugenia Kim
- Brioni
- Morgenthal Frederics
- Eres
- Chopard
- Christian Louboutin
- Bottega Veneta
- Selima Optique
- Catimini
- Little Eric*
- **27** La Perla
- Tartine et Chocolat
- Ascot Chang
- Diane von Furstenberg*
- Robert Talbott*
- Sergio Rossi
- Chanel
- Alain Mikli
- Ermenegildo Zegna*
- Yohji Yamamoto
- Allen Edmonds
- Bergdorf Goodman
- Jimmy Choo
- John Lobb
- Sigerson Morrison
- Carolina Herrera
- Tiffany & Co.
- Kiehl's
- Oxxford Clothes
- La Petite Coquette
- Robert Marc
- Anne Fontaine
- Wempe*
- Bonpoint

By Category

Accessories
- **28** Eugenia Kim
- **27** Bergdorf Goodman
- Bergdorf Men's
- **25** Barneys
- Saks Fifth Avenue

Activewear
- **26** Patagonia
- **25** Paragon
- Super Runners Shop
- **24** Puma
- **22** Lacoste

Bridal
- **26** Vera Wang
- Bergdorf Goodman
- Yumi Katsura
- Michelle Roth
- **25** Saks Fifth Avenue

Clothing: Children's
- **28** Catimini
- **27** Tartine et Chocolat
- Bonpoint
- Au Chat Botte
- **25** Jacadi

Clothing: Designer (Men's)
- **27** Ermenegildo Zegna
- Giorgio Armani
- Paul Smith
- **26** Hugo Boss
- **24** John Varvatos

Clothing: Designer (Men's/Women's)
- **28** Hermès
- **27** Yohji Yamamoto
- Etro
- Issey Miyake
- Gucci

---

* Tied with store directly above it

10 subscribe to zagat.com

Top Merchandise

Clothing: Designer (Women's)
- 27 Diane von Furstenberg
  Chanel
  Carolina Herrera
- 26 Christian Dior
  Chloé

Clothing: Discount
- 22 Century 21
  Find Outlet
- 21 Aaron's
  S&W
- 19 Nice Price

Clothing: Men's (Classic)
- 28 Brioni
- 27 Oxxford Clothes
  Bergdorf Men's
- 26 Paul Stuart
  Saks Fifth Avenue

Clothing: Men's (Contemporary)
- 26 Barneys
- 24 Ted Baker
- 23 99X
  Jeffrey
- 20 Stussy NYC

Clothing: Women's (Boutiques)
- 26 Language
- 25 Ibiza
  Hedra Prue
  Kirna Zabête
  Foley & Corinna

Consignment/Vintage
- 25 Fisch for the Hip
- 24 Amarcord Vintage Fashion
  Resurrection
- 23 Ina
- 22 Encore

Cosmetics/Toiletries (Dept. Stores)
- 28 Bergdorf Goodman
- 27 Barneys
  Bergdorf Men's
  Henri Bendel
- 26 Saks Fifth Avenue

Cosmetics/Toiletries (Specialists)
- 29 Creed
- 27 Kiehl's
  Fresh
  Floris of London
  C.O. Bigelow Chemists

Department Stores
- 27 Bergdorf Goodman
  Bergdorf Men's
- 26 Barneys
  Saks Fifth Avenue
- 25 Takashimaya

Eyewear
- 28 Morgenthal Frederics
  Selima Optique
- 27 Alain Mikli
  Robert Marc
- 26 Oliver Peoples

Fashion Chain: Men's
- 25 Rochester Big & Tall
- 22 Brooks Brothers
- 20 Sisley
  Banana Republic Men's
  Club Monaco

Fashion Chain: Women's
- 23 Eileen Fisher
- 21 Anthropologie
- 20 Sisley
  Banana Republic
  Ann Taylor

Handbags (Specialists)
- 28 Bottega Veneta
- 25 Prada
  Anya Hindmarch
- 24 Coach
  Furla

Hosiery/Lingerie
- 28 Eres
- 27 La Perla
  La Petite Coquette
- 26 Wolford
  Fogal

Jeans
- 27 Barneys
- 25 Diesel Denim Gallery
  What Comes/Goes Around
  Henri Bendel
- 24 Earl Jean

Jewelry: Classic
- 29 Harry Winston
  Graff
  Van Cleef & Arpels
  Cartier
- 28 Mikimoto

Jewelry: Contemporary
- 28 Reinstein Ross
- 27 Bergdorf Goodman
  Fragments
  Aaron Faber
- 25 Barneys

Maternity
- 26 Liz Lange Maternity
- 22 A Pea in the Pod
- 21 Mimi Maternity
- 20 Bloomingdale's
- 17 Maternity Works

vote at zagat.com · 11

Top Merchandise

Newcomers/Rated
28 Marni*
27 Jean Paul Gaultier*
　　Hollywould
26 Tag Heuer
25 Hickey Freeman
　　Petit Bateau
　　Chanel Fine Jewelry*

Newcomers/Unrated
　　Adidas
　　Agent Provocateur
　　Alexander McQueen
　　Jil Sander
　　Stella McCartney

Shirts/Ties
29 Turnbull & Asser
28 Hermès
27 Ascot Chang
　　Robert Talbott**
25 Thomas Pink

Shoes: Children's
28 Little Eric
26 Shoofly
23 Harry's Shoes
　　Great Feet
22 Tip-Top Shoes

Shoes: Men's
27 Allen Edmonds
　　John Lobb
23 Bergdorf Men's
22 Johnston & Murphy
21 Timberland

Shoes: Men's & Women's
27 Jeffrey
26 Barneys
　　Otto Tootsi Plohound
25 Saks Fifth Avenue
　　Bally

Shoes: Women's
28 Manolo Blahnik
　　Christian Louboutin
27 Sergio Rossi
　　Jimmy Choo
　　Sigerson Morrison

Sneakers
25 Paragon
　　Super Runners Shop
24 Puma
23 Niketown
　　New Balance

Watches
29 Cartier
28 Piaget
　　Cellini
　　Chopard
27 Wempe

---

* Low votes
** Tied with store directly above it

12　　　　　　　　　　subscribe to zagat.com

Top Merchandise

Top Home/Garden

- **29** Steuben
- Pratesi
- **28** Bernardaud
- Christofle
- Ann Sacks Tile
- Artistic Tile
- Baccarat
- Buccellati
- Waterworks
- Avventura
- Lalique*
- **27** Country Floors
- Frette
- Urban Archaeology
- Tiffany & Co.
- Cassina USA
- Bridge Kitchenware
- Scully & Scully
- **26** Schweitzer Linen
- Simon Pearce Glass
- Moss
- B&B Italia
- Simon's Hardware
- Hastings Bath & Tile
- Maurice Villency*

- Zabar's
- Bergdorf Goodman
- Barneys
- Broadway Panhandler
- Dean & Deluca
- Aero
- Gallery Orrefors
- **25** Just Bulbs
- ABC Carpet & Home
- ABC Carpet (Carpets/Rugs)
- Scott Jordan Furniture
- Artemide
- Jonathan Adler
- Gracious Home
- AF Supply
- Bodum*
- Drexel Heritage*
- Georg Jensen*
- Roche Bobois*
- Michael C. Fina
- Williams-Sonoma
- Albee Baby Carriage
- Bellini
- Chelsea Garden
- Einstein-Moomjy*

By Category

Accessories
- **26** Moss
- **25** Jonathan Adler
- **24** Terence Conran
- Mxyplyzyk
- Pierre Deux

Bathroom Fixtures
- **28** Waterworks
- **27** Urban Archaeology
- **26** Hastings Bath & Tile
- **25** AF Supply
- **24** Davis & Warshow**

Cookware
- **27** Bridge Kitchenware
- **26** Zabar's
- Broadway Panhandler
- Dean & Deluca
- **25** Bodum

Department Stores
- **26** Bergdorf Goodman
- Barneys
- **25** ABC Carpet & Home
- Gracious Home
- Takashimaya

Fine China/Crystal
- **29** Steuben
- **28** Bernardaud
- Christofle
- Baccarat
- Avventura
- Lalique*

Furniture
- **27** Cassina USA
- **26** B&B Italia
- Maurice Villency
- Aero
- **25** Scott Jordan Furniture

Garden
- **26** Lexington Gardens**
- **25** Chelsea Garden
- **24** Smith & Hawken
- **21** Bed, Bath & Beyond
- Garden Shop/Hort. Soc.**

Hardware Stores
- **26** Simon's Hardware
- **25** Gracious Home
- **23** Vercesi Hardware
- Pintchik
- **22** Home Depot

---

* Tied with store directly above it
** Low votes

vote at zagat.com 13

Top Merchandise

Linens
- 29 Pratesi
- 28 Porthault*
- 27 Frette
- 26 Schweitzer Linen
- 23 Harris Levy

Lighting
- 25 Just Bulbs
- Artemide
- 24 Lighting by Gregory
- 23 Lee's Studio
- 21 Bowery Lighting

Major Appliances
- 25 Williams-Sonoma
- 24 S Feldman Housewares
- Krups Kitchen & Bath
- Gringer & Sons
- 22 Bed, Bath & Beyond

Newcomers/Unrated
- ABH Design
- Baker
- Clio
- Vitra
- Xukuma

Silver
- 28 Christofle
- Buccellati
- 27 Tiffany & Co.
- 25 Georg Jensen
- Michael C. Fina

Tiles
- 28 Ann Sacks Tile
- Artistic Tile
- 27 Country Floors
- Urban Archaeology
- 23 Nemo Tile

* Low votes

14   **subscribe to zagat.com**

Top Merchandise

Top Lifestyle

- **29** Dempsey & Carroll
  B&H Photo-Video
- **28** Tender Buttons
  Sound by Singer
  Leather Man
  Footlight Records
- **27** Smythson of Bond St.
  Kate's Paperie
  B&J Fabrics
  Joseph Patelson Music
  Crane & Co., Paper
  Fountain Pen Hospital
  Pearl Paint
  FAO Schwarz
  Tumi
  TLA Video
  City Quilter
  M&J Trimming/Buttons
  Tents and Trails
  Louis Vuitton
- **26** Nat Sherman
  T. Anthony
  Bang & Olufsen
  Lyric Hi-Fi
  Clyde's

Fetch*
Saks Fifth Avenue*
Dunhill
Harvey Electronics
Joon
Toys in Babeland
MoMA Design Store
Crouch & Fitzgerald
New York Golf Center
Flight 001
- **25** Manny's Music
  J&R Computer World
  Generation Records
  Montblanc*
  Other Music
  Colony Music
  Hyman Hendler
  New York Central Art
  World of Golf
  Paragon
  Paper Access
  Yarn Co.
  Lincoln Stationers
  Davidoff of Geneva
  Tekserve

By Category

Art Supplies
- **27** Pearl Paint
- **25** New York Central Art
- **24** A.I. Friedman
- **23** Sam Flax
  Lee's Art

Audio/Electronics
- **28** Sound by Singer
- **26** Bang & Olufsen
  Lyric Hi-Fi
  Harvey Electronics
- **24** J&R Music World

Cameras/Video
- **29** B&H Photo-Video
- **25** Adorama Camera
- **21** Olden Camera
- **20** Alkit Pro Camera
- **19** Willoughby's

CDs/Vinyl
- **28** Footlight Records
- **25** Generation Records
  Other Music
  Colony Music
  Virgin Megastore

Computers
- **25** J&R Computer World
  Tekserve
- **22** Best Buy
- **20** CompUSA
  DataVision

Fabrics/Notions
- **28** Tender Buttons
- **27** B&J Fabrics
  City Quilter
  M&J Trimming/Buttons
- **25** Hyman Hendler

Instruments/Sheet Music
- **27** Joseph Patelson Music
- **26** Matt Umanov Guitars**
- **25** Manny's Music
  Colony Music
- **24** Sam Ash

Knitting/Needlepoint
- **25** Yarn Co.
- **23** Downtown Yarns
- **22** Stitches East
  Erica Wilson Needle Works
  Rita's Needlepoint

---

* Tied with store directly above it
** Low votes

vote at zagat.com

Top Merchandise

Luggage/Leather Goods
27 Tumi
    Louis Vuitton
26 T. Anthony
    Saks Fifth Avenue
    Crouch & Fitzgerald

Museum Stores
26 MoMA Design Store
25 Met. Museum of Art
24 AsiaStore/Asia Society
23 American Craft Museum
22 Jewish Museum

Newcomers/Unrated
    Apple Store SoHo
    Neue Galerie
    Purl
    TKNY
    Vespa

Pet Supplies
26 Fetch
24 Beasty Feast
23 Doggie-Do & Pussycats Too
22 Furry Paws
21 Petco

Sex Shops
28 Leather Man
26 Toys in Babeland
22 Eve's Garden
20 Pleasure Chest
19 Pink Pussycat

Sporting Goods
27 Tents and Trails
26 New York Golf Center
25 World of Golf
    Paragon
23 Gerry Cosby & Co.

Stationery
29 Dempsey & Carroll
27 Smythson of Bond St.
    Kate's Paperie
    Crane & Co., Paper
25 Paper Access

Theme Stores
23 NBA Store
    New York Firefighter's
22 Mets Clubhouse Shop
    Yankee Clubhouse Shop
20 Disney

Toys
27 FAO Schwarz
24 Mary Arnold Toys
23 Penny Whistle
    Toys R Us
22 Westside Kids

Videos/DVDs
27 TLA Video
25 Virgin Megastore
    Kim's Mediapolis
24 J&R Music World
    Tower Records

By Location

Chelsea
27 City Quilter
26 New York Golf
25 Myoptics
    AF Supply
    Williams-Sonoma

Chinatown
27 Pearl Paint
24 Kam Man
19 Pearl River Mart

East Village
28 Eugenia Kim
    Footlight Records
    Selima Optique
27 Kiehl's
25 New York Central Art

East 40s
28 Cellini
27 Allen Edmonds
    Robert Marc
    Tumi
26 Nat Sherman

East 50s
29 Harry Winston
    Van Cleef & Arpels
    Cartier
    Dempsey & Carroll
    Turnbull & Asser

East 60s
29 Graff
    Steuben
    Creed
    Pratesi
28 Tender Buttons

Top Merchandise

East 70s
- *29* Creed
- *28* Reinstein Ross
  Morgenthal Frederics
  Christian Louboutin
  Selima Optique

East 80s
- *29* Dempsey & Carroll
- *28* Little Eric
- *27* Tartine et Chocolat
  Au Chat Botte
  Fresh

East 90s & Up
- *28* Catimini
- *27* Robert Marc
  Bonpoint
- *25* Jacadi
  L'Occitane

Financial District
- *27* Fountain Pen Hospital
  Fragments
  Tents and Trails
- *26* Joon
- *25* J&R Computer World

Flatiron District
- *28* Artistic Tile
- *27* Paul Smith
- *26* Bang & Olufsen
  Jo Malone
  Otto Tootsi Plohound

Garment District
- *29* B&H Photo-Video
- *27* B&J Fabrics
  M&J Trimming/Buttons
- *26* Tourneau
  Sephora

Gramercy Park
- *27* Pearl Paint
- *26* Simon's Hardware & Bath
- *23* Vercesi Hardware
- *22* Tokyo Joe
  Furry Paws

Greenwich Village
- *27* Kate's Paperie
  La Petite Coquette
  TLA Video
  C.O. Bigelow Chemists
- *26* Fetch

Lower East Side
- *26* Toys in Babeland
- *25* Foley & Corinna
- *24* Seven New York
  Lighting by Gregory
- *23* Harris Levy

Meatpacking District
- *27* Diane von Furstenberg
- *25* Bodum
- *24* Jeffrey
- *23* Scoop

Murray Hill
- *25* Roche Bobois
- *23* Doggie-Do & Pussycats
- *22* Ethan Allen
  Morgan Library Shop
  LaCrasia

NoHo
- *29* Creed
- *25* Other Music
- *24* Tower Records
- *23* Bond 07 by Selima
  Katayone Adeli

NoLita
- *27* Sigerson Morrison
  Hollywould
  Fresh
- *26* Lunettes et Chocolat
  Language

SoHo
- *28* Reinstein Ross
  Stuart Moore
  Morgenthal Frederics
  Eres
  Selima Optique

South Street Seaport
- *24* Coach
- *21* Sharper Image
  Brookstone
- *19* Guess?
  Talbots

TriBeCa
- *27* Urban Archaeology
  Issey Miyake
- *26* Shoofly
- *24* Bu & the Duck
- *23* P&S Fabrics

Union Square
- *28* Ann Sacks Tile
  Sound by Singer
- *27* Country Floors
- *25* Paragon
  Virgin Megastore

West Village
- *28* Leather Man
- *27* Fresh
- *26* Flight 001
- *25* Myoptics
  Chelsea Garden Ctr.

vote at zagat.com   17

Top Merchandise

West 40s
- **27** Crane & Co., Paper
  Tumi
- **26** Harvey Electronics
- **25** Sephora
  Manny's Music

West 50s
- **28** Manolo Blahnik
- **27** Ascot Chang
  Smythson of Bond St.
  Joseph Patelson Music
  Aaron Faber

West 60s
- **27** Robert Marc
- **25** Paper Access
  Gracious Home
  Lincoln Stationers
  Bonne Nuit

West 70s
- **26** Bang & Olufsen
  Sephora
- **25** Super Runners Shop
- **24** Intermix
  Z. Baby Company

West 80s
- **28** Avventura
- **26** Schweitzer Linen
  Patagonia
  Zabar's
  Shoofly

West 90s
- **25** Albee Baby Carriage
- **21** Equinox
  Metro Bicycles
  Janovic Plaza
- **19** La Brea

Outer Boroughs

Brooklyn
- **28** Little Eric
- **25** ABC Carpet & Home
  Clay Pot
  Jacadi*
  AF Supply
  Boss, The
- **24** William Barthman
  Kleinfeld & Son
- **23** Toys R Us
  Bird

Queens
- **23** Thomasville
  Toys R Us
  Nemo Tile
- **22** Ethan Allen
  Home Depot
  Bed, Bath & Beyond
  Best Buy
  Smiley's
  Costco
- **21** Petco

---

* Tied with store directly above it

subscribe to zagat.com

Top Presentation

- **29** Graff
- Harry Winston
- **28** Steuben
- Creed
- Cartier
- Waterworks
- Turnbull & Asser
- Takashimaya
- Bernardaud
- Van Cleef & Arpels
- Baccarat
- **27** Tartine et Chocolat
- Chopard
- Hermès
- Bulgari
- Carolina Herrera
- Moss
- Smythson of Bond St.
- Fresh
- Buccellati
- Etro*
- Hastings Bath
- Dylan's Candy Bar
- Apartment, The
- Frette
- Piaget*
- Reinstein Ross*
- FAO Schwarz
- Ann Sacks Tile
- Tiffany & Co.
- Lalique
- **26** Stuart Moore
- Christian Dior
- Issey Miyake*
- Bonpoint
- Bang & Olufsen
- Asprey
- Morgenthal Frederics
- Penhaligon's
- Comme des Garçons
- Felissimo
- Brioni
- Fred Leighton
- Manolo Blahnik
- St. John
- A La Vieille Russie
- Dunhill
- Hogan
- Bergdorf Goodman
- Chanel

Architectural Interest

- Adidas
- Alexander McQueen
- Apple Store SoHo
- Baker
- Calvin Klein
- Cartier
- Comme des Garçons
- ddc domus collection
- Destination
- Diesel Superstore
- Donna Karan
- Fred Leighton
- Henri Bendel
- Hugo Boss
- Issey Miyake
- Jean Paul Gaultier
- Lee's Art Shop
- Maurice Villency
- Miss Sixty
- Nicole Farhi
- Niketown
- Prada
- Ralph Lauren
- Rubin Chapelle
- Terence Conran Shop
- Versace
- Vespa
- Vitra

Holiday Decoration

- ABC Carpet & Home
- Barneys
- Bergdorf Goodman
- Bloomingdale's
- Cartier
- Catimini
- Disney
- Dylan's Candy Bar
- FAO Schwarz
- Henri Bendel
- Kate's Paperie
- Lord & Taylor
- Macy's
- Ralph Lauren
- Saks Fifth Avenue
- Sony Style
- Takashimaya
- Tiffany & Co.

---

* Tied with store directly above it

vote at zagat.com

Top Service

- **28** Turnbull & Asser
- Toys In Babeland
- **27** City Quilter
- Graff*
- Piaget
- Van Cleef & Arpels
- **26** Harry Winston
- John Lobb
- Carolina Herrera
- Scott Jordan Furniture
- Ascot Chang
- Tekserve
- Nat Sherman
- Dempsey & Carroll
- **25** T. Anthony
- Buccellati
- Fountain Pen Hospital
- Robert Talbott
- Penhaligon's
- Valentino*
- Jo Malone
- Super Runners Shop
- Dunhill
- Crouch & Fitzgerald
- Art of Shaving
- Beasty Feast*
- Vercesi Hardware*
- Malia Mills Swimwear
- Oxxford Clothes
- Robert Marc
- **24** Fetch
- St. John
- Hickey Freeman
- Davidoff of Geneva
- Kiehl's
- Michael Kors*
- Cartier
- Joon
- Asprey
- Bulgari*
- Avon Salon and Spa
- Mary Arnold Toys
- Bergdorf Men's
- Greenstones
- Baccarat
- Harriet Love
- Brioni
- Ermenegildo Zegna
- Paul Stuart
- Joan Michlin Gallery

Free Delivery in NYC

- Apple Store SoHo
- Assets London
- Chanel Fine Jewelry
- Eric
- Gracious Home
- Paper Access
- Paterson Silks
- Pet Stop
- Planet Kids
- S Feldman Housewares
- Spoiled Brats
- Steinway and Sons
- Stickley, Audi & Co.
- Super Runners Shop

In-Store Dining

- ABC Carpet & Home
- Apartment, The
- Barneys
- Bergdorf Goodman
- Bloomingdale's
- Bodum
- Burberry
- DDC Lab
- Dean & Deluca
- Diesel Superstore
- DKNY
- ESPN Zone
- Lord & Taylor
- Macy's
- NBA Store
- Nicole Farhi
- Saks Fifth Avenue
- Takashimaya
- TKNY
- Virgin Megastore

---

* Tied with store directly above it

Good Values

Savvy New Yorkers not only frequent seasonal sample sales to scoop up bargains throughout the year, they also have a list of affordable stores in their collective back pocket. The following retailers offer outstanding values just about every day.

American Eagle Outfitters
April Cornell
B&H Photo-Video
Bis Designer Resale
Bodum
Body Shop
Boucher
Broadway Panhandler
Century 21
Costco
Crate & Barrel
Dave's Army Navy
David's Bridal
Demeter
Dr. Jays
Enchanted Forest
For Eyes
Fossil
Gerry's Menswear
H&M
Home Depot
Housing Works Thrift Shop
Jam Paper & Envelope
Kam Man
Kiehl's
Kmart
LeSportsac
Liliblue
M.A.C. Cosmetics
M&J Trimming/Buttons
Mavi Jean
Meg
Old Navy
Orchard Corset
Pearl River Mart
Petco
Pookie & Sebastian
Purdy Girl
Ray Beauty Supply
Skechers
Smiley's
Super Runners Shop
Swatch
Syms
Target
Watch World
Westside Kids
William Wayne
Yellow Door
Zara

Directory

| M | P | S | C |

Aaron Basha C   23 | 21 | 20 | VE
680 Madison Ave. (bet. 61st & 62nd Sts.), 4/5/6/N/R/W to 59th St./ Lexington Ave., 212-935-1960; www.aaronbasha.com
■ Many a "most-prized piece of jewelry" comes from this East Side retailer, whose whimsical designs – flowers, "multi-colored" bugs and of course the famed, "absolutely adorable baby shoe" charms – often become "status items"; "celebrity moms" are often spotted here picking up a "customized" gift for a "new grandmother" or themselves; naturally, popularity comes at a price.

Aaron Faber Gallery S C   27 | 25 | 21 | VE
666 Fifth Ave. (53rd St.), E/F to 5th Ave., 212-586-8411; www.aaronfaber.com
■ So what if MoMA's moved temporarily – entering this chic-ly minimalist space on West 53rd Street "is like going into a craft museum"; some know this "true gallery" (they hold exhibitions as well as sell stuff) as a "standby for vintages watches" that has the "best service department around"; to others, the draw is the "eclectic, handcrafted jewelry" that complements the "wonderful estate pieces"; "from antique to ultramodern", it's "the best wearable art in town."

Aaron's   21 | 15 | 18 | E
627 Fifth Ave. (bet. 17th & 18th Sts.), Brooklyn, M/R to Prospect Ave., 718-768-5400; 888-768-5400; www.aarons.com
◪ "Very expensive clothing is now only expensive" at this family-owned "old-timer" "off the beaten path" in south Park Slope where "eager-to-help" salespeople "call you when what you like comes in"; a "comfy" waiting area for "hubby to sit" sipping free coffee and "great purses", accessories, jewelry and womenswear divided into "displays of name designers" like Max Mara and Elie Tahari make this "a shopper's dream" despite the communal dressing room and prices that are "not that cheap."

A. Atelier S C   – | – | – | E
125 Crosby St. (bet. Houston & Prince Sts.), N/R to Prince St., 212-941-8435
At first, this SoHo boutique seems somber, with masonite floors, black leather couches and white marble tables, but the decor provides a dramatic backdrop for presenting cutting-edge clothing talent – mostly pricey European designers – for both men and women.

ABC CARPET & HOME ● S   25 | 24 | 17 | VE
888 Broadway (E. 19th St.), 4/5/6/L/N/Q/R/W to 14th St./Union Sq., 212-473-3000
20 Jay St. (Plymouth St.), Brooklyn, F to York St., 718-643-7400 C
www.abchome.com
■ Each "nook and cranny" of this "dazzling", "dizzying" Flatiron District "decorating wonderland" is crammed with everything from "the most luxurious table and bed linens", "beautiful pillows", "über-chic sofas" and chandeliers to French, Italian, Asian and American "antique-y looking things" and "unique" ephemera from "unknown and well-known designers"; if the eight floors of "ever-changing", "quirky" displays of "pseudo-bohemian elegance" don't make you light-headed, the prices "poking holes in the ozone layer" may; N.B. an equally cavernous new branch has opened in Brooklyn's Dumbo section.

| M | P | S | C |

ABC Carpet & Home (Carpets/Rugs) ◐🅂🅲
 25 | 22 | 17 | E

881 Broadway (bet. 18th & 19th Sts.), 4/5/6/L/N/R/Q/W to 14th St./ Union Sq., 212-473-3000; www.abchome.com

■ Don't go to this "expansive carpeting mecca" in the Flatiron District "looking for presentation" (like you would at its stylish big sister across the street), but do make a pilgrimage for "piles and piles" of "excellent" "upscale" rugs "from around the world"; some say the staff is "willing to bargain", but for a sure thing wallet-watchers head for the basement and check out the clearance items and remnants "for great buys."

ABC Carpet & Home Warehouse Outlet ◐🅂
 21 | 13 | 15 | E

1055 Bronx River Ave. (Bruckner Expwy.), Bronx, 6 to Whitlock Ave., 718-860-0468; www.abccarpet.com

■ Supporters say "the occasional find makes the trek" to this Bronx warehouse outlet of the famed Flatiron District duo "worth it" for "seek and ye shall find" "good deals" on furniture, bed and table linens, textiles and rugs, though they warn "you have to remember how high-end they were to begin with"; still, detractors dis the "hit-or-miss" selection of "random pieces" and caution prices "still ain't cheap."

Abercrombie & Fitch ◐🅂🅲
 16 | 18 | 13 | M

South Street Seaport, 199 Water St. (Fulton St.), 2/3/4/5/A/C/J/M/Z to Fulton St./B'way/Nassau, 212-809-9000
12655 Richmond Ave. (Baltic Ave.), Staten Island, 718-698-9480
888-856-4480; www.abercrombie.com

■ "Get your libido going" at these national chain "playgrounds" for the "pouty young"; the South Street Seaport and Staten Island "hangouts" are "constantly crowded" with "teenyboppers" pawing the "sexy", "rugged" "preppy" wear, even though detractors dis "blaring music" and "eye-candy salespeople" lacking "any ability to fold shirts or keep the store orderly"; bring a "fat allowance from mom and dad", as the "hipness quotient" costs aplenty.

ABH Design 🅲
 – | – | – | E

401 E. 76th St. (bet. 1st & York Aves.), 6 to 77th St., 212-249-2276

Costume designer Aude Bronson-Howard's appealing new Upper East Side store features mostly her own stylish takes on fashion and home accessories, although there are some unusual imports as well; *pour la maison*, there are striped silk napkins, lacy-edged Italian plates, fanciful French candlesticks and terry towels trimmed with pom-poms, and *pour madame*, faux mink slippers, sporty down stoles and cashmere, cotton and cut-velvet robes.

Abracadabra 🅂
 21 | 17 | 17 | M

19 W. 21st St. (bet. 5th & 6th Aves.), N/R to 23rd St., 212-627-5194; www.abracadabrasuperstore.com

■ "You're sure to learn a good trick or two" at this Flatiron hocus-pocus shop that's "full of curiosities" – and "far more than a toy store; "you'll find a myriad of costumes" to buy or rent and "simply incredible masks" (it's "the place to be for Halloween" or even an "offbeat date") plus "sections dedicated to wigs, weapons and fake jewelry"; N.B. check out the weekend magic shows.

vote at zagat.com

| M | P | S | C |

Academy Records & CDs | 23 | 12 | 15 | I |
77 E. 10th St. (bet. 3rd & 4th Aves.), 6 to Astor Pl.; N/R to 8th St., 212-780-9166
12 W. 18th St. (bet. 5th & 6th Aves.), 4/5/6/L/N/Q/R/W to 14th St./Union Sq., 212-242-3000 ◐ S C
www.academy-records.com

■ You'll have to "go elbow-to-elbow with fellow browsers" to "unearth" "musical treasures" at this "ultimate source for used classical" LPs in the Flatiron District; the "tightly packed" selection also turns up jazz, rock and show tune CD "rarities and staples", VHS tapes and DVDs at "rock-bottom prices"; P.S. the East Village outlet sells mostly jazz and a bit of pop.

a.cheng ◐ S C | ▽ 20 | 19 | 23 | M |
443 E. Ninth St. (bet. Ave. A & 1st Ave.), 6 to Astor Pl.; L to 1st Ave., 212-979-7324; www.achengshop.com

■ "Very cute", "girlie creations" rule at this "tiny East Village store", the brainchild of owner and shopkeeper Alice Cheng; her signature "hand-stitching" and vintage "kimono-fabric" touches on tailored jeans, denim jackets and Mandarin-collared dresses ensure "everyone's compliments" when worn.

Active Wearhouse ◐ S | – | – | – | M |
514 Broadway (bet. Broome & Spring Sts.), 6 to Spring St.; N/R to Prince St., 212-965-2284

This hopping SoHo shop features a fly selection of sports and urban streetgear for men and women, from jerseys, team caps and ENYC sweatshirts to Sean Jean jackets, North Face parkas and Baby Phat hoodies and sweatpants; denim is also on display, while sneakers and shoes take center stage in the rear of the store, with a wraparound wall devoted to major playas such as Puma, Timberland and Adidas.

Add ◐ S | 22 | 22 | 20 | M |
461 W. Broadway (bet. Houston & Prince Sts.), F/S/V to B'way/Lafayette; N/R to Prince St., 212-539-1439

■ "Spiffy Manhattanites" fall for the "great shawls", "kitschy handbags", "eclectic costume jewelry" and "unique hats" from a host of fresh, new designers at this SoHo accessories "gem"; the "extremely friendly sales staff" is "happy to let you open the cases to try things on" and will even "offer great gift ideas – even if that gift is for yourself."

Addison on Madison C | 19 | – | 21 | E |
29 W. 57th St., 9th fl. (bet. 5th & 6th Aves.), N/R/W to 5th Ave./59th St., 212-308-2660

■ For "shirts you don't see anywhere else" – including some with "unusual ¼-inch collar sizes" – gents look to this specialty store whose styles favor the "comfortable, baggy American look"; shoppers savor the "accommodating" services: "sleeves are shortened to fit" and "care is taken to get you a tie that works with the shirt"; it moved to temporary Midtown digs post-*Survey*.

Adidas S | – | – | – | M |
136 Wooster St. (bet. Houston & Prince Sts.), N/R to Prince St., 212-777-2001; 800-289-2724; www.adidas.com

Fashionistas and club kids browse alongside bona fide athletes at this sleek SoHo scenester stocked with the Originals Collection –

old-school merchandise from the '60s, '70s and '80s re-colored for a new über-hip generation, legendary logo intact; groove to way-cool tunes while scoping out racks of tees and must-have activewear, classic sneakers, retro bags and bucket hats displayed on low white tables and ultra-futuristic ice-blue counters; boxer Muhammad Ali gets his props with a showcase of brand-name memorabilia.

Adorama Camera S 25 | 12 | 15 | M
42 W. 18th St. (bet. 5th & 6th Aves.), 4/5/6/N/R/Q/W to 14th St./Union Sq., 212-741-0052; 800-223-2500; www.adorama.com

■ "If you want to avoid long lines", this Flatiron photo palace is "the best one-stop shopping for all your camera needs and wants"; you can expect "great prices" on a "very large stock" of new and used equipment for "professional and beginner" shoots and darkroom work, but "don't expect coddling" since the staff "can't be bothered with stupid questions from amateurs."

Adriana's Caravan ●SC 24 | 19 | 23 | M
Grand Central, 4/5/6/7/S to 42nd St./Grand Central, 212-972-8804; 800-316-0820; www.adrianascaravan.com

■ "Like a far-off bazaar", this "convenient" "godsend for cooks who commute via Grand Central Station" was voted No. 1 for Herbs & Spices in our *NYC Marketplace Survey*, but it also boasts a "beautiful" selection of "exotic tableware" that makes for "wonderful gifts"; "this store has it all", including reasonable prices and a "helpful proprietor."

Adrien Linford SC 25 | 25 | 18 | E
927 Madison Ave. (74th St.), 6 to 77th St., 212-628-4500
1339 Madison Ave. (bet. 93rd & 94th Sts.), 6 to 96th St., 212-426-1500

■ Upper East Side duo devoted to Asian-oriented items – from home accessories like pottery, furniture made of abaca (banana fiber) and golden Buddhas to "upscale geegaws" like "handmade jewelry"; since "they have something for everyone", it's a "great place to get a gift."

Aedes De Venustas ●SC ∇ 29 | 27 | 24 | E
9 Christopher St. (bet. 6th Ave. & 7th Ave. S.), 1/9 to Christopher St., 212-206-8674; 888-233 3715; www.aedes.com

■ "The products, packaging and salespeople are all beautiful" at this tiny, gilded-brick-and-burgundy Greenwich Village boutique with "gorgeous and unusual fragrances", including candles and bath and beauty products from the likes of Dyptique, Creed and Christian Tortu; "service is superb" (they'll let you "take home samples to try before you buy"), and gift-wrapping is as chic as the shop's fabulous floral arrangements.

Aero C 26 | 21 | 19 | VE
132 Spring St. (bet. Green & Wooster Sts.), N/R to Prince St., 212-966-1500; www.aerostudios.com

■ Inspired by the élan of '40s French furnishings, "bright, young" interior designer and owner Thomas O'Brien fills his two-story SoHo shop with a "brilliant selection" of his own furniture and lighting designs as well as "well-chosen" vintage items from around the world; aesthetes assert that "he could be this generation's Jean-Michel Frank", but even if he's not, the pieces are "clean, fresh and so very New York."

vote at zagat.com

		M	P	S	C

Aerosoles ◐ S C   18 | 16 | 16 | I
*36 W. 34th St. (bet. 5th & 6th Aves.), B/D/F/N/Q/R/V/W to 34th St./
Herald Sq., 212-563-0610; 800-798-9478; www.aerosoles.com
For additional locations, see Top Chain Stores index*
■ "A whole lotta comfort", "a twinge of style" "and a teeny tiny price" prompt boosters to bellow "bravo", this chain is "finally" "making great strides"; scores of surveyors insist these shoes feel "like you're walking on a cloud", plus they're so "fetching" ("not as unhip as they used to be") it "almost makes you forget your mother would like them"; "how boring" yawn the "blasé", who also find service "so-so" and the decor downright "antiseptic."

AF Supply Corp.   25 | 16 | 14 | E
*22 W. 21st St., 15th fl. (bet. 5th & 6th Aves.), F/V to 23rd St.,
212-243-5400; 800-366-2284* C
*942 Lafayette Ave. (bet. Dr. Sandy F. Ray Blvd. & Stuyvesant Ave.),
Brooklyn, J to Kosciusko St., 718-443-6900
www.afsupply.com*
■ Loyalists of this converted loft space in Chelsea head here "for ideas" and a "fabulous selection" of plumbing and mid- to high-end bath fixtures (from basins to bathtubs and bidets) "in all styles" – just don't forget to make an appointment (the Brooklyn branch is bigger and takes walk-ins); while surveyors are split on service ("informed" vs. imperfect), they agree "prices are high."

Agatha ◐ S C   19 | 18 | 15 | M
*159-A Columbus Ave. (67th St.), 1/9 to 66th St., 212-362-0959
611 Madison Ave. (58th St.), N/R/W to 5th Ave./59th St., 212-758-4301
www.agatha.fr*
■ East Side or West Side, browsing for "cheap and chic", "colorful costume jewelry" is a cinch at these "fashionable" French chain links, which "neatly lay out the wares in glass cases and on the walls"; the "fun-faux", "throwaway" pieces, including the signature Scottish Terrier line, won't "break the bank" – but you also "get what you paid for" say those who quibble over the "quality."

Agent Provocateur S C   – | – | – | E
*133 Mercer St. (bet. Prince & Spring Sts.), N/R to Prince St.,
212-965-0229; www.agentprovocateur.com*
James Bond may be nowhere in sight, but bondage-worthy unmentionables certainly are at SoHo's spanking new British import from Vivienne Westwood's son, Joseph Corre, and his wife, Serena Rees; replete with lace-print wallpaper, a dainty vanity, black lacquered furniture, vitrines filled with frisky riding crops and foxy displays of filmy baby dolls, peekaboo undies and marabou mules, this lascivious boudoir, overseen by pink-clad saleswomen straight out of central casting, is bound to unleash your inner vixen.

Agnès B.   21 | 20 | 15 | E
*13 E. 16th St. (bet. 5th Ave. & Union Sq. W.), 4/5/6/L/N/Q/R/W to
14th St./Union Sq., 212-741-2585; 888-246-3722
103 Greene St. (bet. Prince & Spring Sts.), N/R to Prince St.,
212-925-4649* S
*1063 Madison Ave. (bet. 80th & 81st Sts.), 6 to 77th St., 212-570-9333
www.agnesb.com*
■ "For days when you feel like being French", these "appealing" boutiques beckon with "classic T-shirts", "adorable" separates

and "career clothing with a twist", most of it cut "for the thin crowd"; each can be "a fun place to shop", but bring along *beaucoup* bucks, as the merchandise is often "*très cher.*"

Agnès B. Homme S C | 20 | 20 | 18 | E |
79 Greene St. (bet. Broome & Spring Sts.), N/R to Prince St., 212-431-4339; www.agnesb.com

■ Conveniently close to the chain's female flagship in SoHo, this masculine counterpart is "a must-stop for your man", thanks to the "great selection of shirts, pants and accessories" arrayed in a clean, spare space; the "terrific, sleek designs" of its "offbeat" classics appeal to the "Francophile in all of us."

A.I. Friedman S | 24 | 22 | 19 | M |
44 W.18th St. (bet. 5th & 6th Aves.), 1/9 to 18th St., 212-243-9000

☑ In a "chic, airy" Flatiron space, this "quality" art "warehouse" stocks "for the weekend dabbler"; there's only a "small selection of premium supplies" for "real" painters and sculptors, but it's "great for elegant frames, fancy Italian office furniture, inventive journals" and "interesting knickknacks", plus "they don't treat you like a moron if you don't know exactly what you're looking for."

Alain Mikli S C | 27 | 25 | 20 | VE |
880 Madison Ave. (bet. 71st & 72nd Sts.), 6 to 68th St., 212-472-6085; www.mikli.fr

■ "If you want to be noticed", this Upper East Side eyewear boutique features "gorgeous", "fashion-forward" frames in "stylish palettes" that ensure you "won't see yourself coming and going"; the pale wood–clad interior is "equally beautiful", the "service is impeccable", and even if "people with heart conditions should beware of the sticker shock" that naturally accompanies such "high-end" wares, it's well "worth it" for the "coolest specs in town."

Alan Moss ⇌ C | ▽ 29 | 26 | 19 | VE |
436 Lafayette St. (4th St.), F/S/V to B'way/Lafayette, 212-473-1310

■ East Village stalwart showcasing "museum-quality" 20th-century furniture, art, glass and lighting; loyalists "love" the owner's "great eye" for "fabulous things" but caution that the cost of benefiting from some of the "best taste" in NY can often be "out-of-bounds."

A LA VIEILLE RUSSIE | 28 | 26 | 24 | VE |
781 Fifth Ave. (bet. 59th & 60th Sts.), N/R/W to 5th Ave./59th St., 212-752-1727; www.alvr.com

☑ It's "like shopping in Old St. Petersburg" at this "purveyor of high-end Russian artifacts" where the famed Fabergé eggs, "often-rare" European jewelry and "antique place settings" co-exist in a "luxurious", "museum-like" setting "across from the Plaza"; the staff is "pleasant and professional" (as long as you "dress like the czar" some mutter), and if the prices seem as "royal" as the "beautiful pieces'" pedigrees – well, "just [gazing at] the windows is a turn-on."

Albee Baby Carriage Co. C | 25 | 8 | 19 | M |
715 Amsterdam Ave. (95th St.), 1/2/3/9 to 96th St., 212-662-5740; www.albeebaby.com

■ Family-owned since 1933, this "one-stop-shopping" "old faithful" on the Upper West Side "carries everything you could possibly need for your babe", from furniture, cribs and strollers to toys, all

vote at zagat.com

| M | P | S | C |

"packed into a very tight space"; sure, it can be "chaotic to navigate", but rest assured, the "knowledgeable, helpful staff" "really knows its stuff"; P.S. "free delivery is a dream", plus "they repair Maclaren strollers for a reasonable cost."

Aldo S C
16 | 17 | 15 | M

15 W. 34th St. (bet. 5th & 6th Aves.), B/D/F/N/Q/R/V/W to 34th St./ Herald Sq., 212-594-6255; 888-818-2536; www.aldoshoes.com Additional locations throughout the NY area

■ "Your feet can look good without costing an arm and a leg" applauds the "younger, hipper crowd" that falls head over heels for this "trendy" Canadian chain's "chunky, funky and borderline cheesy" men's and women's footwear; but bashers give it the boot, blasting the "shoes look better than they actually feel" – "boy, do my little piggies hurt" – and find the "psuedo-helpful" staff has all the "personality of a cardboard box."

Alexander McQueen S
– | – | – | VE

417 W. 14th St. (bet. 9th & 10th Aves.), A/C/E/L to 14th St./8th Ave., 212-645-1797; www.alexandermcqueen.com

You can expect the unexpected from this futuristic flagship in the Meatpacking District; its curved walls, vaulted ceilings and mirrored, cylindrical dressing rooms evoke a *Close Encounters of the Third Kind* backdrop for this British bad boy of a design star, whose womenswear currently features exquisitely extreme leather coats, silk chiffon 'harness dresses' and sharply tailored suits.

Alexia Crawford S C
24 | 21 | 22 | M

199 Prince St. (bet. MacDougal & Sullivan Sts.), C/E to Spring St., 212-473-9703; www.alexiacrawford.com

■ "Tucked away on the outskirts of SoHo", this "cute" accessories shop owned by Aussie Alexia offers "great, offbeat" "treasures" "that won't break the bank"; the "trendy but wearable jewelry", made mostly from sterling silver, freshwater pearls and semi-precious stones, and the "unique" colorful handbags "look modern and stylish" – no wonder "young, cost-efficient shoppers" keep coming back for more.

Alice Underground ● S
18 | 15 | 12 | M

481 Broadway (bet. Broome & Grand Sts.), 6/J/M/N/Q/R/W/Z to Canal St., 212-431-9067

■ For an experience akin to "raiding your eccentric aunt's closet", "go ask Alice", whose creaky-floored, "spacious store" in SoHo carries an array of men's and women's vintage threads, toys and home furnishings; prices are "not the cheapest" (though the "old linens are still a bargain") and sophisticates sniff the "leather jackets, formalwear and funky stuff" are "not top-of-the-line – but it's worth checking out" for the occasional "incredible find."

Alife Rivington Club
▽ 24 | 27 | 18 | E

178 Orchard St. (bet. Houston & Stanton Sts.), F/V to Lower East Side/ 2nd Ave., 646-654-0628
158 Rivington St. (bet. Clinton & Suffolk Sts.), F/J/M/Z to Delancey/ Essex Sts., 212-375-8128 S C

■ "Push a buzzer to get into" this "fantastic" Lower East Side "underground" "country club for sneakers" where, once inside, you'll "catch glimpses of people you'd know if you were cooler"; "if you're truly an old-school aficionado", the "limited-edition, imported" and vintage "kicks", displayed in wood cubbyholes,

M P S C

"will bring back tons of memories"; older sibling Alife nearby on Orchard Street feels like an "exhibit space", with artwork in the windows offset by "hip footwear" and an "enticing" assortment of apparel and accessories.

Alkit Pro Camera   20 | 18 | 19 | E
222 Park Ave. S. (18th St.), 4/5/6/L/N/Q/R/W to 14th St./Union Sq., 212-674-1515 S
830 Seventh Ave. (bet. 53rd & 54th Sts.), 1/9 to 50th St., 212-262-2424
820 Third Ave. (50th St.), 6 to 51st St., 212-832-2101
www.alkit.com

◪ There's a lot of contrast to the picture of this camera shop/lab chain: photo buffs impressed with the "professional-quality developing" and "helpful, knowledgeable" service, including free tutorials with digital purchases, say it's "good all-around"; while their Advantage Club offers discounts, others sniff it's "not the best place to buy", given the "expensive but mediocre processing" – perhaps it's all that "arrogance bubbling over" into the chemicals?

Allan & Suzi S   21 | 16 | 17 | E
416 Amsterdam Ave. (80th St.), 1/9 to 79th St., 212-724-7445; www.allanandsuzi.net

◪ "If your style is flamboyant", you'll enjoy exploring this long, narrow Upper West Side consignment/vintage clothing store, "crammed to the gills" with "fashions that range from funky to haute couture", from 1950s prom dresses to last season's Roberto Cavalli; regulars warn "beware the costs" and, occasionally, the owners (who "can be moody", though knowledgeable); still, be it a feather boa or a pair of Jimmy Choos, "everyone needs something from here in his or her closet."

Allen Edmonds C   27 | 22 | 23 | VE
24 E. 44th St. (bet. 5th & Madison Aves.), 4/5/6/7/S to 42nd St./Grand Central, 212-682-3144
551 Madison Ave. (55th St.), E/V to 5th Ave./53rd St., 212-308-8305 S
877-817-7615; www.allenedmonds.com

■ "Without question, some of the most well-made and comfortable shoes on the planet" are walking out of these veteran Midtowners, best known for their handcrafted "quality, conservative" business footwear (though they actually offer a "wide range of styles", from dress to golf), meticulously fitted by "excellent" staffers; yes, the goods are geared to "rich feet", but "for hard-to-find sizes, they're worth the bucks."

Alpana Bawa S C   – | – | – | E
70 E. First St. (bet. 1st & 2nd Aves.), F/V to 2nd Ave., 212-254-1249
41 Grand St. (bet. Thompson St. & W. B'way), A/C/E to Canal St., 212-431-6367
www.alpanabawa.com

The stripped-down interiors of this SoHo shop and its East Village offshoot serve as a blank canvas for the wake-up-call colors of this radiant, directional his-and-her collection of "comfortable" Indian shirts, dresses and separates; splendid fabrics, artfully placed embroidery, whimsical appliqués and fanciful stripes and dots make these "ethnic-inspired" collectibles stand out from the pack, prompting the wistful to wish they could "wear these clothes day in and day out."

vote at zagat.com

			M	P	S	C

Alphabets   23 | 20 | 15 | M
115 Ave. A (bet. 7th St. & St. Marks Pl.), 6 to Astor Pl., 212-475-7250
2284 Broadway (bet. 82nd & 83rd Sts.), 1/9 to 79th St.,
212-579-5702 ●S
47 Greenwich Ave. (bet. Charles & Perry Sts.), 2/3 to 14th St.; 1/9 to Christopher St., 212-229-2966
www.alphabetsnyc.com

■ You'll encounter "kitsch galore" (as well as "upscale candles, bath products and housewares") at this "eclectic", "quirky" mini-chain that caters to "the child within" with loads of "campy" novelties exhibiting a "wink-and-nudge irony" that's catnip to "baby boomers"; those who know their ABCs also revel in the merch "of the decidedly adult variety" that, along with "the best cards", "makes gift-giving so easy."

Altman Luggage S   23 | 11 | 19 | I
135 Orchard St. (bet. Delancey & Rivington Sts.), F/J/M/Z to Delancey/ Essex Sts., 212-254-7275; www.altmanluggage.com

■ Expect "Lower East Side prices and atmosphere" at this Orchard Street luggage "institution" "jammed" with "every type of bag for every type of traveler", "from Andiamo to Tumi" and more; while "all the major brands are always discounted" "below department-store prices", "don't be afraid to ask for a better deal" – insiders insist "there's room for bargaining."

Amarcord Vintage Fashion ●S   24 | 21 | 23 | M
84 E. Seventh St. (bet. 1st & 2nd Aves.), 6 to Astor Pl., 212-614-7133; www.amarcordvintagefashion.com

■ "Very sophisticated vintage shoppers" visit this East Villager for its "wonderful selection" of "witty clothes" and "unusual bags", "mostly by Italian designers" from the 1960s–80s; everything's "reasonably priced and in mint condition", but "luck's in the cards if the owner is around", as he'll "tell you exactly which part of Europe each item came from."

American Craft Museum Shop S C   23 | 21 | 18 | E
40 W. 53rd St. (bet. 5th & 6th Aves.), E/V to 5th Ave./53rd St., 212-956-3535

■ It's easy to "fill the seams between art and craft" in "every room in the house" with "authentic items made in the USA" at this "very small" West 50s "source" "crowded with" "funky" "handmade jewelry, quilts, glassware, baskets" and "good sketchbooks"; "far beyond the typical posters and plastic doodads in most museum shops", its "charming", "extravagant", even "slightly bizarre", merchandise will "make you jealous of the store buyer."

American Eagle Outfitters ●S   15 | 15 | 15 | M
575 Broadway (Prince St.), N/R to Prince St., 212-941-9785
South Street Seaport, 89 South St., 2/3/4/5/A/C/J/M/Z to Fulton St./ B'way/Nassau, 212-571-5354
Staten Island Mall, 2655 Richmond Ave., Staten Island, 718-494-2885
www.ae.com

◪ If their producers ever cut them off, the "young, cute cast of *Dawson's Creek*" might shop for "weekend duds" at this "Abercrombie-esque" chain "for teens with a smaller budget" and "less attitude"; cop that "rumpled, wrinkled" "classic look" "for frat boys and the girls who love them" at South Street Seaport, on Staten Island and, now, in SoHo.

| M | P | S | C |

American Folk Art Museum ⬤🅂   19 | 19 | 17 | M
2 Lincoln Sq., Columbus Ave. (bet. 65th & 66th Sts.), 1/9 to 66th St., 212-595-9533
45 W. 53rd St. (bet. 5th & 6th Aves.), E/V to 5th Ave./53rd St., 212-265-1040 🅲
www.folkartmuseum.org

▄ "Descend through the new jewel box of a building" designed by Tod Williams Billie Tsien & Associates in Midtown "to the store tucked into a ground-floor corner and shop for bottle-cap bowls", "pine cone, corncob and starfish Santas" and other "fun stuff" "from the heartland"; "they know their merchandise and give you history" as well as an artist's bio with your purchase, but the "uneven" collection has antagonists arguing "you'll do better at a craft fair"; there's another branch in the museum's Upper West Side gallery.

American Kennels ⬤🅂   18 | 14 | 15 | E
798 Lexington Ave. (bet. 61st & 62nd Sts.), 4/5/6/N/R/W to 59th St./Lexington Ave., 212-838-8460

▄ At this East 60s pet shop, you'll find just about "anything you need" for the "pampered" pooch, including "fashionable dog collars" and "cute clothes", and the "knowledgeable staff" can help guide you; however, wallet-watchers warn it's strictly for those with "endless budgets."

American Museum of Natural History 🅂   21 | 20 | 16 | M
79th St. & Central Park West, B/C to 81st St., 212-769-5100; www.amnh.org

■ With a main store and "many theme boutiques" throughout the museum, treasure hunters "don't have to dig too hard" for riches here; the "extensive selection" of "innovative and educational toys" makes it "one of the best places to shop for kids' gifts" – though there's "stuff that's equally fascinating for their parents", such as "nifty" "archaeological models", "nature books, videos", "unique jewelry" and "assorted decorative items"; best of all, the purchases "won't break the bank", "especially with a member's discount."

Amsale   24 | 23 | 20 | VE
625 Madison Ave. (bet. 58th & 59th Sts.), N/R/W to 5th Ave./59th St., 212-583-1700; www.amsale.com

■ Amsale Aberra "fulfills every woman's Grace Kelly–inspired wedding dream" at her "airy", by-appointment-only "Madison Avenue bridal boutique" with "classic", "elegant gowns" that are "feminine without being frothy" and finished with "unique details"; while a bevy of betrothed applauds the "phenomenal service provided by patient, no attitude saleswomen", a few find the staff a "bit haughty"; N.B. as a bonus, the designer also creates enviable eveningwear.

Amy Chan 🅂🅲   – | – | – | M
247 Mulberry St. (bet. Prince & Spring Sts.), 6 to Spring St., 212-965-9907; 212-966-3524

Established at the forefront of the NoLita boom, this designer's groovy shop boasts old-world tiled floors and fresco-like walls, a "cool" backdrop for her "hippie rock star" handbags, functional shapes swathed in super-luxe fabrics like Chinese brocade, suede and paillettes (one of her signature looks), "hip"-ster belts,

vote at zagat.com

accessories and "cute" casual clothing; the "friendly staff" is so welcoming, "you don't even mind that everyone in there is a size 0."

Amy Downs Hats ⇗ C ▽ 24 | 26 | 21 | E
227 E. 14th St. (bet. 2nd & 3rd Aves.), L to 3rd Ave., 212-358-8756
■ "Charming and shapely *chapeaux* to grace any face" "attract passersby" to this "fun shop" "on an otherwise unremarkable section of 14th Street"; the "ne plus ultra of hatters", this "truly original" designer concocts "fabulous", "fanciful", "funky styles that are always fresh" and "never fail to make" shoppers "smile" – ask for the "whimsical", "colorful" Sushi topper and you'll catch on to her "sense of humor" too.

An American Craftsman ●S C 22 | 21 | 18 | E
317 Bleecker St. (Grove St.), 1/9 to Christopher St., 212-727-0841
Rockefeller Ctr., 60 W. 50th St. (bet. Rockefeller Plaza & 6th Ave.), F/V to 47-50th Sts./Rockefeller Ctr., 212-307-7161
790 Seventh Ave. (52nd St.), 1/9 to 50th St., 212-399-2555
www.anamericancraftsman.com
■ Fans of these gallery-style stores say their "handmade" home furnishings – many of them crafted of "wood or ceramic" and ranging from trickling fountains and wind chimes to "decorative boxes", bowls, chopping blocks and "beautiful art glass" – make for "unique gifts", but some critics call them "knickknacks" that are "kitschy" and "common."

Andy's Chee-Pees ●S 15 | 9 | 10 | M
691 Broadway (bet. 3rd & 4th Sts.), 6 to Bleecker St.; F/S/V to B'way/Lafayette, 212-420-5980
■ "An enormous selection of old Levi's, corduroys, [rock] T-shirts and other typical thrift-store fare" – plus "Cinderella-style prom dresses from the 1950s" and '60s – fills this NoHo retailer, itself a veteran of the vintage scene; however, many reviewers rant it's "not so chee-pee", given the "quality of the merchandise" and its "cramped" presentation.

Angela's Vintage Boutique ●S – | – | – | M
330 E. 11th St. (bet. 1st & 2nd Aves.), L to 1st Ave.; 6 to Astor Pl., 212-475-1571
Though barely bigger than a shoebox, this East Village vintage clothier boasts a 20th-century–spanning, well-displayed array of merchandise for madame; the offerings range from fun (1950s ballerina bags) to formal (1920s flapper dresses), with an emphasis on party clothes and sportswear from status-y names like Dior and Geoffrey Beene.

Angelo & Maxies ●S 20 | 19 | 18 | E
233 Park Ave. S. (19th St.), 4/5/6/L/N/Q/R/W to 14th St./Union Sq., 212-220-9200
1285 Sixth Ave. (52nd St.), E/V to 5th Ave./53rd St., 212-459-1222
www.angelo-maxies.com
■ Arguably "the most manly places to buy cigars in the city", these Midtown and Gramercy Park twin chop houses popular with the suspenders-and-power-tie set boast a "quality" selection, a "knowledgeable staff" and a downstairs lounge that can be privately booked; while some grumbling is heard regarding "overpriced" merchandise, satisfied supporters state "what's better than steak" and a stogie?

| M | P | S | C |

Angel Street Thrift Shop ⑤ | 16 | 15 | 16 | I |
118 W. 17th St. (bet. 6th & 7th Aves.), 1/9 to 18th St., 212-229-0546; www.angelthriftshop.org

◪ "You have to dig and go often", but this Chelsea thrift shop yields "great finds", particularly "excellent furniture", "gently worn designer" threads and "fun records", with proceeds benefiting the Lower East Side Service Center; the "setup" in a 19th-century industrial building and "low prices" are heavenly, but the service veers from "friendly" to "unhelpful."

Anik ●⑤ | – | – | – | E |
1122 Madison Ave. (bet. 83rd & 84th Sts.), 4/5/6 to 86th St., 212-249-2417
1355 Third Ave. (bet. 77th & 78th Sts.), 6 to 77th St., 212-861-9840

"For the more conservative trendsetter" as well as "the working woman looking for clothes for work and play", this Upper East Side duo is a destination offering a "great selection of suits by top designers", plus weekend-wear from labels like Juicy Couture and Joie Jeans and evening options "for anything from a cocktail party to a black-tie event"; the original location, set beside a "row of hip stores on Third Avenue", is a bit more fashion-forward than its Madison Avenue counterpart.

Anna Sui ⑤Ⓒ | 22 | 22 | 18 | E |
113 Greene St. (bet. Prince & Spring Sts.), N/R to Prince St., 212-941-8406

■ "Adventurous" SoHo shoppers dig the "fanciful bohemian chic" (think purple walls and red floors) in this "funky little boutique" that takes you "back in time", "blasting '60s music" as a backdrop for the eponymous designer's "girlie, sexy" "hippyish clothing"; prices are "a little high", but the "attentive" service isn't overbearing, so feel free to "sit, shop, browse" or "check out the really fun cosmetics."

Anne Fontaine ⑤ | 27 | 25 | 24 | E |
610 Fifth Ave. (bet. 49th & 50th Sts.), F/V to 47-50th Sts./Rockefeller Ctr., 212-489-1554
93 Greene St. (bet. Prince & Spring Sts.), C/E to Prince St., 212-343-3154
791 Madison Ave. (67th St.), 6 to 68th St., 212-639-9651
www.annefontaine.com

■ Lovers of this Parisienne trio, furnished with European antiques and fabrics, call it the "ultimate store for the classic white blouse" with "a zillion styles" (in black too!), each "so well made it's worth every penny"; ooh-la-las also go to the "big-sizes range for us not-so-skinny people" and "nicest-ever" sales associates who "give honest opinions about the fit"; so, no wonder "you can't resist purchasing three or four at one go."

Anne Klein ⑤ | – | – | – | E |
417 W. Broadway (bet. Prince & Spring Sts.), C/E to Spring St.; N/R to Prince St., 212-965-9499; www.anneklein.com

For its first retail venture, this long-standing design house (now helmed by Charles Nolan) has opened a spacious SoHo store that sports high ceilings and an elegant central staircase, which leads up to the collection's sportier clothes and secondary AK line; down below, it's the eye-catching accessories and shimmery eveningwear that prevail.

vote at zagat.com   **35**

| M | P | S | C |

Annie & Company Needlepoint C   — | — | — | M
1325 Madison Ave. (bet. 93rd & 94th Sts.), 6 to 96th St., 212-360-7266; www.annieandco.com
"Sit and stitch" in one of the "comfy areas" at this large, "lovely, brightly lit" Upper East Side needlepoint newcomer with a "great" French country feeling and "very friendly service"; in addition to "starter projects for the beginner", custom accessories, baby motifs and "intricate painted canvases" from Trubey, this "excellent shop" is "rapidly stocking up on cross-stitch and embroidery supplies in response to customer request."

ANN SACKS TILE & STONE   28 | 27 | 16 | VE
204 E. 58th St. (bet. 2nd & 3rd Aves.), 4/5/6/N/R/W to 59th St./ Lexington Ave., 212-588-1920
5 E. 16th St. (bet. 5th Ave. & Union Sq. W.), 4/5/6/L/N/R/W to 14th St./ Union Sq., 212-463-8400
800-278-8453; www.annsacks.com
▣ "You can do some serious damage to your back account" at these "pricey", "stylish" stores near Union Square and in the East 50s showcasing "absolutely amazing tile", including versions in copper or mosaic glass, and "cool", "up-to-the-moment" fixtures like faucets and sinks; still, a few naysayers throw cold water on things by commenting that the wares are "stunning but so is the attitude."

ANN TAYLOR ◐ S C   20 | 20 | 18 | M
645 Madison Ave. (60th St.), N/R/W to 5th Ave./59th St., 212-832-9114; 800-342-5266; www.anntaylor.com
For additional locations, see Top Chain Stores index
■ "The mother ship" for NYC's crew of "businesswomen" carries a cargo of "day-to-night frocks" with "a look that's sharp but not edgy"; "conservative", "classic", "clean" and "friendly", the city's innumerable outlets offer "cuts to fit a real woman's body", whether she's petite or size 16, and though the goods might be too "bland" for "hanging out on an East Village stoop", if you're in the job market, the clearance rack "doesn't disappoint" for a "great bargain" on the "perfect corporate interview suit."

ANN TAYLOR LOFT ◐ S C   18 | 19 | 17 | M
150 E. 42nd St. (Lexington Ave.), 4/5/6/7/S to 42nd St./Grand Central, 212-883-8766; www.anntaylor.com
For additional locations, see Top Chain Stores index
■ Go "on the fly", "check out the sales" at this "no-frills" but "appealing" Ann Taylor alternative "catering to the 30s crowd"; you'll "walk out with money in your pocket" and a bagful of "really cute", "good-quality, basic things that will not go out of style"; it's "more trendy, more casual and a better value" than its namesake, so there are "massive lines at lunch hour."

ANTHROPOLOGIE   21 | 24 | 16 | E
85 Fifth Ave. (16th St.), 4/5/6/L/N/Q/R/W to 14th St./Union Sq., 212-627-5885 ◐ S
375 W. Broadway (bet. Broome & Spring Sts.), C/E to Spring St., 212-343-7070
www.anthropologie.com
▣ "Bohemians at heart" hanker after the "fantasy-driven designs" at these Flatiron and SoHo national chain links with their "shabby chic", "flea-market feel"; the "fab merch for a fab crowd" features "street-meets-runway fashions", "whimsical" jewelry and

| M | P | S | C |

"home furnishings with European flair and funk" – all of it carrying irritatingly "eye-popping price tags"; still, "from the delicate lingerie to the wrought-iron table lamps", the scene "makes you feel like a fairy princess", so it's impossible to "walk out empty-handed."

Antiquarium
| – | – | – | VE |

948 Madison Ave. (bet. 74th & 75th Sts.), 6 to 77th St., 212-734-9776
Specializing in original Greco-Roman, Egyptian and Near Eastern art and antiquities, this Upper East Side boutique seems "a gallery more than a store"; each piece is delivered with a certificate of authenticity and origin, and while the number of zeroes in an item's price roughly equals the number of zeroes in its date, "where else can you find a 5th-century BC ring?"

Anya Hindmarch C
| 25 | 21 | 18 | E |

29 E. 60th St. (bet. Madison & Park Aves.), N/R/W to 5th Ave./59th St., 212-750-3974
115 Greene St. (bet. Prince & Spring Sts.), N/R to Prince St., 212-343-8147 S
www.anyahindmarch.com

■ You can always spot this British designer's "adorable" purses – just "look for the telltale little bow", her dime-size logo; the "sweet shops" in SoHo and on the Upper East Side also stock luggage and small leather goods that are "gorgeous in a sleek, cool sort of way", a newly introduced line of "whimsical shoes", plus "clever accessories", all at "heart-stopping prices"; fans with a healthy sense of self also "love the 'be-a-bag' service" that puts "your picture on" your tote.

APARTMENT, THE S C
| 20 | 27 | 17 | E |

101 Crosby St. (Prince St.), N/R to Prince St., 212-219-3066; www.theapt.com

■ Attention, "trendy housewares shoppers", this "hip", "well-edited" SoHo store serves up "funky", albeit pricey, European furniture by Edra and Michael Sodeau with an "interactive" twist – grab a bite in the "kitchen cafe" while browsing for tabletop items or shop for "cool" bathroom accessories in the fully decked-out restroom downstairs.

Apartment 48 S C
| ▽ 26 | 28 | 24 | M |

48 W. 17th St. (bet. 5th & 6th Aves.), 1/2/3/9/F/L/V to 14th St./6th Ave., 212-807-1391

■ "Warm and inviting" Flatiron home-furnishings "gem" where "items are displayed" as if they're in an actual apartment (albeit the seven-room one "you wish you had"); "every piece of furniture is for sale", along with vases, glassware and a "great assortment" of both contemporary and classic accessories for every space in the house, including must-haves for that mudroom in the country.

A.P.C. S C
| 20 | 19 | 15 | E |

131 Mercer St. (bet. Prince & Spring Sts.), N/R to Prince St., 212-966-9685; www.apc.fr

◪ "Definitely a stop" worth making, this airy SoHo loft with rough-hewn wood-plank floorboards and "surprisingly friendly" service houses the "minimalist" French line of men's and women's "just yummy" crisp shirts, tees, low-rise jeans, suits and sweaters, providing "staples for any New Yorker"; while these "great basics look simple", they're "cut to perfection" and "very well made"; those less spellbound find the "fit limited" and the staff "snippy."

vote at zagat.com

| | | | M | P | S | C |

A Pea in the Pod S C   22 | 21 | 20 | E
860 Madison Ave. (70th St.), 6 to 68th St., 212-988-8039; 877-273-2763; www.apeainthepod.com
◪ "You can still feel cool while pregnant" at this Madison Avenue flagship of the national chain, a "fantastic one-stop shopping source for work-to-play wardrobes" where "it's all about maternity Seven jeans", "very current styles" from such designers as Anna Sui, Three Dots and Elie Tahari" for label-conscious moms-to-be and "fun, fashionable" store-brand threads; while there's "not a grosgrain bow to be seen", wallet-watchers whine that it's "a little pricey for about four months of wear."

Apple Store SoHo ◗ S   – | – | – | E
103 Prince St. (Greene St.), N/R to Prince St.; C/E to Spring St., 212-226-3126; 800-692-7753; www.apple.com
In a former SoHo post office, this visually arresting Macintosh boutique offers every configuration of Apple products, from computers to operating systems; from the first floor's displays of software and hardware (geared toward gaming, video editing or any purpose in between), ascend the glass staircase to the theater offering daily classes for beginners and pros, the kiddie corner and the Genius Bar, where the staff pours out on-the-spot tech support.

April Cornell ◗ S   21 | 22 | 20 | M
487 Columbus Ave. (bet. 83rd & 84th Sts.), B/C to 81st St., 212-799-4342; www.aprilcornell.com
◪ "Take a step back to the Victorian era" at this Upper Westsider abloom with "sweet and romantic" attire, "darling baby clothes", "gorgeous linens" and gifts galore; while devotees delight in the "floral dresses" and "matching mother-daughter" outfits, urbanites call the "country charm" "a little corny" – but even they confirm the "high quality" of the goods.

Arche S C   21 | 19 | 19 | E
10 Astor Pl. (bet. B'way & Lafayette St.), 6 to Astor Pl.; N/R to 8th St., 212-529-4808
995 Madison Ave. (77th St.), 6 to 77th St., 212-439-0700
1045 Third Ave. (bet. 61st & 62nd Sts.), F to Lexington Ave./63rd St.; 4/5/6/N/R/W to 59th St./Lexington Ave., 212-838-1933
128 W. 57th St. (bet. 6th & 7th Aves.), N/R/Q/W to 57th St., 212-262-5488
123 Wooster St. (Prince St.), N/R to Prince St., 646-613-8700
www.arche-shoes.com
◪ "Arty, hippie", "all-purpose" shoes with "primarily nubuck uppers" in "wild colors for all seasons" and "ultra-comfy", "squishy soles" are "served up with French attitude" and a "Cartier price tag" at this Manhattan outfit; admirers declare they're a "delight to walk in" and especially "great for new moms and baby boomers looking for something different", but detractors denounce the "slightly bizarre" designs, concluding "I'd rather go barefoot."

Armani Casa S   22 | 26 | 20 | VE
97 Greene St. (bet. Prince & Spring Sts.), N/R to Prince St., 212-334-1271; www.armanicasa.com
■ This "architecturally cool" and "calming" "minimalist slice of heaven" in SoHo showcases "beautiful", "highbrow home fashions" drawn from "the master's aesthetic" and "translated into wood, ceramic and glass"; fashionistas feel you "can't go wrong"

38   subscribe to zagat.com

| M | P | S | C |

with the signature subdued colors and "clean" lines, evidenced in shagreen side tables and pillows made of luscious leathers; of course, these "creature comforts" come at couture-like prices.

Arnold Tobacco Shop
▽ 24 | 20 | 24 | E

323 Madison Ave. (bet. 42nd & 43rd Sts.), 4/5/6/7/S to 42nd St./Grand Central, 212-697-1477; www.arnoldstobacco.com

■ The "service comes with a smoke and a smile" at this "genteel" 92-year-old emporium with a walk-in humidor that draws kudos for its "knowledgeable staff" and the "best selection" of "top-of-the-line" cigars and accessories, pipes and tobaccos; "convenient" to Grand Central Station, it "makes Father's Day shopping a breeze."

Art and Tapisserie S
– | – | – | E

1242 Madison Ave. (bet. 89th & 90th Sts.), 4/5/6 to 86th St., 212-722-3222

It may be "small", but this Madison Avenue infants' and children's wonderland crams in quite an array of "unique gifts and toys", from whimsical costumes to special nursery items; your child's name can live on in infamy, as many of the items, including jewelry and furniture, can be personalized, plus they also carry chess sets – in case you're raising the next Bobby Fisher.

Artbag C
– | – | – | VE

1130 Madison Ave. (84th St.), 4/5/6 to 86th St., 212-744-2720; www.artbag.com

Nestled in an East 80s brownstone, this family-run shop features an eponymous collection of quilted, woven and one-of-a-kind bags and belts; while customers covet these creations, service also takes center stage: the European-trained craftsmen can copy a favorite piece, custom-design a couture number in an array of leathers and exotic skins and repair, restitch or remodel almost anything.

Artemide C
25 | 23 | 14 | VE

46 Greene St. (bet. Broome & Grand Sts.), A/C/E to Canal St., 212-925-1588; www.artemide.com

◪ "If you delight in contemporary lighting", this SoHo showroom of the Italian-based company will "inspire" you with its "gorgeous", "high-tech" offerings, including iconic "modern classics" such as Richard Sapper's Tizio desk lamp; opponents call it "overpriced" and service can be a bit "snooty", but "if you're concerned about quality" and "great design", "this store will satisfy your cravings."

Arthur Brown & Brothers C
22 | 15 | 18 | M

2 W. 46th St. (bet. 5th & 6th Aves.), 7 to 5th Ave.; B/D/F/V to 42nd St., 212-575-5555; 800-772-7367; www.artbrown.com

■ "Just walking in makes me feel creative" profess pals of this pen shop in Midtown that's a "reliable" "resource for all things" related to writing instruments (both new and antique); the staff is "helpful and knowledgeable", as befits a 75-year-old establishment, and it's "very good for picture framing as well."

ARTISTIC TILE
28 | 25 | 20 | VE

150 E. 58th St. (bet. Lexington & 3rd Aves.), 4/5/6/N/R/W to 59th St./Lexington Ave., 212-838-3222
79 Fifth Ave. (bet. 15th & 16th Sts.), 4/5/6/L/N/Q/R/W to 14th St./Union Sq., 212-727-9331
800-260-8646; www.artistictile.com

■ An "incredible selection" of "truly artistic tiles" in a variety of "quality" materials, from metal and marble to glass, pebbles and

vote at zagat.com   39

even leather, along with bathroom fixtures like faucets and sinks, are showcased at these East 50s and Flatiron stores; while surveyors are split over service ("very informed" vs. "spotty"), they agree that prices are "high."

Art of Shaving   25 | 25 | 25 | E
141 E. 62nd St. (bet. Lexington & 3rd Aves.), F to Lexington Ave./ 63rd St., 212-317-8436
373 Madison Ave. (bet. 45th & 46th Sts.), 4/5/6/7/S to 42nd St./ Grand Central, 212-986-2905
www.theartofshaving.com

■ "Ladies, spoil your men" at this "wonderful source" for grooming products, "hard-to-find items" that they'll "love even if they won't admit it" and "the best shave in town"; an "attentive and friendly" staff runs this duo of "upscale", "beautiful stores" that "take you back in time", except for the very contemporary "steep prices"; P.S. consider a "gift certificate" for the guy "who has everything or for the groomsmen at your wedding."

ASCOT CHANG   27 | 25 | 26 | VE
7 W. 57th St. (bet. 5th & 6th Aves.), F to 57th St.; N/R/W to 59th St./ 5th Ave., 212-759-3333; 800-486-9966; www.ascotchang.com

■ "If you find a man who wears Ascot Chang, marry him" advise the enamored of this beige-walled, wood-paneled shirt maker on 57th Street; you'll be "pampered like a prince" as, from "thousands of fabric choices", you "pick the pattern, collar and cuff and let them craft" "the best [garment] you will find in the world" (there are "equally fantastic off-the-rack" models too); of course, "with exclusivity comes a hefty" tab, but "when you can't get to Hong Kong", this is "the cat's meow in bespoke."

A Second Chance Designer Resale   17 | 12 | 15 | M
1109 Lexington Ave., 2nd fl. (bet. 77th & 78th Sts.), 6 to 77th St., 212-744-6041

◪ "If you hit it right, you can score still-respectable designer or designer-ish clothes, shoes and bags" say supporters of this East 70s crammed-to-the-gills consignment store; but second-story surroundings that are "kind of scruffy" and prices that are "kind of expensive" (for "ordinary" pieces) stop skeptics from coming back for seconds.

AsiaStore in the Asia Society and Museum S   24 | 21 | 19 | E
725 Park Ave. (70th St.), 6 to 68th St., 212-288-6400; www.asiasociety.org

◪ "The best place to find unique things from Central Asia" is this "recently renovated" and "enlarged" Park Avenue shop boasting a "lovely presentation" of merchandise that is "custom-made or usually found only in the East", plus "books that no one else has", many of which are set on "the best half-price table in the business"; nevertheless, "the selection and prices are not as great as before the redo", and intrepid shoppers would rather "fly to Thailand and buy it themselves for the cost of some items."

ASPREY   28 | 26 | 24 | VE
725 Fifth Ave. (bet. 56th & 57th Sts.), E/V to 5th Ave./53rd St.; S to 57th St., 212-688-1811; www.asprey.com

■ "A taste of upper-class England can be had strolling" through this "elegant, precious" Midtown staple that's held in the "highest regard" by most who shop here; browsing among the "exquisite" jewels and the "finest silver and leather goods" is made easy by the "beautiful" displays as well as by the "proper British service" dispensing the "royal treatment" ("if they don't carry it, they'll custom-order it"); "hefty prices" prevail, but it's rather nice "not having to cross the pond to pick up a bauble or two."

Assets London ●🄲   23 | 21 | 19 | E
464 Columbus Ave. (bet. 82nd & 83rd Sts.), B/C to 81st St., 212-874-8253 🅂
152 Franklin St. (bet. Hudson & Varick Sts.), 1/9 to Franklin St., 212-219-8777

☑ "Fun and funky" pair that's "a must" for women desiring a wide selection of "stylish"-to-"trendy" clothing and accessories; though some feel the Zen-ish "TriBeCa branch has more interesting stock", the pink-and-lilac "Upper West Side shop has better sales"; they're worth waiting for, lest the "exorbitant prices" lead you to liquidate your own assets.

A. Testoni 🅂   – | – | – | E
665 Fifth Ave. (bet. 52nd & 53rd Sts.), E/V to 5th Ave./53rd St., 212-223-0909; www.testoniusa.com

A Fifth Avenue standby, this swanky shop, run by a 74-year-old Bologna-based, family-owned company, caters to meticulous gents (i.e. Ronald Reagan, Mikhail Gorbachev and Jean-Paul Belmondo) and ladies seeking handmade luxury shoes, handbags and luggage steeped in an old-world leather-making tradition; well-heeled upscale couples choose from a wide collection including classic loafers, pretty pumps, strappy sandals, half-brogues and wing tips with flair.

Athlete's Foot ●🅂   17 | 14 | 13 | M
46 W. 34th St. (B'way), B/D/F/N/Q/R/V/W to 34th St./Herald Sq., 212-629-8200; 888-801-9157; www.theathletesfoot.com
Additional locations throughout the NY area

☑ Mega-chain that's "a treasure trove of inexpensive sneakers, but only if you are lucky in timing your visit" – if so, you'll find "a decent selection" of "all the major sports brands" alongside "your basic activewear" and you'll be "in and out in no time"; flip a coin and it's a "very disorganized" "disaster" of "middle-of-the-road" merchandise with "no personality" and a "staff that works at the speed of molasses."

At the Gryphon ●🅂🄲   ∇ 24 | 12 | 24 | M
233 W. 72nd St. (bet. B'way & West End Ave.), 1/2/3/9 to 72nd St., 212-874-1588

■ "Be sure to check out the window display, as there is always a theme" at this "one-of-a-kind" Upper West Side music store where you won't find just "any ol' recording"; the classical, jazz and soundtrack LPs, CDs and books are "rare", so – "depending on the luck of the draw" and the help of the "knowledgeable" staff – you may stumble upon a "long-lost friend" among the stacks.

Au Chat Botte 🄲   27 | 25 | 19 | VE
1192 Madison Ave. (bet. 87th & 88th Sts.), 4/5/6 to 86th St., 212-722-6474

■ "Ooh-la-la" fawn fans of this Upper East Side infants' shop where "you pay for the fabulous" "French fashions for babies", "precious" outfits that mirror the latest in mom-size Parisian styles; the "great selection" of "beautiful classics includes European shoes", tot accessories, bedding and nursery furniture; but a few faultfinders

vote at zagat.com

feel that it's only worth a visit "if you can get past the attitude wafting from the salespeople."

A-Uno – | – | – | E
198 Spring St. (bet. Sullivan & Thompson Sts.), C/E to Spring St., 212-343-2040
123 W. Broadway (Duane St.), 1/2/3/9/A/C/E to Chambers St., 212-227-6233
Advocates attest this women's boutique is A-one indeed, given its smartly edited selection of "interesting clothing for grown-ups" from such labels as Marithé + François Girbaud, Elm Design Team and the intriguing Pier Antonio Gaspari, whose sweaters look chic either right-side-up or upside-down; the decor at both its TriBeCa and SoHo locations may seem stark, but the "unparalleled service" warms things up.

auto S C – | – | – | E
805 Washington St. (bet. Gansevoort & Horatio Sts.), A/C/E/L to 14th St./8th Ave., 212-229-2292; www.thisisauto.com
This tiny, "minimalist" space in the Meatpacking District displays a decidedly eclectic assortment of gifts like sweater-clad rocks, porcelain pigs, retro trays and Christian Tortu candles, along with colorful bed linens; devotees defend the seemingly "random" selection as being "paired down to what you now find you cannot live without" after shopping here.

Aveda Environmental Lifestyle Store 24 | 22 | 21 | E
140 Fifth Ave. (19th St.), 4/5/6/L/N/Q/R/W to 14th St./Union Sq., 212-645-4797 ● S
509 Madison Ave. (bet. 52nd & 53rd Sts.), E/V to 5th Ave./53rd St., 212-832-2416
1122 Third Ave. (bet. 65th & 66th Sts.), 6 to 68th St.,, 212-744-3113
866-823-1425; www.aveda.com
■ You "come away feeling refreshed from shopping" at this "environmentally conscious" beauty pioneer offering a vast array of "wonderful-smelling natural products" that include "can't-live-without-them" cosmetics, aromatherapy oils, hair and skincare lines, as well as custom-blended versions; "just walking in here takes the stress meter down, although paying for items takes it back up a bit"; N.B. appointments can also be made for a variety of spa services, including facials, waxing and massage at another division of the company, Aveda Salons and Spas.

Avirex S C ▽ 25 | 22 | 18 | M
652 Broadway (bet. Bleecker & Bond Sts.), 6 to Bleecker St., 212-254-3030; www.avirex.com
◪ "Wow! It's worth going just to see the store" exclaim aviation aficionados of this NoHo newcomer known for its reproduction WWII leather bomber jackets, pilots' scarves and collectibles; it's also a source for "quality" men's and women's sportswear, including jeans, T-shirts and dancewear, all at "great prices."

Avon Salon and Spa ● S 22 | 24 | 24 | M
Trump Tower, 725 Fifth Ave. (57th St.), 4/5/6/F/N/R/W to 59th St./Lexington Ave., 212-755-2866; www.avoncompany.com
■ "No more ding-dongs for me because now you can get your Skin-So-Soft in a store" is what surveyors say about the Fifth Avenue retail shop beneath the spa offshoot of this 1939 cosmetics pioneer; the company's reasonably priced makeup and skincare and body treatments are all showcased here – from the best-

M | P | S | C

selling Pack Your Bags depuffing eye gel to Brad Johns hair potions; N.B. appointments can also be made for a variety of spa services, particularly with the popular eyebrow-grooming gurus.

AVVENTURA 🅢🅒 28 | 23 | 21 | VE
463 Amsterdam Ave. (bet. 82nd & 83rd Sts.), C/E to 81st St.; 1/9 to 79th St., 212-769-2510; 888-640-9177; www.forthatspecialgift.com

■ The "best place to shop for art glass and ceramics" assert aesthetes about this "must-see" Upper Westsider with "stunning windows" and three large museum-like rooms filled with "one-of-a-kind", "beautiful handmade items" like Venini vases, Venetian chandeliers and Deruta pottery that make for "memorable gifts"; while it can be "annoying that it's not open on Saturdays", the fact that they "gift-wrap and ship anywhere" in the U.S. helps offset the inconvenience.

A.W. Kaufman 22 | 7 | 18 | M
73 Orchard St. (bet. Broome & Grand Sts.), F/J/M/Z to Delancey/Essex Sts., 212-226-1629

■ "Worth the pilgrimage" and the "Lower East Side atmosphere" laud lingerie lovers who uncover "great prices on expensive" bras and panties from the "finest-quality brands" like Chantelle, La Perla, Hanro and Joelle at this "jam-packed" 79-year-old, family-run standby; the "sales staff must know every piece they carry", since there's "no hands-on" browsing allowed and no "trying on" either – unless you consider the storage area a dressing room.

A/X Armani Exchange 🌑🅢 18 | 19 | 16 | E
568 Broadway (Prince St.), N/R to Prince St., 212-431-6000
645 Fifth Ave. (51st St.), E/V to 5th Ave. & 53rd St., 212-980-3037
www.armaniexchange.com

☑ "Sleek basics" and "fashionable jeans" satisfy the "slim, trendy" "club kids" who "pack" these "hip" SoHo and Midtown stores, finding logo-laden "clothes with attitude" at "more reasonable prices" than the designer's Emporio and Collezioni lines (even so, sticker-shocked savants say "wait for the sales"); but while devotees deem it perfect for "Armani wanna-bes", others axe it as a "glorified Gap."

Baby Bird 🌑🅢🅒 - | - | - | E
428 Seventh Ave. (bet. 14th & 15th Sts.), Brooklyn, F to 7th Ave., 718-788-4506

Nestled next to Bird, a fave of stylin' Park Slopers, this hip little boutique offers infants' and tots' togs that are just as snazzy as mom's; staples like Petit Bateau T-shirts layer wonderfully well with Levi's, and for future artists and rock stars, there are limelight-worthy onesies in colorful prints and whimsical bibs, plus novelty knockouts from pet lines like Electric Polka Dot and Lucky Wang; P.S. there are toys to entertain little ones while mother shops.

BabyGap 🌑🅢🅒 22 | 19 | 15 | M
60 W. 34th St. (B'way), B/D/F/N/R/Q/W to 34th St./Herald Sq., 212-760-1268; www.gap.com
For additional locations, see Top Chain Stores index

■ "A godsend for all those baby showers" (and it's "easy to exchange") and "cute, practical" infants clothes, this ubiquitous chain is such a "perennial favorite" fans can't imagine "where we would be today without it"; this is "clothing that can last and be handed down", so "stock up on the basics" and "check back

vote at zagat.com 43

M | P | S | C

often" – "things go on sale frequently"; but the jaded jab "if you want your child to literally wear what every other New York City child is wearing, shop here."

BACCARAT C   28 | 28 | 24 | VE
625 Madison Ave. (59th St.), N/R/W to 5th Ave./59th St., 212-826-4100
■ This "classic", 173-year-old French manufacturer of "gorgeous" fine crystal "has branched out into colors and diversified their merchandise", so their "superb" stemware, decanters, rings and other "lovely things" continue to "wow" the crowds; it's also clear that the "beautiful" Upper East Side venue with a new second-floor showroom is "as good as the one in Paris – without the jet lag."

Bag House, The S C   22 | 17 | 17 | M
797 Broadway (bet. 10th & 11th Sts.), N/R to 8th St.; 6 to Astor Pl., 212-260-0940
■ A "cornucopia of possibilities" awaits at this Village "one-stop shop" specializing in luggage and leather goods; customers get carried away over the "extensive" selection of school bags, travel bags and just everyday bags", including "backpacks galore", at "prices that seem competitive"; but it's not an open-and-shut case for all – a handful feel they "can be beat with a little legwork."

Bagutta S C   – | – | – | VE
402 W. Broadway (bet. Broome & Spring Sts.), C/E to Spring St., 212-925-5216
Downtown divas and dudes find happiness at this luxurious two-floor SoHo boutique that's "perfect if you have lots of money" to spend; label-conscious customers thumb through the well-edited, "super" collection, snapping up European designer wear from bold-faced names like Alexander McQueen and Jean Paul Gaultier; the men's clothing, also a study in sartorial splendor, is housed upstairs; but cynics less swayed by its charms toss it off as "trendoid."

Baker ● S   – | – | – | E
129-133 Hudson St. (Beach St.), 1/9 to Franklin St., 212-343-2956; www.bakerfurniture.com
After over 100 years of producing furniture for the American consumer, this "tried-and-true" Midwestern-based manufacturer opened a new 12,000-sq.-ft., two-story store in TriBeCa designed by Bill Sofield; his sophisticated collection along with that of California-based interior decorator Barbara Barry is on the first floor, while more traditional designs dominate the second.

Ballantyne Cashmere C   – | – | – | E
965 Madison Ave. (bet. 75th & 76th Sts.), 6 to 77th St., 212-988-5252
It's all cashmere all the time at this East 70s boutique, which for years has been offering men and women the plush two-ply stuff, not just in the usual sweater suspects, but in pants, hats and gloves; it now exclusively carries the venerable Scottish label, and once you finger the merchandise, it might be hard to escape without a twinset or two (one in a classic intarsia, another in the firm's new cooler hues or stripes).

Bally S C   25 | 23 | 20 | E
628 Madison Ave. (59th St.), N/R/W to 5th Ave./59th St., 212-751-9082; www.bally.com
◪ "Gotta love the Swiss" for the "buttery-soft leather" in the "fine handbags, belts and shoes" at this streamlined East 50s boutique;

subscribe to zagat.com

| M | P | S | C |

"excellent quality", "comfort and luxury" combined is the "novel concept" ballyhooed by "serious shoppers", but despite efforts to "update the image", hipper heels huff that the merchandise is "still too conservative."

BANANA REPUBLIC ●S   20 | 20 | 16 | M
626 Fifth Ave. (bet. 50th & 51st Sts.), E/V to 5th Ave./53rd St., 212-974-2350; 888-277-8953; www.bananarepublic.com
For additional locations, see Top Chain Stores index

◪ Service "can barely keep up" with the "yuppie" "hordes" going bananas over "Garanimals" for grown-ups at the "ubiquitous" "Starbucks of retail"; the "reliable classics" can be a bit costly, but "keen-eyed bargain hunters" stalk the "awesome" sale racks "in the back" of the "well laid-out" stores; fashionistas who find the "four-color repertoire" "not as ripe" as it once was warn "standing next to someone on the train who's wearing your exact same outfit" might make you wanna peel off the "cookie-cutter" clothes.

Banana Republic Men's ●S   20 | 20 | 16 | M
114 Fifth Ave. (17th St.), 4/5/6/L/N/Q/R/W to 14th St./Union Sq., 212-366-4691
528 Broadway (Spring St.), N/R to Prince St., 212-334-3034
888-277-8953; www.bananarepublic.com

◪ If he's a "professional on a budget", these chain "staples" in the Flatiron and SoHo might be your "husband's favorite stores"; the "helpful, friendly" clerks guide him through the "ever-changing selection of casual shirts, pants, shorts", "stylish shoes" and accessories, and if he "waits for sales, it's almost like getting free clothes"; though they publicly call the threads "bland", even iconoclasts whisper "I wish the Banana Republic clone look would go out of fashion so I could wear it again."

B&B Italia   26 | 25 | 18 | VE
150 E. 58th St. (bet. Lexington & 3rd Aves.), 4/5/6/N/R/W to 59th St./ Lexington Ave., 212-758-4046; 800-872-1697; www.bebitalia.it

■ For "modern furniture" fanatics, this gleaming, white two-story space by Antonio Citterio in the East 50s is the apotheosis of "cool", "clean" Italian design; contemporary seating by Jeffrey Bernett, pieces from Gaetano Pesce and the "elegant" accessories and linens upstairs are "drool"-worthy, but far from "minimal" prices leave some frugal fans out in the cold.

B&H PHOTO-VIDEO PRO AUDIO S   29 | 20 | 19 | M
420 Ninth Ave. (bet. 33rd & 34th Sts.), A/C/E to 34th St./Penn Station, 212-444-6600; 800-947-9950; www.bhphotovideo.com

■ This shutterbug's "Wonkaland", with purchases in "little baskets whizzing on overhead tracks", spans a Garment District block; "New York's photographic supermarket" "runs like a well-oiled machine" in which the "vast selection" of new and used equipment and film may be "overwhelming", but the "surly yet efficient staff" "can help anyone from a newbie homeboy to a grizzled war photographer find what they need at a reasonable price"; just "don't go Friday night or Saturday", when it's closed for Shabbat.

B&J Fabrics   27 | 19 | 20 | E
263 W. 40th St. (bet. 7th & 8th Aves.), 1/2/3/7/9/A/C/E/N/Q/R/S/W to 42nd St./Times Sq., 212-354-8150

■ "Anything your heart desires is here" at this textile "lover's dream" in the Garment Center, "along with a very knowledgeable

vote at zagat.com

staff to help"; "don't judge when you walk in the door" – "it's well worth" a stop just to "poke around" one of the "best selections of fine European fabrics", including "current fashions" you may "recognize from designer" collections, "at reasonable prices"; N.B. the store was slated to move at press time.

BANG & OLUFSEN S | 26 | 26 | 22 | VE
927 Broadway (bet. 21st & 22nd Sts.), N/R to 23rd St., 212-388-9792
330 Columbus Ave. (bet. 75th & 76th Sts.), 1/2/3/9 to 79th St., 212-501-0926
952 Madison Ave. (75th St.), 6 to 77th St., 212-879-6161
www.bang-olufsen.com
■ "Is it art, or is it a stereo?" – the "friendly" staff at this "museum of audio" might say it's both; the "avant-garde" Danish company has been creating "sleek and functional" home entertainment products for "design-minded" "well-to-do's" for over 70 years, and if the "gorgeous" "gadgets" exceed your budget, there's always the "cool, cool" pleasure of "walking in just to dream."

Barami Studio | 16 | 16 | 15 | M
136 E. 57th St. (Lexington Ave.), 4/5/6/N/R/W to 59th St./Lexington Ave., 212-980-9333
535 Fifth Ave. (bet. 44th & 45th Sts.), 4/5/6/7/S to 42nd St./Grand Central, 212-949-1000
375 Lexington Ave. (41st St.), 4/5/6/7/S to 42nd St./Grand Central, 212-682-2550
1404 Second Ave. (73rd St.), 6 to 77th St., 212-988-3470
485 Seventh Ave. (36th St.), 1/2/3/9 to 34th St/Penn Station, 212-967-2990
www.barami.com
■ "Upcoming professionals" purchase career clothes at these all-around-town women's apparel shops; but while advocates applaud their "feminine and refined", "perfect-fit suits" as "worth it for the money", cons complain the goods "used to be nicer"; service, too, can range from "attentive" to "practically on top of you."

Barbara Bui S C | 26 | 24 | 20 | VE
115-117 Wooster St. (bet. Prince & Spring Sts.), N/R to Prince St., 212-625-1938; www.barbarabui.com
■ "Unusual" window displays "entice" you into the "hushed galleries" of this SoHo shop, where "East meets West" in "Zen-like designs" that appeal to women who want "wearable" yet "sophisticated, cutting-edge" clothing, especially in pants ("the best"); just expect to pay dearly for the "details and quality" when the "helpful salespeople" ring up the bill.

Barbara Feinman Millinery S C | ▽ 23 | 20 | 22 | M
66 E. 7th St. (bet. 1st & 2nd Aves.), F/V to 2nd Ave., 212-358-7092; www.feinmanhats.com
■ Fans flip their lids for "toppers in all shapes and sizes" with glamorous names like Bogie, Bacall and Ingrid at this "frilly and flowery", modern yet retro East Village atelier; "wonderful" Barbara "remembers her customers" and "knows her hats", in fact, she'll "pick out the most unlikely thing and it will look good on you", plus "most can be customized"; P.S. it's also "good for costume jewelry."

Barclay-Rex | 23 | 21 | 22 | E
75 Broad St. (bet. Marketfield & S. William Sts.), 4/5 to Bowling Green, 212-962-3355
70 E. 42nd St. (Vanderbilt Ave.), 4/5/6/7/S to 42nd St./Grand Central, 212-692-9680

M | P | S | C

(continued)
Barclay-Rex
570 Lexington Ave. (bet. 50th & 51st Sts.), 6 to 51st. St., 212-888-1015

■ "They know their stuff" at this trio of stogie stalwarts (established in 1910) where they also "seem to stock everything" in the way of accessories; although the "excellent variety" of combustibles tends to be "a bit pricey", "everyone is nice and friendly", which makes for "a great place to stop by and have a smoke."

Bardith ♯ — | — | — | VE
31 E. 72nd St. (Madison Ave.), 6 to 68th St., 212-737-8660
901 Madison Ave. (bet. 72nd & 73rd Sts.), 6 to 68th St., 212-737-3775

Since 1965, this Madison Avenue purveyor of posh 18th- and 19th-century English porcelain and pottery has offered complete sets of formal china service by all the legendary companies, as well as beautiful Spanish majolica; around the corner, its sibling sells Dutch delft and English papier-mâché trays and glassware.

Bark **S C** — | — | — | E
369 Atlantic Ave. (bet. Bond & Hoyt Sts.), Brooklyn, A/C/G to Hoyt/Schermerhorn Sts., 718-625-8997

Sharing the same space and address as the hip Boerum Hill store Breukelen is this home-furnishings shop selling handblown crystal from Mexico and Scandinavia, along with sumptuous Italian sheets and silk comforters.

Barking Zoo ●S ∇ 24 | 22 | 25 | M
172 Ninth Ave. (bet. 20th & 21st Sts.), E to 23rd St., 212-255-0658

■ "Stylish" canines crave the "cute accessories" (yes, "even Burberry") on offer at this Chelsea pet boutique where a "great variety of toys" and other "nice merchandise" also get tails wagging; humans "love" the "extremely helpful staff" and the fact that "they deliver" to the neighborhood; it also offers zoo-tably fashionable hard-to-find premium cat and dog foods.

Barkley **S C** ∇ 24 | 24 | 21 | E
215 E. 76th St. (bet. 2nd & 3rd Aves.), 6 to 77th St., 212-734-9373; 866-522-7553; www.barkleydog.com

■ This "proverbial pooch Disneyland" on the Upper East Side provides the "hottest items for Fido", including the "perfect ostrich leather collar with sterling-silver bone"-shaped tags and an "excellent assortment of sweaters and leashes"; it's "great" for gifts for cat- and "dog-loving friends", though a few are petulant about the "expensive" offerings.

Barneys Co-op 22 | 19 | 15 | E
236 W. 18th St. (bet. 7th & 8th Aves.), 1/9 to 18th St., 212-593-7800
116 Wooster St. (bet. Prince & Spring Sts.), C/E to Spring St.; N/R to Prince St., 212-965-9964 **S C**

☑ "Wild and unpredictable", this "decadent emporium of fun" for "trendier-than-thou shoppers" in the heart of SoHo and Chelsea is familiar to fans of its floors in parent Barneys; its airy, "well laid-out" interior is a clean backdrop for "a hodgepodge of retro-futuristic designs" from the likes of Helmut Lang, Prada Sport and Marc by Marc Jacobs, arrayed alongside a "scoopful of small international labels", shoes and the "best cosmetics" and jeans; just remember, "Downtown doesn't mean downscale, so don't expect a bargain" –

vote at zagat.com

or co-operation from salespeople who seem "more interested in themselves" than you.

BARNEYS NEW YORK ●S   26 | 25 | 19 | VE
660 Madison Ave. (61st St.), N/R/W to 5th Ave., 212-826-8900; 888-822-7639; www.barneys.com
◪ A "fantasyland for the well-heeled", this "free-flowing" East 60s department store "exerts a gravitational pull" on "chic urbanites" with its "premier men's shop" ("grab that wild Commes Des Garçons shirt while heading for an Armani suit"), "ultra-hip-to-traditional" designer duds for dames, "the best jeans in NYC" ("free" hemming too), "unique [Goyard] handbags", "great jewelry", "fabulous footwear" ("from Blahnik to their own brand") and a "new beauty floor"; from the reservations-only restaurant (at lunchtime) to Simon Doonan's "genius" window displays, "taste, luxury and humor" abound – even the "outrageous prices are good for a laugh" – except perhaps with the infamously "self-important" salespeople (though they are trying harder "to be civil").

Barton-Sharpe   – | – | – | VE
200 Lexington Ave., Ste. 914 (bet. 32nd & 33rd St.), 6 to 33rd St., 646-935-1500; www.bartonsharpe.com
Murray Hill furniture maker employing traditional cabinetmaking techniques such as tenon and mortise joints, which turn up in "well-made" reproductions of 18th-century American furniture; in addition, French-Canadian–style pieces and English Georgian and Regency replicas are available.

Bath & Body Works ●S   18 | 20 | 18 | I
141 Fifth Ave. (bet. 20th & 21st Sts.), N/R to 23rd St., 212-387-9123; 800-395-1001; www.bathandbodyworks.com
Additional locations throughout the NY area
◪ For a "flowery, fruity" "pick-me-up present", teens and "tweens" hit this "sweet-smelling" toiletries chainlet for "all kinds" of soap, bath gels, lotions, candles and perfumes at "inexpensive prices"; but sophisticates simply sniff at the "cutesy" "limited merchandise" and "overwhelming mixture of scents."

Bath Island ●SC   21 | 21 | 21 | M
469 Amsterdam Ave. (bet 82nd & 83rd Sts.), 1/9 to 79th St., 212-787-9415; www.bathisland.com
■ This "oasis on the Upper West Side" has "no fancy bottles, just simple, great products", like "unique bath items", candles, custom-blended skincare lines and scented lotions, making it "the perfect place to buy a gift for someone who has very specific tastes."

BCBG by Max Azria   23 | 20 | 17 | E
770 Madison Ave. (66th St.), 6 to 68th St., 212-717-4225 **SC**
120 Wooster St. (bet. Prince & Spring Sts.), N/R to Prince St., 212-625-2723
www.bcbg.com
◪ "Phenomenally fitting", "flashy", "feminine and sexy" clothing – "what the young, single man-hunter wears to stalk her prey" – takes center stage at this Upper East Side and SoHo duo that offers everything from "bathing suits and business suits" to formal gowns (the scene is "prom dress central come June"); "service varies" ("nice if they think you'll shell out money, rude if not"), and definitely love it before you buy it, warn those who decry the "no-refund policy" (store credit/exchange for 10 days only).

| M | P | S | C |

BDDW
_| _ | _ | VE

5 Crosby St. (bet. Grand & Howard Sts.), 6/J/M/N/Q/R/W/Z to Canal St., 212-625-1230; www.bddw.com

Soaring SoHo space that's a "cathedral" for handcrafted wood furniture like stunning dining tables, gorgeous platform beds and cool, wood-encased speakers; whether purchasing a piece off the showroom floor or custom-ordering one, the converted pay a pretty penny for such purchases.

Beacon's Closet ●S
_| _ | _ | I

110 Bedford Ave. (N. 11th St.), Brooklyn, L to Bedford Ave., 718-486-0816
220 Fifth Ave. (bet. President & Union Sts.), Brooklyn, N/R to Union St., 718-230-1630
www.beaconscloset.com

It can be "difficult to find good" used clothing at "reasonable prices", and that's why this "great trade-and-buy thrift store" (they offer on-the-spot sellers cash or store credit) seems such "a treasure" to Williamsburgers; the clothing – primarily recent, casual chain-store brands – rarely costs above $20, while leather coats average about $40; all's neatly arranged amid an industrial-chic warehouse setting of concrete floors and hanging metallic lamps; N.B. the Park Slope branch was set to open at press time.

Beads of Paradise ●SC
23 | 20 | 18 | M

16 E. 17th St. (bet. B'way & 5th Ave.), 4/5/6/L/N/Q/R/W to 14th St./Union Sq., 212-620-0642

■ "Go to relax and dream" at this "transporting little store" in the Flatiron District, "a bead wonderland where wanna-be children" are busy "stringing trinkets" in the back, while others peruse the "one-of-a kind" African artifacts up front; experienced jewelry makers say "there are less expensive suppliers", but neophytes can benefit from the "make-your-own" workshops or simply buy one of the finished pieces made by the "soft-spoken staff."

Bear's Place, A SC
▽ 24 | 19 | 20 | E

789 Lexington Ave. (bet. 61st & 62nd Sts.), 4/5/6/N/R/W to 59th St./Lexington Ave., 212-826-6465

■ Barely a bear to be had, still, there's a "varied selection" of "unique", "good-quality toys", especially for "younger children", at this Upper East Side plush-animal-and-puppet pad, as well as hand-painted kids' tables and chairs; let the "knowledgeable sales help" guide you – "the store's layout can be cramped."

Beasty Feast
24 | 17 | 25 | M

237 Bleecker St. (bet. Carmine & Leroy Sts.), 1/9 to Christopher St., 212-243-3261 ●
630 Hudson St. (bet. Horatio & Jane Sts.), A/C/E/L to 14th St./8th Ave., 212-620-7099 ●SC
680 Washington St. (Charles St.), A/C/E/S/V to W. 4th St., 212-620-4055
www.beastyfeast.com

■ If you "prefer to give your business to the little guys", this long-time trio of Downtown pet shops will reward you with "great personalized service" from "friendly" owners and staff ("if they don't have it, they'll order it"), "healthier food than you'd find in the superstores" and a "very homey feel"; there's also a "good selection" of accessories, and more important, "all sales are inspected by house cats."

vote at zagat.com 49

Beau Brummel 🆂 🅲   23 | 21 | 20 | E

421 W. Broadway (bet. Prince & Spring Sts.), N/R to Prince St.; C/E to Spring St., 212-219-2666; www.beaubrummel.com

▪ When you want to "dress like Regis", head to this "classy store" in SoHo for "superb" dress and casualwear with "lots of funk and color" (their own label as well as others of the Byblos/Cerruti/Zegna ilk); while there are "attentive" – some say "aggressive" – people "to help you shop", opponents opine the offerings "often seem overpriced", which is why the savvy wait to "hit the sales."

Bebe 🆂   16 | 17 | 14 | M

100 Fifth Ave. (15th St.), 4/5/6/L/N/Q/R/W to 14th St./Union Sq., 212-675-2323
1044 Madison Ave. (79th St.), 6 to 77th St., 212-517-2323
1127 Third Ave. (66th St.), 6 to 68th St., 212-935-2444
805 Third Ave. (50th St.), E/V to Lexington Ave./53rd St., 212-588-9060
www.bebe.com

▪ "Perfect body required" (read: "size 0") at this women's fashion chain, where "gear for girls' night out" "with a wild streak" appeals to "trashy high school" and "twentysomething" "babes" who plunk down dough for "sexy" eveningwear, sparkly jewelry, "slutty" shoes and active apparel "too cute for the gym"; frank-talking foes dub it "harlotwear", but who's to say that's not a compliment?

Bebe Thompson 🅲   – | – | – | E

1216 Lexington Ave. (bet. 82nd & 83rd Sts.), 4/5/6 to 86th St., 212-249-4740

Jam-packed with European clothing for wee ones and big kids (newborn to size 16), this Upper East Side boutique offers groovy goodies from high-end lines like Lili Gaufrette, Malina and Sonia Rykiel; many a little girl goes ga-ga for the wide selection of sparkly barrettes, while moms mark their calendars for the excellent off-season sales.

Beckenstein 🆂   22 | 11 | 14 | M

257 W. 39th St. (bet. 7th & 8th Aves.), A/C/E to 42nd St./Port Authority, 212-475-6666; 800-221-7272

▪ "If you're looking to match a designer fabric", this Garment District shop "is the place" fawn fans who bolt over for the "great selection" of "fine-quality" cloth at "good prices."

Beckenstein Fabrics & Interiors 🆂   21 | 16 | 14 | M

4 W. 20th St. (bet. 5th & 6th Aves.), F/V to 23rd St., 212-366-5142; 800-348-1327; www.beckenstein.com

▪ Interior decorators and do-it-yourselfers rely on this Flatiron fabric destination for its "great selection" of "interesting", "good-quality" home-furnishings textiles at "reasonable" prices; "they do wonderful work with upholstery" and custom draperies, but pressed patrons take heed: "special orders can take a long time."

BED, BATH & BEYOND 🅲   22 | 18 | 15 | M

410 E. 61st St. (1st Ave.), 4/5/6/N/R/W to 59th St./Lexington Ave., 646-215-4702
620 Sixth Ave. (bet. 18th & 19th Sts.), 1/9 to 18th St., 212-255-3550 ● 🆂
96-05 Queens Blvd. (63rd Dr.), Queens, G/R/V to 63rd Dr., 718-459-0868
800-462-3966; www.bedbathandbeyond.com

▪ "The one-stop shopping spot for furnishing a dorm room or first apartment" ("or whenever the urge to redo gets overwhelming"),

| M | P | S | C |

this "football-field-size" trio is a "household treasure chest"; "whether for bathroom, bedroom, kitchen or garden", fans find it "truly goes beyond", with "interesting new" appliances ("even the gadgets you see on TV"), "fresh and fun" toiletries and "all manner of seasonal, holiday-specific items"; however, its "vastness" "can be a mixed blessing – there's no such thing as a quick trip" through the "meandering displays", and while "every single salesperson says hello to you", "they need more help."

Belgian Shoes | 24 | 16 | 20 | E |
110 E. 55th St. (bet. Lexington & Park Aves.), E/V to 53rd St., 212-755-7372; www.belgianshoes.com

☒ "It's worth it indeed" to "wait up to a year" for "handmade", "built-to-last" shoes from this Midtown "home of the pink-and-green loafer" (founded by Henri Bendel in 1956) laud loyalists who flip for the "most comfortable flats in the world" that "feel every inch like slippers"; you'll find a "limited selection" in stock – "only a couple of styles with dozens of color combinations" – and "tassels, tassels everywhere", but cutting-edge critics sniff it's "not for fashionistas."

Bellini S C | 25 | 25 | 21 | VE |
1305 Second Ave. (bet. 68th & 69th St.), 6 to 68th St., 212-517-9233; www.bellini.com

■ "Great Italian imports made to last and grow with your child" abound at this two-story Upper East Side branch of a furniture chain offering "very high-quality", "solidly made timeless designs" "at a price"; choose from a "wide selection" of "cream-of-the-crop" cribs, chairs, bedding and nursery accessories "to decorate the little one's room", plus "beautiful" stuff for kids and teens; N.B. custom-made goods are also available.

Benetton | 16 | 17 | 15 | M |
749 Broadway (bet. 8th St. & Waverly Pl.), 6 to Astor Pl., 212-533-0230 ◐ S
597 Fifth Ave. (bet. 48th & 49th Sts.), E/V to 5th Ave./53rd St., 212-317-2501 ◐ S C
South Street Seaport, 10 Fulton St. (bet. South & Water Sts.), 2/3/4/5/A/C/J/M/Z to Fulton St./Broadway/Nassau., 212-509-3999
120 Seventh Ave. (17th St.), 1/9 to 18th St., 646-638-1086
www.benetton.com

☒ "They're not just sweaters anymore", but the "rebirth" of the people's place for "classic Italian cool" still has shoppers asking if it's "evolved enough" to deliver "sharp, simple" essentials at "decent prices"; some are "pleasantly surprised" by "bright" cotton tops and suits for "working girls with style", while those who say "controversial ads are no substitute for good clothes" cite "larges that fit like smalls" and "complete lack of service."

Ben Kahn Furs | – | – | – | VE |
150 W. 30th St., 2nd fl. (bet. 6th & 7th Aves.), B/D/F/N/Q/R/V/W to 34th St./Herald Sq., 212-279-0633

With its cream moiré curtains and rose-colored marble entrance, this well-appointed Garment District showroom makes it clear why celebrities in search of the perfect pelt book appointments here; though established in 1920, the family-owned furrier keeps up with the times with its best-selling reversible sheared-mink coats and accessories, as well as classic sable concoctions.

vote at zagat.com   51

| | | | **M** | **P** | **S** | **C** |

Ben's for Kids C
| | | | 19 | 12 | 18 | E |

1380 Third Ave. (bet. 78th & 79th Sts.), 6 to 77th St., 212-794-2330
◪ You'll find "lots of goodies packed into" this "small" store on the Upper East Side where "it's a pleasure to shop" for strollers, cribs and baby necessities; while Ben's buddies applaud the "good selection" and advise it's "better for toys than for clothes", the less-smitten snap that choices are "limited"; N.B. the store was temporarily closed at press time due to a fire.

BERGDORF GOODMAN S
| | | | 27 | 26 | 22 | VE |

754 Fifth Ave. (bet. 57th & 58th St.), N/R/W to 5th Ave./59th St., 212-753-7300; 800-558-1855
■ "Posh and classy", this "grande dame" overlooking the Plaza Hotel retains its "charming old-school vibe", but has a "new edge and flair" with "every designer label your heart desires" and a "subterranean dream" of a cosmetics department (whose "madcap beauty" events are "like disco night with your girlfriends"); "you could spend all day staring" at the "delectable accessories" like the "great assortment of dainty-to-chunky" modern jewelry and the recently expanded "stellar shoe selection", while brides can seek out "sleek or fairy-tale dresses"; the "courteous", "professional" salespeople "actually follow up", and while the price tags are (of course) "outlandish", end-of-the-season "serious markdowns make it affordable."

Bergdorf Men's S
| | | | 27 | 26 | 24 | VE |

745 Fifth Ave. (58th St.), N/R/W to 5th Ave./59th St., 212-753-7300; 800-558-1855
◪ "An essay in understated elegance", this "dignified" (some say "stuffy") "island of calm in Midtown" is "as complete a men's store as exists anywhere in the world", offering "superior" suits and "high-end" sportswear ("the prominent designers are all on board"), "English shirts", "custom-made Italian shoes", seemingly "500 kinds of cufflinks" and a "massive tie selection"; of course, you'll "pay top dollar" for "upscaling the man in your life", and while the atmosphere "borders on the elitist" – you may "spot a star from Broadway or Hollywood" among the "posh displays" – "dress well and you'll be treated right."

Berkley Girl S
| | | | – | – | – | M |

410 Columbus Ave. (bet. 79th & 80th Sts.), B/C to 81st St., 212-877-4770
Tween-friendly to the max, this bright white Upper West Side newcomer (named after the owner's golden retriever) outfits trendy girls from top to bottom; kicky T-shirts are arranged on an easy-access display cube flanked by racks of bright, funky togs from labels like Lucky Brand Dungarees and Betsy & Babs, while whimsical handbags, barrettes and accessories fill the shelves above; as daughter browses, mom can kick back on the way-cool comfy chair and ottoman in the corner.

BERNARDAUD C
| | | | 28 | 28 | 22 | VE |

499 Park Ave. (59th St.), 4/5/6/F/N/R/W to 59th St./Lexington Ave., 212-371-4300; 800-884-7775; www.bernardaud.net
■ "If you entertain elegantly", this Eastsider is "a wonderful source" for this "fabulous" French manufacturer's Limoges porcelain patterns like Constance and Fusion White, which are accented with gold and platinum; the "beautiful shop" also offers

| | | | **M** | **P** | **S** | **C** |

crystal and silver flatware, along with furniture; just be prepared to pay an "arm and a leg for the privilege of shopping here."

Best Buy   22 | 19 | 16 | M
60 W. 23rd St. (6th Ave.), F/V to 23rd St., 212-366-1373 ◐ S
50-01 Northern Blvd. (bet. 50th St. & Newtown Rd.), Queens, G/R/V to 46th St., 718-626-7585
2795 Richmond Ave. (Platinum Ave.), Staten Island, 718-698-7546 ◐ S
888-237-8289; www.bestbuy.com

☒ "All the toys are out", and "there's nothing better than being able to test" LCD monitors, notebook computers, TVs and other stuff before you buy at these "huge stores" glutted with "competitively priced" electronics; "though it's merely a chain, they've managed to make the experience almost pleasant" – just "don't expect the royal treatment" from the staff.

Betsey Bunky Nini C   ▽ 23 | 21 | 22 | E
980 Lexington Ave. (bet. 71st & 72nd Sts.), 6 to 68th St., 212-744-6716

■ Open since 1969, this relaxed, elegant and comfortable Upper East Side boutique was founded by designer Betsey Johnson and two friends (who all cashed out a while back); loyalists say it's "still great after all these years" for its "interesting clothes" – the Piazza Sempione line is a big seller – that, while "pricey, are usually worth it for something different."

Betsey Johnson S C   21 | 21 | 20 | E
248 Columbus Ave. (bet. 71st & 72nd Sts.), 1/2/3/9/B/C to 72nd St., 212-362-3364
251 E. 60th St. (bet. 2nd & 3rd Aves.), 4/5/6/N/R/W to 59th St./Lexington Ave., 212-319-7699
1060 Madison Ave. (bet. 80th & 81st Sts.), 6 to 77th St., 212-734-1257
138 Wooster St. (bet. Houston & Prince Sts.), N/R to Prince St., 212-995-5048
www.betseyjohnson.com

■ "Mainstream funky" sums up the "ever-eclectic stylings of Ms. Johnson" that are popular with (and seem primarily sized for) "well-heeled teenagers" who "dare to stand out" in her "frivolous", "flirty" party clothes; "it's a blast" to browse these "upbeat", pink-walled shops, especially as the "sweet staffers" will "run over in a second" to "help you get over any inhibitions."

Betwixt S C   – | – | – | E
245 W. 10th St. (bet. Bleecker & Hudson Sts.), 1/9 to Christopher St., 212-243-8590

Packed to the rafters with designer brands like Miss Sixty, Diesel, Juicy Couture and Nicole Miller, this West Village boutique appeals to tweens trying to live up to Mary Kate and Ashley's cool factor; fledgling fashionistas plow through piles of purses, backpacks, sleepover bags and tons of sparkly costume jewelry and pore over the makeup station stocked with glosses, while mom takes it easy on the couch; a hefty allowance may be needed to pick up the rockin' school clothes here.

Beyul S   – | – | – | VE
353 W. 12th St. (bet. Greenwich & Washington Sts.), A/C/E/L to 14th St./8th Ave., 212-989-2533

Way west on a quiet block in the Village, an old warehouse space has been transformed into a Far East temple – a traditional moongate guards the front of the store, and in the rear a Tibetan

vote at zagat.com

| M | P | S | C |

shrine watches over its wares, which consist of 18th-, 19th- and 20th-century Asian antiques; standouts include a collection of Chinese ancestral portraits, nearly life-size scroll paintings integral to honoring the spirits of long-gone family members.

Bicycle Habitat ⓢⓒ   24 | 16 | 22 | M
244 Lafayette St. (bet. Prince & Spring Sts.), N/R to Prince St.; 6 to Spring St., 212-431-3315; www.bicyclehabitat.com

■ "Fair dealing, excellent mechanics" and a "good selection" of bicycles and "accessories, especially for the urban" cyclist, make this SoHo "standout" a "pedal-pusher's delight"; "it's a great place to shop" for everything from Trek to BMX models, plus they're "really helpful in repairs and ordering parts for special models – service the way we all want it."

Bicycle Renaissance ⓢ   24 | 15 | 18 | E
430 Columbus Ave. (bet. 80th & 81st Sts.), 1/9 to 79th St.; B/C to 81st St., 212-724-2350

◪ "A busy bike store" in a "convenient Upper West Side location" within pedaling proximity to Central Park, this "comfortable" 30-year-old stalwart is where "cyclists in-the-know" turn for a "good selection" of bicycles (including wheels for kids), apparel and accessories; while some surveyors salute the service, others opine "make sure you've got one of the top guns working with you."

Big Drop ⓞⓢⓒ   23 | 18 | 14 | E
174 Spring St. (bet. Thompson St. & W. B'way), C/E to Spring St., 212-966-4299
1321 Third Ave. (bet. 75th & 76th Sts.), 6 to 77th St., 212-988-3344
425 W. Broadway (bet. Prince & Spring Sts.), C/E to Spring St., 212-226-9292
www.bigdropnyc.com

◪ "Always on target with trends", this sleek trio of women's boutiques (the lollipop-bright West Broadway locale's the latest) showcases "unusual selections from up-and-coming" designers (plus "favorites" like Rebecca Taylor and Seven) whose wares often have a handcrafted appeal; however, a Big Drop between the Merchandise and Service scores suggests the staff needs to mend its alternately "pushy" and "too-cool-to-help" ways.

Billy Martin's Western Wear ⓢⓒ   ▽ 23 | 21 | 18 | E
220 E. 60th St. (bet. 2nd & 3rd Aves.), 4/5/6/N/R/W to 59th St./Lexington Ave., 212-861-3100; www.billymartin.com

■ "Yee-haw", the vintage bar and Coca-Cola machine aren't the only reasons everyone from Billy Bob Thorton to Jewel to good ol' Western-wear aficionados find this East 60s retailer "a fun place to shop"; patrons pony up big bucks for some of the "best" colorful, novelty alligator "boots in town", "great" silver and turquoise jewelry, belts, buckles and rodeo-ready rhinestone cowboy shirts.

Bird ⓞⓢⓒ   23 | 25 | 21 | E
430 Seventh Ave. (bet. 14th & 15th Sts.), Brooklyn, F to 7th Ave., 718-768-4940; www.shopbird.com

■ "Style-starved Slopers" pigeonhole this Brooklyn boutique as "providing SoHo fashion without the attitude"; the "color-coded" stock is "an addiction" for "boho girls with a French flair" who want "intelligent", "whimsical" yet "utilitarian clothing and accessories" (exclusive labels "complement the store's own design"); however, even high-fliers warn prices aren't "cheap-cheap."

| M | P | S | C |

Birnbaum & Bullock — | — | — | VE
27 W. 20th St., Ste. 703 (bet. 5th & 6th Aves.), N/R to 23rd St., 212-242-2914; www.birnbaumandbullock.com
"If the bride wants something special", this by-appointment-only Flatiron showroom is "the place to go"; these "two very talented designers" create clean-lined "gorgeous gowns", plus components comprised of interchangeable bodices, including corset and tank styles, and skirts that go the gamut from full silhouettes to satin A-lines; the icing on the cake: "wonderful and caring service."

Biscuits & Baths Doggy Village C — 18 | 18 | 20 | E
227 E. 44th St. (bet. 2nd & 3rd Aves.), 4/5/6/7/S to 42nd St./Grand Central, 212-692-2323 ● S
1535 First Ave. (bet. 80th & 81st Sts.), 6 to 77th St., 212-794-3600
www.biscuitsandbath.com
■ An "adorable day camp for dogs", this East 40s pet spa and its Upper East Side satellite ensure its clients "live better than most New Yorkers", offering a "nice array" of "luxury items" and "great toys" for sale, as well as "fun" activities like a canine "cocktail hour that's a treat", jazz concerts or a dip in the pooch pool; it's the "ultimate in pampering" for pups and kitties too, but a few wonder if four-legged friends "really need a birthday party?"

Bis Designer Resale S — 22 | 21 | 21 | M
1134 Madison Ave. (bet. 84th & 85th Sts.), 4/5/6 to 86th St., 212-396-2760; www.bisbiz.com
■ This "tiny treasure" is a "temple of temptation" to consignment shopaholics for its often-"brilliant designer finds" – "everything from Ralph Lauren loafers to Hermès pullovers" – plus a "nicely edited collection of bric-a-brac"; a "refined" setting makes this ladies' place "the next best thing to shopping retail on Madison Avenue – at about a quarter of the price."

Bisou-Bisou ● S C — 20 | 20 | 18 | E
474 W. Broadway (bet. Houston & Prince Sts.), N/R to Prince St., 212-260-9640; www.bisou-bisou.com
■ "Sexy" sells at this "hip" SoHo boutique specializing in "kinda trashy", "good-for-clubbing" womenswear and lingerie for "those with a figure" (especially a "teeny-tiny" one); the staff takes time to "match the perfect dress to the perfect accessories" – as they should, given the "this-is-expensive!" prices.

Blacker & Kooby S C — 22 | 14 | 16 | E
1204 Madison Ave. (88th St.), 4/5/6 to 86th St., 212-369-8308
■ On the Upper East Side, this "convenient" family-owned shop has been "meeting the needs of the neighborhood" for nearly 40 years with a "good selection of stationery, pens and novelty items" and "great office supplies and prepacked invitations"; "locals" love it for "pickups in a pinch", "competitive" prices and an "always helpful "staff.

Blades Board and Skate — 22 | 16 | 21 | M
659 Broadway (bet. Bleecker & 3rd Sts.), 6 to Bleecker St., 212 477-7350 ● S
160 E. 86th St. (bet. Lexington & 3rd Aves.), 4/5/6 to 86th St., 212-996-1644
Pier 62 (23rd St.), C/E to 23rd St., 212-336-6299

(continued)

vote at zagat.com

M | P | S | C

(continued)

Blades Board and Skate
120 W. 72nd St. (bet. B'way & Columbus Ave.), 1/2/3/9 to 72nd St., 212-787-3911
888-552-5233; www.blades.com
■ "If you are into extreme skating and surfing" or "just looking for" an "awesome" selection of "cool stuff" like in-line blades, snowboards and accessories, gyrate over to this Northeast chain; the "knowledgeable", "genuinely interested" staff may "!look like the kids you avoided in high school" (i.e. "tattooed, pierced skate rats"), but "who better to buy from than those who live" the rad life?

Bleecker Bob's Golden Oldies Record Shop ●S   22 | 10 | 14 | M
118 W. Third St. (bet. MacDougal St. & 6th Ave.), A/C/E/F/V/S to W. 4th St., 212-475-9677; www.bleeckerbobs.com
◪ "Browse" through the "dust-filled bins" at this Greenwich Village "institution" "for all those records you thought were lost forever", from "hard-to-find rock" "imports" and "out-of-print" "goodies" to "old vinyl", especially "super-rare punk LPs" (and CDs); while the staff can be difficult, they "know everything they have and where it is."

Bleecker Street Records ●S   22 | 15 | 16 | M
239 Bleecker St. (bet. Carmine & Leroy Sts.), A/C/E/F/S/V to W. 4th St., 212-255-7899
■ "A must-visit when you're strolling down Bleecker Street", this "no-frills" Village CD and LP haunt is "perfect for hunting down" "something you're not likely to hear on the radio", as well as "good bargains, especially in jazz and blues"; the staff is "beyond informed" – they really "know the obscure and offbeat artists" – so chances are you'll "never leave empty-handed."

bliss   23 | 23 | 20 | E
568 Broadway (bet. Houston & Prince Sts.), F/S/V to B'way/Lafayette, 212-219-8970 ●
19 E. 57th St., 3rd fl. (bet. 5th & Madison Aves.), 4/5/6/N/R/W to 59th St./Lexington Ave., 212-219-8970
888-243-8825; www.blissworld.com
◪ The retail arm of this buzzing SoHo spa and its Midtown offshoot offers an "enticing stock of delicious creams, washes and waxes", "great soaps" and "yummy skincare products" like the famous Lemon & Sage Body Butter moisturizer that almost "make you want to eat them rather than slather them all over your legs"; though most maintain they'd "spend their entire salary here if they could" ("you find yourself asking, rent or body lotion?"), critics counter it's "overpriced and overhyped"; N.B. appointments can also be made for a variety of spa services, including facials, but some say it may be "easier to get an audience with the Pope."

Blockbuster Video   18 | 15 | 10 | M
835 Eighth Ave. (51st St.), C/E to 50th St., 212-765-2021;
www.blockbuster.com
Additional locations throughout the NY area
◪ "You have the best chance of getting a newly released movie" at "the McDonald's of video stores", "a family values–oriented", "convenient" chain where you "can't beat the selection" of "the latest blockbusters"; but critics bash a "staff that knows nothing

56   subscribe to zagat.com

| M | P | S | C |

about film and couldn't care less" and the "mainstream" monolith's "very Hollywood" "pop fluff" titles ("don't go here for any obscure cinema" – it's "not for the arthouse set.")

Bloom C — 20 | 22 | 18 | M
361 Madison Ave. (bet. 45th & 46th Sts.), 4/5/6/7/S to 42nd St./ Grand Central, 212-370-0068

■ Asian flair and pristine lines prevail in this "well laid-out" "Midtown find", a New York City branch of a Japanese jeweler, where those in-the-know buy a "wide variety" of "sleek" silver, titanium and white-gold creations at "all price ranges"; the staff "really knows the pieces", but make sure to inquire about the stringent return policies.

BLOOMINGDALE'S ●S — 23 | 18 | 14 | E
1000 Third Ave. (bet. 59th & 60th Sts.), 4/5/6/N/R/W to 59th St./ Lexington Ave., 212-355-5900; www.bloomingdales.com

◪ "From cheap to couture", nearly "everything the discerning shopper needs" lies within this most "upscale" of the "all-around department stores" ("it even has its own subway stop" on 59th); there's "almost too much choice" among the "wide variety" of clothing", "fashionable necessities", "astonishing gadgets", "high-end" cookware, "well-presented" furniture, "luxury sheets" and "wowza array of cosmetics" that's worth running the "perfume-spritzing gauntlet" for; critics cry over a "no-show sales force" that's "rarer than rain in the Mojave", but for better or worse, "nothing in NY comes close" to this "landmark", and maybe that's why it's ranked this *Survey*'s Most Popular store.

Blue S — ▽ 21 | 13 | 18 | E
125 St. Marks Pl. (bet. Ave. A & 1st Ave.), 6 to Astor Pl., 212-228-7744

■ Owner-designer Christina Jara is a "godsend" to fans who make tracks to her East Village boutique for retro-cool "custom-made" cocktail dresses, suits and formalwear "in every imaginable pattern"; the "funky" threads put oh-so-groovy bridesmaids and those seeking stand-out-in-a-crowd party garb in the pink at prices that won't bring on the blues; "leave your inhibitions behind", as there's "no room for modesty" in this tiny storefront.

Blue Bag — 24 | 24 | 22 | E
266 Elizabeth St. (Houston St.), 6 to Spring St., 212-966-8566

■ "Why bother flying to France" when you can breeze over to this NoLita boutique for "totally charming" European accessories, including "fabulous bags" from an array of independent designers that "span all styles" and "dictate trends before they happen on the street", all displayed on easy-access wood shelves; staffed with "extremely nice salespeople", it's "a wonderful place for special gifts" that can "create covetousness."

Bodum SC — 25 | 24 | 20 | M
413-415 W. 14th St. (bet. 9th & 10th Aves.), A/C/E/L to 14th St./8th Ave., 212-367-9125; 800-232-6386; www.bodum.com

■ "Chic design ideas combined with practicality and modest pricing" make this "hidden gem" in the Meatpacking District "a hit" "for the home"; it's a "supermarket" for the European company's "cool", "sleek" stuff like glass teapots, steel fondue sets and "French-press coffeemakers galore", plus there's a "nice" little in-store cafe too.

vote at zagat.com 57

Bodyhints ◐ⓈⒸ — | — | — | M
462 W. Broadway (bet. Houston & Prince Sts.), C/E to Spring St., 212-777-8677; 866-334-3433; www.bodyhints.com
Take a hint from this "wonderful" SoHo mega-boutique – two spacious floors filled with walls of bras (no drawers), "irresistible lingerie" and swimwear, and a "down-to-earth staff" add up to double the browsing fun; no matter your heart's desire – low-rise undies from Lilo, satin chemises from Mary Green or camis and hangout pants by James Perse – it's all here for the lusting; P.S. "the dressing rooms are so plush you'll wish you could rent" one.

Body Shop, The ◐Ⓢ 20 | 19 | 18 | M
747 Broadway (bet. 8th St. & Waverly Pl.), N/R to 8th St.; 6 to Astor Pl., 212-979-2944; 800-263-9746; www.thebodyshop.com
For additional locations, see Top Chain Stores index
■ Devotees declare that this U.K.-based chain is "the one that started it all" in 1976 in terms of "non-animal-tested toiletries" and "environmentally conscious" products that "don't look as if they belong on a rural commune"; "yummy-smelling", natural-ingredient bath-and-body items, massage creams and cosmetics are "well priced" and displayed in "cheerful", "well-organized" shops.

Boffi SoHo Ⓒ — | — | — | VE
31½ Greene St. (Grand St.), 6 to Spring St., 212-431-8282; www.boffi.com
This Milan-based international bath-and-kitchen chain opened a sprawling showroom in SoHo in 2000, and it's a mecca for loft-dwellers who covet the custom-made cabinets, appliances, sinks and lighting; the minimalist, high-tech style incorporates concrete, steel, glass and wood, and several designs have been shown at the Louvre and MoMA.

Bolton's ◐Ⓢ 11 | 9 | 9 | I
27 W. 57th St. (bet. 5th & 6th Aves.), F to 57th St., 212-935-4431; 800-414-8000
Additional locations throughout the NY area
◪ "Moderately fashionable", "matronly clothing" makes this "zero-atmosphere" discount chainster a "good low-end place" for "older types" to solve "pantyhose crises" and other "workwear" dilemmas, since "there are so many" "small, easily negotiated" branches "that if you cannot find your size, you can walk around the corner to the next one and they'll have it" – if you're in the average range, that is, as "they stopped carrying plus sizes", and "the smalls aren't so small."

Bombalulus ⓈⒸ 24 | 18 | 22 | M
244 W. 72nd St. (bet. B'way & West End Ave.), 1/2/3/9 to 72nd St., 212-501-8248
101 W. 10th St. (bet. Greenwich & 6th Aves.), 1/2/3/9/F/L/V to 14th St./6th Ave., 212-463-0897
www.bombalulus.com
■ "Absolutely adorable and just a little offbeat", this colorful Greenwich Village children's boutique and its more spacious sibling on the Upper West Side are crammed with "cute, bright" clothing and "different baby gifts" "for the chic city kid"; most of the merchandise is made in-house, "so you won't find it in many other stores", plus there are toys on-site to busy little ones while you browse.

| | | | M | P | S | C |

Bombay Company, The S   17 | 18 | 15 | M
Beekman Townhouse, 1062A Third Ave. (bet. 62nd & 63rd Sts.), 4/5/6/N/R/W to 59th St./Lexington Ave., 212-759-7217
900 Broadway (20th St.), N/R to 23rd St., 212-420-1315 ●
441 Columbus Ave. (81st St.), 1/9 to 79th St., 212-721-1417
Staten Island Mall, 2655 Richmond Ave., Staten Island, 718-494-0426
800-829-7789; www.bombaycompany.com

■ "If you're looking for things for the home that aren't expensive", this chain is "the place for you" praise penny-pinchers in pursuit of "reproduction" "traditional-style" "dark wood" furniture and "interesting accent pieces" like prints, mirrors, frames and lamps; but snobs simply sniff at the "same old, same old" "faux upscale" furnishings and "kitschy bric-a-brac."

Bond 07 by Selima S C   23 | 26 | 18 | VE
7 Bond St. (bet. B'way & Lafayette St.), 6 to Bleecker St., 212-677-8487; www.selimaoptique.com

■ Owned by the lady behind Selima Optique, this "eye-catching" NoHo boutique sells the designer's "ultra-chic" frames, plus a jolly "jambalaya" of "kooky", "cutting-edge" "bohemian dresses", "beautiful handbags", lingerie and "even some vintage stuff"; "original is the operative word here", but "beware – you might have to sell your goldfinger to afford" the "sumptuous array."

Bonne Nuit ● S C   25 | 21 | 19 | E
30 Lincoln Plaza (bet. 62nd & 63rd Sts.), 1/2 to 66th St., 212-489-9730

■ Tucked away in a "hidden location" in Lincoln Plaza, this "unique" lingerie-and-childrenswear boutique with a "frank but delicate staff" offers a "carefully chosen selection of beautiful items" you don't "see anywhere else", from long lacy nightgowns and novelty robes to velvet peignoir sets and brazen bustiers; if you can tear yourself away from the unmentionables, take a peek at the "excellent mix of unusual" European clothing "for little ones."

BONPOINT C   27 | 26 | 19 | VE
1269 Madison Ave. (91st St.), 4/5/6 to 86th St., 212-722-7720
811 Madison Ave. (68th St.), 6 to 68th St., 212-879-0900

■ "Classic and stylish (not trendy)", the "fabulous" French finery for kids found at these Upper East Side shops comes in "the most luxurious textures and exquisite colors", all "nicely displayed" in Provençal-style cases; it's "great for special occasions" if you want to spend "a small fortune", but the sticker-shocked quip that "therapy might be a better way to spend the cash" and find the vibe "snobby and stuffy."

Borealis S C   – | – | – | VE
229 Elizabeth St. (bet. Houston & Prince Sts.), F/V to 2nd Ave., 917-237-0152

This Northern (as in NoLita) light shines with an "original", "eclectic mix of jewelry", many pieces handcrafted by rising stars and highlighting large, unfaceted, earthy stones; it's an "interesting" array "for the Downtown crowd", but "be careful" – despite the often-understated looks, it's "very expensive."

Boss, The S   25 | 23 | 20 | E
849 Flatbush Ave. (bet. Linden Blvd. & Martense St.), Brooklyn, F to Church Ave., 718-287-4979

■ Not to be confused with Hugo Boss, this specialty shop sports a selection of "sleek stylish wear" with a Euro-Caribbean twist; a

vote at zagat.com

"nice selection" of colorful Jean Mercius sport shirts, along with the odd Armani, lines the long walls, while a vast assortment of highly detailed dress trousers and colorful shoes fills the center aisle; Flatbush fans appreciate the "wide cuts with good tailoring", though the service sometimes seems on island time.

BOTTEGA VENETA C   28 | 26 | 22 | VE
635 Madison Ave. (bet. 59th & 60th Sts.), N/R/W to 5th Ave./59th St., 212-371-5511; www.bottegaveneta.com
■ A "recent upgrade in style" and an "excellent staff" create an "enjoyable shopping experience" for fashionistas who zip over to this Madison Avenue outpost for "unique Italian goods", including "soft and lovely" shoes, accessories and status woven handbags, plus a new luxe line of apparel for men and women, all "priced for the elite"; kvetchers quibble it's "not the same since Gucci" became a backer, but supporters snap back "they still have it."

Botticelli S C   – | – | – | E
666 Fifth Ave. (53rd St.), 6 to 51st St.; E/V to 53rd St., 212-586-7421
620 Fifth Ave. (49th St.), 6 to 51st St.; E/V to 53rd St., 212-632-8300
522 Fifth Ave. (bet. 43rd & 44th Sts.), 4/5/6/7/S to 42nd St./Grand Central, 212-221-9075
www.botticellishoes.com
Sporting a logo as curvy as its wares – from sexy kitten pumps to sleekly pointed slingbacks and buckled boots – this Italian-based Fifth Avenue footwear phenom knows a thing or two about keeping its patrons pampered; the luxe collection includes classic men's shoes, office-worthy handbags and totes with unexpected pocket detailing and a range of high-end leather and shearling coats for men and women.

Boucher S   – | – | – | M
9 Ninth Ave. (Little W. 12th St.), A/C/E/L to 14th St./8th Ave., 212-206-3775; 866-623-9269; www.boucherjewelry.com
With its dainty teardrop earrings and lariat necklaces, this aptly named ('*boucher*' means 'butcher') Meatpacking District jewelry shop has a rep for the finest, "fun" bridesmaids' gifts around – at least among discriminating, Vera Wang–worshipping wives-to-be; "friendly service" supplements the "absolutely wonderful" wares.

Bowery Kitchen Supplies S C   21 | 12 | 14 | M
Chelsea Mkt., 460 W. 16th St. (9th Ave.), A/C/E/L to 14th St./8th Ave., 212-376-4982; www.bowerykitchens.com
■ "If they don't have it, it doesn't exist" declare devotees of this commercial cooking equipment and supplies store in Chelsea Market that stocks a "wide-ranging selection" of all the "weird and wonderful" items "you'll ever need" – from convection ovens to cake rings – "if you love to cook or you just want to pretend to be a chef"; "good buys" abound, and there are also inexpensive glasses and dinner plates fit for frugal, first-time apartment-dwellers.

Bowery Lighting S C   21 | 13 | 15 | M
132 Bowery (bet. Broome & Grand Sts.), J/M/Z to Bowery, 212-941-8244
◪ "An extensive selection of lighting fixtures and lamps" in styles from art deco to contemporary is "crammed" into this "terrific" Lower East Side institution; "good prices" make it worth it to sift through the "big jumble", but be sure you "know what you want" before you buy because of the "no-returns policy."

| M | P | S | C |

Boyd's Madison Avenue ◐ S C   25 | 16 | 17 | E
655 Madison Ave. (bet. 60th & 61st Sts.), N/R/W to 5th Ave./59th St., 212-838-6558; 800-683-2693; www.boydsnyc.com

■ "Everything imaginable for beauty", including makeovers, makeup, perfume, an "amazing" inventory of "hard-to-find European items" and one of "the largest selections of hair accessories", keeps customers coming to this Upper East Side establishment – despite its "cluttered" setting and "overly attentive" salespeople; it started as an apothecary back in 1940, and today there is still a pharmacy in the back of the store.

Bra Smyth S C   25 | 16 | 23 | E
905 Madison Ave. (bet. 72nd & 73rd Sts.), 6 to 68th St., 212-772-9400; www.brasmyth.com

■ "The mother of lingerie stores", this "helpful", family-owned Upper Eastsider is one of the "only places where you can be assured of getting the exact fit" whether you're buying a "lacy, racy French bra-and-panty set" or a "beautiful nightgown"; the "professional" corsetieres and seamstresses "make sure you're securely hugged by their European" unmentionables and "alter in a flash"; P.S. they also have a "good selection" of bathing suits, activewear and kids PJs.

Brass Center, The   ∇ 25 | 15 | 22 | E
248 E. 58th St. (bet. 2nd & 3rd Aves.), 4/5/6/N/R/W to 59th St./Lexington Ave., 212-421-0090; www.thebrasscenter.com

■ This "great neighborhood store" in the East 50s has a misleading moniker, since an array of materials, from chrome to porcelain, is used to produce the "quality" bathroom fixtures, plumbing, hardware and architectural fittings purveyed here; the "friendly, helpful" staff will help you select "imported items you won't find elsewhere" that are often "cheaper than mail-order" prices.

Breukelen S ⇌ C   ∇ 21 | 22 | 17 | E
369 Atlantic Ave. (bet. Bonds & Hoyt Sts.), Brooklyn, A/C/G to Hoyt/Schermerhorn, 718-260-0024; www.breukelenny.com

■ While this hip Boerum Hill shop takes its name from the 17th-century Dutch appellation for the outer borough, the wares here are strictly contemporary – gorgeous two-tone glass by Japan-based Sugahara, handmade ceramic mirrors, candles and cast-silver-and-gold jewelry by local artists – and are "great for gifts"; a tabletop-and-linen purveyor called Bark is located in the rear.

Bridal Atelier by Mark Ingram   – | – | – | VE
127 E. 56th St. (bet. Lexington & Park Aves.), 4/5/6/N/R/W to 59th St./Lexington Ave., 212-319-6778

"The absolute nicest bridal experience" sigh the blissful who head to this East 50s townhouse for "beautiful" gowns from lines like Wearkstatt and Angel Sanchez; the "helpful staff listens to what you want" and "brings out dresses that match your description"; sure, it's by appointment only, but lucky ladies have found this shop "pretty flexible about making last-minute" arrangements, "not an easy task in this city."

Bridal Garden, The ◐   13 | 8 | 13 | M
122 E. 29th St. (bet. Lexington & Park Aves.), 6 to 28th St., 212-252-0661

■ You "gotta hit it just right" at this by-appointment-only, non-profit bridal store in Gramercy Park, benefiting the Sheltering

vote at zagat.com   **61**

M | P | S | C

Arms Children's Services charity, but it's "worth a peek if you're on a budget"; the "wide selection" includes "used", worn-just-once creations, samples and extra inventory from designers like Vera Wang and Carolina Herrera; but critics caution "don't bother if you're not a model-size" "waif", plus gowns may "need to be altered elsewhere", bumping up the cost.

Bridge Kitchenware C | 27 | 13 | 17 | M
214 E. 52nd St. (bet. 2nd & 3rd Aves.), 6 to 51st St.; E/V to 53rd St./Lexington Ave., 212-688-4220; 800-274-3435; www.bridgekitchenware.com

■ The "best kitchenware store in the city" say supporters of this East 50s legend where "all the chefs shop"; the "astounding volume of merchandise" includes cutlery, "cake pans", copper pots and a "cornucopia of gizmos and gadgets" that could lead to "sensory overload"; you also may have to "blow the dust off" some items, but most maintain that's a small price to pay for "classic bargains" for the cook.

Brief Encounters S C | ▽ 23 | 14 | 21 | E
239 Columbus Ave. (71st St.), 1/2/3/9 to 72nd St., 212-496-5649

■ They've "always carried Cosabella" confide customers who gush over the "great selection" of European designer name undies and sleepwear at this "small", cramped Columbus Avenue corner shop stocked with "better stuff than it looks like they would have from their window displays"; service is equally uplifting thanks to a "very patient", "very knowledgeable staff" – "you can actually feel confident with a bra fitting here."

BRIONI C | 28 | 26 | 24 | VE
55 E. 52nd St. (bet. Madison & Park Aves.), E/V to 5th Ave./53rd St., 212-355-1940
57 E. 57th St. (bet. Madison & Park Aves.), 4/5/6/N/R/W to 59th St./Lexington Ave., 212-376-5777 S
888-778-8775; www.brioni.com

■ "When price is not an issue", these Midtown representatives of the veteran fashion house are "unequalled" for their "fine men's clothing that's made to last a lifetime"; "discriminating buyers" salivate over the "eye-catching selection" that ranges from the "perfect Italian suit" to "flashy" "casual clothes", "great ties and beautiful shirts", all in a "Naples-in-New-York" setting; though "very knowledgeable", the service can be slightly "snooty" – but if "James Bond shops here, how can you go wrong?"

British American House S | 22 | 18 | 18 | E
488 Madison Ave. (51st St.), 6 to 51st St., 212-752-5880

▰ Those searching "for the continental look" can cast their eyes toward Midtown, where (despite the name) this 24-year-old retailer offers up an all-Italian range of men's clothing and accessories, arranged by color and designer; but while some applaud the "great quality" and "helpful service", skeptics sniff it's "nothing special."

Broadway Panhandler S C | 26 | 20 | 18 | M
477 Broome St. (bet. Greene & Wooster Sts.), A/C/E to Canal St., 212-966-3434; 866-266-5927; www.broadwaypanhandler.com

■ Both "novice and experienced" types throng to this "Disneyland for cooks" in SoHo for "good deals" on a "plethora" of "everyday" pots and pans, "specialty bakeware", utensils and appliances from "low-end to high", all sold by a "knowledgeable staff" that

62   **subscribe to zagat.com**

| M | P | S | C |

doesn't "mind answering questions"; on weekends the expansive, columned space gets "crowded", but that doesn't keep wallet-watchers from the "not-to-be-missed" "annual yard sale" in June.

Brooklyn Museum Shop 🆂🅲 | 22 | 17 | 16 | M |
200 Eastern Pkwy. (Washington Ave.), Brooklyn, 2/3 to Eastern Pkwy., 718-638-5000; www.brooklynmuseum.org

■ Come on, "Manhattanites, Brooklyn isn't that far away", so hop the subway and get in on "the best-kept secret in town for gifts"; "the shop is like the museum – unpretentious, interesting, occasionally surprising", with a "nice blend of quality goods" "reflecting its strong collections in African, Asian and American art", as well as its borough identity; though "interestingly quirky" stuff is "jumbled together" with "fairly standard fare", brave the clutter and you're sure to find "excellent clearance-sale items."

Brooklyn Public Couture 🆂 | – | – | – | E |
198 Court St. (Wyckoff St.), Brooklyn, F/G to Bergen St., 718-237-8508

Stepping into this Cobble Hill "hidden gem", decorated with old hatboxes, is like entering the peach-walled closet of a lady who loved swing coats in the '50s, Anne Fogarty and Halston dresses in the '60s and '70s and Gigli tops in the '80s – and stores some Paul Stuart suits for her boyfriend too; some say the "vintage finds" are pricey, but the on-site owner's willing to negotiate.

BROOKS BROTHERS ◐🅲 | 22 | 21 | 20 | E |
666 Fifth Ave. (bet. 52nd & 53rd Sts.), E/V to 5th Ave./53rd St., 212-261-9440
346 Madison Ave. (44th St.), 4/5/6/7/S to 42nd St./Grand Central, 212-682-8800 🆂
800-274-1815; www.brooksbrothers.com

■ "Nine-to-fivers" insist this "granddaddy of preppy" "lives up to its reputation" for "conservative but stylish" business suits and "country club" duds that make even a "frumpy-looking guy into a GQ model in minutes"; society types "swear by" "timeless" blue blazers and "superb" "dress shirts", only regretting that women's apparel gets "a fraction of the floor space"; "unbeatable" service makes shopping "a pleasure", which is as it should be when these "razor-sharp clothes" "cut a big hole in your wallet"; N.B. digital tailoring is available – but, alas, at the flagship on Madison Avenue only.

Brookstone | 21 | 21 | 19 | E |
South Street Seaport, 19 Fulton St. (Front St.), 2/3/4/5/C/J/M/Z to B'way/Nassau/Fulton St., 212-344-8108
16 W. 50th St. (bet. 5th & 6th Aves.), B/D/F/V to 47-50 Sts./Rockefeller Ctr., 212-262-3237 ◐🆂
20 W. 57th St. (bet. 5th & 6th Aves.), F to 57th St., 212-245-1405
JFK Int'l Airport, Concourse Level, Queens, 718-244-0192
LaGuardia Airport, Departure Level Concourse D, Queens, 718-505-2440
800-926-7000; www.brookstone.com

■ Stressed-out surveyors who stop at these "big playgrounds" for a "free massage" in their auto-reclining Shiatsu lounge chair "always find something irresistible" to buy; chockablock with "clever" "gizmos, widgets and tchotchkes" like voice-recording pens, talking thermometers and video-camera watches that "seem too gadgety to work well – but do", the chain is "good for impulse shopping" for "James Bond wanna-bes."

vote at zagat.com 63

| M | P | S | C |

Bruce Frank Beads ◑ S C   ▽ 20 | 17 | 19 | M
215 W. 83rd St. (bet. Amsterdam Ave. & B'way), 1/9 to 86th St., 212-595-3746; 877-232-3775; www.brucefrankbeads.com
☒ They "take beaders seriously" at this retailer that offers "plenty of choice" among a "superior" assortment of new and vintage varieties "from around the world", with an especially "good selection of semi-precious" stones; but critics carp the "hip staff can be standoffish", particularly on "crowded weekends", and the "prices are high" – perhaps reflecting its "great location on the Upper West Side."

Bruno Magli S C   24 | 21 | 20 | VE
677 Fifth Ave. (bet. 53rd & 54th Sts.), E/V to 53rd St., 212-752-7900; www.brunomagli.it
☒ "What's not to love?"; "beautiful Italian leather and that classic look" make this Midtown shop's "quality" shoes some of the "best and most comfortable ever worn" – "just don't look at the tag" – plus there's a "good selection" of leather goods and outerwear to fall for; but not everyone feels like a sole-mate – it's "boring" yawn the less-impressed, who find it "tailored for an older set", with "prices that make it into a gallery for many New Yorkers."

Bu & the Duck S C   24 | 23 | 22 | E
106 Franklin St. (bet. Church St. & W. B'way), 1/9 to Franklin St., 212-431-9226; www.buandtheduck.com
■ "Slightly quirky", vintage-inspired kids' clothes (up to age 8) "with a personal touch", cuddly rag dolls and furniture, that's what this "very fashionable" TriBeCa boutique has to offer; the selection is "completely original" – they even carry suspenders – and "service is very personal", but (gasp) be "prepared to break the bank."

BUCCELLATI   28 | 27 | 25 | VE
46 E. 57th St. (bet. Madison & Park Aves.), 4/5/6/F/N/R/W to 59th St./Lexington Ave., 212-308-2900; www.buccellati.com
■ It "makes you feel like a Medici" to shop at this Italian "icon" in Midtown, a "class act" known for the "original, extraordinary workmanship" of its "signature pieces" of silverware and its "truly exclusive", Renaissance-inspired "exquisite jewels and settings"; the fittingly "elegant" surroundings and staff can be "intimidating", but it's a "feast for the eyes" – and if you're not careful, it can feast on your wallet too.

Built by Wendy S C   23 | 19 | 19 | E
7 Centre Market Pl. (bet. Broome & Grand Sts.), 6 to Spring St., 212-925-6538; www.builtbywendy.com
■ On the SoHo-NoLita border, this "great little" boutique "rocks" with a beige-and-white interior that provides backup for owner Wendy Mullin's "edgy, but pretty" "urban cowgirl" clothes and accessories, including the "coolest guitar straps" (a hint at the designer's beginnings – selling her wares in record stores).

BULGARI   28 | 27 | 24 | VE
730 Fifth Ave. (57th St.), F to 57th St., 212-315-9000 C
783 Madison Ave. (bet. 66th & 67th Sts.), 6 to 68th St., 212-717-2300
800-285-4274; www.bulgari.com
☒ For those "over-the-top" moments, bauble-seekers with big budgets head toward this "luxe Italian goldsmith", whose Fifth and Madison Avenue venues provide "lovely showcases" for

| **M** | **P** | **S** | **C** |

"stunning jewelry" and trendy watches ("great diamond settings"); "service is sometimes haughty", but "always helpful" and "prompt" (hint: be "dressed to kill when you walk in"); of course, "for the price, everything should be gorgeous – and it is."

Bumble and bumble   – | – | – | M
146 E. 56th St. (Lexington Ave.), 4/5/6/N/R/W to 59th St./Lexington Ave., 212-521-6500; www.bumbleandbumble.com
Known for over 25 years of work with models and magazines, this influential East 50s salon is still hopping, and its "great products that do as they promise", from the classic Gentle Shampoo to the new Thickening Conditioner, along with hair accessories, remain at the head of the class; the bonus for tracking down these somewhat hard-to-find items at the source: possible star sightings.

Burberry   25 | 24 | 21 | VE
131 Spring St. (Greene St.), 6 to Spring St., 212-925-9300
9 E. 57th St. (bet. 5th & Madison Aves.), 4/5/6/N/R/W to 59th St./Lexington Ave., 212-371-5010 **S**
www.burberry.com
■ Once known for its "classic" "famed trench coats" ("even one for your dog!"), this venerable Brit brand recently "reinvented" its image, stamping its familiar plaid on "super-expensive" his-and-hers clothes, "scarves, gloves, handbags and anything else your little English-loving heart desires" ("overexposed" sneer a few fashionistas); however, since everyone from "urban hipsters" to "the society set" now "stops 'n' shops" at the "well laid-out" Midtown and SoHo stores, at times the "excellent sales staff can get a little overwhelmed" and "arrogant" (too much plaid-itude?); N.B. at 57th Street, refresh yourself with a stop at the new Tea Cup.

Burlington Coat Factory ●SC   14 | 8 | 7 | I
707 Sixth Ave. (bet. 22nd & 23rd Sts.), F/V to 23rd St.., 212-229-2247; www.coat.com
■ "When you're broke and need a gray wool skirt for an interview" or you otherwise "couldn't afford a coat that keeps you very warm", this "self-service" Chelsea flagship "offers a possibility" for "something basic", with the "occasional" chance of a discount designer "adventure" on the side; citing merchandise ranging from "fantastic to phooey" and the "slowest cashiers in the Western hemisphere", "Bette Davis" wanna-bes pout "what a dump!"

Butter SC   – | – | – | E
407 Atlantic Ave. (bet. Bond & Nevins Sts.), Brooklyn, A/C/G to Hoyt/Schermerhorn, 718-260-9033
You may get toasted sampling the "*luxer*-than-usual" womenswear at this white-walled boutique in Boerum Hill, where a mix of "cleanly edited basics" by local and out-of-town labels line up on the racks and salespeople serve you selections in your size; your snack's complete when you head down the block to Jelly, their companion shoe store.

buybuy Baby ●SC   – | – | – | M
270 Seventh Ave. (bet. 25th & 26th Sts.), 1/9 to 23rd St.; 1/9 to 28th St., 212-645-0187; www.buybuybaby.com
Suburban shopping ease comes to Chelsea with the arrival of this new two-floor offshoot of a national chain, providing everything baby and toddler need; shelves are stocked floor to ceiling with furniture, strollers, car seats and gear plus bottles and bibs, while

vote at zagat.com

the high-end layette area is chockablock with big-name basics from labels like Carter's and Baby Jockey; nursery purchases like lamps, rocking chairs or cribs can be personalized by staff artists.

Cadeau 🅢 🅒 | – | – | – | E |

254 Elizabeth St. (bet. Prince & Houston Sts.), N/R to Prince St., 212-674-5747; 866-622-3322; www.cadeaumaternity.com
For stylish maternity clothes with an urban attitude, head to this new luxe NoLita boutique, the brainchild of former Barney's execs turned designers; expecting fashionistas treat themselves to Italian-made apparel, including hip workwear like fitted blazers and cashmere sweaters, casual funky options and even lingerie, plus all-natural prenatal skincare lines from Selph as well as Erbaviva; there's also a made-for-impulse-purchasing lovely layette section – why resist?; N.B. pregnancy-related seminars are held monthly.

California Closets | 21 | 16 | 21 | E |

1625 York Ave. (86th St.), 4/5/6 to 86th St., 212-517-7877; 888-336-9709; www.californiaclosets.com
■ If you live in a typical NYC "small apartment", a complimentary "in-home consultation" from this "good" "custom-closet" pioneer on the Upper East Side specializing in space-saving designs will "make you want to start spring cleaning"; the company also comes up with storage solutions for garages and offices.

Calling All Pets 🅢 | ∇ 23 | 17 | 24 | M |

301 E. 76th St. (bet. 1st & 2nd Aves.), 6 to 77th St., 212-734-7051
1590 York Ave. (bet. 83rd & 84th Sts.), 4/5/6 to 86th St., 212-249-7387 🅒
■ "When you see the store cats", you know the "lovely" sister-owners and "helpful staff" "care" at these two Upper East Side pet shops that "cater to the many pooches and kitties in the area" with "gourmet food" and a "variety of treats and toys"; prices are "competitive", and though the interiors are "small", they "have everything you need."

Calvin Klein 🅢 | 25 | 25 | 19 | VE |

654 Madison Ave. (60th St.), N/R/W to 5th Ave./59th St., 212-292-9000
◪ Less costs more at this Madison Avenue "minimalist mecca" designed by architect John Pawson, whose "sleek" all-white setting and concrete floors create a Calvinistic "fashion temple" for Klein's signature "tasteful, unadorned look" in his-and-hers "classic, elegant" apparel and accessories (high-end collection only – no CK here, ma'am), cosmetics and "fabulous" home furnishings; some snipe the service can be "as cool as the design", but "if you love Calvin, this is the place to get it."

Calypso | 21 | 21 | 17 | E |

424 Broome St. (bet. Crosby & Lafayette Sts.), 6 to Spring St., 212-274-0449
935 Madison Ave. (74th St.), 6 to 77th St., 212-535-4100
280 Mott St. (bet. Houston & Prince Sts.), N/R to Prince St., 212-965-0990 🅢 🅒
◪ "New Yorkers sick of black" make a beeline to these "breezy, beachy" boutiques for "flirty, Caribbean-inspired" sarongs and "teeny bikinis", "floaty" "gypsy" skirts (some with bustles) and cotton tops, all "arranged by" "lush tropical color"; some pout that "prices could be lower", given that the "clothes are best suited for summer" or "trips to the tropics."

66   **subscribe to zagat.com**

| M | P | S | C |

Calypso Bijoux 🆂🅲 — | — | — | E
252 Mott St. (bet. Houston & Prince Sts.), N/R to Prince St., 212-334-9730
The folks behind the über-hot chain of Caribbean-inspired clothing turn their hands to jewelry, augmented by a few accessories, with this little NoLita boutique down the block from one of their women's stores; the designers range from the ethereal Erickson Beamon to the Asian-inspired Chan Lu to the Victorian-influenced Becky Kelso.

Calypso Enfant & Bebe 🆂🅲 ▽ 26 | 25 | 24 | E
426 Broome St. (bet. Crosby & Lafayette Sts.), 6 to Spring St., 212-966-3234
■ Laid-back and homey, this SoHo boutique is filled with "sweet", baby and kids' clothes "that are also hip" – and, in some instances, just like the "beautiful", colorful Caribbean-inspired outfits mom buys herself at Calypso's women's counterparts around town; the "unique merchandise", including French-label goods and hand-crocheted sweaters and booties, is "not cheap, but it's so adorable you'll occasionally overlook the prices."

Calypso Homme 🆂🅲 — | — | — | E
405 Broome St. (bet. Centre & Lafayette Sts.), 6 to Spring St., 212-343-0450
"Sensitive alpha-males can get their chick-magnet attire here", while "girlfriends can buy their sartorially challenged companions" a gift at this SoHo counterpart to the Caribbean-inspired women's boutiques; these colorful, "casual clothes" can also serve as "something that's a little different for vacations", while playfully helpful, Continental-accented service gets you in a holiday mood.

Camera Land 🅲 ▽ 23 | 16 | 22 | M
575 Lexington Ave. (bet. 51st & 52nd Sts.), 6 to 51 St., 212-753-5128; www.cameralandny.com
■ "Big-city selection and small-town service make a great combo" at this "solid local camera store" in the East 50s; the "excellent" offerings include all the latest gear, the East Coast's only do-it-yourself full-processing digital machine and a "great picture framing" department where homegrown mogul Donald Trump gets his photos" matted.

Camouflage 🆂🅲 ▽ 22 | 23 | 24 | E
139 Eighth Ave. (17th St.), A/C/E/L to 14th St./8th Ave., 212-691-1750
141 Eighth Ave. (17th St.), A/C/E/L to 14th St./8th Ave., 212-741-5173
■ Situated side-by-side in Chelsea, this "hip" pair "does a great job of interpreting trends with clothes that men want to wear", with labels that range from pattern-happy Etro to monochromatic Helmut Lang; 139 Eighth Avenue carries outerwear and sporty styles, while 141 has dressier goods, but the "always chic" yet "conservative" merchandise, backed up by the "best service", makes each address a "favorite."

Camper ⬤🆂 25 | 25 | 17 | E
125 Prince St. (Wooster St.), N/R to Prince St., 212-358-1841; www.camper.com
◪ "European originality started" the bowling-shoe "craze", moving these "sassy" *zapatos* from "Spanish grandfather's closets to the runways", but it's the "comfort and style wrapped in" "adorable" looks that prompt patrons to profess their "love" and sigh, "wish they weren't so popular"; happy campers adore the "minimalist" brick-red SoHo shop's "interesting presentation" of "cool shapes and colors", but cynics snipe they're "not as hip as they were three

vote at zagat.com 67

years ago", call the staff "über-snooty" and find the "steep" cost "almost as much as a cheap ticket" to Madrid.

Canal Hi-Fi Inc S C   – | – | – | M
319 Canal St. (bet. Greene & Mercer Sts.), 6/J/M/N/Q/R/W to Canal St., 212-925-6575; www.canalhifi.com
A Chinatown staple since 1977, this labyrinthine store is packed floor to ceiling with everything from the newest DVD players for your home entertainment setup to turntables and microphones for the DJ in you, as well as a staff that can help you negotiate all the tricky technical information; as for negotiating prices, that can be tricky too: it "has the rep of being a bargain mecca", but reputations aren't always reliable.

Canal Jean Company   19 | 13 | 11 | I
2236 Nostrand Ave. (bet. Aves. H & I), Brooklyn, 2/5 to Flatbush Ave., 718-421-7590; www.canaljean.com
◾ Though smaller than its legendary but now-defunct SoHo sibling, this Flatbush "haven" still pulls in "starry-eyed" teens and twentysomethings with its "discount, baby, discount" jeans ("especially Levi's"), "off-the-wall" vintage threads, "funky club clothes" and lingerie; if you're willing to "dig into" "mounds of stuff", you may "be rewarded" with "spectacular deals."

Capezio   19 | 14 | 17 | M
1776 Broadway, 2nd fl. (bet. 57th & 58th Sts.), 1/9/A/B/C/D to 59th St./ Columbus Circle, 212-586-5140
1650 Broadway (51st St.), 1/9 to 50th St., 212-245-2130 S
678 Broadway, 2nd fl. (bet. Bond & Great Jones Sts.), N/R to 8th St., 212-254-4018 S
136 E. 61st St. (Lexington Ave.), 4/5/6/N/R/W to 59th St./Lexington Ave., 212-758-8833
1651 Third Ave. (bet. 92nd & 93rd Sts.), 6 to 96th St., 212-348-7210
877-532-6237; www.capeziodance.com
◾ "Good-quality" men's, women's and kids' "dancers' essentials from apparel to footwear" are the *pointe* of this chain that dates back to 1857; it's "not just for ballerinas", though, as it offers an "almost overwhelming selection" of "great work-out" gear as well, and though a few find the prices tutu "high", insiders divulge they "give discounts" to performers with appropriate ID.

Capitol Fishing Tackle Co. C   – | – | – | M
218 W. 23rd St. (bet. 7th & 8th Aves.), 1/9 to 23rd St.; C/E to 23rd St., 212-929-6132; 800-528-0853
If the kitschy, cool neon sign and fishing bric-a-brac in the windows don't lure you into this 105-year-old institution, a fixture on 23rd Street since 1969, perhaps the range of product lines will; aimed at all levels, from novice to pro, this experienced angler stocks top-notch brand names in rods, reels and lines for freshwater, saltwater, surf casting and fly-fishing, plus the dedicated staff takes their hobby seriously – they're determined not to have their customers tell the dreaded tale of 'the one that got away.'

Cappellini Modern Age   – | – | – | VE
102 Wooster St. (bet. Prince & Spring Sts.), N/R to Prince St., 212-966-0669; www.cappellininewyork.com
Hipsters seeking the sleekest innovative contemporary furniture from today's hottest international designers head to the SoHo store of this Milanese manufacturer; the gallery space displays chairs

68   subscribe to zagat.com

		M	P	S	C

covered in pebbles by Marcel Wanders, whimsical plastic rainbow seating from Patrick Nourguet and curvy benches by Jean-Marie Massaud; don't miss the colorful hand-knotted rugs designed by Christine Van Der Hurd in the back.

Cap Sud C — | — | — | E
218 Lafayette St. (bet. Broome & Spring Sts.), N/R to Prince St.; 6 to Spring St., 212-219-8508
Distinctly French in sensibility – starting with the woven bistro chairs for sale outside – this SoHo store features lighting by Julie Prisca and Les Migrateurs, along with accessories and furniture from the Christian Liaigre school of design.

Carapan Urban Spa & Store ●SC — 20 | 20 | 19 | M
5 W. 16th St. (bet. 5th & 6th Aves.), 4/5/6/L/N/R/Q/W to 14th St./ Union Sq., 212-627-2265; www.carapan.com
■ Located near the trendy Flatiron District, this "relaxing", sweet-smelling stalwart offers a "good selection" of bath and beauty products with a Native American accent at "moderate" prices; N.B. appointments can also be made for a variety of spa services, including facials and massage.

Carlyle Custom Convertibles S — 23 | 18 | 19 | E
1066 Third Ave. (bet. 62nd & 63rd Sts.), 4/5/6/N/R/W to 59th St./ Lexington Ave., 212-838-1525
1375 Third Ave. (bet. 78th & 79th Sts.), 6 to 77th St., 212-570-2236
122 W. 18th St. (bet. 6th & 7th Aves.), 1/2/3/9/F/L/V to 14th Ave./6th Ave., 212-675-3212
www.carlylesofa.com
■ "It's as comfortable as a bed", "but it's a beautiful couch" declare devotees of this chainlet's convertible sofas; you can choose from the stock available or use your own material and specs and have a "splendid" custom-made version constructed; it's "a little more expensive" than some others, but for the "very good quality", it's "worth it", and the Chelsea Custom Clearance Center on 18th Street offers discounts on premade pieces.

Carmine Street Guitars C — | — | — | M
42 Carmine St. (bet. Bedford & Bleecker Sts.), 1/9 to Houston St., 212-691-8400; www.carminestreetguitars.com
"A master woodworker who makes his own" reasonably priced Kelly custom line is the man behind the counter at this "low-key" spot in a former Village speakeasy; "lots of unexpected" new, used and consigned strummable instruments and a "great selection of resonators" await purchase by "cool" cats who come for "quality and knowledge instead of a big name" only.

Carnegie Cards & Gifts ●SC ▽ 23 | 19 | 16 | M
56 W. 57th St. (bet. 5th & 6th Aves.), F to 57th St., 212-977-2494
■ "Cluttered but cute" Midtown shop where you're likely to find everything from "lotions, potions and handbags" to "little home things"; it's "the perfect place for thoughtful presents", and there's a "great selection of cards" to accompany them.

CAROLINA HERRERA 27 | 27 | 26 | VE
954 Madison Ave. (75th St.), 6 to 77th St., 212-249-6552; www.carolinaherrera.com
■ Though the wedding dresses are "one-of-a-kind", brides-to-be aren't the only ones given "the most individualized attention in

vote at zagat.com 69

town" at this "beautifully furnished flagship" on the Upper East Side; a "wonderful, caring staff" epitomizes the "grace and style" of the designer herself, making sure the "gorgeous, sexy gowns" and other "well-made" clothes are "discreetly displayed" in an "elegant" space with a "Guggenheim Museum–like" spiral stair.

Caron Boutique C | - | - | - | VE

675 Madison Ave. (bet. 61st & 62nd Sts.), 4/5/6/N/R/W to 59th/ Lexington Ave., 212-319-4888

This nearly one-century-old French perfumery has opened its first New York boutique on Madison Avenue, bringing a tradition of luxurious, "rare fragrances", which are even available in Baccarat crystal bottles, and exceptional service to Upper Eastsiders, who presumably can afford to support the sumptuous space, accented in faux marble, glass and gold filigree, that's a replica of the original on Avenue Montaigne in Paris.

CARTIER | 29 | 28 | 24 | VE

653 Fifth Ave. (52nd St.), E/V to 5th Ave./53rd St., 212-753-0111; www.cartier.com

■ When you crave the "*crème de la crème*", this "legendary" French jeweler is one of *les musts*; within its "magnificent townhouse" – a Fifth Avenue fixture since 1917 – lie "glittering display cases" full of "exquisite", "classy and understated" icons, like the "incomparable" Trinity rings and "the best tank watches", along with "younger, edgier" pieces; the staff is "well trained", "but the service department is truly extraordinary"; P.S. a recent "marvelous renovation" has created new space for the burgundy-colored leather goods and bridal registry.

Casa Amadeo Antigua Casa Hernandez | - | - | - | M

786 Prospect Ave. (bet. Longwood Ave. & 160th St.), Bronx, 2/5 to Prospect Ave., 718-328-6896

An integral player in New York's music scene since 1927, when it first opened in East Harlem, this fabled phenom, now located in Longwood, Bronx, features a staggering collection of Puerto Rican and Latin titles on CD and vinyl; set in a turn-of-the-century building, the store takes its name from its present owner, songwriter Mike Amadeo, and its original proprietor, Victoria Hernandez, sister of famed composer Rafael, and has long been a community hangout for performers, including Eddie Palmieri and Ray Barretto.

Cassina USA | 27 | 25 | 21 | VE

155 E. 56th St. (bet. Lexington & 3rd Aves.), 4/5/6/N/R/W to 59th St./ Lexington Ave., 212-245-2121; www.cassinausa.com

■ "*Ciao, bella*" salute supporters of this East 50s furniture store showcasing the "best" "modern, sleek", "to-drool-over" designs by Piero Lissoni and Philippe Starck, as well as the cream of the classic crop, with seating, desks and tables by masters Frank Lloyd Wright, Le Corbusier, Charles Rennie Mackintosh and Gerrit Rietveld; dramatic Flos lighting by Jasper Morrison and a "surprisingly warm" staff are added turn-ons.

Castor & Pollux ●SC | - | - | - | E

67½ Sixth Ave. (Bergen St.), Brooklyn, 2/3 to Bergen St., 718-398-4141

On an unlikely Prospect Heights block, two Martha Stewart alums have set up this cute-as-a-button boutique where many of the impeccably stylish goods – a succinct selection of women's and baby clothing, jewelry, handbags, toys and beauty products – are

M | P | S | C

designed and crafted by the owners themselves; a hipster-chick's best friend, this yearling has been known to lure discriminating Manhattanites for its one-of-a-kind wares.

Casual Male Big & Tall   15 | 13 | 19 | M
291 Third Ave. (bet. 22nd & 23rd Sts.), 6 to 23rd St., 212-532-1415 ● S
527 86th St. (bet. 5th Ave. & Fort Hamilton Pkwy.), Brooklyn, R to 86th St., 718-921-9770
2435 Flatbush Ave. (bet. Aves. T & U), Brooklyn, 2/5 to Flatbush Ave., 718-252-1313
1110 Pennsylvania Ave. (bet. Cozine & Flatlands Aves.), Brooklyn, 718-649-2924
Bay Plaza Shopping Ctr., 2094 Bartow Ave. (CoOp City Blvd.), Bronx, 6 to Pelham Bay Park, 718-379-4148
945 White Plains Rd. (bet. Bruckner Blvd. & Story Ave.), Bronx, 718-239-0761
2295 Richmond Ave., Staten Island, 718-370-7767
www.casualmale.com

◼ "Just when you thought you could never find quality in your size – presto!" you come across "a whole store [actually, a whole chain] full of dressy, comfy stuff" expressly made for men of stature; malcontents mutter about "the poor merchandise selection" – "some good fashions, some polyester nightmares" – but most maintain the business-, casual- and activewear represent "the best buys for big guys" and laud the "affable help."

Caswell-Massey S C   24 | 22 | 22 | M
518 Lexington Ave. (48th St.), 4/6/E/V to 51st St./Lexington Ave., 212-755-2254; www.caswell-massey.com

◼ "Polished wooden counters and shelves" and chandeliers give this "classic" in the East 40s an "elegant ambiance from another age", and indeed the company claims to be America's oldest (1752) chemist/perfumer; "beauty products with a timeless appeal" like the popular Almond & Aloe line reside alongside "toiletries for babies and people with sensitive skin", shaving accessories and colognes that are said to have been favored by the founding father George Washington.

Catherine Malandrino S C   26 | 23 | 19 | VE
468 Broome St. (Greene St.), C/E to Spring St., 212-925-6765; www.catherinemalandrino.com

◼ SoHo "cool" merges with "frilly femininity" at this Broome Street boutique, a favorite of celebrities and hip stylists for its "fun, flirty" dresses and "well-cut" women's separates; while even disciples deplore the "limited selection" and the fact that the "floaty" "pieces are so heavy on the wallet", most praise the "friendly staff" and "neat artwork" on the "trademark" chartreuse walls.

CATIMINI S C   28 | 25 | 19 | VE
1284 Madison Ave. (bet. 91st & 92nd Sts.), 6 to 96th St., 212-987-0688; www.catimini.com

◼ "This is where those kids who look like city kids shop" pronounce proponents who head to this Upper East boutique, the only U.S. branch of the French chain, for "adorable", "fun", "stylish" clothing "with a European flair"; the "beautiful but pricey" collection, which also includes footwear, whimsical bedding and cups and saucers, is "very cute" for "wee little ones" as well as children up to size 12.

vote at zagat.com

	M	P	S	C

CCS Counter Spy Shop C | – | – | – | E |
444 Madison Ave. (49th St.), E/V to 5th Ave./53rd St., 212-688-8500; 866-779-4843; www.spyzone.com
The only store in New York among seven global locations, this East 40s outlet brings all your secret-agent dreams to life with "just what you want" in gas masks and gadgets; the "pretty cool" if slightly "creepy" merchandise, like a camera the size of your thumbnail, is a novelty to novices but a necessity to spy novelists.

Cécile et Jeanne ⏺ S C | – | – | – | M |
1100 Madison Ave. (bet. 82nd & 83rd Sts.), 4/5/6 to 86th St., 212-535-5700
436 W. Broadway (bet. Prince & Spring Sts.), C/E to Spring St., 212-625-3535
www.cecileetjeanne.com
"Satisfy any craving for whimsical jewelry" at this SoHo hangout (with a new Madison Avenue *cousine*) of a Paris-based designer, whose limited U.S. distribution makes the handmade pieces – especially the signature doves – coveted by career women who like bold, resin-studded baubles; a change of store management last year has increased the profile of this exclusive line.

Celine C | 25 | 23 | 21 | VE |
667 Madison Ave. (bet. 60th & 61st Sts.), N/R/W to 5th Ave./59th St., 212-486-9700; www.celine.com
■ Marrying an American sensibility to a "tasteful", established French label, designer "Michael Kors delivers" designs that "dreams are made of" – constructed from the "best fabrics" with "unbeatable" tailoring – "for the pampered woman" who patronizes this "clean, sleek" Upper East Side boutique; complementing the "classy" clothes are "expensive accessories", perfume and leather goods, including the signature Inca loafer.

CELLINI | 28 | 24 | 23 | VE |
509 Madison Ave. (bet. 52nd & 53rd Sts.), E/V to 5th Ave./53rd St., 212-888-0505
Waldorf-Astoria, 301 Park Ave. (49th St.), 6 to 51st St., 212-751-9824
◪ Wristwatch worshipers say whether it's the Waldorf-Astoria location or the East 50s branch, "for pure selection, no one is better" than this establishment, a "fabulous" place for "hard-to-find" and "limited editions", especially of "luxury brands" like Franck Müller; "prices are high", but it's possible to "get deals" from the "tough", yet highly "knowledgeable staff"; N.B. there's a strong selection of European jewelry as well.

CENTURY 21 ⏺ S | 22 | 10 | 9 | I |
22 Cortlandt St. (bet. B'way & Church St.), 2/3/4/5/A/C/J/M/Z to Fulton St./B'way/Nassau, 212-227-9092 C
472 86th St. (bet. 4th & 5th Aves.), Brooklyn, R to 86th St., 718-748-3266
www.c21stores.com
◪ "Support Downtown" by "bargain shopping" for "divine" "designer duds", "upscale" bed linens and cosmetics at this "madhouse" discount "goldmine" (with a branch in Brooklyn); women vie for space in the "scary" communal dressing rooms, "men can't try on clothes" at all and everyone "battles" "throngs" of "fashion hounds" "inspecting for flaws" in the aisles, but in the end, "who cares if the salespeople treat you like cows" and check-out takes a century? – it's all "sooo worth it", 'cause "when you hit, you hit big!"

72   subscribe to zagat.com

| M | P | S | C |

Ceramica 🆂🅲   _- | - | - | M_
59 Thompson St. (bet. Broome & Spring Sts.), C/E to Spring St., 212-941-1307; 800-228-0858; www.ceramicadirect.com
Umbria and Tuscany come to the table with the 20 imported, hand-painted majolica patterns sold at this SoHo ceramic shop; Italian craftsmen (mainly from the famed village of Deruta) employ 600-year-old techniques to create dinnerware, pasta bowls, platters and pitchers that have a traditional look but are lead-free and dishwasher-safe to suit contemporary life.

Cerruti 🅲   ∇ 23 | 23 | 23 | VE
789 Madison Ave. (bet. 66th & 67th Sts.), 6 to 68th St., 212-327-2222; www.cerruti.com
■ As "one of the best suit-makers around", it's reassuring that the Italian design house lives up to its reputation (since 1881) as a premier tailor in this high-ceilinged boutique in the East 60s; just be sure to 86 the budget when fondling the fashionably conservative goods in wool, silk and suede for both the *signore* and *signora*.

Cesare Paciotti 🅲   ∇ 24 | 26 | 18 | VE
833 Madison Ave. (bet. 69th & 70th Sts.), 6 to 68th St., 212-452-1222; www.cesare-paciotti.com
■ Strut your stuff in these sexy stilettos and you'll "definitely find a sugar daddy" quip customers who hail Cesare on the Upper East Side for its "superb selection" of the "finest footwear with an edge" (certain to tempt the "splurge impulse in all of us"); still, a handful huff that "service has decreased over the years", shrugging "why bother?"

Champagne Video ●🆂   16 | 13 | 15 | I
1577 First Ave. (82nd St.), 4/5/6 to 86th St., 212-772-2058
1194 First Ave. (bet. 64th & 65th Sts.), 6 to 68th St., 212-517-5050
1416 Third Ave. (bet. 80th & 81st Sts.), 6 to 77th St., 212-517-8700
213 W. 79th St. (bet. Amsterdam Ave. & B'way), 1/9 to 79th St., 212-873-4600
www.champagnevideo.com
■ A predominantly Upper East Side "local" "independent chain featuring enough of what you need (including porn) without censorship"; while the "selection is limited", it's "good for VHS and DVD buys."

Champs ●   16 | 13 | 13 | M
South Street Seaport, Pier 17, 89 South St. (John St.), 2/3/4/5/A/C/J/M/Z to Fulton St./B'way/Nassau, 212-406-6944 🆂
1381 Sixth Ave. (56th St.), F to 57th St., 212-757-3634 🆂
1 W. 34th St. (5th Ave.), 6 to 33rd St., 212-239-3256 🆂
Staten Island Mall, 2655 Richmond Ave. (Ring Rd.), Staten Island, 718-698-1560
www.champssports.com
■ "Good-for-basics" chain where you can "pick up sneaks, Yanks jerseys, socks", activewear and "athletic gear" "in season" from "big-name sure sellers" like Adidas, Puma, Spalding, Vans, Louisville and the like; but those seeking high-end products jab at the "weak selection" and nix it as an "excuse for a full-service sporting-goods store."

vote at zagat.com   73

| M | P | S | C |

Chanel
| 27 | 26 | 21 | VE |

15 E. 57th St. (bet. 5th & Madison Aves.), N/R/W to 5th Ave./59th St., 212-355-5050 S C
139 Spring St. (bet. Greene & Wooster Sts.), N/R to Prince St., 212-334-0055
800-550-0005; www.chanel.com

◪ "What tops Chanel?" – not much assert enthusiasts who call the 57th Street flagship and its newer SoHo sibling "the ultimate in luxury", giving high-fives to the "classic beauty and workmanship" of the women's apparel and accessories – now "modern and sexy" thanks to designer Karl Lagerfeld, who's taken "über-branding" to a whole new level; "label-conscious" ladies opt for those "timeless" quilted bags or the "always-in-fashion" suits, while others settle for lipstick, "perfume or a scarf"; still, even Coco would go loco at the "iffy service" ("intimidating" vs. "impeccable") and "elitist" prices.

Chanel Fine Jewelry
▽ | 25 | 25 | 22 | VE |

733 Madison Ave. (64th St.), F to 63rd St./Lexington Ave., 212-535-5828; 800-550-0005; www.chanel.com

■ "Finally, the jewelry gets a store of its own" laud lovers of this new "luxe paradise" in the East 60s, designed by Peter Marino, with the fashion house's signature beige-and-black color scheme; the hedonistic baubles "exude the class and style" of Mlle. Coco's "original designs" (the signature matelassee pieces are quilted, just like the purses), as does the label-clad staff that "treats you like royalty"; P.S. walk through the adjoining bag-and-shoe boutique to check out "the ladies' room where Chanel perfumes are available for freshening up."

Charles Jourdan
| 23 | 23 | 20 | E |

155 Spring St. (bet. W. B'way & Wooster St.), C/E to Spring St., 212-219-0490; www.charles-jourdan.com

◪ "My tootsies love this store" swoons a "made-it crowd" that coos over the "variety of styles from fancy-schmancy to basic everyday" to super-"sexy" at this SoHo boutique; these "shoes last" insist some surveyors who swear they "never go out of style", but a few beg to differ, asserting "they never change and we wish they did."

Charles P. Rogers Brass Bed Co. ●S
| 23 | 20 | 20 | E |

55 W. 17th St. (bet. 5th & 6th Aves.), 4/5/6/L/N/Q/R/W to 14th St./Union Sq., 212-675-4400; 800-582-6229; www.charlesprogers.com

■ This manufacturer began making "beautiful" brass, wrought-iron and wooden beds in the mid-19th-century and continues to sell a "fabulous" selection ranging from canopied to contemporary styles at "great prices" at its store in the Flatiron District; "excellent personalized service" also helps shoppers rest easy.

Charles Tyrwhitt S
| – | – | – | E |

377 Madison Ave. (46th St.), 4/5/6/7/S to 42nd St./Grand Central, 212-286-8988; 866-797-2701; www.ctshirts.com

Newly arrived among the Midtown men's clothiers, this British-based store offers a contemporary spin on classic Jermyn Street styling (albeit actually manufactured in Italy); the matte-black shelves brim with colorful cotton dress shirts (both his and hers) with distinctive removable brass stays, as well as silk ties and cuff links for handy coordination; most models retail at $80, but such

subscribe to zagat.com

| M | P | S | C |

accoutrement as spacious fitting rooms and knowledgeable staffers harken to higher-priced haberdashers.

Cheap Jack's ●S | 17 | 10 | 11 | E |
841 Broadway (bet. 13th & 14th Sts.), 4/5/6/L/N/Q/R/W to 14th St./ Union Sq., 212-777-9564; www.cheapjacks.com

■ "If you have time to search the racks" (they stretch up to the ceiling), "you'll almost always find something to ring your chimes" at this Union Square used-clothing warehouse, crammed with "well-preserved winter coats", "vintage denim", Eisenhower-era dresses and tons of ties and T-shirts; but cons counter "this place should be called Overpriced Jack's", given the "ridiculous" tags.

Chelsea Garden Center Home ●SC | 25 | 25 | 20 | E |
435 Hudson St. (bet. Leroy & Morton Sts.), 1/9 to Canal St., 212-727-7100; www.chelseagardencenter.com

■ "A veritable oasis in the city", this "huge loft space" in the West Village offers "high-quality" "gorgeous plants, pots and furniture", as well as "tinkling waterfalls", inspiring "lust" in even the most "die-hard urbanite"; though service is "attentive" and the "blooms are lovely and well cared for", many find the wares "overpriced"; N.B. all botanicals are cultivated in its sister nursery in Chelsea.

Chelsea Second Hand Guitars C | – | – | – | M |
220 W. 23rd St. (bet. 7th & 8th Aves.), 1/2/C/E to 23rd St., 212-675-4993

Salivate over a secondhand Les Paul sitting in the window of this crowded storefront that rents, sells and consigns used vintage guitars, basses, amps and equipment next door to the fabled Chelsea Hotel; there's "no place to stand, it's impossible to browse", and "if you're not a famous rock star, be prepared not to be spoken to", but work up your nerve because assertive strummers can score bargains here.

Chelsea Wholesale Flower Market SC | 24 | 19 | 18 | M |
75 Ninth Ave. (bet. 15th & 16th Sts.), A/C/E/L to 14th St./8th Ave., 212-620-7500; www.chelseaflowersny.com

■ "Amateur botanists" classify this "wholesale wonderland" in the Chelsea Market as "a piece of the country in the middle of NYC"; devotees dig the "incredible selection" of "beautiful flowers" and "great plants" as well as "good pots and supplies" at "fair prices"; bouquets are also bestowed upon the "helpful service."

Cherry ●S   ▽ | 20 | 16 | 16 | M |
19 Eighth Ave. (bet. Jane & W. 12th Sts.), A/C/E/L to 14th St./8th Ave., 212-924-1410

■ Nestled amid a row of boutiques, this small Villager offers an array of his-and-hers apparel that looks "ultra-trendy", even though it dates from the 1950s–80s; mostly daywear, the "designer merch" includes early Calvin Klein and Anne Klein, plus glitzy footwear from shoemaker-to-the-stars Joseph LaRue; however, skeptics snap the stuff's "slightly overpriced", given the humble digs.

Children's General Store SC   ▽ | 20 | 20 | 18 | M |
2473 Broadway (bet. 91st & 92nd Sts.), 1/2/3/9 to 96th St., 212-580-2723
Grand Central, 107 E. 42nd St., 4/5/6/7/S to 42nd St./Grand Central, 212-682-0004 ●

■ "If you take your kids to the Playspace playground" on the Upper West Side or commute to Grand Central Terminal, "you can't avoid

vote at zagat.com   75

a stop" at these "nicely set up" toy stores; the puzzles, books, educational games and sundry items are organized by category, and while the "selection is limited", it's well-edited so you may discover "stuff you won't find elsewhere" inlcuding "smaller less expensive items."

Children's Place, The ●🅢🅒   17 | 16 | 14 | I
22 W. 34th St. (bet. 5th & 6th Aves.), B/D/F/N/Q/R/V/W to 34th St./ Herald Sq., 212-904-1190; 800-527-5355; www.childrensplace.com
For additional locations, see Top Chain Stores index
◰ "Inexpensive but real cute clothes" for little ones that "meet the need for trendy stuff" can be found at this chainster with locations in all five boroughs; "your dollar goes a long way here" – "the prices won't leave you wondering whether you can throw in a few socks" – plus "sales are frequent"; some shoppers find that "not the best quality materials are used, but for a little kid, it's not a big deal" – just "don't expect it to last more than two children."

Chloé 🅒   26 | 24 | 21 | VE
850 Madison Ave. (70th St.), 6 to 68th St., 212-717-8220; www.chloe.com
■ Designer Phoebe Philo brings a "British cheekiness" to this 50-year-old French label, and her "cutting-edge" sensibility shows up in this Upper East Side boutique filled with "effortlessly chic" dresses and "flamboyant" T-shirts; "sophisticated shoppers" suggest that, since celebrities and "insiders get the pick of the fab stuff, get there pre-season" before everything (especially the "great-fitting pants") is gone.

CHOPARD 🅒   28 | 27 | 23 | VE
725 Madison Ave. (bet. 63rd & 64th Sts.), 6 to 68th St., 212-218-7222; www.chopard.com
■ Fitted with mahogany and a marble fireplace, this East 60s jewel box of a "blinding gem" boutique is a veritable "candy store for big girls" whose sweet tooth runs to "nice, large-sized stones", "exquisitely intricate" designs and the "beautiful" signature Happy Diamond timepieces (the loose jewels float inside the face); this is a pretty "great spot for indulgence", though "not *everything* is prohibitively expensive."

CHRISTIAN DIOR 🅢🅒   26 | 26 | 22 | VE
21 E. 57th St. (bet. 5th & Madison Aves.), N/R/W to 5th Ave./59th St., 212-931-2950; www.dior.com
■ From perfume to purses, "the pleasures of Dior are many", and this "beautiful store for the beautiful people" on 57th Street carries most of 'em; the logo-obsessed love designer John Galliano's "cutting-edge glam" ("crazy, fun clothes" that the *Sex and the City* gals made "surprisingly wearable"), as well as the "of-the-moment" accessories and "good-quality makeup"; yes, it's "high-style at high prices", but "impeccable service that's never snotty" makes the expenditure worthwhile.

Christian Dior Joaillerie 🅢🅒   – | – | – | VE
17 E. 57th St. (bet. 5th & Madison Aves.), N/R/W to 5th Ave./59th St., 212-207-8448; www.dior.com
Located next door to its namesake clothing boutique on 57th Street is this colorful precious and semi-precious jewelry collection, also overseen by designer John Galliano; Dior devotees say it offers "the coolest styles with outstanding quality", whether one's fancy runs to whimsically named pieces like Vampire's Fiancée

| M | P | S | C |

(diamond-skull pendants), molten-gold Nougat rings or the big-rock Miss Dior line.

CHRISTIAN LOUBOUTIN C | 28 | 26 | 21 | VE |
941 Madison Ave. (bet. 74th & 75th Sts.), 6 to 77th St., 212-396-1884
■ "The French certainly don't fail when it comes to shoes", and this "truly creative" designer is a prime example – he "knows how to take something fabulous and make it even better; his "Parisian-style" Madison Avenue "super-chic boutique" "with a floor-to-ceiling chandelier in the alcove" showcases "elegant", feminine" "sky-high heels" adorned with the "notorious" "scarlet sole" that "make you feel beautiful the moment you put them on" – "like a courtesan to Louis XIV."

CHRISTOFLE C | 28 | 26 | 22 | VE |
680 Madison Ave. (62nd St.), N/R/W to 5th Ave./59th St., 212-308-9390
■ For the "finest sterling place settings in the world" and "well-designed silver plate", tony types tout the Upper East Side branch of this über-upscale French silversmith whose flatware, though stratospherically priced, is "well worth" it; it also offers crystal, porcelain and table linens, making it a "great place to shop for weddings" or your own "elegant" entertaining.

Chrome Hearts | – | – | – | VE |
159 E. 64th St. (bet. Lexington & 3rd Aves.), 6 to 68th St., 212-327-0707
Calling all "billionaire bikers": on the Upper East Side, this very "hip spot" showcases "top-of-the-line silver" and the "most amazing leather" goods in "everything from belts to jewelry", much of it "custom-work for celebrities"; some say it's the "coolest retail space in NYC", but to properly reflect the prices, "there should be a VVE category."

Chuckies ●SC | 26 | 20 | 16 | VE |
1073 Third Ave. (bet. 63rd & 64th Sts.), F to 63rd St./Lexington Ave., 212-593-9898
399 W. Broadway (bet. Broome & Spring Sts.), N/R to Prince St., 212-343-1717
■ "It's always a joy to see what's on the rack" at these "hip" slices of "heaven for shoe mavens" in SoHo and the East 60s chockablock with "awesome" "designer" footwear "from Jimmy Choos" on down the line; the "high style" extends from the "crazy" setting – (think velvet couches and chandeliers) to the attitude ("snobby staff" sigh the snubbed); P.S. "you better be a trust-fund baby to shop here" – unless you "stop by during sale" time for "bargains."

Circuit City | 20 | 17 | 14 | M |
2232 Broadway (80th St.), 1/9 to 79th St., 212-362-9850 ●S
232 E. 86th St. (bet. 2nd & 3rd Aves.), 4/5/6 to 86th St., 212-734-1694
52 E. 14th St. (bet. 4th & 5th Aves.), 4/5/6/L/N/Q/R/W to 14th St./Union Sq., 212-387-0730
625 Atlantic Ave., 2nd fl. (Fort Greene Pl.), Brooklyn, 2/3/4/5/N/Q/R/W to Atlantic Ave./Flatbush Ave., 718-399-2990
136-03 20th Ave., Queens, 7 to Main St., 718-961-4246
96-05 Queens Blvd. (Junction Blvd.), Queens, G/R/V to 63rd Dr./Queens Blvd., 718-275-2077

(continued)

vote at zagat.com   77

M | P | S | C

(continued)
Circuit City
Staten Island Mall, 2505 Richmond Ave., Staten Island, 718-982-1182
800-843-2489; www.circuitcity.com

▪ "If it requires an outlet, batteries or a player of any sort, they have it" at this national chain of "electronic wonderlands", and "the price is good, though you'd better find it yourself" – "they have few sales reps on the floors" and not enough folks behind the registers; instead of cooling your jets in the "frustratingly" "long checkout line", try "ordering it online and picking it up right in the store whenever you want."

C.I.T.E. Design S   ▽ 18 | 17 | 14 | M
100, 108, 120 Wooster St. (bet. Prince & Spring Sts.), 6 to Spring St./ N/R to Prince St., 212-431-7272; www.cite-design.com

▪ This "interesting series" of three SoHo stores clustered on one side of Wooster Street starts at the southern end with a shop offering an assortment of "whimsical" gifts like kitschy plastic grass, along with practical Pyrex jars; the next space houses a collection of "groovy" mid-century furniture, followed by one featuring items and accessories with a Danish bent; the selections "can be hit or miss", but most "keep going back."

City Opera Thrift Shop S   20 | 18 | 16 | M
222 E. 23rd St. (bet. 2nd & 3rd Aves.), 6 to 23rd St., 212-684-5344

▪ Boasting the "most pleasant atmosphere of any thrift shop in town" – and it's on a Gramercy Park "block loaded with 'em" – this store offers "unusual furniture", "designer duds" and "idiosyncratic items", like the "occasional vintage opera costume"; some sigh over the "overpriced", "limited stock", but converts clap hands over their "classy finds."

City Quilter, The S   27 | 25 | 27 | M
157 W. 24th St. (bet. 6th & 7th Aves.), 1/9 to 23rd St., 212-807-0390; www.cityquilter.com

■ "It's amazing what they cram into this tiny", "cozy" Chelsea "quilters' heaven" that "does a great job of displaying" its 1,300 bolts of "special", contemporary cotton fabrics and "supplies such as books, notions" and "interesting patterns"; the nimble-fingered make a beeline for "wonderful" "classes that cover a variety of hand and machine techniques" and give a thumbs-up to the "friendly, funny crew."

City Sports ●SC   18 | 15 | 15 | M
153 E. 53rd St. (bet. Lexington & 3rd Aves.), E/V to 53rd St./ Lexington Ave., 212-317-0541; www.citysports.com

▪ You'll find "nothing fancy" at this Midtown athletic retreat, but you will find a "fair selection and fair prices" on "clothing specific to different sports", including "excellent women's workout wear", "activity-related footwear" and sporting goods for every season; "check out their sale section for amazing deals on still current styles", but since the staff can be "invisible", you may have to be game to go it alone.

Claire's Accessories S   12 | 11 | 11 | I
1385 Broadway (bet. 37th & 38th Sts.), B/D/F/N/Q/R/V/W to 34th St./ Herald Sq., 212-302-6616 ●
755 Broadway (bet. 8th St. & Waverly Pl.), N/R to 8th St.; 6 to Astor Pl., 212-353-3980 ●

78   subscribe to zagat.com

| | | | | M | P | S | C |

(continued)
Claire's Accessories
720 Lexington Ave. (58th St.), 4/5/6/N/R/W to 59th St./Lexington Ave., 212-644-8665 ◐
1381 Sixth Ave. (56th St.), F to 57th St., 212-977-9294 ◐
2133 86th St. (Bay Pkwy.), Brooklyn, M/W to Bay Pkwy., 718-333-9631 ◐
476 86th St. (bet. 4th & 5th Aves.), Brooklyn, R to 86th St., 718-630-5895 ◐
Bay Terrace Shopping Ctr., 21201 26th Ave. (212th St.), Queens, Q13 or Q28 bus, 718-225-8392 ◐
107-29 71st Ave. (Austin St.), Queens, E/F/G/R/V to Forest Hills/71st Ave., 718-261-1680
www.claires.com

▰Anyone "who is or acts like a 12-year-old" enjoys indulging in the "dirt-cheap", "disposable jewelry" and "lots of hair thingies" displayed by this chain, aka the "goody-bag capital of the world"; fans find it the "perfect spot to shop for little sisters" or a "quick trend fix", but foes fume that the fads will outlast the merchandise and deplore the "indifferent service by gum-smacking teens."

Classic Sofa S ∇ | 24 | 16 | 18 | E |
5 W. 22nd St. (bet. 5th & 6th Aves.), N/R to 23rd St., 212-620-0485; www.classicsofa.com

■ "If you want a good, comfortable sofa that doesn't look like every other one, shop here" say supporters of this Flatiron custom-couch company that offers hardwood frames, down-fill and a "great fabric selection" that ranges from suede to chenille and canvas; moreover, you can "have it your way", including "odd sizes and shapes", in as little as two weeks turnaround time.

Clay Pot ◐SC | 25 | 23 | 21 | E |
162 Seventh Ave. (bet. 1st St. & Garfield Pl.), Brooklyn, Q to 7th Ave., 800-989-3579; www.clay-pot.com

▰"Everyone loves getting gifts" from this "Park Slope staple", which carries a "bit pricey" "collection of works by artisans in all mediums", "from pottery and [handblown glass] to funky jewelry and elegant wedding bands"; "be prepared to fight a crowd on weekends" and holiday seasons, but the "helpful staff" makes waiting "worth it."

Clea Colet | – | – | – | VE |
960 Madison Ave. (bet. 75th & 76th Sts.), 6 to 77th St., 212-396-4608; www.cleacolet.com

"Feminine designs and atmosphere" are found at this designer's by-appointment-only Madison Avenue bridal boutique; made of exquisite, top-of-the-line silk and lace, these classic gowns range from "charmingly fanciful" with regal trains and sweeping skirts to glamorous and seductive with curve-enhancing silhouettes; headpieces are created in-house, while all of the handcrafted detailing is done in Europe.

Clio SC | – | – | – | M |
92 Thompson St. (bet. Prince & Spring Sts.), C/E to Spring St., 212-966-8991; www.clio-home.com

Named after the Greek muse of history, this small SoHo newcomer inspires with an eclectic selection of home accessories that ranges from whimsical to worldly; horn salad servers, handblown glasses, cheese plates, colorful contemporary ceramics and

vote at zagat.com

clean cylindrical lighting are displayed on farm tables and in cupboards that are also for sale.

Cloisters, The S C | 21 | 20 | 18 | M |
The Cloisters, Fort Tryon Park, A to 190th St., 212-650-2277
■ "If you love Medieval" goodies, feed your Dungeons-and-Dragons fetish with "classy trinkets from the Dark Ages" at this "pleasant" boutique in the "beautiful" "castle"-like branch of the Met in Fort Tryon Park; it's "such a tiny space", its "limited selection" doesn't lure wanna-be knights and damsels "out of their way to shop", but if you're far Uptown, "it's worth a look-see."

CLUB MONACO | 20 | 20 | 16 | M |
2376 Broadway (87th St.), 1/9 to 86th St., 212-579-2587
520 Broadway (bet. Broome & Spring Sts.), C/E to Spring St., 212-941-1511
160 Fifth Ave. (21st St.), N/R to 23rd St., 212-352-0936 ● S
121 Prince St. (bet. Greene & Wooster Sts.), N/R to Prince St., 212-533-8930
1111 Third Ave. (65th St.), 6 to 68th St., 212-355-2949
8 W. 57th St. (5th Ave.), N/R/W to 5th Ave./59th St., 212-459-9863
888-580-5084; www.clubmonaco.com
■ "For the budding fashionista" who isn't yet "so label conscious", this "minimal, chic" Canadian Club serves up everything from "clean, spare" (some say "bland") "black and white basics" to "smart Prada and Helmut Lang imitations" "from the latest runway", all at "an affordable price"; "inventory is switched monthly, so you never get bored", and their "absolutely fab" threads are "easy to wear", provided you're both hip and "hipless."

Clyde's ● S | 26 | 22 | 22 | E |
926 Madison Ave. (74th St.), 6 to 77th St., 212-744-5050;
800-792-5933; www.clydesonmadison.com
■ "You can pick up your Joey New York Facial Scrub and your potassium iodide tablets in one trip" at this "boutiquey, little" Upper East Side pharmacy that also has an "outstanding selection of beauty products", along with other "pretty pricey notions" like Rigaud candles; if you need help, the "salesgirls know it all."

Coach ● S | 24 | 23 | 20 | E |
620 Fifth Ave. (50th St.), E/V to 5th Ave./53rd St., 212-245-4148
79 Fifth Ave. (16th St.), N/R/W/Q/4/5/6 to 14th St./Union Sq., 212-675-6403
595 Madison Ave. (57th St.), N/R/W to 5th Ave./59th St., 212-754-0041
342 Madison Ave. (44th St.), 4/5/6/7/S to 42nd St./Grand Central, 212-599-4777
143 Prince St. (bet. W. B'way & Wooster St.), N/R to Prince St., 212-473-6925
South Street Seaport, 193 Front St. (Water St.), 2/3/4/5/A/C/J/M/Z to Fulton St./B'way/Nassau, 212-425-4350
888-262-6224; www.coach.com
■ "Always the gold standard for leather goods" chorus customers who canter over to this chain for "every kind of bag you could want", "trendsetting accessories" and "indestructible" shoes, all of "unsurpassed quality" that "lasts for years"; the "knowledgeable staff" "treats you like royalty" plus they offer a "wonderful repair policy", but the less-impressed maintain that it's "become too mainstream" – "it seems like everyone and their mother have one of their" purses.

subscribe to zagat.com

| | | M | P | S | C |

C.O. Bigelow Chemists ◐🅂🅒   27 | 22 | 20 | M
414 Sixth Ave. (bet. 8th & 9th Sts.), A/C/E/F/S/V to W. 4th St., 212-533-2700; 800-793-5433; www.bigelowchemists.com
■ "About as chic as a drugstore gets" sums up this "atmospheric" 1838 West Village classic where "old-time remedies and beauty products co-exist with the latest New Age aromatherapy and herbal cures", "hard-to-find", "offbeat imported items", "terrific hair ornaments" and "cool cosmetics and trinkets" that make for nifty little stocking stuffers; just note that "while it exudes nostalgia, the prices are wholeheartedly 2003"; still, supporters are "happy it's still here" and proclaim "may it never fall to Duane Reade."

Coconut Company   – | – | – | E
131 Greene St. (bet. Houston & Prince Sts.), N/R to Prince St., 212-539-1940
With an eclectic, albeit somewhat schizophrenic, mix of French antiques and Asian-inspired chairs and tables, this SoHo store strives for a kind of vague colonial elegance; one of the highlights here is Ian Mankin's collection of subtly striped fabrics.

Cohen's Fashion Optical ◐🅂🅒   15 | 14 | 14 | M
767 Lexington Ave. (60th St.), 4/5/6/N/R/W to 59th St./Lexington Ave., 212-751-6652; 800-393-7440; www.cohensfashionoptical.com
Additional locations throughout the NY area
◪ "Glasses for the masses" alongside "designer" numbers add up to an eyewear chain with "something for everyone"; but service that veers from "clueless" and "disinterested" to "very good" and "helpful", and all the "wheeling and dealing" ("don't forget your coupon"), make a few feel framed.

Cole Haan   23 | 22 | 20 | E
620 Fifth Ave. (50th St.), B/D/F/V to 47-50th Sts./Rockefeller Ctr., 212-765-9747
667 Madison Ave. (61st St.), 4/5/6/N/R/W to 59th/Lexington Ave., 212-421-8440; www.colehaan.com 🅂
■ "Treat your feet" to "butter soft", "comfortable", "solidly crafted shoes – you'll wear out before they do"; the "fabulous selection" of "beautiful", "classic" footwear and "basic leather goods" is "stylish but conservative", plus the men's choices "have a nice edge", including Nike Air-tech soles; "from free replacement laces to friendly smiles", the "pleasant atmosphere" makes this Fifth and Madison Avenue pair "necessary stops" on any walking tour.

Colony Music ◐🅂🅒   25 | 13 | 19 | E
1619 Broadway (49th St.), 1/9 to 50th St., 212-265-2050;
www.colonymusic.com
◪ Housed "in the Brill building, an icon "synonymous with American songwriting", this 50-plus-year-old "institution" is a "great" "source for music and memorabilia that's theatrical in nature"; it's "the place to go for sheet music", Broadway and pop and "tough-to-find stuff", plus there's a "huge karaoke selection"; still, "they'll charge you for the convenience of having it" wail the wallet-pinched, who shriek at the "comically high prices."

COMME DES GARÇONS 🅂🅒   24 | 26 | 20 | VE
520 W. 22nd St. (bet. 10th & 11th Aves.), C/E to 23rd St., 212-604-9200
■ Even if you're "not destined to wear" Rei Kawakubo's "edgy" designs, visiting her "super space-age" "jewel" is "well worth

vote at zagat.com

the hike" to the edge of the Chelsea gallery district; from the brushed-aluminum entryway to the bright, white interior of steel booths, it seems "more museum than store" until you note the "outrageously expensive" prices on the "Japanese avant-garde clothing that could double as art."

CompUSA ◐S   20 | 16 | 11 | M
420 Fifth Ave. (37th St.), B/D/F/N/Q/R/V/W to 34th St., 212-764-6224
1775 Broadway (57th St.), A/B/C/D/1/2 to 59th St./Columbus Circle, 212-262-9711
97-77 Queens Blvd. (64th Rd.), Queens, R/G/V to 63rd Dr., 718-286-4798
800-653-3831; www.CompUSA.com
◨ A "comprehensive" selection of software, scanners, PCs, Macs and handhelds, as well as a "remarkable choice of games", is at your fingertips in these "busy" "warehouse" "musts for the computer geek" in you; "shabby service" might have you feeling you've "been through hell and back", but techies with "help-yourself attitude" find "all the minutiae" you and your desktop "could ever need."

Constança Basto S C   – | – | – | E
573 Hudson St. (bet. Bank & 11th Sts.), A/C/E/L to 14th St./8th Ave., 212-645-3233; www.constancabasto.com
Known for her slithery, sky-high jeweled sandals and sleek, vibrant-colored heels – the barer, the better – Brazilian designer Constança Basto brings a riot of Rio to her new West Village shop; brilliant orange stripes and gilded mirrors line the walls of this bright, boudoir-like boutique that serves up substance and eye candy alike.

Cooper-Hewitt National Design   22 | 17 | 16 | M
Museum Shop S C
Cooper-Hewitt, 2 E. 91st St. (5th Ave.), 4/5/6 to 86th St., 212-849-8355; www.si.edu/ndm
■ "Don't let the old-school architecture" of the "gorgeous mansion it's housed in" "fool you" – this Upper East Side design "store has lots of cool, modern, funky items, from jewelry to wrapping paper to alarm clocks and ear-shaped paper clips"; the staff "does not rush you" as you browse the shelves "in Andrew Carnegie's library" for "a range of items you probably don't need at a range of prices you're willing to pay."

Cose Bella   – | – | – | VE
7 E. 81st St. (bet. 5th & Madison Aves.), 6 to 77th St., 212-988-4210
"Beautiful designs and wonderful service that makes every bride feel like a princess" coo customers who throw the "wonderful" designer and staff at this East 80s shop bouquets; there's more than walk-the-aisle-wear, however – discriminating shoppers also fall for the "couture" ready-to-wear "at semi-couture prices" (including "gorgeous dresses"), "with simple but elegant tailoring in an incredible array of beautiful silks" and sumptuous fabrics.

Cosmophonic Sound   – | – | – | E
1622 First Ave. (84th St.), 4/5/6 to 86th St., 212-734-0459; www.cosmophonic.com
If you're looking for service on your large-screen TV projector, head downstairs to this "friendly" East 80s electronics store where "discriminating" shoppers can see the latest plasma TVs and customized remote controls and get "knowledgeable, attentive" guidance in planning their multi-room automation system.

| M | P | S | C |

COSTCO WHOLESALE ●S | 22 | 12 | 9 | I |
976 Third Ave. (39th St.), Brooklyn, M/N/R/W to 36th St., 718-965-7603
32-50 Vernon Blvd. (B'way), Queens, N/W to Broadway, 718-267-3680
2975 Richmond Ave. (Staten Island Expwy.), Staten Island, 718-982-9000
800-774-2678; www.costco.com
☑ For "one-stop" "bulk" "shopping like the Brady Bunch could've used", these outer borough, members-only "leviathans" sell "almost anything", from "massive tubs of condiments" to "clothes and electronics" – "they even do vacations and prescriptions"; if you have the patience for "insanely long lines", the "mandatory car" to cart the goods and "an extra apartment to hold it all", you can "stock up" on "great-deal" "quality brands" like Calvin Klein and Levi's, and if you're particularly "gluttonous", "you can have a [free] lunch with all the tastings they offer."

Costume National S C | 24 | 24 | 17 | VE |
108 Wooster St. (bet. Prince & Spring Sts.), N/R to Prince St., 212-431-1530; www.costumenational.com
■ There's nothing costumey in this "austere", midnight-hued SoHo shop with its luminescent borders – just a "well-made, modern" collection by Italian designer Ennio Capasa of his-and-hers tailored jackets, separates and "some of the world's most beautiful" shoes; the "down-to-earth" staff keeps its distance as you traverse racks filled with "basic black", "streamlined-but-not-too-minimal" clothing that's "flattering if you have less than 3 percent body fat."

Council Thrift Shop S | 15 | 10 | 12 | I |
246 E. 84th St. (bet. 2nd & 3rd Aves.), 4/5/6 to 86th St., 212-439-8373; www.ncjwny.org
☑ "An occasional jewel can be found" among the "quality" designer clothes and "great household goods" at this Upper East Side thrift shop that benefits programs provided by the National Council of Jewish Women; though it's sometimes "a little more expensive than others", cognoscenti counsel there are "off-seasonal sales" that make it "worth a stop."

COUNTRY FLOORS | 27 | 25 | 18 | VE |
15 E. 16th St. (bet. 5th Ave. & Union Sq. W.), 4/5/6/L/N/Q/R/W to 14th St./Union Sq., 212-627-8300; www.countryfloors.com
■ "Definitely not your run-of-the-mill store", this "gorgeous" Union Square showroom sells a "beautiful" and "unique" "assortment" of "upper-end" floor and wall "tiles from all over the world", including handmade ones from Portugal, Provence and Morocco; the staff is "helpful" and "knowledgeable", but don't be floored by the prices.

Country Home & Comfort S | – | – | – | M |
43 W. 22nd St. (bet. 5th & 6th Aves.), N/R to 23rd St., 212-675-2705; www.countryhomeandcomfort.com
Not just for admirers of Americana, as the name implies, the "well-displayed" sofas, cupboards and tables at this Flatiron home-furnishings store are also imported from Indonesia, Holland and Hungary; styles range from contemporary to Asian-inspired.

Crabtree & Evelyn | 21 | 22 | 19 | M |
1310 Madison Ave. (bet. 92nd & 93rd Sts.), 6 to 96th St., 212-289-3923
520 Madison Ave. (bet. 53rd & 54th Sts.), E/V to 5th Ave./53rd St., 212-758-6419 C

(continued)

vote at zagat.com

(continued)
Crabtree & Evelyn
Rockefeller Ctr., 620 Fifth Ave. (bet. 49th & 50th Sts.), B/D/F/V to 47th-50th Sts./Rockefeller Ctr., 212-581-5022
800-272-2873; www.crabtreeandevelyn.com
■ The Anglo-oriented amble over to this toiletries trio to locate "lovely gifts for the hostess, grandma or mom" at "reasonable prices"; a "friendly, helpful" staff will help you choose from a "great selection" of "good quality" bath products, candles, home fragrances, potpourri and English-accented teas, cookies, lemon curd and chutney.

Craft Caravan – | – | – | E
63 Greene St. (bet. Broome & Spring Sts.), N/R to Prince St., 212-431-6669
A favorite haunt of fashion editors and stylists, this SoHo pioneer showcases a collection of cultures – from Japanese kimonos and African caftans to Native American cuffs – plus functions as a paradise for fabric and bead aficionados with its well-edited home furnishings collection; the low-key staff is more than happy to describe the origin of each exquisitely crafted piece.

Crane & Co., Paper Makers S C   27 | 22 | 20 | E
Rockefeller Ctr., 59 W. 49th St./30 Rockefeller Plaza (bet. 5th & 6th Aves.), B/D/F/V to 47-50 Sts./Rockefeller Ctr., 212-582-6829; www.crane.com
■ For stationery that makes a simple "thank-you note seem like presidential correspondence", this Rockefeller Center store provides "possibly the most well-made paper on the planet" that's "perfect for any occasion"; though style mavens maintain the stock's "conservative", more insist that "new designs and colors" provide "arty" alternatives at prices that range from "reasonable" to "top-end."

CRATE & BARREL ● S   23 | 23 | 18 | M
Cable Bldg., 611 Broadway (Houston St.), F/S/V to B'way/Lafayette, 212-308-0011
650 Madison Ave. (60th St.), N/R/W to 5th Ave./59th St., 212-308-0011
800-967-6696; www.crateandbarrel.com
■ "If you need to start from scratch", this Midtown "must for any Manhattan apartment" is a "one-stop shop" whose "practical" housewares and handsome, "sturdy" furniture are "perfect for those on a budget who don't want to show it"; "it's also the place to stock up before a party" or for "wedding presents" (the "whole reason to get married is to register" here); N.B. there's a new 40,000-sq.-ft. branch in SoHo, a stone's throw from the Angelika Film Center, in the historic Cable building.

CREED   29 | 28 | 22 | VE
9 Bond St. (bet. B'way & Lafayette St.), 6 to Bleecker St., 212-228-1732 ● S
680 Madison Ave. (61st St.), N/R/W to 5th Ave./59th St., 212-838-2780
897 Madison Ave. (72nd St.), 6 to 68th St., 212-794-4480
■ Since 1760, this Anglo-Franco firm has been making "the most luxurious" scents, which have come to be "relished" by the "rich and famous" ("Audrey Hepburn's" signature "Spring Flowers is a perennial favorite", and Grace Kelly and Natalie Wood were also fans), as well as "fashionistas"; just an ounce of caution: "mix-and-match only if your wallet allows, otherwise go with the non-personalized" perfumes.

| | | | | M | P | S | C |

Crouch & Fitzgerald ⓢ   26 | 21 | 25 | E
400 Madison Ave. (48th St.), B/D/F/V to 47-50th Sts./Rockefeller Ctr., 212-755-5888
■ Established in 1839, this "old-time leather store" on Madison Avenue still thrives thanks to "excellent quality" and a "wide selection" including "staples like Tumi and Hartmann" business cases, with "refined, old-world" "service to match"; the "products may not always have the highest styling, but classic and long lasting are better attributes anyway", and traditionalists take note: they carry "the gentleman's comb-and-file case for the breast pocket"; P.S. mark your calendar for their "super summer sale."

Crunch ●ⓢ   ▽ 18 | 14 | 12 | M
54 E. 13th St. (bet. B'way & University Pl.), 4/5/6/L/N/Q/R/W to 14th St./Union Sq., 212-475-2018
404 Lafayette St. (bet. Astor Pl. & 4th St.), 6 to Astor Pl., 212-614-0120
888-227-8624; www.crunch.com
☑ After your endorphin fix, you can get a shopper's high at these "nice" Village gyms purveying "cool", "comfortable workout wear" as well as yoga mats, candles, skincare products, videos and CDs, all at "better prices if you're a member"; while critics carp about their "boring", "walking-billboard" branded gear, they carry other "funky" lines like Marika and Hardtail as well.

Crush ●ⓒ   – | – | – | E
860 Lexington Ave. (bet. 64th & 65th Sts.), 6 to 68th St., 212-535-8142
Think pink at this effervescent East 60s boutique (previously of Brooklyn), whose slogan is 'hip stuff you'll want' – and you probably will, given the mix of mint-condition vintage and new "kitschy, fun clothing", "girlie gifts", children's toys and even delightful dog carriers, as sported in the movie *Legally Blonde*.

Cynthia Rowley ⓢⓒ   23 | 21 | 22 | E
112 Wooster St. (bet. Prince & Spring Sts.), N/R to Prince St., 212-334-1144
■ Girls just wanna have fun in this "girlie-girl emporium", its quilted pastel walls a breath of "fresh air" in oh-so-boho SoHo; admirers applaud the store's "spunky vibe" with its rows of "whimsical", "flirty" clothing, accessories and cosmetics from the "queen of swell", and laud the "low-pressure" sales staff that's "honest" with "helpful suggestions."

DAFFY'S ●ⓢ   16 | 9 | 8 | I
1775 Broadway Ave. (57th St.), 1/9/A/B/C/D to 59th St., 212-294-4477
1311 Broadway (34th St.), B/D/F/N/Q/R/V/W to 34th St./Herald Sq., 212-736-4477
462 Broadway (Grand St.), 6/J/M/N/Q/R/W to Canal St., 212-334-7444
125 E. 57th St. (bet. Lexington & Park Aves.), 4/5/6/N/W/R to 59th St./Lexington Ave., 212-376-4477
111 Fifth Ave. (18th St.), 4/5/6/L/N/Q/R/W to 14th St./Union Sq., 212-529-4477
335 Madison Ave. (44th St.), 4/5/6/7/S to 42nd St./Grand Central, 212-557-4422
8801 Queens Blvd. (bet. 55th & 56th Aves.), Queens, G/R/V to Grand Ave., 718-760-7787
877-933-2339; www.daffys.com
☑ Bargain predators find it "impossible to resist" "regular" "fishing and hunting" expeditions at this "zoo" for "broke" fashion animals; "Daffaholics" say "the key is knowing when the new shipments

vote at zagat.com   **85**

| M | P | S | C |

come in" so you can "paw through" "stylish" "Italian clothing", "deep-discount designer underwear", the "greatest baby gifts", "adorable European children's" apparel, "occasional killer shoes" and other "treasures"; otherwise, you might find only a "hodgepodge" of "schlock" "picked over like a desert carcass."

Dana Buchman S 24 | 22 | 21 | E
65 E. 57th St. (bet. Madison & Park Aves.), N/R/W to 5th Ave./59th Sts., 212-319-3257; 800-522-3262

■ For those fashionably attuned to the "corporate world" of "conservative" "outfit dressing", this Midtown boutique holds a bull market's worth of "businesswoman" clothing in fabrics that "feel much more expensive than they are"; their "perfect fit" pleases all sizes, including petites, while the service scores points for its "high-end" professionalism "without the pretension."

D & G ◐ S C 23 | 24 | 19 | VE
434 W. Broadway (bet. Prince & Spring Sts.), C/E to Spring St., 212-965-8000; www.dolcegabbana.it

◪ An "outpost for the see-and-be-seen crowd" on SoHo's main drag, these "minimalist", "trippy" digs house "all the glitter and glam" that Domenico Dolce and Stefano Gabbana can capture in their "zany", "very Euro" designs, including "amazingly cut" jeans; but the parsimonious pout it's "way too expensive" for a diffusion line, claiming the goods are "more eye candy than real clothing."

Danskin ◐ S 21 | 17 | 14 | M
159 Columbus Ave. (bet. 67th & 68th Sts.), 1/9 to 66th St., 212-724-2992; 800-288-6749; www.danskin.com

■ This "original", "old standby" in the West 60s sells "long-lasting", "high-quality gear" that's "designed for dancers, but wonderful for any workout", thanks to the "great textiles" used and the "beautiful" styles that the *jeté* set deems "good enough to wear to lunch"; with lines ranging from girls' to plus sizes, it's "for the ballerina in everyone."

Darryl's S C ▽ 22 | 21 | 25 | M
492 Amsterdam Ave. (bet. 83rd & 84th Sts.), 1/9 to 86th St., 212-874-6677

■ "More than just a neighborhood place", this "sweet shop" in an Upper West Side area "without much choice in women's clothing" is "just the right size" to find fashionable, European-designed "items you've searched far and wide for" – from party clothes to work-out gear – thanks to the "great eye" of the eponymous owner.

DataVision ◐ S C 20 | 15 | 12 | M
445 Fifth Ave. (bet. 39th & 40th Sts.), 4/5/6/7/S to 42nd St./Grand Central, 212-689-1111; www.datavis.com

◪ "While the product range is good" at this branch of a chain store near Gramercy Park, the "crowded presentation" of computers, printers and projectors is "pushed" by an aggressive staff quoting "the highest ticket prices out there"; "however, savvy shoppers have the little-known option of haggling with sales reps" for "competitive" coin.

Daum C ▽ 25 | 26 | 25 | VE
694 Madison Ave. (bet. 62nd & 63rd Sts.), N/R/W to 5th Ave./59th St., 212-355-2060; www.daum-france.com

■ "Even if you are not into glass", this "expensive" shop in the East 60s is "a must" declare devotees of its "wonderful workmanship", which consists primarily of *pate de verre* vases, candlesticks, stemware and such; while a few feel that some of the animal- and insect-bedecked designs from the long-standing French manufacturer are "over the top", "helpful salespeople" can assist you in "finding something simpler."

Dave's Army Navy S | 21 | 12 | 17 | I
581 Sixth Ave. (bet. 16th & 17th Sts.), 1/2/3/9/F/L/V to 14th St./6th Ave., 212-989-6444; 800-543-8558
■ "Selling everything the working person (or person that wants to look like a working person) needs", from "Levi's to Carhartt [clothes] to Red Wing shoes" along with army surplus, this Flatiron favorite is "a place every guy wants to shop at"; although there is "no floor plan" and the store's "not a lot to look at", a "friendly staff and almost unbeatable prices" ensure that most "don't leave empty-handed."

David Aaron ●S | 20 | 18 | 16 | M
529 Broadway (bet. Prince & Spring Sts.), N/R to Prince St., 212-431-6022
◪ When you "can't afford Gucci and Prada but still want to look fashionable", slip into some "fantastic", "high-quality knock-off" shoes from Steve Madden's "bustling" SoHo "store for grown-ups"; while mavens are mad for the "cool", "stylish" selection that's "tamer" than his teen line, the less-impressed pout they're "too trendy to be carried past a couple of seasons" and lace into the "lackadaisical help."

Davide Cenci | 25 | 19 | 17 | VE
801 Madison Ave. (bet. 67th & 68th Sts.), 6 to 68th St., 212-628-5910; www.davidecenci.com
◪ "Wonderful Italian style" is well represented by the "great suits, jackets, slacks" and accessories ("the only place for silk socks") at this boutique in a Madison Avenue townhouse; it helps to "have the right body" for the "slim-fitting" wear, but if not, there's always the made-to-measure option; some mutter that "you could better afford to fly to Rome and buy from the source" – or simply "go during the sales"; P.S. ladies, don't overlook the "women's department on the 4th floor", especially the coats.

Davidoff of Geneva S C | 25 | 26 | 24 | VE
535 Madison Ave. (54th St.), E/V to 5th Ave./53rd St., 212-751-9060; www.davidoff.com
■ You'll be as "pampered as if you were buying diamonds" at this "awesome" Swiss stogie Midtown establishment where the "super" staff is "absolutely professional about everything"; understand that "you'll pay full price" for the custom-made, handcrafted cigars, as well as for the ties, luggage and leather goods, but the "wonderful humidor" alone ("great smell") makes it "fun to stop in."

David Saity Jewelry C | 24 | 19 | 23 | VE
450 Park Ave. (bet. 56th & 57th Sts.), 4/5/6/N/R/W to 59th St./Lexington Ave., 212-223-8125
◪ Offering the "absolute last word on Native American jewelry", this Midtown "store is on the wish list of everyone" for whom there's no such thing as "too much turquoise", silver or coral – especially when it's featured in "gorgeous handmade designs"; some sigh the "displays are too crowded to appreciate the detailed work", "but if you can't get to Santa Fe, this is the place."

vote at zagat.com

| M | P | S | C |

David's Bridal ●S
| – | – | – | M |

502 86th St. (bet. 5th & 6th Aves.), Brooklyn, R to 86th St., 718-238-1633; 888-480-2743; www.davidsbridal.com
Covering every bridal base under the sun, this 50-year-old national chain offers everything from size-2 strapless, crystal-beaded A-line gowns to figure-flattering plus-size sheaths to frilly flower-girl dresses, all at prices that won't put parents in hock; guys also get in the act with tuxedoes that go hand-in-hand with bridesmaids' sweet special-occasion wear; N.B. there's also a mega-selection of bright, buoyant styles for the prom-bound.

David Webb C
▽ | 27 | 28 | 25 | VE |

445 Park Ave. (bet. 56th & 57th Sts.), 4/5/6/N/R/W to 59th St./ Lexington Ave., 212-421-3030; www.davidwebb.com
■ Since 1948, this Park Avenue veteran has been satisfying the nature lover in all of us with its impressive array of animal-shaped fine jewelry in bold colors and enamels; though best known for its golden tiger brooches and sapphire-eyed horse clips, it also carries a collection of diamond-studded watches and Etruscan-inspired pieces.

David Yurman C
| 24 | 23 | 21 | VE |

729 Madison Ave. (64th St.), 6 to 68th St., 212-752-4255; 877-226-1400; www.davidyurman.com
◪ "Cultish" describes the clientele of this modernistic "Madison Avenue boutique" that's "small in size but has lots of merchandise" from a "master jewelry designer"; loyalists "love the styling" of his "silver-and-gold combinations" adorned with "colorful stones", but skeptics snap the "trendsetting" two-toned pieces "are so everywhere that individuality is nonexistent."

David Z. C
| 21 | 16 | 15 | M |

821 Broadway (12th St.), 4/5/6/L/N/Q/R/W to 14th St./Union Sq., 212-253-5511 ●S
556 Broadway (bet. Prince & Spring Sts.), 6 to Spring St.; N/R to Prince St., 212-431-5450 ●S
451 Broome St. (Mercer St.), N/R to Prince St.; 6 to Spring St., 212-625-9391
384 Fifth Ave. (bet. 35th & 36th Sts.), 6 to 33rd St.; S/4/5/6/7 to 42nd St./ Grand Central, 212-253-5511
655 Sixth Ave. (21st St.), F/V to 23rd St., 212-807-8546 ●S
■ "Quick to move on fashion trends", this Manhattan chain is "the place" for "casual, sporty", "urban footwear", including "new, hot sneaks for the hip-hop set"; it's a "sensible shoe paradise" with "choices galore" "in all the right flavors at the right price", plus "service is extremely helpful, not pushy"; but a few find fault with the "young sales force that keeps its distance" and sometimes "has a little attitude."

Davis & Warshow, Inc.
▽ | 24 | 20 | 17 | E |

A&D Building, 150 E. 58th St., 4th fl. (bet. Lexington & 3rd Aves.), 4/5/6/N/R/W to 59th St./Lexington Ave., 212-980-0966; www.daviswarshow.com
■ Since 1925, this showroom that's now located in the A&D Building has sold "quality" kitchen and bathroom fixtures (specializing in established American-made brands like Kohler), as well as plumbing and heating supplies; proponents praise the "good" merchandise and "long-standing reliability."

88 subscribe to zagat.com

M | P | S | C

ddc domus design collections   – | – | – | E
181 Madison Ave. (34th St.), 6 to 33rd St., 212-685-0800; www.ddcnyc.com
Designed by the firm overseen by famed architect Philip Johnson, this airy, white space in Murray Hill boasts a striking wall of undulating angles as well as Italian furniture by masters like Massimo Vignelli and Achille Castiglioni; the leather futon-like sleeper sofa sells well, while the soaring suspended shelving that stretches from floor to ceiling by Carlos Scarpa catches the eye.

DDC Lab **S C**   – | – | – | E
180 Orchard St. (bet. Houston & Stanton Sts.), F/V to 2nd Ave., 212-375-1647; www.ddclab.com
Quench your craving for caffeine, new "fitted jeans" and way-cool accessories in one fell swoop at this hip, high-ceilinged shop on the Lower East Side with an espresso bar in front, denim bar in back and the "well-designed" men's and women's collections by Roberto Crivello and Savania Davies-Keiller in between; blood-red dressing rooms add color to the white-washed brick space, and just-friendly-enough salespeople are so cool they don't have to act it.

Dean & Deluca ● **S C**   26 | 23 | 19 | E
560 Broadway (Prince St.), N/R to Prince St., 212-226-6800; 800-781-4050; www.deandeluca.com
■ Loyalists love the "unusual" kitchen-oriented items, from caviar servers and Italian copper to sterling-silver salt cellars and top-of-the-line Laguiole knives, that are displayed in the rear of this statusy SoHo gourmet food mecca; but the miserly can only moan about "overpriced objects for those who obviously order in."

Deco Jewels ● **S C**   – | – | – | E
131 Thompson St. (bet. Houston & Prince Sts.), N/R to Prince St., 212-253-1222
"Specializing in vintage handbags made of Lucite", this "adorable little store" in SoHo is also "quite a find" for "well-curated costume jewelry" and "the best cuff links ever"; owner "Janice Berkson knows her stuff – and what looks best on you" too.

De La Concha Tobacconist ● **S C**   25 | 24 | 23 | E
1390 Sixth Ave. (bet. 56th & 57th Sts.), F to 57th St., 212-757-3167; www.delaconcha.com
■ "They often have what you can't get elsewhere" at this "well-stocked", "family-owned" "cigar-smokers' paradise" where you'll also find a "great selection of tobaccos" and "exotic cigarettes"; added attractions like a "knowledgeable" staff, "reasonable prices" and a hand-roller on-premises once a week make this Midtown mainstay "a complete winner."

DeMask **S**   – | – | – | E
135 W. 22nd St. (bet. 6th & 7th Aves.), 1/9 to 23rd St., 212-352-2850; www.demask.com
"Personalized service compensates" for the skin sensation you might get from this boutique's own line of specialized couture; with stores in Europe and Chelsea, plus recent spreads in mainstream fashion mags, it's the hottest place to purchase all things rubber, from gowns and tux tails for the ballroom to hoods and mitts for the dungeon; perch on the red round banquette and flip through the rack of high-end fetish publications while your special someone wriggles in and out of prospective purchases.

vote at zagat.com

| | | | M | P | S | C |

Demeter 🆂🅲   25 | 22 | 22 | I
83 Second Ave. (bet. 4th & 5th Sts.), F/V to 2nd Ave., 212-473-3450; 800-482-0422
■ "The most unusual perfumes" award probably has to go to this East Village fragrance boutique – after all, "who else has something called Funeral Home", much less Dirt, Tomato, Grass, Laundromat and Holy Water?; more conventional, "pretty" florals like Sweet Pea round out the selection of 150 "great single-note scents", ensuring that there's "at least one for everyone."

Demolition Depot/   – | – | – | VE
Irreplaceable Artifacts ⌀
216 E. 125th St. (bet. 2nd & 3rd Aves.), 4/5/6 to 125th St., 212-777-2900; www.irreplaceableartifacts.com
Four floors of salvaged goods from mansions to Masonic lodges crowd this Harlem warehouse whose architectural remnants range from church alters to entire wood-paneled rooms, making it the "best stop for that hard-to-find antique piece to complete your home"; for porcelain bathroom fixtures, hit the third floor, where much more than just a kitchen sink can be snagged.

DEMPSEY & CARROLL 🅲   29 | 25 | 26 | VE
110 E. 57th St. (bet. Lexington & Park Aves.), 4/5/6/N/R/W to 59th St./Lexington Ave., 212-486-7526
1058 Madison Ave. (80th St.), 6 to 77th St., 212-249-6444
800-444-4019; www.dempseyandcarroll.com
■ "One box of the embossed stationery" purveyed at these "*très exclusive*" East Side shops makes you "feel like *la crème de la crème* of NY"; its "beautifully done, traditional engraved" goods, voted No. 1 in this *Survey*'s Lifestyle category, are a "must-have" if you're "mailing to people who care" and are "nicely presented" in "lovely" settings; customers "needing help with matters of etiquette" receive "excellent guidance" from the "incredible staff", and even though it's "verrry expensive", it's "worth it" at these "bastions of civilized living."

Dernier Cri ◐🆂🅲   – | – | – | E
869 Washington St. (bet. 13th & 14th Sts.), A/C/E/L to 14th St./8th Ave., 212-242-6061
For chicks about to rock, owner Stacia Valle, MTV alum and former manager of the band Third Eye Blind, salutes you at her funky industrial-looking Meatpacking District boutique strewn with animal-skin rugs and packed with cult-fave labels like Gauge, Luella Bartley and Twinkle; this slick music-minded mecca (dig the Ramones on the stereo) gets goth, alternative and punk princesses to walk this way with shirred blouses, Avril Lavigne-esque culottes, minis and, of course, killer jeans and tees – get-down gear that says yeah baby, 'I'm with the band.'

Designer Resale 🆂   22 | 20 | 17 | M
324 E. 81st St. (bet. 1st & 2nd Aves.), 6 to 77th St., 212-734-3639; www.resaleclothing.org
■ "Nothing like buying an Anna Sui suit for one-third the price" gloat groupies of this spacious consignment store that stretches across several brownstones' ground floors; "arranged in neat, well-edited racks", the "delectable items in all sizes" "range from Chanel and Armani to [relative] cheapies like Eileen Fisher and Ellen Tracy Company"; what with the affiliated Gentleman's Resale store

M | P | S | C

adjacent and a Children's Resale shop just up the block, this concern threatens to "take up nearly all of East 81st Street."

Design Source By Dave Sanders C — | — | — | E
115 Bowery (bet. Grand & Hester Sts.), 6/J/M/N/Q/R/W to Canal St., 212-274-0022
Dave-otees tout the "great selection" of decorative hardware, tubs, sinks and plumbing fixtures at this Lower East Side bathroom source; "reliable" salespeople don't hesitate to "recommend reasonably priced" options, but hardworking folk might find the hours daunting, as it's "closed weekends" and otherwise open only till 5 PM.

Desiron S C ∇ 21 | 21 | 17 | VE
111 Greene St. (bet. Prince & Spring Sts.), N/R to Prince St., 212-966-0404
204 Park Ave. S. (bet. 17th & 18th Sts.), 4/5/6/L/N/Q/R/W to 14th St./Union Sq., 212-979-5777
139 W. 22nd St. (bet. 6th & 7th Aves.), 1/9/F/V to 23rd St., 212-414-4070
www.desiron.com
■ The Carfaro brothers custom-make "stylish", "user-friendly" mid-century-inspired furniture like bookcases, beds, bureaus and tables out of metal, wood and Lucite and showcase them in their trio of shops; minimalist-mavens maintain items are "expensive but worth it."

Destination ● S C — | — | — | VE
32-36 Little W. 12th St. (bet. Ninth Ave. & Washington Sts.), A/C/E/L to 14th St./8th Ave., 212-727-2031; www.destinationny.net
"Art meets fashion" in this cavernous Meatpacking District shop lauded for its chic display of "fantastic, one-of-a-kind" antique and fine jewelry and drool-worthy European handbags and shoes from a "unique" selection of "great designers", many "unheralded", with an attached gallery space that keeps the smooth groove rollin'; N.B. at press time, uptown designer Jackie Rogers had just opened a tony shop with red lacquered walls within this top-flight destination, featuring her made-to-order eveningwear at high-altitude prices.

Details 22 | 17 | 12 | M
347 Bleecker St. (10th St.), 1/9 to Christopher St., 212-414-0039 ● S C
188 Columbus Ave. (bet. 68th & 69th Sts.), B/C to 72nd St., 212-362-7344
142 Eighth Ave. (16th St.), A/C/E/L to 14th St./8th Ave., 212-366-9498
■ This "cute", "crowded" trio of home-furnishings shops boasts more bathroom accessories (from shower curtains to toiletries), "scented candles" and "decorative kitchen accents" like "unique glassware" and placemats than "you can shake a stick at", making it a sensible source for "decorating and gifts."

df S C — | — | — | M
248 Smith St. (bet. DeGraw & Douglass Sts.), Brooklyn, F/G to Bergen St., 718-935-9490
Located on the coolest *calle* in Carroll Gardens, this newcomer specializes in contemporary home furnishings from Mexico City, or what locals there refer to as '*Distrito Federal*'; the goods here look more haute than hacienda and range from colored glasses and bowls to versatile veneered cubes in white or walnut; the mostly exclusive collection is housed in a small but airy space that was converted from an old barber shop.

vote at zagat.com

Dialogica S   – | – | – | E
59 Greene St. (bet. Broome & Spring Sts.), C/E to Spring St., 212-966-1934; www.dialogica.com
Cavernous, columned furniture store in SoHo owned by a husband-and-wife design team that sells contemporary cabinets, beds, tables and lighting along with expansive sofas, chairs and chaises that can be upholstered in over 200 shades of chenille, velvet or faux suede.

DIANE VON FURSTENBERG S C   27 | 24 | 22 | E
385 W. 12th St. (bet. Washington St. & West Side Hwy.), A/C/E/L to 14th St./8th Ave., 646-486-4800; www.dvf.com
■ It's a "labor of love" to get to this intimate, mirror-ceilinged boutique on a tree-lined street in the Meatpacking District, but DVF disciples declare it's "worth the trip" for the "sleek, sexy" wrap dresses in "distinct patterns" that look "flattering" whether you're "a 15-year-old girl or a 50-year-old woman"; no crowd-control problem here, so if it's "overwhelming personal attention" you want as you navigate the clothes, shoes and accessories – you got it.

Diesel Denim Gallery S   25 | 24 | 19 | E
68 Greene St. (bet. Broome & Spring Sts.), 6 to Spring St.; N/R to Prince St., 212-966-5593; www.diesel.com
◪ "Not for the meek or mild", this "beautifully styled" jean "lover's paradise" offers a "myriad" of men's and women's "cuts, and washes" – enough to "drive you crazy"; "offering a semblance of exclusivity", this SoHo "outpost" features Karl Lagerfeld's special collection and items you won't find at its sister stores; sure, the "denim bar" can "be quite intimidating", but "fear not" – the "knowledgeable staff" "helps you" search for "your perfect pair" of "pricey", "mmm... feel so good" blues.

Diesel Style Lab ◐ S C   22 | 24 | 19 | E
416 W. Broadway (bet. Prince & Spring Sts.), N/R to Prince St., 212-343-3863; www.diesel.com
◪ In addition to "very hot" jeans, this "great-looking" SoHo "spin-off" of the "populist, avant-garde" denim label carries an edgier mix than its "counterparts", including a "wonderful selection of wild and fun urban night wear" for men and women; while devotees delight in the "cool stuff for Generation X", infidels indicate you have to be "Italian model" thin and "think it's normal to spend" oodles on "bizarre items" to shop here; a few crab about the Lab's staff that seems cast from "failed-actor central."

Diesel Superstore   23 | 22 | 17 | E
770 Lexington Ave. (60th St.), 4/5/6/N/R/W to 59th St./Lexington Ave., 212-308-0055 ◐ S
1 Union Sq. W. (14th St.), 4/5/6/L/N/Q/R/W to 14th St./Union Sq., 646-336-8552
www.diesel.com
■ A "postmodern superstore to overwhelm the senses", this "hypermarket" for "vintage-look" "Euro jeans" with a "flattering" fit and all of the collections (including Style Lab and Diesel Kids) "pumps up the volume" – literally – with a DJ booth plus a cafe in the Lexington Avenue store; while "not as personal as the Denim Gallery", it's still where "scenesters and hippies live in peace", "coughing up the dough" for "trendy" "streetwear" "at trendy prices"; the "hip factor" extends to the "very helpful" staff.

| M | P | S | C |

Dimitri Nurseries 🅢🅒 ▽ 21 | 14 | 18 | M
1992 Second Ave. (bet. 102 & 103rd Sts.), 6 to 103rd St., 212-876-3996; www.dimitrisgardencenter.com
■ Fans are "perennial" at this Spanish Harlem greenhouse, nursery and "best-quality garden-service center" that's "worth the trek", since it's the only place in Manhattan that has 15,000 sq. ft. of "reasonably priced" plants and a vast variety of "outdoor trees" that come with "helpful advice" from a staff that's so friendly it makes up for the "inconvenience" of the long trip Uptown.

Disc-O-Rama Music World 20 | 9 | 14 | I
40 Union Sq. E. (bet. 16th & 17th Sts.), 4/5/6/L/N/Q/R/W to 14th St./Union Sq., 212-260-8616
186 W. 4th St. (bet. 6th & 7th Aves.), 1/9 to Christopher St.; A/C/E/F/S/V to W. 4th St., 212-206-8417 🌙🅢🅒
146 W. 4th St. (6th Ave.), 1/9 to Christopher St.; A/C/E/F/S/V to W. 4th St., 212-477-9410
866-606-2614; www.discorama.com
■ "You won't find better deals" than at these three "extremely cramped" music stores, in the Village and Union Square, where "new releases", including DVDs, "top 40 and popular radio hits", plus classical and "popular catalog items" "can be had very cheaply"; "while they may not have everything" and "the used rock selection varies greatly by location", the staff is "generally very friendly" and "if it isn't there, they'll get it for you."

Disney 20 | 23 | 18 | M
147 Columbus Ave. (66th St.), 1/9 to 66th St., 212-362-2386 🌙🅢
711 Fifth Ave. (55th St.), E/V to 5th Ave./53rd St., 212-702-0702 🌙🅢
300 W. 125th St. (bet. Frederick Douglass Blvd. & St. Nicholas Ave.), A/B/C/D to 125th St., 212-749-8390
218 W. 42nd St. (bet. 7th & 8th Aves.), 1/2/3/7/9/N/Q/R/S/W to 42nd St./Times Sq., 212-302-0595 🌙🅢
Kings Plaza, 5100 Kings Plaza (Ralph Ave.), Brooklyn, 718-677-1860 🌙🅢
800-328-0368; www.disneystore.com
☑ "If you love the Mouse, you must visit his house[s]", "where adults can be kids", "kids go wild" and "wallets get vacuumed"; the Fifth Avenue store, in particular, is like "a short trip to the Magic Kingdom", with an "animation gallery" and "multiple levels" "well stocked" with "everything Disney", plus the "lines and high prices that make it as much a headache as the theme park" itself; "it's a world of happiness" for Mickey junkies, but a "nauseating typhoon of color and noise" for the "rodent"-phobic.

DKNY 🌙🅢🅒 21 | 22 | 17 | E
655 Madison Ave. (60th St.), N/R/W to 5th Ave./59th St., 212-223-3569
420 W. Broadway (bet. Prince & Spring Sts.), C/E to Spring St., 646-613-1100
www.dkny.com
☑ Like the Big Apple itself, Donna Karan's "lower-end line" has "a little something for everyone" say natives and tourists "of different ages" and both genders who sail into the "huge, multi-floor" Madison Avenue store or the "spacious" SoHo shop, "highly focused on their hunt" "for those staples with a modern edge" or "making a beeline for the housewares and accessories"; however, opponents opine it's "a bit overhyped", saying the quality of the clothes is just "DKOK."

vote at zagat.com

Doggie-Do & Pussycats Too C   23 | 23 | 22 | E
567 Third Ave. (bet. 37th & 38th Sts.), 4/5/6/7/S to 42nd St./Grand Central, 212-661-9111; www.doggiedo.com
◪ "Pampered" Murray Hill "pets with a Fifth Avenue complex" are gratified by the "unusual" "designer" accessories ("best outerwear for dogs in the city") supplied by this "cute" store; pooches having a bad-fur day can avail themselves of "great grooming" as owners "browse", assisted by the "friendly staff"; however, cat fanciers lament the "small selection" for felines, and penny-pinchers posit that "pricewise, it's way out of line."

Dö Kham ●SC   – | – | – | E
19 Christopher St. (bet. Greenwich Ave. & 7th Ave. S.), 1/9 to Christopher St., 646-486-4064
304 E. Fifth St. (bet. 1st & 2nd Aves.), F/V to 2nd Ave., 212-358-1010
48 Greenwich Ave. (bet. Charles & Perry Sts.), 1/9 to Christopher St., 212-255-9572
51 Prince St. (bet. Lafayette & Mulberry Sts.), 6 to Spring St., 212-966-2404
Why hitch to the Himalayas for "ethereal" his-and-hers clothing, pashmina shawls, mountain-ready fox-fur hats, ethnic jewelry and embellished bedspreads when it's available at its "real-thing"-Tibetan best at these Downtown siblings; customers cotton to the "quality" embroidered gauze and raw silk shirts in a wide range of "amazing" high-intensity colors and lengths, concurring that it's an appealing "addition to the vast world of fashion."

Dolce & Gabbana C   25 | 26 | 21 | VE
825 Madison Ave. (bet. 68th & 69th St.), 6 to 68th St., 212-249-4100; www.dolcegabbana.it
■ Step into *la dolce vita* at this airy Upper East Side boutique filled with the "body-flattering" men's and women's clothes that the D & G guys do so seductively well; all the trappings of the "Euro jet-set" are on display – "22nd-century jeans, the best sunglasses on the planet", "elegant, but not uptight" suits and the famed animal prints ("only they could make leopard spots and flowers on the same blouse work"); "crazy", maybe, but "it's hard to argue with such creativity" – so just say *arrivederci*, bank account.

Domain SC   21 | 22 | 18 | E
938 Broadway (22nd St.), N/R to 23rd St., 212-228-7450
Trump Palace, 1179 Third Ave. (69th St.), 6 to 68th St., 212-639-1101
101 West End Ave. (65th St.), 1/9 to 66th St./Lincoln Ctr., 917-441-2397
www.domain-home.com
■ "Plumper-than-plump" furniture like couches, chairs and chaises, along with "classic", "casually elegant", European-inspired dining tables and armoires, abounds at the Flatiron, East and West Side branches of this chain; most find the prices "fair", adding that there are "good sales" as well.

Domsey's S   16 | 7 | 7 | I
431 Broadway (bet. Hewes & Hooper Sts.), Brooklyn, J/M/Z to Hewes St., 718-384-6000; www.domsey.com
Domsey's Express S
1609 Palmetto St. (Wyckoff Ave.), Brooklyn, L/M to Myrtle/Wycoff Aves., 718-386-7661; www.domsey.com
◪ "Patience is a necessary virtue at this Downtown warehouse setting", a veritable "shopping mall of used clothes organized by type" or "sorted by the pound" – anything from "old (looking) jeans"

to "Army/Navy" surplus to "vintage leather"; malcontents mutter the "ultra-cheap" merchandise is "now too picked-over by local Brooklyn hipsters", but fans find you can still "hit pay dirt" – just "be prepared to sift and sift and sift"; N.B. the Bushwick Express is somewhat smaller.

Donna Karan
23 | 25 | 21 | VE

819 Madison Ave. (bet. 68th & 69th Sts.), 6 to 68th St., 212-861-1001; www.donnakaran.com

■ Murmur "om" as you step inside this "serene oasis" on Madison Avenue, whose "Zen-like" setting (complete with Japanese sculptures and a bamboo garden) complements the "*crème de la crème*" collection clothing (no DKNY here) and extensive home furnishings; in keeping with the mood ("like a world-class spa when you walk in"), the "knowledgeable" sales staff guides males and females in pursuit of shopping nirvana, be it "beautifully sophisticated" basics or more "imaginative" garments.

Donzella
– | – | – | VE

17 White St. (bet. 6th Ave. & W. B'way), 1/9 to Franklin St., 212-965-8919; www.donzella.com

A mid-century-modern collector's dream, this TriBeCa store sells stunning "rare pieces" by heavy-hitters like Paul Frankl, Edward Wormley, T.H. Robsjohn-Gibbings and Tommi Parzinger at "fair prices"; its selection of desks and cocktail tables is estimable, and custom-seating based on old European and American designs is also available.

Dooney & Bourke
22 | 22 | 18 | E

20 E. 60th St. (bet. Madison & Park Aves.), 4/5/6/F/N/R/W to 59th St./Lexington Ave., 212-223-7444; 800-347-5000; www.dooney.com

◪ The "distinctive structured bags" "last for years and years" assert admirers who also frequent this chain's flagship on the Upper East Side for totes, luxury apparel, gloves, shoes and scarves; though the collection has expanded and "become current and relevant", critics consider it "too conservative" and "too expensive."

Door Store 🅂
16 | 15 | 16 | M

601 Amsterdam Ave. (89th St.), 1/9 to 86th St., 212-501-8699
1 Park Ave. (33rd St.), 6 to 33rd St., 212-679-9700
969 Third Ave. (bet. 58th & 59th Sts.), 4/5/6/N/R/W to 59th St./Lexington Ave., 212-421-5273
123 W. 17th St. (bet. 6th & 7th Aves.), 1/9 to 18th St., 212-627-1515
877-366-7867; www.doorstorefurniture.com

◪ "If you walk through the door of this store", you'll find "real furniture" – from dining and bedroom sets to bookcases – at "affordable prices"; frugal folks who are not looking for cutting-edge design make this long-standing East Coast chain their choice for "setting up a first household."

Dosa 🅂 🅒
– | – | – | E

107 Thompson St. (bet. Prince & Spring Sts.), C/E to Spring St., 212-431-1733

Far ahead of its time, this spare boutique started in SoHo in the mid-1980s; furnished with bamboo fixtures and a cement floor, this standard-bearer still attracts attention from lovers of the "hippie-chic look", who embrace its distinctive silk separates in "amazing colors" and textures as staples to layer, mix and match.

vote at zagat.com

Downstairs Records S | - | - | - | M |
1026 Sixth Ave. (bet. 38th & 39th Sts.), B/D/F/N/R/V/W to 34th St./ Herald Sq., 212-354-4684; www.downstairsrecords.com
Though originally located, where else, below street level, this family-owned record store, specializing in oldies, rare titles and vinyl, is now tucked away in a second-floor shop in the Garment District; music buffs thumb through 45s, new and old, from Elvis to Coldplay, 12-inch records, from Cher to Busta Rhymes, and albums, from Funkmaster Flex to Fatboy Slim.

Downtown Yarns C | 23 | 23 | 23 | M |
45 Ave. A (bet. 3rd & 4th Sts.), F/V to 2nd Ave., 212-995-5991
■ "Homey" and "friendly", this "purl of a yarn store in the East Village" feels like it could be "in the Berkshires" with "a pet dog lying about", "a knitting guru to help with questions", a "super-helpful staff" and a "small but nice selection" of "funky, fun stuff"; P.S. there are "great classes for beginners as well as experts."

Drexel Heritage S | 25 | 21 | 19 | E |
32 W. 18th St. (bet. 5th & 6th Aves.), 4/5/6/L/N/R/Q/W to 14th St./ Union Sq., 212-463-0088; www.drexelheritage.com
■ Flatiron branch of a "reputable" 100-year-old manufacturer that sells "high-quality" "traditional furniture" along with more contemporary living room, dining room and bedroom sets inspired by everything from Californian to African influences; just be aware that part of the Heritage of this "fine old name" includes "expensive" price tags.

Drimmers S | ▽ 26 | 13 | 19 | M |
1608 Coney Island Ave. (bet. L & M Sts.), Brooklyn, Q to Ave. M, 718-773-8483; www.drimmers.com
■ The folks at this "friendly" Coney Island "appliance heaven" won't take you for a ride when it comes to their "modest to high-end" merchandise, which is offered at "probably the cheapest price you can get"; you'll find the big stuff (Sub-Zero refrigerators and Thermador professional stoves) on the first floor and smaller items (Miele vacuum cleaners and Krups coffeemakers) on the second; delivery to the five boroughs is included in the sticker price.

Dr. Jays ●SC | - | - | - | M |
33 W. 34th St. (bet. 5th & 6th Aves.), B/D/F/N/Q/R/V/W to 34th St./ Herald Sq., 212-695-3354; www.drjays.com
Additional locations throughout the NY area
With scores of stores throughout Brooklyn, The Bronx, Queens and Manhattan, this urban outfit reels in customers who prefer their kicks and clothing with a hip-hop flava; athletic gear runs the gamut from team caps and sneakers to jerseys and sweatpants from labels like Puma, Pony and Outkast, while stylin' streetwear ranges from Phat Farm and Baby Phat to Timberland and Tommy Girl.

Dune SC | - | - | - | VE |
88 Franklin St. (bet. B'way & Church St.), 1/9 to Franklin St., 212-925-6171; www.dune-ny.com
This stark TriBeCa space showcases sexy steel tables by graphics guru Fabien Baron, wood seating from David Khouri, Michael Solis' colorful storage units and rugs by Harry Allen and Richard Shemtov; everything is made-to-order, and all upholstered pieces are available in the store's award-winning textiles.

| M | P | S | C |

DUNHILL S   26 | 26 | 25 | VE
711 Fifth Ave. (bet. 55th & 56th Sts.), E/V to 53rd St., 212-753-9292; www.dunhill.com

■ "Nothing like a cigar shop where you can also get custom-fitted suits and shirts" attest aficionados who enjoy this "oh-so-English" Midtown "temple of luxe" celebrated for its "great selection" of stogies and "upscale accoutrement" ("the Rolls-Royce of smoke" stores) as well as its "beautiful" clothes and watches; Anglophiles also admire the "fine service" at this century-old, two-floor "true gentleman's paradise" that "makes shopping fun, even for guys."

DYLAN'S CANDY BAR ●SC   24 | 27 | 15 | E
1011 Third Ave. (60th St.), 4/5/6/N/R/W to 59th St./Lexington Ave., 646-735-0078; www.dylanscandybar.com

■ "A real-life Willy Wonka fantasy come true (minus the Oompa-Loompas)", Dylan (daughter of Ralph) Lauren's "whimsical" two-story East 60s "soda shop for the 21st century" has "something for kids of any age", from "not-sold-elsewhere M&M colors" to "vintage Pez dispensers", all "deliciously presented and dazzling in every way" – including the "designer price tags"; N.B. they host kids' birthday parties downstairs.

Earl Jean SC   24 | 21 | 18 | E
160 Mercer St. (bet. Houston & Prince Sts.), N/R to Prince St.; F/V/S to B'way/Lafayette, 212-226-8709; www.earljean.com

■ The "down-to-earth" salespeople may give "you the once over" at this SoHo flagship that feels like a mod rec room, but they're just scoping out which "worth dieting for" jeans work for your big bad bod; this king of "low-riders" gets high-fives for "sexy, Western-style" denim and cords that "make anyone's butt look great" – indeed, combined with the "simply fab" shirts and jackets, it's the uniform of "hipsters, urban cowgirls and uptown well-to-do's"; N.B. there's now a men's collection too.

East Side Kids C   ▽ 20 | 18 | 19 | E
1298 Madison Ave. (92nd St.), 6 to 96th St., 212-360-5000

◪ Parents who find everything here from baby shoes to "real Mary Janes" to tween-friendly boots, plus even a few styles in adult sizes (and free popcorn) want to "tell everyone" about this Upper Eastsider that's also equipped with a stroller-friendly entrance; but don't dillydally during prime time, because the footwear "sells out early each season" (read: back-to-school and bound-for-camp) and may not be reordered.

E.A.T. Gifts SC   21 | 18 | 15 | E
1062 Madison Ave. (80th & 81st Sts.), 6 to 77th St., 212-861-2544; www.elizabar.com

◪ "A wonderful place to pick up little knickknacks" and "silly whatnots" "for care packages, party favors", "stocking stuffers or a "gift for yourself", this Upper Eastsider turns "everyone into a kid"; but cynics sound off that it's "small and crowded", adding they "can't stand Eli Zabar's *meshugge* prices."

E. Braun & Co. C   – | – | – | VE
717 Madison Ave. (bet. 63rd & 64th Sts.), F to Lexington Ave./63rd St., 212-838-0650

Loyalists who like luxe linens head to this Madison Avenue grande dame purveying fine sheets, hand-embroidered tablecloths,

vote at zagat.com

napkins and placemats, plus towels and throws – all imported from Europe; custom-sizes and colors are also available.

Eddie Bauer 17 | 16 | 16 | M
1976 Broadway (bet. 66th & 67th Sts.), 1/9 to 66th St., 212-877-7629 ◐ S
578 Broadway (bet. Houston & Prince Sts.), N/R to Prince St., 212-925-2179
1172 Third Ave. (bet. 68th & 69th Sts.), 6 to 68th St., 212-737-0002
711 Third Ave. (bet. 44th & 45th Sts.), 4/5/6/7/S to 42nd St./Grand Central, 212-808-0820
7000 Austin St. (69th Ave.), Queens, E/F/G/R/V to Forest Hills/71st Ave., 718-459-2270
800-426-8020; www.eddiebauer.com

☑ "Some things never change", but that doesn't bother "outdoorsy types" who "love" the "slow-down style" of "crunchy-granola staples" like "good weekend" chinos, "durable" polo shirts and "warm fleeces" at these "unisex" purveyors of "anti-Manhattan fashion"; stock up on "unique travel gadgets", backpacks and "camping doodads", but "Bauer beware" of "limited service."

Edith Weber & Assoc. – | – | – | VE
994 Madison Ave. (77th St.), 6 to 77th St., 212-570-9668; www.antique-jewelry.com

Though tiny, this boutique offers "fantastic finds" in antique and vintage jewelry – anything from a Georgian mourning brooch to an Edwardian diamond tiara to an art deco wedding band; the tabs reflect the Upper East Side address, but the "friendly" mother-and-son owners, both known educators in the field, are discreetly "willing to adjust prices."

Edmundo Castillo S C – | – | – | E
219 Mott St. (bet. Prince & Spring Sts.), 6 to Spring St., 212-431-5320

Sleek, sophisticated and sliver-sized – think ultimate shoe closet – this acclaimed designer's NoLita shop vaunts its vampy wares with élan; vividly colored suede boots, breathtaking backless ankle-strap, sexy T-strap and bombshell-esque open-toed stilettos, all made for negotiating cab rides, not pavement, are displayed in gray cubbyholes and red shelves, with a few standouts reserved for the front window; long gray curtains, retro-modern lamps and seats and a friendly staff complete the uplifting shopping experience.

e. Harcourt's S C – | – | – | M
219 Mott St. (bet. Prince & Spring Sts.), 6 to Spring St., 212-226-8028

This little gem nestled on trendy Mott Street in NoLita might easily be overlooked if it weren't for the lit candles and fresh flowers floating in a pool in the front window; inside, a small selection of fragrance, soaps, incense and candles – all made in-house – should satisfy those in search of something different.

Eidolon S C ∇ 23 | 25 | 27 | M
233 Fifth Ave. (bet. Carroll & President Sts.), Brooklyn, M/N/R to Union St., 718-638-8194

■ 'Eidolon' means 'ideal image' in Greek, and that's the aim of this fashion-forward Park Slope boutique, a co-operative where local designers are given a pretty, pink-toned showcase for "eclectic", often "handmade" women's apparel and "unique accessories" (including handbags and the "best shoes ever"); the "very friendly owners" ensure there's "always something fun" to try on.

| | | | **M** | **P** | **S** | **C** |

Eight Ball Records ◐ⓈⒸ ─ | ─ | ─ | M
105 E. Ninth St. (bet. 3rd & 4th Aves.), N/R to 8th St.; 6 to Astor Pl., 212-473-6343; 800-699-6343; www.eightballshop.com
Boasting "one of the best selections of vinyl for club DJs", this "East Village standby record shop" sells its own label, rare imports and domestic discs; dance-music connoisseurs clued in to genres like acid jazz, deep trance and drum & bass take their cues here, as do purists who like their oldies and blues on wax; aficionados who prefer to listen first, buy afterward, bring their treasures to the DJ booth and get down to the bitchin' sound system.

Eileen Fisher 23 | 22 | 21 | E
341 Columbus Ave. (bet. 76th & 77th Sts.), 1/9 to 79th St., 212-362-3000
314 E. Ninth St. (bet. 1st & 2nd Aves.), 6 to Astor Pl., 212-529-5715
166 Fifth Ave. (bet. 21st & 22nd Sts.), N/R to 23rd St., 212-924-4777
1039 Madison Ave. (bet. 79th & 80th Sts.), 6 to 77th St., 212-879-7799
521 Madison Ave. (bet. 53rd & 54th Sts.), E/V to 5th Ave./53rd St., 212-759-9888
395 W. Broadway (bet. Broome & Spring Sts.), C/E to Spring St., 212-431-4567 ◐Ⓢ
800-345-3362; www.eileenfisher.com
■ "Over 40s" "get hooked" on the "beautiful simplicity" of this "comfortable" clothing in "understated tones" "typifying womanly elegance"; a "non-threatening" staff "stands ready to assist" at the SoHo flagship where "exemplary urban architecture relates Japanese principles to the designer's clear vision" of "timeless style" – "if you like the potato-sack look" sniff "slim figures"; N.B. the 9th Street store stocks samples you won't find elsewhere.

Einstein-Moomjy Ⓢ 25 | 20 | 20 | E
141 E. 56th St. (bet. Lexington & 3rd Aves.), 4/5/6/N/R/W to 59th St./Lexington Ave., 212-758-0900; 800-864-3633; www.einsteinmoomjy.com
■ From tribal to Tibetan and hand-knotted to broadloom, this "well-lit", "reliable" emporium in the East 50s stocks a "great selection" of "beautiful", "long-lived" "quality" rugs; if the "many one-of-a-kind" carpets don't suit your style, you can call your own shots with custom-made, and there are home furnishings as well.

Elgot ▽ 21 | 11 | 16 | E
937 Lexington Ave. (bet. 68th & 69th Sts.), 6 to 68th St., 212-879-1200; www.elgotkitchens.com
■ Upper Eastsiders who cry Wolf (as well as Sub-Zero, Miele and other "high-end kitchen appliances") call this "convenient" kitchen-and-bath showroom "the only place to go"; the staffers "know their merchandise" and can help design and install custom cabinetry, countertops and plumbing fixtures, but a few who've been burned warn of service ranging from "pushy" to indifferent.

Elizabeth Arden ⓈⒸ ─ | ─ | ─ | M
691 Fifth Ave. (bet. 54th & 55th Sts.), E/V to 5th Ave./53rd St., 212-829-0664; www.elizabetharden.com
Behind the iconic red door on Fifth Avenue lies an extensive selection of this cosmetics-and-skincare pioneer's products – from its best-selling Visible Difference Eight-Hour Cream to the newer ceramide anti-aging treatments; the elegant blond-wood-and-marble-floored townhouse setting is the result of a 2001 makeover designed to keep up with the Joneses (and the Bergdorf Goodmans) down the luxury-goods-lined street; N.B. appointments can also

vote at zagat.com

M P S C

be made for a variety of spa services, including facials, waxing and massage, or with hairdresser Oribe.

Elizabeth Locke C — | — | — | VE
968 Madison Ave. (bet. 75th & 76th Sts.), 6 to 77th St., 212-744-7878
This tiny Upper East Side "jewel box" offers "a piece for every age" – and from every age, since the designer uses anything from ancient coins to 18th-century Chinese objets to 19th-century Venetian glass to fashion her "well-made, distinctive" wares, which are also known for the "wonderful color of the 19 karat gold" she favors.

El Museo Del Barrio S — | — | — | M
1230 Fifth Ave. (104th St.), 6 to 103rd St., 212-831-7272; www.elmuseo.org
At the top of Museum Mile, *amantes de las artes* can browse for books, CDs and posters by and about Puerto Rican, Caribbean and Latin American artists, plus hard-to-find handmade crafts from the islands and Central and South America; the knowledgeable staff is eager to help you navigate through esoterica like *fiestas patrones* masks, wooden santos, mundillo embroidery and porcelain figurines lodged inside *ajote* pods.

Emanuel Ungaro C 26 | 25 | 20 | VE
792 Madison Ave. (67th St.), 6 to 68th St., 212-249-4090; www.emanuelungaro.fr
■ "Perfection" blooms as abundantly as the signature floral prints at this long-standing Madison Avenue boutique, home to the French designer's sensual collection of silk dresses, suits and separates; shoppers sum up its newly renovated interior (starring a fuchsia glass staircase) and sales staff in one word – "beautiful"; sure, everything is "extremely expensive", but "if you can afford it, you have no choice but to buy it" the pampered purr.

Emilio Pucci C 26 | 24 | 22 | VE
24 E. 64th St. (bet. 5th & Madison Aves.), 6 to 68th St., 212-752-4777; www.emiliopucci.com
■ 'Let's do the time warp again' could be the motto of this legendary, "so retro" Upper East Side shop with its "psychedelic" prints beloved by Marilyn Monroe and Jackie O back then, and countless chic women right now (thanks to "seasonal updates" by Christian Lacroix); "if you aren't afraid of color, nothing beats" "splurging" on these "notoriously bright" "classics" – anything from g-strings to men's ties to "beach towels, a don't-miss for summer."

Emporio Armani S 24 | 23 | 20 | E
110 Fifth Ave. (bet. 16th & 17th Sts.), 4/5/6/L/N/Q/R/W to 14th St./Union Sq., 212-727-3240
601 Madison Ave. (bet. 57th & 58th Sts.), N/R/W to 5th Ave./59th St., 212-317-0800
410 W. Broadway (Spring St.), C/E to Spring St., 646-613-8099
www.emporioarmani.com
■ Groupies go gaga over Giorgio's bridge-line emporia where both genders "can buy anything Armani, from underwear to shoes" to "timeless suits" and "comfy jeans", all bearing the trademark "good quality, details and elegant design" at "affordable prices" (well, compared with the designer's high-end collection, anyway); "personalized service" also helps "cultivate customers."

| M | P | S | C |

EMS (Eastern Mountain Sports) ●S | 22 | 18 | 20 | M |
591 Broadway (bet. Houston & Prince Sts.), N/R to Prince St., 212-966-8730
20 W. 61st St. (B'way), 1/9/A/B/C/D to 59th St./Columbus Circle, 212-397-4860
888-463-6367; www.ems.com

■ "Heaven for outdoor junkies" and "crunchy urbanites who yearn" for valleys and streams, these SoHo and Upper West Side chain offshoots stock "high-quality" "hiking and more adventurous equipment" for sports like kayaking and mountaineering, plus some of the "best wicking clothes", "fantastic backpacks" and bicycles; "they've got the goods" (much of it tested by the EMS Climbing School in Mount Washington), plus "they've got smart people behind the counter to help" "novices and the experienced alike."

Enchanted Forest SC | – | – | – | M |
85 Mercer St. (bet. Broome & Spring Sts.), N/R to Prince St., 212-925-6677

Spellbinding from top to bottom, this gallery/toy boutique in SoHo bewitches parents and children alike with its unique collection of puppets, marionettes, soft sculptures, musical instruments and craft kits, all presented in a faux-forest setting that's "truly original"; cross the bridge that serves as an upstairs to reach "one of the best collections of stuffed animals in the city" (say hello to Esmerelda the Warthog) – indeed, unless you're a Grinch, it's hard to leave empty-handed.

Encore S | 22 | 15 | 14 | M |
1132 Madison Ave. (bet. 84th and 85th Sts.), 4/5/6 to 86th St., 212-879-2850; www.encoreresale.com

☒ Since 1954, this Madison Avenue "grandmommy of resale shops" has kept the consignment-minded coming back encore and encore for its "ever-changing selection" of "current styles" ("very Uptown girl – lots of Chanel – but they cram in trendier labels too", plus some menswear); some hiss it's "a hit-or-miss place", but the majority rules it's "one of the best bets for finding a bargain."

Enelra ●SC | ▽ 22 | 17 | 16 | E |
48½ E. Seventh St. (bet. 1st & 2nd Aves.), 6 to Astor Pl., 212-473-2454

■ Sure, this "small" pink-and-red store stocked with "high-end lingerie, boas and robes" and owned by a "very funny East Villager" has "been around forever, but once you discover it, you wanna keep it secret" confide insiders; the "large selection of unique items and old standbys ranges from demure to sporty" to "kinky" to "beautiful, lacy and sexy"; the "knowledgeable" "employees even help lost boyfriends choose well."

Enzo Angiolini S | 20 | 18 | 16 | M |
551 Madison Ave. (55th St.), E/V to 5th Ave./53rd St., 212-339-8921
331 Madison Ave. (bet. 42nd & 43rd Sts.), 4/5/6/7/S to 42nd St./Grand Central, 212-286-8726
Manhattan Mall, 901 Sixth Ave. (bet. 32nd & 33rd Sts.), 1/2/3/9/A/C/E to 34th St./Penn Station; B/D/F/N/Q/R/W to 34th St./Herald Sq., 212-695-8903

■ For "finely crafted", "long-lasting" "treats for your feet" that "won't set you back a pretty penny" head to this national chain; the "leather is usually soft", and styles range from "sophisticated", "classic" and "work appropriate" ("good for climbing the corporate

vote at zagat.com

ladder") to "fashionable and comfortable at the same time"; but a few trendoids lament "it hasn't quite got today's chic" look and complain about "weird sizing."

Equinox Energy Wear ◐ C   21 | 15 | 15 | E
344 Amsterdam Ave. (76th St.), 1/9 to 79th St., 212-721-2171 S
2465 Broadway (92nd St.), 1/2/3/9 to 96th St., 212-721-6384 S
1633 Broadway (50th St.), 1/9 to 50th St., 212-315-9299
897 Broadway (bet. 19th & 20th Sts.), N/R to 23rd St., 212-674-5880 S
205 E. 85th St. (3rd Ave.), 4/5/6 to 86th St., 212-717-8826 S
140 E. 63rd St. (Lexington Ave.), 4/5/6/N/R/W to 59th St./Lexington Ave., 212-752-5360 S
250 E. 54th St. (2nd Ave.), 6/E/V to Lexington Ave./53rd St., 212-753-2793 S
97 Greenwich Ave. (12th St.), 1/2/3/9/F/L/V to 14th St./7th Ave., 212-620-0103 S
420 Lexington Ave. (44th St.), 4/5/6/7/S to 42nd St./Grand Central, 646-227-1074
14 Wall St. (Nassau St.), 3/4 to Wall St., 212-587-7113
www.equinoxnyc.com
▼ "I will not sweat in these threads" vow vaunters of the "great work-out clothes" purveyed at these upscale gyms; "anyone who likes to exercise in style" wearing "stuff that'll take a beating" declares the duds "cute" and "fun", but jaded Gothamites gripe the designs are "too California" and the prices "outrageous."

Erbe S   – | – | – | E
196 Prince St. (bet. MacDougal & Sullivan Sts.), C/E to Spring St., 212-966-1445; www.erbedermocosmetica.com
SoHo stalwart showcasing their own brand of all-natural skincare from Italy that uses only pure plant essences, distillations and oils (like lavender and chamomile) for its bath-and-body products, masks, moisturizers, cleansers and toners; sensitive-skin types will be especially soothed, since everything is also pH balanced and hypo-allergenic; N.B. appointments can also be made for a variety of spa services, including facials, waxing and massage.

ERES C   28 | 24 | 22 | VE
621 Madison Ave. (bet. 58th & 59th Sts.), 4/5/6/N/R/W to 59th St./Lexington Ave., 212-223-3550
98 Wooster St. (Spring St.), C/E to Spring St., 212-431-7300 ◐ S
800-340-6004; www.eresparis.com
■ Ooh-la-la – with "high-style" sleek shops on Madison Avenue and in SoHo, there's "no need to fly to Paris" for this French chain's "very chic" swimwear and intimate apparel that's "always sexy without being overt"; supporters tout the "superb quality, comfort" and "great fit" of these "upscale pieces", including some of the "simplest, well-made bathing suits" and "lovely, sheer" bras, panties and seamed stockings; *oui*, it's "expensive, but it's so beautiful" and "lasts forever."

Eric S C   23 | 20 | 17 | E
1222 Madison Ave. (bet. 88th & 89th Sts.), 4/5/6 to 86th St., 212-289-5762
1333 Third Ave. (bet. 76th & 77th Sts.), 6 to 77th St., 212-288-8250
▼ "Watch out for the drool outside the windows" quip customers who skip over to this "expensive" Upper East Side shoe duo for a "right-on selection" of "the latest designerwear"; "Eric knows what NYC women want", from "the yummiest sandals" to house-label "upscale knockoffs", plus the "quality" "cannot be beat";

while a few find the "staff helpful", others opine they're full of "attitude"; N.B. sibling stores like Little Eric sell kids' footwear.

Erica Tanov S C ▽ 25 | 22 | 22 | E
204 Elizabeth St. (bet. Prince & Spring Sts.), 6 to Spring St., 212-334-8020; www.ericatanov.com

■ With its white walls and hanging bulbs, a "peaceful", "soothing atmosphere" permeates this NoLita space; the designer's "crisp, fresh", "well-made ensembles", often trimmed with "great [vintage] fabrics", "make you feel like a girl", while the "adorable baby gear" caters to your maternal side; the "charming sales help" ensures you will also "fall in love" with an assortment of jewelry, handbags and "epitome-of-cool" sneakers.

Erica Wilson Needle Works C 22 | 19 | 16 | VE
717 Madison Ave. (bet. 63rd & 64th Sts.), 6 to 68th St., 212-832-7290; 800-973-7422

◪ Established in 1965 by Erica Wilson, the "British-trained" "grande dame of needlepoint", this Upper East Side stalwart is still one of "the best sources for high-quality canvases"; while it "stocks everything you need", worked-up stitchers say you "may need to take out a mortgage" to shop here and deem the "service snooty."

Ermenegildo Zegna S 27 | 24 | 24 | VE
743 Fifth Ave. (bet. 57th & 58th Sts.), N/R/W to 5th Ave./59th St., 212-421-4488; www.zegna.com

◪ Some perhaps "have problems pronouncing the name, but [no one] questions" the quality at this Fifth Avenue haberdasher, known for the "best-fitting suits" in "gorgeous" wools, the "finest" ties and other "luxe looks", Italian style; perhaps the "beautiful things are sometimes buried" in the "small" space, but the service is as "impeccable" as the tailoring, making this "the place to buy all your clothes – right after you hit the Lotto", that is.

Erwin Pearl S C – | – | – | M
677 Fifth Ave. (bet. 53rd & 54th Sts.), E/V to 5th Ave./53rd St., 212-207-3820; 800-379-4673
697 Madison Ave. (bet. 62nd & 63rd Sts.), 4/5/6/N/R/W to 59th St./ Lexington Ave., 212-753-3155
Rockefeller Ctr., 70 W. 50th St. (bet. Madison & Park Aves.), B/D/F/V to 47-50th Sts./Rockefeller Ctr., 212-977-9088
www.erwinpearl.com

Amid Midtown's priciest purveyors, this chain offers an oasis of "wonderful costume jewelry that's often mistaken for the real thing" – case in point: their 'Jackie O' three-strand necklace – so convincing are its concoctions of cubic zirconia and glass pearls; there is some "kitschy stuff" too, like the Adorable Pooches line of enamel dogs, all served up by a charmingly attentive staff.

Escada S 26 | 26 | 23 | VE
715 Fifth Ave. (56th St.), N/R/W to 5th Ave./59th St., 212-755-2200; www.escada.com

■ Fashionable *femmes fatales* keep tabs on the "drop-dead gorgeous" inventory at this "ultra-chic" Fifth Avenue boutique, with its "curvaceous" clothing, "wonderful shoes" and tasteful accessories that are "oh, to dream" for; naturally, when buying such things as "beautifully hand-beaded gowns, you pay by the bead" – but the salespeople "treat you as if you matter whether [you purchase] full-price or on sale."

vote at zagat.com

			M P S C

ESPN Zone ●🅂 — | — | — | M
1472 Broadway (42nd St.), 1/2/3/7/9/S to 42nd St./Times Sq., 212-921-3776; www.espn.go.com
Downstairs from the big screens in the same-named Times Square restaurant is an emporium that may bring sports widows as much grief as play-off season; guys and gals glued to the games can swaddle themselves head to foot in ESPN merchandise, from boxers and leather pants to BBQ mitts and rain ponchos, and there are even tiny sizes for cheering chips-off-the-old-block.

Estella 🅂🄲 — | — | — | E
493 Sixth Ave. (bet. 12th & 13th Sts.), 1/2/3/9/F/L/V to 14th St., 212-255-3553
Brightly lit with stark white walls, an antique display table and a minimalist gallery feel, this Village newcomer features a tight collection of finely made, pricey childrenswear from edgy European designers; while the handpicked selection is limited, with more of an emphasis on girls than boys, each piece is special and subtly offbeat, making it well worth exploring.

Ethan Allen 🅂 22 | 22 | 19 | E
192 Lexington Ave. (32nd St.), 6 to 33rd St., 212-213-0600 ●
1107 Third Ave. (65th St.), 4/5/6/N/R/W to 59th St./Lexington Ave., 212-308-7703
103 West End Ave. (bet. 64th & 65th Sts.), 1/9 to 66th St., 212-201-9840
112-33 Queens Blvd. (76th Rd.), Queens, F to 75th St., 718-575-3822
Heartland Shopping Ctr., 2275 Richmond Ave. (Nome Ave.), Staten Island, 718-983-0100
888-324-3571; www.ethanallen.com
■ Fans of this furniture company say it's "come a long way" since it started in 1932, now offering not only "high-quality" "traditional" pieces and accessories but also more "modern" looks; there's also a "good design service" on hand to help "make decorating easy."

ETRO 🄲 27 | 27 | 23 | VE
720 Madison Ave. (bet. 63rd & 64th Sts.), F to Lexington Ave./63rd St., 212-317-9096; www.etro.it
■ Those seeking "true Milanese style" should Ferrari-it to the "sumptuous setting" of this East 60s outpost of the luxury-goods maker known for being "very forward colorwise"; its men's and women's clothing in "luxe fabrics" and "brilliant hues", including "nearly blinding shirts" and trademark paisleys, represents a "fine distillation of vibrant Italian" design, so "wear it with panache."

EUGENIA KIM ●🅂 28 | 24 | 23 | E
203 E. Fourth St. (bet. Aves. A & B), F/V to 2nd Ave., 212-673-9787; www.eugeniakim.com
■ "Everyone who walks through the door" of this "hip" milliner's "intimate" red-and-blue-colored East Village shop is "treated like a star, even if they happen to be one" (she's "adorned the likes of J. Lo" and Janet Jackson); "super, super helpful", "with great taste" and "style", this hat honcho "clearly cares about" "what is right for your head" – no wonder the cap-tivated claim the "completely original designs" fashioned from felt, straw, fur or corduroy "are worth the price"; "Elsa Schiaperelli can rest easy now that Eugenia is around."

| M | P | S | C |

Eva ◐ S C
-|-|-| E

227 Mulberry St. (bet. Prince & Spring Sts.), 6/J/M/N/Q/R/W to Canal St., 212-925-3208

Rows of beautifully dressed mannequins line this NoLita boutique, its pale colors and neutral palette a subdued backdrop for the "fabulous quality" women's tops, jeans and dresses; the focus is on emerging stylemakers, so be open to new names.

Eve's Garden
22 | 18 | 23 | M

119 W. 57th St., Ste. 1201 (bet. 6th & 7th Aves.), F/N/Q/R/W to 57th St., 212-757-8651; 800-848-3837; www.evesgarden.com

☒ "Ladies, start your engines", 'cause this "great place for women, by women" has the tools to tune your gears, albeit discreetly; "started a quarter-century ago as an exercise in equality and freedom", the erotica store remains "hidden" "on the 12th floor of an office building" on 57th Street, and "shy" shoppers appreciate its "nice, quiet privacy", though it's "a little too timid" and "low on fun" for feistier fetishists.

EXPRESS ◐ S
14 | 15 | 14 | I

584 Broadway (bet. Houston & Prince Sts.), N/R to Prince St.; F/S/V to B'way/Lafayette, 212-625-0313; www.expressfashion.com
Additional locations throughout the NY area

☒ "Upbeat" fashion chain where a "strange customer mix" of "high-schoolers to power-lunching corporate chicks" and, in some locations, "hip", "young" guys "can find almost anything" from "cute to sexy to glam to casual" in clothing and accessories "without a hefty tag", provided they "don't need it to last for more than one season"; the sales help is "nice", but "slower than it should be" for the "trend-driven" pace of a place called Express.

Express Men (fka Structure)
18 | 18 | 16 | M

7 W. 34th St. (bet. 5th & 6th Aves.), B/D/F/N/Q/R/V/W to 34th St., 212-967-5093 ◐ S
89 South Street Seaport, Pier 17 (Fulton St.), 1/2/4/5/A/C/J/M/Z to Fulton St./B'way Nassau, 212-766-5709
Kings Plaza Shopping Ctr., 5100 Kings Plaza, Brooklyn, 718-377-6334
www.expressfashion.com

☒ "Nice, fun", "safe clothes for safe boys" dominate this recently renamed chain where "decent", "durable" duds are "moderately priced"; Europhiles "disappointed" with a re-Structuring that "traded Italian-inspired tailoring" for "average Americana" yawn it's the "fashion equivalent of narcolepsy."

Eye Candy ◐ S C
-|-|-| M

329 Lafayette St. (bet. Bleecker & Houston Sts.), 6 to Bleecker St.; F/V/S to B'way/Lafayette, 212-343-4275; www.eyecandystore.com

"You can always find something in this grandma's attic" of a NoHo must-see for "great vintage handbags" and costume jewelry, along with "funky" eyewear, shoes and one-of-a-kind items; it's a "small shop", but "with tons to look at", it definitely "lives up to its name."

Eye Man, The
-|-|-| E

2264 Broadway (bet. 81st & 82nd Sts.), 1/9 to 79th St., 212-873-4114; www.eyeman.com

"First-time customers become lifelong customers" at this cozy Upper West Side optician thanks to its "knowledgeable" staff,

vote at zagat.com

| M | P | S | C |

"optometric expertise" and "excellent array" of "hip-and-trendy", "high-fashion" and "tried-and-true frames" from names like Oliver Peoples, Paul Smith and Martine Sitbone; the "dedicated" optometrists show "meticulous concern for vision problems and needs" – the "kind of service that hardly exists anymore."

Fab 208 NYC ●S ▽ | 17 | 14 | 18 | M |
75 E. Seventh St. (bet. 1st & 2nd Aves.), F to 2nd Ave., 212-673-7581; www.fab208nyc.com

■ "'70s retro fab" is always in at this "rocking and rolling" bubble-gum-pink-and-red East Village shop, which specializes in "modified vintage clothes" and T-shirts with logos we can't print in a family guide; some feel the "one-of-a-kind items" "look better on the rack than on you", but owners Allen and Jo Smith "treat each customer like a friend", and "hey, you've got to get your leopard-print panties somewhere, right?"

FACE Stockholm S | 20 | 22 | 16 | M |
226 Columbus Ave. (bet. 70th & 71st Sts.), 1/2/3/9/B/C to 72nd St., 212-769-1420
687 Madison Ave. (62nd St.), F to Lexington Ave./63rd St., 212-207-8833 C
110 Prince St. (Greene St.), N/R to Prince St., 212-966-9110
www.facestockholm.com

■ Swedish cosmetics company founded by a mother-and-daughter duo that's a "great place for colors, cool evening makeup and everything that shines and glitters", as well as skincare and foundation products "with tones named after the months of the year"; prices are certainly "reasonable", but some say, Face it, the "service varies" ("carry your Marc Jacobs bag with you if you want help").

Facets ●SC | – | – | – | M |
97A Seventh Ave. (bet. President & Union Sts.), Brooklyn, M/N/R to Union St., 718-638-3898

"In Park Slope, this gorgeous shop" is "destined to give" some much-needed diversity to the neighborhood's artisanal jewelry options; the "constantly changing", "small selection" of "uniquely crafted" pieces from independent designers "constantly changes", so "if you see it, you better grab it."

Facial Index S | – | – | – | VE |
104 Grand St. (bet. Greene & Mercer Sts.), 6/J/M/N/Q/R/W to Canal St., 646-613-1055

A "great selection" of "edgy, hip, fab and funky" frames for fashionista faces are proffered at this SoHo eyewear boutique where the glasses are accessibly presented in a minimalist setting; the "fantastic" staff is "discreet" and "patient, even when they know you aren't going to buy anything", which makes it fun to "play" with the "pricey" wares.

Façonnable S | 24 | 23 | 23 | E |
689 Fifth Ave. (54th St.), E/V to 5th Ave./53rd St., 212-319-0111; www.nordstrom.com

■ It's "tempting to keep" this plush-carpeted store "one of the best-kept secrets" in Midtown, but word is out about its "comfortable clothes" whose "loud colors, bold patterns" and highly visible logo betray its Gallic roots (kind of a "French answer to Ralph Lauren"); gentlemen enjoy the "fine neckwear" and "gorgeous shirts", which

| M | P | S | C |

"still look new after a year of wear", while ladies march up the stairs to a "well-made, classic" "selection of basics"; for both sexes, the "knowledgeable, unobtrusive" "service is everything."

Family Jewels, The S ▽ 23 | 19 | 17 | E

130 W. 23rd St. (bet. 6th & 7th Aves.), F/V to 23rd St., 212-633-6020; www.familyjewelsnyc.com

■ "Alluring window displays" hint at the "fun browsing" that awaits within this long, low-ceilinged Chelsea vintage store; "if you dig, you can find the perfect item" among the men's and women's clothes, accessories and lingerie, with a "great selection of '50s cocktail dresses" and beaded bags particular standouts; some, however, huff "you'd have to hock the family jewels to buy here"; N.B. most of the merch is mid-century, but antique hounds should sniff out the stash of '20s gowns behind the counter.

FAO SCHWARZ S C 27 | 27 | 18 | E

767 Fifth Ave. (bet. 58th & 59th Sts.), N/R/W to 5th Ave./59th St., 212-644-9400; www.fao.com

■ "Its wrapping paper is the little blue box of children's gifts" and like its Fifth Avenue neighbor, it's "a New York experience", but more important, it's a "toy mecca" "for kids of all ages"; "who can resist the endless charm of Barbie world" and "giant stuffed bears to snuggle with"? – it "rivals an amusement park" – plus, the "hands-on policy is a child's delight"; while the wide-eyed call it a "wonderland at Christmastime", cynics counsel "don't go over the holidays" "when it's a zoo" and "tourists move like snails."

Fat Beats ● S – | – | – | M

406 Sixth Ave. (bet. 8th & 9th Sts.), A/C/E/F/V/S to W. 4th St., 212-673-3883

If rap is your flava, this "legendary shop" in the Village is your crib; a "hip-hop DJ's mecca" "with retail stores in Amsterdam and LA" as well, "NYC's premier" spot for def sounds "continues to impress" with a phat selection of CDs, vinyl, videos, magazines and "T-shirts with their own logo"; the only beef you might have is with the "snotty clerks."

FELISSIMO ● S 25 | 26 | 20 | E

10 W. 56th St. (5th Ave.), N/R/W to 5th Ave./59th St., 212-247-5656; www.felissimo.com

■ Puzzled patrons aren't quite sure if this "beautiful" space is "a store or a gallery" after its drastic re-focusing two years ago; to clarify the confusion, note that the top four floors of the stunning East Side townhouse are "serene" exhibition areas with ever-changing design displays, while the ground-floor gift shop offers a limited selection of "creative new products" and jewelry.

Fenaroli by Regalia C – | – | – | E

501 Seventh Ave., Ste. 416 (37th St.), 1/2/3/9/A/C/E to 34th St./Penn Station, 212-764-5924; www.fenarolinewyork.com

After you've found 'the dress', finish off your Cinderella-for-a-day look with "classy" bridal accessories from this Garment Center showroom; shoppers solemnly swear by the "beautiful headpieces", ranging from elegant veils to pearl-encrusted tiaras, as well as the "fabulous wedding shoes", Italian silk handbags, jewelry and childrenswear; the "wonderful" staff is "very helpful and willing to go out of its way" "to please"; N.B. appointments suggested.

vote at zagat.com

| | | | M | P | S | C |

Fendi ⑤ⓒ   24 | 23 | 19 | VE
720 Fifth Ave. (57th St.), N/R/W to 5th Ave./59th St., 212-767-0100
☑ Season after season, fashionistas feed their "Fendi-trendi" fetish with an "instantly recognizable" baguette, bauble or sable from this "impressive", "neatly organized" Fifth Avenue shop that "rocks" if you've got "attitude" and can afford the "skyscraper prices" for the "best leather goods", "amazing" accessories and "the furs, oh, the furs"; though you may have to fend for yourself, the "salespeople are friendlier than you might expect."

Ferragamo, Salvatore ⑤   27 | 25 | 23 | VE
661 Fifth Ave. (bet. 52nd & 53rd Sts.), E/V to 5th Ave/53rd St., 212-759-3822
124 Spring St. (Greene St.), E/C to Spring St., 212-226-4330
800-628-8916; www.salvatoreferragamo.it
☑ When in need of "shopping therapy", "treat yourself" to the "comfort and status" of this Italian brand in its Fifth Avenue flagship (furnished with "classy" leather couches) and newer SoHo sibling; though they carry his-and-hers clothes, "quality scarves" and the "best ties in the world", most say "nothing else matters" but the "hardworking" yet "soft-as-butter shoes" that come in "sizes for everyone" and actually are "a great value", given they "wear like iron"; some sigh "styles are a bit staid", but an "inviting staff" keeps the footwear a "favorite."

Fetch ●⑤ⓒ   26 | 25 | 24 | E
43 Greenwich Ave. (bet. 6th & 7th Aves.), A/C/E/F/V/S to W. 4th St., 212-352-8591; www.fetchpets.com
■ For the "utmost in upper-crust pet accessories" without the "froufrou pretentiousness" of Uptown shops, this "decidedly Downtown" Greenwich Village store has "everything for the spoiled NYC" domestic companion, including an annual doggie "ice cream social"; the "helpful" staff is abetted by an owner who's "frequently on-site, as is Ali, the big Newfie that's often mistaken for a rug", and though "practical it's not", it's "perfect" for "gifts."

FILENE'S BASEMENT ●⑤   15 | 8 | 8 | I
2220-26 Broadway (79th St.), 1/9 to 79th St., 212-873-8000
620 Sixth Ave. (18th St.), F/L/V to 14th St./6th Ave., 212-620-3100
18704 Horace Harding Expwy. (188th St.), Queens, 718-479-7711
www.filenesbasement.com
☑ You may be "eternally grateful" for the "incredible buys" you dredge up here, but you "can't be shy about combing through" "mounds of clothing", and "you have to be lucky" to unearth "diamonds in the rough" like "sale Valentino and Bulgari ties" or "hand-embroidered designer sweaters", since the New York branches are "not up to snuff" with the "famed Boston bargain-center" flagship; spelunking insiders don't expect guidance from a "staff that's permanently on break."

Filth Mart ⑤   21 | 17 | 16 | M
531 E. 13th St. (bet. A & B Aves.), L to 1st Ave., 212-387-0650
■ It's "great digging" for dirt at this incense-scented, East Village vintage clothes and novelties store that "specializes in '60s, '70s and '80s" "finds of all kinds", including "tons of tees", "denim and leather jackets", plus rhinestones, "patches and iron-on" decals (this "is the birthplace of the bedazzled rock shirt"); "the owners make no bones about the fact that the merchandise is mostly used", but it's "perfectly priced."

| M | P | S | C |

Find Outlet S | 22 | 18 | 19 | M |
361 W. 17th St. (bet. 8th & 9th Aves.), A/C/E/L to 14th St./8th Ave., 212-243-3177
229 Mott St. (bet. Prince & Spring Sts.), F/S/V to B'way/Lafayette Sts.; 6 to Spring St., 212-226-5167
■ There's "a sample sale every day" at this "appropriately named", "little" bargain "boutique" that makes "scrounging for designer discounts manageable" for its "edgier", "hip" clientele in Chelsea and NoLita; "pretty up-to-date styles" are "arranged by color", the sales help is "laid-back" and "friendly" and "e-mail notifications" keep you in on the "scoop."

Finyl Vinyl S C | – | – | – | I |
204 E. Sixth St. (Cooper Sq.), 6 to Astor Pl.; N/R to 8th St., 212-533-8007; www.finylvinyl.com
For that elusive '70s R&B album or folkie single, this East Village store might be the finyl spot; they specialize in obscure vinyl of all genres, including blues, funk, jazz, Latin, even spoken word; one caveat: day-trippers might find out that the Beatles riff on the door, 'Open Eight Days A Week', is a big teaser – hours are a bit more helter-skelter than that.

Fisch for the Hip S C | 25 | 22 | 19 | E |
153 W. 18th St. (bet. 6th & 7th Aves.), 1/9 to 18th St., 212-633-6251; www.fischforthehip.com
☑ Wise men and women fish here at this Chelsea consignment store, with its "carefully selected inventory of hot designer garb" and "display cases bulging with Birkins, Kellys", Chanel, Vuitton and other status bags; a "friendly staff helps you unearth retail treasures" in the neatly ordered, burgundy-and-mustard setting; however, even some hipsters hiss "prices are high" by used-clothing standards.

Fishs Eddy ◐ S | 21 | 20 | 16 | I |
2176 Broadway (77th St.), 1/9 to 79th St., 212-873-8819
889 Broadway (19th St.), N/R to 23rd St., 212-420-9020
877-347-4733; www.fishseddy.com
☑ "Funky, fun" and "inexpensive kitchen- and tableware" that is "good for starting out" "jam-pack" both these Upper West Side and Flatiron District locations where commercial-quality "vintage" china and glass "from cruise ships, boarding schools and defunct restaurants" along with new patterns by name designers like Cynthia Rowley are so "precariously stacked" you "sometimes feel like a bull" in a you-know-what shop; it can be "hit-or-miss", and you might have "to dig hard to find the good stuff."

Flight 001 ◐ S C | 26 | 25 | 20 | E |
96 Greenwich Ave. (bet. Jane & 12th Sts.), 1/2/3/9/L to 14th St., 212-691-1001; www.flight001.com
■ Even "non-jet setters" and "people who only fantasize" about making a getaway advise "don't leave the gate without" a visit to this "Bond-esque", "funky" "traveler's haven" in the West Village; the "clever, quirky selection" runs the gamut from "practical" "paraphernalia" like luggage and CD cases to "neat little doodads" "you didn't even know you needed", like Travel Scrabble, plus the "smart and informed" staff knows a thing or two about "creative gift wrap."

Flirt ●🅢🅒　▽ 16 | 20 | 22 | M

252 Smith St. (bet. DeGraw & Douglass Sts.), Brooklyn, F to Bergen St., 718-858-7931; www.flirtdesign.com

■ The "name says it all" at this "Smith Street star" that seduces with its "cute, offbeat" "girlie" wear in a "friendly environment"; a dizzyingly shabby-chic decor – pink-and-yellow checkerboard floors, silver-striped walls, old cabinets – is the backdrop for local designers' work, much of it in vintage threads; they'll also artfully embellish old jeans.

Floris of London　27 | 25 | 23 | E

703 Madison Ave. (bet. 62nd & 63rd Sts.), 4/5/6/F/N/R/W to 59th St./Lexington Ave., 212-935-9100; 800-535-6747; www.florisoflondon.com

■ This "tiny" Madison Avenue outlet of the London perfumer that's been purveying scents since 1730 offers "lovely gifts" like "beautiful bath accessories" that evoke an "English garden", men's toiletries, room sprays and candles, along with "potpourri and pieces to put it in."

Florsheim Shoe Shops　19 | 17 | 18 | M

444 Madison Ave. (50th St.), 6/E/V to 51st St./Lexington Ave., 212-752-8017
101 W. 35th St. (6th Ave.), B/D/F/N/Q/R/V/W to 34th St./Herald Sq., 212-594-8830 ●🅢
www.florsheim.com

▣ These "reliable" chain offshoots in the Garment District and East 50s are "good for moderately priced nice shoes", especially when you want "service instead of do-it-yourself shopping" say a smattering of surveyors; but most find that "hit or miss" is more the name of the game, convinced that the staff and quality are "not the same as in days gone by."

Flou 🅢　– | – | – | E

44 Greene St. (bet. Broome & Grand Sts.), 6 to Spring St., 212-941-9101; www.flou.com

New SoHo flagship of an Italian 'bedroom lifestyle' store that carries everything to make that area more inviting – from ingenious space-saving beds that lift up to reveal easily accessible storage space underneath to luxe linens, leather furniture and sleek lighting.

Fogal 🅢🅒　26 | 20 | 23 | VE

510 Madison Ave. (53rd St.), E/V to 53rd St., 212-355-3254; www.fogal.com

■ "Va-va-voom – a real head turner" exclaim enthusiasts of the "exquisite beyond belief" French couture legwear and lingerie sold at this Madison Avenue chain offshoot; while these "sheer delights" "cost a fortune, they wear like iron" – indeed, "hosiery does not have to be a disposable item" insist insiders who deem the "amazing selection" "a lady's must in every color, and texture, of the rainbow"; P.S. the staff is also "magnificent."

Foley & Corinna ●🅢🅒　25 | 20 | 23 | E

108 Stanton St. (bet. Essex & Ludlow Sts.), F to 2nd Ave., 212-529-2338; www.foleyandcorinna.com

■ "Keep this one a secret" beg boosters of this Lower East Side boutique that offers some of "the best shopping on the planet"; its "exclusive" mix of Anna Corinna's "vintage finds" and Dana Foley's "genius" new designs "blends seamlessly" into a stew of "sexy, hip, gorgeous" dresses, tops and trousers; salesgirls are "super-friendly", as are the owners, who are often "there to give advice."

FOOTLIGHT RECORDS 🅂🅲   28 | 18 | 23 | M
113 E. 12th St. (bet. 3rd & 4th Aves.), 4/5/6/L/N/Q/R/W to 14th St./ Union Sq., 212-533-1572; www.footlight.com
■ If you're "looking for an obscure Morricone soundtrack or a Japanese *Chorus Line*", "out-of-print cast albums" or "the best of the crooners (and crooonerettes)" and pre-rock vocalists, sashay over to this Village "show-tune mecca", where a "fantastic selection" from "the world" of "theater, cabaret, television", Broadway "and more is on proud display"; a round of applause for the staff, please – they're "fellow fanatics of musicals" and "vintage music" and really "know their stuff."

Foot Locker ●🅂🅲   18 | 14 | 13 | M
120 W. 34th St. (bet. 6th & 7th Aves.), A/C/E/1/2/3 to 34th St./ Penn Station, 212-629-4419; 800-991-6815; www.footlocker.com
Additional locations throughout the NY area
◪ "Why go anywhere else" than this shoe-shop chain when you can track down the "largest selection" of "decent exercise gear" and "lots and lots" of "great cheap kicks" that may not "always be the coolest" but "can't be beat for sports"; still, some stomp on the "dodgy" service and "cluttered presentation" ("mounds of clothes on the dressing room floor"), leaving cynics to conclude "when it comes to charm, these stores may as well be drive-thrus."

For Eyes 🅲   21 | 18 | 16 | M
Graybar Bldg., 420 Lexington Ave. (bet. 43rd & 44th Sts.), 4/5/6/7/S to 42nd St./Grand Central, 212-697-8888; www.foreyes.com
■ "If you need to own multiple pairs and styles" of eyewear, this East 40s link of a chain sells a "great selection" of "designer frames" that are "inexpensive without looking cheap" (two pairs for $99 is the "best deal in NYC"); with "quick turnaround", it's a "godsend" for folks who "tend to lose their glass."

Forman's 🅂   18 | 15 | 15 | M
145 E. 42nd St. (Lexington Ave.), 4/5/6/7/S to 42nd St./Grand Central, 212-681-9800
560 Fifth Ave. (bet. 45th & 46th Sts.), 4/5/6/7/S to 42nd St./Grand Central, 212-719-1000
59 John St. (bet. Dutch & William Sts.), 2/3/4/5/A/C/J/M/Z to Fulton St., 212-791-4100
82 Orchard St. (bet. Broome & Grand Sts.), F/J/M/Z to Delancey St., 212-228-2500
◪ It's "like shopping with your grandmother" at this "discounter worth visiting" around town, where "everything looks good on you, dahlink", and you might be "pushed" into purchasing it; it's "not exactly bargain territory", and the "aggressive" help isn't for the faint of heart, but both "the plus-sized crowd" and "the petite businesswoman need look no further" for "work staple" "fashions at a slightly lowered price."

Forréal 🅂🅲   – | – | – | M
1200 Lexington Ave. (bet. 81st & 82nd Sts.), 4/5/6 to 86th St., 212-717-0393
1369 Third Ave. (bet. 78th & 79th Sts.), 6 to 77th St., 212-396-0563
1335 Third Ave. (bet. 76th & 77th Sts.), 6 to 77th St., 212-734-2105
www.forrealnyc.com
For an "incredible selection of the latest denims" (Miss Sixty, Juicy et al.) and "T-shirts in all the brand names", blue-jean babes try

this trio of boutiques; the 1369 Third Avenue location also offers "up-to-the-minute fashion imports"; a "wide variety of prices" is an additional plus.

Fortunoff   23 | 19 | 18 | M
681 Fifth Ave. (54th St.), E/V to 53rd St./5th Ave., 212-758-6660; 800-367-8866; www.fortunoff.com
■ "Prices are fair" on the "massive selection" of silver, china and crystal at this "reliable" "New York institution" on Fifth Avenue, making it a "great place" for gifts; the "bridal registry is top-notch" and there's also an "excellent selection" of "quality" "high-end jewelry" at a "decent price."

48th Street Custom Guitars C   – | – | – | E
170 W. 48th St. (bet. 6th & 7th Aves.), C/E to 50th St., 212-764-1364; www.48thstcustomguitars.com
"A cut above the guitar malls" nearby, this small, instrument-glutted Midtown shop specializing in vintage American axes caters to rock stars and well-heeled electric guitar and bass collectors with hundreds of "cool Teles, Strats and hollow bodies", plus new custom beauties by masters like James Tyler and John Suhr, all at high-strung prices.

42nd Street Photo ●SC   19 | 10 | 12 | M
378 Fifth Ave. (bet. 35th & 36th Sts.), B/D/F/N/Q/R/V/W to 34th St./ Herald Sq., 212-594-6565; www.42photo.com
☒ It may "still be one of the best places to get photo equipment after all these years", but – "oy" – you "better know what you're doing when you visit this store"; for starters, it's no longer on its eponymous thoroughfare, but in the West 30s, and though "these guys have the merchandise, they are very fast talkers"; but "don't be put off by their attitude", "don't settle" and you can get a "good price" on "many selections."

Fossil ●S   19 | 18 | 16 | M
541 Broadway (bet. Prince & Spring Sts.), N/R to Prince St., 212-274-9579
530 Fifth Ave. (bet. 44th & 45th Sts.), 4/5/6/7/S to 42nd St./Grand Central, 212-997-3978
103 Fifth Ave. (bet. 17th & 18th), 4/5/6/L/N/Q/R/W to 14th St./Union Sq., 212-243-7296
www.fossil.com
■ The name's definitely a misnomer at this trendy watch chainlet that offers a "fantastic way to find the latest fashion-magazine styles without the high prices"; the almost "overwhelming displays" of tickers range from classic to "colorful" to cutesy ("where else can you find a Felix the Cat" model?), but all are infinitely "wearable" and of "great quality" to boot; the SoHo store also carries womens- and menswear.

Foundation S   – | – | – | M
329 Atlantic Ave. (bet. Hoyt & Smith Sts.), Brooklyn, A/C/G to Hoyt/ Schermerhorn; F/G to Bergen St., 718-403-9757; www.foundationny.com
Hip home-furnishings-and-accessories store in the heart of Boerum Hill that's stocked with "trendy" storage and seating from Pure Design, Blu Dot and Offi, along with colorful silk pillows and glasses; for the design-impaired, an on-site consulting service can help you plan your next place or shop for you.

| M | P | S | C |

Fountain Pen Hospital | 27 | 19 | 25 | M |
10 Warren St. (bet. B'way & Church St.), N/R to City Hall, 212-964-0580; 800-253-7368; www.fountainpenhospital.com
■ "Everything you ever needed or wanted to know about pens" is contained in this "amazing" "sliver of a store" that's been in the Financial District since 1946; it's a "mecca" for belletrists, whether they prefer to use contemporary limited editions or vintage styluses, and the "approachable" staff is "terrific" and "knowledgeable", whether you're looking to "buy, sell or fix" a writing instrument.

Four Paws Club, The ●🅂🅲 | ▽ 25 | 23 | 25 | M |
387 Bleecker St. (Perry St.), 1/9 to Christopher St., 212-367-8265
■ The "super-helpful staff" knows "dogs by name" and "really cares about animals" at this West Village yearling that supplies "great snacks", a "wonderful selection of collars and unique" accessories as well as books and gifts for bipeds; though the store may be "small", it manages to accommodate a "friendly four-legged ambassador" in the form of a "huge cat" that's "worth checking out."

Fourteen Wall Street Jewelers | – | – | – | M |
14 Wall St. (bet. Broad St. & B'way), 2/3 to Wall St., 212-732-3788
Entering its third decade, this small, family-owned store is a typical mom-and-pop shop that Wall Streeters find "good for a fast gift" among its inventory of gold chains, birthstone jewelry and dress watches; the moderate prices are appreciated during these bear-market days.

Fragments 🅲 | 27 | 24 | 16 | E |
116 Prince St. (bet. Greene & Wooster Sts.), N/R to Prince St., 212-334-9588 🅂
53 Stone St. (S. Williams St.), N/R to Whitehall St., 212-269-3955
888-637-2463; www.fragments.com
◪ A "hipster's *Breakfast at Tiffany's*" shopping experience can be had at these SoHo and Financial District showroom/retailers, which give both "established" and "up-and-coming designers" space to show "one-of-a-kind" "jewelry treats" that "range from arty to dramatic to refined"; for 20 years they've "set the trends" ("if Julia or J. Lo is wearing it, they sold it"), and if sometimes the staff "could not care less", well, at least that makes the browsing easy.

Frank Stella Ltd. ●🅂 | 22 | 20 | 23 | E |
440 Columbus Ave. (81st St.), B/C to 81st St., 212-877-5566
NY Athletic Club, 921 Seventh Ave. (58th St.), N/R/Q/W to 57th St., 212-957-1600
◪ Though founded in 1976, this haberdasher "constantly maintains its trendiness, even bringing back the horizontal-striped dress shirt" applaud advocates of its tailored garb, "nice choice of accessories" and "helpful, no-pressure service"; a few foes call it a fallen star ("used to be special"), but most feel it's still "worth the trip" either to the NY Athletic Club flagship or the Columbus Avenue branch.

Fratelli Rossetti 🅂 | 24 | 19 | 18 | VE |
625 Madison Ave. (58th St.), 4/5/6/F/N/R/W to 59th St./Lexington Ave., 212-888-5107; www.rossetti.it
■ For "great Italian shoes" in "classic styles" with an unexpected fashion twist, "very beautiful leather bags", plus outerwear and

accessories, make tracks to this East Side boutique; the "well-made" merchandise "never seems to wear out" – in fact it's played a wardrobe role in some stylesetters' lives "since forever"; while some surveyors insist that the "staff is always polite and helpful", a handful feels that service borders on "indifferent."

Frédéric Fekkai Style De Provence Boutique 24 | 24 | 20 | E

15 E. 57th St. (bet. 5th & Madison Aves.), 4/5/6/F/N/R/W to 59th St./Lexington Ave., 212-583-3350; www.fredericfekkai.com

■ Followers are "hooked" on the famed coiffeur's "luxurious" and "pricey" namesake haircare products (the "Apple Cider rinse is great") and accessories that are tucked into a boutique section of his East Side salon; N.B. appointments can also be made for a variety of spa services, including facials, waxing and massage.

FRED LEIGHTON 25 | 26 | 23 | VE

773 Madison Ave. (66th St.), 6 to 68th St., 212-288-1872

☑ Some of the "best window-shopping on Madison Avenue" can be had at this estate jeweler *par excellence*, "famous for loaning to Hollywood" stars his "spectacular selection" of "showstopping" sparklers; housed in an appropriately art deco–like setting (marble floors, exotic-wood cases and lacquered panels), "some [pieces] are antique, some are antique-style" (e.g. old stones in new settings), but all represent "glitz to the nth", albeit at "dazzling" prices; "lookyloos" beware, though – "they take jewelry seriously here and you better too."

French Connection ●⬛ 19 | 19 | 15 | M

700 Broadway (4th St.), 6 to Astor Pl.; N/R to 8th St., 212-473-4486
304 Columbus Ave. (bet. 74th & 75th Sts.), 1/2/3/9 to 72nd St., 212-496-1470
1270 Sixth Ave. (bet. 50th & 51st Sts.), F/V to 47-50th Sts./Rockefeller Ctr., 212-262-6623
435 W. Broadway (Prince St.), N/R to Prince St., 212-219-1139
888-741-3285; www.frenchconnection.com

☑ "Funky" fellas and femmes connect with "chic Euro" style in "durable" materials at this "sometimes innovative" British-based chain of "very clean" stores with "lovely displays"; "great basic tees" and "sleek" pants appeal to "young, nubile" "urbanites", but the "inflated price tags" don't, and the FCUK logo on T-shirts and shopping bags has prisses tsking "enough" – "who wants to wear what looks like a curse word?"

French Corner ●⬛C ▽ 21 | 17 | 18 | M

464 W. Broadway (bet. Houston & Prince Sts.), N/R to Prince St., 212-505-1980

■ Ladies looking for that "killer look" love the "affordable-for-everyone" offerings at this "well-organized" SoHo boutique, which corners the market on European designer diffusion lines; it's possible to "pick up something hot for an [impromptu] night on the town" here, as the "overeager, but honest" staff has "perfected the art of the quick sale."

French Sole C ▽ 18 | 17 | 22 | M

985 Lexington Ave. (71st St.), 6 to 68th St., 212-737-2859

■ "A real gem" purr patrons who pirouette over for "cute", "classic but stylish" "ballet flats in every color, texture" and "pattern" that leave you "speeding through the sidewalks of the Upper East Side in comfort and European grace"; the "charming, old-world way to

subscribe to zagat.com

| M | P | S | C |

shop for shoes" ("wouldn't have it any other way") includes "hoping that your size will be stored way up high so you can watch the assistant climb to precarious heights on the pink ladder."

FRESH | 27 | 27 | 22 | E |
388 Bleecker St. (Perry St.), 1/9 to Christopher St., 917-408-1850
1061 Madison Ave. (bet. 80th & 81st Sts.), 6 to 77th St., 212-396-0344 S C
57 Spring St. (bet. Lafayette & Mulberry Sts.), 6 to Spring St., 212-925-0099
800-373-7420; www.fresh.com

■ Head here "if you're on a diet, as you can inhale the divine scents of milk, sugar and chocolate without gaining a pound!" assert admirers about these toiletries stores with the "perfect name because that's how their products make you feel"; the beauty, bath and body lines, which rely mainly on natural home remedies whenever possible (like the best-selling Brown Sugar Body Polish), are "expensive" but "worth the splurge", and the "sweet" staff is "super-generous with free samples"; N.B. Gywneth Paltrow and Julianne Moore are among the celeb clientele.

FRETTE C | 27 | 27 | 22 | VE |
799 Madison Ave. (bet. 67th & 68th Sts.), 6 to 68th St., 212-988-5221; www.frette.com

■ "If Queen Elizabeth isn't sleeping on" "the Rolls-Royce" of sheets, she should be declare devotees of this "dreamland" on the Upper East Side selling "ultra-luxe bed and table linens from Italy" with "the highest thread count" to customers like the Vatican; those who Frette over "paying through the nose" should hit the store's "fabulous" 30–40 percent off sales in January and July.

Frick Collection S | 20 | 18 | 19 | M |
1 E. 70th St. (5th Ave.), 6 to 68th St., 212-288-0700; www.frick.org

◪ Housed in the "spectacular" 1914 Upper East Side digs of industrialist and avid collector Henry Clay Frick, this "real gem" of a museum's "pocket-size shop" has a "very fine selection of books", prints and "lovely" "mementos" "corresponding to the collection" of 15th- through 19th-century Western art; it's "staffed by polite people who will help if they can", and though it's a bit "limited" and "stodgy" for expansive Downtown tastes, it's "enough to satisfy those who love the Frick."

Frida's Closet S C | 22 | 24 | 23 | M |
296 Smith St. (bet. 2nd & Union Sts.), Brooklyn, F/G to Carroll St., 718-855-0311

■ Worshiped by Madonna and the subject of a Salma Hayek movie, Mexican artist Frida Kahlo inspires this "slightly bizarre concept" shop in Carroll Gardens; inside the red-and-mustard-colored "tiny" space, adorned with the painter's portrait, each item is treated as a piece of art and each exclusive piece of "cute" clothing numbered, so you know you're getting something "unique" from the "low-key" staff.

Furla S C | 24 | 23 | 17 | E |
727 Madison Ave. (64th St.), 6 to 68th St., 212-755-8986
430 W. Broadway (bet. Prince & Spring Sts.), C/E to Spring St.; N/R to Prince St., 212-343-0048
www.furla.com

◪ Customers croon over the "outstanding selection" of "beautiful leather goods" at these SoHo and Upper East side branches of

vote at zagat.com

| M | P | S | C |

the Bologna, Italy–based chain, lauding the "stylish" bags done up in "clean lines and funky shapes" and "sophisticated" shoes and gloves at "semi-reasonable prices"; but critics sigh that the "snotty" staff can put a damper on their shopper's high; N.B. the Madison Avenue branch was renovated post-*Survey*.

Furry Paws ●⦿S 22 | 17 | 19 | M
141 Amsterdam Ave. (66th St.), 1/9 to 66th St., 212-724-9321 C
120 E. 34th St. (bet. Lexington & Park Aves.), 6 to 33rd St., 212-725-1970 C
310 E. 23rd St. (bet. 1st & 2nd Sts.), 6 to 23rd St., 212-979-0920 C
1039 Second Ave. (bet. 54th & 55th Sts.), 4/5/6/F/N/R/W to 59th St./Lexington Ave., 212-813-1388
1705 Third Ave. (bet. 95th & 96th Sts.), 6 to 96th St., 212-828-5308

■ A "good selection of merchandise" that includes "great stuff you can't find elsewhere" makes this chainlet a "one-stop shopping" destination for petaphiles; supporters also cite the "easy-to-browse" displays, a "helpful", "friendly" staff and "free delivery" that's "critical for a 20-pound bag of dog food" as factors that fuel their fur-vor for this "reliable" litter of "neighborhood stores."

Fye ●S C 19 | 17 | 14 | M
716 Lexington Ave. (bet. 57th & 58th Sts.), 4/5/6/N/R/W to 59th St./Lexington Ave., 212-826-3500
1290 Sixth Ave. (51st St.), N/R/W to 49th St., 212-581-1669
405-407 Sixth Ave. (8th St.), A/C/E/F/V/S to W. 4th St., 212-243-1446
5540 Broadway (Kimberly Pl.), Bronx, 1/9 to 231st St., 718-432-6884
2188A White Plains Rd. (Underhill Ave.), Bronx, 2 to Pelham Pkwy., 718-792-4233
800-540-1242; www.fye.com

■ "Awesome! you can listen to some tracks before you buy" the CD – "gotta love that" gush tunesmiths who also applaud this chain's "pretty good selection of DVDs", games and videos, all at "better prices than Coconuts, its predecessor"; still, cynics are not entertained by this "typical" mega-outfit.

Galileo ●S C – | – | – | E
37 Seventh Ave. (13th St.), 1/2/3/9 to 18th St., 212-243-1629; www.galileonyc.com

"Pricey but perfectly packaged" glassware – vessels, vases and Venetian varieties – populates shelf upon shelf of this Greenwich Village corner shop that also displays lamps, pillows and other home accessories; the "salespeople are helpful", and even the most persnickety person will "always find a gift here."

Gallery of Wearable Art – | – | – | VE
34 E. 67th St. (bet. Madison & Park Aves.), 6 to 68th St., 212-570-2252; www.galleryofwearableart.com

"One of the best-kept fashion secrets in NYC", this opulent by-appointment-only East 60s boutique, lushly decorated to resemble a Parisian atelier, carries some of the "most glamorous, one-of-a-kind" bridal and evening gowns, fabulous antique finds and lavishly embellished artisinal coats, all at stratospheric prices; made mostly from vintage textiles and embroidery, the unique creations channel spirits of eras past, from siren-esque satin numbers à la Jean Harlow to regal Victorian-inspired knockouts.

	M	P	S	C

Gallery Orrefors Kosta Boda C   26 | 23 | 22 | E
685 Madison Ave. (62nd St.), 4/5/6/F/N/R/W to 59th St./Lexington Ave., 212-752-1095; www.orrefors.com

■ "Beautiful art glass" from this over 100-year-old Swedish glassmaker can be had at its East 60s offshoot, where vases and votives, as well as one-of-a-kind, signed-and-limited-edition ornamental pieces make it an "excellent", albeit "pricey", "source for gifts."

Gant S   – | – | – | E
645 Fifth Ave. (bet. 51st & 52nd Sts.), B/D/F/V to 47-50th Sts./Rockefeller Ctr., 212-813-9170
77 Wooster St. (bet. Broome & Spring Sts.), C/E to Spring St., 212-431-9610
www.gant.com

Originally known as the label inside Ivy Leaguers' button-down and rugby shirts, this now-international brand has evolved into a complete collection of business "casual clothing" for the new traditionalist; a "wonderful sales staff helps you navigate the many choices", which include neo-preppy women's sportswear at the cherry-wood-accented flagship store convenient to Rockefeller Center; there's a SoHo sibling too.

GAP ●SC   16 | 16 | 15 | M
60 W. 34th St. (B'way), B/D/F/N/Q/R/W to 34th St./Herald Sq., 212-760-1268; www.gap.com
For additional locations, see Top Chain Stores index

☛ "Diehards" return again and again to this "old reliable" for a "quick, basic fix" of "classic, clean", "all-American" attire for "the whole family", including "the best jeans", khakis, white tees, denim jackets and "no-nonsense" bras and undies "at good prices"; nevertheless, traditionalists lament "recent seasons'" "disco trends", while snobs "overwhelmed by blandness" coupled with a "significant" "gap" in service sniff that it might be "as convenient as the corner deli", but there's "always more promise than delivery."

GAPKIDS ●SC   21 | 19 | 15 | M
60 W. 34th St. (B'way), B/D/F/N/Q/R/W to 34th St./Herald Sq., 212-760-1268; www.gap.com
For additional locations, see Top Chain Stores index

■ "You'll never leave empty-handed" from this "tried-and-true" chain that has "some of the cutest children's clothes around", with "designs that are a bit more adventurous and hipper than the adult" offerings ("this is how the cool kids dress"); "both parents and kids will be happy" with the "durable" clothing that "really takes the test of rough-and-tumble" boys and girls and "won't break the bank"; "sales are the way to go" say seasoned shoppers, who find that some items are "perfect for petite women too!"

Garden Shop at the Horticultural Society of New York, The C   ▽ 21 | 22 | 21 | M
128 W. 58th St. (bet. 6th & 7th Aves.), N/R/Q/W to 57th St., 212-757-0915; www.hsny.org

■ A "hidden gem" in Midtown, this century-old nonprofit provides a "great resource" for would-be horticulturalists with advice from its "helpful, knowledgeable staff"; it's also abloom with indoor and outdoor plants, an "interesting selection of bulbs" and "surprisingly nice gift items."

vote at zagat.com

Gas Bijoux 🅢🅒 – | – | – | M
238 Mott St. (Prince St.), 6 to Spring St., 212-334-7290
Owned by the folks behind Blue Bag, this tiny NoLita newcomer (colored cotton-candy pink, with a huge chandelier) features jewelry handmade by designer André Gas; his clever, one-of-a-kind concoctions are characterized by semi-precious gems and beads in base-metal or silver settings.

Gateway Country 🅢🅒 19 | 20 | 16 | M
4 Columbus Circle (bet. 57th & 58th Sts.), 1/9/A/B/C/D to 59th St./Columbus Circle, 212-246-5575
244 E. 86th St. (bet. 2nd & 3rd Aves), 4/5/6 to 86th St., 212-988-4425
200 Park Ave. S. (17th St.), 4/5/6/L/N/Q/R/W to 14th St./Union Sq., 212-982-4140
www.gateway.com
◪ They're fazing out the bovine-and-silo theme at the stores for this computer company started on an Iowa farm, but customers "satisfied" with their "great PCs" and third-party printers, scanners and digital cameras still invoke the Holstein-print packaging, bellowing "mooove on over", you other chains; but critics simply counter bull and cite "poor service."

Generation Records ●🅘🅢 25 | 18 | 15 | M
210 Thompson St. (bet. Bleecker & W. 3rd Sts.), A/C/E/F/S/V to W. 4th St., 212-254-1100
■ New York's "funky", "fun" "punk headquarters" and "hideaway" in the Village is also a "Brit-pop and indie haunt" offering music "aficionados" everything from "avant-garde doom metal" to "rare imports"; while the resident "store cats are always happy to share their opinions on the music" and "spin any CD on their in-store system", "don't expect warm and fuzzy service."

George Smith ▽ 25 | 18 | 16 | VE
75 Spring St. (Crosby St.), 6 to Spring St., 212-226-4747; www.georgesmith.com
■ Long-standing, statusy SoHo store whose "pricey", "beautiful" bespoke English furniture – the pieces are handmade to order, from the birch or beech wood frame to the down-filled cushions – will "only get better" with wear; customers can choose from 70 styles of seating, including the signature sofa with turned wooden legs, and from a variety of fabrics that range from florals to solids and stripes.

Georgette Klinger ●🅘🅢🅒 – | – | – | E
501 Madison Ave. (bet. 52nd & 53rd Sts.), E/V to 5th Ave./53rd St., 212-838-3200; 800-554-6437; www.georgetteklinger.com
It's been over 60 years since this grande dame of the beauty industry first opened her doors on Madison Avenue, and the flagship store recently got its own gray-and-gold makeover; the retail section of the shop features the company's classic skincare lines, along with new additions like Vincent Longo cosmetics and AromaFloria spa products; N.B. appointments can also be made for a variety of spa services, including facials, waxing and massage.

Georg Jensen 🅒 25 | 24 | 21 | VE
683 Madison Ave. (bet. 61st & 62nd Sts.), 4/5/6/N/R/W to 59th St./Lexington Ave., 212-759-6457; www.georgjensen.com
■ This "upscale" Upper East Side branch of the nearly 100-year-old Scandinavian silversmith showcases the company's "fabulous"

118   subscribe to zagat.com

M | P | S | C

clean-lined designs in cutlery, candlesticks and containers by mid-century masters like Arne Jacobsen and Henning Koppel; there's also jewelry that ranges from art-nouveau–inspired items to more modern takes on brooches and bracelets; N.B. it shares space with Royal Copenhagen Porcelain, which has been favored by Danish royalty ever since its kilns were first fired up in 1775.

Geppetto's Toy Box S C — | — | — | M
10 Christopher St. (bet. Gay St. & Greenwich Ave.), A/C/E/F/V/S to W. 4th St.; 1/9 to Christopher St., 212-620-7511; 800-326-4566; www.nyctoys.com

You'll "feel like a kid again" at this "superb toy store" tucked away in the Village, where the "helpful staff" is always ready to offer suggestions; a large selection of "creative" puppets surround their very own stage, while "adorable" marionettes mix with jack-in-the-boxes and a good number of enchanting dolls.

Geraldine ● S C — | — | — | E
246 Mott St. (bet. Houston & Prince Sts.), 6 to Spring St., 212-219-1620; www.geraldinenyc.com

Don't let the air-tight feel of this minimalist, cream-colored NoLita boutique fool you – Hedra Prue's sister store is home to an eye-catching array of cheeky sandals, revved-up pumps and rockin' cowboy boots that suit urban ladies just fine; come for well-known designs by the likes of Christian Louboutin, Emma Hope and Marc by Marc Jacobs and stay to discover young European talents that have just hit the scene.

Gerry Cosby & Co. ● S 23 | 13 | 16 | E
Madison Square Garden, 3 Penn Plaza (7th Ave. & 32nd St.), 1/2/3/9/A/B/C/D to 34th St./Penn Station, 212-563-6464

■ "Shopping here can be more exciting than the actual games at Madison Square Garden" upstairs declare diehards who deem this "convenient" shop, stocked with one of the "best selections of sporting goods", a "must-go before events"; whether you're trying to "track down that hard-to-find" "authentic" "Rangers or Knicks jersey", "real hockey equipment" or "related stuff", this is the "place to go for the genuine article"; while some cynics would rather take a puck in the teeth than deal with the "intimidating service", supporters shoot back it's a "venerable New York experience."

Gerry's Menswear ● S — | — | — | M
353 Bleecker St. (bet. Charles & 10th Sts.), 1/9 to Christopher St., 212-691-0636 C
110 Eighth Ave. (bet. 15th & 16th Sts.), A/C/E/L to 14th St./8th Ave., 212-243-9141

Can a store be "trendy and classic both"? – this one can, thanks to its two locations: in Chelsea, sparse-yet-slick decor sets off boldly styled Armand Basi and Theory leather jackets and pants, Ariano Goldschmied jeans and Ra-Re shirts that are rare indeed – all geared to gay, modish men; the West Village branch caters to a more conservative clientele, with Armani sportswear and Pringle of Scotland sweaters.

Ghost S C ▽ 22 | 19 | 18 | E
28 Bond St. (bet. Bowery & Lafayette St.), 6 to Bleecker St., 646-602-2891; www.ghost.co.uk

■ There's nothing scary here – except maybe "how much" this British brand's "light and glowy dresses" cost; nevertheless, this

vote at zagat.com   **119**

NoHo spot with a Parisian flea-market feel works "for society gals" and anyone else who craves the kind of "clothes that flow" "in a fantasy."

Ghurka ▽ 25 | 25 | 24 | VE
41 E. 57th St. (Madison Ave.), N/R to 5th Ave., 212-826-8300; 800-587-1584; www.ghurka.com
■ "Some of the most beautifully tanned leather" comes "safari-style" at this Midtown mecca where you also find "top-notch help and presentation" ("only the finest for those with money"); disciples fall into line for the "durable, high-quality bags", "classic luggage" and trunks and lifestyle apparel and accessories inspired by the gear that Ghurkas, young men who served in Nepal in British military regiments, wore in the 1800s.

Gianfranco Ferré C ▽ 23 | 25 | 25 | VE
845 Madison Ave. (bet. 70th & 71st Sts.), 6 to 68th St., 212-717-5430; www.gianfrancoferre.it
■ Once an architect, always an architect: this Italian-born designer has translated his first love into "beautifully constructed" men's and women's clothing, as well as precisely conceived accessories and fragrances ("great cologne!") at his sleek Upper East Side boutique; influenced by his early travels to India, even his tailored suits often possess a fluid drape.

Giorgio Armani 27 | 25 | 23 | VE
760 Madison Ave. (65th St.), 6 to 68th St., 212-988-9191; www.giorgioarmani.com
■ *Grazie,* Giorgio! grin groupies who insist the Italian "master of design" "deserves his reputation" for his "ultimate-in-chic" couture, shown off in this Madison Avenue boutique; the exquisite ("are they real?") "employees glide across hushed, wide-open spaces" to assist with the rows of signature "sleek, minimalist" suits and separates, superb shoes and "stunning" eveningwear, a favorite of stars (both male and female) on award-show nights; these "casually elegant" threads, accessories and cosmetics can induce "sticker shock" – but for the "beautiful people", they're "the uniform for all occasions, except the gym."

Giraudon ●S C ▽ 23 | 20 | 22 | M
152 Eighth Ave. (bet. 17th & 18th Sts.), 1/2 to 18th St., 212-633-0999; 800-278-1552; www.giraudonnewyork.com
☑ "If I designed shoes, they would look like this" gush ardent admirers of the French footwear at this small Chelsea shop; while fashion-forward fans flip for the "really nice selection" of "fun options" with a healthy dose of "attitude", gripers grouse they are simply "uncomfortable."

Girl Props ●S 19 | 16 | 14 | I
33 E. Eighth St. (University Pl.), N/R to 8th St.; 6 to Astor Pl., 212-533-3240
153 Prince St. (bet. Thompson St. & W. Broadway), N/R to Prince St.; C/E to Spring St., 212-505-7615 C
www.girlprops.com
■ 'Inexpensive . . . we *never* say cheap' runs the slogan of this "urbanized" accessories pair in Greenwich Village and SoHo; "teens (and anyone else who likes to glitter)" enjoy the "best collection of cool-now, passé-in-an-hour jewelry", "funky, trendy trinkets" and wigs at "unbeatable prices" for costume parties or those "occasions when only a boa will do."

Givenchy ⓈⒸ ▽ 22 | 23 | 19 | VE
710 Madison Ave. (63rd St.), 4/5/6/N/R/W to 59th St./Lexington Ave., 212-688-4338; www.givenchy.com
■ In its sleek East 60s outpost, this renowned Parisian house still offers "classic clothes", including "wonderful suits" that "will last a lifetime"; but in the hands of young designer Julien Macdonald, the collection has gained a more colorful edge, even as it retains the "tailored-to-fit" sophistication that makes each "elegant", "*très* expensive" piece "worth the money."

Global Table ⓈⒸ ▽ 27 | 25 | 18 | M
107 Sullivan St. (bet. Prince & Spring Sts.), C/E to Spring St., 212-431-5839; www.globaltable.com
■ "You can always find something to buy" at Nathalie Smith's SoHo "tabletop heaven" where the "eclectic assortment of dishes", Capiz-shell bowls, tea sets and trays "from around the world" "are great pieces" that are elegant enough "to mix" with your "granny's china" without costing the family jewels; the space is "small", so watch that "huge tote bag" you're probably schlepping.

Goldin-Feldman – | – | – | E
150 W. 30th St., 5th fl. (7th Ave.), B/D/F/N/Q/R/W to 34th St./Herald Sq., 212-239-0512
In a fifth-floor Garment District loft, this "well-established" third-generation furrier (a favorite with personal shoppers) prides itself on service, "asking what you want" in the way of "stylish" coats and, "if they don't have it, gladly making" your heart's desire; some say "don't be fooled" by the "showroom [atmosphere] – these are retail prices") (though less marked-up than those of the stores they sell to).

Goodwill Industries ❶Ⓢ 12 | 7 | 8 | I
220 E. 23rd St. (3rd Ave.), 6 to 23rd St., 212-447-7270 Ⓒ
2196 Fifth Ave. (bet. 132nd & 135th Sts.), 2/3 to 135th St., 212-862-0020 Ⓒ
514 W. 181st St. (Amsterdam Ave.), 1/9 to 181st St., 212-923-7910
217 W. 79th St. (Amsterdam Ave.), 1/9 to 79th St.; C/D to 81st St., 212-874-5050 Ⓒ
258 Livingston St. (Bond St.), Brooklyn, A/C/G to Hoyt St., 718-923-9037 Ⓒ
52 W. Fordham Rd. (Davidson Ave.), Bronx, 4 to Fordham Rd., 718-733-2453 Ⓒ
32-36 Steinway St. (Broadway), Queens, R/V to Steinway St., 718-932-0418 Ⓒ
www.goodwill.org
◪ "From clothing to books to housewares, you never know what you may find" at this historic thrift-shop chain; naturally, "you're not going for a classy experience", and "you'll have to look hard" to find treasure, but who can resist when "a shirt may run you less than breakfast at Starbucks"?

Gotham Bikes ⓈⒸ ▽ 25 | 19 | 26 | M
112 W. Broadway (bet. Duane & Reade Sts.), 1/2/3/9 to Chambers St., 212-732-2453; www.gothambikes.com
◪ One of the "most courteous bike shops in town", this TriBeCan is staffed with avid, active, "very friendly" cyclists "without an air of snobbery", who are eager to help "bikers of all levels" (including Mayor Michael Bloomberg) choose the right vehicle from the "wide selection of prices and styles"; N.B. under the same ownership as Toga Bikes.

vote at zagat.com

| | | | M | P | S | C |

Gothic Cabinet Craft 🆂🅲   15 | 8 | 14 | I
715 Ninth Ave. (49th St.), C/E to 50th St., 212-246-9525;
www.gothiccabinetcraft.com
Additional locations throughout the NY area
◪ "Budget-conscious folks" and "students" head to this multi-branched seller of finished and unfinished wooden furniture for "basic stuff" like bookcases, beds, dressers and storage units, along with custom-built pieces; while the sophisticated sniff at the "so-so selection and quality", the frugal feel the "cheap" prices at this chain make it fine for furnishing a "first apartment."

Gotta Knit 🆂🅲   20 | 17 | 14 | E
498 Sixth Ave., 2nd fl. (bet. 12th & 13th Sts.), F/V to 14th St.; L to 6th Ave., 212-989-3030; 800-898-6748
◪ A "very current", "colorful" selection of "pricey yet gorgeous yarns" awaits at this small, second-floor Greenwich Village knitting-and-needlepoint destination that's "always crowded" with hobbyists; while a smattering insist that the "knowledgeable staff" "holds your hand and helps you through whatever you need", most snarl that pals "of the house are well treated but unknowns" are "made to feel like intruders in an unfriendly knitting circle."

Gown Company, The   ∇ 15 | 12 | 19 | M
312 E. Ninth St. (bet. 1st & 2nd Aves.), L to First Ave.; 6 to Astor Pl., 212-979-9000; www.thegowncompany.com
◪ "It's all about the service and the chance you'll luck out" at this "tiny", by-appointment-only East Village bridal shop where "if you can find" a sample dress from the likes of Lazaro or Helen Morley, or pull a one-off gown that never made it into production from the "off-the-rack rack, you've got yourself a steal"; it's "limited in sizes", so if you're pining for a "large selection, keep looking."

GRACIOUS HOME ●🆂   25 | 17 | 20 | E
1992 Broadway (67th St.), 1/9 to 66th St./Lincoln Ctr., 212-231-7800
1217 & 1220 Third Ave. (70th St.), 6 to 68th St., 212-517-6300
1201 Third Ave. (bet. 69th & 70th Sts.), 6 to 68th St., 212-517-6300
www.gracioushome.com
■ "From dimmers to doilies", these "bursting-at-the-seams" Lincoln Center and East Side stores make supporters "swoon" with an "amazing selection of everything for the home at all prices", including hardware, kitchenware, bedroom and bathroom accessories; the staff is "unbelievably knowledgeable" ("they have more and better answers than the Sears tool guy and constantly pull miracles from the ceiling-high shelves") and "free delivery is a nice added bonus"; a new branch devoted to lamps, lighting products and custom-made shades makes for a Third Avenue trio.

GRAFF   29 | 29 | 27 | VE
721 Madison Ave. (bet. 63rd & 64th Sts.), 6 to 68th St., 212-355-9292;
www.graffdiamonds.com
■ A dazzling array of "gems in every imaginable color and shape", including "drop-dead diamonds to drool over", makes this London-based outfit the "ultimate for jewelry"; many a passerby stops to gaze at the "most incredible window displays" on Madison Avenue, which – along with the "exquisite wood" interior – cause reviewers to vote the place No. 1 for Presentation; "prices are beyond expensive, they're astronomical", but the "courteous and helpful" staff "always wears a smile."

| M | P | S | C |

Grand Central Racquet C
– | – | – | E

Grand Central, 45th St. Passageway (Vanderbilt Ave.), 4/5/6/7/S to 42nd St./Grand Central, 212-856-9647
341 Madison Ave. (44th St.), 4/5/6/7 to 42nd St./Grand Central, 212-292-8851
www.grandcentralracquet.com

An "excellent all-around tennis store", this Madison Avenue maven courts customers with tennis and squash racquets, shoes and accessories from hard-hitting brands like Head, Wilson and Prince, while its tiny kiosk in Grand Central "terminal by the Roosevelt Passageway" carries a "smaller selection"; the "knowledgeable" staff may make you feel like you're part of the pro tour – "if you need your racquet strung quickly", it'll be back in your hands in no time, "usually on the same day"; N.B. no weekend hours.

Granny-Made S C
▽ 24 | 19 | 22 | E

381 Amsterdam Ave. (bet. 78th & 79th Sts.), 1/9 to 79th St., 212-496-1222; 877-472-6691

◪ Stacks and stacks of imported handknit "stuff", plus a "nice selection" of "homemade" sweaters and hats for adults, children and babies inspired by a real grandmother can be found at this "small" Upper West Side boutique; while the choices "range from traditional to funky", the cost can be out of the loop for wallet-watchers who quip "hope some portion of the high prices is going to granny herself"; N.B. during the holidays, they also sell cookies baked by another nurturing nana.

Great Feet S C
23 | 19 | 19 | M

1241 Lexington Ave. (84th St.), 4/5/6 to 86th St., 212-249-0551; www.striderite.com

■ "The place to go for your child's first pair" of Stride-Rites, this fun, large, "popular" Upper East Side store also offers one of the "best selections of kids' shoes, boots, sandals" and sneakers around; while it's "always crowded", you usually "don't have to wait long at off-times", since the "staff knows what they're doing" and can "handle the volume" – just "don't go on weekends, unless you're a masochist."

Green Onion, The C
– | – | – | M

274 Smith St. (bet. DeGraw & Sackett Sts.), Brooklyn, F/G to Carroll St., 718-246-2804

"Little" and "cute", this cheery yellow Cobble Hill kids' clothing shop is kitted out to the max with "unique, quality stuff", including Malina knitwear and other high-end lines, exclusive 'BKLN' baby tees and super-cool accessories (Astroturf Mary Janes, anyone?), plus an assortment of toys, books and blankets made for gift-giving; check store hours before you set out – they're a bit inconvenient if you don't live in the area.

Greenstones C
25 | 19 | 24 | E

442 Columbus Ave. (bet. 81st & 82nd Sts.), B/C to 81st St., 212-580-4322 S
1184 Madison Ave. (bet. 86th & 87th Sts.), 4/5/6 to 86th St., 212-427-1665

■ "Quality"-seekers "love to shop" for "beautiful European clothing and accessories" (primarily French lines like Catimini and Deux par Deux) for babies and children (up to age 10) at these stylish siblings, a lengthy stone's throw away on the Upper East and

vote at zagat.com

Upper West Sides; the "great" "staff helps you select your trendy kids' wardrobe" of "cute, playful but not overly sophisticated" clothing, and to top it off, you'll find one of "the best selections of hats in town."

Gringer & Sons S | 24 | 9 | 16 | M |
29 First Ave. (2nd St.), F to Second Ave., 212-475-0600
■ "For Viking, Sub-Zero", Garland, Gaggenau and other choice kitchen-appliance manufacturers, loyalists look no further than this East Village storefront; the "crowded quarters" don't allow for "all models" to be "displayed on the floor", but they do carry a "large selection", so ask; while some sigh "it's easier to get a reservation at Nobu than get help" here, the staff does "know its stuff" once you do.

Gucci S | 27 | 26 | 21 | VE |
685 Fifth Ave. (54th St.), 6/E/V to 53rd St./Lexington Ave., 212-826-2600
840 Madison Ave. (bet. 69th & 70th Sts.), 6 to 68th St., 212-717-2619
www.gucci.com
■ "Check your balance" (both financial and physical) before dipping into these Fifth and Madison Avenue dens of desire, where it's not if, but what, you want – and "everybody wants something" from the "flashy" luxury label revamped by designer Tom Ford; in Midtown, the multi-floor, "sleek, renovated interior" is a "fun maze to explore" and the salespeople are thankfully "unpushy" ("if you can get them"); still, it's a "zoo", as logo-lovers and "massive amounts of tourists" "drool over" the "amazing purse collection", traditionalists embrace "status loafers" ("leather heaven on earth") and movie stars and "super-trendies" storm the glam his-and-hers sportswear.

Guess? ●S | 19 | 20 | 17 | M |
537 Broadway (bet. Prince & Spring Sts.), N/R to Prince St.; 6 to Spring St., 212-226-9545
South Street Seaport, 23-25 Fulton St. (Water St.), 2/3/4/5/A/C/J/M/Z to Fulton St./B'way/Nassau, 212-385-0533
Kings Plaza, 5351 Kings Plaza, Brooklyn, 718-421-5075
2655 Richmond Ave. #209, Staten Island, 718-370-1594
800-394-8377; www.guess.com
■ "No guesswork here" – this chain hits the "what's hot, what's not" spot with "fantabulous" jeans with an "unbeatable" fit, "very sexy tops" and "party clothes" for "young New Yorkers"; while the nostalgic question its currency – "reminds me of the '80s and Anna Nicole Smith" – defenders shoot back "these latest trends last longer than most."

Guggenheim Museum Stores S C | 19 | 18 | 14 | E |
Guggenheim Museum, 1071 Fifth Ave. (89th St.), 4/5/6 to 86th St., 212-423-3615; 800-329-6109; www.guggenheimstore.org
■ Architecture buffs "guess Frank Lloyd Wright didn't include a gift shop in his plans" because the "baubles", books, "art posters and postcards" at this Upper East Side museum are stuffed into a "cramped" space, though there's nothing "little" about the "high prices"; style snobs sniff that the "cool factor" on "Calderesque art mobiles", "funky magnets" and "recycled license-plate Filofaxes" "expired in the '80s", and if "those tourists from Iowa don't know that", it seems as though the "bored staff" does.

Gumbo ⑤◉   – | – | – | M

493 Atlantic Ave. (bet. Nevins St. & 3rd Ave.), Brooklyn, 2/3/4/5/N/Q/R to Atlantic Ave., 718-855-7808

A sumptuous stew of kids' and women's clothing and accessories from faraway lands draws customers to this cavernous Atlantic Avenue shop replete with a wee table for crayon sessions, African drums and an airy art gallery to the rear; fanciful onesies, blankets and infants' apparel from labels like Zutano and Oink!baby greet shoppers, with the racks bursting with toddler's and children's one-of-a-kind dresses, fleece pants and tees and bright Peruvian sweaters for both little ones and fuzzy-loving adults.

Gymboree ⑤◉   20 | 20 | 17 | M

2271 Broadway (81st St.), 1/2 to 79th St., 212-595-9071 ●
2015 Broadway (69th St.), 1/9 to 68th St./Lincoln Ctr., 212-595-7662
1120 Madison Ave. (83rd St.), 4/5/6 to 86th St., 212-717-6702
1332 Third Ave. (bet. 76th & 77th Sts.), 6 to 77th St., 212-517-5548
1049 Third Ave. (62nd St.), 4/5/6/N/R/W to 59th St./Lexington Ave., 212-688-4044
2655 Richmond Ave., #121 (Ring Rd.), Staten Island, 718-370-8679
877-449-6932; www.gymboree.com

■ Customers turn cartwheels for this "happy place to shop" and its "cute as a button", "color-themed" tots' clothing at "affordable prices"; the "adorable" selection is "great for coordinating a look", plus it's "generally durable" enough to "stand up through multiple washings" and maybe even "through siblings"; but less-adventurous shoppers pout that the "bright" shades are "always so flashy", concluding it's "better for babies and younger kids."

Gym Source ⑤◉   ▽ 27 | 21 | 22 | E

40 E. 52nd St. (bet. Madison & Park Aves.), 6 to 51st St., 212-688-4222; 800-496-7687; www.gymsource.com

■ The source indeed "for good-quality" cardio equipment from brands like Cybex, Nautilus and True, for the home, office or commercial gym, this two-floor Midtown mecca also features a "great selection" of free weights, benches, strength machines and accessories; the knowledgeable staff also provides "good service" – just ask Madonna or Henry Kissinger, said to be among the satisfied customers.

Hable Construction ⑤◉   – | – | – | M

230 Elizabeth St. (bet. Houston & Prince Sts.), N to Prince St., 212-343-8555; www.hableconstruction.com

The Hable sisters opened up their new NoLita boutique in a cozy space with tin ceilings and a garden out back, but their merch – bold-patterned felt-appliqué pillows and playful, printed tablecloths, rugs, runners and fabric – is of the moment; every fashionista needs one of their magazine bags – from demure ones, which hold this month's issues, to giant totes that can contain a year's worth.

Hammacher Schlemmer & Co.   24 | 23 | 20 | VE

147 E. 57th St. (bet. Lexington & 3rd Aves.), 4/5/6/N/R/W to 59th St./Lexington Ave., 212-421-9000; 800-421-9002; www.hammacher.com

■ "Techno geeks dream" of "clearing their first million to shop daily" at this "toy store for the rich and unconventional" in the East 50s, where "all the things you'll never need", including two-

vote at zagat.com   **125**

way radio wristwatches and hats with programmable LCD displays, are "tested for quality, presented with abundant information" and come with a "lifetime warranty"; "take visitors" and show them "what people are capable of inventing" – along with what they're "prepared to spend."

H&M | 15 | 13 | 8 | I |
1328 Broadway (34th St.), B/D/F/N/Q/R/V/W to 34th St./Herald Sq., 646-473-1165
558 Broadway (bet. Prince & Spring Sts.), N/R to Prince St., 212-343-2722
640 Fifth Ave. (bet. 51st & 52nd Sts.), E/V to 5th Ave./53rd St., 212-489-0390 ◗ S
435 Seventh Ave. (34th St.), 1/2/3/9 to 34th St./Penn Station, 212-643-6955
125 W. 125th St. (Lenox), 2/3 to 125th St., 212-665-8300 ◗ S
Kings Plaza Mall, 5100 Kings Plaza, Brooklyn, 2 to Brooklyn College/Flatbush Ave., then take B41 bus, 718-252-5444
90-15 Queens Blvd. (bet. 90th & 91st Aves.), Queens, G/R/V to Woodhaven Blvd., 718-592-4200
www.hm.com

▪ The "crazy throngs" and "horrendous lines" might make you "feel you're at an 'N Sync concert" when you "jump into" this Swedish "madhouse" of fashion, but all the "disposable designer wanna-be clothing" is "trashy, flashy and so dirt cheap it doesn't matter"; avoid "peak" weekends, "buy in bulk" and indulge in a "guilt-free" "scavenger hunt" for all sizes of threads "du jour" for "punk rock clubs" and "last minute outfits" without "going broke" – translation: "$1.50 for earrings? I'm sold!"

Hard Rock Cafe ◗S | 12 | 16 | 15 | M |
221 W. 57th St. (bet B'way & 7th Ave.), 1/9/A/B/C/D/E to 59th St./Columbus Circle; N/Q/R/W to 57th St., 212-459-9320; www.hardrock.com

▪ "Rock and roll", hoochie-coo! – this "traditional souvenir store with a Manhattan flair" on West 57th is "always fun for people who have never been to the city and need that all-important T-shirt" or some other piece of "overpriced merchandise that promotes the chain"; but just "try to find a New Yorker" inside – "last time I purchased anything here I was in the 6th grade" harrumph locals, though slumming fashionistas confide "they have denim shirts that last for years."

Harley Davidson of NY ◗S C | 16 | 19 | 16 | M |
686 Lexington Ave. (bet. 56th & 57th Sts.), 4/5/6/F/N/R/W to 59th St./Lexington Ave., 212-355-3003; www.nycharleydavidson.com

▪ Get your motor running and head to the East 50s for "all the Harley stuff" an easy rider needs; the "attire for interesting people" (and four-wheeling wanna-bes) includes the requisite T-shirts, leather, bandannas and helmets, plus belt buckles, purses, eyewear and teeny-tiny duds for the recently born-to-be-wild; some might think this "silly trend needs to be stopped", but don't tell that to the aging bruisers buying logo shot glasses.

Harriet Love S C | 23 | 20 | 24 | E |
126 Prince St. (bet. Greene & Wooster Sts.), N/R to Prince St., 212-966-2280

■ One of "SoHo's pioneers", this "teensy-weensy" store is still a must-stop for its "unusual selections" of ladies' European-designed duds and accessories "with a vintage/retro twist"; "really nice staffers try to please" with "very Stevie Nicks" – style "wonderful

| M | P | S | C |

surprises" that include "cute bags and hats", "casual and dressy knits" and jewelry.

Harris Levy S | 23 | 12 | 19 | M
278 Grand St. (bet. Eldridge & Forsyth Sts.), S to Grand St., 212-226-3102; 800-226-3102; www.harrislevy.com

■ "Madison Avenue linens at less than Madison Avenue prices" is the mantra at this 1894 "Lower East Side landmark" where four "generations of [Levy] family pictures grace the walls"; savvy shoppers head here for a "beautiful selection of the best linens" – from 600-thread-count imported sheets to "special orders"; just don't let the queue at the counter or the "ask-for-it method of shopping" deter you.

Harry's Shoes S C | 23 | 17 | 20 | M
2299 Broadway (83rd St.), 1/9 to 86th St., 212-874-2035; 866-442-7797; www.harrys-shoes.com

■ A "great example of a family shoe store", this "hectic" "Upper West Side institution" stocks a "multitude" of "premium brands", "pricey British and Italian imports" and a "good selection for the little ones"; the "amazingly old-school" "sassy" "salespeople seem to actually know something about footwear – what a concept!" and "just like when you were a kid" will even "measure your feet" ("if you have any fit or comfort issues these are the people to see"); just "avoid it on weekends", when it can be a "footloose" "madhouse" and "more crowded than Jones Beach in July."

HARRY WINSTON | 29 | 29 | 26 | VE
718 Fifth Ave. (56th St.), E/V to 5th Ave./53rd St.; N/R/W to 5th Ave./ 59th St., 212-245-2000; 800-988-4110; www.harrywinston.com

■ "Jeweler to the stars", Academy Awards–night regular and the *Survey*'s No. 1 for Fashion/Beauty, this neo-classical Midtown icon's "name carries [as much] weight" as its celebrated sparklers ("who knew diamonds could be so big?") "that leave many speechless"; the "pinnacle of elegance" for the "elite, celebrities and moguls" may seem "a little snobbish" to mere mortals just looking, but "serious customers" who "have the money to spend" find "service impeccable."

Harvey Electronics S C | 26 | 21 | 20 | VE
2 W. 45th St. (bet. 5th & 6th Aves.), F/B/D to Rockefeller Ctr., 212-575-5000; 800-254-7836; www.harveyonline.com

❏ "Serious listeners" and those who "need hands-on guidance" through the full-frequency spectrum of 7.1 channel surround processors, integrated amplifiers and belt-driven turntables shop for the "ultimate gear" at this Midtown "high-end" "Disney World of flat-screen TVs", home theaters and "major stereo systems"; but since it's priced "for that wealthy electronics guy", it's "a great place" only "if you're Bill Gates."

HASTINGS BATH & TILE | 26 | 27 | 20 | VE
230 Park Ave. S. (19th St.), 4/5/6/L/N/Q/R/W to 14th St./Union Sq., 212-674-9700; www.hastingstilebath.com

■ "Out-of-the-ordinary" and "up-to-the-moment" bathroom tiles as well as a "gorgeous selection" of sinks and fixtures attract "informed" customers to this "terrific" showroom off Union Square Park; the staff can "help you design your space", and the products are "nicely presented" in an "inspirational" fashion, but, alas, for wallet-watchers the prices are purely "aspirational."

vote at zagat.com 127

Hat Shop, The 🆂🅲 ▽ 25 | 25 | 25 | E
120 Thompson St. (bet. Prince & Spring Sts.), C/E to Spring St., 212-219-1445
■ There's "something for everyone" at this tiny Thompson Street atelier teeming with topper temptations; the "fantastic selection" from milliners galore covers every nook and cranny and ranges from the practical to the all-out indulgent; the "amazing Linda" Pagan and her "terrific" staff will help you select the look that's right for your face, and don't forget: "hats can be made to measure."

Hattitude – | – | – | M
93 Reade St. (bet. Church St. & W. B'way), 1/2/3/9 to Chambers St., 212-571-4558
"You can't walk out of" this "fun", ultra-feminine TriBeCa hat outpost "without buying something fabulous" fawn fans, especially "if you're into the Emily Brontë heroine look"; owner Wendy Carrington's "unique" lids are made from "gorgeous" fabrics, many vintage, and they not only "fit and cover your ears", they also "pack wonderfully."

Hedra Prue 🆂🅲 25 | 18 | 18 | E
281 Mott St. (bet. Houston & Prince Sts.), N/R/ to Prince St.; 6 to Bleecker St., 212-343-9205; www.hedraprue.com
■ Presenting a "well-edited collection" of "harder-to-find" young designers like MRS and Martin, this "tiny" "Mott Street gem" has the "flawless knack" of nailing what's on the "cusp of avant-garde" for the "girl who doesn't like to dress like everyone else"; "prices are high, but hit them at sale time and you'll be a happy hipster."

Heights Kids 🆂 – | – | – | E
85 Pineapple Walk (bet. Cadman Plaza & Henry St.), Brooklyn, 2/3 to Clark St., 718-222-4271
The height of convenience for mamas and papas, this Pineapple powerhouse carries everything but furniture for wee ones; parents praise the small but carefully chosen selection of strollers from brands like Peg Perego and Maclaren, car seats and baby gear that's the best of the best and also reach for the newborn–toddler apparel, from popular lines like Catimini, Baby Dior and Absorba, as well as the high-quality wooden and educational toys from brands like Brio and Sassy.

Helena Rubenstein Beauty Gallery ●🆂 ▽ 22 | 21 | 20 | E
135 Spring St. (bet. Greene & Wooster Sts.), C/E to Spring St.; N/R to Prince St., 212-343-9963; www.helenarubenstein.com
■ "Welcome back" say supporters of this cosmetics grande dame that opened its first beauty salon in 1902 and three years ago turned up in this "beautiful", sleek SoHo space with a two-floor shop; a "gallery" setting is the backdrop for a "great selection" of updated products – perfume, makeup and skincare – that belies its rep for "colors your mother wears"; N.B. appointments can also be made for a variety of spa services downstairs, including facials, waxing and massage.

Helene Arpels – | – | – | VE
470 Park Ave. (bet. 57th & 58th Sts.), 4/5/6/N/R/W to 59th St./Lexington Ave., 212-755-1623
Proudly impervious to trends, this ladies' shoe salon of a certain age caters to "the Park Avenue set" with a collection of "original"

M | P | S | C

pumps, loafers and boots; no pointy toes or sky-high heels here – just colorful leather for day and jewel-encrusted satin and suede for night, along with a few suits and alligator purses; a plush gray-and-pale-blue showroom filled with Oriental rugs and tapestried chairs displays these emblems of elegant good taste.

Helen Woodhull at James Robinson C — | — | — | VE
480 Park Ave. (58th St.), 4/5/6/N/R/W to 59th St./Lexington Ave., 212-826-1212 for studio; 212-752-6166 for James Robinson
Many a groupie loves the "gorgeous", one-of-a-kind pieces made by this artisan, now within the Park Avenue antique jeweler James Robinson; it's an appropriate home, as her forte has always been using historic crafting techniques and ancient intaglios, amulets and cabochons in gold bezel-set rings, earrings and bracelets.

Helmut Lang S C 24 | 25 | 16 | VE
80 Greene St. (bet. Broome & Spring Sts.), N/R to Prince St., 212-925-7214; www.helmutlang.com
■ Once you get the hang of Lang, admirers say, this is one of those SoHo stores that "justifies an expensive purchase", as "you'll be wearing it years later"; the immediate gratification lies in an "unfussy", "minimal interior" filled with "S&M-meets-career" suits, T-shirts and jeans for men and women – mostly black, white or neutrals – made in high-tech, stretchy "used-by-NASA materials"; "prices are in outer space too."

Helmut Lang Parfums S — | — | — | E
81 Greene St. (bet. Broome & Spring Sts.), N/R to Prince St., 212-334-3921; www.helmutlang.com
The well-known designer opened this freestanding store directly across from his flagship boutique in SoHo as a showcase for his own line of perfumes, bath-and-body products and men's colognes; while the setting evokes the aesthetic of an old-world apothecary, performance artist Jenny Holzer's LED tribute to scent pulsing atop one of the walls adds an avant-garde element.

HENRI BENDEL S 24 | 24 | 20 | VE
712 Fifth Ave. (56th St.), E/V to 53rd St.; N/R/W to 5th Ave./59th St., 212-247-1100; 800-423-6335
◪ Enter the "extravagant" realm of this Fifth Avenue "jewel box" (complete with landmarked Lalique windows), which combines the "cachet" of a "small boutique" with the "selection of a large" emporium; it's famed for its "gold-standard cutting-edge beauty brands", on the main floor (also the site of "kitschy" "novelty gifts" and "fabulous private-label sweaters"); up the winding staircase lies an "eclectic mix" of hairclips and hats, the "latest and greatest" jeans and womenswear from emerging designers "high-styled for the young and the young-at-heart – and size"; however, some grouse it's gotten "too far-out" and say the staff, though "helpful", can turn "hoity-toity" before handing over the "legendary" brown-and-white-striped shopping bag.

Henry Lehr S C 24 | 17 | 22 | E
232 Elizabeth St. (bet. Houston & Prince Sts.), F/V/S to B'way/Lafayette St.; 6 to Spring St., 212-274-9921
268 Elizabeth St. (bet. Houston & Prince Sts.), F/V/S to B'way/Lafayette St.; 6 to Spring St., 212-343-0567
■ These "cool and casual" NoLita lairs capture a lion's worth of "genuinely buyable stuff" for "young, slick shoppers", who like to

vote at zagat.com 129

browse among their "great selection of [designer] jeans", "hip" boy/girl T-shirts and "cute gloves" to construct the ultimate more-in-the-know-than-thou uniform; P.S. bargain-hunters wait for the "season's-end sale racks outdoors" (in summer).

Here Comes the Bridesmaid 18 | 7 | 12 | M
238 W. 14th St. (bet. 7th & 8th Aves.), A/C/E/L to 14th St./8th Ave., 212-647-9686; www.bridesmaids.com
◪ "A bride looking to save her girls some money should visit" this Chelsea shop of "cheapie treasures" where bridesmaid dresses featured in "typical bridal magazines" await; but critics counter that the "sad presentation", "cast sloppily on racks", "looks like the backstage of a high school theater dressing room", adding that "appointments are overbooked."

HERMÈS ◉ 28 | 27 | 23 | VE
691 Madison Ave. (62nd St.), N/R/W to 5th Ave./59th St., 212-751-3181; 800-441-4488; www.hermes.com
■ For "posh" Parisian "perfection", nobody outdoes this "open and airy" Upper Eastsider for "quality, style and status" goods, especially when it comes to "superbly made" scarves ("are eight too many?"), "ties that are the stuff of legend" and the much-"lusted"-after Kelly and Birkin bags, available to the few who make the waiting list; "don't be intimidated by the hype" – a doorman welcomes you in and salespeople are "extremely approachable", if sometimes cobbled by the "crowds of tourists"; in the land of luxury, "this store is king", so prepare to "overpay at the palace."

H. Herzfeld ◉ ▽ 25 | 18 | 21 | VE
507 Madison Ave. (bet. 52nd & 53rd Sts.), E/V to 53rd St./5th Ave., 212-753-6756; www.herzfeldonline.com
◪ Offering a "well-edited" selection of "high-end menswear" and accessories since 1890, this "reliable" Midtown shop represents "one of the last of the classics, with European quality and tradition" (e.g. the custom-made shirt service); perhaps its "fashion sense is a bit stuck in a rut" – "nothing purchased here will ever scare the horses" – but most "gottaluvit" for its "stuffy, timeless" appeal.

Hickey Freeman ◉ 25 | 24 | 24 | VE
666 Fifth Ave. (bet. 52nd & 53rd Sts.), E/V to 5th Ave./53rd St., 212-586-6481; 888-603-8968; www.hickeyfreeman.com
■ In its "beautiful" young Fifth Avenue store, this "old standby" (since 1899) offers up "conservatively stylish", "well-constructed" "American tailored suits" "made from the finest material" and proffered by "expert help" who understands "that corporate look"; whether you opt for custom-made, off-the-rack or something from the "Bobby Jones collection of country-club lifestyle sportswear", the garments will "fit like a glove" (as indeed they should, given the "eye-popping prices"); P.S. suit buyers, "make sure to spring for the second pair of pants."

H.L. Purdy ◉ – | – | – | E
1195 Lexington Ave. (bet. 81st & 82nd Sts.), 6 to 77th St., 212-737-0122
1171 Madison Ave. (bet. 85th & 86th Sts.), 4/5/6 to 86th St., 212-249-3997
971 Madison Ave. (76th St.), 6 to 77th St., 212-794-2020
501 Madison Ave. (52nd St.), E/V to 53rd St./5th Ave., 212-688-8050
www.hlpurdy.com
From the "meticulous", "prompt" and "willing" opticians "with a smile" to the Lexington Avenue location's children's center with

M | P | S | C

pint-sized furniture and fixtures, it's all about service at this eyewear outfit; "this is the place to go if you need new specs" praise patrons who are also purdy pleased that prescriptions can be filled for everything from solid gold and jeweled frames to binoculars, opera glasses and even telescopes.

HMV ●S 21 | 18 | 13 | M
565 Fifth Ave. (46th St.), 4/5/6/7/S 42nd St./Grand Central, 212-681-6700
308 W. 125th St., A/B/C/D to 125th St., 212-932-9619
www.hmv.com

☐ "More of an event than a music/video/book" emporium, with an "open layout and listening stations" where you can tune into "popular stuff", these chainsters stock "everything you might ever want to listen to or watch"; while fans find it a "favorite" source for "cool imports" with a "terrific" classical department too, mega-store cynics sniff it's "a bit pricey", offering "nothing special or different."

HOGAN S C 23 | 26 | 23 | VE
134 Spring St. (bet. Greene & Wooster Sts.), C/E to Spring St., 212-343-7905

■ Bringing a "little boho to SoHo", this "interesting" shop (Tod's "exciting" sibling) dispenses "downtown conservative-hip chic" by way of "sublimely comfy" "funky footwear" and "terrific bags"; it's "always worth a visit" fawn fashionistas, who hotfoot it over for a host of "uncommon products" from "fabulous sneakers" to "great everyday loafers"; sure, the merchandise is "very expensive", but most insist it's "worth the money."

Hold Everything S 19 | 19 | 16 | M
1309 Second Ave. (69th St.), 6 to 68th St., 212-879-1450 ●
104 Seventh Ave. (16th St.), 1/9 to 18th St., 212-633-1674
800-421-2264; www.williams-sonomainc.com

☐ "Everything you need to get your ducks in order", and your closet, kitchen, bathroom and bookshelves too, is the point of these Chelsea and East Side stores providing "practical" "storage" "solutions" for "obsessive-compulsive people" and anyone living in a "cramped New York City apartment"; but penny-pinchers find them "pricey" and suggest you "use shoeboxes instead."

Holland & Holland C ▽ 28 | 27 | 24 | VE
50 E. 57th St. (bet. Madison & Park Aves.), N/R/W to 5th Ave./59th St., 212-752-7755; www.hollandandholland.com

■ Founded in 1835 as a firearms maker, this venerable British company aims "for the horsey set" (or "well-off wanna-bes") who set their sights on "truly top-of-the-line" tweedy threads, "safari clothes" and "sporting books and accessories"; P.S. "even if you don't shoot, don't miss the bespoke guns on the top floor" of the East 50s townhouse.

Hollywood Video S 18 | 13 | 11 | I
535 Columbus Ave. (86th St.), B/C to 86th St., 917-441-3561; 877-325-8687;
www.hollywoodvideo.com
Additional locations throughout the NY area

■ Those who like to watch "love the five night" rental policy at this video/DVD chain that's "good for big Hollywood flicks", with a mondo biography and documentary section as well; but some serious cineastes say "it's not for specialty or foreign films" and "not as good as the independents."

vote at zagat.com

		M	P	S	C

Hollywould ❶   27 | 25 | 23 | E
198 Elizabeth St. (bet. Prince & Spring Sts.), 6 to Spring St., 212-343-8344; www.ilovehollywould.com
■ "As the name suggests", LA-based designer Holly Dunlap's "NoLita treasure", decorated with blue walls, awning-striped benches and a luxe chandelier, is "all about glamour"; the "whimsical", "fun party shoes", "flashy heels" in "wild patterns" and "sexy" stilettos with "cute, fuchsia foil linings" are not only "eye-catching, they're actually comfortable" to boot; the "to-die-for" selection appeals to "dollar-laden ladies with pooches as small as their purses" and celebs like Britney and J. Lo.

Holy Cow ❶ S   - | - | - | M
442 Ninth St. (7th Ave.), Brooklyn, F to 7th Ave., 718-788-3631
On the parlor floor of a brownstone, the only store of its kind in the wilds of Park Slope is a grazer's green pasture of new and used rock, reggae, jazz and blues vinyl and CDs, including promo rarities; the friendly, knowledgeable folks behind the counter will even let you take your prospective purchases for a spin on their turntable.

Home Depot S C   22 | 13 | 15 | I
50-10 Northern Blvd. (bet. 49th & 50th Sts.), Queens, R to Northern Blvd., 718-278-9031; 800-430-3376; www.homedepot.com
For additional locations, see Top Chain Stores index
◪ "Bigger is better" boast buffs of these "über-hardware stores" in Brooklyn and Queens that are a "DIYer's dream", with "everything you could ever need", even "the little thingy that goes with the whatsit"; critics complain of "chaos" caused by "long lines at checkout" ("bring your overnight bag") and a staff that's adept at "playing deaf"; still, the "tremendous selection" and "great prices" lead many to plead "please come to Manhattan."

Homer   - | - | - | VE
939 Madison Ave. (bet. 74th & 75th Sts.), 6 to 77th St., 212-744-7705; www.homerdesign.com
After hitting the Whitney, the design-driven can pop a few doors down to this East 70s contemporary furniture store where accent pieces by Chuck Price, Tony Duquette and Jeremiah Goodman are displayed among the dark-stained chaises, shelves and beds designed by the owner, architect/designer Richard Mishaan.

Hooti Couture ❶ S   - | - | - | M
321 Flatbush Ave. (7th Ave.), Brooklyn, Q to 7th Ave., 718-857-1977
"Always a fun stop when in Park Slope", this small antique-clothing store specializes in daytime (and some dressy) duds from the 1940s on, with an especially "terrific selection of vintage bags" and costume jewelry; the "free-spirited" "owner is always sweet and helpful", and the little messages she scrawls on the tags of each garment (e.g. 'the dress I turned Ed down in') are, well, a hoot.

Hotel Venus by Patricia Field ❶ S C   20 | 23 | 17 | M
382 W. Broadway (bet. Broome & Spring Sts.), C/E to Spring St., 212-966-4066; www.patriciafield.com
■ Check into SoHo's "dominatrix-wear" dominion, owned by *Sex and the City* costumer Patricia Field; it's "like shopping at a circus" as you peruse the "eccentric, over-the-top club" and "drag queen" garb, plus (slightly) more sedate pieces from labels like Miss Sixty, J. Lindberg and House of Field; other features include a Hello Kitty

| M | P | S | C |

section and a beauty salon, "the best place to get your eyebrows plucked by real professionals – men who want to be women"; N.B. it now also carries inventory from the designer's late namesake boutique (not reflected in the Merchandise score).

Hot Toddie 🆂🅲   – | – | – | E
741 Fulton St. (bet. S. Elliott Pl. & S. Portland Sts.), Brooklyn, C to Lafayette Ave., 718-858-7292
Cool styles for wee hipsters (infants through size 6) abound at this fairy-tale-esque Fort Greene boutique aglow with chandeliers, gilt-framed mirrors and displays made from old French carriages; stylin' mamas coddle their sons with Sean John clothing and offbeat must-haves like Fifi & Fido's bowling shirts and their fashionistas-in-training with trendy wear from Betsey Johnson and D&G; there's even a small selection of baby's first jewelry, educational toys from Germany – and a friendly staff to help stumped gift-givers.

House of Oldies 🅲   – | – | – | M
35 Carmine St. (bet. Bleecker St. & 6th Ave.), A/B/C/D/E/F to W. 4th St., 212-243-0500; www.houseofoldies.com
Your house would need a basement a city block long if you were storing 700,000 discs too; this thirtysomething labor of love hawks near-mint, mint and still-sealed vinyl of every conceivable non-classical genre, including out-of-print 45s and LPs; if you've got a hankering for Elvis Presley's original Sun Studio singles or a *Sgt. Pepper* picture disc, they've got 'em, but you can only pick 'em up noon–5 PM Tuesday–Saturday, when they're open.

Housing Works Thrift Shop 🆂   20 | 17 | 16 | I
306 Columbus Ave. (bet. 74th & 75th Sts.), 1/2/3/9/B/C to 72nd St., 212-579-7566
202 E. 77th St. (bet. 2nd & 3rd Aves.), 6 to 77th St., 212-772-8461
157 E. 23rd St. (bet. Lexington & 3rd Aves.), 6 to 23rd St., 212-529-5955
143 W. 17th St. (bet. 6th and 7th Aves.), 1/2 to 18th St., 212-366-0820
www.housingworks.org
■ If such a thing as a posh thrift is possible, this "quirky, mod" quartet certainly qualifies for its "great cross-section" of "high-quality merchandise" (particularly "cool picks" in furniture), often arrayed in "amusing window displays"; the seasoned say "for the best selection, shop early" in the day.

Howard Kaplan Bath Shop 🅲   – | – | – | VE
827 Broadway (bet. 12th & 13th Sts.), L/N/Q/R/W/4/5/6 to 14th St./Union Sq., 212-674-1000; www.howardkaplanantiques.com
The beautiful facade of this Village store seems straight out of Paris' Left Bank, and inside you'll find French antique and reproduction bathroom fixtures, plumbing, mirrors, lighting and accessories, from *grande* copper tubs to *petite* soap dishes; though its unique wares inspire *amour*, alas, it's "way too expensive" for many budgets.

H. Stern 🅲   24 | 24 | 22 | VE
645 Fifth Ave. (51st St.), E/V to 5th Ave./53rd St., 212-688-0300; 800-747-8376
■ Boasting over 100 stores worldwide, this Brazilian-based firm carries "classically creative", "artistic" jewelry that "you can actually picture wearing"; the modern space makes it "comfortable to walk in and browse" among the "color-coded" precious and semi-precious stones, and the "passionate salespeople" are quite "customer-friendly"; while pieces can be pricey, many are "more reasonable than most Fifth Avenue jewelers."

vote at zagat.com

| M | P | S | C |

H20 Plus   20 | 20 | 17 | M
650 Madison Ave. (60th St.), 4/5/6/N/R/W to 59th St./Lexington Ave., 212-750-8119
460 W. Broadway (bet. Houston & Prince Sts.), N/R to Prince St., 212-505-3223 ●〇S
800-242-2284; www.h2oplus.com

■ These white-and-blue Madison Avenue and SoHo toiletries stores feature a "sleek", mostly water-based line of bath-and-body products, along with perfumes, that "make you feel like you're on a tropical island"; reasonable prices also make them "great for gifts" for girls of all ages.

Hugo Boss S   26 | 25 | 22 | VE
717 Fifth Ave. (56th St.), N/R/W to 5th Ave./59th St., 212-485-1800; www.hugoboss.com

■ A recent "landmark on Fifth Avenue", this multi-floor flagship with a striking facade and endless staircases invites you in for the "penultimate in cool men's [and women's] fashions"; some favor the "great suits" from the luxury Baldessarini line ("a grown-up brand for grown-up style"), while others say it's "the place to go for casual", avant-garde goods from the HUGO label; whichever, there's clearly a little bit of bad boy in every Boss ("so sexy I want to devour my boyfriend when he's wearing it!").

Hunting World S C   ▽ 18 | 18 | 20 | VE
118 Greene St. (bet. Prince & Spring Sts.), N/R to Prince St., 212-431-0086; www.huntingworld.com

■ What started as the elite "safari look" in the '60s with functional expedition-worthy gear continues for a new generation of "urban gorillas" willing to shell out big bucks at this granite-walled SoHo shop; admirers snag bounty like "quality" Battue nylon handbags and luggage that meet the cold-weather challenge and durable canvas and leather duffles, totes and pouches; but a handful feel poached upon, opining "no reason to pay these prices."

Hyman Hendler and Sons   25 | 10 | 13 | E
67 W. 38th St. (bet. 5th & 6th Aves.), B/D/F/N/Q/R/V/W to 34th St./Herald Sq., 212-840-8393

■ "One of a vanishing breed", this 103-year-old Garment Center stalwart spanning three generations carries trimmings plus "all the ribbon you could ever imagine"; "tell them what you are looking for" and a "beautiful selection" ranging from lengths of grosgrain and velvet to novelty and vintage finds "starts to magically appear", in what feels like a "scene out of Harry Potter."

Ibiza ●S C   25 | 23 | 21 | E
46 University Pl. (bet. 9th & 10th Sts.), N/R to 8th St., 212-533-4614
42 University Pl. (bet. 9th & 10th Sts.), N/R to 8th St., 212-505-9907
56 University Pl. (10th St.), N/R to 8th St., 212-375-9984

■ "A fun place to shop for funky", "phenomenal" women's clothing that "works for all ages and occasions", with an emphasis on "luscious fabrics" and "hippie"-chick styles (channel your inner Stevie Nicks), this Village boutique doubles as a "wonderful" spot to pick up "adorable prints and styles" for little ones, from Zutano separates to Petit Bateau T-shirts; Ibiza Kidz a few doors down is "packed with toys" and "an amazing selection of shoes" for wee ones, mostly European imports like Elefanten.

| **M** | **P** | **S** | **C** |

Ideal Tile   – | – | – | M
405 E. 51st St. (1st Ave.), E/V to Lexington Ave.; 6 to 51st St., 212-759-2339; www.idealtileimporting.com
This outpost of a national chain located in a small space in the East 50s packs a wallop with its "wonderful selection" of granite, marble and ceramic kitchen-and-bath tiles that include the most current Italian designs; idealists also exult in the "good craftsmanship" of the wares and the "great", "helpful" staff.

IF ⓈⒸ   – | – | – | VE
94 Grand St. (bet. Greene & Mercer Sts.), N/R to Canal St., 212-334-4964
A pioneer (established 1974) in SoHo, this unadorned, loft-like space keeps its cutting-edge reputation firmly intact with a "wonderful" array of "avant-garde" European designer wear for women (Dries Van Noten, Veronique Branquinho, et al.) – "typically a better selection than at larger" venues.

Il Bisonte ⓈⒸ   – | – | – | E
120 Sullivan St. (bet. Prince & Spring Sts.), C/E to Spring St., 212-966-8773; 877-458-4166; www.ilbisonte.com
Antique fixtures and bison figurines set the tone for this Florence-based company's artisanal men's and women's leather handbags, briefcases, backpacks, totes and small leather goods, available in all shapes and sizes at this airy SoHo haven; ask for the natural vegetable-tanned vacchetta leather – it starts out as a rich honeyed shade and gets deeper, darker and richer-looking with age.

Illuminations   21 | 23 | 18 | M
873 Broadway (18th St.), 4/5/6/L/N/Q/R/W to 14th St./Union Sq., 212-777-1621
Rockefeller Ctr., 46 W. 50th St. (bet. 5th & 6th Aves.), B/D/F/V to 47-50th Sts./Rockefeller Ctr., 212-582-8850
54 Spring St. (bet. Lafayette & Mulberry Sts.), 6 to Spring St., 212-226-8713 ◐ Ⓢ
800-621-2998; www.illuminations.com
■ "As trendy wax shops go, no one holds a candle to" this chain whose "beautifully lit", "tranquil" interiors "provide an excellent antidote to city craziness"; partisans are positively glowing about the "splendidly presented", "lovely displays" of merchandise and the "addictive", "amazing scents", and if your funds are tapering, "head to the sale items in the back for great deals."

Il Makiage ⓈⒸ   – | – | – | M
107 E. 60th St. (Park Ave.), 4/5/6/N/R/W to 59th St./Lexington Ave., 212-371-0551; 800-722-1011
Owner Ilana Harkavi opened this pioneering East Side cosmetics boutique back in 1972, and it's still a good destination if you want an enormous selection of colors – over 500 shades of nail polish, lipstick, eyeshadow and blush – textures and formulas, plus expert advice.

Il Papiro Ⓒ   – | – | – | E
1021 Lexington Ave. (bet. 73rd & 74th Sts.), 6 to 77th St., 212-288-9330
Fans of flame-stitched designs declare "very few stationery stores [match] the quality" of this small Upper Eastsider, one of the first purveyors of fine Florentine papers in NYC (and still "the place to go if you don't want traditional monograms" on your letterhead); available in a cornucopia of colors, its marbelized designs decorate

vote at zagat.com

M | P | S | C

a variety of objects – desk sets and date books, picture frames and pencils, even wastebaskets and Kleenex boxes; but if you don't pant for peacock-feathered prints, there are solid-hued, hand-bound leather accessories too.

Ina S — 23 | 18 | 13 | E
208 E. 73rd St. (bet. 2nd & 3rd Aves.), 6 to 68th St., 212-249-0014
262 Mott St. (bet. Houston & Prince Sts.), 6 to Spring St., 212-334-2210
21 Prince St. (bet. Elizabeth & Mott Sts.), F/V/S to B'way/Lafayette, 212-334-9048
101 Thompson St. (bet. Prince & Spring Sts.), C/E to Spring St., 212-941-4757

◪ Clotheshorses who "really wanted, but couldn't afford, that Prada suit" last year head to these "high-end designer hideouts", consignment shops "well stocked" with "recent-season castoffs" that are "definitely still in style" (not much "funky fashion" here); loyalists laud the "attention to display" (especially for the "amazing shoes") and disregard "the unhelpful staff"; N.B. the Mott Street branch is men's only.

Industrial Plastic Supply — 23 | 11 | 14 | I
309 Canal St. (Mercer St.), 6/J/M/N/Q/R/W/Z to Canal St., 212-226-2010; www.yourplasticsupermarket.com
■ The "funky interior designer", "nightclub" owner or "artist in you" "can find the weirdest things and get some creative ideas" at this "cool mini-museum of plastic products" on Canal Street; the "cavernous", "worn-out" shop "is your place for pink duck cut-outs" and other "quirky but useful" "cheap, delightful crap" – just "make sure they" "cut to [your] specifications."

Infinity C — – | – | – | E
1116 Madison Ave. (83rd St.), 4/5/6 to 86th St., 212-517-4232
Private-"school princesses" jet over to this Madison Avenue shop that resembles the inside of an overstuffed closet for "flashy, trendy" pre-teen and teen-sized clothing to wear once school uniforms come off; fashionistas in their formative years get their fill of fashion fun thanks to the hot selection of jeans, tees and casualwear from such labels du jour as Juicy Couture and Miss Sixty; P.S. when it's time to kick it up a notch for dressy social events, there's a small section devoted to formalwear.

Ingo Maurer Making Light S C — – | – | – | VE
89 Grand St. (Greene St.), A/C/E/ to Canal St., 212-965-8817; www.ingo-maurer.com
This lighting store in a landmarked SoHo building showcases the eponymous German-born designer's lyrical creations like the "exploding china chandelier" and his signature 'Lucellino Lamp', a bulb with wings; the "intriguing concepts" and use of unusual materials and technology have led to collaborations with luminaries like Issey Miyake and exhibitions at MoMA and the Philadelphia Museum of Art.

Innovation Luggage ☽ S — 19 | 13 | 14 | M
2001 Broadway (68th St.), 1/9 to 66th St., 212-721-3164
1755 Broadway (bet. 56th & 57th Sts.), 1/9/A/B/C/D to 59th St./Columbus Circle, 212-582-2044
300 E. 42nd St. (2nd Ave.), 4/5/6/7/S to 42nd St./Grand Central, 212-599-2998

| M | P | S | C |

(continued)
Innovation Luggage
521 Fifth Ave. (bet. 43rd & 44th Sts.), B/D/F to 42nd St.; 4/5/6/7/S to 42nd St./Grand Central, 212-986-4689
670 Sixth Ave. (bet. 20th & 21st Sts.), 1/9 to 23rd St., 212-243-4720
866 Third Ave. (bet. 51st & 52nd Sts.), E/V to 5th Ave./53rd St., 212-832-1841
www.innovationluggage.com
◪ "Soft-sided, hard, inexpensive and expensive, there's something for everyone" at this mini-chain of luggage emporiums; but the less-impressed can't handle the "cloying service" and carry on that it's "priced for businessmen", advising "look elsewhere" or wait for the "good buys on close-outs."

Innovative Audio ◉   ▽ 27 | 21 | 21 | VE
150 E. 58th St. (bet. Lexington & 3rd Aves.), 4/5/6/N/R/W to 59th St./Lexington Ave., 212-634-4444 Ⓢ
76 Montague St. (bet. Hicks St. & Montague Terr.), Brooklyn, 2/3 to Clark St., 718-596-0888
www.innovativeaudiovideo.com
■ With stores in the East 50s and the Heights, this home-entertainment "favorite" has sold the hottest devices via the "soft-sell approach" for 30 years; the "superlative" staff "just hooks up the equipment in a listening room and leaves you alone" for your date with "that special speaker", component or VCR/DVD combo.

Intérieurs ◉   — | — | — | E
149-151 Franklin St. (bet. Hudson & Varick Sts.), 1/9 to Franklin St., 212-343-0800
Beautiful exposed-brick TriBeCa store featuring plush upholstered contemporary furniture and lighting from the French company Modenature, along with Chinese antiques, Asian-inspired tables and chairs and furry flokatis.

INTERMIX   24 | 20 | 16 | E
210 Columbus Ave. (bet. 69th & 70th Sts.), B/C to 72nd St., 212-769-9116
125 Fifth Ave. (bet. 19th & 20th Sts.), N/R to 23rd St., 212-533-9720
1003 Madison Ave. (bet. 77th & 78th Sts.), 6 to 77th St., 212-249-7858 Ⓢ
◪ "Label-conscious" "FITs (fashionistas-in-training)" "won't go home empty-handed" from this "dangerously enticing" chain with its "discriminating", "well-edited" mix of "I-can't-believe-how-much-I-spent-but I-had-to-have-it" women's clothing and accessories; an "easy-to-navigate" layout ("by color scheme") encourages you to "max out daddy's AmEx", but beware the "brutally honest" staffers, especially if you're "above a size 4."

International Center of Photography Ⓢ ◉ — | — | — | M
1133 Sixth Ave. (43rd St.), B/D/F/V to 47-50th Sts./Rockefeller Ctr., 212-857-9725; 800-688-8171; www.icp.org
Shutterbugs get a buzz on at the ICP's shop in Midtown; though the store doesn't sell prints, noteworthy photographers' work shows up in posters, postcards, videos, handmade jewelry and books, including limited editions and volumes autographed at Friday evening signings; buffs can also score funky equipment like the Frycam (a sort of fast-food spycam with a lens peering out from a bag of plastic *frites*), the camera bag to tote it in and the frames and albums to show off the results.

vote at zagat.com

M P S C

International Cutlery (fka Hoffritz) ▽ 23 | 21 | 19 | E
367 Madison Avenue (bet. 45th & 46th Sts.), 4/5/6/7/S to 42nd St./ Grand Central, 212-924-7300; 866-487-6164; www.internationalcutlery.com
■ "There's no place like" this East 40s castle of cutlery sprawled over 15,000 sq. ft. with over 2,000 products, including 60 different pairs of scissors; though it's no longer affiliated with Hoffritz, it still carries "great knives" and other "good-quality" specialty items that are crafted in Germany.

In the Market – | – | – | E
150 W. 28th St. (bet. 6th & 7th Aves.), 1/9 to 28th St., 212-255-6290
This new Chelsea shop is the perfect marriage of pottery studio and plant store, combining custom-made ceramics with unusual greenery for the home, particularly bonsai trees, as well as "floral products for designers and decorators" and garden accessories; a kiln in the back has fired up future plans to provide classes for would-be mud-slingers.

Intrepid Sea-Air-Space Museum S 20 | 18 | 19 | M
Pier 86 (46th St.), C/E to 50th St.; A/C/E to 42nd St./Port Authority, 212-245-0072; www.intrepidmuseum.org
■ The fleet is in with a cargo-hold full of "fun clothes" and "good trinkets for kids", "ex-Navy wives (they just love those hats)" and uniform fetishists at this "unbelievable" museum store for military-history paraphernalia; the duplex space is located in the Visitor's Center next to the Hudson River aircraft carrier, so landlubbers don't have to board ship to shop.

IS: Industries Stationery S C – | – | – | E
91 Crosby St. (bet. Prince & Spring Sts.), N/R to Prince St., 212-620-0300; www.industriesstationery.com
Update "your stationery wardrobe" with the "nice selection" of date books, journals, calendars and photo albums at this shop that's recently relocated to SoHo; you'll find a "limited range", but one with a "specific color and print point of view" in designs featuring bold geometrics and cool graphics that will make you want to "start writing immediately."

ISSEY MIYAKE C 27 | 26 | 22 | VE
119 Hudson St. (bet. Franklin & Moore Sts.), 1/2 to Franklin St., 212-226-0100 S
992 Madison Ave. (77th St.), 6 to 77th St., 212-439-7822
www.isseymiyake.com
■ "Is it clothing or sculpture?" – a little bit of both insist acolytes of the "truly innovative", "immensely wearable" men's and women's garb by the boundary-breaking Japanese designer; whether it's displayed in the "art-world" setting of the new TriBeCa flagship (a Frank Gehry–designed "21st-century" space that's a "wonder to behold") or the original Madison Avenue location, prices are "higher than the sun", but the "unpretentious" salespeople let you browse the "wild styles" and "eye-catching" accessories, always "there if you need them."

Jacadi C 25 | 23 | 19 | VE
1296 Madison Ave. (92nd St.), 6 to 96th St., 212-369-1616 S
787 Madison Ave. (bet. 66th & 67th Sts.), 6 to 68th St., 212-535-3200 S

M | P | S | C

(continued)
Jacadi
1260 Third Ave. (bet. 72nd & 73rd Sts.), 6 to 68th St., 212-717-9292
5005 16th Ave. (bet. 50th & 51st Sts.), Brooklyn, B to 50th St., 718-871-9402 **S**
www.jacadiusa.com

☑ "Pretend you live in Paris and dress your child accordingly" at these "well-appointed" Upper East Side and Brooklyn chain links where it's a "delight to shop" for "classic", "European-style" baby and children's apparel, "beautiful bedding, accessories" and playthings ("there are no softer soft toys in NYC"); while touters trumpet the "top-notch" togs as "worth every dime", scoffers rebel against the "fussy clothes", "hefty prices" and "snobby" staff.

Jack Spade **S C**   22 | 23 | 20 | E
56 Greene St. (Broome St.), C/E to Spring St.; N/R to Prince St., 212-625-1820; www.jackspade.com

■ "More props than actual goods" make Andy Spade's "cool, but not contrived" SoHo "jewel box of updated schoolboy nostalgia" – think "model airplanes and hi-fis" – a "special place to visit"; the "manly hunks of leather and canvas" – "good-looking stuff, from bags and wallets" to luggage and briefcases – sport the "minimal" "look of a Kate" design, "but for dudes"; while ambiance-seekers swoon over the "overall aesthetic", modernists muse it should "move into the next century."

Jaded **S C**   ▽ 21 | 19 | 17 | M
1048 Madison Ave. (80th St.), 6 to 77th St., 212-288-6631; 800-576-9116

■ Jaded jewelry lovers may be rejuvenated by the "different items" at this Madison Avenue boutique; the handmade, "interesting semiprecious" works and "good copies of serious pieces" use 22 karat gold-plate and the historic lost-wax casting process to make meticulous replicas of antiquarian and Renaissance designs.

Jaeger   ▽ 24 | 24 | 25 | E
818 Madison Ave. (bet. 68th & 69th Sts.), 6 to 68th St., 212-628-3350

■ "Conservative" dressers know something fickle fashionistas don't – "a breath of fresh air", in the person of designer Bella Freud, has rejuvenated this "venerable" British brand on the Upper East Side without losing the "worth-the-price" quality; Jaegermeisters dub the his-and-hers clothes, leather goods and accessories (even umbrellas) "wearable classics" that "last for years"; the staff puts on a "helpful and friendly" show too.

James Robinson   – | – | – | VE
480 Park Ave. (58th St.), 4/5/6/N/R/W to 59th St./Lexington Ave., 212-752-6166; www.jrobinson.com

In a hushed, museum-like setting, this green-carpeted Midtown mecca for antique silver, glassware and jewelry is pricey but "worth it" for the privilege of owning a patrician piece of the past, be it belle epoque baubles by Cartier and Tiffany, art nouveau and art deco cuff links, or designs from Helen Woodhull; it also offers Georgian and Victorian porcelain dinner sets from Spode and Minton.

James II Galleries Ltd. **C**   – | – | – | E
11 E. 57th St., 4th fl. (bet. 5th & Madison Aves.), 4/5/6/N/R/W to 59th St./Lexington Ave., 212-355-7040; www.james2.com

Situated since the '40s on the fourth floor of an East 57th Street building, this boutique aims for an antique English-townhouse feel,

---
vote at zagat.com   139

with an interior staircase and walls adorned with needlepoint and mirrors; an expert in 19th-century decorative arts, antiques and fine jewelry, it caters to clients seeking something unique – perhaps a gold-mounted seal necklace?

Jamie Ostrow C — | — | — | E
876 Madison Ave. (bet. 71st & 72nd Sts.), 6 to 68th St., 212-734-8890
Bright colors, bold graphics and contemporary typefaces are the stock in trade at this stationer, set in an airy glass-fronted shop; for 20 years, Madison Avenue matrons and celebrities have been captivated by its mold-breaking custom-printed invitations, writing paper and cards.

Jammyland ●SC — | — | — | M
60 E. Third St. (bet. 1st & 2nd Aves.), F to 2nd Ave., 212-614-0185; 888-664-7369; www.jammyland.com
Hey mon, dis is de "real" 'ting for vintage reggae in the East Village, with fresh-off-the-boat British and Jamaican reissues in cassettes, CDs and platters from Marley to (Eek-a) Mouse, plus some new African and Latin sounds; the staff is "knowledgeable and always willing to help out", and you can pick up a T-shirt or sweatshirt for those cold nights in Jamaica (Queens).

Jam Paper & Envelope S 19 | 11 | 15 | I
11 Third Ave. (bet. 13th & 14th Sts.), 4/5/6/N/Q/R/W to 14th St./ Union Sq.; L to 3rd Ave., 212-473-6666
611 Sixth Ave. (bet. 17th & 18th Sts.), F/V to 14th St.; 1/9 to 18th St., 212-255-4593
www.jampaper.com
■ The "quirky selection" is the star at these East Village and Flatiron "no-frills" "warehouses for paper" where some "digging" through the "cluttered shelves" yields "beautiful" stationery, envelopes, bags and "fun office supplies" at "bargain" prices; the goods are "great for spurring creative ideas", particularly for "do-it-yourself" projects involving "neon colors."

Jamson Whyte SC — | — | — | E
25 Mercer St. (bet. Canal & Grand Sts.), A/C/E to Canal St., 212-965-9405
316 Bleecker St. (bet. Christopher & Grove Sts.), 1/9 to Christopher St., 212-255-6420
www.jamsonwhyte.com
Escape the hustle and bustle of city life and "go to the island" of Indonesia when you visit this SoHo store whose owner stocks it with handmade home furnishings – like chairs, beds and tables, mostly made from reclaimed teak – found or inspired by trips throughout Southeast Asia; the small Bleecker Street branch, simply dubbed Jamson's, stocks accessories (such as birdcages, clocks and candles) only.

J&R COMPUTER WORLD S 25 | 17 | 17 | M
15 Park Row (bet. Ann & Beekman Sts.), N/R to City Hall, 212-238-9100; 800-806-1115; www.jandr.com
■ This "fabulous" "family-owned" "institution" "has taken over Park Row" to become a "one-stop" "electronics nirvana" for "everything you need and want", including "all the newest gadgets" hawked by "knowledgeable" staffers who "won't take you to the cleaners"; the "crowds" "are not for the faint of heart", however, so "pick an off-time to go."

| M | P | S | C |

J&R MUSIC WORLD S C
24 | 16 | 17 | M

23 Park Row (bet. Ann & Beekman Sts.), N/R to City Hall, 212-238-9000; www.jandr.com

■ One of the "largest of the little guys", this "Downtown institution" near the Financial District "cannot be kept down"; it's "worth the trip for a long sojourn in entertainment heaven", thanks to a "vast selection" of CDs from "a wide range of periods" (including "straight-ahead jazz" and classical recordings), DVDs and videos at "decent prices"; it's "likely to have what you're looking for", and it's "staffed by people who actually know music."

Janet Russo S C
– | – | – | E

262 Mott St. (bet. Houston & Prince Sts.), 6 to Spring St.; N/R to Prince St., 212-625-3297; www.janetrusso.com

"100 percent girl" sums up this NoLita boutique whose dusty-rose walls and crystal chandeliers light up the Victorian-inspired dresses and separates in "beautiful fabrics" that "fit very well", although some say there "aren't too many different cuts" to choose from; still, such whimsical extras as vintage purses, Vietnamese good-luck dolls and cashmere tights make up for any lack on the racks.

Janet Sartin Institute S C
– | – | – | E

500 Park Ave. (bet. 58th & 59th Sts.), 4/5/6/N/R/W to 59th St./Lexington Ave., 212-751-5858; www.sartin.com

Any place that can call both Nancy Reagan and Jennifer Lopez clients must have a mind-bogglingly wide appeal, and apparently this half-century-old Park Avenue grooming grande dame does; its signature skincare products include superfatted soaps, sunblocks, lift lotions, moisturizers and astringents, and there's also a small selection of makeup; N.B. appointments can also be made for a variety of spa services, including facials and waxing.

Jane Wilson-Marquis
– | – | – | E

130 E. 82nd St. (bet. Lexington & Park Aves.), 4/5/6 to 86th St., 212-452-5335
155 Prince St. (bet. Thompson St. & W. B'way), C/E to Spring St., 212-477-4408 S
www.bridalgowns.net

"If you want something richly elegant", make an appointment at this English designer's SoHo and Upper East Side boutiques, "recommended for every bride-to-be" searching for the "dress of her dreams"; the "one-of-a-kind" silk "couture creations" are turned out in "exquisite designs", many in "Elizabethan and Renaissance-type" styles, and embellished with embroidery and appliquéd roses; "everyone from the salespeople to the seamstress is pleasant, helpful and supportive", and they'll even "tailor specifically to your requests."

Janovic Plaza S
21 | 15 | 18 | M

2475 Broadway (92nd St.), 1/2/3/9 to 96th St., 212-769-1440
136 Church St. (bet. Murray & Warren Sts.), A/C to Chambers St., 212-349-0001
80 Fourth Ave. (10th St.), 4/5/6/L/N/Q/R/W to 14th St./Union Sq., 212-477-6930
771 Ninth Ave. (bet. 51st & 52nd Sts.), C/E to 50th St., 212-245-3241
215 Seventh Ave. (bet. 22nd & 23rd Sts.), 1/9 to 23rd St., 212-645-5454
161 Sixth Ave. (Spring St.), C/E to Spring St., 212-627-1100

(continued)

(continued)
Janovic Plaza
1153 Third Ave. (87th St.), 4/5/6 to 86th St., 212-289-6300
1150 Third Ave. (67th St.), 6 to 68th St., 212-772-1400
292 Third Ave. (23rd St.), 6 to 23rd St., 212-777-3030
159 W. 72nd St. (bet. Columbus & B'way), 1/2/3/9 to 72nd St., 212-595-2500
800-772-4381; www.janovicplaza.net

◪ "Go nowhere else" fawn followers of these paint, wallpaper and window-treatment stores that provide the "best places for decorating ideas", offering "easy, do-it-yourself" solutions, a "good selection" and "great value"; service, however, "ranges from pleasant and helpful to downright rude", and some dis the product display's "disorganization."

Jay Kos ◉ — | — | — | VE
986 Lexington Ave. (bet. 71st & 72nd Sts.), 6 to 68th St., 212-327-2382

Step into this East 70s haven of colorful chaos to enter "the most original men's store in New York"; while there's a "fine" array of the house brand's unique twist on traditional suits and shirts, the place offers "much more than clothing" regulars rhapsodize – e.g. Borsalino hats, Liberty of London accessories and Brigg umbrellas; "great follow-through" from the "nice salespeople" ensures everything's jake.

Jazz Record Center — | — | — | M
236 W. 26th St., 8th fl. (bet. 7th & 8th Aves.), 1/9 to 28th St., 212-675-4480; www.jazzrecordcenter.com

Hidden in an eighth-floor Chelsea suite is a "jazz lover's paradise" thick with "unbelievable" vinyl, "unusual CDs", posters, books, magazines and such endangered species as musicians' one-sided, homemade acetate platters; the staff knows its stuff, riffing on inventory from compilations to Charlie Parker's *The Bird Blows the Blues*, the very first LP ever pressed.

J.CREW ◉⬛ 19 | 18 | 16 | M
91 Fifth Ave. (bet. 16th & 17th Sts.), 4/5/6/N/Q/R/W to 14th St./Union Sq., 212-255-4848
347 Madison Ave. (45th St.), 4/5/6/7/S to 42nd St./Grand Central, 212-949-0570
99 Prince St. (bet. Green & Mercer Sts.), N/R to Prince St., 212-966-2739
30 Rockefeller Plaza (bet. 5th & 6th Aves.), B/D/F/V to 47-50th Sts./Rockefeller Ctr., 212-765-4227
South Street Seaport, 203 Front St. (Fulton St.), 2/3/4/5/A/C/J/M/Z to Fulton St./B'way/Nassau, 212-385-3500
800-562-0258; www.jcrew.com

◪ "Conservatives" Crew-sing for the "perfect preppy fix" of "well-done", "white-bread" T-shirts, chinos, belts, sweaters, bathing suits and flip-flops gush "if I could die in a clothes store, it would be" in this "orderly, appealing" chain; "mellow colors" and "nice styles that stick around for more than one season" evoke "a drive through the country in a convertible with a dog in the backseat", a scenario that cosmopolitan style-mavens call a "snoozefest."

Jean Paul Gaultier ▽ 27 | 24 | 20 | VE
759 Madison Ave. (bet. 65th & 66th Sts.), 6 to 68th St., 212-249-0235; www.jeanpaul-gaultier.com

■ Fashion's original bad boy – he's the man who clad Madonna in her cone corset – favors the Starck (as in über-architect Philippe)

142 subscribe to zagat.com

approach in his Upper East Side shop (think crystal fixtures, quilted, flesh-toned taffeta walls and a movie-screen entrance flickering with exotic imagery 24/7; it all creates a sexy boudoir of "terrific" men's and women's clothing, accessories and JPG jeans, but some argue the selection doesn't represent "the best" of this "visionary."

Jeffrey ●S 24 | 23 | 20 | VE
449 W. 14th St. (bet. 9th & 10th Aves.), A/C/E/L to 14th St./8th Ave., 212-206-1272
☑ With its concrete floors and hip-hop music, this is clearly not your mother's department store, but an "ultra-mod" Meatpacking District pioneer that inspires raves for its "godlike" footwear (from Gucci to Prada, the "most comprehensive selection of high-fashion lines" in town) and "packed racks" of "unique", "slick" menswear; there's also a "carefully selected", "eclectic" array of women's designers ("not always wearable by actual humans") plus cosmetics and fine, contemporary jewelry for those "impulse purchases"; of course, "cool comes with a cost", but most pay up for the "best of the current season's best."

Jelena Behrend (fka Oxygène Collectif) - | - | - | M
188 Orchard St. (bet. Houston & Stanton Sts.), F to 2nd Ave., 212-995-8497
This pioneering Lower Eastsider dazzles its disciples (who range from retailers to rock stars) with "beautiful", intricate silver and gold bands, bracelets and pendants, which can be custom-engraved with messages; if it seems to have "little stock", be patient – the goods are being hand-hammered in the back room.

Jelly S C - | - | - | E
389 Atlantic Ave. (bet. Bond & Hoyt Sts.), Brooklyn, A to Hoyt St., 718-858-8214
White walls, a calm, gallery-like atmosphere and artfully placed bamboo-and-wood shelves filled with super-cool men's and women's shoes – little wonder Atlantic Avenue is hipper than ever; the sister to neighboring girl-shop Butter, this yummy newcomer features a sweet array of everything from embellished flip-flops, Birkenstocks and to-die-for numbers by Marc Jacobs, plus delicious cashmere scarves from Lutz & Patmos.

Jennifer Convertibles 15 | 13 | 13 | M
902 Broadway (20th St.), N/R to 23rd St., 212-677-6862;
www.jenniferfurniture.com
Additional locations throughout the NY area
☑ "Functional furnishings at a reasonable price" is what supporters say about this sofa-bed chain that offers an "above-average selection of fabric choices" for hideaway beds that come in handy for "unexpected and expected quests" alike; but the unconverted complain about the lack of design "style", less than sterling service and the strict return policy – it's verboten.

Jennifer Tyler S C - | - | - | E
986 Madison Ave. (bet. 76th & 77th Sts.), 6 to 77th St., 212-772-8350;
www.jennifer-tyler.com
If cashmere is your weakness, the hip takes on classic sweater sets in this East 70s boutique may be your downfall; persuasive staffers display a deft hand selecting luxe, brightly colored components for both male and female wardrobes, so come prepared to plunk down some bucks for the plush stuff.

| | | | M | P | S | C |

Jensen-Lewis S 21 | 19 | 19 | M
89 Seventh Ave. (15th St.), 1/2/3/9 to 14th St., 212-929-4880; www.jensen-lewis.com
■ Chelsea stalwart selling "funky", "very modern furniture and accessories" at "less-than-you-would-find-elsewhere" prices; design devotees dote on its American Leather Collection and "cool" tables and beds from Baronet and dub the "interesting", appropriately "apartment-sized" home furnishings here "New York living friendly."

Jewish Museum S C 22 | 21 | 19 | M
1109 Fifth Ave. (92nd St.), 6 to 96th St., 212-423-3211; www.jewishmuseum.org
■ The shops at this Upper East Side museum perform "a mitzvah in themselves", "offering very special" "tchotchkes" and "gorgeous Judaica", from "books, housewares, decorations", music and toys to "unusual jewelry" and "elegant, expensive religious items" just perfect for "bar mitzvah and wedding gifts."

Jill Stuart S C ▽ 22 | 21 | 13 | E
100 Greene St. (bet. Prince & Spring Sts.), C/E to Spring St.; N/R to Prince St., 212-343-2300
■ This young NYC native's "feminine" style grabbed the spotlight in *Clueless*, but her "sexy" dresses, denims and doodads actually have an in-the-know twist; the two-story SoHo store, her only retail outlet, has lots of "funky" merchandise – though not much in "real-people sizes" say regulars who avoid the "less-than-friendly" staff and tramp downstairs to the vintage collection below.

Jil Sander – | – | – | VE
11 E. 57th St. (bet. 5th & Madison Aves.), E/F to 5th Ave.; 6 to 51st St., 212-838-6100; www.jilsander.com
Step into the stripped-down elegance of this new East 57th Street flagship of the renowned German design house (now owned by Prada, its namesake founder having departed); the white-walled, limestone-floored space and gray-clad staff provide an appropriate backdrop to the coolly modern, understated his-and-hers clothing, arranged by color on floating racks.

Jimmy Choo C 27 | 25 | 19 | VE
645 Fifth Ave. (bet. 51st & 52nd Sts.), E/V 53rd St./Lexington Ave., 212-593-0800; www.jimmychoo.com
■ For "hot, hot, hot, high-heeled high-end" stilettos that impart "an instant *Sex and the City* look", slither over to this Fifth Avenue "nirvana"; the "drop-dead", "fabulous" "fairy-tale" "foot jewels" (created by Tamara Mellon and Sandra Choi) "aren't shoes, they're works of art" and so "coveted" that just "being seen in them is exhilarating"; while Choo-aholics claim these "must-haves" are "worth a pinch or two on the foot" and the wallet, even they admit that "dealing with the snooty service" can bring you down to earth.

Jimmy Jazz S C ▽ 19 | 17 | 12 | M
86 Delancey St. (Orchard St.), F to Delancey St., 212-505-8969 ●
132 W. 125th St. (Malcolm X Blvd.), 2/3 to 125th St., 212-665-4198
■ Phat Farm, Sean Jean, Ecko Unlimited and Roca Wear are some of the hot urban-designer labels attracting jazz hounds to this Uptown and Downtown duo that's especially "great for jeans and other casual clothes that cost more elsewhere"; admirers applaud

M | P | S | C

the extensive "range of sizes, in addition to a big-and-tall section" in most locations, along with a wall of name-brand athletic shoes; "that rap music has to go", though.

Jimmy's S C — | — | — | VE
1226 King's Hwy. (bet. 12th & 13th Sts.), Brooklyn, F/Q to Kings Hwy., 718-645-9685
Sure, it's out of the way, but this boutique off Coney Island Avenue ain't no sideshow to loyalists enticed by its "wide-ranging", well-edited inventory of "expensive, but pretty great" European designer clothes; expect a bit of naughty-haughty attitude from the staff – these folks are serious about high fashion, whether it's delivered in a cocktail dress, men's jacket or extravagant little bauble.

Jim Smiley S — | — | — | M
128 W. 23rd St., 2nd fl. (bet. 6th & 7th Aves.), 1/9/C/E to 23rd St., 212-741-1195
On the second floor of a Chelsea townhouse, a cozy living room–like setting surrounds an array of elegant women's (and some men's) vintage clothing – much of it bearing the original sales tags – mainly from the 1940s–1960s; mint-condition Norell and Balenciaga pieces fetch four figures, but most of the merch, from old-time emporiums like Gus Mayer and La Maison Blanche, costs under $200.

J.J. Hat Center C ▽ 24 | 19 | 25 | E
310 Fifth Ave. (bet. 31st & 32nd Sts.), B/D/F/N/Q/R/V/W to 34th St./ Herald Sq., 212-239-4368
■ "The real thing for classic men's" toppers with a few women's tossed in for good measure, this Garment Center favorite "keeps you well covered" (along with bigwigs like Rod Stewart) with everything from "gangster styles" to "sexy Latin panamas"; this "old-timey" standby has been peddling hats since 1911, so it's no wonder the "experienced staff knows and loves" their *chapeaux*.

J. Lindeberg Stockholm S C ▽ 22 | 23 | 18 | E
126 Spring St. (Greene St.), C/E to Spring St.; N/R to Prince St., 212-625-9403
■ "Adventurous fashion types" find a "fantastic, sexy European line" at this "very trendy" 1970s-style store in SoHo, "primarily stocked with men's clothes" by a Swedish designer; devotees dig the "fairly tight-fitting" duds that are "way too hip for work, but good for the weekend", especially if you "want to be a rock star, baby!"

J. Mavec & Company C — | — | — | VE
946 Madison Ave. (74th & 75th Sts.), 6 to 77th St., 212-517-7665; www.jmavec.com
Originally designed by Kitty Hawks in 1986, this small, serene Upper East Side boutique showcases a dainty collection of precious pieces; though some think it offers "the most beautiful antique jewelry to be found" (mostly 19th- and early 20th-century), it also carries vintage-inspired works by designers Otto Jakob, Gabriella Kiss and the eponymous Janet Mavec herself.

J. McLaughlin C 20 | 20 | 17 | E
1311 Madison Ave. (bet. 92nd & 93rd Sts.), 6 to 96th St., 212-369-4830
1343 Third Ave. (77th St.), 6 to 77th St., 212-879-9565 ◗ S
www.jmclaughlin.com
◪ No *"Preppy" Handbook* required when it comes to shopping at this warm, homey, "tasteful" Upper East Side standby; the button-

vote at zagat.com 145

down-and-khakis set asserts that it's "perfect for that business-casual" look and "good" "updated" "basics", plus they have "a ton of women's clothes too"; still, wallet-watchers wail that it's "wildly overpriced" "for the product offered.

J. Mendel C | ▽ 20 | 23 | 21 | VE |

723 Madison Ave. (bet. 63rd & 64th Sts.), 4/5/6/N/R/W to 59th St./Lexington Ave.; 6 to 68th St., 212-832-5830

■ "Ask your sugar daddy to buy you a present" at this "wonderful" East 60s fur salon with its champagne-colored walls and grand chandelier; despite its "many years" in business, its coats and accessories (luxe hats, gloves and even purses) are "always cutting-edge"; of course, "the prices are pure retail, but hey – it costs to look this stylish."

J.M. Weston C | – | – | – | VE |

812 Madison Ave. (68th St.), 6 to 68th St., 212-535-2100; www.jmweston.com

A pair of handcrafted shoes from this 110-year-old, French men's and women's footwear line may set you back a pretty euro, but those who splurge at this Madison Avenue shop find that with proper care and costly resoling by expert cobblers in Limoges, their investment may last a lifetime; the timeless styles range from traditional loafers and riding boots to wing tips, and there's even a new men's collection designed by Michel Perry, the acclaimed footwear designer.

Joan Michlin Gallery S C | 25 | 24 | 24 | E |

449 W. Broadway (bet. Houston & Prince Sts.), N/R to Prince St., 212-475-6603; 800-331-1335; www.joanmichlin.com

■ Joan Michlin "goes back to the earliest Lincoln Center crafts fairs", but she "remains one of the best contemporary" jewelers, creating wearable "works of art" that are "impeccably" designed; manned by a "hard-selling, but very pleasant staff", her Victorian-style SoHo store's "a great place for gifts and peace offerings."

Jobson's Luggage S C | 22 | 14 | 21 | M |

666 Lexington Ave. (bet. 55th & 56th Sts.), E/F/V to 51st St., 212-355-6846

■ "Anything you need to go anywhere" can be had at this East 50s luggage establishment boasting a "huge selection" of "high-quality", "mid-market" suitcases and garment bags; it's "so cramped you literally have to walk over the merchandise", but you'll be rewarded with "knowledgeable" "helpful" salespeople who go the extra mile.

Joël Name Optique de Paris C | – | – | – | VE |

65 W. Houston (Wooster St.), N/R to Prince St., 212-777-5888

Blonde and sleek, as in wood and lighting, this SoHo eyewear shop is home to a high-end selection of designer frames as well as super-glam ones from Judith Lieber ensconced with crystals and semiprecious stones; many styles are out of sight – such is the price of looking good.

Joe's CDs ◐ | ▽ 21 | 15 | 15 | I |

96 Christopher St. (Bleecker St.), 1/9 to Christopher St., 212-414-4099
11 St. Marks Pl. (bet. 2nd & 3rd Aves.), 6 to Astor Pl., 212-673-4606 S

■ "You'll definitely find something you want" at these Downtown "bargain hunter's dream CD" shops featuring "used and promo" items at a "great price"; you'll "feel like you got your workout for

| M | P | S | C |

the day" when you head "up the stairs to" the East Village location, but you'll be rewarded with a wider selection of DVDs than its West Village sibling carries.

Joe's Fabric Warehouse S ▽ 24 | 12 | 16 | I
102 Orchard St. (Delancey St.), F to Delancey St., 212-674-7089
■ A "terrific selection" of designer fabrics for upholstery and draperies, plus trimmings imported from France and Italy, all "at rock-bottom prices", abounds at this "super" store on the Lower East Side; "the help is really helpful" – and "if they don't have it, they'll get it" for you.

John Derian S C | - | - | - | E |
6 E. Second St. (Bowery), F/V to 2nd Ave., 212-677-3917; www.johnderian.com
Decoupage devotees descend on the East Village on-site studio and shop of this eponymous owner for his "fabulous" vases, plates and paperweights decorated with vintage prints of flora, fauna and old letters; also adding to the atmosphere is a cache of charming Indian linens and French quilts, antique Chinese mirrors and carefully chosen odds and ends with "a twist on traditional style."

John Fluevog ●S 23 | 21 | 19 | M
250 Mulberry St. (Prince St.), N/R to Prince St., 212-431-4484; 800-381-3338; www.fluevog.com
■ Whether you're "a teen who hangs out" Downtown, "young at heart" or "bold and brazen" like Fluev-fan Marilyn Manson, this Canadian mini-chain's NoLita offshoot is bound to help you "stand out from the crowd"; the "funkiest" "shoes with more personality than should be legal" are hawked by "tough, but amiable" sales folk, many sporting "different color hair every time" you pop by, in a cool setting that "makes you feel at home."

John Lobb C 27 | 25 | 26 | VE
680 Madison Ave. (bet. 61st & 62nd Sts.), 4/5/6/N/R/W to 59th St./ Lexington Ave., 212-888-9797; www.johnlobb.com
■ "If you have to ask how much, don't even come" to this Madison Avenue "pinnacle" of "hands-down", the "best men's footwear available"; this subsidiary of Hermès offers ready-to-wear styles alongside handmade English versions created "the way shoes are supposed to be made"; sure, they're "obscenely expensive", but they'll "make you look like a million bucks."

Johnston & Murphy S 22 | 19 | 20 | E
520 Madison Ave. (54th St.), E/V to 5th Ave./53rd St., 212-527-2342
345 Madison Ave. (44th St.), 4/5/6/7/S to 42nd St./Grand Central, 212-697-9375
888-324-6189; www.johnstonmurphy.com
◪ This grand East 40s and East 50s set of "standbys" offers a "solid, but unremarkable" range of "good basic material for your feet" that just may "satisfy the unadventurous"; the "durable", "well-made business and casual work shoes" are doled out with "service that ranges from professional to pretentious."

John Varvatos S 24 | 25 | 23 | VE
149 Mercer St. (bet. Houston & Prince Sts.), N/R to Prince St.; 800-689-0151; www.johnvarvatos.com
■ Rapidly rising toward the "top of the fashion food chain", this men's designer (whose resumé includes Ralph Lauren and Calvin

vote at zagat.com 147

| M | P | S | C |

Klein) offers "understated", "distinctly American" but decidedly stylish suitings, plus a "good selection of modern sportswear" and "must-have shoes" in his oak-and-blackened-steel "minimalist store" in SoHo; the "very friendly staff is willing to go the extra mile even if you're not P. Diddy."

Jo Malone ●◐S   26 | 26 | 25 | E
Flatiron Building, 949 Broadway (23rd St.), N/R to 23rd St., 212-673-2220; www.jomalone.com

■ "One whiff and you're hooked" at this Flatiron sophomore, a "minimalist" store with a "complex concept of layering fragrance" created by British scent-smith Jo Malone (but now under the Estée Lauder umbrella); "light", "natural" "fragrances are made from grocery-store items" like grapefruit and ginger and turned into "top-notch" products for the "body, face and home"; the "sleek" cream-and-black "packaging is also perfect for that special gift."

Jonathan Adler S C   25 | 25 | 18 | E
465 Broome St. (Greene St.), 6 to Spring St., 212-941-8950; 877-287-1910; www.jonathanadler.com

■ "Original" and "interesting", the handcrafted ceramics and textiles sold at this SoHo shop have established the eponymous owner/designer nationally (he also has stores in East Hampton and LA); while admirers "adore" his "simple" organic shapes and praise his Peruvian-inspired pillows as "cult items", wallet-watchers whine his star power inspires "astronomical prices"; N.B. a new Upper East Side offshoot is set to open this spring.

Joon C   26 | 20 | 24 | E
Grand Central, 107 E. 42nd St. (Park Ave.), 4/5/6/7/S to 42nd St./Grand Central, 212-949-1700 ●S
782 Lexington Ave. (61st St.), 4/5/6/N/R/W to 59th St./Lexington Ave., 212-935-1007
Trump Tower, 725 Fifth Ave. (57th St.), 4/5/6/N/R/W to 59th St./Lexington Ave., 212-980-3932
Winter Garden Atrium, 3 World Financial Ctr. (Vesey St.), 1/2/3/9/A/C/E to Chambers St., 212-227-0557 S
800-782-5666; www.joon.com

■ "If it writes and it's beautiful, you'll find it here" say supporters of this mini-chain purveying a "great selection" of "pens as art"; "excellent service" from a "knowledgeable staff" ("if they don't have it, they'll order it") and prices set at "every budget" also get high marks; pen-sive surveyors insist they're "easy to overlook, but worth the effort to find."

Joovay S C   – | – | – | E
436 W. Broadway (bet. Prince & Spring Sts.), C/E to Spring St., 212-431-6386

Shimmy into slinky slips, silk chemises, kimono-style robes, luxe pajamas and other "sexy" siren-wear (à la said customer Jennifer Lopez) at this "real lingerie store", a "tiny" top-drawer SoHo standby that offers European labels like Cosabella and La Perla; the "staff is wonderful" and "prices are good."

Jos A. Bank S   18 | 17 | 19 | M
366 Madison Ave. (46th St.), 4/5/6/7/S to 42nd St./Grand Central, 212-370-0600; www.josabank.com

■ Fondly known as the "poor man's Brooks Brothers", this Midtown outpost of a national chain specializes in "solid-quality, standard-

148 subscribe to zagat.com

M | P | S | C

issue business and business-casual" garb; but while "entry-level" executives applaud it as a "reliable source" and "good value", the more fashion-forward sniff the "selection's uninspiring" and chafe at extra costs ("you have to pay for cuffs" on pants).

Joseph S C   25 | 19 | 18 | E

106 Greene St. (bet. Prince & Spring Sts.), C/E to Spring St.; N/R to Prince St., 212-343-7071 ●
816 Madison Ave. (bet. 68th & 69th Sts.), 6 to 68th St., 212-570-0077

☑ "Six-foot-tall supermodels" pack into the American outposts of this British brand, but don't be put off – although "long legs are encouraged", "you can always find a great fit" in the "exciting clothing", particularly the "pretty" "pants that can't be beat"; while the "quality and fabrics are gorgeous", critics complain about "staff that doesn't offer much assistance"; N.B. the SoHo flagship carries womens- and menswear, but Madison Avenue is for ladies only.

Joseph Edwards S C   ▽ 24 | 20 | 24 | M

500 Fifth Ave. (42nd St.), 7 to 5th Ave.; 4/5/6/7/S to 42nd St./Grand Central, 212-730-0612

■ A Fifth Avenue fixture for over 20 years, this Midtowner offers an extensive selection of watches, ranging from Baume & Mercier and Breitling to Tag Heuer and Omega, all at very "fair prices"; but what really makes things tick is the "excellent customer service" and "superb repair" department.

Joseph Patelson Music House   27 | 16 | 21 | M

160 W. 56th St. (bet. 6th & 7th Aves.), N/R/Q to 57th St./7th Ave., 212-582-5840; www.patelson.com

■ "You might bump into the next Horowitz" roaming through the stacks in the "dusty, old-world insides" of the "last bastion of civilization" across the street from Carnegie Hall's stage door; "the only game in town for sheet music for serious musicians" of a classical bent, it's a "great source for obscure and one-of-a-kind" scores and librettos ferreted out by an "extremely knowledgeable staff" whose "specialty is special orders."

Joyce Leslie ● S   9 | 8 | 7 | I

20 University Pl. (8th St.), N/R to 8th St., 212-505-5419
2147 86th St. (Bay Pkwy.-21st St.), Brooklyn, M/W to Bay Pkwy., 718-266-0100
2109 Ralph Ave. (Ave. K), Brooklyn, 718-251-3219
Kings Plaza Mall (Flatbush Ave.), Brooklyn, 718-252-6488
37-28 Main St. (38th Ave.), Queens, 7 to Main St., 718-353-8419
56-48 Myrtle Ave. (Cornelia St.), Queens, L to Myrtle Ave., 718-381-3031
Staten Island Mall, Staten Island, 718-370-1705
www.joyceleslie.com

☑ "If you want a one-off trashy dress to wear to that party", you'll find "funky runway look-alikes" galore at this "hootchie-wear" chain in the Village and the boroughs; "great for high-schoolers", "club kids" and "drag queens", the "slightly slutty" merchandise "won't even take a nibble of your wallet", though deeper pockets say it's "good for cheap but too cheap to be good."

J. Press   23 | 22 | 23 | E

7 E. 44th St. (bet. 5th & Madison Aves.), 4/5/6/7/S to 42nd St./Grand Central, 212-687-7642; 800-765-7737; www.jpressonline.com

■ "A classic" praise preppies who proclaim that this Midtown "store is like an alumni visit to your college campus", where you can

vote at zagat.com   149

find "the finest Wasp wear", from "madras jackets" to the "best Ivy League scarves"; seemingly, "the styles never change", so "if you buy a new wardrobe here, people will think you've had it forever."

JR Cigar S C | 25 | 20 | 21 | M |
562 Fifth Ave. (46th St.), B/D/F/V to 47th-50th Sts./Rockefeller Ctr., 212-997-2227; www.jrcigar.com

■ "Every cigar imaginable" ("from low- to high-end") is stockpiled in the Midtown vault of this former bank-turned-"Disney World" for stogie smokers that scores for its "inexpensive knockoffs" and "weekly specials"; toss into the ring "knowledgeable service", and puff-essors of "unbeatable quality" ask "why go anywhere else?"

Judith Leiber C | 26 | 25 | 23 | VE |
987 Madison Ave. (bet. 76th & 77th Sts.), 6 to 77th St., 212-327-4003; www.judith-leiber.com

■ When the Upper East Side status-minded need to make a "sparkling entrance", they're usually clutching one of these evening purses of hand-glued Austrian crystal, exotic- or animal-shaped "little jewels" that have represented the "epitome of accessories" for 40 years; "whimsical", "beautiful", "gaudy", "these bags are everything except practical", but "if money isn't an issue", why not indulge "the movie star in you."

Judith Ripka C | 25 | 24 | 20 | VE |
673 Madison Ave. (61st St.), 4/5/6/N/R/W to 59th St./Lexington Ave., 212-355-8300

☑ Fair warning – "you can't own just one piece" of the "addictive", "ultra-feminine jewelry" sold in this tiny East 60s boutique; all agree the "unique" pieces, especially the signature loop-and-toggle bracelets, convey "such status", but while some claim they "treat you like a queen", others say the "salespeople don't seem to care."

Juilliard Bookstore, The ● C | ▽ 23 | 20 | 16 | E |
60 Lincoln Center Plaza (B'way at 65th St.), 1/9 to 66th St., 212-799-5000 ext. 237; www.bookstore.juilliard.edu

☑ At the northern end of Lincoln Center Plaza atop Alice Tully Hall is this little store "crowded" with an "excellent stock of classical music books", plus CDs and T-shirts", mugs and other items sporting Juilliard's logo; though prodigies pout that the institution "deserves a bigger and better shop", budding Bernsteins insist you can find "almost any score you need in a pinch" here.

Julian and Sara ● S C | ▽ 26 | 19 | 13 | VE |
103 Mercer St. (Spring St.), N/R to Prince St.; C/E to Spring St., 212-226-1989

☑ Small and sweet, this SoHo kids' boutique boasts a "wonderful selection" of "unique French clothing" that's to "be used daily, not just for special occasions"; but the jaded jab that it's just "another chance" for parents and grandparents "to spend too much on children's clothes" and maintain that the "staff can be rude."

Juno ● S C | 19 | 19 | 18 | E |
543 Broadway (bet. Prince & Spring Sts.), N/R to Prince St., 212-625-2560
426 Broadway (bet. Prince & Spring Sts.), C/E to Spring St., 212-219-8002
866-586-6746; www.junoshoes.com

☑ Fashionable men and women snap up "very funky", "exciting" "European shoes" at these SoHo sister shops, including "nice nightlife styles", while hipster kids jet over for "unique" kicks; but not everyone jumps for Juno – the less-impressed find the collection "too clunky" and "expensive for what it is"; P.S. wallet-watchers "wait for the sales" and scoop 'em up by the armload.

Just Bulbs S | 25 | 14 | 17 | M |
936 Broadway (bet. 21st & 22nd Sts.), N/R to 23rd St., 212-228-7820
◪ "The name says it all" – there's "every bulb under the sun" (possibly even "a few Edison models in the back") at this Flatiron favorite once affectionately lampooned by Letterman; the store's "cramped", but it's "the only place" for "odd-sized" incandescent items, European fixtures and "fun, funky" stuff like novelty string lights; still, critics counter it's just "pricey."

Just for Tykes SC | – | – | – | E |
83 Mercer St. (bet. Broome & Spring Sts.), N/R to Prince St., 212-274-9121; www.justfortykes.com
Spacious and stylish, befitting its smart setting, this SoHo shop spotlights a special selection of kids' apparel, toys and gear in colorful cubes and on accessible rolling racks; aesthetes adore the broad range of top-drawer clothing collections like Catimini, Deux Par Deux, Cherry Pie and Cakewalk, as well as the unique nursery furniture and high-end bedding, including quilts from Judi Boisson.

Just Shades C | ▽20 | 14 | 18 | M |
21 Spring St. (Elizabeth St.), 6 to Spring St., 212-966-2757
◪ This "reliable" NoLita store is "still the tops" to touters seeking toppers for their lamps; it supplies "plain, garden-variety" shades and will also custom-make versions for "hard-to-fit" fixtures or fashion them "from your own fabric"; however, a few doubters are left in the dark by a less than sparkling selection.

Jutta Neumann ●SC | – | – | – | E |
158 Allen St. (bet. Rivington & Stanton Sts.), F to 2nd Ave., 212-982-7048; www.juttaneumann-newyork.com
Craftsmanship is key to this "fantastic" Lower East Side leather guru who creates crunchy couture sandals ("the perfect summer flats" that "last forever") in a vast range of colors and styles to your every specification – think Birkenstock meets Balenciaga for hipsters of all stripes; this designer also stitches up "amazing leather cuffs and bracelets" and a colorful mix of "beautiful, modern bags, belts and wallets."

Kam Man ●S | 24 | 11 | 9 | I |
200 Canal St. (Mulberry St.), 6/J/M/N/Q/R/W/Z to Canal St., 212-571-0330
■ "It's an education just walking down the aisles" of this Chinatown supermarket" with its cans of quail eggs and barrels of dehydrated fish, but the store's basement also offers "cool stuff" like the "largest selection of everyday Asian dinnerware, tea sets", woks and rice cookers "this side of Beijing", all at "inexpensive" prices.

Karen's for People and Pets C | 21 | 20 | 16 | VE |
1195 Lexington Ave. (bet. 81st & 82nd Sts.), 6 to 77th St.; 4/5/6 to 86th St., 212-472-9440; www.karensforpets.com
◪ "There's no place like Karen's" claim two-legged loyalists of this longtime pet shop and salon in the East 80s, where there's a "great selection" of "high-quality" accessories that include alligator and faux-fur clothes and carriers; but detractors deem it too dog-centric and caution "be prepared to spend."

vote at zagat.com

			M P S C

Kar'ikter ●🆂🄲   – | – | – | M
19 Prince St. (bet. Elizabeth & Mott Sts.), N/R to Prince St.;
A/C/E to Spring St., 212-274-1966; 888-484-6846;
www.karikter.com
Sweetly schizophrenic NoLita store that aims at adults as well as *enfants*: the front of the shop sells grown-up amusements like fly swatters and gnome stools from Philippe Starck and "whimsical gadgets from Alessi", while the back features children's books, toys and merchandise inspired by the antics of fictional European characters like Babar, Tintin and Le Petit Prince.

Karkula (fka Breukelen) 🆂⇘🄲   ▽ 21 | 22 | 17 | E
68 Gansevoort St. (bet. Greenwich & Washington Sts.), A/C/E/L to
14th St./8th Ave., 212-645-2216
■ One look at the leather exterior of this home-furnishings shop in the Meatpacking District lets you know you're in for a "unique" experience; the "selection" of contemporary art, sculpture and porcelain lighting, along with felt seating and rugs from Paola Lenti, "feels very personal."

Kartell 🆂🄲   – | – | – | M
45 Greene St. (bet. Broome & Grand Sts.), C/E to Spring St.,
212-966-6665; 866-854-8823; www.kartell.com
Get "cutting-edge plastic furniture" at "surprisingly low prices" given this store's SoHo location and its mostly Italian pedigree; among the best-sellers here are Philippe Starck's Ero chair (they carry his new Ghost chair too), along with colorful storage from Piero Lissoni and shelving by Ron Arad; small-ticket items like desk accessories and bins also offer affordable splashes of color.

Katayone Adeli 🄲   23 | 21 | 17 | E
35 Bond St. (bet. Bowery & Lafayette St.), F/S/V to B'way/Lafayette;
6 to Bleecker St., 212-260-3500
🞅 You can never be too skinny – or have too many super-skinny slacks from this cool, contemporary designer, a fave of celebs and Downtown types, who go-go to NoHo to troll the "spartan, modern" shop for "sexy things to slip into" (including those "amazingly flattering pants"); but critics cavil at the "crazy prices."

KATE SPADE 🆂🄲   23 | 24 | 19 | E
454 Broome St. (Mercer St.), N/R to Prince St., 212-274-1991;
www.katespade.com
🞅 "Nothing says classic American girl" (right "down to the first edition Salingers enshrined in cubbies") like this designer's "minimum-presentation-maximum-goods" SoHo "accessory museum"; "sweetly sophisticated" "Nantuckety" "classic bags with a kick" and "fabulous jewelry", shoes, paper, PJs and scents appeal to the "modern" woman "who still has time to handwrite a thank-you note" and keeps "spare change in the hundreds"; but patrons put off by the "aloof" service and "pricey stuff" pout "puh-lease, isn't everyone over the phenomenon by now?"

Kate Spade Travel 🆂🄲   23 | 22 | 18 | E
59 Thompson St. (bet. Broome & Spring Sts.), C/E to Spring St.,
212-965-8654; www.katespade.com
🞅 "If you have to travel, why not do it in style" say Spade-philes who saunter over to this SoHo satellite store for satchels, duffels, wheeled suitcases and garment bags kitted out in "trendy" prints,

| M | P | S | C |

solids and stripes; while aesthetes agree that the pieces are "so refined and expensive you'd be afraid to check them", cynics snap back they're "flimsy and faddish."

KATE'S PAPERIE   27 | 26 | 19 | E
561 Broadway (bet. Prince & Spring Sts.), N/R to Prince St., 212-941-9816 S
1282 Third Ave. (bet. 73rd & 74th Sts.), 6 to 77th St., 212-396-3670 S
8 W. 13th St. (bet. 5th & 6th Aves.), F/V to 14th St., 212-633-0570
888-941-9169; www.katespaperie.com

■ "E-mail? what e-mail" ask "serious scribes" of this "fabulous" trio of stationers that the pulp faction calls a "spiritual awakening"; these "magnificent emporiums" abound with "stylish", "unique" goods for the "paper fetishist", as well as "beautiful journals", the "latest and greatest in invitations" and "cool stamps" – plus a gift-wrapping service; ranters ream "ridiculous" prices, but addicts aver "I'd like to send them a thank-you note"; N.B. a West 57th Street branch was scheduled at press time.

Kavanagh's   – | – | – | E
146 E. 49th St. (bet. Lexington & 3rd Aves.), 6 to 51st St., 212-702-0152
"Blass, Beene, de la Renta – the clothes are all top-of-the-line" at what mavens call the "Mercedes of Manhattan resale shops" in the East 40s, whose antique-furnished space is also littered with "previously owned Manolos" on the floor and "carefully selected" Chanel and Hermès purses on the walls; "it's all fairly pricey, especially for consignment", but few match ex Bergdorf Goodman personal shopper "Mary Kavanagh's service" and contacts ("she really does know every uptown girl in New York").

KB Toys   16 | 9 | 9 | I
2411 Broadway (89th St.), 1/9 to 86th St., 212-595-4389
Manhattan Mall, 901 Sixth Ave. (bet. 32nd & 33rd Sts.), B/D/F/N/Q/R/V/W to 34th St./Herald Sq., 212-629-5386 ● S
1411 St. Nicholas Ave. (bet. 180th & 181st Sts.), 1/9 to 181st St., 212-928-4816
www.kbtoys.com

■ The "basic" toy "selection is limited but the prices are great" at this national chain where you'll find "bargains all around" (they "tend to reduce the prices on slow-moving merchandise pretty quickly"); it helps to "go in here knowing what you want, since service is limited to ringing up purchases" lob the less game, who also find it "very cramped" and "messy."

KD Dance & Sport ● S C   – | – | – | M
339 Lafayette St. (Bleecker St.), 6 to Bleecker St., 212-533-1037; www.kddance.com
Designed by two former dancers, "the clothes here can make anyone feel like" a corps member declare devotees who dash over to this "great" NoHo shop for wrap tops, jazz pants and fitted shorts in a variety of knit yarns and textures; the om-crowd oohs and ahs over the yoga collection of capris, camis, midriff tees and bodysuits in colors so calm they may send you into a Zen state.

Keiko S C   – | – | – | E
62 Greene St. (bet. Broome & Spring Sts.), 6 to Spring St., 212-226-6051; 888-534-5669; www.keikonewyork.com
Whether you want to make waves in a "custom-designed" or an "off-the-rack" directionally styled tankini, bikini or maillot done

vote at zagat.com

up in vibrant solids, stripes or Op-Art patterns, chances are this Japanese designer carries "your perfect", oh-so-flattering suit at her SoHo boutique; men also get in the swim with trunks and so-brief bottoms in eye-popping shades, but looking like a bathing beauty "doesn't come cheap", so "be prepared" to shell out.

Kelly Christy S C — | — | — | E
235 Elizabeth St. (bet. Houston & Prince Sts.), N/R to Prince St.; 6 to Spring St., 212-965-0686
When milliner Kelly Christy makes magic behind the white curtain in her tiny NoLita atelier, the results include everything from updated cloches and elegant-shaped fedoras to fancier feathered numbers or a custom-creation for a wedding day.

Ken Hansen Photographic ▽ 28 | 23 | 27 | E
509 Madison Ave., 18th fl. (53rd St.), E/V to 53rd St./Lexington Ave., 212-317-0923
■ The shopping is "good for high-line equipment" high up on the 18th floor of a Madison Avenue building where this family of "professional photographers" "pre-selects the cream of the crop" to fill the fine-looking cabinets of their "established, enviable" store; "while the stock is not as extensive as the discounters'" and prices are not as low, the place sets the "gold standard" for new and vintage Hasselblads, Contax and other "top-notch" stuff.

Kenjo C ▽ 22 | 19 | 20 | E
40 W. 57th St. (bet. 5th & 6th Aves.), N/R/Q/W to 57th St., 212-333-7220
■ Though not well known by our voters, this West 57th store offers a "wonderful selection of watches" for fans of handmade mechanical chronographs or perpetual calendars, including "fine collectors' brands" such as Daniel Roth and Gerald Genta; "decent prices" and "personal service" keep the cognoscenti content.

Kenneth Cole ● S 21 | 20 | 18 | E
597 Broadway (Prince St.), N/R to Prince St., 212-965-0283
353 Columbus Ave. (bet. 76th & 77th Sts.), B/C to 81st., 212-873-2061
Grand Central, 107 E. 42nd St., 4/5/6/7/S to Grand Central, 212-949-8079
95 Fifth Ave. (17th St.), 4/5/6/L/N/Q/R/W to 14th St./Union Sq., 212-675-2550
Rockefeller Ctr., 610 Fifth Ave. (49th St.), B/D/F/V to 47th-50th Sts./Rockefeller Ctr., 212-373-5800
800-536-2653; www.kennethcole.com
■ Best known for "trend-of-the-moment" footwear that "fits like a glove" ("no cruel shoes here"), this chain is also "a good stop" for "comfortable", "corporate casual" clothes ("black is always the default color of choice"); "granted, they won't win points for originality" – except for their "activist" ads – but "the ordinary chap [or chick] can find something" here; P.S. the "styles are a steal when on sale."

Kentshire Galleries 25 | 26 | 23 | VE
Bergdorf Goodman, 754 Fifth Ave. (bet. 57th & 58th St.), N/R/W to 5th Ave. & 59th St., 212-872-8653; 800-558-1855 S
37 E. 12th St. (bet. B'way & University Pl.), 4/5/6/L/N/Q/R/W to 14th St./Union Sq., 212-673-6644 ⇌ C
www.kentshire.com
■ It's "fun to just wander in and add to the wish list" at this British antiques-and-decorative-arts specialist; the Village flagship offers a range of furniture, silver and porcelain – primarily Georgian and

| M | P | S | C |

Regency – arranged in period room settings; the Bergdorf Goodman outpost focuses on smaller "wonderful finds", such as tabletop knickknacks and Victorian, Edwardian and art deco jewelry.

Kenzo S C   24 | 26 | 23 | VE
80 Wooster St. (bet. Broome & Spring Sts.), N/R to Prince St., 212-966-4142; www.kenzo.com

■ "Viva Kenzo!" cry longtime followers of the Japanese designer, whose heart belongs to Paris and whose fan base is international; this SoHo boutique reflects his "eclectic" sensibility in "men's and women's everything", including exuberant scarves and ties that are "a little way out, but nice" too; salespeople are eager to help, so ask for a spritz of the famed perfume if they seem "ready to pounce."

Kerquelen S C   22 | 24 | 18 | E
430 W. Broadway (bet. Prince & Spring Sts.), 6/C/E to Spring St., 212-965-8910; www.kerquelen.com

◪ For "interesting" men's and women's footwear from Spain that strikes "a nice balance between trendy and conservatively with-it", supporters skip over to this modern SoHo shop; but a few fret that the "wacky" shoes just don't "look right on your feet."

Kidding Around S C   ▽ 23 | 19 | 24 | M
60 W. 15th St. (bet. 5th & 6th Aves.), 1/2/3/F/L/V to 14th St., 212-645-6337

■ No kidding around, this newly expanded child-"friendly" Flatiron fun house is stocked with "imaginative toys for infants and up" "not found in department stores"; it's a "great place for gifts", and if you don't know what to buy, "the staff will work with you."

Kids R Us   17 | 13 | 13 | I
8973 Bay Pkwy. (Shore Pkwy.), Brooklyn, 718-373-0880
4818 Northern Blvd. (48th St.), Queens, 7 to 46th St., 718-626-5437 ◐ S
2795 Richmond Ave. (Platinum Ave.), Staten Island, 718-983-7100 ◐ S
www.kidsrus.com

◪ "For that inexpensive gift or play clothes" at "good value" prices, head to one of these borough offshoots of a national chain; while mavens say it's "great for that trendy stuff" and newborn staples, particularly the "preemie-size section", a few feel that "as the sizes go up the quality goes down."

Kid's Supply Co. S C   – | – | – | E
1343 Madison Ave. (94th St.), 6 to 96th St., 212-426-1200; www.kidssupplyco.com

"If you've got the bucks", this Madison Avenue destination is "the place" to go for kids' bedding, lamps and furniture, which ranges from modular desks to pine bunk beds; these investment pieces (for ages two and up) are made to last a childhood, and almost all of the merchandise can be custom-designed – including linens.

KIEHL'S S   27 | 21 | 24 | M
109 Third Ave. (13th St.), L to 3rd Ave.; 4/5/6/L/N/Q/R/W to 14th St./ Union Sq., 212-677-3171; 800-543-4571; www.kiehls.com

■ "Absolutely the best beauty products" make this "authentic" 1851 East Village "institution" the "ultimate" favorite of surveyors for skin, hair and body booty in "no-frills packaging", including the "world-famous" Lip Balm #1 and the Blue Astringent Herbal Lotion that's "guaranteed to make your zits vanish"; there's a generous "try-before-you-buy" policy, so an "incredibly knowledgeable staff" is "happy to hand out" "plentiful free samples."

vote at zagat.com

M | P | S | C

Kimara Ahnert ⑤ⓒ — | — | — | E
1113 Madison Ave. (83rd St.), 4/5/6 to 86th St., 212-452-4252; 800-452-9802; www.kimara.com
Posh salon on the Upper East Side specializing in custom-designed makeup and skincare that's been something of a secret address for models, socialites and Hollywood types like Catherine Zeta-Jones, who had them do her wedding-day makeup; still, it strikes some mere mortals as "snobby" and "high priced"; N.B. appointments can also be made for a variety of spa services, including facials, waxing and massage.

Kimera ⑤ⓒ — | — | — | M
366 Atlantic Ave. (bet. Bond & Hoyt Sts.), Brooklyn, A/C to Hoyt St., 718-422-1147
274 Fifth Ave. (bet. 1st & Garfield Sts.), Brooklyn, N/R to Union St., 718-965-1313
www.kimeradesign.com
Back when Park Slope's Fifth Avenue was on the cusp, pioneering Yvonne Chu established a shoebox stuffed with her own Asian-inspired line of raw-silk separates and dresses, accessories from Brooklyn designers and vintage finds; now with an additional larger, two-room shop, she's created a brave new Caribbean-colored world on burgeoning Atlantic Avenue, bringing all of the above, plus furniture, pillows and throws from the Far East, to cutting-edge customers.

Kim's Mediapolis/Mondo/Underground ●⑤ⓒ 25 | 15 | 14 | M
85 Ave. A (bet. 5th & 6th Sts.), L to 1st Ave.; F/V to 2nd Ave., 212-529-3410
144 Bleecker St. (bet. La Guardia Pl. & Thompson Sts.), A/C/E/F/V/S to W. 4th St., 212-260-1010
2906 Broadway (bet. 113th & 114th Sts.), 1/9 to 110th St., 212-864-5321
6 St. Marks Pl. (3rd Ave.), 6 to Astor Pl.; N/R to 8th St., 212-505-0311
www.kimsvideo.com
◼ On Avenue A, in the Village and up in Morningside Heights are the "coolest" "CD and DVD meccas", where audiovisual "junkies" "fulfill their cravings" for "anything out of the ordinary in movies and music", scoring "gems in the used section"; as for the "punker-than-thou" staff, who "will sneer at you no matter what you ask for", they should know that their "rude" schtick "has become a cliché by now."

Kirna Zabête ⑤ⓒ 25 | 24 | 20 | VE
96 Greene St. (bet. Prince & Spring Sts.), N/R to Prince St., 212-941-9656; www.kirnazabete.com
◼ A candy-colored supermarket of SoHo style, this "brilliant" showcase for "the next big thing in fashion" is a "Downtown shopping must" proclaim cultists who praise the "devastatingly cool" offerings from "known-and-unknown" designers, as well as the "fun, bright, eclectic" baby and "dog stuff"; walk downstairs to "buy gifts for girlfriends" (e.g. candles, Anya Hindmarch change purses), or check your e-mail at the in-house Macs.

Kiwi Design ⑤ⓒ — | — | — | E
179 Berkeley Pl. (7th Ave.), Brooklyn, 2/3 to Grand Army Plaza; Q to 7th Ave., 718-622-5551
Cozy as a country cottage, with a juicy green exterior and butter-yellow walls within, this Park Slope newcomer, owned by Marlene

| M | P | S | C |

Siegel, a seasoned retailer, and Christine Alcalay, an emerging designer, is chockablock with wonderful womenswear; but while luscious-colored tees, hoodies and ultra-femme blouses from fab lines tempt, it's Kiwi's own 'couture' ready-to-wear – kicky A-line wool skirts, a Dior-esque coat – that jumpstarts constant cravings.

Kleinfeld & Son ⬤🆂🅲   24 | 16 | 17 | E

8202 Fifth Ave. (82nd St.), Brooklyn, R to 86th St., 718-765-8500; www.kleinfeldbridal.com

☑ "If you can envision" your designer gown, "they've got it" at this "crazy busy" Bay Ridge "bridal haven" where "helpful" consultants who know their merchandise "backwards and forwards" "bring the dresses in to you"; "go after you've gotten an education", "otherwise you'll be dazed and confused" by the "outstanding selection"; it's "not the fairy-tale mecca" expected pout the put-off, who proclaim the "pushy staff" may make you "run back to boutique-land"; N.B. by appointment only.

KMART   12 | 8 | 6 | I

770 Broadway (10th St.), 6 to Astor Pl.; N/R to 8th St., 212-673-1540
250 W. 34th St. (bet. 7th & 8th Aves.), A/C/E/1/2/3 to 34th St./ Penn Station, 212-760-1188 ⬤🆂
8973 Bay Pkwy. (Shore Pkwy.), Brooklyn, R to 86th St., 718-372-0022
1998 Bruckner Blvd. (bet. Pugsley Ave. & White Plains Rd.), Bronx, 6 to Parkchester/E. 177th St., then 36 bus to White Plains Rd., 718-430-9439
300 Baychester Ave. (bet. Bartow Ave. & Hutchinson River Pkwy.), Bronx, 6 to Pelham Bay Park, then 12 bus to Bay Plaza, 718-671-4758
66-26 Metropolitan Ave. (bet. Audley St. & Grosvenor Rd.), Queens, M to Metropolitan Ave., 718-821-2412
6111 188th St. (Horace Harding Expwy.), Queens, J to Jamaica Ave., then 30 bus to 188th St., 718-264-2320
2660 Hylan Blvd. (Lindbergh Ave.), Staten Island, 718-351-8500
800-635-6278; www.kmart.com

☑ For "those on a budget", this "tacky-but-tolerable" "discount chain" provides a "giant" place to "spend a little, get a lot" of household staples and toiletries, "no-frills basics" apparel, "dirt-cheap" orchids and "DVD bargains"; for fans, the "nice range of appliances" and hardware and the Martha Stewart Collections can "actually make it a worthwhile shopping stop"; still, "service is lacking", as evidenced by often "poorly stocked" shelves, "messy" aisles and "unbearable" crowds at checkout.

Knits Incredible 🅲   – | – | – | VE

971 Lexington Ave., 2nd fl. (bet. 70th & 71st Sts.), 6 to 68th St., 212-717-0477; 800-371-0477

Co-owned by yarn wholesaler Stacy Charles, this Upper East Side shop is primarily stocked with the proprietor's line – "the best of the best from a real knitter" – offering a "good selection of high-end" skeins, plus "great buttons" and "creative designs"; while some admirers applaud the staff that's "always there to help", a few get unraveled by the "attitude with a capital A."

Knitting Hands 🆂🅲   – | – | – | M

398 Atlantic Ave. (bet. Bond & Hoyt Sts.), Brooklyn, 2/3/4/5 to Nevins St., 718-858-5648; www.knittinghands.com

Offering the "best classes in town, hands down", this "new kid in town is trying, successfully, to win friends" in its sprawling space

vote at zagat.com

on edgy Atlantic Avenue; you'll find all the yarns you need, from Red Heart to cashmere, plus a cache of books unlike anywhere else.

Knitting 321 C — | — | — | E
321 E. 75th St. (bet. 1st & 2nd Aves.), 6 to 77th St., 212-772-2020
Stocked with a "beautiful selection of yarns", including natural fibers, plus European and fashion-forward skeins, books and supplies and decorated with a maple table made for gathering, this "friendly" Upper East Side newcomer feels like a "secret discovery"; the "helpful owners" offer "hand-holding through early projects", making it especially worth a stop "for novice knitters."

Knoll — | — | — | VE
105 Wooster St. (bet. Prince & Spring Sts.), N/R to Prince St., 212-343-4000; www.knoll.com
This SoHo showroom shows off some of the groundbreaking furniture designs it originally commissioned – Tulip chairs by Eero Saarinen, Cyclone tables from Isamu Noguchi and wire seating by artist Harry Bertoia – that have now become mid-century classics, along with new contemporary pieces for the home and office.

Koos & Co. — | — | — | VE
1283 Madison Ave. (bet. 91st & 92nd Sts.), 6 to 96th St., 212-722-9855
As close to a couture atelier as you'll get on the Upper East Side, this unstuffy second-floor shop warmly welcomes both browsers and buyers to view veteran Dutch designer Koos van den Akker's one-of-a-kind, richly embellished, collaged wool and fur coats, jackets and dresses, a look beloved by devotees of (but costing much more than) his Koos Of Course! collection seen on QVC.

Kors Michael Kors S C 24 | 23 | 22 | E
159 Mercer St. (bet. Houston & Prince Sts.), F/S/V to B'way/ Lafayette, 212-966-5880
■ "Girlie girls need not apply (or shop)" at this SoHo boutique with its red lacquered interior that heats up the heart (and wallet) with cool clothes and cabana classics; among the "well-made" wares, the best-selling item is a traditional turtleneck, but those with more dash than cash content themselves with a belt, scarf or bottle of perfume.

Kraft — | — | — | E
315 E. 62nd St. (bet. 1st & 2nd Aves.), 4/5/6/N/R/W to 59th St./ Lexington Ave., 212-838-2214
Since it opened in 1935, this purveyor of high-end plumbing fixtures, cabinet hardware and bathroom accessories in the East 60s has won a host of acolytes who "worship" the "exceptional custom" work that's delivered "on time"; the "great selection" ("if you can't find it, you aren't looking") and "informative staff" also elicit praise.

Kreiss Collection ▽ 23 | 22 | 20 | VE
215 E. 58th St. (bet. 2nd & 3rd Aves.), 4/5/6/N/R/W to 59th St./ Lexington Ave., 212-593-2005; 800-573-4771; www.kreisscollection.com
■ This very beige showroom near Bloomies features "ultra-posh" upholstered furniture collections that range from European-elegant to California-casual, as well as luxe Italian bed linens; their "big" sectional sofas rival only the size of the "pocketbook" needed to buy them, but for smaller-scaled chairs, chaises and tables, there's the slimmer Sierra Towers Condo line.

| M | P | S | C |

Kremer Pigments — | — | — | M
228 Elizabeth St. (bet. Houston & Prince Sts.), N/R to Prince St., 212-219-2394; 800-995-5501; www.kremer-pigmente.com
Kremer is a scientist, but he isn't mad; while powders of every hue make the "small" NoLita shop look "like a candy store for artists", the only U.S. outlet for the German doc's "excellent" pigments is a sober place where "educated sales help" "gives personal attention to each" painter, restorer, instrument or furniture maker in search of color concentrates, binders, brushes and other raw materials.

Krizia C — | — | — | VE
769 Madison Ave. (bet. 65th & 66th Sts.), 6 to 68th St., 212-879-1211; www.krizia.net
Think high-fashion Fellini, and you'll know what to expect at this East 60s boutique, home of high-end men's and women's collections designed by Mariuccia Mandelli – synonymous since 1957 with timeless classics with a twist; her embraceable style is reflected in the amiable salespeople, who make it a "pleasure to shop here."

Krups Kitchens & Bath C 24 | 11 | 16 | M
11 W. 18th St. (bet. 5th & 6th Aves.), 1/9 to 18th St., 212-243-5787
■ This "small", family-owned Flatiron shop is "stuffed to the ceiling" with such "top appliances" as Wolf and La Cornue stoves, along with bathroom fixtures from Kohler and Toto; "prices are very good for Manhattan", and they also offer a free design service.

La Belle Epoque S ▽ 23 | 19 | 18 | E
280 Columbus Ave. (73rd St.), 1/2/3/9 to 72nd St., 212-362-1770; www.vintageposters.us
■ If you've been seduced by the Paris flea market look, you can replicate it by decorating your walls with "vintage" posters from this Upper West Side store purveying an "enormous selection" of "pricey but amazing" European advertising prints devoted to products ranging from champagne to chocolate.

La Boutique Resale S 21 | 15 | 13 | M
1045 Madison Ave., 2nd fl. (bet. 79th & 80th Sts.), 6 to 77th St., 212-517-8099; www.laboutiqueresale.com
■ Like many of its ilk, this second-floor shop offers an array of recent-season clothes "for the classy woman", with labels like Alaïa and Plein Sud co-mingling with Chanel and St. John; however, it's "their collection of vintage wear" that makes them stand out among the "Madison Avenue resale crowd", though even fans find the staff *un peu* "pushy"; N.B. Downtowners can check out Consignment City, its new, funkier sister on St. Marks Place.

La Brea ●S C 19 | 15 | 12 | M
2440 Broadway (90th St.), 1/9 to 86th St., 212-724-2777
Beacon Hotel, 2130 Broadway (bet. 74th & 75th St.), 1/2/3/9 to 72nd St., 212-873-7850
1575 Second Ave. (bet 81st & 82nd Sts.), 6 to 77th St., 212-772-2640
1321 Second Ave. (bet. 69th & 70th Sts.), 6 to 68th St., 212-879-4065
www.labrea.com
■ "Last-minute" gift shoppers appreciate this mini-chain of "neat novelty shops" known for "unusual cards", "fun T-shirts" and "gag items that are perfect for the person you sort of know"; though some sniff it's full of "middle-of-the-road tchotchkes", more insist "you

vote at zagat.com

can't find the same stuff anywhere else"; P.S. the fact that they're "open late is a plus."

La Cafetière ◐ S C — | — | — | M
160 Ninth Ave. (bet. 19th & 20th Sts.), A/C/E/L to 14th St./8th Ave., 646-486-0667
The cheery "everyday French household" wares like table linens, pitchers and bowls stocked at this Chelsea store recall sun-drenched days in Southern France, which is where most of its home accessories are imported from; sheets and quilts are gorgeous and demand a pretty price to match.

Lacoste S C 22 | 21 | 20 | E
543 Madison Ave. (bet. 54th & 55th Sts.), E/V to 5th Ave./53rd St., 212-750-8115; 800-452-2678; www.lacoste.com
■ "Making a comeback – or has it always been in vogue?" ask "retro-preps" shopping this East 50s boutique, who know the "classic" ("hasn't changed in years") polo shirt with "that little green gator" (actually, a crocodile) remains the "real" Wasp uniform; pick up a few in "all those beautiful colors", and try on some shoes too, before hitting the country club with Bootsie.

LaCrasia 22 | 18 | 21 | M
304 Fifth Ave. (31st St.), 6 to 28th St./33rd St., 212-695-0347; www.wegloveyou.com
■ "Gold can be found" among the dross at this handy "no frills" shop near the Empire State Building that "makes gloves more interesting"; boosters give the "beautiful, original accessories" a thumbs-up, applauding the "amazing collection" that ranges "from fancy to funky" and from cotton to calfskin, "providing perfect accents to any ensemble"; N.B. there's an unrelated LaCrasia in Grand Central Terminal that sells similar merchandise.

LaDuca Shoes C — | — | — | E
534 Ninth Ave. (bet. 39th & 40th Sts.), A/C/E to 42nd St./Port Authority, 212-268-6751; www.laducashoes.com
A dancer who's worked with everyone from Twyla Tharp to Ann Reinking, choreographer/footwear guru Phil LaDuca offers a showstopping selection of round-toed, flexible character, jazz and tap numbers and custom-made designs in his tiny, tin-ceilinged shop in the shadow of Port Authority; while the colorful T-, X- and Y-strap shoes, can-can boots and platform sandals attract fashion groundbreakers like Björk, it's Broadway and Hollywood hoofers like *Hairspray* phenom Marissa Jaret Winokur and *Chicago* stars Catherine Zeta-Jones and Renée Zellweger who really like to strut their stuff in these stageworthy creations.

Lady Foot Locker S C 19 | 16 | 13 | M
1504 Second Ave. (bet. 78th & 79th Sts.), 6 to 77th St., 212-396-4567
120 W. 34th St. (B'way), B/D/F/N/R/Q/V/W to 34th St./Herald Sq., 212-629-4626 ●
5314 Fifth Ave. (bet. 53rd & 54th Sts.), Brooklyn, R to 53rd St., 718-439-4669
King's Plaza, 5364 King's Plaza Blvd., Brooklyn, 718-253-9631
Queens Fashion Ctr., 90-15 Queens Blvd., Queens, 718-760-3271
800-991-6815; www.ladyfootlocker.com
◪ "Know your stuff before you set foot in" this chain and you just may find a winning combination of "fitness and casual" "shoes to walk, run, hop, skip and jump in", plus a "modest selection" of athletic apparel from national brands like Reebok and Nike; but

naysayers nix this "nothing special" outfit, deeming the "variety and sizes too limited" and the "frazzled" staff "poorly informed."

Lafco ⑤ ⓒ — | — | — | E

200 Hudson St. (bet. Canal & Vestry Sts.), 1/9 to Canal St., 212-925-0001; 800-362-3677; www.lafcony.com

Spare, serene TriBeCa lifestyle store with a split personality: scattered among the soaps and skincare lines from Florence's Santa Maria Novella (one of the oldest pharmacies in the world), the Greek-made Korres and the Japanese-inspired Kimono Collection are exquisite accessories from Arte Cuoio and leather beds, chairs and ottomans by Triangolo coupled with steel-and-wood furniture.

Laina Jane ⑤ ⓒ 25 | 21 | 23 | E

416 Amsterdam Ave. (bet. 79th & 80th Sts.), 1/9 to 79th St., 212-875-9168

35 Christopher St. (Waverly Pl.), 1/9 to Christopher St., 212-727-7032

45 Christopher St. (bet. Waverly Pl. & 7th Ave.), 1/9 to Christopher St., 212-807-8077

■ When your significant other prefers you in states of undress, head to these "lovely little" lingerie shops in the Village and the Upper West Side to uncover the "cutest bras, thongs, hot pants and sleepwear", "including the latest in Cosabella" and "very pretty" unmentionables from labels like Eberjey and Only Hearts; N.B. a branch opened at 45 Christopher Street post-*Survey*, and the original at 35 Christopher Street is slated to close in June.

Lalaounis ⓒ ▽ 28 | 26 | 20 | VE

739 Madison Ave. (bet. 64th & 65th Sts.), 6 to 68th St., 212-439-9400

■ "You'll feel like a goddess [wearing] a piece" of "unique Greek- and Roman-style jewelry" from this Upper East Side boutique, whose light-wood setting showcases its "extensive collections" of highly stylized, hand-hammered 18 and 22 karat gold pieces; admirers attest this is craftsmanship "to rival the Ancients" – even if prices rival airfare to the Mediterranean.

LALIQUE ⓒ 28 | 27 | 21 | VE

712 Madison Ave. (63rd St.), 6 to 68th St., 212-355-6550; www.lalique.com

■ If you're going for "gorgeous", you'll clearly find it at this sliver of Parisian posh transplanted to Madison Avenue, where the famed French crystal maker displays designs that range from perfume bottles and paperweights to "beautiful" museum-quality bowls, vases, sconces and screens, many with the company's signature satin finish; if you're looking for something less fragile, they also offer jewelry and leather goods like belts and briefcases.

Lana Marks — | — | — | VE

645 Madison Ave. (60th St.), N/R to 5th Ave., 212-355-6135; www.lanamarks.com

Luxury knows no bounds at this Madison Avenue boutique where 150 ladylike styles of Italian-made alligator, crocodile, ostrich and lizard handbags are offered in 100 vibrant shades; prices are also "out of this world", but this Palm Beach–based designer keeps good company – popular namesakes include the Farrah Fawcett tote and the Princess Diana handbag, and she also counts Oprah Winfrey and Reese Witherspoon among her celeb clients.

| M | P | S | C |

Language 🆂🅲   26 | 23 | 19 | VE
238 Mulberry St. (bet. Prince & Spring Sts.), N/R to Prince St.; 6 to Spring St., 212-431-5566; 888-474-5566; www.language-nyc.com
◼ "Beautifully combining art, fashion and beauty" in one space, this "NoLita original" speaks volumes with its "so-cool" designer threads ("all the Chloé you want"), plus jewelry, housewares and "the latest copy of *Visionaire*; "hot" goods translate into "flaming prices" ("ouch"), so "shop with your sugar daddy."

LA PERLA 🆂🅲   27 | 24 | 20 | VE
93 Greene St. (bet. Prince & Spring Sts.), C/E to Spring St., 212-219-0999
777 Madison Ave. (bet. 66th & 67th Sts.), 6 to 68th St., 212-570-0050
866-527-3752; www.laperla.com
◼ Even "if you don't look like Marilyn Monroe, you certainly will feel like her" after the "unpretentious staff" "gets through with you" at this Madison Avenue outpost and its new, spacious, sleek SoHo sibling; "how can you not feel extraordinary and sexy" when you "splurge" on "the best in luxury lingerie" (as well as "beautiful bathing suits and clothing")?; "oh, that I could afford to wear" these "exquisite" "delicates" "every day" wail the wistful, to which pragmatists retort "get your boyfriend to buy it."

La Petite Coquette 🆂🅲   27 | – | 20 | VE
51 University Pl. (bet. 9th & 10th Sts.), 6 to Astor Pl., 212-473-2478; 800-240-0308; www.thelittleflirt.com
◼ "You could spend hours pawing the lacy next-to-nothings" from "crème de la crème" labels like Aubade and Le Mystere and "still not be bored" at Rebecca Apsan's "très feminine" "lingerie classic" on University Place; "this is where stars" like Sarah Jessica Parker shop for "really nice scanties" – indeed "you'll find" everything from "reasonably priced thongs to $400 merry widows" to swimwear that's certain "to make someone's heart beat faster"; P.S. it's no longer a "shoebox" thanks to a post-*Survey* expansion.

La Petite Etoile 🆂🅲   – | – | – | VE
746 Madison Ave. (bet. 64th & 65th Sts.), 6 to 68th St., 212-744-0975; www.lapetiteetoile.com
After dropping major bucks at Chanel, pop across Madison Avenue to this high-end infant- and childrenswear shop to scoop up layette items and togs from European and American lines like Petit Bateau, Floriane, I Pinco Pallino and Sonia Rykiel for that little star in your life; P.S. the friendly sales staff helps with sizing questions.

La Petite Princesse 🆂🅲   – | – | – | M
203 Lafayette St. (bet. Broome & Spring Sts.), 6 to Spring St., 212-965-0535; www.sohoprincess.com
At this SoHo insider's secret, French clothing and jewelry designer Carole Lebris sells celebrities like Penelope Cruz a wide selection of one-of-a-kind costume pieces studded with semi-precious stones, Italian glass or colorful enamels – plus some apparel – at prices that let even the parsimonious feel like princesses.

Laundry by Shelli Segal 🆂🅲   23 | 21 | 19 | E
97 Wooster St. (bet. Prince & Spring Sts.), C/E to Spring St.; N/R to Prince St., 212-334-9433
◼ Sure, "the label is available at department stores", but this streamlined SoHo shop often carries creations you won't "see

elsewhere"; meant for the "young or young at heart", the laundry list of temptations includes "romantic, cutting-edge" dresses and "well put-together" separates that go from "basics that fit normal women" to "very foo-foo" to "NYC nightlife" looks "you won't regret in the morning."

Laura Ashley S | 18 | 20 | 17 | E |
398 Columbus Ave. (79th St.), B/C to 81st St., 212-496-5110; 800-463-8075; www.laura-ashley.com

A "comfy" "English-country" interior blooms with everything for "conservative prim girls", including signature mother-daughter dresses and "homey" furnishings ("they coordinate everything", from lamps to bed linens); but while this veteran Upper West Side emporium "stands the test of time" for those who love all things "frilly" and "feminine", it wins no fans among folk who feel "floral is out."

Laura Biagiotti C | – | – | – | VE |
4 W. 57th St. (5th Ave.), 4/5/6/F/N/R/W to 59th St./Lexington Ave., 212-399-2533; www.laurabiagiotti.it

At the crossroads of the 57th-Street-and-Fifth-Avenue shopping hub, this woodsy Italian boutique fulfills the expectations of its chic clientele – it's "great for cashmere" separates, flowing silk dresses, scarves and leather goods, all priced to empty even the plumpest wallets.

Layla S C | – | – | – | E |
86 Hoyt St. (bet. Atlantic & State Sts.), Brooklyn, A/C/G to Hoyt-Schermerhorn Sts., 718-222-1933

Light and lovely, with flowing curtains in the windows, pristine white walls and a stark black floor, this Hoyt Street shrine to the home boasts shelves jammed with quilted silk coverlets, pillows and soft embroidered throws in brilliant colors, most imported from Turkey, India and Morocco; for those who prefer to wear their ethnic exotica, there's a selection of embellished shirts and vibrant skirts.

Laytner's Linens & Home ●S | 20 | 14 | 14 | M |
2270 Broadway (82nd St.), 1/9 to 79th St., 212-724-0180
237 E. 86th St. (bet. 2nd & 3rd Aves.), 4/5/6 to 86th St., 212-996-4439
800-690-7200; www.laytners.com

Fans of these Uptown home-furnishings emporiums pronounce them a "reliable" "place to find baskets, shower curtains", "300-thread-count sheets" and Mission- and Shaker-style furniture at "moderate" prices; but critics carp about the "limited selection" of "pretty basic merchandise" that can be a "little dated."

LEATHER MAN, THE ●S C | 28 | 20 | 23 | E |
111 Christoper St. (bet. Bleecker & Hudson Sts.), 1/9 to Christopher St., 212-243-5339; www.theleatherman.com

■ "Breathe in" swoon skin enthusiasts dizzy over the aromatic, "excellent assortment" of "custom and off-the-rack" "fine leather goods" at this Christopher Street boutique; there are "no lingerie, boas and the like" here – just loads of high-end hides tailored on-site, plus a "vast selection of toys and implements" to feed your "fetish"; "the shaved-head staff" might look "scary", but "they're so friendly and knowledgeable, you'll find yourself recommending the place", that is if you're not "bound and gagged."

vote at zagat.com

| M | P | S | C |

Le Chien Pet Salon 🛇🅒 ▽ 18 | 23 | 12 | VE
Trump Plaza, 1044 Third Ave. (bet. 61st & 62nd Sts.), 4/5/6/N/R/W to 59th St./Lexington Ave., 212-861-8100; 800-532-4436; www.lechiennyc.com

◪ Located in the Trump Plaza in the East 60s, this pet salon and boutique will "make even the most affluent person wish they were a dog for a day"; the selection, from rhinestone collars to poochy perfume, is supplied by "the finest designers" on the furry fashion scene; however, it's "way overpriced" to some, and others growl about the staff's "snobbery."

Le Corset by Selima 🛇🅒 ▽ 25 | 20 | 24 | E
80 Thompson St. (bet. Broome & Spring Sts.), C/E to Spring St., 212-334-4936

◼ If Selima Salaun's "tiny little" charmer in SoHo "isn't your favorite lingerie store, it should be" insist insiders who fall for her own "hip and slinky" wares, as well as a "wonderful mix" of "contemporary designer items" from ooh-la-la labels like Aubade, Fifi Chanchil and Chloé; retro-babes also cinch up "unique vintage" corsets, baby dolls and gowns; N.B. Salaun also owns Bond 07 by Selima and Selima Optique.

Le Décor Français 🅒 – | – | – | VE
1006 Lexington Ave. (bet. 72nd & 73rd Sts.), 6 to 68th St., 212-734-0032; www.ledecorfrancais.com

Though known for its colorful fabrics, ranging from silks and taffetas to cottons and horsehair, this "very small, elegant" Upper East Side shop also sells some select home furnishings; pillows, exotic candles, vintage table lamps and retro-inspired upholstered furniture help transform city pads into pieds-à-terre.

Lee's Art Shop Inc. 🛇🅒 23 | – | 17 | E
220 W. 57th St. (bet. B'way & 7th Ave.), N/Q/R/W to 57th St.; 1/9/A/B/C/D to 59th St./Columbus Circle, 212-247-0110; www.leesartshop.com

◪ "Tony Bennett" and other West 50s "art-supply junkies" "can kill an hour or more browsing" through this "recently expanded", "almost gallery-like store"; "though they stock professional supplies, they're also for the hobbyist", as "they carry beautiful journals, stationery, photo albums", "frames of all sizes" and some genuine "oddball things."

Lee's Studio 🛇🅒 23 | 15 | 16 | E
1755 Broadway (56th St.), 1/9/A/B/C/D to 59th St., 212-371-1122

◼ "Tightly packed" Midtown store "crowded" with furniture, but mostly "imaginative lamps and fixtures"; since the "varied and robust" lighting collection ranges from "funky" to contemporary to Mission- and Tiffany-styles, there's "something for every home"; still, shoppers are split on the staff, with some giving glowing reports about "knowledgeable" service, but others taking a dimmer view; N.B. as we go to press, plans are afoot for a move into the same space as its sibling, Lee's Art Shop.

Le Fanion 🅒 – | – | – | E
299 W. Fourth St. (Bank St.), 1/9 to Christopher St., 212-463-8760; www.lefanion.com

Sweet little slip of a West Village tabletop shop showcasing "beautiful" pottery and earthenware ranging from café au lait cups to pitchers glazed in the warm colors of the south of France; adding

M | P | S | C

to the atmosphere are antique armoires and fanciful contemporary chandeliers cascading with colored crystal fruit.

Legs Beautiful Hosiery   20 | 16 | 16 | M
Citigroup Ctr., 153 E. 53rd St. (bet. Lexington & 3rd Aves.), E/F/V to 53rd St./Lexington Ave., 212-688-9599
MetLife Bldg., 200 Park Ave. (bet. 42nd & 45th Sts.), 4/5/6/7/S to 42nd St./Grand Central, 212-949-2270 ●
1025 Third Ave. (bet. 60th & 61st Sts.), 4/5/6/F/N/R/W to 5th Ave./59th St., 212-750-3730 ● S
2 World Financial Ctr. (Vesey St.), E to World Trade Center, 212-945-2858

▫ "The place to buy everything you need for your legs (and then some)", these gam-havens about town stock a "nice selection of designer hosiery" and are "great for socks and undies too"; while it's "not exciting" and can feel "overcrowded" and "cramped", most admit they're darn "convenient."

Leonard Poll   – | – | – | E
1264 Third Ave. (bet. 72nd & 73rd Sts.), 6 to 68th St., 212-535-1222
40 W. 55th St. (bet. 5th & 6th Aves.), F to 57th St., 212-246-4452 C

With over 4,000 "really unique and unusual eyeglass frames" to choose from, patrons can't help but put Poll on a pedestal, anointing this Eastside-Westside duo as a "godsend"; the "fabulous service" is a "throwback to old-fashioned artisanal opticians", with licensed professionals "grinding lenses on-premises"; sure, the "prices are high", but it's "many cuts above the chains" – indeed, "you get what you pay for."

Léron   – | – | – | VE
750 Madison Ave. (65th St.), 6 to 68th St., 212-753-6700; www.leron.com

Since 1910, this tony, family-owned shop housed in a pink East 60s townhouse has been selling "delectable" bed-, bath- and table linens and lingerie; there's a choice of over 5,000 designs, and they can custom-make anything, like putting your favorite pooch's picture on pillows or sheets; just be aware that such "amazing personalization" comes at a "heart-pounding price."

Les Copains C   22 | 22 | 20 | VE
807 Madison Ave. (bet. 67th & 68th Sts.), 6 to 68th St., 212-327-3014

■ Though the parent company's in Italy, a "very French" sensibility permeates this "elegant" East 60s women's store, whose signature sweater sets and "pretty" dresses are "a little on the grown-up side", with prices to match; the staff "couldn't be nicer", and there's now a small but significant collection of men's sportswear too.

Les Migrateurs S C   – | – | – | E
188 Duane St. (bet. Greenwich & Hudson Sts.), 1/2/3/9 to Chambers St., 212-966-8208; www.lesmigrateurs.com

Gallic owner Henri Personnaz designs most of the colorful furniture and accessories sold at his TriBeCa store, like leather-topped game tables and stunning colored-glass consoles, which are all made back home; curvaceous vases from fellow Frenchman Christian Tortu can be found downstairs, along with Personnaz's ingenious table lights.

vote at zagat.com

| M | P | S | C |

LeSportsac 🅂🅲   19 | 18 | 19 | M

1065 Madison Ave. (81st St.), 6 to 77th St., 212-988-6200
176 Spring St. (bet. Thompson St. & W. B'way), C/E to Spring St., 212-625-2626
www.lesportsac.com

■ If "lightweight is the criteria", then these signature ripstop parachute-nylon goods all done up in "cool designs" (some from Diane von Furstenburg) with fun patterns updated every four-to-six weeks are "the best travel bags around"; the modern Upper East Side and SoHo chain branches are lined with "inexpensive, sporty little fashion statements" "you gotta have", from totes to wallets, as well as pricier newbies trimmed with shearling mink.

Lester's 🅂🅲   22 | 17 | 21 | E

1522 Second Ave. (80th St.), 6 to 77th St., 212-734-9292
2411 Coney Island Ave. (Ave. U), Brooklyn, Q to Ave. U, 718-645-4501

■ "Sure to please the most picky child", this Gravesend stalwart and Upper East Side sibling carry a "cutting-edge" "selection of what's trendy this week for kids", including "some European labels" and layette items, dressing everyone from babies to teens; "the shoe department is always busy" (and stocks labels like Aster and Shoe Be Do), but the "friendly" "staff handles the chaos well"; while a few fume it's "crowded" with "pushy moms", supporters retort "why go elsewhere?"

Lexington Gardens 🅲   ▽ 26 | 25 | 19 | E

1011 Lexington Ave. (bet. 72nd & 73rd Sts.), 6 to 68th St., 212-861-4390

■ "Beautiful items" line the windows at this cozy Lexington Avenue "shop for decorative accessories for the garden" that caters to the "green thumb and clotheshorse" alike with a surprising selection of "midpriced items" (from trowels to trousers) and "custom-made dried arrangements."

Lightforms 🅂🅲   ▽ 21 | 18 | 12 | M

509 Amsterdam Ave. (bet. 84th & 85th Sts.), 1/9 to 86th St., 212-875-0407
168 Eighth Ave. (bet. 18th & 19th Sts.), A/C/E/L to 14th St./8th Ave., 212-255-4664

■ "From traditional to contemporary to funky", these Chelsea and Upper West Side lighting stores "carry it all", including period reproductions and hard-to-find "shades for sconce lamps", plus bulbs and household accessories; the "good selection and prices" please partisans, but a few detect an "attitude" from the staff.

Lighting by Gregory 🅂🅲   24 | 16 | 14 | M

158 Bowery (bet. Broome & Delancey Sts.), J/M/Z to Bowery; 6 to Spring St., 212-226-1276; 888-811-3267; www.lightingbygregory.com

◪ Gregorians chant that this "mack-daddy of generic lighting" boasts "the best selection in the city", with over 150 different product lines at "prices that can't be beat"; however, the service at this "vast" Lower East Side "destination" fluctuates from "knowledgeable" and "helpful" to "impatient" and "ungracious" (though the staff will "recommend great electricians").

Lighting Center, The 🅲   ▽ 22 | 17 | 15 | E

240 E. 59th St. (2nd Ave.), 4/5/6/N/R/W to 59th St./Lexington Ave., 212-888-8383; www.lightingcenter-ny.com

◪ On the fringe of the design district in the East 50s, this lighting store specializes in "nicely presented" modern fixtures from Lutron

166   subscribe to zagat.com

| M | P | S | C |

Ligne Roset S
| 24 | 25 | 20 | VE |

250 Park Ave. S. (20th St.), 6 to 23rd St., 212-375-1036
1090 Third Ave. (64th St.), 6 to 68th St., 212-794-2903
115 Wooster St. (bet. Houston & Prince Sts.), N/R to Prince St., 212-253-5629
www.ligne-roset-usa.com

■ "Ooh, who wouldn't want to live in these spaces?" ask acolytes about these French furniture showrooms filled with the company's "modern", "sleek" sofas, chaises and tables – the epitome of "form and function"; you'll need "a fat wallet", but the lauded delivery service and "approachable staff" may ease the separation anxiety.

Liliblue S C
| – | – | – | M |

955 Madison Ave. (75th St.), 6 to 77th St., 212-249-5356

An Upper East Side newcomer, the store offers a "fun", selective collection of French accessories ranging from "very cute" bags and hats to scarves and "fabulous-looking" costume jewelry – including some "real showstopper pieces" at such "reasonable prices" you won't mind if they last only a season; "gracious service" leaves a lingering afterglow.

Lilliput S C
| – | – | – | E |

265 Lafayette St. (bet. Prince & Spring Sts.), 6 to Spring St., 212-965-9567
240 Lafayette St. (bet. Prince & Spring Sts.), 6 to Spring St., 212-965-9201
www.lilliputsoho.com

Set just a block apart, these SoHo havens for fashion-forward Lilliputians stock an exciting mix of very dressy outfits, fantasy dress-up options and punchy play clothes from the likes of Diesel and Lili Gaufrette, plus fun, funky footwear, from rubber boots to ruby slippers; the smaller original shop at 265 Lafayette focuses on newborn through 8 years while its larger sibling dresses hipster babies through hipster tweens and teens (up to size 18), with a limited but interesting toy selection in both.

Lincoln Stationers ● S C
| 25 | 19 | 17 | E |

1889 Broadway (63rd St.), 1/9 to 66th St., 212-459-3500; 800-298-9367; www.lincolnstationers.com

■ "One of the only stationery stores left on the Upper West Side", this "well-stocked" shop elicits bravos from boosters of its "personalized" writing paper and other "great stuff" like "floral-patterned file folders" that "make you want to open a home office"; it's "a bit cluttered", and service can be "negligent, if pleasant", but the "fabulous selection" of "fine merchandise" pleases loyalists.

Linda Dresner C
| ▽ 21 | 20 | 24 | VE |

484 Park Ave. (bet. 58th & 59th Sts.), 4/5/6/N/R/W to 59th St./ Lexington Ave., 212-308-3177

◪ You may have to "work up the courage" to enter this spacious, marble-floored Park Avenue women's boutique, whose spare, "understated" looks seem "a bit sterile" to some; but once inside, the reward is an "unusual selection" of "upscale" European and Japanese notables – including a large Jil Sander collection – chosen by the eponymous owner, a much-respected style maven; the highly rated, "helpful" staff reflects the "taste and quality" of the boss' picks.

vote at zagat.com

Lingerie on Lex S C ▽ 21 | 15 | 19 | E
831 Lexington Ave. (bet. 63rd & 64th Sts.), 6 to 68th St., 212-755-3312
■ An "excellent stop for the bridal bound" as well as seekers of sensuous scanties, this "lovely" "little gem near Bloomies" has a great selection of color-coordinated, "top-of-the-line lingerie" including "all the best" labels, from "Gosamer and Cosabella to Hanky Panky", plus pantyhose from Italy, France and Germany; the staff is not only "very helpful and knowledgeable", they're also "husband-friendly."

Links of London 24 | 23 | 20 | E
535 Madison Ave. (bet. 54th & 55th Sts.), 6 to 51st St., 212-588-1177; 800-210-0079
Metropolitan Life Bldg., 200 Park Ave. (44th St.), 4/5/6/7/S to 42nd St./Grand Central, 212-867-0258
www.linksoflondon.com
■ With their woody, eggshell-colored interiors, this "visually pleasing" Midtown duo is a "wonderful place to pick up silver gifts with pizzazz" (check out the cuff links in particular); fans are unfazed by the platinum prices for the sterling items, but "personnel who are a bit snobby" tarnish the experience a tad.

Lion & the Lamb C 18 | 18 | 13 | E
1460 Lexington Ave. (bet. 94th & 95th Sts.), 6 to 96th St., 212-876-4303
■ The "needlework selection shines" at this "little shop in an unlikely neighborhood" on the Upper East Side, which also carries embroidery, beads and a recently expanded yarn selection – "everything you need for a knitting project"; while acolytes adore the "excellent service and classes", others opine the owner should tame his woolly ways – "smoking in the store? not cool!"

Lisa Shaub S C – | – | – | E
232 Mulberry St. (bet. Prince & Spring Sts.), N/R to Prince St., 212-965-9176; www.lisashaub.com
"So chic, but not pretentious" sums up this natty NoLita hat haven where owner "Lisa is often" on hand "giving the place a mom-and-pop-shop feel"; whether made from soft felt, wool or polar fleece, this designer's "unique styles" offset "high-fashion ensembles" and are "lovely for every season", plus she will "custom-make anything to fit your color, material or size preference."

LITTLE ERIC S C 28 | 22 | 18 | VE
1118 Madison Ave. (bet. 83rd & 84th Sts.), 4/5/6 to 86th St., 212-717-1513
1331 Third Ave. (bet. 76th & 77th Sts.), 6 to 77th St., 212-288-8987
226 Atlantic Ave. (bet. Boerum Pl. & Court St.), Brooklyn, 2/3/4/5 to Borough Hall, 718-254-0106
■ Decorated with paintings and pictures of children, these "fabulous", brightly colored Upper East Side footwear siblings carry an "excellent assortment" of "fantastic" "upscale kids'" loafers, Mary Janes, boots and Superga sneakers, "all made in Italy"; "they stand by their product", including their own "adorable" collection; while most items are "both stylish and age-appropriate", some of the offerings may be more for "special occasions" "unless your little one is a lady who lunches"; N.B. the Brooklyn branch opened post-*Survey*.

| M | P | S | C |

Little Folk Art 🆂🅲
| – | – | – | E |

159 Duane St. (bet. Hudson St. & W. B'way), 1/2/3/9 to Chambers St., 212-267-1500

Treasure trove in TriBeCa for hand-painted nursery and kid-room furniture, plus decorative items with a distressed country look and beautiful bedding from companies like Nilaya; shower-bound shoppers seeking the ultimate gift and parents of means also swoon over the very special layette pieces, those all-important first books for a baby's library and other charming cherishables.

Livi's Lingerie 🆂
| ∇ 21 | 8 | 25 | M |

1456 Third Ave. (bet. 82nd & 83rd Sts.), 6 to 86th St., 212-879-2050

■ A "good old-fashioned bra store" offering "old-world service", this "New York treasure" on the Upper East Side carries an "interesting assortment" of "unique items", including bridal bustiers and lingerie; the "genuinely helpful" "mavens" "fit you personally" "to a tee" – indeed, they "know what they're doing", and what's more, they're "honest with you."

Liz Claiborne 🆂
| 19 | 18 | 17 | M |

650 Fifth Ave. (52nd St.), E/F to 5th Ave./53rd St., 212-956-6505; www.lizclaiborne.com

▪ "Whether dressing up or taking it easy", "refined", mature gals find "classic clothes made nicely" at this East 50s "top-of-the-line boutique"; the layout is "easy to shop", the staff is "attentive" and the styles are cut "to fit a woman's body", making it "dependable" for shopping in the "real world", even if "the department stores have better selections and sales prices on Liz."

Liz Lange Maternity 🆂🅲
| 26 | 25 | 23 | E |

958 Madison Ave. (bet. 75th & 76th Sts.), 6 to 77th St., 212-879-2191; 888-616-5777; www.lizlange.com

■ "Fashionable" females "who want to maintain" "their sleek New York look even though they're pregnant" head to this Upper East Side designer boutique for "chic" mix-and-match looks a "world away from blah maternity wear"; the "stretch jeans rock" and the "elegant trousers show how beautiful pregnant women can be", plus for active moms-to-be, there's even a new Liz Lange for Nike line of athletic wear; it's "costly, but worth it" – especially "if the grandparents are paying."

Liz O'Brien 🅲
| – | – | – | VE |

800A Fifth Ave. (61st St.), N/R/W to 5th Ave./59th St., 212-755-3800

Aficionados of this Upper East Side shop trust the eponymous owner's "wonderful eye" for "fabulous" American and French furniture from the 1930s, '40s and '50s, so they "shop here often" to get first dibs on coveted, costly pieces by such masters as Billy Haines, James Mont, Jean Royère and Maison Jensen.

L'Occitane ●🆂🅲
| 25 | 24 | 21 | E |

247 Bleecker St. (bet. Carmine & Leroy Sts.), A/C/E/F/V/S to W. 4th St., 212-367-8428
2303 Broadway (bet. 83rd & 84th Sts.), 1/9 to 86th St., 212-496-1967
198 Columbus Ave. (69th St.), B/C to 72nd St., 212-362-5146
42nd St. & Lexington Passage, 4/5/6/7/S to Grand Central, 212-557-6754
1288 Madison Ave. (bet. 91st & 92nd), 6 to 96th St., 212-987-8987
1046 Madison Ave. (bet. 79th & 80th Sts.), 6 to 77th St., 212-639-9185

(continued)

vote at zagat.com

M | P | S | C

(continued)
L'Occitane
510 Madison Ave. (53rd St.), E/V/6 to Lexington Ave./51st St., 212-826-5020
146 Spring St. (bet. W. B'way & Wooster St.), C/E to Spring St., 212-343-0109
1188 Third Ave. (69th St.), 6 to 68th St., 212-585-1955
101 University Pl. (12th St.), 4/5/6/L/N/Q/R/W to Union Sq., 212-673-8630
www.loccitane.com
■ Francophiles seeking a "little bit of Provence in New York" head for these "sweet retreats" where they are "transported by the scents of lavender and verbena wafting around them"; the chain's "pricey" but "wonderful skin products" include "luxurious" soaps, fragrances, cosmetics and lotions, like the popular Shea Butter Hand Cream, as well as what some consider "the best men's grooming toiletries", all "beautifully packaged" for you or a friend.

LOEHMANN'S ●S C   19 | 10 | 8 | M
101 Seventh Ave. (bet. 16th & 17th Sts.), 1/9 to 18th St., 212-352-0856; 800-241-5689
5740 Broadway (236th St.), Bronx, 1/9 to 238th St., 718-543-6420
2807 21st St. (Emmons Ave.), Brooklyn, Q to Sheepshead Bay, 718-368-1256
www.loehmanns.com
◪ "Look like a countess but spend like a clerk", "just as your mom and grandma" did, at the city's "original" discounter in Chelsea and the boroughs, where "women of all walks" "dig through the racks" in the Back Room for "steals and deals" on "up-to-the-minute" "catwalk" garb, "from Prada to Nicole Miller"; the loyalty program is nice", but "oy", "it can be stressful" "climbing over" the "unorganized" merchandise while clerks "yell at you to hang clothes back up" and the oldsters tut it "ain't what it used to be."

London Jewelers S C   – | – | – | VE
37-15 Junction Blvd. (bet. Roosevelt & 37th Aves.), Queens, 7 to Junction Blvd., 718-639-7636
Cuban-link chains and gold medallions are just some of the "gorgeous but extremely expensive jewelry" on offer at this Corona specialist (no relation to the East Hampton outfit of the same name); the ample glass-case displays of diamonds and gemstones make browsing easy, but dress "well-to-do" if you want them to "pay attention to you."

Longchamp   24 | 20 | 18 | E
713 Madison Ave. (bet. 63rd & 64th Sts.), 6 to 68th St., 212-223-1500;
www.longchamp.com
■ These "super-lightweight" nylon French bags, available in "every color of the rainbow", are "perfect for traveling, lugging gym clothes and books" or just "schlepping around"; Long-lovers also champion this Madison Avenue shop's "wonderfully styled and well-made" luggage, leather goods and backpacks, all well priced for what they are.

Loom ●S C   – | – | – | M
115 Seventh Ave. (bet. Carroll & President Sts.), Brooklyn, Q to 7th Ave.; F to 7th Ave., 718-789-0061
From its stroller-friendly aisles to its custom-made wooden display cases brimming with tempting tchotchkes and indulgences, everything about this new gift-giver's nirvana in Park Slope

| M | P | S | C |

beckons browsers; special is the byword, as evidenced by French notebooks, Italian stationery, Jutta Neumann leather handbags, wool purses by local designer Sofie Becket and Kiln enamel jewelry; covetable items for the home also abound, including hand-thrown pottery and funky glass vases.

LORD & TAYLOR S
| 21 | 17 | 17 | M |

424 Fifth Ave. (bet. 38th & 39th Sts.), 4/5/6/7/S to 42nd St./Grand Central, 212-391-3344; www.lordandtaylor.com

◪ "Orderly, organized and quiet", this "good, classic department store" remains an "old-time favorite" for many a Murray Hiller, who applauds the "consistent quality" and "reasonable prices" of its "fancy and practical" "real woman's clothes", menswear, a "wide selection of kid stuff" and accessories ("get your Easter bonnet here"); however, while it's "trying to escape the grandma stigma with new designers", modernists still find it "kind of frumpy", with "crammed aisles" and "uneven service"; still, "since it's not a tourist attraction" (except for the "terrific Christmas windows"), there are "no long register lines" – and oh, those "bargains on coupon days!"

LORO PIANA C
| 28 | 25 | 23 | VE |

821 Madison Ave. (bet. 68th & 69th Sts.), 6 to 68th St., 212-980-7961

■ Enter "cashmere heaven" at this Upper East Side retailer, home of a 19th-century Italian purveyor of "conservative, high-quality knitwear" for men, women and children; go ahead, "spoil yourself" with the "touch and feel" of "awesome" wool scarves, robes or throws; the staff makes the "extra effort to find articles", as "not everything is on display."

Louis Féraud
| – | – | – | VE |

3 W. 56th St. (5th Ave.), 4/5/6/F/N/R/W to 59th St./Lexington Ave., 212-956-7010

Just off Fifth Avenue in the West 50s, this tony, flatteringly lit boutique keeps its sophisticated clientele of ladies who lunch supplied with just the right amount of rich colors, ooh-able fabrics and softly tailored classics; polished and pretty salespeople are willing and able to assist.

Louis Vuitton
| 27 | 25 | 20 | VE |

703 Fifth Ave. (55th St.), E/V to Fifth Ave./53rd St., 212-758-8877 ⦿ S
116 Greene St. (bet. Prince & Spring Sts.), 6 to Spring St.; N/R to Prince St., 212-274-9090
www.vuitton.com

◪ The "snob factor", "little thank-you notes for shopping", the logo bags that "last forever" and the "ultimate luggage indulgence" ("where else can a girl purchase a steamer trunk?") – ah, the list of why folks "love Louis" goes on and on, which is about how long you'll wait for this luxury firm's most-desirables, and sometimes service too at the Fifth Avenue flagship; still, the Marc Jacobs-designed mens- and womenswear is "top quality and beautiful to boot" (especially the boots), so shop the SoHo location ("less inundated with tourists") or wait for a 57th Street mega-store to open (scheduled for summer 2003).

Love Saves the Day ⦿ S
| 20 | 19 | 14 | M |

119 Second Ave. (7th St.), 6 to Astor Pl., 212-228-3802

■ "Kitsch rules" at this "East Village vintage shop", "full of novelty items galore" – "that old, now-defunct board game you loved as

vote at zagat.com

a child, collectible action figures, unopened packages of baseball cards"; the colorful, "crowded" premises also contain old "books and records to sift through", plus a "small clothing section" of casualwear ("great used jeans") and new, libidinous gag gifts that'll titillate "out-of-town friends."

Lowell/Edwards C   – | – | – | VE
979 Third Ave., 5th fl. (bet. 58th & 59th Sts.), 4/5/6/N/R/W to 59th St./ Lexington Ave., 212-980-2862; www.lowelledwards.com
As every interior decorator knows, the Upper East Side's D&D Building is stuffed to its guilded gills with high-end showrooms, and this store is one of the sexiest, displaying remote-controlled, custom home-entertainment systems, including Runco cabinets that magically open onto Denon plasma TVs, or Kent stereo speakers that descend from the ceiling on cue; if you don't have a bring-your-own, they'll set you up with an in-house designer.

Luca Luca S C   22 | 23 | 22 | VE
1011 Madison Ave. (78th St.), 6 to 77th St., 212-288-9285
690 Madison Ave. (62nd St.), 4/5/6/N/R/W to 59th St./Lexington Ave., 212-755-2444
■ Strap on the stilettos for trawling these Upper East Side shops, home to the "hottest" cashmeres, shearlings and shiny, slinky separates for oh-so-"sexy" "matrons"; some won't Luca twice at the "trashy-flashy" threads (too "way out"), but for most, the "ridiculously great service" ("in-store alterations" and free, same-day delivery) outweighs the "ridiculously priced" frocks.

Lucky Brand Dungarees ● S   21 | 20 | 21 | M
172 Fifth Ave. (22nd St.), N/R to 23rd St., 917-606-1418
260 Columbus Ave. (70th St.), 1/2/3/9 to 72nd St.; B/C to 72nd St., 212-579-1760
38 Greene St. (Grand St.), A/C/E to Canal St., 212-625-0707
1151 Third Ave. (67th St.), 6 to 68th St., 646-422-1192
800-964-5777; www.luckybrandjeans.com
■ Even the "most picky of jean connoisseurs" feels 'lucky' at this "retro" yet "streetwise" denim "mecca" where the "cool" "consistent-for-fit" jeans slither over "teenyboppers of all ages" and "don't cost as much as some other trendy" brands; sure there are "thousands of options", but it's not like looking for a needle in a haystack – the "service with a smile" "demystifies the art of buying" and helps "you find that perfect pair."

Lucy Barnes ● S C   – | – | – | E
117 Perry St. (bet. Greenwich & Hudson Sts.), 1/9 to Christopher St., 212-647-0149
It's refreshing to see a romantic rebel, and that's just the spirit of this cozy boutique in the heart of the Village; whitewashed brick walls and a simple tin ceiling set the stage for "floaty, fancy, fabulous threads" for women and brides-to-be, in "eclectic" floral prints and embroidered vintage cottons – all embodying "deliciously new ideas."

Lulu Guinness S C   ▽ 23 | 26 | 19 | E
394 Bleecker St. (bet. W. 11th & Perry Sts.), 1/9 to Christopher St., 212-367-2120; www.luluguinness.com
■ Burgeoning Bleecker Street is more "adorable" than ever thanks to this "quaint" girlie shop that "beams with personality" and "whimsical" murals "splashed across the walls"; "the employees'

| M | P | S | C |

accents make you feel like you're across the pond with Lulu herself", and the "crazy", "colorful", "clever designs and shapes" of the handbags, cosmetic cases and, now, footwear "put a smile on your face"; indeed, "the roses on the black satin purse are so red you want to water them."

Lunettes et Chocolat 🅂🅲 | 26 | 24 | 22 | E |
25 Prince St. (bet. Elizabeth & Mott Sts.), 6 to Spring St.; N/R to Prince St., 212-925-8800

■ "Even if you're not in the market" for eyewear, this "quirky" "little shop" embodies an "interesting concept" – an oh-so-French marriage of "cool" Selima Salaun glasses and "divine" MarieBelle chocolates – that's worth a "stop-in" when you're cruising NoLita; it also purveys "chic hats", and if the "minimal" selection of goods "isn't earth-shattering, the "cute" decor and "to-die-for" cocoa keeps a lunettic fringe coming back.

L'Uomo 🌒🅂🅲 | ▽ 20 | 23 | 22 | E |
383 Bleecker St. (Perry St.), 1/9 to Christopher St., 212-206-1844

■ Male clients claim you "can't miss" with this veteran Villager, which blends a comprehensive collection of Hugo Boss with exclusive Orlando casual clothing, Moreno Martini de Firenza spread-collar sport shirts and uncommon leather outerwear in an easy-to-shop space staffed by "exceptional" salespeople; if the labels seem too "pricey", just "wait until the goods go on sale."

Luxury Brand Outlet 🅲 | 12 | 5 | 9 | M |
2503 Broadway (bet. 93rd & 94th Sts.), 1/2/3 to 96th St., 212-866-8458
355 E. 78th St. (bet. 1st & 2nd Aves.), 6 to 77th St., 212-988-5603 🌒🅂

■ "Hey, you never know" what "chic brands" of "designer clothes" you'll find "lurking under all the mess" at this Upper East and West Side discounter; "patient" burrowers "especially love the shoes", bags and belts, but pout that the "poor selection" and "expensive" prices keep this duo from "rising to its potential."

Lyric Hi-Fi 🅂🅲 | 26 | 20 | 18 | VE |
1221 Lexington Ave. (bet. 82nd & 83rd Sts.), 4/5/6 to 86th St., 212-439-1900; www.lyricusa.com

■ "Whether you're stopping in to chat about budget phono pre-amp options or to audition some serious stereo equipment", the goods at this sound-and-vision specialty store are "stellar"; the folks on the floor at the East 80s flagship of the country's first high-end audio/video retailer are highly informed and seasoned, but antagonists argue that "snooty doesn't begin to describe them."

M.A.C. Cosmetics | 24 | 23 | 19 | M |
14 Christopher St. (Gay St.), 1/2 to Christopher St., 212-243-4150
Flatiron Bldg., 1 E. 22nd St. (B'way), N/R to 23rd St., 212-677-6611
113 Spring St. (bet. Greene & Mercer Sts.), 6 to Spring St., 212-334-4641;
800-387-6707 🅂
www.maccosmetics.com

■ A long-standing "beauty staple" for professionals, this cosmetics company showcases a "wide variety of colors and shades", particularly when it comes to lipstick, "can't-live-without-it" Lipglass and eyeshadow, to "bring out your inner drag queen", "glam girl" or "grown-up"; while "reasonable prices" make it "a bargain next to other comparable lines", it can be "hit-or-miss with the salespeople" 'cause "it's kind of cool but also kind of scary that the entire staff wears makeup – including the men."

vote at zagat.com

MacKenzie-Childs C | 23 | 23 | 18 | VE

824 Madison Ave. (69th St.), 6 to 68th St., 212-570-6050; 888-665-1999; www.mackenzie-childs.com

■ "Alice in Wonderland is in there somewhere" assert observers of this "labyrinth" of a Madison Avenue home-furnishings shop whose "unique" and "eccentric" items range from "incredibly colored" "hand-painted ceramics" to "whimsical" furniture like fish-shaped chairs and candy-striped tuffets; but while pros praise the "sensory overload" here, a few find the "busy" merch and "expensive" prices make them "dizzy."

MACY'S ●S | 18 | 13 | 9 | M

151 W. 34th St. (bet. Broadway & 7th Ave.), 1/2/3/9/N/R/W/B/D/F/Q to 34th St., 212-695-4400; www.macys.com
Additional locations throughout the NY area

■ This 101-year-old "king of the department stores" and a "must-see for tourists" can be "hard to navigate" (the Herald Square flagship "spans a full city block"); but if you "have a compass and the patience", you'll find an "impressive variety" of "moderately priced, durable" merchandise, including "high-energy" cosmetics counters, a "canyon" of appliances ("the Cellar is stellar!"), "a hidden treasure" trove of kids' furniture, "quality beds" and an "expansive" shoe selection; critics claim it's a "miracle on 34th Street" if the "chaotic" scene on sale days and "disgruntled" salespeople don't "scare you away"; still, for sheer "variety" you "can't beat the behemoth" – and besides, who else would sponsor Thanksgiving Day parades and July 4th fireworks?

Madina Milano SC | – | – | – | E

151 Spring St. (bet. W. B'way & Wooster St.), C/E to Spring St., 646-613-0838; 866-623-4626; www.madina.it

Relatively new SoHo outpost of a chic Italian cosmetics company that's the brainchild of Madina Ferrari, a former theatrical designer with a passion for color; innovative workstations invite customers to play with thousands of shades (over 350 lipsticks and 160 eyeshadows), and expert makeup artists stand by ready to rescue overly avid appliers.

Magic Windows SC | 23 | 20 | 21 | E

1186 Madison Ave. (87th St.), 4/5/6 to 86th St., 212-289-0028; www.magic-windows.com

■ "Worth a trip Uptown for beautiful" domestic and imported children's clothing that spans the ages, this Madison Avenue boutique offers a "varied selection" ranging from layette to "top-quality classics" for boys and girls to "inviting dresses" and "gorgeous prom gowns"; styles tend to be "very conservative for younger kids, but more fashion-forward into the pre-teen years"; still, the less spellbound sigh that the merchandise tends to be "too girlie."

Magry Knits | – | – | – | E

80 E. Seventh St. (bet. 1st & 2nd Aves.), F/V to 2nd Ave., 212-674-6753; www.magryknits.com

Renee Burrows, the "very friendly and approachable" owner of this "great little find" in the East Village not only "dyes and hand-spins" her own skeins, turning out some of the "most varied" and "creative yarn in the city", she also "carries hand-knit garments that are stylish and hip"; "personalized classes" are also offered

| M | P | S | C |

(the proprietor's "patience" with newbies "is a virtue"), and "weekly stitch parties round out the fun."

Make Up For Ever S ▽ 26 | 21 | 25 | M
409 W. Broadway (bet. Prince & Spring Sts.), N/R to Prince St.; C/E to Spring St., 212-941-9337; 877-757-5175; www.makeupforever.fr
■ Paris-based cosmetics company that started in 1984 as a line of professional theatrical makeup, whose SoHo branch draws civilians as well with "everything you could ever need", including a "huge variety" of "great, custom colors" with a "massive amount of pigmentation" and moderate prices.

Malia Mills Swimwear S 26 | 20 | 25 | E
199 Mulberry St. (Spring St.), 6 to Spring St., 212-625-2311; 800-685-3459; www.maliamills.com
■ Savvy swimmers set a course for this NoLita bikiniland of "mix-and-match sizes" for "every shape" in silky solids or cool prints; a "super-knowledgeable, friendly" staff (including the designer herself) knows how to make you "feel comfortable about your body", and if you need an even more Malia-ble fit, they'll custom-design you a "sexy, figure-flattering" (and, yes, "pricey") suit.

Malo C ▽ 27 | 22 | 23 | VE
814 Madison Ave. (68th St.), 6 to 68th St., 212-396-4721
125 Wooster St. (bet. Prince & Spring Sts.), N/R to Prince St., 212-941-7444 S
■ Whether in the East 60s or SoHo, there's nothing shallow about Malo – on the contrary, the Italian designer specializes in ultra-thick, four-ply "classic cashmere" for men and women that "lasts a lifetime"; a "most wonderful" staff "really takes the time to help you" with your "pricey" purchase, be it a "beautiful sweater" or a bomber jacket.

M&J Trimming/Buttons C 27 | 19 | 17 | M
1000-1008 Sixth Ave. (bet. 37th & 38th Sts.), B/D/F/N/Q/R/V/Q to 34th St./Herald Sq., 212-391-6200; 212-842-5050; 800-965-8746; www.mjtrim.com
■ "Wow!" – this Garment District notions emporium is "like crawling into a cool granny's knitting basket" say handy hobbyists with a "DIY bent"; "prepare to be dazzled" by the "floor-to-high-ceiling array of ribbons, fringe, lace" and "other doodads" – you'll think you've "died and gone to button-and-trim heaven"; it's "inspiring and overwhelming" – "whatever madness you want to indulge" "you'll find it here."

Mandolin Brothers – | – | – | E
629 Forest Ave. (Oakland Ave.), Staten Island, 718-981-8585; www.mandoweb.com
If you've scoured Manhattan for a mandocello, don't fret – just ferry over to Staten Island, where this "guitar player's paradise" for new, used and vintage esoterica awaits; it's out of the way for straphangers without limousine budgets, but some axemen insist it's "the only place to go when you're serious about buying."

Manfredi C – | – | – | VE
702 Madison Ave. (bet. 62nd & 63rd Sts.), 4/5/6/N/R/W to 59th St./Lexington Ave., 212-734-8710
In the East 60s, this Italian maestro creates "fun watches" and light, "wonderfully designed fine jewelry" that emphasizes the

vote at zagat.com

reflective nature of the gold and colorful gemstones; some of his creations, like the single jewels suspended between lariat-like chokers, "you won't see anywhere else" devotees declare.

Manny's Music S — 25 | 19 | 22 | M
156 W. 48th St. (bet. 6th & 7th Aves.), N/R/W to 49th St.; B/D/F/V to 47th-50th Sts./Rockefeller Ctr., 212-819-0576; 866-776-6266; www.mannysmusic.com

◾ "Shop where the pros do" at this septuagenarian Midtown "classic" with two-story walls covered in autographed photos of the jazzmen and rockers who've patronized it; "you may be intimidated that the guy showing you" a "reasonably priced" guitar, bass, keyboard or drum kit "can outplay you, but they know their stuff", and they're "modest" enough not to gloat; perhaps they just agree with snobby songsters who sniff the place is "not what it used to be" since it changed ownership.

MANOLO BLAHNIK C — 28 | 26 | 21 | VE
31 W. 54th St. (bet. 5th & 6th Aves.), E/V to 5th Ave./53rd St., 212-582-3007

◾ "Dip into your trust fund" before heading over to Midtown's "holy grail" of "ultimate high heels" made even more "famous by Sarah Jessica Parker in *Sex in the City*"; this "chichi" "shrine" seduces "fashionistas" with "divine", "beautifully crafted" "masterpieces", in other words, "definitely cab shoes – no walking allowed, unless you're making your way from bar to table, then sashay away"; while a handful hails service as "good", many maintain it's nearly "non-existent unless the salesperson recognizes you or your handbag."

Maraolo ☾S — 19 | 19 | 16 | E
782 Lexington Ave. (61st St.), 4/5/6/F/N/R/W to 59th St./ Lexington Ave., 212-755-9687
1321 Third Ave. (bet. 75th & 76th Sts.), 6 to 77th St., 212-988-4726

◾ A "favorite for many years", these Upper East Side "havens" stock "well-designed, simple Italian shoes" that "wear quite well", providing a "nice everyday alternative to Jimmy Choo and Bruno Magli" that "even a working girl" or guy "can afford", plus leather handbags and briefcases; while admirers adore the "great selection", others opine there are "some good styles, but it's not consistent."

Marc by Marc Jacobs ☾SC — – | – | – | E
403-5 Bleecker St. (W. 11th St.), 1/9 to Christopher St., 212-924-0026; www.marcjacobs.com

Denim devotees lay claim to the boy wonder's secondary line at these understated West Village adjoining men's and women's boutiques, home to the rich rocker/hippie chick/trustafarians who adore Jacobs' brand of insouciant style at a (comparatively) affordable price; regulars rub elbows with lanky models and languourous movie stars, who perk up only to snatch the cool-cooler-coolest threads.

Marc Jacobs SC — 26 | 23 | 20 | VE
163 Mercer St. (bet. Houston & Prince Sts.), N/R to Prince St., 212-343-1490; www.marcjacobs.com

◾ New Yorkers of all sexes worship Marc "major-splurge" Jacobs, long a design wunderkind on Seventh Avenue and now a veritable force of fashion-forward fancies that fans "can't get enough of"; at his spare SoHo boutique, he's "cornered the market" on "fresh, uncomplicated, cool" clothing – half-"Minnie Mouse, half-Edie

| M | P | S | C |

Sedgwick" – and reinvented classic shoes and bags into "hot, hot, hot" must-haves that make up for some staff "attitude, attitude."

Marc Jacobs Accessories ❶🆂🅲   – | – | – | E

385 Bleecker St. (Perry St.), 1/9 to Christopher St.; A/C/E/L to 14th St., 212-924-6126; www.marcjacobs.com

Fashionistas swear by this iconic designer's 'it' accessories at this Greenwich Village corner shop, part of his Bleecker Street empire, which inspire a feeding frenzy wherever you go; tiptoe into this eye-catching boutique for a feast of goodies, from retro-inspired shoes to heavenly, gotta-have-it clutches and buttery leather shoulder bags – chances are you won't leave empty-handed.

Mare ❶🆂   ▽ 23 | 21 | 20 | E

426 W. Broadway (bet. Prince & Spring Sts.), C/E to Spring St., 212-343-1110; www.mare.com

◪ With its sea-foam-colored walls, curvy surfaces and "beautiful Italian shoes", this little bit of the Mediterranean in SoHo is always "worth a stop", especially if you're on the prowl for "high-fashion" "Downtown" footwear including some of the "most comfortable stiletto-heel boots ever made"; while a smattering of sidesteppers demur at "designs that shy away from being too original", sole-mates maintain "you never know what you'll find."

Mariko 🅲   – | – | – | M

998 Madison Ave. (77th St.), 6 to 77th St., 212-472-1176

Ladies who lunch and socialite wanna-bes alike shop at this cluttered, beige-and-cream-colored Upper Eastside jeweler, a "great choice for fabulous fakes", whether one's taste runs to of-the-moment styles or timeless looks, like a copy of the three-strand pearl choker made popular by Jackie O.

Marimekko 🆂   ▽ 22 | – | 20 | E

1262 Third Ave. (bet. 72nd & 73rd Sts.), 6 to 68th St., 212-628-8400; 800-527-0624; www.kiitosmarimekko.com

■ "Bold, graphic stripes" and designs infused with a "little bit of Finland", like the "wonderful, splashy" prints "we knew in the '70s" and '60s can still be found at this Upper Eastsider; the "timeless stuff", including textiles, tablecloths, bedding, "great totes" and accessories, plus "beautiful cotton" apparel for adults and kids, is "still great after all these years"; N.B. the store moved post-*Survey*.

Mario Badescu Skin Care 🆂   – | – | – | M

320 E. 52nd St. (bet. 1st & 2nd Aves.), 6 to 51st St./Lexington Ave., 212-758-1065; www.mariobadescu.com

For more than 35 years, this pale-pink-and-green Upper East Side specialty retailer has been catering to a clientele that includes "high-profile celebrities" like Sarah Jessica Parker and Martha Stewart, with its "great" all-natural skincare line that "won't break the bank"; the face is the focus – with zit-zapping Drying Lotion the best-seller among 200 other products – but there are bath-and-body potions too; N.B appointments can also be made for a variety of spa services, including facials, waxing and massage.

Marni 🆂🅲   ▽ 28 | 26 | 23 | VE

161 Mercer St. (bet. Prince & Houston Sts.), N/R to Prince St., 212-343-3912

■ Fashion purists scoop up "lovely" designs at this distinctively "beautiful" SoHo boutique, furnished with a milky-glass floor and

vote at zagat.com

chrome 'tree-limb' fixtures, knowing they'll be one season ahead of the pack in Consuelo Castiglioni's creations; using rich fabrics, this Italian designer cultivates a "combination of ease, romance and toughness" that keeps her brand of "feminine" chic from being "too girlie"; there's "great stuff" for guys too, but "be ready to spend."

Marsha D.D. S C   ▽ 23 | 17 | 20 | E
1574 Third Ave. (bet. 88th & 89th Sts.), 4/5/6 to 86th St., 212-831-2422

■ "*The* place" for tween clothing and accessories, this large Upper East Side "kids' favorite from age 10 on" exudes a "very hip" vibe with a red rubber floor, snowboard benches and zebra-striped carpeting in the dressing rooms; the owner is "on top of the trends", so the "stuff is way-cool" – "mostly jeans, T-shirts" and sweaters from "hot" labels like Diesel, Juicy and Quiksilver; yeah, it's "expensive", but they have "everything" this age group wants.

Marshall's S C   – | – | – | M
125 W. 125th St. (Lenox Ave.), 1/9 to 125th St., 212-866-3963 ●
625 Atlantic Ave. (Hanson Pl.), Brooklyn, 2/3/4/5/M/N/Q/R/W to Atlantic Ave., 718-398-5254 ●
48-18 Northern Blvd., Queens, R/Q to Northern Blvd., 718-626-4700
888-MARSHALLS; www.marshallsonline.com

What's "a little trip into Queens", Brooklyn or, now, Harlem when you can experience "the rush" of scoring "last season's styles" by designers like Donna Karan, Ralph Lauren and Tahari "at wonderfully low prices", plus "linens, gourmet cooking items, glasses, etc." at this "great place to find" the goods for less?; "go with an open mind and you'll be pleasantly surprised."

Martin ● S C   – | – | – | M
206 E. 6th St. (bet. 2nd & 3rd Aves.), 6 to Astor Pl., 212-358-0011

Behind an East Village storefront lies a "tiny" shop, "kind of like a friend's bedroom", filled with much-raved-over pants and jeans ("the be-all and end-all for anyone tall") and "offbeat, but not too weird" jackets, tops and dresses with a sexy, edgy rock 'n' roll energy (to complement the collage of musicians on the tin ceiling).

Mary Adams, The Dress S   – | – | – | E
138 Ludlow St. (bet. Rivington & Stanton Sts.), F/V to 2nd Ave.; F to Delancey St., 212-473-0237; www.maryadamsthedress.com

"*Très* funky" custom-made and off-the-rack party frocks, wedding dresses and gowns are this Lower East Side designer's raison d'être; if you're "not the typical bride", this is the "stuff that dreams are made of", with "original" girlie get-ups turned out in vibrant shades or white with a burst of bright detailing, offset by romantic ruffles, loads of flouncy layers or "baroque" bustle-backs.

Mary Arnold Toys C   24 | 20 | 24 | E
1010 Lexington Ave. (bet. 72nd & 73rd Sts.), 6 to 68th St., 212-744-8510

■ "Recommending gifts for specific ages" may be a "lost art" elsewhere, but not at this "excellent, cute toy store" on the Upper East Side, where the "staff is helpful" and "knowledgeable"; the "very nice selection" includes dolls, crafts and early-development choices and even special "things you can't find in other larger chain stores"; N.B. ask about the birthday wish list.

| M | P | S | C |

Mason's Tennis Mart 🆂🅲   21 | 18 | 18 | E
56 E. 53rd St. (bet. Park & Madison Aves.), 6 to 51st St./Lexington Ave., 212-755-5805

■ A popular stop for U.S. Open attendees, this "been-around-forever" Midtown shop "always has the latest tennis stuff", including designer attire from the likes of Ellesse and Fila, a "great selection of equipment" and a "staff that has great patience" to help you score what you need; while they certainly "know" their game here, "they sure do charge you for the knowledge" declare the price conscious, but even they say the "deals are terrific" if you "catch the 50 percent off sale" twice a year.

Maternity Works 🆂🅲   17 | 11 | 16 | I
16 W. 57th St. (bet. 5th & 6th Aves.), F to 57th St., 212-399-9840; www.maternitymall.com

■ "From cheapo to primo, there are great deals to be found" at this Midtown maternity mecca where "high-end brand names" such as Mimi Maternity and Pea in the Pod (all owned by the same parent company) are sold "at a fraction of the price"; there's "not much ambiance", the "space is small and the merchandise crammed" together, but "you'll feel like you're searching for hidden treasure and you'll be rewarded . . . sometimes."

Matt Umanov Guitars 🆂🅲   ▽ 26 | 22 | 22 | E
273 Bleecker St. (bet. Cornelia & Jones Sts.), 1/2 to Christopher St., 212-675-2157; www.umanovguitars.com

■ There may be "no bargains" and "no smiles" at this Village "landmark", but if you're a "musician" (not just a "famous" one), you're "automatically a friend" of "the guitar gods behind the counter" offering an "interesting mix" of new and vintage fretted instruments and sheet music; the eponymous "Matt is great to do business with" – he's "down-to-earth and knows his stuff."

Maurice Villency   26 | 25 | 22 | VE
200 E. 57th St. (3rd Ave.), 4/5/6/N/R/W to 59th St./Lexington Ave., 212-725-4840; www.villency.com

■ This 71-year-old company's new blocklong, glass-fronted flagship on East 57th Street is the backdrop for "well-constructed", "pricey" contemporary custom-made furniture – some fabricated in "leather like butter"; the store has also made its first foray into home accessories ranging from sheets to lamps and pillows.

Mavi Jean 🌑🆂🅲   – | – | – | M
510 Broome St. (W. B'way), C/E to Spring St., 212-625-9454; www.mavi.com

You don't have to be a "5'10" anorexic model type" or even a trust-fund baby to shop at this "cool jeans" haunt in SoHo; though known for perfect-fit pants that come in the "softest fabrics" and the newest washes and "look good on almost any" stylish woman or man, this denim dynamo also offers scads of skirts ranging from micro-mini to ankle-length plus Western-style jackets; N.B. a bi-level flagship in Union Square was slated to open at press time.

Maxilla & Mandible 🆂🅲   ▽ 24 | 23 | 18 | E
451 Columbus Ave. (bet. 81st & 82nd Sts.), B/C to 81st St., 212-724-6173; www.maxillaandmandible.com

■ "If you're dying to buy junior a trilobite for his birthday", "putter around" this Upper West Side osteological shop "after the Museum

vote at zagat.com   **179**

of Natural History" – "for the kid" or even the photographer, collector or naturalist "interested in skulls and skeletons, there is no where else like it."

Max Mara C — | — | — | VE
813 Madison Ave. (68th St.), 6 to 68th St., 212-879-6100
450 W. Broadway (bet. Houston & Prince Sts.), N/R to Prince St.; C/E to Spring St., 212-674-1817 S
The clean white walls of this "highly recommended" store evoke the pure luxury of the clean-lined Italian clothing collection with its "gorgeous, classic" rich-woman coat-and-suit silhouettes that "cost more but will last you forever"; though Madison Avenue's the flagship, for Maximum choice, fans should fast-track it to the SoHo concept shop, which sells one-of-a-kind items.

Max Studio S — | — | — | E
415 W. Broadway (bet. Prince & Spring Sts.), N/R to Prince St.; C/E to Spring St., 212-941-1141; www.maxstudio.com
While the decor of this bi-level SoHo boutique pales in comparison with its chichi neighbors', the shop's inventory holds its own with a "nice mix of work, fun and dressy clothes" in neutrals and subtle prints from this widespread label; compounded by the background techno music, the hustle-bustle makes it fun to browse both the new offerings and the perpetual-sale items downstairs.

Mayle S C 24 | 23 | 19 | E
252 Elizabeth St. (bet. Houston & Prince Sts.), F/S/V to B'way/ Lafayette St., 212-625-0406
■ Set up to feel like designer Jane Mayle's closet, the "adorable atmosphere" of this NoLita boutique "draws you in, but the clothes make you stay" sigh stalwarts who save up for the "vintage-inspired" femme-fatale sheaths, signature cotton T-shirts and "whimsical" wares; fans feel it's "what shopping should be – fun, relaxed and beautiful."

Me & Ro S 24 | 25 | 19 | E
239 Elizabeth St. (bet. Houston & Prince Sts.), 6 to Spring St., 917-237-9215; www.meandrojewelry.com
◪ Designed by the architects ShoP with a red plaster wall and a floating flower pond in the window, this "tiny" NoLita space aims to be "spiritually stylish" to reflect the East-meets-West feel of its dangling, beaded jewelry that often carries "Sanskrit-inscribed" "messages of peace, fearlessness and love"; "everything here is delicate – except for the prices" and perhaps the "laissez-faire" staff (maybe they should study the inscriptions).

Mecox Gardens S C — | — | — | E
962 Lexington Ave. (bet. 70th & 71st Sts.), 6 to 68th St., 212-249-5301; www.mecoxgardens.com
It's an indoor-outdoor haute hodgepodge at this Upper East Side furniture store for house and garden; from global scavenger hunts, these folks bring back and daringly arrange an eclectic collection of modern pieces, antiques and reproductions into object lessons for clientele; fin-de-siècle Chinese demi-lune tables are topped with handmade, contemporary ceramic lamps while Syrian mother-of-pearl inlaid chests share corners with Grande San Juan hurricane lanterns; at their original Hamptons digs, there's lawn space to show off Vienna urn planters and French iron benches.

Medici ○🅂🄲   18 | 17 | 18 | M
420 Columbus Ave. (bet. 80th & 81st Sts.), B/C to 81st St., 212-712-9342
24 W. 23rd St. (bet. 5th & 6th Aves.), F/V to 23rd St., 212-604-0888
☒ Worth checking into now and again, this footwear outfit is known for colorful "fashionable shoes, at good prices", that oftentimes sport "very inventive" heels and detailing, as well as "cute" handbags and accessories; but stylesetters scoff that they're either "a few seasons ago" or just plain "wanna-be."

Meg ○🅂🄲   – | – | – | M
312 E. Ninth St. (bet. 1st & 2nd Sts.), 6 to Astor Pl., 212-260-6329
"Made for real women, not dolls" marvel mavens about designer Meghan Kinney's modus operandi, the results of which are displayed in her East Village boutique; her "totally wearable" womenswear may be Downtown hip, but it's always flattering with its unusual textiles and sexy, siren necklines.

Memorial Sloan-Kettering Cancer Center Thrift Shop   17 | 15 | 14 | M
1440 Third Ave. (bet. 81st & 82nd Sts.), 4/5/6 to 86th St., 212-535-1250
☒ "My friends would faint if they knew it's where I get my gorgeous clothes" confide the "cheapskate ladies who lunch" and shop at this "spacious" Upper East Side thrift store that's the beneficiary of "the highest-quality donations", including "great home furnishings"; even opponents who opine it's "overpriced" admit "there are bargains to be had."

Mendel Goldberg Fabrics 🅂🄲   – | – | – | E
72 Hester St. (bet. Ludlow & Orchard Sts.), F/J/M/Z to Delancey & Essex Sts., 212-925-9110
The fabric selection, while limited, is "great", and the Lower East Side store is so small if you blink you may miss it, but the service is huge – "they remember your name, and everything you ever bought"; no wonder it's a must-stop for serious sewing circles.

Men's Wearhouse ○🅂   19 | 19 | 21 | M
115 Broadway (Cedar St.), 1/2/4/5/6/A/C to Fulton St./B'way/Nassau, 212-233-0675
380 Madison Ave. (46th St.), 4/5/6/7/S to 42nd St./Grand Central, 212-856-9008
655 Sixth Ave. (20th St.), F/V to 23rd St., 212-243-3517
2021 Bartow Ave. (Ash Loop), Bronx, 6 to Pelham to #12 Bus, 718-320-8347
Circuit City Mall, 2535 Richmond Ave. (bet. Platinum Ave. & Richmond Hill Rd.), Staten Island, 718-982-5751
800-776-7847; www.menswearhouse.com
☒ "Men who hate to shop" can get "a whole wardrobe", including rented formalwear, in "one easy day" at this "inexpensive" fashion chain, with a flagship (aptly enough) in the Financial District; "good tailoring" and "helpful" service make it "worth a visit" for most, though a few kvetch it's "not the classy store it promotes."

Metro Bicycles 🅂🄲   21 | 15 | 21 | M
417 Canal St. (6th Ave.), 1/9 to Canal St., 212-334-8000
332 E. 14th St. (bet. 1st & 2nd Aves.), 4/5/6/N/R/Q/W to 14th St./Union Sq., 212-228-4344
1311 Lexington Ave. (88th St.), 4/5/6 to 86th St., 212-427-4450
546 Sixth Ave. (14th St.), F/L to 14th St., 212-255-5100

(continued)

M | P | S | C

(continued)
Metro Bicycles
231 W. 96th St. (B'way), 1/2/3/9 to 96th St., 212-663-7531
360 W. 47th St. (9th Ave.), A/C/E to 42nd St./Port Authority, 212-581-4500
92-64 Queens Blvd. (Woodhaven), Queens, G/R/V to Woodhaven, 718-478-3338
www.metrobicycles.com

◪ "They stand behind their" "excellent selection" of accessories, parts and "bikes for all members of the family" at this chainlet in Manhattan and Queens; the "helpful" staff "really knows its stuff" and is "willing to lend a hand" to steer you toward a bevy of brands including Trek, Raleigh and Klein – "the only thing they won't do is take you for a ride."

Metropolitan Lumber & Hardware S | 21 | 11 | 18 | M |
617 11th Ave. (bet. 45th & 46th Sts.), A/C/E to 42nd St./Port Authority, 212-246-9090
175 Spring St. (bet. Thompson St. & W. B'way), C/E to Spring St., 212-966-3466
108-20 Merrick Blvd. (109th Ave.), Queens, E/J/Z to Jamaica Ctr. Parsons/Archer, 718-657-0100
108-56 Roosevelt Ave. (108th St.), Queens, 7 to 111th St., 718-898-2100
34-35 Steinway St. (bet. 34th & 35th Aves.), Queens, N/W to 36th Ave., 718-393-4441

◪ "Great selection" is the draw at these "local" hardware standbys purveying "high-quality tools, specialty parts" and "lumber to go" for "minor to major construction projects"; service fluctuates from "the most helpful on the planet" to "lacking" ("you'd better know what you're looking for"), but home improvers appreciate that these "solid" stores are "close" by.

METROPOLITAN MUSEUM OF ART | 25 | 23 | 18 | M |
GIFT SHOP S
1000 Fifth Ave. (81st St.), 6 to 77th St., 212-570-3894
Macy's Herald Sq., 151 W. 34th St. (bet. 6th & 7th Aves.), B/D/F/N/Q/R/V/W to 34th St./Herald Sq., 212-268-7266
113 Prince St. (bet. Greene & Wooster Sts.), N/R to Prince St., 212-614-3000
Rockefeller Ctr., 15 W. 49th St. (5th Ave.), B/D/F/V to 47th-50th Sts./Rockefeller Ctr., 212-332-1360
www.metmuseum.org

■ What "could be amazing individual jewelry, art print, stationery and book stores", as well as an "educational children's" boutique, gets "rolled into one" at the "granddaddy of museum shops"; you can "do most of your holiday shopping" amid a "treasure trove" "covering all prices and tastes" from "cerebral" and "expensive" to "cute" and on "clearance"; "the only problem is fighting the crowds" of "tourists with fanny packs."

Mets Clubhouse Shop ●S | 22 | 20 | 17 | M |
143 E. 54th St. (bet. Lexington & 3rd Aves.), E/V to 53rd St./Lexington Ave., 212-888-7508
11 W. 42nd St. (bet. 5th & 6th Aves.), 7 to 5th Ave., 212-768-9534
www.sportsavenue.com

■ If you're cultivating the look that says "let's go, Mets", try these "meccas" in Times Square and the East 50s for "a cap, a T-shirt, a yearbook" and such from "a large selection in all price ranges" – at least, if you're a guy ("female fans want to see more cute items"

| M | P | S | C |

for themselves); however, everyone's "amused by the discount rack of jerseys with the names and numbers of traded players."

Michael Anchin Glass Co. S C — | — | — | M
245 Elizabeth St. (bet. Houston & Prince Sts.), 6 to Spring St., 212-925-1470; www.michaelanchin.com
Some of the "most exciting glass in New York" and a "kaleidoscope of shimmering color" light up this little NoLita gallery whose owner, Michael Anchin, blows all the "beautiful pieces" that crowd the shelves himself; his long-necked vases and orb lamps are one-of-a-kind items "you'll never find anywhere else."

Michael Ashton C — | — | — | VE
933 Madison Ave. (74th St.), 6 to 77th St., 212-517-6655
This small Upper Eastsider positively glitters with the grandiose estate and period jewelry filling its cases; it's elegantly adorned with antique furniture, the better to get you in the mood to blow a bundle on an early 20th-century parure or an art deco watch.

Michael C. Fina S 25 | 22 | 19 | E
545 Fifth Ave. (45th St.), 4/5/6/7/S to 42nd St./Grand Central, 212-557-2500; 800-289-3462; www.michaelcfina.com
■ "Wend your way past the newly engaged couples registering" at this Midtown emporium and you'll find "fantastic prices" on an "amazing assortment" of china, crystal, silver, stainless steel and giftware in styles that "range from traditional to trendy" (i.e. from Spode to Calvin Klein); since "they have everything under the sun", it's a "wonderful source" for "wedding presents" and "baby gifts."

Michael Dawkins C — | — | — | E
33 E. 65th St. (Madison Ave.), 6 to 68th St., 212-639-1540; www.michaeldawkins.com
Darling of the department stores, Michael Dawkins has a "great eye" and it shows in his "very wearable, very chic" jewelry in which the "design excels"; his gallery-like East 60s boutique shines with pieces demonstrating his signature silver granulation technique (affixing miniscule spheres in patterns onto a metal surface).

Michael Eigen C — | — | — | VE
Grand Central, Lexington Passage, 4/5/6/7/S to 42nd St./Grand Central, 212-949-0170
1200 Madison Ave. (bet. 87th & 88th Sts.), 4/5/6 to 86th St., 212-996-0281
800-780-3861; www.michaeleigen.com
Those meandering Upper Madison Avenue or rushing through Grand Central can peruse this jeweler, who offers more than "a few lovely things" from various designers; the well-displayed lines range from the dainty Erica Courtney to Indian-inspired Me & Ro; watches, wedding bands and traditional fine diamond pendants are on hand too.

Michael Kors 26 | 23 | 24 | VE
974 Madison Ave. (76th St.), 6 to 77th St., 212-452-4685
■ There's something deliciously over-the-top about the fabrics, cut and (sigh) cost of Kors' carefree classics, "designed with love for women" (and men too); the "great location" (the East 70s) of his subtly colored flagship boutique – the work of architect Dan Rowen – and "personal service" ensure the return of regulars who devour the "oh, yum" sportswear.

vote at zagat.com

Michael's – | – | – | M
1041 Madison Ave. (bet. 79th & 80th Sts.), 6 to 77th St., 212-737-7273; www.michaelsconsignment.com
Even those who think "consignment shops aren't all they're cracked up to be" say "try this one", a presence in the field since 1954; in a spacious duplex, it caters to the Upper East Side lady with tapestry-covered seats, large dressing rooms and well-organized rows of "gently worn clothing and accessories" from all the Big Names (entire racks are devoted to Chanel alone); there's also a wedding-gown section that "could be your last stop on the bridal train."

Michelle Roth 26 | 25 | 23 | VE
24 W. 57th St. (bet. 5th & 6th Aves.), F to 57th St., 212-245-3390; www.michelleroth.com
■ It's a "Cinderella experience" at this Midtown "bridal dream" thanks to "charming" brother and sister co-owners Michelle Roth and Henry Weinreich and their "super-friendly staff", who "treat you like the belle of the ball"; the "beautifully crafted gowns", "ranging from simple and elegant to non-traditional", are presented in a "environment that's very comfortable for an overwhelming task" – "a real treat" for the aisle-bound.

Michel Perry ⊡ ▽ 26 | 26 | 25 | VE
320 Park Ave. (51st St.), E/V to 53rd St./Lexington Ave., 212-688-4968
■ Whether he makes them ruched, pointy or spike-heeled, this Frenchman knows a few things about creating come-hither shoes; nestled in his girlie pink Park Avenue "salon" decorated with 18th-century mirrors and modern art is a "drool-worthy" selection for the fairy-tale day you decide that you "already have enough Manolos."

Midnight Records – | – | – | M
263 W. 23rd St. (bet. 7th & 8th Aves.), C/E to 23rd St., 212-675-2768; www.midnightrecords.com
If you're yearning for that lost Canned Heat disc from your youth, check out this Chelsea storefront, a jumble of obscure grunge and psychedelia, including "imports you'll never see again"; the owner buys on whim, so you might also stumble across a hot patch of mambo or a bitchin' swell of surf rock in the dusty digs of what claims to be the world's largest indie and reissue CD and LP mail-order house; N.B. shuttered Monday, Wednesday and Sunday.

Mika Inatome – | – | – | VE
11 Worth St. (bet. Hudson St. & W. B'way), 1/9 to Franklin St., 212-966-7777; www.mikainatome.com
"You feel as if you're getting your money's worth" at this Tribeca by-appointment-only bridal shop where Mika Inatome and her designers "work with you to" custom-"make a dress that fits your personality"; the contemporary styles, like an elegant silk jacquard gown with ruched detailing, adventurous one-shoulder number with detachable train and made-for-the-red-carpet satin crêpe confection, can all be adjusted to taste.

MIKIMOTO ⊡ 28 | 25 | 23 | VE
680 Fifth Ave. (bet. 53rd & 54th Sts.), N/R to 5th Ave., 212-457-4501
730 Fifth Ave. (bet. 56th & 57th Sts.), N/R to 5th Ave., 212-457-4600
888-701-2323; www.mikimoto.com
■ "Pearl people" profess the "only place to buy" "the definitive necklace" is at this Japanese master, credited with creating the

first cultured strands in 1893; at both light-wood, contemporary Midtown sites, the "classic beauties" – "some so big they could be gumballs" – are "beautifully displayed", and a "knowledgeable" staff describes how they're "exquisitely made"; "you'll have them for life, and be paying for them that long as well."

Mimi Maternity C 21 | 18 | 21 | M
Winter Garden, 2 World Financial Ctr., 225 Liberty St., 2nd level (South End Ave.), 212-566-1382 S
2005 Broadway (69th St.), 1/2/3 to 72nd St., 212-721-1999 S
1125 Madison Ave. (84th St.), 4/5/6 to 86th St., 212-737-3784
1021 Third Ave. (bet. 60th & 61st Sts.), N/R/W to 59th St./Lexington Ave., 212-832-2667
2655 Richmond Ave. (Ring Rd.), Staten Island, 718-761-0097
877-646-4666; www.mimimaternity.com

◪ "What a relief!" sigh expectant moms – "you can buy your pregnancy wardrobe" at this chain "without breaking the bank"; "the styles are fun", and the staff helps you find "great basics" that "fit and wear well"; the "only downside is the price" retort the budget conscious – "how long are you gonna wear these" items?

Mini Mini Market ●SC ▽ 20 | 21 | 20 | M
218 Bedford Ave. (bet. N. 4th & 5th Sts.), Brooklyn, L to Bedford Ave., 718-302-9337; www.mini-mini-market.com

■ A "Brooklyn girl's dream", especially for "Williamsburg hipsters", this "fantastic find" is loaded with a "cute selection of fashionable" accessories, apparel, shoes, body products and gifts from local talents as well as designers from afar; "good prices", a "varied selection" and a decidedly cool retro vibe (pink-and-red floors) all make it "worth the trip" on the L train.

Mish – | – | – | VE
131 E. 70th St. (bet. Lexington & Park Aves.), 6 to 68th St., 212-734-3500

"Where all the bright young things shop" for all the bright things they can don is this East 70s jewel box for exclusive designs by bowtie-bedecked namesake Mish Tworkowski (ex Sotheby's); whimsy, color and craftsmanship combine in limited-edition and unique multi-hued sapphire and diamond briolette necklaces, baroque South Sea pearl cuff links and gold-and-semiprecious-stone signature pagoda brooches, all of which go like hotcakes.

Missoni C 23 | 23 | 21 | VE
1009 Madison Ave. (78th St.), 6 to 77th St., 212-517-9339; www.missoni.com

■ In this understated Upper East Side boutique, the well-respected Italian knitwear-maker known for "colorful beauty" "stays fresh" year after year by coming up with lively and "highly original" textured patterns in men's, women's and accessories collections; so if you feel "dizzy" with desire, dig deep into your pocket for "one or two pieces to jazz up your Calvins and Armanis."

Miss Sixty C 21 | 20 | 17 | E
246 Mulberry St. (bet. Prince & Spring Sts.), F/V/S to B'way/Lafayette, 212-431-6040 ●S
386 W. Broadway (bet. Broome & Spring Sts.), C/E to Spring St., 212-334-9772
www.misssixty.com

■ "Poke around" these SoHo and NoLita '70s-flashback emporia "especially known" for "cheeky", "radical" Italian jeans (the

vote at zagat.com

Miu Miu C   22 | 22 | 18 | E

831 Madison Ave. (bet. 69th & 70th Sts.), 6 to 68th St., 212-249-9660
100 Prince St. (bet. Greene & Mercer Sts.), N/R to Prince St., 212-334-5156 S

◪ The Madison Avenue and flagship SoHo locations of this line for women and "rich teens" feel much like any "typical space", but just "browsing" the "sexy, see-through, stylish" sheaths and separates makes you feel like an "ever-cute" "hipster"; however, while "less pricey than [parent] Prada, it still puts pressure on the pocketbook" – too much for basically "playful" purses and shoes, some sniff.

Mixona ●SC   ▽ 26 | 26 | 23 | E

262 Mott St. (bet. Houston & Prince Sts.), 6 to Spring St., 646-613-0100; www.mixona.com

■ "A nice airy shop with friendly service" and "beautifully displayed merchandise", this "fun" "fave" in NoLita coaxes coquettes to come hither with its "unique collection" of "gorgeous gossamer little things" "for every taste, from basic Hanro and wacky leather items" to lust-worthy lacy bras and panties from Leigh Bantivolgio; "sexy and wearable", this "great selection" of unmentionables "should be at the top of any girl's drawer."

Modell's ●SC   17 | 12 | 11 | I

1293 Broadway (34th St.), B/D/F/N/Q/R/V/W to 34th St./Herald Sq., 212-244-4544; 800-275-6633; www.modells.com
Additional locations throughout the NY area

◪ A "New York institution" since 1889, this "basic, no-frills", "all-purpose sporting goods" chain "aims to please" with a "good" "mix" of "exercise clothing and gear", "team paraphernalia", "great buys on equipment" and "bargains on athletic shoes" – "if you can't find it here, give up"; but bashers boo at the "cramped" quarters and cite "disinterested" and "inexperienced" service.

Modernica SC   – | – | – | E

57 Greene St. (bet. Broome & Spring Sts.), 6 to Spring St., 212-219-1303; www.modernica.net

For those "doing the mid-century thing", this SoHo showroom is a "must-see", since its reissues of modern furniture classics by Charles and Ray Eames and Herman Miller, as well as George Nelson's bubble lamps, are offered at "great value" "compared with other neighborhood stores" with the same aesthetic.

Modern Stone Age SC   ▽ 22 | 20 | 20 | E

54 Greene St. (Broome St.), N/R to Prince St., 212-219-0383; www.modernstone.com

■ Step off the crowded SoHo sidewalks and into this "soothing, Zen-like store" where "beautiful" babbling fountains form a "serene" backdrop for "unusual" furniture and bath-and-kitchen accessories made out of stone, such as "stunning" fireplaces, sinks, frames and otherworldly onyx lamps; the owners, a former conceptual artist and an ex-interior architect, will also custom-make pieces for any room in the house.

186   subscribe to zagat.com

| M | P | S | C |

MOMA DESIGN STORE ⓈⒸ   26 | 23 | 17 | E
81 Spring St. (Crosby St.), 6 to Spring St., 646-613-1367 ☻
44 W. 53rd St. (bet. 5th & 6th Aves.), E/V to 5th Ave./53rd St., 212-708-9669
www.momastore.org

■ "A fabulous place to spend money" on "have-it-all" pals is this destination for "cutting-edge design"; amid the "authorized Corbu and Eames reproductions", "minimalist housewares", ergonomic gizmos, "offbeat jewelry", "graphically arresting" stationery and "funky" art books, "you won't see yourself coming and going" (and neither will the "ditzy" staff), but "the look in people's eyes when you give them a gift from MoMA" says "groovy, baby" – "you're the coolest cat in town."

Mommy Chic ⓈⒸ   – | – | – | E
235 Mulberry St. (bet. Prince & Spring Sts.), 6 to Spring St.,
646-613-1825; 866-244-2666; www.mommychic.com

This NoLita boutique houses designer/co-owner Angela Chew's own sophisticated collection of "fabulous, fun" maternity fashions, ranging from "yummy" knits and elegant hand-beaded evening gowns to more casual urban looks, weekend wear and denim pieces; the newly introduced baby-and-children's line (newborns through age 6), made primarily from fine European cottons, appeals to stylish little ones.

Montblanc ⓈⒸ   25 | 25 | 22 | VE
120 Greene St. (bet. Prince & Spring Sts.), N/R to Prince St., 212-680-1300;
866-828-4810
595 Madison Ave. (bet. 57th & 58th Sts.), N/R/W to 5th Ave./59th St.,
212-223-8888; 800-581-4810
www.montblanc.com

■ "For those who demand the best", these "quiet" shops in SoHo and on Madison Avenue are the peak of "self-pampering", providing the "ultimate writing instrument" ("everyone wants one, two . . . and then there are the collector's editions"), as well as "great cuff links", watches, leather goods and stationery; the "friendly, knowledgeable staff" provides "outstanding service" that matches the "excellent quality" of the merchandise.

Montmartre ☻ⓈⒸ   – | – | – | E
2212 Broadway (79th St.), 1/9 to 79th St., 212-875-8430
247 Columbus Ave. (71st St.), B/C to 72nd St., 212-721-7760
225 Liberty St. (S. End Ave.), N/R/W to Rector St., 212-945-7858
1157 Madison Ave. (85th St.), 4/5/6 to 86th St., 212-988-8962

Savvy shoppers head to these "neighborhood stores" – those "on the Upper West Side" have been fixtures for 20 years – that remain mighty "good places" for "always-hip New York and European designers" (typical labels include BCBG, Theory and the best-selling Rebecca Taylor) in a well-edited mix of casual-, career- and eveningwear for madame; the staff is helpful but needs reminding that "browsing should be encouraged."

Mood Fabrics Inc. Ⓒ   – | – | – | M
225 W. 37th St., 3rd fl. (7th Ave.), 1/2/3 to 34th St./Penn Station,
212-730-5003

Psst, Mick Jagger, "you can get whatever you" want, including "any and every fabric you can think of" from high-end and up-and-coming designers, plus "exotic trims" and some "surprises" at this Garment Center textile titan; "the prices and selection

vote at zagat.com

Mood Indigo 🅢🅒 – | – | – | E
181 Prince St. (bet. Sullivan & Thompson Sts.), C/E to Spring St., 212-254-1176
Take "a trip back in time" at this "salt-and-pepper-shaker heaven" in SoHo, where the kitschy array of "retro items" mostly from the '30s, '40s and '50s also includes a huge collection of colorful Fiestaware, Russel Wright dinnerware, whimsical barware and Depression-glass plates and bowls.

Moon River Chattel 🅢🅒 – | – | – | M
62 Grand St. (bet. Kent & Wyeth Aves.), Brooklyn, L to Bedford Ave., 718-388-1121
Williamsburg home-furnishings shop where you can wax nostalgic over weathered farm tables and shelves, vintage table linens and old-fashioned appliances, along with mostly reproduction toys and enamelware; in an annex across the street, the owners offer architectural salvage from old buildings and signage from long-gone carnivals.

Morgane Le Fay 🅒 26 | 25 | 23 | VE
746 Madison Ave. (bet. 64th & 65th Sts.), 212-879-9700
67 Wooster St. (bet. Grand & Spring Sts.), C/E to Spring St., 212-219-7672 🅢

■ Walking into these East 60s or SoHo stores feels like visiting a chic cathedral, with their "architectural" dresses and "ethereal" gowns lending a magical air to the high-ceilinged rooms; the "ever-unique", "fantasy" clothing "makes you wish you had a ball to attend every night", but chances are you'll need a fairy godmother to afford it.

Morgan Library Shop 🅢🅒 22 | 19 | 19 | M
29 E. 36th St. (Madison Ave.), 6 to 33rd St., 212-590-0390; www.morganlibrary.org/shop

■ Amid the workaday bustle in Murray Hill, one of NY's "most underrated museums" is "an oasis of calm" for "discerning" bibliophiles, and its "nicely designed" shop follows suit; "laid out as if Mr. Morgan planned it as well as he planned his exquisite library", it offers "tasteful" "little gifts" and "excellent-quality" cards and books "you can't find elsewhere", all mirroring the rare printed matter and drawings on display; the staff is "personable", "maybe because few people" browse this "well-kept secret."

MORGENTHAL FREDERICS 28 | 26 | 23 | VE
699 Madison Ave. (bet. 62nd & 63rd Sts.), 4/5/6/N/R/W to 59th St./Lexington Ave., 212-838-3090 🅢
944 Madison Ave. (bet. 74th & 75th Sts.), 6 to 77th St., 212-744-9444
399 W. Broadway (Spring St.), C/E to Spring St., 212-966-0099 ●🅢
www.morgenthal-fredericsny.com

■ "The Rolls-Royce" of opticians sports three Manhattan locations, all with "great" David Rockwell–designed interiors that provide appropriate showrooms for "traffic-stopping" eyewear designs that combine a "molto-trendy" look with the "latest technology"; the "wonderfully seasoned staff" is "genuinely interested in helping you find suitable frames" and create an "unusually un-stressful shopping experience"; the only catch: "you'll really think you need glasses when you see the prices."

---

188 subscribe to zagat.com

| M | P | S | C |

Morris Brothers 🆂   22 | 15 | 18 | M
2322 Broadway (84th St.), 1/9 to 86th St., 212-724-9000
■ "A mainstay for the camping set" for generations, this Upper Westsider is also an "old standby" for "anything and everything for kids" and teens, from "pajamas and gym clothes to sporting clothes" to all of the "trendy" "essentials" (think Juicy Couture and Mavi); but the less-enthralled pout that the "presentation could use a boost."

Moschino   24 | 24 | 20 | VE
803 Madison Ave. (bet. 67th & 68th Sts.), 6 to 68th St., 212-639-9600; www.moschino.it
■ Check your pulse upon entering this Upper East Side shop – it's racing from the "wacky" women's jackets, jeans, dresses and accessories, most carrying the designer's signature heart logo; "humorous decor" and "unusual window displays" "keep you smiling for hours" (especially the restroom "decorated with LEGOs"); prices can make a pretty "wild statement" too.

MOSS 🆂🅲   26 | 27 | 21 | VE
146 Greene St. (bet. Houston & Prince Sts.), N/R to Prince St., 212-226-2190; 866-888-6677; www.mossonline.com
■ All hail Murray Moss and his "cutting-edge" SoHo "shrine to good design", a "pristine citadel of modern taste" with "unusual, museum-quality merchandise"; everything – from "drop-dead beautiful" Moser crystal and Nymphenburg porcelain to vases by Hella Jongerius and "clever" lighting by Droog – is "preciously priced" and "strikingly" displayed behind glass in a "gorgeous white-walled space" where salespeople serve as well-versed curators of what's "cool."

Motherhood Maternity 🆂   17 | 12 | 16 | I
1449 Third Ave. (82nd St.), 6 to 77th St., 212-734-5984
36 W. 34th St. (bet. 5th & 6th Aves.), B/D/F/Q/R/V/W to 34th St./Herald Sq., 212-695-9106; www.motherhood.com
🗹 "Nice for the price", this nationwide maternity chain comes in handy for "casual, utilitarian" "inexpensive basics like T-shirts and jeans" – in short, "not too hip clothes at reasonable prices"; though you can "save a lot of money" initially, many miffed moms moan that the styles are "frumpy."

Movado 🆂   25 | 23 | 22 | E
Rockefeller Ctr., 610 Fifth Ave., ground level (bet. 49th & 50th Sts.), F to 47-50th Sts./Rockefeller Ctr., 212-218-7555
138 Spring St. (Wooster St.), C/E to Spring St., 212-431-0249 ●🅲
www.movado.com
🗹 Known for the "sleek, simple designs" of its oft-imitated "classic timepieces", this venerable company keeps on ticking amid the "welcoming atmosphere" of its Rockefeller Center and SoHo homes; the "service is somewhat snobbish but helpful", however even fans find the "watches are more creatively styled than the [newer] jewelry" and housewares lines.

Mrs. John L. Strong 🆂   25 | 22 | 19 | VE
Barneys, 699 Madison Ave., 2nd fl. (60th St.), N/R/W to 59th St./Lexington Ave., 212-833-2060
■ What insiders insist is the "Bentley of the society stationers" recently changed hands, but the previous owner stayed on as

vote at zagat.com   189

president to ensure the "high-end", "traditional" letter paper and invitations remain "some of the best in the world"; tucked away on the second floor of Barney's, it still purveys the same "gorgeous", "classic" products, and if some whisper the "service is less than friendly", more "love it for the fact that it represents seven decades of moneyed Manhattan."

MTV Store S | 10 | 15 | 11 | M |
1515 Broadway (44th St.), 1/2/3/7/N/Q/R/S/W to 42nd St./Times Sq., 212-846-5655; www.mtv.com

If "this is a store, where are they hiding the merchandise?" crank kiddies hot for "cute", "tiny V-necks, CDs, DVDs" and other "cheesy stuff" for the newest MTV generation; what "looks like it might've been a bathroom before remodeling" is right below the Times Square studio where *Total Live Request* is shot, so it's "crowded" with teenybopper tourists pawing the "thrown-together" merch, particularly "after spring break", when the shop gets "cleaned out."

Munder-Skiles | – | – | – | E |
799 Madison Ave., 3rd fl. (bet. 67th & 68th Sts.), 6 to 68th St., 212-717-0150

"Garden furniture takes on a new elegance" at this "Hamptons-crowd choice" in the East 60s where designer John Danzer offers unique outdoor (and some indoor) chairs, tables and accessories; many items are based on originals from Monticello and Edith Wharton's home, The Mount, for which he has the exclusive license, and others display modern influences; N.B. consultation is also available.

Museum of the City of New York, The S | – | – | – | M |
1220 Fifth Ave. (103rd St.), 6 to 103rd St., 212-534-1672, ext. 227; www.mcny.org

Whether tourist or local, nearly "every kid and adult will find things to rave about" at this museum shop dedicated to all things Gotham; from inexpensive "period-style toys to books", maps and pricey, framed Bernice Abbott reproductions, there's all sorts of bites of The Apple to nurture your NYC nostalgia – it might be the only place in the five boroughs where you can still buy a spaldeen and a stickball bat.

Music Inn C | – | – | – | M |
169 W. Fourth St. (bet. Cornelia & Jones Sts.), A/C/E/F/V/S to W. 4th St., 212-243-5715

They usually "charge you a dollar to walk in", "they treat you like a piece of dirt, and you go away" "loving" it: this world-music instrument store is one of those "strange" Greenwich Village institutions that makes NY unique, and "if you can get the owner and persuade him to let you look", you "can grab a great" find at a "reasonable price" – just "expect to go back several times before you find him in."

Mxyplyzyk S C | 24 | 20 | 14 | M |
125 Greenwich Ave. (Horatio & 13th Sts.), A/C/E to 14th St./8th Ave., 212-989-4300; www.mxyplyzyk.com

"Cool, cool, cool" West Village "boutique of fun and fancy" featuring hip tabletop, kitchen and bath items with a "high-design quotient" for almost low-rent prices; a rather "brusque" staff presides over the "crowded" space "crammed" with "random" and "funky gift" ideas – see-through scales and doggie banks – "that you won't find anywhere else."

subscribe to zagat.com

| M | P | S | C |

Myoptics S | 25 | 23 | 22 | E |
82 Christopher St. (bet. Bleecker St. & 7th Ave.), 1/9 to Christopher St., 212-741-9550 C
123 Prince St. (bet. Greene & Wooster Sts.), N/R to Prince St., 212-598-9306
96 Seventh Ave. (bet. 15th & 16th Sts.), 1/2/3/9/F/V/L to 14th St./ Union Sq., 212-633-6014
42 St. Marks Pl. (bet. 1st & 2nd Aves.), 6 to Astor Pl., 212-533-1577 C
www.myoptics.com
■ "Edgy glasses for the urban-chic geek" are the trademark of this "funky" outfit where a "fabulous selection" of "wonderful" frames is matched by "impeccable workmanship"; the salespeople "really like their jobs" and "have a great eye – no pun intended – for what looks best on you", and though a few warn that "some locations are better than others", most are satisfied with the "mix of style and quality."

Nancy & Co. S C | 20 | 17 | 16 | E |
1242 Madison Ave. (89th St.), 4/5/6 to 86th St., 212-427-0770
◪ Women seeking an "interesting selection" of tasteful, "classy" sportswear, "gorgeous knits" and "unusual" accessories find this Upper Eastsider "worth a visit" when "in the neighborhood"; but malcontents mutter over the "frumpy", "overpriced basics" and suggest the staff isn't such great company, either.

Nancy Geist S C | ▽ 24 | 23 | 21 | E |
107 Spring St. (Mercer St.), N/R to Prince St.; 6 to Spring St., 212-925-7192
■ "Strategically plan your walk home" so you can "pass by the windows" of this gallery-esque SoHo footwear shop with curvy, cushy benches and "ogle" the "gorgeous" creations within; the "stylish" handmade Italian sandals and shoes come in lots of "cute" colors, and they're so "lovely" they make you "want to maintain your pedicure"; while the wistful "wish I could afford more" (they're a "bit pricey"), others opine the tags are "right for the quality."

Nancy Koltes at Home S | – | – | – | VE |
31 Spring St. (bet. Mott & Mulberry Sts.), 6 to Spring St., 212-219-2271; www.nancykoltes.com
This "lovely, little" "find" on Spring Street sells "gorgeous stuff" like "beautiful bedding"(600-thread-count) made in Italy, table linens and towels; it's also the only place in New York where you can find coveted Scandia Down comforters.

Nanette Lepore S C | 25 | 21 | 22 | E |
423 Broome St. (bet. Crosby & Lafayette Sts.), 6 to Spring St., 212-219-8265; www.nanettelepore.com
■ "On a skinny day", stop by this "pretty" SoHo boutique with its "bright" pink floor, birdcages and chandelier to try on "crisp, colorful" "delicate and beautifully patterned" dresses or one of the "well-made", "flirty" separates; converts "swoon" about the "relatively light price tag" (compared with other designers), calling this "a sure winner for extremely feminine clothing."

National Wholesale Liquidators ● S | 15 | 7 | 7 | I |
632 Broadway (Houston St.), F to B'way/Lafayette St., 212-979-2400
691 Co-Op City Blvd. (bet. Carver Loop & Peartree Ave.), Bronx, 6 to Pelham Bay Park, 718-320-7771

(continued)

vote at zagat.com

(continued)
National Wholesale Liquidators
2901 59th St. (bet. Bay Pkwy. & 23rd Ave.), Brooklyn, N to 23rd Ave., 718-256-9200
4802-22 New Utrecht Ave. (48th St.), Brooklyn, W to 50th St., 718-438-2604
71-01 Kissena Blvd. (71st Ave.), Queens, 7 to Main St., 718-591-3900
www.nationalwholesaleliquidators.com

☒ "For this and that from here and there", it's a "riot to shop in" this "dollar store on steroids" in NoHo and the boroughs; "students moving in for the semester" "fill carts up quickly" with "candles, cleaning products, picture frames, salted mixed nuts, batteries, face wash, sponges" and other "dorm-room chic" "essentials", some with "brand names"; it's "sloppy, dumpy" and the staff is "rude", but "do you really care when the prices are this cheap?"

Nat Sherman ⓢ | 26 | 26 | 26 | E |
500 Fifth Ave. (42nd St.), 4/5/6/7/S to 42nd St./Grand Central, 212-764-5000; www.natsherman.com

■ It's always "a treat to visit" this "comfortable" Midtown "mecca for smokers" where "everything is first class", from the "unparalleled service" to the "great accessories" and "fab signature brands"; while "the best doesn't come cheap" at this "landmark" family-owned establishment, "anyone who is serious about tobacco needs to pay homage here at least once."

Nautica ●◐ⓢⓒ | 19 | 20 | 18 | E |
Rockefeller Plaza, 50 Rockefeller Plaza (bet. 5th & 6th Aves.), 1/2/F to 47th-50th Sts./Rockefeller Ctr., 212-664-9594; 877-628-8422; www.nautica.com

☒ "More Cape Cod than Ocean City", the "something-white" "classics" at this West 50s chainster service men and women who've sailed "above and beyond the J. Crew yacht wanna-bes and Tommy Hilfiger preppy" set; if the merchandise is similar to everything else "you already have in your closet", at least it's "good quality", though money-wise mates say "save money" and stay on the lookout "until they have a sale."

NBA Store ⓢⓒ | 23 | 25 | 16 | E |
666 Fifth Ave. (52nd St.), 6/E/V to 53rd St./Lexington Ave., 212-515-6221; www.nbastore.com

☒ "Your one-stop shop for all your NBA gear" is this East 50s store that's "great for gifts for the basketball aficionados" on your list; sportswear includes jerseys, T-shirts, warm-up jackets and sneakers emblazoned with "lots of different team" logos, and the interior's a "playland for kids of all ages", with a "great court inside"; the service, however, gets a penalty for "indifference", and others cry foul over the "expensive" merchandise.

NBC Experience ⓢ | 17 | 21 | 15 | M |
30 Rockefeller Ctr. (49th St.), 1/9/B/D/F/N/R/Q to 47-50 Sts./Rockefeller Ctr., 212-632-3975; 800-884-2212; www.shopnbc.com/nbcstore

☒ "If you're the type who can't live without logo items from your favorite TV shows, you'll love this" "colorful, playful experience complete with tours, interactive exhibits, souvenirs of NY, *Today*, *Will and Grace*, *Friends*, *SNL* T-shirts" and "scrubs from *ER*"; the tri-level Rockefeller Center mega-store is "great for tourists", boob-tube "freaks" and "children, as there's so much to see", do

M P S C

and buy, but high-minded surveyors huff "if only what they spent on this junk would go into their ever-softening news division."

Nemo Tile Company | 23 | 19 | 19 | M |
48 E. 21st St. (bet. B'way & Park Ave. S.), 6 to 23rd St., 212-505-0099
177-02 Jamaica Ave. (Liberty Ave.), Queens, F to Hillside, 718-291-5969
800-636-6845; www.nemotile.com

■ These family-owned "low-key stores" in the Flatiron and Jamaica are "the places" to go for tile, offering the "full range, from basics to luxury styles", as well as plumbing and bathroom accessories; the "helpful service" ("if you get the right salesperson, the advice is golden") and "great prices" make this pair among the "best" resources for budget-minded DIYers.

Nest S | – | – | – | M |
396A Seventh Ave. (bet. 12th & 13th Sts.), Brooklyn, F to 7th Ave., 718-965-3491; 866-231-1900

Perched on a growing stretch of Park Slope, this home-furnishings newcomer, owned by two former graphic designers, aims to feather the nests of fellow dwellers; the orange store sign and perky blue exterior feel like an urban welcome wagon, inviting customers to enter and explore the Japanese stoneware, retro-modern lamps, Indian bedspreads, fuzzy throws and colorful terry-cloth towels, all arranged in cool cubes against a backdrop of painted brick walls and a groovy green fireplace.

Neue Galerie S C | – | – | – | E |
1048 Fifth Ave. (86th St.), 4/5/6 to 86th St., 212-628-6200;
www.neuegalerie.org

Upper Fifth Avenue's newest museum – Ronald Lauder's lavish gift – boasts a shop as "elegant" as the gallery's edifice and Viennese-style cafe and as interesting as its innovative 19th- and 20th-century art; "beautiful books, prints" and items inspired by artists like Hoffman and Loos are hawked by English- and "German-speaking staffers who really know what they're doing", though some patrons plead "please find more glass and porcelain."

New Balance S | 23 | 17 | 19 | M |
821 Third Ave. (50th St.), 6/E/V to 53rd St./Lexington Ave., 212-421-4444
51 W. 42nd St. (bet. 5th & 6th Aves.), 7/B/D/F/V to 42nd St./6th Ave., 212-997-9112
www.newbalance.com

■ Perhaps they're "not as flashy" as some of the other sneaker stores, but these "cool" emporiums in the East 50s and West 40s sell "the greatest shoes on the planet" according to admirers (chief among them "runners"); the "seasoned staff" will "help you find the best pair for your foot type", with lots of options for "odd sizes", and they "always carry the latest models before anyone else."

New Museum Store C | – | – | – | E |
583 Broadway (bet. Houston & Prince Sts.), N/R to Prince St., 212-219-1222; www.newmuseum.org

Hip culture-vultures go underground to this ample SoHo museum shop for edgy postmodern gifts and lit; a nice chunk of the extensive selection of artist's monographs and books on design theory are marked down as much as 70 percent, and the only appropriate response to a Keith Haring domino set or a Yoshitomo Nara snow globe is a resoundingly positive "snap!"

vote at zagat.com

| M | P | S | C |

New York Central Art Supply 🆂🅲   25 | 15 | 21 | M
62 Third Ave. (11th St.), 4/5/6/L/N/Q/R/W to 14th St./Union Sq., 212-473-7705; 800-950-6111
■ The "encyclopedic assortment" of "quality" paper and "general printmaking supplies" gives bookmakers the "shivers" at this "old-school" "king of art-supply" stores in the East Village; the family-run sixtysomething joint is "cramped and ugly", but their stock is "beautiful", "the staff knows what they're doing" and "you can't go wrong with the place where Andy Warhol bought his supplies."

New York Doll Hospital ⌀🅲   – | – | – | E
787 Lexington Ave., 2nd fl. (bet. 61st & 62nd Sts.), 4/5/6/N/R/W to 59th St./Lexington Ave., 212-838-7527
A "hole-in-the-wall" tucked away on the second floor, this 100-year-old Upper East Side shop not only purveys antique and collectible dolls, it's also the "cutest trauma center" for teddies and inanimate moppets – and it's piled high with parts to prove it; owner Irving Chais "knows what he's doing" – and parents confronted with emergency situations are "thrilled this store exists."

New York Elegant Fabric   – | – | – | E
222 W. 40th St. (bet. 7th & 8th Aves.), 1/2/3/7/N/Q/R/S/W to 42nd St./Times Sq., 212-302-4980
Though its offerings may be "on the expensive side for the district", this West 40s stop is worth investigating, as it "always has some very unique fabric" finds on hand that you "don't seem to see anywhere else", particularly piece goods for men's suits.

New York Firefighter's Friend   23 | 18 | 22 | M
263 Lafayette St. (bet. Prince & Spring Sts.), 6 to Spring St., 212-226-3142; 800-229-9258; www.nyfirestore.com
■ An "excellent way to pay tribute" "since 9/11" is to spend your "money where it helps to support the heroes" at "NY's Bravest" store in SoHo; it's "authentically run-down" but well stocked with "firefighter's garb", including T-shirts, sweatshirts and BBQ aprons for both sexes and all ages; a variety of gift items – calendars and keychains, blankets and books – completes the collection.

New York Golf Center ◐🆂🅲   26 | 22 | 17 | E
131 W. 35th St. (bet. B'way & 7th Ave.), B/D/F/N/Q/R/V/W to 34th St./Herald Sq., 212-564-2255

Golf Club at Chelsea Piers ◐🆂🅲
Pier 59 (18th St. & West Side Hwy.), A/C/E to 14th St., 212-242-8899 www.newyorkgolf.com
■ Covering 9,000 sq. ft., this "huge" Garment Center chain offshoot "feels like you're in the clubhouse of a really nice" golf facility; the "helpful staff" guides you through the "great selection" of "single clubs and full sets", apparel, shoes and accessories at a cost that's "par for the course"; its smaller sibling on the main floor of the Golf Club at Chelsea Piers also has "excellent equipment" from brands like Callaway and Cobra, but wallet-watchers warn about "Pebble Beach prices on the Hudson", advising "just go to hit golf balls."

New York Look, The 🅲   21 | 16 | 13 | E
2030 Broadway (69th St.), 1/2/3/9 to 72nd St., 212-362-8650
551 Fifth Ave. (45th St.), 4/5/6/7/S to 42nd St./Grand Central, 212-557-0909 ◐🆂

194   **subscribe to zagat.com**

| **M** | **P** | **S** | **C** |

(continued)
New York Look, The
*30 Lincoln Plaza (bet. B'way & 62nd St.), 1/9/A/B/C/D to 59th St./
Columbus Circle, 212-245-6511* ●S
*570 Seventh Ave. (41st St.), 1/2/3/7/N/Q/R/S/W to 42nd St./Times Sq.,
212-382-2760*
468 W. Broadway (Houston St.), C/E to Spring St., 212-995-5488 ●S
◪ "Ignore the cheesy name" say fans of this women's apparel chain, whose branches "look like tourist marts from the outside" but on the inside contain "decent-quality" contemporary "career and dress-up" threads, "well-made shoes" and "stunning costume jewelry" by "small designers from all over the world"; "good sales" mitigate the "extortionate prices", but wear "armor to fend off" the "overbearing" staff, "legendary for being pushy."

New York 911 S | – | – | – | I |
*263 Lafayette St. (bet. Prince & Spring Sts.), 6 to Spring St.,
212-219-3907; www.ny911.com*
Shoppers stop in the name of the law at this SoHo sister to the Firefighter's Friend where the Finest stash can be had for a steal; a space as tight as a holding cell is packed with shirts, patches, magnets, coffee mugs, ashtrays, shot glasses and even golf balls, all related to the men and women in blue; there's even a squishy toy patrol car and an Emergency Service Unit action figure for your brood of little crime-busters at home.

New York Public Library Shop | 21 | 18 | 17 | M |
*455 Fifth Ave. (40th St.), 4/5/6/7/S to 42nd St./Grand Central,
212-340-0839*
42nd St. & Fifth Ave., 7 to 5th Ave., 212-930-0641
*Schomburg Ctr., 515 Malcolm X Blvd. (135th St.), 2/3 to 135th St.,
212-491-2206*
www.thelibraryshop.org
■ Take a study break at the Library shops to "find the perfect gift for that fussy aunt in Wisconsin", particularly if she's of a "scholarly" bent; "lovely books", "good kids'" stuff and "fun NY memorabilia" are "expertly presented and reasonably priced"; N.B. the Schomburg Center's boutique specializes in African handicrafts and literature by and about African-American writers.

New York Replacement Parts Corp. | ▽ 22 | 5 | 17 | M |
*1456 Lexington Ave. (bet. 94th & 95th Sts.), 6 to 96th St., 212-534-0818;
800-228-4718; www.nyrp.com*
■ What some boast is the "best plumbing supply house around" may be this "reliable" East 90s store, with a "fine showroom for bath fixtures" and a general store "next door that has everything"; the staff is "incredibly knowledgeable" and the "prices are great", and though you should "prepare to wait", if you're "patient", you "can get what you want."

New York Transit Museum ●SC | 19 | 17 | 16 | M |
*Grand Central, Main Concourse, 4/5/6/7/S to 42nd St./Grand Central,
212-878-0106; www.mta.nyc.ny.us/museum*
◪ Next stop, Grand Central for an underground spree at "the deepest store you'll ever visit", "selling everything subway-related"; "token cuff links, transit-map ties" and "MetroCard tote bags" are part of the "fun, weird stuff" the city is made of, but the shop does "need a better selection of merchandise."

		M	P	S	C

Nice Price 🆂🅲   19 | 10 | 14 | I
493 Columbus Ave. (bet. 83rd & 84th Sts.), 1/9 to 86th St., 212-362-1020; www.clothingline.com
▱ Some stylish skinflints say this "bare-bones" Upper Westsider is a "sure thing" for "savings well below wholesale" on duds "you drooled over in other stores", including "random finds" from Diane von Furstenberg and Cynthia Rowley; though "bargains" for "every bodytype and taste" continue to "end up triaged here", the "disarray" has those who knew it when waxing "18 years ago, this place was wonderful – or was I much poorer and less fussy?"

Nicole Farhi 🆂🅲   23 | 25 | 19 | VE
10 E. 60th St. (bet. 5th & Madison Aves.), N/R/W to 59th St./Fifth Ave., 212-223-8811
■ When London's calling, *au courant* Anglophiles head to this hip, East 60s lifestyle shop, whose floors – a stylish series of floating glass, walnut and bluestone platforms – display male and female "classic" clothes, accessories and "especially well-done leather" goods, plus "wonderful home furnishings" and antique trifles; those hungry for more hit the "excellent restaurant" downstairs.

Nicole Miller 🅲   22 | 20 | 20 | E
780 Madison Ave. (bet. 66th & 67th Sts.), 6 to 68th St., 212-288-9779
134 Prince St. (bet. W. B'way & Wooster St.), N/R to Prince St., 212-343-1362; www.nicolemiller.com 🆂
■ Play "dress up" at these small SoHo and Upper East Side boutiques where "from the [scarf] to the purse, they get it right every time", whether your ideal "special-occasion outfit" is "that little black dress you've been looking for forever" or something in the designer's signature "wild patterns and colors"; the fun is enhanced by "helpful employees", particularly on Prince Street.

Niketown ●🆂   23 | 24 | 17 | M
6 E. 57th St. (bet. 5th & Madison Aves.), 4/5/6/N/R/W to 59th St./Lexington Ave., 212-891-6453; www.niketown.com
▱ The "Shangri-la of Nike-ness" may be this "mega-store" in the East 50s that's a "wonderland for fans" of the swoosh-buckling brand; the "presentation is mind-blowing", with five floors filled with "up-to-the-minute merchandise", including the "newest" sneakers and the "best work-out clothes"; though a few feel it's "a little light on the women's selection" and the "service is harried", more maintain it provides a "great shopping experience."

1950 ⌿   – | – | – | VE
440 Lafayette St. (bet. Astor Pl. & E. 4th St.), 6 to Astor Pl., 212-995-1950
Airy, expansive and expensive East Village furniture store offering "beautiful", hard-to-find mid-century French pieces like Jean Prouvé tables and Charlotte Perriand bookshelves, along with tables and chairs by George Nakashima, the Japanese-American craftsman whose graceful, organic wood furniture is rarely spotted for sale outside his home state of Pennsylvania.

99x 🆂🅲   23 | 19 | 18 | M
84 E.10th St. (bet. 3rd & 4th Aves.), N/R to 8th St.; 6 to Astor Pl., 212-460-8599; www.99xny.com
■ "Anglophile heaven", whether you're a "mod, a punk or just your regular indie kid", this "super-friendly" British-owned East Village boutique "rocks" one step beyond with its "not for poseurs" "funky

196   **subscribe to zagat.com**

footwear" like TUK creepers, "hard-to-find Doc Martens" and "old-school Pumas" and hipster clothing with "retro charm" from labels like Ben Sherman and Fred Perry; scenesters also dig the pork-pie hats and oh-so-New-Wave skinny ties.

NINE WEST ⬤S | 18 | 17 | 14 | M |

675 Fifth Ave. (bet. 53rd & 54th Sts.), E/V to 5th Ave./53rd St., 212-319-6893; www.ninewest.com
For additional locations, see Top Chain Stores index

◼ "Go West – you can't go wrong" at this "jam-packed" "safe bet" if you need "attractive" "everyday workhorse" shoes "at everyday prices" or the "latest runway knockoffs"; "a perfect combo of style and comfort", the "fashionable footwear" inspires "average Janes" "all across America" to "follow the trends while going easy on the pocketbook"; but the less enthused point to "spotty service" that "takes a lifetime" and conclude this "generic" chain is "for those who miss suburban malls."

Nisa S | – | – | – | E |

250 Elizabeth St. (bet. Houston & Prince Sts.), 6 to Spring St., 212-925-4772
"Really sexy little numbers" reveal revelers who rejoice in the "pretty, frilly" one-of-a-kind lingerie and "beautiful bathing suits" "for women with real bodies" at this "hidden treasure" in NoLita; from the "small, intimate space" with tin ceilings, antique furniture and air of romance to the "nicest staff ever", it's "one of those finds you can't resist."

Noir et Blanc...Bis C | – | – | – | M |

19 W. 23rd St. (bet. 5th & 6th Aves.), N/R to 23rd St., 212-627-1750
Despite the name, not everything is 'black and white' in this Flatiron store – *au contraire*, the goods are arranged by color, the jewel-like tones sparking up the women's tailored separates (plus a beaded top or two) from a range of U.S., European and British designers like Ghost; semiprecious jewelry, velvety scarves and purses round out the ensembles.

Noose, The ⬤C | – | – | – | M |

261 W. 19th St. (bet. 7th & 8th Aves.), 1 to 18th St., 212-807-1789 S
409 W. 13th St. (bet 9th Ave. & Washington St.), A/C/E to 14th St./8th Ave., 212-807-7297
For 20 years, all walks of New Yorkers have been fit to be tied at this little hard-core boutique on a quaint Chelsea side street where latex bondage suits can run up to $2,000; the well-regarded store is stuffed to the gills with custom-made and European imported toys for serious players who go in for the P.E.S. electrical system and other only slightly less shocking accoutrement; the 13th Street branch is conveniently located inside the gay leather bar The Lure.

Norman's Sound & Vision ⬤SC | 20 | 12 | 16 | I |

67 Cooper Sq. (bet. 7th & 8th Sts.), 6 to Astor Pl., 212-473-6599
33 St. Marks Pl. (bet. 2nd & 3rd Aves.), 6 to Astor Pl., 212-253-6162

◼ The "excellent stock" of CDs, vinyl, videos and DVDs at these sibs in the East Village reflects proprietor "Norman's encyclopedic knowledge" and his connections – "he often gets discs before they're released"; the goods are "jammed into the displays so tight, it takes an effort to pull them out", but when you do, you too might boast "I love paying $10 for the same brand-new item my friends bought for $18 at HMV."

| M | P | S | C |

North Beach Leather S C | 21 | 21 | 22 | E |
523 Broadway (Spring St.), N/R to Prince St., 212-625-8668; www.northbeachleather.com
■ "Always rockin'", soft as "butter" creations rule at this SoHo haunt, "fully stocked" for girls and guys lookin' to "get leathered up from head to toe"; skin hues range from basic black to knockout colors, with innovative pieces that go the gamut, from spaghetti-strap dresses to low-waist pants to collectibles that go a "little overboard" (remember Elvis' studded cape and Elton's fringe jacket?); the "dedicated staff" is just one more reason it's "stayed ahead of the pack."

N. Peal C | – | – | – | E |
5 W. 56th St. (5th Ave.), N/R/W to 5th Ave./59th St., 212-333-3500; www.npeal.com
Peel off that old merino crewneck and try on one of the plush puppies in this West 50s boutique, with its rows of classy, clingy cashmere sweaters and stacks of scarves (say 'pashmina, please') on curvy blonde-wood shelves, all from the venerable Scottish firm; the salespeople are as warm and fuzzy as the merchandise.

NYCD ● S | ∇ 21 | 15 | 22 | I |
426 Amsterdam Ave. (bet. 80th & 81st Sts.), 1/9 to 79th St., 212-724-4466; www.nycd-online.com
■ "Reminiscent of Village stores", this "mom-and-pop shop" is "legendary on the Upper West Side" as "the best place for cheap, used CDs", with an "excellent mix" of rock, jazz, soundtracks, "hard-to-find" and import titles; go for gridlock surfing through the über-bargain boxes "on the sidewalks on weekends."

Oculus 20/20 ● | – | – | – | E |
189 Bedford Ave. (bet. N. 6th & 7th Sts.), Brooklyn, L to Bedford Ave., 718-666-0040 S
522 Henry St. (Union St.), Brooklyn, F/G to Carroll St., 718-852-9871
"Great glasses" from tight collections of high-end designers like Lunor and Frances Klein are the focus at these Brooklyn siblings where the chic goods are displayed in bright "jewel-box spaces"; eyewear isn't the only "find" – during the holiday season the stores also stock a small selection of fashionable hats and necklaces; much like the neighborhood, the Williamsburg shop is a bit funkier.

Oilily S C | 24 | 23 | 20 | VE |
870 Madison Ave. (bet. 70th & 71st Sts.), 6 to 68th St., 212-628-0100; www.oililyusa.com
◪ "Pippi Longstocking lives!" exclaim enthusiasts who head to the Upper East Side branch of this Netherlands-based chain for "cute", "funky" infants', children's and women's "clothes with bright, fun, happy dispositions" in a "kaleidoscope of colors" and patterns; the styles are so "unique", with "amazingly high prices", that some surveyors say it's "just not my bag" – "considering how fast kids grow you may be better off investing in college."

OK Cigars ● ● S C | – | – | – | E |
383A W. Broadway (bet. Broome & Spring Sts.), C/E to Spring St., 212-965-9065; www.ok-cigars.com
More than just ok, this SoHo cigar shop's welcoming interior resembles an old-fashioned apothecary, with its wooden shelving, art-covered walls and cozy jumble of stock featuring a large

M | P | S | C

selection of imported humidors and both new and antique lighters, cutters and ash trays; the large range of well-kept, hand-rolled stogies includes both major and boutique brands.

O'Lampia Studio 🆂🅲   ▽ 27 | 20 | 23 | E
155 Bowery (bet. Broome & Delancey Sts.), 6 to Spring St., 212-925-1660; www.olampia.com

■ It's "the best on the Bowery" brag boosters of this lighting store that shines with its "simple", "beautiful", custom-made designs that are "well crafted" by folks who "know how to handle their materials"; all this "great style" is "worth the price", especially when you factor in the "strong service" that "goes the extra mile."

Olde Good Things 🆂   – | – | – | VE
19 Greenwich Ave. (W. 10th St.), A/C/E/F/V to W. 4th St., 212-229-0850 🅲
124 W. 24th St. (bet. 6th & 7th Aves.), F/V to 23rd St., 212-989-8401 🅲
400 Atlantic Ave. (Bond St.), Brooklyn, N/R to DeKalb Ave., 718-935-9742
888-551-7333; www.oldegoodthings.com

"Prepare to dig in and get your hands dirty" at this four-floor Chelsea warehouse, a "great" "treasure trove of salvaged past grandeur" ranging from doorknobs and sconces to mirrors, marble mantels, humongous iron gates and every pediment and ornament in between; vintage building materials like tin ceilings and wood beams are also part of the pickings; N.B. the Brooklyn branch is open only on weekends and is slowly being phased out, while the Greenwich Avenue offshoot is new.

Olden Camera 🅲   21 | 9 | 16 | M
1265 Broadway (32nd St.), B/D/F/N/Q/R/V/W to 34th St./Herald Sq., 212-725-1234

◪ This "leftover from the old camera neighborhood" near Herald Square pretty much sells just that – old cameras; "hard-to-find gear" including antique folding types, '50s Brownies and 8 and 16mm film equipment make for "interesting" rummaging, and it might be the "best place to go for used Leicas and accessories" on the cheap, but with an "aged" setting and "gruff staff", it's "surely a pale reflection of its once-glorious self."

OLD NAVY ●🆂🅲   15 | 14 | 14 | I
149-150 W. 34th St. (bet. 6th & 7th Aves.), B/D/F/N/Q/R/V/W to 34th St./ Herald Sq., 212-594-0115; 800-653-6289; www.oldnavy.com
Additional locations throughout the NY area

◪ Its crew of fans insists there's "no better place" to scoop up "super-duper", "cheap" but "durable", "casual" "necessities like tanks, sweats, pajamas", jeans, jackets and flip-flops "for the whole family" than this "fast-food" fashion chain; its fleet of foes feel "rock-bottom pricing" doesn't make up for "old styles no sailor would ever wear" and "service that sometimes stinks."

Olive and Bette's 🅲   22 | 17 | 17 | E
252 Columbus Ave. (72nd St.), 1/2/3 to 72nd St., 212-579-2178
1070 Madison Ave. (bet. 80th & 81st Sts.), 6 to 77th St., 212-717-9655
158 Spring St. (bet. W. B'way & Wooster St.), C/E to Spring St., 646-613-8772 🆂
www.oliveandbettes.com

◪ "Trendy teenyboppers" beat a fast track to these "adorable" boutiques, tempted by their "quintessential tops shop" reputation ("keep the cute T-shirts coming!") and "fresh", "super-fun" attitude;

vote at zagat.com   **199**

prices are "awfully steep", but "girl power" prevails thanks to a "knowledgeable" staff "always full of suggestions."

Oliver Peoples C — 26 | 24 | 22 | VE
755 Madison Ave. (bet. 65th & 66th Sts.), 6 to 68th St., 212-585-3433 S
366 W. Broadway (Broome St.), N/R to Prince St., 212-925-5400
888-568-1655; www.oliverpeoples.com

■ "The originator of the modern 'cool glasses' scene" presents a "huge" selection of "gorgeous" frames that are "cutting-edge trendy, but not to the point that they'll be out of style next season"; the SoHo and Upper East Side branches are "beautifully designed", the staff is "helpful" and the "quality" of the eyewear "makes it easier to see your empty wallet after you pay their prices."

OM Boutique S C — _ | _ | _ | VE
134 E. 27th St. (Lexington Ave.), 6 to 28th St., 212-532-5620 ●
100 Lexington Ave. (27th St.), 6 to 28th St., 212-684-5194

Film buffs bowled over by Bollywood, the thrillingly over-the-top cinema from India, and enthusiasts of ethnic goods covet the colorful striking wares at this Lexington Avenue shop filled with gorgeous silk saris, sarongs, men's *kurtas*, patterned bedspreads, statues of deities and Indian CDs; venture around the corner to OM Saree Palace for more treasures or to be fitted by a staff tailor in the warm, enveloping atmosphere.

OMO Norma Kamali C — 20 | 22 | 16 | E
11 W. 56th St. (bet. 5th & 6th Aves.), N/Q/R/W to 57th St., 212-957-9797; 800-852-6254; www.normakamalicollection.com

◪ The designer who "brought shoulder pads and sneakers into fashion" is still going strong in her cool, museum-like West 50s boutique, all of whose rooms (and you, when you leave) "smell like her fantastic fragrance"; citing the "beautiful swimwear" and "eclectic vintage pieces", supporters say "her stuff never goes out of style", but critics counter there's "little innovation here" – the "best characteristic is the store itself"; P.S. OMO stands for 'On My Own'.

OM Yoga ● S C — _ | _ | _ | M
826 Broadway, 6th fl. (12th St.), 4/5/6/L/N/Q/R/W to 14th St./Union Sq., 212-254-9642; www.omyoga.com

"Zen in a store" sigh a smitten handful who head to this handy nook in the popular yoga destination, now located above the Strand, for colorful logoed T-shirts, strike-a-pose yoga pants (some made of hemp blends), mats and books and kits by owner Cyndi Lee; but not everyone is flexible about the cost, claiming it's "expensive for clothes and paraphernalia you can find elsewhere at better prices."

1 on G ● S C — _ | _ | _ | M
55 Great Jones St. (bet. Bowery & Lafayette St.), 6 to Bleecker St., 212-505-6610; www.oneong.com

Iconoclasts of both sexes hotfoot it to Japanese stylist Midori "Dreamy" Nakagawa's huge high-tech hub in NoHo for offbeat designer wear from an international (with an accent on the Far East) roster of labels, unique tees designed by tattoo artists and cartoonists, funky handmade jewelry and tchotchkes from India and beyond; fittingly enough, the way-out wares are displayed on a ceiling conveyor belt reminiscent of a dry cleaner's implement.

	M	P	S	C

One Shubert Alley ●SC   20 | 15 | 14 | M
1 Shubert Alley (bet. 44th & 45th Sts.), A/C/E to 42nd St./Port Authority, 212-944-4133; 800-223-1320; www.broadwaynewyork.com

■ One singular shopping sensation, and you can forget the rest, for surveyors say this tiny store for "all things Broadway" is second best to none, son; located in the Theater District's heart, it's a "must for tourists and local theater queens" lusting "for novelties from [current] shows", and since the "staff doesn't bat an eyelash when you enter", you can hum along to the score of *Thoroughly Modern Millie* without embarrassment while you browse; its sister at 1535 Broadway also carries Big Apple souvenirs.

Only Hearts ●◗SC   21 | 21 | 19 | M
386 Columbus Ave. (bet. 78th & 79th Sts.), 1/9 to 79th St.; B/C to 81st St., 212-724-5608
230 Mott St. (bet. Prince & Spring Sts.), 6 to Spring St., 212-431-3694
www.onlyhearts.com

■ "Lingerie that's comfy and sexy – who knew?" coo coquettes aquiver over these "cute little shops" on the Upper West Side and NoLita; it's "fun to browse" through the jewelry cases and the "crowded racks" filled with "good basic" "staples" and "lots of sassy", lace-trimmed "colorful" camis and chemises "you can even wear out clubbing"; P.S. there's also an innerwear-inspired line of "adorable clothes" and a new yoga-oriented 'spa' line.

On Stage Dance Shop C   – | – | – | M
197 Madison Ave. (bet 34th & 35th Sts.), 6 to 33rd St., 212-725-1174

The no-frills ambiance at this compact Murray Hill may not prompt rounds of applause, but the neatly organized dancewear from labels like Capezio, Danskin and Danza may elicit encore visits; it's a bonanza for basics as well as hip street-inspired looks, with loads of leggings, camis, tights and jazz pants underscored by a small selection of ballet slippers, dance shoes and kids' tutus.

On Your Toes Dancewear C   – | – | – | M
2090 Hylan Blvd. (bet. Hamden & Hunter Aves.), Staten Island, 718-980-4880

One of the "best stores on Staten Island for dancewear" hail a handful of hoofers who head to this accessible shop for leotards, activewear and tights from top brands like Capezio and Danskin balanced by a showstopping selection of jazz, tap and *pointe* shoes; would-be performers and center-stagers who like to test the goods first can pivot and *relevé* away on the wood floor.

Orchard Corset SC   – | – | – | M
157 Orchard St. (bet. Rivington & Stanton Sts.), F/J/M/Z to Delancey/Essex Sts., 212-674-0786; www.orchardcorset.com

"No naughty nighties here, just good everyday lingerie" and "spot-on fitting" from a "family of pros" opine patrons who "come on down" to this 73-year-old Lower East Side institution; the "selection and prices can't be beat", with "great deals on nice bras" in "every size", but the less-enthused lace into the "makeshift changing room" and "run-down" decor, declaring "oy! what an experience."

Oriental Lamp Shade Co. C   ∇ 27 | 19 | 21 | E
816 Lexington Ave. (bet. 62nd & 63rd Sts.), 4/5/6/N/R/W to 59th St./Lexington Ave., 212-832-8190

(continued)

vote at zagat.com

| M | P | S | C |

(continued)
Oriental Lamp Shade Co.
223 W. 79th St. (bet. Amsterdam Ave. & B'way), 1/9 to 79th St., 212-873-0812
www.orientallampshade.com
■ "Try the silk" lampshades at these "friendly neighborhood merchants" in the East 60s and West 70s, and "you'll never go back to poly" posit proponents, who include the "finest designers"; "they make anything" "you could possibly imagine", and the "helpful" staff can rewire and repair your treasures as well; the enlightened insist the "good quality" is "worth the price."

Original Leather Store ●⑤   – | – | – | M
256 Columbus Ave. (72nd St.), 1/2/3/9 to 72nd St.; B/C to 72nd St., 212-595-7051
1100 Madison Ave. (bet. 82nd & 83rd Sts.), 4/5/6 to 86th St., 212-585-4200
176 Spring St. (Thompson St.), C/E to Spring St., 212-219-8210
171 W. Fourth St. (bet. 6th & 7th Aves.), A/C/E/F/V/S to W. 4th St., 212-675-2303
www.originalleather.com
Beauty is skin deep at this chainlet of Manhattan hide houses where a menagerie from basic lambskin to genuine python is fashioned into the hottest ready-to-wear cuts; 'destroyed' leather flight jackets for him share racks with low-waisted bell-bottoms for her, plus shearlings and sheddings from Seraphin and other high-end European manufacturers.

Original Levi's Store ●⑤ⓒ   21 | 18 | 18 | M
536 Broadway (bet. Prince & Spring Sts.), N/R to Prince St., 646-613-1847
750 Lexington Ave. (59th St.), 4/5/6/N/R/W to 59th St./Lexington Ave., 212-826-5957; 800-872-5384
www.levi.com
■ Go "back to basics" at this "trusty" denim giant on Lex and its spanking new sibling in SoHo; worshipers "love the low-riders", the "classic Red Tab" line and the "made-to-order option" for "hard-to-fit bodies", plus, guess what, a pair of jeans here doesn't "require all of your food money for a week"; but while some praise the "polite" staff, others opine they need a 911 to fetch the 501s; N.B. the Broadway site opened post-*Survey*.

Origins   22 | 22 | 21 | M
2327 Broadway (bet. 84th & 85th Sts.), 1/9 to 86th St., 212-769-0970
Flatiron Bldg., 175 Fifth Ave. (22nd St.), N/R to 23rd St., 212-677-9100
Grand Central (42nd St. & Vanderbilt Ave.), 4/5/6/7/S to 42nd St./Grand Central, 212-808-4141
Rockefeller Ctr., 44 W. 50th St. (bet. 5th & 6th Aves.), B/D/F/V to 47-50th Sts./Rockefeller Ctr., 212-698-2323
402 W. Broadway (Spring St.), C/E to Spring St., 212-219-9764 ●⑤
800-674-4467; www.origins.com
■ "What's better than looking good, smelling great" and being environmentally friendly at the same time? ask acolytes of this chain that's "an oasis from the concrete jungle"; fans "love" the "East-meets-West, Zen-type scents" and the "great range" of plant-based skincare and bath-and-body products ("Oprah's endorsement of the Ginger Soufflé Whipped Body Cream" didn't hurt either); a "great, no-pressure sales staff" and moderate prices help make "you feel like you're doing yourself a favor by shopping here."

| | | | **M** | **P** | **S** | **C** |

Orvis Company S   21 | 23 | 19 | E
522 Fifth Ave. (44th St.), 4/5/6/7/S to 42nd St./Grand Central, 212-827-0698; 888-548-9548; www.orvis.com
■ Track down "country bumpkin clothing" for men and women, including "sporting wear for the well-heeled" "trout fisherman and his Labrador retriever" and "everything anyone could want for fly-fishing" and hunting, from rods and reels to traps and clays, at this Midtown offshoot of this 147-year-old Vermont-based chain; while you may want to "take up" angling or shooting "just to shop here", armchair outdoorsmen opine "it's fun to just look around."

Oshkosh B'Gosh SC   22 | 19 | 18 | M
586 Fifth Ave. (bet. 47th & 48th Sts.), B/D/F/V to 47-50th Sts./Rockefeller Ctr., 212-827-0098; www.oshkoshbgosh.com
■ "Every kid needs a pair of overalls" from this "good source of staples" that also "sets the standard" for "sturdy", "everyday" baby and children's clothes, as well as shoes, bedding and plush toys; head to the Midtown branch of this chainster to shop for "excellent quality" "tough stuff" little ones will "wear again and again", all at "reasonable prices."

Other Music ●SC   25 | 20 | 21 | M
15 E. Fourth St. (bet. B'way & Lafayette St.), 6 to Astor Pl.; F to B'way/Lafayette, 212-477-8150; www.othermusic.com
■ Opposite Tower Records (geographically and philosophically) is the Village's "adventurous music-lover's paradise", specializing in "ultra-obscure" indie and underground sounds on CD and vinyl hawked by staffers "who actually know something about what they're selling"; a customer base representing the "highest concentration of DJs per square foot" in the city means "you won't find any of that teenybopper mall crap here."

Otto Tootsi Plohound ●SC   26 | 23 | 17 | E
38 E. 57th St. (Madison Ave.), N/R/W to 5th Ave./59th St., 212-231-3199
137 Fifth Ave. (bet. 20th & 21st Sts.), N/R to 23rd St., 212-460-8650
273 Lafayette St. (Prince St.), F/V/S to B'way/Lafayette; N/R to Prince St., 212-431-7299
413 W. Broadway (bet. Prince & Spring Sts.), N/R to Prince St., 212-925-8931
■ "If you've got a shoe fetish", this "fab" foursome, overflowing with a "dizzying selection" of "what's next" – "all designer, all the time" – is a "lovely place to drool"; the "just-so gal" and her guy swoon for "swanky", "offbeat", "fancy schmancy", "Downtown footwear" from labels like Costume National, Freelance and Prada, as well as lesser-known "hip, chic European" names; sure, the staff can be "indifferent", but few "fashion-forward" fans seem to care, as this "temple" has some of the "most stylish kicks around."

Out of the Closet Thrift Shop ⌀   ▽ 16 | 11 | 12 | E
220 E. 81st St. (bet. 2nd & 3rd Aves.), 6 to 77th St., 212-472-3573
◪ Set in an 1838 farmhouse on the Upper East Side, "this is no ordinary thrift shop", but one that offers 10,000 books, Meissen and Flora Danica porcelain and the occasional Rodin watercolor, as well as clothes and records; as could be expected, "these knickknacks cost a paddy-whack and a half", but it all goes to a "great cause" (direct services for AIDS patients) and there are frequent sales of "up to 90 percent off – honest!"

vote at zagat.com

Oxxford Clothes   27 | 24 | 25 | VE

36 E. 57th St. (bet. Madison & Park Aves.), 4/5/6/N/R/W to 5th Ave./ 59th St., 212-593-0204; www.oxxfordclothes.com

■ Although it opened in 1998, this 57th Street haberdasher bears an "older, distinguished look" befitting its historic label, since 1916 a synonym for traditional but "fashionable" menswear; privileged patriots pursuing "perfection" prefer it for selling "completely handmade American suits", "custom-made" to their physiques ("off-the-peg" is available too); prices for the clothing and "top-notch shoes" are "in the stratosphere", but high-fliers insist this is "the best the U.S. has to offer."

Palazzetti S   ▽ 23 | 21 | 19 | VE

515 Madison Ave., 2nd fl. (53rd St.), E/V to 5th Ave./53rd St., 212-832-1199; 888-881-1199; www.palazzetti.com

■ Madison Avenue "must" for high-end "contemporary" and "classic" furniture like "gorgeous" reproduction chairs by Mies van der Rohe, Marcel Breuer and Harry Bertoia, along with new designs for sectionals and bathrooms; the showroom is "upstairs, folks – if you're watching the street, you'll miss it" – just look for the big baseball mitt–shaped sofa in the window.

Pan Aqua Diving S C   ▽ 25 | 19 | 24 | E

460 W. 43rd St. (bet. 9th & 10th Aves.), A/C/E to 42nd St./Port Authority, 212-736-3483; 800-434-0884; www.panaqua.com

■ For "a wonderful selection" of scuba diving and snorkeling gear and "expert servicing on the premises", paddle over to this Hell's Kitchen shop; fans flip for "great classes" at Manhattan health clubs and group trips and also give the "friendly, helpful staff" a fins-up; sure, "top quality isn't cheap, but if you are 100 feet underwater you might ask yourself, what is your life worth?"

P&S Fabrics S   23 | 12 | 18 | I

355 Broadway (bet. Franklin & Leonard Sts.), 1/9 to Franklin St., 212-226-1534; www.psfabrics.com

■ Tucked in TriBeCa, this "huge" "favorite" is "filled with every fabric you could possibly want" for "clothing and home" (you'll "want to reupholster everything!"), plus "lots of notions, craft supplies", a "good selection of patterns" and "great yarns"; the "owners are very pleasant" and so is the "friendly, helpful" staff; P.S. "rummage through the basement" for deals "on a rainy day."

Paper Access   25 | 20 | 16 | M

2030 Broadway (bet. 69th & 70th Sts.), 1/2/3/9 to 72nd St., 212-799-4900
23 W. 18th St. (bet. 5th & 6th Aves.), 1 to 18th St., 212-463-7035 ☽ S
800-727-3701; www.paperaccess.com

■ "Tons and tons of paper" "as far as the eye can see" fills these Flatiron and Upper West Side "one-stop shops" that fulfill "all your stationery needs" with a "wide variety of invitations and cards" and "great craft supplies" that are an "artist's delight"; they're "better-priced" than much of the competition, and "you can always find what you need" amid the "seemingly mile-long" shelves.

Papivore S C   – | – | – | E

233 Elizabeth St. (bet. Houston & Prince Sts.), 6 to Bleecker St., 212-334-4330; www.papivore.com

Those with a creative block may wish to patronize this "gorgeous", recently relocated NoLita specialty store where the "amazing

M P S C

selection of paper and journals" will "make you want to write every day"; in addition to "great stationery" and "excellent printing" services, it also offers pens, books and household accessories, and even if "prices are steep", its devotees would "travel to NYC just to shop" here.

PARAGON SPORTING GOODS ●S 25 | 18 | 16 | M
867 Broadway (18th St.), 4/5/6/L/N/Q/R/W to 14th St., 212-255-8036; 800-961-3030; www.paragonsports.com

◪ "A four-season sporting goods" "adventureland", this three-floor Union Square "Shangri-La" offers a "complete inventory" of "the highest-quality equipment for whatever sport takes your fancy", from skiing and tennis to rock climbing and kayaking, "and the clothing to go with it"; "it's athletically inspiring just to be" in this "virtual playground" that makes you feel "like a kid in a really expensive candy store" – "you could spend days browsing the merchandise"; but the less-enthused gripe that "service may be hard to find", especially on weekends, when it's "as crowded as a World Cup soccer match."

Park Avenue Audio C – | – | – | E
425 Park Ave. S. (29th St.), 6 to 28th St., 212-685-8101; www.parkave.com
Three generations of hi-fi enthusiasts have run this Gramercy Park establishment, and they're still ready to work with you or your interior designer to customize and install your "top-of-the-line" audio or theater setup; these "great" folks "don't oversell and really seem to want to match the customer to the right system."

Parke & Ronen ●SC – | – | – | E
176 Ninth Ave. (21st St.), C/E to 23rd St., 212-989-4245; www.parkeandronen.com
Chelsea-ites love to roam this charmingly sleek boutique that pays equal attention to men and women with neatly tailored pants and jackets in wool, leather or Ultrasuede, stand-out-in-a-crowd print shirts and love-thy-body T-shirts, all designed by Parke Lutter and Ronen Jehezkel; sweet staffers amiably attend customers.

Paron Fabrics 23 | 15 | 17 | M
855 Lexington Ave. (bet. 64th & 65th Sts.), F to 63rd St., 212-772-7353
56 W. 57th St. (bet. 5th & 6th Ave.), F to 57th St., 212-247-6451
240 W. 40th St. (bet. 7th & 8th Aves.), A/C/E to 42nd St./Port Authority, 212-768-3266
www.paronfabrics.com

■ "Anything you could want in fashion fabrics" for apparel is here at this textile trio, the "first place to go" for "discounted bargains"; the Midtown flagship upstairs on 57th Street boasts a "terrific half-price section", the cozy, Upper East branch stocks "great designer fabrics", from Ralph Lauren to Bill Blass, and the newest "Annex on 40th Street" offers a "beautiful" choice of goods; P.S. "if they don't have it, they'll get it."

Patagonia S 26 | 22 | 22 | E
426 Columbus Ave. (81st St.), B/C to 81st St., 917-441-0011
101 Wooster St. (bet. Prince & Spring Sts.), N/R to Prince St.; C/E to Spring St., 212-343-1776
800-638-6464; www.patagonia.com

■ Whether you're taking an "adventure trip" or "keeping warm on the subway", these "great" Upper West Side and SoHo stores provide "the world's best outdoor clothing", including "cool baby"

vote at zagat.com   205

| M | P | S | C |

and kids' stuff, according to the fleece police, who also rave about the chain's "environmentally conscious" corporate mission; the "classic styling" means the "long-lasting products" "never become outdated", and the staff makes it a "pleasure to shop."

Patch NYC S C   22 | 24 | 18 | E
17 Eighth Ave. (bet. Jane & W. 12th Sts.), A/C/E to 14th St., 212-807-1060; www.patchnyc.com
■ "Quirky" with "a patch of whimsy", this Village accessories boutique is "perfect for the girl-next-door hoping to add something kitschy to her solid colors"; most of the "adorable" items, from vintage-inspired hats and T-shirts to "purses so cute you're afraid to carry them", sport "fun appliqués" ("animal lovers can wear their favorite pals" on their bags); P.S. service is "attentive."

Paterson Silks   14 | 7 | 9 | M
300 E. 90th St. (2nd Ave.), 4/5/6 to 86th St., 212-722-4098
151 W. 72nd St. (bet. Amsterdam & Columbus Aves.), 1/2/3/9 to 72nd St., 212-874-9510
215-22 73rd Ave. (Bell Blvd.), Queens, Q 75 Bus, 718-776-5225
◪ A "neighborhood necessity", this textile trio on the Upper West Side, Upper East Side and Queens can be "convenient for fabric for a children's school project", notions, apparel and upholstery purposes; but most patrons are put off by the "surly service" and "high prices", advising "compare, and you'll go elsewhere."

Patina S   – | – | – | M
451 Broome St. (bet. B'way & Mercer St.), 6 to Spring St., 212-625-3375
Situated on a SoHo side street, this pink space seems less a store than a room filled with someone's favorite things – if one's favorites were a 1930s Fortuny perfume bottle, a 1940s crocodile purse or a 1960s Yves Saint Laurent car coat; despite the tiny digs, the accessories and housewares are neatly displayed in wall-unit cubicles; though not bargain-basement, prices are reasonable given the unique nature of the period pieces.

Paul & Joe ●S C   ▽ 25 | 22 | 19 | VE
2 Bond St. (bet. B'way & Lafayette St.), 6 to Bleecker St.; N/R to 8th St., 212-505-0974
■ "Adorable and French", with the "expensive price tag" to match, the well-cut men's and women's clothing in this NoHo boutique has a vintage air that's as familial as its name (Paul and Joe are designer Sophie Albou's sons); feel free to scrawl on the shop's chalkboard, *s'il vous plaît*, if, like some fans, you "want more stuff to choose from."

Paul & Shark S C   24 | 24 | 22 | VE
772 Madison Ave. (66th St.), 6 to 68th St., 212-452-9868; www.paulshark.it
■ "Before that yachting weekend", savvy sailors set course for the Madison Avenue member of this global fleet, which specializes in "great outdoor apparel" made in Italy; yes, the water-repellent knits, coats and shoes cost "stratospheric" amounts – but given their high-tech quality, most don't find them "overpriced."

Paul Frank Store S C   – | – | – | M
195 Mulberry St. (Spring St.), 6 to Spring St., 212-965-5079; www.paulfrank.com
How much is that monkey in the window ask tweens, teens and twentysomethings who flock to this California designer's colorful,

modular NoLita boutique where Frank's brainchild, Julius, the wide-mouthed primate, plus other whimsical cartoon characters, adorns everything from T-shirts, hoodies and pajamas to novelty watches, wallets, sneakers and snowboards; cultists also go ape for jeans, twill pants and casual shirts with barely a noticeable logo, vintage-inspired eyewear and, soon to come, Paul Frank furniture.

Paul Smith 🅂🄲 | 27 | 23 | 18 | VE
108 Fifth Ave. (bet. 15th & 16th Sts.), 4/5/6/L/N/Q/R/W to 14th St./Union Sq., 212-627-9770; www.paulsmith.co.uk

■ A Flatiron hot spot for "snappy" menswear, this British import with bubble-gum pink walls relies on a sly sense of color and "eye-catching" stripes to create "quirky takes on classic silhouettes"; the staff is "dandy" at helping, and "though you will pay the price for looking so cool", most say it's worth it for a "shirt with a little something special" or some "irreverent" accessories ("who thought cuff links could be fun?").

Paul Stuart 🅂🄲 | 26 | 25 | 24 | VE
45th St. & Madison Ave., 4/5/6/7/S to 42nd St./Grand Central, 212-682-0320; 800-678-8278; www.paulstuart.com

■ "For the classic English look, look no further" than this family-owned Midtown haberdasher – "one of the few full-service men's stores left in NYC" – where the "great colors, workmanship" and "lofty quality" of the clothes and furnishings "round out a traditional wardrobe with flair and style"; advocates also applaud the "retro-modern interiors" patrolled by a "helpful sales staff"; it's all pretty "pricey", but why not splurge, "if you've got the jack"; P.S. they offer similarly "distinguished" womenswear upstairs.

Payless Shoe Source ●🅂 | 11 | 10 | 9 | I
1 Herald Sq., 1293 Broadway (34th St.), B/D/F/N/Q/R/V/W to 34th St./Herald Sq., 212-947-0306; www.payless.com
Additional locations throughout the NY area

◪ "If you're looking for knockoff styles at inexpensive prices", "you can find some real deals" on "footwear for the entire family" at this national chain with branches in all five boroughs; it's a "great place to get" "trendy, summer stuff" "you'll trash on vacation" and kids' shoes, since they'll grow out of them so fast", but critics quickly counter "pay less . . . get less."

P.C. Richard & Son ●🅂 | 16 | 12 | 12 | M
120 E. 14th St. (bet. 3rd & 4th Aves.), N/R/4/5/6 to 14th St./Union Sq., 212-979-2600; 800-369-7915; www.pcrichard.com
Additional locations throughout the NY area

◪ This family-run giant with stores in most of the boroughs is known for its "good prices" and broad selection, but it "sabotages itself with horrendous service" and "bad presentation" of electronics "scattered on shelves"; many reviewers relate that it's more of a "source for basic household appliances like stoves, refrigerators and air conditioners" than for monitors, scanners and PCs.

Peanutbutter & Jane 🅂🄲 | – | – | – | E
617 Hudson St. (bet. Jane & W. 12th Sts.), A/C/E/L to 14th St., 212-620-7952

"Crammed full" of "fun, funky, one-of-a-kind" infant, toddler and big kid togs and "unique educational toys", this Villager feels like you're "shopping in a very nice attic"; temptation abounds, from poodle purses and vintage clothing to Betsey Johnson infant dresses; sure, it's all sandwiched together ("don't bring strollers

vote at zagat.com 207

or large shopping bags"), but a friendly staff is on hand to help you choose the right thing.

Pearldaddy ◐ S C — | — | — | M

202A Mott St. (bet. Kenmare & Spring Sts.), 6 to Spring St., 212-219-7727
At this NoLita insider's secret, the world is your oyster, since every item in the narrow, exposed-brick space is made from freshwater pearls; the large, varied selection ranges from simple, traditional pearl studs to the best-selling multi-strand necklaces dyed bronze or baby-blue, while pearl-hungry daddies can choose from a variety of cuff links.

PEARL PAINT S 27 | 16 | 16 | I

308 Canal St. (bet. B'way & Church St.), A/C/E to Canal St.; 6/J/M/N/Q/R/W/Z to Canal St., 212-431-7932
207 E. 23rd St. (bet. 2nd & 3rd Aves.), 6 to 23rd St., 212-592-2179
www.pearlpaint.com
■ "Could you ever beat" the "enormous stock" at this "Pearl in the oyster bed of art supplies"?; a "crazy" six-story "walk-up tenement" on Canal Street "organized like a rabbit warren" "jammed with people and excellent merchandise", it's "cheap and nasty", "joyful" and "inspiring"; the "stairs'll kill ya", as "the elevator never comes", and "the staff can be helpful or condescending depending on the moon's rotation", but you'll "thank the Lord it's around" because "if it ain't here, it ain't"; N.B. Gramercy is home to a smaller sibling.

Pearl River Mart ◐ S C 19 | 10 | 9 | I

277 Canal St. (B'way), J/M/N/Q/R/W/Z/6 to Canal St., 212-431-4770
200 Grand St. (bet. Mott & Mulberry Sts.), J/M/N/Q/R/W/Z/6 to Canal St., 212-966-1010
800-878-2446; www.pearlriver.com
■ "Exotic fun" is yours for the taking at this Chinatown department store duo, two "treasure troves" of "fun, funky and functional" items you "suddenly, desperately need"; what it "lacks in presentation", it "makes up for in quantity" with an "astonishing" "grab bag" of "all things Asian-inspired", much like what's in "rarified SoHo or NoLita boutiques" – only at "dirt-cheap" prices; sure, it's "a little grimy and the staff has attitude", but cool fashionistas know its "exquisite" embroidered slippers, silk "Suzy Wong" cheongsams and "subtle ceramics" make it a no-brainer for bargain-priced styling; plus, it's "close to great food"; N.B. at press time, the Canal Street branch was scheduled to move to Broadway.

Peck & Goodie Skates ◐ S C — | — | — | E

917 Eighth Ave. (bet. 54th & 55th Sts.), 1/9/A/C/E to 59th St./Columbus Circle, 212-246-6123
"'The' place to go" for the puck-and-rink set since 1940, this "tiny", no-frills family-owned Midtowner "has whatever you could ask for in ice skates", from figure and speed to hockey, as well as a smaller selection of roller, in-line and quad skates and even skateboards; the "dedicated salespeople will be with you for as long as it takes to get the right equipment that fits perfectly", and they'll also sharpen those blades.

P.E. Guerin ⌐ — | — | — | VE

23 Jane St. (bet. 8th & Greenwich Aves.), A/C/E/L to 14th St., 212-243-5270; www.peguerin.com
Since 1857, the Guerin family has provided metalwork for public buildings and parks as well as residences all over the country;

| M | P | S | C |

plated brass hinges, knobs and plumbing and lighting fixtures are made either at the company's Valencia, Spain foundry or on-site in the West Village, and its artisans can reproduce period pieces; N.B. by appointment only.

PENHALIGON'S S | 26 | 26 | 25 | E |
870 Madison Ave. (71st St.), 6 to 68th St., 212-249-1771; 877-736-4254; www.penhaligons.com

■ Founded in 1870, this British bastion of toiletries has been making pricey perfumes and "long-lasting" colognes for the likes of Winston Churchill, and its tiny Madison Avenue offshoot continues the tradition with the "finest fragrances", along with shaving sets, silver scent bottles, soaps and candles.

Penny Whistle S C | 23 | 20 | 19 | M |
448 Columbus Ave. (bet. 81st & 82nd Sts.), B/C to 81st St., 212-873-9090
1283 Madison Ave. (bet. 91st & 92nd Sts.), 6 to 96th St., 212-369-3868

■ "The bear blowing bubbles outside is a giveaway" – there are "great little things for little hands" at this "charming" Upper West Side toy store, and a smaller selection of "unique, intelligent" merchandise at its Upper East Side sibling; full of "clever gifts", like marionettes and choo-choo accessories, "these lovely boutiques" are "fun for kids and adults"; while it "may not have the best selection in town, it's always worth a visit."

Perfumania ● S C | 18 | 12 | 12 | I |
Empire State Bldg., 20 W. 34th St. (bet. 5th & 6th Aves.), B/D/F/N/Q/R/V/W to 34th St./Herald Sq., 212-736-0414; 800-927-1777; www.perfumania.com
Additional locations throughout the NY area

◪ It's the "large selection" of "discounted" "designer and drugstore perfumes" and men's colognes that's the draw at this chain of "no-frills stores" located throughout the city; they claim to guarantee the lowest price or they pay you.

Perlier Kelemata S C | – | – | – | M |
436 W. Broadway (bet. Prince & Spring Sts.), N/R to Prince St., 212-925-9999; 877-737-5353; www.perlier.com

A little, light-filled SoHo space is the serene setting for five all-natural Italian and French bath-and-body collections from Perlier, Kelemata, Cerealia, Imaginez and Victor; fragrances like Honey and White Almond, Orange Blossom and Vetiver fill the air, inspiring some weary shoppers to head home to a warm scented bath.

Petco | 21 | 17 | 14 | M |
860 Broadway (17th St.), 4/5/6/L/N/Q/R/W to 14th St./Union Sq., 212-358-0692 ● S
147 E. 86th St. (bet. Lexington & 3rd Aves.), 4/5/6/to 86th St., 212-831-8001
560 Second Ave. (bet. 31st & 32nd Sts.), 6 to 33rd St., 212-779-4550
157-20 Cross Bay Blvd. (157th Ave.), Queens, Q41 Bus, 718-845-3331
1756 Forest Ave. (Morningstar Rd.), Staten Island, 718-370-8820
800-571-2952; www.petco.com

◪ A "one-stop shop for all pet needs", this superstore chain carries "most major brands of food", a "large variety of accessories and gifts" and "staple" "supplies for every critter imaginable"; alas, "what it gains in size, it loses in personal service", and there are oftentimes "long lines at checkout" – still, there's praise for the "good prices" ("don't forget to apply" for 'Pals', its "frequent-buyer's card").

vote at zagat.com

| M | P | S | C |

Peter Elliot S
24 | 20 | 21 | VE

1070 Madison Ave. (81st St.), 6 to 77th St., 212-570-2300
☑ "Still tweedy after all these years", this "small but exquisite" East 80s haberdasher offers a "focused selection of some of the best men's fashion"; critics cry "cool it on the markups", but most feel warmly about a staff that "turns the most hopeless into respectable citizens"; P.S. across the street, "the women's store is fab too."

Peter Fox Shoes S C
24 | 22 | 22 | VE

105 Thompson St. (bet. Prince & Spring Sts.), C/E to Spring St., 212-431-7426; www.peterfox.com
■ "Unusual" "wedding shoes" "you won't scoff at" for "brides who would like something other than the typical" fare, plus "funky" footwear for off-the-aisle occasions, some with "Victorian flair", are all in store at this small, girlish SoHo shop; the "friendly" staff ensures a "pleasant shopping experience."

Peter Hermann S C
– | – | – | M

118 Thompson St. (bet. Prince & Spring Sts.), C/E to Spring St., 212-966-9050
As tightly packed as a Jamin Puech purse, since 1987 this small SoHo store's been a must-stop for his-and-hers accessories – from bags and backpacks to belts and billfolds – in leather, vinyl or rubber; Mandarina Duck and Strenesse are other big brands.

Peters Necessities for Pets S C
▽ 18 | 15 | 19 | M

236 E. 75th St. (bet. 2nd & 3rd Aves.), 6 to 77th St., 212-988-0769
■ "These guys are great" – "especially Pete, who runs the show" rave regulars of this East 70s pet shop where the "good service" extends to "free treats" for furry noshers; the selection's "not terribly big", but it carries a few items you "won't find elsewhere."

Petit Bateau S
25 | 21 | 19 | E

1100 Madison Ave. (82nd St.), 4/5/6 to 86th St., 212-988-8884; www.petit-bateau.com
■ "The perfect tee is hard to find, but the French have done it right", coming up with "arguably the most comfortable" ones "in the world", or at least the "best darn T-shirt this side of Madison Avenue"; though intended for babies and children (check out the "lovely cotton pajamas and onesies" as well), the "little" tops are also "cult favorites" for "small women"; P.S. the Europe-bound "wait to shop for them in Paris" "for a fraction of the price."

Petland Discounts ●S
17 | 12 | 14 | I

530 E. 14th St. (bet. Aves. A & B), L to 1st Ave., 212-228-1363; www.petlanddiscounts.com
Additional locations throughout the NY area
☑ "If you're on a budget, your pet won't be able to tell you shop" at this large discount chain that's "well stocked" with "everything you need for your little beasties" at "dirt-cheap prices"; however, while the staff at some locations is "friendly", others are so "surly, they should be whacked with a rolled-up newspaper."

Pet Stop S C
21 | 16 | 17 | M

564 Columbus Ave. (bet. 87th & 88th Sts.), 1/9/B/C to 86th St., 212-580-2400
■ "Everyone's helpful" at this "very decent neighborhood pet store" in the West 80s, where an "excellent selection of dog food" and "reliable delivery service" keep both local canines and their humans happy.

M P S C

Phat Farm S C   19 | 20 | 14 | E
129 Prince St. (bet. W. B'way & Wooster St.), N/R to Prince St., 212-533-7428; www.phatfarmstore.com; www.babyphat.com
■ "Great hip" apparel that's "pfine pfor" "young people" jonesing for "Wasp clothes three sizes too big" can be found at this SoHo shop done up with classic American country decor including wooden barn doors; this "perfect locale" showcases hip-hop entrepreneur Russell Simmons' line of jeans, logo tees, sweats and sneakers and also spotlights his wife Kimora Lee's hot Baby Phat collection; better bring along a phat wallet – a phew phind it a "little overpriced."

Philosophy di Alberta Ferretti S C   24 | 23 | 19 | VE
452 W. Broadway (bet. Houston & Prince Sts.), C/E to Spring St., 212-460-5500; www.aeffeusa.com
■ Despite the name, there are no bookish babes here; on the contrary, a "Ferretti fox can be seen from miles away" in "dreamy clothes" from this "dreamy store" on SoHo's main drag that's dedicated to the Italian designer's younger line of "richly woven" women's jackets and ethereal dresses; a cascading waterfall runs through the museum-like interior, a lush accent to the luxe space with its "twentysomething staff."

PIAGET C   28 | 27 | 27 | VE
730 Fifth Ave. (bet. 56th & 57th Sts.), N/R/W to 5th Ave./59th St., 212-246-5555; 800-359-4538; www.piaget.com
■ "Many a favorite dress watch" has come from this longtime Geneva concern, whose Midtown outpost bears a striking midnight-blue and natural-maplewood decor; timepieces that some call "the best in the world" complement the "painstakingly crafted" fine jewelry; just "watch out" (pun intended) for "high-end luxury" price tags as well.

Pieces ● S   – | – | – | E
671 Vanderbilt Ave. (Park Pl.), Brooklyn, Q to 7th Ave.; 3 to Grand Army Plaza, 718-857-7211; www.piecesofbklyn.com
'Fashion That Turns Heads' says the slogan on the awning, and once within this happening corner Prospect Heights shop owned by a retail-schooled married couple, customers register that the sexy threads for women (and a smattering for men) do all that and more, with a friendly coffee klatch vibe to boot; the strut-your-stuff wear includes standouts from Cynthia Steffe and Single, unusual labels like Ya-Ya and Cultura, plus a few fabulous hats, accessories and shoes – hey, what's a 'piece' without a head-to-toe look?

Pier 1 Imports ● S   18 | 18 | 14 | I
461 Fifth Ave. (40th St.), 4/5/6/S to 42nd St./Grand Central, 212-447-1610
71 Fifth Ave. (15th St.), 4/5/6/L/N/Q/R/W to 14th St./Union Sq., 212-206-1911
1550 Third Ave. (87th St.), 4/5/6 to 86th St., 212-987-1746
800-245-4595; www.pier1.com
■ The "budget-minded" make a beeline for these "jam-packed" branches of a chain brimming with "practical" wicker, rattan and bamboo baskets and furniture, "funky candleholders", "place mats and plates", "colorful" pillows and "odd knickknacks"; the stylish may sniff at the store's "basic", "cookie-cutter" merchandise, but pros praise its "cost-effective home-decor solutions."

vote at zagat.com

Pierre Deux S | 24 | – | 18 | E
625 Madison Ave. (bet. 58th & 59th Sts.), 4/5/6/F/N/R/W to 59th St./ Lexington Ave., 212-521-8012; www.pierredeux.com

■ "Toile, toile and more toile" – Madison Avenue's "ultimate source of French country style" appeals to "the Francophile in all of us"; the famous "pretty prints" turn up in "*très* beautiful fabrics", "soft, sturdy carryalls", "colorful tablecloths" and upholstered furniture, plus there are plenty of "lovely touches for the home", from glassware to rugs; the "ever-expanding" selection of "goods doesn't come cheap" but "it's nice to browse"; N.B. the store moved to larger quarters 12 blocks down post-*Survey* and is not related to Pierre Deux Antiques on Bleecker Street.

Pilar Rossi | – | – | – | VE
784 Madison Ave. (bet. 66th & 67th Sts.), 6 to 68th St., 212-288-2469
When it's knock-'em-dead time, many a femme fatale turns to this Spanish specialist in sequins and chiffon; inside her minimalist jewel box in the East 60s lies a perfectly edited collection of dramatic, well-cut suits and beautifully embellished evening wear; so go with a gala in mind, and the obliging staff will offer one-on-one service.

Pink Pussycat ●SC | 19 | 16 | 17 | M
167 W. Fourth St. (bet. 6th & 7th Aves.), A/B/C/D/E/F/Q to W. 4th St., 212-243-0077
355 Fifth Ave. (bet. 4th & 5th Sts.), Brooklyn, F/M/R to 4th Ave./9th St., 718-369-0088
www.pinkpussycat.com

◪ "Tourists, drag queens" and "pimply" "first-time buyers" "come together" at a "naughty", "entertaining" "pit stop for props" at West Fourth Street's "famed" "landmark" of "smut" that's also "valued for its people-watching potential"; design fetishists fret the "decor is clinical, but how much can you do with vibrators and plastic butts?", despite connoisseurs' critique that "the inventory" "isn't living up to its illustrious" 38-year rep; N.B. a tamer, lingerie-heavy branch across from a junior high has caused a stir with the Park Slope PTA.

Pink Slip ●S | 22 | 14 | 19 | M
Grand Central, 107 E. 42nd St. (bet. Lexington & Park Aves.), 4/5/6/ 7/S to 42nd St./Grand Central, 212-949-9037; 866-816-7465; www.thepinkslip.com

◪ "Definitely the place to go to add spice to your bedroom", "this little store" carries an "amazing selection" of come-hither wear, from cami-corsets by Arianne to "beautiful" chemises and bra sets from Mary Green; while it's "surprisingly classy considering its Grand Central location", shy flowers give it the slip, claiming "it's a little embarrassing trying on lingerie in the train station."

Pintchik SC | 23 | 15 | 17 | M
478 Bergen St. (Flatbush Ave.), Brooklyn, 2/3 to Bergen St., 718-783-3333

■ "You can buy your items, go home and complete the entire job before you can even get out of" the bigger chain stores maintain mavens of this "true neighborhood" hardware purveyor in Park Slope; it's "tough to beat for paint and supplies", the "salespeople are knowledgeable and friendly", and if the layout feels a "bit cramped", the fact that it has "everything you could possibly want" more than compensates.

P.J. Huntsman | – | – | – | M |

36 W. 44th St. (bet. 5th & 6th Aves.), 7/B/D/F/V to 42nd St./6th Ave., 212-302-2463; 800-968-3418; www.pjhuntsman.com

Entering this mini-sporting shop, surrounded by Midtown university clubs, is like visiting a cozy gentlemen's study filled with hunting clothes, gear and gifts for the gentry (or those aspiring); owner/manager Pat Colombo provides personal attention for patrons perusing his properly priced 'performance' articles made in the U.S., U.K. and Europe.

Planet Kids S C | 21 | 14 | 14 | M |

2688 Broadway (103rd St.), 1 to 103rd St., 212-864-8705
247 E. 86th St. (bet. 2nd & 3rd Aves.), 4/5/6 to 86th St., 212-426-2040 ◐

■ "A must for baby shopping", these two Uptown boys' and girls' galaxies offer a "great selection" of a "wide range of items" at "reasonable" prices; the original Upper East Side shop sells toys, furniture, strollers, swings, high chairs and clothing from layette to age two, while the newer, smaller satellite on the Upper West Side carries apparel for sizes right up through the teens.

Pleasure Chest ◐ S | 20 | 19 | 18 | M |

156 Seventh Ave. (bet. Charles & Perry Sts.), 1/9 to Christopher St., 212-242-2158; 800-316-9222; www.adulttoyexpress.com

◪ It's "porn for the masses" at this Village "pleasure" purveyor that's "as essential as Costco" for all your "bridal shower gag gift" needs, including that popular little dynamo, the Pocket Rocket; "the nice thing about the place is that they have the toys out so you can handle them, turn them on" and "giggle away"; you might find the "prices high", the "variety limited" and the sales help hit-or-miss, but you'll "always want to rush home afterward" to give the goods a whirl.

Pleats Please S C | ∇ 25 | 25 | 18 | E |

128 Wooster St. (Prince St.), N/R to Prince St., 212-226-3600; www.pleatsplease.com

■ Patrons will be pleat-ing for more when they enter this glass-encased SoHo shop with its "admirably bold" line of high-tech, super-pleated polyester pieces imbued with "Issey Miyake's artistry"; somewhat "cheaper" than the designer's main line, the easy-to-pack dresses, tops and witty accessories – such as the best-selling, felt fortune-cookie bag – shine in "lovely colors and textures" sure to "stop traffic."

Plein Sud S C | ∇ 26 | 24 | 19 | VE |

70 Greene St. (bet. Broome & Spring Sts.), C/E to Spring St., 212-431-8800

■ Join the colorful caravan at this SoHo boutique, a true hot spot for "gorgeous", "very sexy, special-occasion dresses" and other clingy, "out-there-but-lots-of-fun" garments from a Moroccan-French designer whose heritage influences the store interior as well as the clothing; just make sure your camel is carrying buckets of gold to cover the cost of these silk, fur and leather creations.

Poggenpohl U.S. Inc. | – | – | – | VE |

230 Park Ave. S. (19th St.), 4/5/6/L/N/Q/R/W to 14th St./Union Sq., 212-228-3334; www.poggenpohl-usa.com

Europe's oldest kitchen manufacturer offers high-tech innovations and "unusual, modern" style that incorporates tinted glass, stainless steel, aluminum and lacquered woods; on-site designers at its Flatiron showroom help customize its ergonomically correct cabinetry and appliances; N.B. by appointment only.

Poli Fabrics S | – | – | – | I |
227 W. 40th St. (bet. 7th & 8th Aves.), A/C/E to 42nd St./Port Authority, 212-768-4555
"Beautiful fabrics for reasonable prices" and "frank, honest salespeople" make this Garment District store a "favorite" for those in-the-know; move quickly, advise insiders, "because those special designer" textiles "get snapped up fast."

Pompanoosuc Mills S | – | – | – | M |
124 Hudson St. (Ericsson Pl.), 1/9 to Franklin St., 212-226-5960; www.pompy.com
Every simple, well-constructed piece of wood furniture sold at this long-standing TriBeCa store, which just jumped from Broome to Hudson Street, is made to order in Vermont; most of the tables, sofas, consoles, chairs, bookshelves and beds are available in a choice of hardwoods like birch, oak, maple, cherry or walnut.

Pondicherri ●SC | – | – | – | M |
454 Columbus Ave. (bet. 81st & 82nd Sts.), 1/9 to 79th St.; B/C to 81st St., 212-875-1609; 800-813-6456; www.pondicherrionline.com
For 35 years the owners of this West 80s emporium have been producing hand-blocked textiles in New Delhi; when it comes to women's clothing, there are "good, basic Indian imports", but traditional Shahjahan table linens and Bengali embroidered pillows outshine any of the seasonal or Westernized designs.

Pookie & Sebastian ●SC | ▽ 26 | 19 | 24 | M |
249 E. 77th St. (bet. 2nd & 3rd Aves.), 6 to 77th St., 212-717-1076
■ It's "worth fighting through the crowd" at this "top-notch" boutique (an increasingly less "well-kept secret on the Upper East Side") that allows shoppers to "stay hip without spending a fortune" on up-to-the-minute styles and looks, including the "first wave of mania" for the jeans du jour; the "very-much-on-top-of-things" salespeople are "kind enough to call" when new shipments arrive.

Pop Shop SC | 24 | 26 | 19 | M |
292 Lafayette St. (E. Houston St.), F/V to B'way/Lafayette, 212-219-2784; 800-542-7464; www.haring.com
■ Hip-hop into SoHo's "fun tribute to the late, great Keith Haring", the '80s artist who "still rules" with shirts, housewares, "lots of great postcards" and kids' furniture bearing his familiar dancing figures, "radiant babies, barking dogs and wolves, oh my!"; proceeds benefit the Keith Haring Foundation, which supports AIDS-related and children's charities.

Porthault C | ▽ 28 | 24 | 23 | VE |
18 E. 69th St. (Madison Ave.), 6 to 68th St., 212-688-1660; www.dporthault.fr
■ "These are sheets you'll want to pass down from generation to generation – after you frame them", of course, sigh sybarites about these "ultimate-in-luxury" "linens from France" housed in a charming Upper East Side townhouse; this "wonderland" of pretty prints also offers beautiful bath towels and a "lovely" selection of "gifts" like children's clothing, candles and china.

Portico S | 23 | 22 | 16 | E |
903 Broadway (20th St.), N/R to 23rd St., 212-473-6662

214 subscribe to zagat.com

M | P | S | C

(continued)
Portico
450 Columbus Ave. (bet. 81st & 82nd Sts.), B/C to 81st St., 212-579-9500
72 Spring St. (bet. Crosby & Lafayette Sts.), 6 to Spring St., 212-941-7800
233 10th Ave. (bet. 23rd & 24th Sts.), C/E to 23rd St., 212-807-8807
www.porticohome.com
◪ Home-furnishings shops featuring a "limited" but "stylish" selection of beds, "chic towels", luxe Egyptian cotton linens and "lovely scented things" for those who want to live like "kings and queens"; minimalists maintain that the "clean"-looking merch isn't "overdesigned", making it "perfect for real city life", but wallet-watchers whine about the "expensive" big-city prices; N.B. the small Tenth Avenue outlet offers discounts on overstocked or slightly damaged items.

Pottery Barn ◐ S   21 | 22 | 17 | M
1965 Broadway (67th St.), 1/9 to 66th St., 212-579-8477
600 Broadway (Houston St.), N/R to Prince St.; B/D/F/Q to B'way/Lafayette; 6 to Bleecker St., 212-219-2420
127 E. 59th St. (Lexington Ave.), N/R/W/4/5/6 to 59th St./Lexington Ave., 917-369-0050
www.potterybarn.com
■ "Every apartment in New York has something" from this home-furnishings "staple" offering "mainstream chic" and a "mix" of "stylish" "quality goods" that "will work with any decor"; "don't expect to be unique if you shop here", but the more conventional claim that "moderate prices" make it a "great place for gifts" and "seasonal items to perk up your home."

Prada C   25 | 25 | 18 | VE
575 Broadway (Prince St.), N/R to Prince St., 212-334-8888 S
45 E. 57th St. (bet. Madison & Park Aves.), 4/5/6/N/R/W to 59th St./Lexington Ave., 212-308-2332
724 Fifth Ave. (bet. 56th & 57th Sts.), N/R/W to 5th Ave./59th St., 212-664-0010 S
841 Madison Ave. (70th St.), 6 to 68th St., 212-327-4200
www.prada.com
◪ This "ultra-cool" line "still has bite" for "die-hard designer fans", and although it's found in several "shopping destinations", its "epicenter" lies in the "electrifying" Rem Koolhaas–designed SoHo flagship – a "masterpiece" to many, a "well-dressed amusement park" to others; still, you "can't miss" a trip (preferably mid-week to avoid "gawkers"), if only to ogle the "awesome skateboarding-ramp" interior, "classic-yet-edgy" fashions and much-ado-about-Miuccia footwear and purses; service veers from "business-like" to "hard-to-get", and "black nylon has never sold for so much", but neither gives pause to the patrons who pant "Prada, please"; N.B. the 57th Street store sells shoes and bags only.

PRATESI C   29 | 24 | 21 | VE
829 Madison Ave. (69th St.), 6 to 68th St., 212-288-2315;
www.pratesi.com
■ For "beautiful Italian linens and towels" "without flying to Italy", hedonists head to this long-standing Upper East Side specialty shop purveying additional "high-end" items "you could just melt in", like "yummy bathrobes"; "there's nothing like sleeping in a bed" made with their sheets – it's just the prices that will give you nightmares.

vote at zagat.com

| M | P | S | C |

Prato Fine Men's Wear ▽ 16 | 11 | 14 | I
8508 Fifth Ave. (85th St.), Brooklyn, R to 86th St., 718-491-1234 S
41 John St. (bet. Dutch & Nassau Sts.), 2/3/4/5/A/C/J/M/Z to Fulton St./ B'way/Nassau, 212-619-9017
122 Nassau St., 1st fl. (Ann St.), 2/3/4/5/A/C/J/M/Z to Fulton St./ B'way/Nassau, 212-349-4150 S
492 Seventh Ave. (bet. 36th & 37th Sts.), 1/2/3/9 to 34th St., 212-564-9683 ◐
28 W. 34th St. (bet. B'way & 5th Ave.), B/D/F/N/Q/R/W to 34th St./ Herald Sq., 212-629-4730 ◐ S
30-48 Steinway St. (bet. 30th & 31st Aves.), Queens, G/R/V to Steinway St., 718-274-2990 ◐ S
888-467-7286; www.pratooutlets.com

◪ Scattered throughout the city, this men's discount clothing chain can be a "good enough place for cheap stuff" – more specifically, "bargain"-priced bridgewear labels, including leather jackets, coats and "decent suits" that can often be "tailored in a day"; but critics claim "you get what you pay for, and not one bit more."

Princeton Ski Shop ◐ S C 18 | 15 | 14 | M
21 E. 22nd St. (bet. B'way & Park Ave. S.), N/R to 23rd St., 212-228-4400; www.princetonski.com

■ "If you're a winter freak", slalom over to this Flatiron sporting-goods store and "stock up on ski essentials"; the "nice selection" featuring brand names like Columbia and Salomon "may not be large, but they can seriously outfit" the slope bound; insiders confide there are "great late-season bargains" – in fact you may want to "hold out until their annual sale"; N.B. they also offer ski and snowboard tune-ups.

Print Icon ◐ S C – | – | – | M
7 W. 18th St. (bet. 5th & 6th Aves.), 4/5/6/L/N/Q/R/W to 14th St./ Union Sq., 212-255-4489; www.printicon.com

This airy Flatiron warehouse is reaching for iconic status as a combination print shop and paperie; pick up pre-made cards and personalized stationery or choose from over a thousand high-quality papers from the likes of Strathmore and Saint-Armand for your custom letter-press, offset and computer-produced creations.

Puma ◐ S 24 | 21 | 15 | M
521 Broadway (bet. Broome & Spring Sts.), 6 to Spring St.; N/R to Prince St., 212-334-7861; www.puma.com

■ "Very cool and fresh in that 'I'm-so-funky-Euro-sporty' way", this "trendy yet athletic" brand boasts a "new attitude" at this spacious two-floor SoHo "museum" that's a "lot of fun to shop"; "start collecting your" edgy and "old-school Pumas here" advise "fashion concious" sneaker diehards, who track down "phat" "hard-to-find models" downstairs before moving up to street level for the "great lookin'" "retro-hip work-out and go-out wear."

Pumpkin Maternity S C ▽ 23 | 22 | 21 | M
407 Broome St. (bet. Centre & Lafayette Sts.), N/R to Prince St.; 6 to Spring St., 212-334-1809; 800-460-0337; www.pumpkinmaternity.com

■ "The funkiest pregnancy store on the planet" rave fans who give "thanks to Pumpkin" Wentzel, a jack-o'-many-trades indie rocker turned designer and SoHo boutique owner for her "comfortable, fun" maternity clothes "geared toward downtown sensibilities";

216 subscribe to zagat.com

in addition to her signature shirred little black dress with an expanding waistline, moms and moms-to-be scoop up "cute" kids clothes and "offbeat" alt-rock CDs featuring fave artists like Dan Zanes; N.B. live kids concerts are held on occasion.

Purdy Girl ⓢⓒ | 21 | 18 | 22 | M |

540 LaGuardia Pl. (bet. Bleecker & W. 3rd Sts.), 4/5/6 to Bleecker St.; A/C/E/F to W. 4th St., 646-654-6752
220 Thompson St. (bet. Bleecker & W. 3rd Sts.), 4/5/6/ to Bleecker St.; A/C/E/F to W. 4th St., 212-529-8385 ●

■ For "frilly", "flirty" dresses and "girlie gear" that's "as feminine as can be", this Village duo is "a find" indeed; "darling collections" "at fair prices" guarantee a Lolita-age clientele, drawn to the mix of "mainstay designers like Nanette Lepore" and "lesser-knowns", all presented by salespeople who exude a "super-friendly" vibe.

Purl ⓢⓒ | – | – | – | E |

137 Sullivan St. (bet. Houston & Prince Sts.), C/E to Spring St., 212-420-8796; www.purlsoho.com

Knitting trendsetters and wanna-bes alike fill this bright, spacious new SoHo yarn store, soaking up the owner's sunny vibes and stylish selection, including antique needles and crochet hooks; the primarily natural fibers and sophisticated supplies range from basic wools and luxury cashmeres to hand-painted yarns, with lots of chunky options, all wrapped to go with a skein of friendly advice.

Purple Passion/DV8 ⓢⓒ | – | – | – | M |

211 W. 20th St. (bet. 7th & 8th Aves.), C/E to 23rd St., 212-807-0486; www.purplepassion.com

It used to be that "the store was tighter than their smallest rubber shorts", but now that this "must" for "serious fetish clothing and equipment" has moved to an ample duplex location in Chelsea, there's room enough for the furthest stretches of hard-core fantasy shopping, from dominatrix gear and role-playing costumes to a vast collection of over 500 corsets, plus all the usual gadgets; downstairs, the bigger hardware shares its showroom with an erotic art gallery.

Push ⓢⓒ | ▽ 23 | 27 | 25 | E |

240 Mulberry St. (bet. Prince & Spring Sts.), 6 to Spring St.; F/S/V to B'way/Lafayette St., 212-965-9699; www.pushjewelry.com

■ Owner-designer Karen Karch operates this "treasure" of a NoLita shop, which clients coo is "the coolest" for its carved-wood facade, aquarium, exposed pipes and jewelry "displayed on dollhouse furniture" or hollowed-out radios; the "friendly, accommodating" staff doesn't have to push to sell her "fantastic, hip designs" to happy couples (the braided, bejeweled wedding and engagement rings are particularly big-sellers).

Quark Spy | – | – | – | E |

537 Third Ave. (bet. 35th & 36th Sts.), 4/5/6/7/S to 42nd St./Grand Central, 212-889-4353; 800-343-6443; www.quarkfiles.com

"Entering this store feels like Mission Impossible", and well it should, since this Murray Hiller stocks state-of-the-art surveillance and counter-surveillance systems to make Agent Q throw in the combination laser/camera/body shield towel; whether you're staving off corporate espionage or just wanna make sure no one rips off your bodega, they're "a little more helpful than other" outfits in servicing your needs.

vote at zagat.com

| M | P | S | C |

Quiksilver S | 19 | 20 | 14 | M |
109-111 Spring St. (Mercer St.), N/R to Prince St., 212-334-4500; 800-576-4004; www.quiksilver.com
🗹 "Surf's up, dude" declare devotees who get stoked at this "colorful" SoHo shop with red boards slung on the sidewalk and the "feel of a resort" within; surfers, snowboarders and skaters make waves for the "cool stuff" including awesome board shorts, T-shirts, "good comfy jeans" and the Roxy line for women – all from the Australian team responsible for creating Ugg boots and Rip Curl wet suits; the staff sometimes "works at its own pace", so the time-pressed may find it a wipeout.

Radio Shack ●S | 14 | 11 | 14 | M |
139 E. 42nd St. (bet. Lexington & 3rd Aves.), 4/5/6/7/S to 42nd St./Grand Central, 212-953-6050; www.radioshack.com
🗹 With 7,200 shacks throughout the nation, this "oldie but goodie" has been "reliable, cheap" and expanding since 1919; though its "inept" staff "may not be classy" and "you can do better elsewhere" on big-ticket items, its multiple locations serve up parts, cables and other "small" bytes for "various electronic needs"; besides, "some of this stuff you just can't get anywhere else."

Rafe SC | – | – | – | E |
1 Bleecker St. (Bowery), F/V to 2nd Ave., 212-780-9739; 800-486-9544; www.rafe.com
Against a signature blue backdrop, this vast NoHo shop owned by designer Ramon Felix (nickname: Rafe) overflows with "gorgeous and creative" shoulder bags, clutches and totes for up-to-date girls (like Cameron Diaz); the ante of classic shapes is upped by a mega-dose of retro-detailing such as embroidery, ribbons and beading, eye-catching colors and durable craftsmanship – which explains the otherworldly prices; N.B. check out the new men's luggage.

R.A.G. ●SC | – | – | – | M |
1501 Broadway (43rd St.), 1/2/3/7/9/N/Q/R/S/W to 42nd St./Times Sq., 212-768-8751
Port Authority, basement level (42nd St.), A/C/E to 42nd St./Port Authority, 212-279-1829
225 W. 34th St. (bet. 7th & 8th Aves.), 1/2/3/9/A/C/E to 34th St./Penn Station, 212-971-0338
At this men's mini-chain, colorful, casual knitwear, shirts and pants with high-end designer flair (but low price tags) are displayed and stacked in compact spaces throughout Midtown, including the Port Authority; the friendly staff helps sort through the supplies, whose best-sellers include a classic American flag sweater.

Rags-A-Go-Go SC | – | – | – | I |
218 W. 14th St. (bet. 7th & 8th Aves.), A/C/E to 14th St.; 1/2/3/9 to 14th St., 646-486-4011; www.ragsagogo.com
On 14th Street, a bare-bones basement is enlivened by stuffed animals on the walls and a "rainbow of vintage" casualwear – cowboy and T-shirts, jeans and corduroys – "organized by color" and "priced by type"; it's "a sure thing for cheap" finds, if you bear in mind this is "truly used clothing."

Ralph Lauren S | 24 | 24 | 19 | VE |
888 Madison Ave. (72nd St.), 6 to 68th St., 212-434-8000
867 Madison Ave. (72nd St.), 6 to 68th St., 212-606-2100

218   subscribe to zagat.com

| M | P | S | C |

(continued)
Ralph Lauren
271 Mulberry St. (bet. Houston & Prince Sts.), 6 to Bleecker St., 212-343-0841
379 W. Broadway (bet. Broome & Spring Sts.), C/E to Spring St., 212-625-1660
800-475-7674; www.polo.com
■ Welcome to "American Classics" 101, a "monument" to a "middle-class [ideal of] haute couture" for men, women and children that "gets high grades for consistency" and an "A+ for window" displays; though "each store has its own vibe", most kudos go to the "gorgeous" Rhinelander Mansion flagship (867 Madison Avenue), which makes you feel "you've entered someone's private" estate, with its "portrait-lined staircases", seemingly "million-dollar-a-year flower budget" and cases of "exquisite" antique jewelry and silver knickknacks; the "helpful staff" makes it easy to navigate the "well-showcased" "tasteful, timeless" apparel, "crisp accessories" and housewares collections; N.B. the Mulberry Street branch is called RRL because it carries only that line.

Rampage ❍ S | – | – | – | I |
127 Prince St. (Wooster St.), N/R to Prince St., 212-995-9569
Packed to the max with über-trendy juniors' clothing, this SoHo offshoot of the national chain is like a candy store for cute young things on a shoestring budget; fans go wild for flirty party dresses, body-hugging tops and edgy jeans in the latest washes with novelty touches like lace-up seams and pin-tucking.

Ray Beauty Supply C | 23 | 8 | 14 | I |
721 Eighth Ave. (bet. 45th & 46th Sts.), A/C/E to 42nd St./Port Authority, 212-757-0175; 800-253-0993; www.raybeauty.com
◪ "Don't expect service or atmosphere" at this "hidden secret of the haircare industry", a "mecca for glamour girls and drag queens alike", located in the West 40s; it's all about "incredible bargains" on "hard-to-find items" and "serious, professional quality" hair and beauty supplies, from straighteners, shampoos and scissors to "high-end appliances" (like the touted SuperSolano hair-dryer).

RCS Computer Experience S C | 20 | 18 | 13 | E |
575 Madison Ave. (56th St.), E/V to 5th Ave./53rd St., 212-949-6935; www.rcseshop.com
◪ "Be sure to try out whatever you are buying first", and you too might think that the "selection of current technology products" at this East 50s "hands-on" outlet "blows other electronics stores away"; but then you might also wonder why the "rude" floor staff insists on such a "hard sell" – after all, "who wants to have a computer shoved down his throat?"

Reaction by Kenneth Cole ❍ S | 18 | 18 | 16 | M |
130 E. 57th St. (Lexington Ave.), 4/5/6/F/N/R/W to 59th St./ Lexington Ave., 212-688-1670; www.kennethcole.com
■ East 57th Street is home to the "hip, young" "more reasonable cousin" of the signature collection, which gets favorable reactions for "good-quality", "wearable" his-and-hers clothing; "loud colors are not welcome here", but for those seeking "black and brown basics", "comfy, trendy" shoes and "affordable leather goods", these are the "designer duds" for you.

| M | P | S | C |

Really Great Things S C　　▽ 25 | 25 | 25 | VE
284 Columbus Ave. (bet. 73rd & 74th Sts.), B/C to 72nd St., 212-787-5354

■ Upper Westsiders know the "masters of temptation" at this "spa-like shop" include "hard-to-find" European and Japanese women's (and a little men's) wear, including the elusive French designer Tara Jarmon, and even "better shoes" ("the real winner here"); while it lives up to its name and has "attentive salespeople" who aim to please, wags wager "with those tags, it should be renamed Really Expensive Things."

Rebecca Moss Ltd. C　　▽ 25 | 19 | 19 | E
510 Madison Ave. (53rd St.), E/V to 5th Ave./53rd St., 212-832-7671; 800-465-7367; www.rebeccamoss.com

■ Owner-designer Sam Zagoory named this "little gem" of a Madison Avenue shop after his grandmother, but his line of "unique" pens and "colorful leather goods" (from agendas to condom holders) is anything but old-fashioned; the store also carries other brands of writing instruments, as well as "great cards and stationery."

Rebel Rebel ● S　　24 | 16 | 21 | M
319 Bleecker St. (bet. Christopher & Grove Sts.), 1/9 to Christopher St., 212-989-0770

■ "When you have the money to buy that prized David Bowie on vinyl", pop down to Bleecker Street and "dig, dig, dig" through the "British imports (and a little Irish), music magazines and memorabilia" at this "small" CD and LP shop; manager/"hottie" David and his "knowledgeable staff make great suggestions", it's one of "the best record stores for celeb sightings", and now that she's Mrs. Guy Ritchie, the "Anglophilic" shop's "Madonna fixation" isn't so "inexplicable."

Record Explosion C　　16 | 8 | 11 | I
176 Broadway (bet. John St. & Maiden Ln.), 1/2/4/5/6/A/C/E/J/M/Z to Fulton St./B'way/Nassau, 212-693-1510 ●
2 Broadway (Stone St.), N/R to Whitehall St.; 4/5 to Bowling Green, 212-509-6444
142 W. 34th St. (bet. 6th & 7th Aves.), 1/2/3/9 to 34th St., 212-714-0450

■ "The 42nd Street Photo of CD stores", this Midtown-Downtown trio is a "picker's delight" "for the occasional bargain", especially on "non-mainstream" music and "old and used movies"; the "neon-lit" stores can be an "abrasive" "mess", but the "surprisingly creative selection" of merchandise makes them "a good source for salsa" and "cheap porn."

Reebok Store ● S　　18 | – | 15 | M
160 Columbus Ave. (bet. 67th & 68th Sts.), 1/9 to 66th St./Lincoln Ctr., 212-595-1480; www.reebok.com

■ "Stylish and functional" men's and women's activewear for everything from golf to running and dance fill this mammoth, futuristic-looking Upper West Side outpost downstairs from the "celebrity hot spot Sports Club"; the footwear is just as wide-ranging, plus there's even a podiatrist on-site once a week to answer footwear questions; prices can be "too expensive", but insiders confide it's a "great deal if you get the gym-membership discount"; N.B. the store was remodeled post-*Survey*.

REINSTEIN ROSS C | 28 | 27 | 22 | VE

29 E. 73rd St. (bet. 5th & Madison Aves.), 6 to 68th St., 212-772-1901
122 Prince St. (bet. Greene & Wooster Sts.), N/R to Prince St., 212-226-4513

■ This "small" all-white jewelry store on the Upper East Side, with a SoHo branch, showcases "beautiful Byzantine-like designs" in "unique shades" of "brushed gold" and "incredible fancy-colored sapphires" and other gemstones; "handmade in homage to ancient goldsmiths", the "intricate" pieces can also be made-to-order in your honor for a particularly precious, "expensive delight."

Religious Sex ◐ S C | – | – | – | E

7 St. Marks Pl. (bet. 2nd & 3rd Aves.), 6 to Astor Pl.; N/R to 8th St., 212-477-9037; www.religioussex.com

"A good girl's place to be bad", this "just plain cool" East Village haunt meets "all your fetish needs" with outrageous lingerie and fantasy wear, from fishnet body stockings and rubber thigh-high boots to the "most beautiful medieval-Renaissance-style clothes" (the "friendly staff is more than happy to lace you into one of their sexy corsets", and if "you're into role-playing", they'll help you "find your costume"); P.S. the "innovative" selection extends to dudewear – think frock coats, PVC jeans and ruffled shirts.

Reminiscence ◐ S C | 17 | 18 | 15 | M

50 W. 23rd St. (bet. 5th & 6th Aves.), F/N/R/V to 23rd St., 212-243-2292; www.reminiscence.com

■ "Step into a shopping time warp" when you enter this "pop-culture" paradise that offers an "eclectic" "mix of seasonal '60s and '70s [casualwear] and new retro-style clothing" from the store's own label; up front, "the perfect party favors, inappropriate gag gifts" and other novelties nestle alongside lunchboxes and "kitschy toys"; despite the name, there's "not much real vintage" here, but it's definitely "worth a gander" if you're cruising Chelsea.

Repêchage: Spa de Beauté | – | – | – | E

Galleria Bldg., 115 E. 57th St. (bet. Lexington & Park Aves.), 4/5/6/N/R/W to 59th St/Lexington Ave., 212-319-1770; 800-284-5044; www.repechage.com

Day spa in the Galleria whose French name translates as "to rescue", which is what its unique sea-based line of skincare and cosmetics claims it does for the skin by relying on seaweed and other hydrating botanicals; N.B. appointments can also be made for a variety of spa services, including facials, waxing and massage.

Repertoire C | – | – | – | E

75 Grand St. (bet. Greene & Wooster Sts.), A/C/E to Canal St., 212-219-8159; www.repertoire.com

The repertoire of home furnishings at this SoHo store ranges from elegant wood-topped tables by Casamilano and comfortable upholstered seating by Flexform and DePadova to playful pieces from Driade and woven-paper floor coverings.

Replay Store S C | – | – | – | E

109 Prince St. (Greene St.), N/R to Prince St.; F/V to B'way/Lafayette, 212-673-6300; www.replay.it

From the county fair–like fixtures to the men's, women's and children's jeans and casual sweatshirts, this two-floor SoHo store looks like it was born in the U.S.A., but the covetable collection, "favored by Europeans", comes straight from Italy; "a fresh alternative", the denim is done up in every fashionable silhouette and "special" wash imaginable and, "like the Energizer Bunny, lasts a long time", making it "worth the extra expense"; N.B. at press time the store was due to undergo a renovation.

Restoration Hardware ●S | 22 | 23 | 18 | M |
935 Broadway (bet. 21st & 22nd Sts.), N/R to 23rd St., 212-260-9479; 800-762-1005; www.restorationhardware.com

☑ "Doorknobs, furniture polish and leather sofas" along with lighting, "clever kitsch" like "retro" "gadgets" (e.g. a 1955 hand warmer) and other "vintage-looking stuff" are sold at this Flatiron branch of the home-furnishings-and-hardware chain; "nostalgia"-obsessed fans feel the "weird mix works" and makes for "old-fashioned" "fun", but critics counter it's a "pricey" "mixed bag."

Resurrection S | 24 | 21 | 16 | E |
217 Mott St. (bet. Prince & Spring Sts.), N/R to Prince St.; 6 to Spring St., 212-625-1374; www.resurrectionvintage.com

■ If "Pucci's your thing" or you think "Courrèges is to die for", this Lower East Side specialist in '60s and '70s "high-quality couture" "in very good condition" will provide "the perfect piece to cause a buzz"; appropriately decorated with Space Age–style chandeliers, round blue chairs and blood-red walls, the "nice digs" make for pleasant browsing, "but be ready to drop some major cash" for the "collectible" goods (e.g. $125 for period Levi's).

Reva Mivasagar S | ▽ 25 | 25 | 23 | E |
28 Wooster St. (bet. Canal & Grand Sts.), A/C/E to Canal St., 212-334-3860; www.revadesigns.com

■ "Very chic", "but still festive enough" for the big day, these retro-inspired yet modern, ivory or colored creations are made "for the not-too-bridey bride" who "can't stand the sugary-sweetness of the wedding industry"; "a pleasure to work with", the "very talented" Singapore-born designer is often at his SoHo shop, where he also turns out eveningwear that "delivers consistently classy looks."

Richard Metz Golf C | ▽ 21 | 19 | 19 | E |
12 E. 46th St. (Madison Ave.), 4/5/6/7/S to 42nd St./Grand Central, 212-599-7252; 888-737-4659; www.richardmetzgolf.com

☑ Go on, "take a mulligan" – the high ceilings at this 34-year-old family-owned "golfer's dreamworld" tucked into a second-floor Midtown location are made for swinging; while some applaud the "nice selection of woods and irons", apparel, shoes and bags, a few find it "limited", particularly the putters and balls.

Ricky's | 24 | 15 | 12 | I |
718 Broadway (bet. Astor Pl. & Washington St.), 6 to Astor Pl., 212-979-5232
590 Broadway (bet. Houston & Prince Sts.), F/V/S to B'way/Lafayette, 212-226-5552
44 E. Eighth St. (Greene St.), N/R to 8th St., 212-254-5247
988 Eighth Ave. (58th St.), 1/2/A/B/C/D to 59th St./Columbus Circle, 212-957-8343
509 Fifth Ave. (bet. 42nd & 43rd Sts.), 7 to 5th Ave., 212-949-7230 ●S
1189 First Ave. (64th St.), 6 to 68th St., 212-879-8361
466 Sixth Ave. (bet. 11th & 12th Sts.), F/L/V to 14th St./Union Sq., 212-924-3401

M | P | S | C

(continued)
Ricky's
112 W. 72nd St. (bet. B'way & Columbus Ave.), 1/2/3 to 72nd St., 212-769-3678
www.rickys-nyc.com

■ "Duane Reade meets the Pink Pussycat" sums up this "naughty" but nice chain "crammed full of kitsch and beauty booty", from "the great selection" of hair products and makeup to "novelty items" like "fake tattoos", "pink wigs and vibrators with kangaroos on them"; be prepared for a "totally New York experience", right down to the salespeople who sometimes seem to "see customers as an annoying distraction from figuring out what club to go to that night"; P.S. if you're feeling "funky" and looking for a costume "on Halloween, this is the place to be."

Rico 🆂🅲
— | — | — | M

372 Atlantic Ave. (bet. Bond & Hoyt Sts.), Brooklyn, A/C/G to Hoyt-Schermerhorn, 718-797-2077; www.shoprico.com

Owner Rico Espinet showcases his lamps and lighting solutions as well as furniture from Mitchell Gold and Dellarobia and modern art and ceramics at this Boerum Hill studio and store; originally a sculptor and a stage-lighting professional, the designer taps into both retro and modern inspirations, using materials like hand-blown frosted glass and polished chrome to create his moderately priced line.

Rita's Needlepoint 🅲
22 | 19 | 23 | E

150 E. 79th St., 2nd fl. (bet. Lexington & 3rd Aves.), 6 to 77th St., 212-737-8613

■ "An unpretentious shop" that "feels like a little club with constant coffee klatches", this Upper East Side boutique tempts with a "good merchandise mix" ranging from "cute, simple and inexpensive to grand, gorgeous projects" that may call for one of Rita's "fabulous custom-painted" canvases; the "sage owners" and their "knowledgeable staff" lend "superior advice", making it "a joy to shop here."

Ritz Furs
∇ 17 | 15 | 13 | E

107 W. 57th St. (bet. 6th & 7th Aves.), F/N/Q/R/W to 57th St., 212-265-4559; www.ritzfurs.com

■ For "those who know furs", there are "excellent bargains" to be had at this West 50s salon, which showcases "gently used designer" coats and accessories; by pelt standards, "prices are for plebeians" – especially in the everything-under-$1,000 basement – whether you're getting a "sumptuous" sable, a mink bikini or a fox cell-phone holder.

RK Bridal
19 | 9 | 13 | M

318 W. 39th St. (bet. 8th & 9th Aves.), A/C/E to 42nd St./Port Authority, 212-947-1155; 800-929-9512; www.rkbridal.com

✔ "You want to get married twice so you can buy two dresses instead of one" at this "no-frills" Garment District "supermarket of bridalwear" "crammed" with "hidden gems" that are "worth a trip for the thrifty bride", plus bridesmaid dresses and "accessories you don't want to spend a lot on"; "bring your armor to fight through the crowds" on weekends complain critics who find the "help way too snooty for the factory outlet" environs, hissing "not for the couture girl."

vote at zagat.com

Roberta's Lingerie C ▽ 22 | 18 | 19 | E
1252 Madison Ave. (90th St.), 4/5/6 to 86th St., 212-860-8366
◼ Whether you go to this "lovely" peach-colored "neighborhood shop" on Madison for "your first bra" or "your honeymoon outfit", "make sure you check in with the experts to get the right fit" and cup size; while boosters big on little nothings claim the "choices are wonderful", "with a broad price range" to boot, a handful shrug that they've "never understood the appeal of this store."

Robert Clergerie S 25 | 22 | 21 | VE
681 Madison Ave. (bet. 61st & 62nd Sts.), N/R to 5th Ave./59th St., 212-207-8600
◼ "Comfort reigns" and "wonderful quality" rules at this Madison Avenue outpost where some of the "best" shoes "the French have to offer" can be found, along with handbags and accessories; the "great styles", including the "popular" wedgie, range from "chunky" to "out there" to just plain "fab" – little wonder loyalists "want more and more"; service is "friendly", prompting patrons to opine "every store in the world should be run as well."

Robert Lee Morris S C 22 | 22 | 17 | E
400 W. Broadway (bet. Broome & Spring Sts.), C/E to Spring St., 212-431-9405; 800-829-8444; www.robertleemorris.com
◼ The "standard bearer for high-end", "serious, modern" sterling-silver jewelry since the '70s is still going strong at his SoHo boutique, turning out "statement-making" designs, like the signature Knuckle rings, that are "not for the meek" (but are often in 18 karat gold nowadays).

Robert Marc 27 | 25 | 25 | VE
190 Columbus Ave. (bet. 68th & 69th Sts.), 1/9 to 66th St./Lincoln Ctr., 212-799-4600 S
1300 Madison Ave. (bet. 92nd & 93rd Sts.), 6 to 96th Sts., 212-722-1600
1046 Madison Ave. (bet. 78th & 79th Sts.), 6 to 77th St., 212-988-9600
782 Madison Ave. (bet. 66th & 67th Sts.), 6 to 68th St., 212-737-6000
575 Madison Ave. (bet. 56th & 57th Sts.), N/R/W to 5th Ave./59th St., 212-319-2000 S
400 Madison Ave. (bet. 47th & 48th Sts.), E/V to 5th Ave./53rd St., 212-319-2900
www.robertmarc.com
◼ La "crème de la crème" of spectacle shops may well be this Uptown Manhattan chain that purveys products that help you "get over bad memories of those big plastic frames you had to wear in the 4th grade"; the "unbelievable selection" of "beautiful", "up-to-the-minute" eyewear is "well organized" and "presented", and the "discerning", "talented" staff "helps you find flattering" glasses that give "you a new outlook on life" that's "worth the price."

Roberto Cavalli S C 25 | 23 | 22 | VE
711 Madison Ave. (bet. 63rd & 64th Sts.), 4/5/6/N/R/W to 59th St./Lexington Ave., 212-755-7722; www.robertocavalli.it
◼ "Prepare to be pampered" by the "accommodating, friendly staff" at this East 60s boutique, whose namesake designer "knows how to flatter the female form" with "gorgeously bold", "big-bucks" dresses, coats and "sexy" jeans; body-hugging and bedecked with furs, feathers and silk appliqués, his "top-notch hippie chic" is "not made for a shy person" but is "so right for a *Sex and the City* night."

| | | | | M | P | S | C |

ROBERT TALBOTT C   27 | 26 | 25 | VE
680 Madison Ave. (bet. 61st & 62nd Sts.), N/R/W to 5th Ave./59th St., 212-751-1200; 800-747-8778; www.roberttalbott.com

■ "The only place for shirts and neckwear" ("they actually have bow ties!") swoon supporters about this compact but "lovely Madison Avenue store", an "upper-class gem" for its "gorgeous" garb in "fab colors"; "although the prices are steep", "where else can one find a seven-fold necktie, at least outside of Italy?"

Roche Bobois S   25 | 25 | 20 | VE
200 Madison Ave. (35th St.), 6 to 33rd St., 212-725-5513; www.rochebobois.com

■ At this East 30s furniture store, the "good-quality", "modern" sofas, beds and tables "wear well", especially seating upholstered in leather that's "like buttah"; for the more traditionally oriented, the Les Provinciales collection contains overstuffed couches and sensuous armchairs with a French feel.

Rochester Big & Tall   25 | 23 | 24 | E
1301 Sixth Ave. (52nd St.), B/D/F/V to 47th-50th Sts./Rockefeller Ctr., 212-247-7500; 800-282-8200; www.rochesterclothing.com
Additional locations throughout the NY area

■ Jolly in-the-green giants "love" the fact that "large men have a place to go where they don't have to settle on something" they don't really want; "one of the few plus-size men's shops in Manhattan", this "upscale" Midtowner carries all the best-known designer brands, and their salespeople, who "remember you and the size you wear", are "unsurpassed"; however, the skinny on the "hefty prices" is "your wallet better be as big as your waistline."

Rocks in your Head ●S   ∇ 22 | 17 | 21 | I
157 Prince St. (bet. Thompson St. & W. B'way), N/R to Prince St., 212-475-6729; www.rocksinyourhead.com

■ "Lord knows how they afford the rent" given the "good prices", but somehow this SoHo "sleeper" manages; a "friendly" "indie-record haven" "behind whose doors are some of the hardest-to-find albums in the city", it's "fun, eclectic, and you'll likely see a rock star" cruising for a rare CD – it's so hip, "the guys from *High Fidelity* would look like Michael Bolton in here."

Rogue Music ●C   – | – | – | I
251 W. 30th St., 10th fl. (bet. 7th & 8th Aves.), 1/2/A/C/E to 34th St./Penn Station, 212-629-5073; www.roguemusic.com

"Everyone from Madonna to Michael Jackson has stopped by" this Garment District store in the Recording and Rehearsal Arts Building to rummage amid the "daily-changing stock" of "hard-to-find" used and consigned instruments and sound equipment, all at "rock-bottom prices"; rappers from sessions upstairs say "it's worth checking often" for new acquisitions and consistently "mind-boggling expertise."

Room   – | – | – | VE
182 Duane St. (bet. Greenwich & Hudson Sts.), 1/2/3/9 to Chambers St., 212-226-1045; 888-420-7666; www.roomonline.com

What began life as a stylish magalog is now a "smart" TriBeCa purveyor of "fresh"-looking furnishings that include contemporary sofas by S. Russell Grove, warm wood tables by e15, colorful John Pomp vases and urban tool kits displayed in a sparse loft setting.

vote at zagat.com

| | | M | P | S | C |

Rooms & Gardens S — | — | — | VE
7 Mercer St. (bet. Canal & Grand Sts.), N/R to Canal St., 212-431-1297; www.roomsandgardensantique.com
Even if you weren't to the manor born, this SoHo purveyor of vintage furniture and European antiques (mostly French) from the 18th to mid-20th century lets you live like you were by providing the proper trappings like ornate garden urns and mercury-glass mirrors; new shipments arrive every three or four months, so don't give up on that 19th-century oak convent table you've always wanted.

Rosen & Chaddick Textiles ▽ 27 | 21 | 19 | M
246 W. 40th St. (bet. 7th & 8th Aves.), A/C/E to 42nd St./Port Authority, 212-869-0142; 800-225-3838
■ Heralded as one of the "top fabric suppliers to Broadway and the entertainment industry", this "all-purpose" textile shop "in the heart of the Garment District" also offers the home-sewing set an "impressive selection of top-quality" goods, particularly "great menswear" options.

Roslyn S C 22 | 19 | 19 | E
276 Columbus Ave. (73rd St.), 1/2/3/9 to 72nd St., 212-496-5050
■ "Whether it is the latest fad or a classic piece" of jewelry, an "antique ring" or kicky, funky "adorable hats and bags", this "small boutique" – "one of the best finds on the Upper West Side" – is "sure to have it"; the eclectic mix of fine collectibles from owner Roslyn Grent as well as other talented designers is matched by "salespeople who accommodate special requests."

Rothman's S 20 | 18 | 19 | M
200 Park Ave. S. (17th St.), 4/5/6/L/N/Q/R/W to 14th St./Union Sq., 212-777-7400; www.rothmansny.com
■ Those who "seek value for name-brand quality" head to the top of Union Square, where they can "get designer men's clothes at discount prices" – both tailored togs (Hickey Freeman, Hugo Boss, etc.) and casuals like Bill's Khakis, plus coats and accessories; the "informed, friendly staff" is geared toward "guys who don't like to shop."

Rubin Chapelle S C — | — | — | E
410 W. 14th St. (bet. 9th Ave. & Washington St.), A/C/E/L to 14th St./8th Ave., 212-647-8636; www.rubinchapelle.com
On West 14th Street's new designer row, this spare, sleek arrival holds its own with a thin Lucite-paneled 'curtain' and curvy white racks that showcase Sonja Rubin's and Kip Chapelle's intriguing blend of masculine-feminine tailoring; the asymmetrical separates and leather jackets for both sexes have avant-garde 'look-at-me' details that ensure everyone will.

Rudy's Music Shop C — | — | — | E
169 W. 48th St. (bet. 6th & 7th Aves.), N/R/W to 49th St., 212-391-1699; www.rudysmusic.com
Midtown "music store without equal" where you can ogle "great vintage and hard-to-find" guitars and basses, including owner Rudy Pensa's own electric brand of "artistic pieces", plus what acoustic aficionados call "the best selection of Taylors in New York"; if you do a Jimi Hendrix, the shop can repair your abused instrument, but "keep in mind this is not a store to find your first guitar."

M | P | S | C

Rue St. Denis ●S   ▽ 23 | 19 | 18 | M
174 Ave. B (11th St.), L to 1st Ave., 212-260-3388
■ From winter coats to cords, there are "great finds every time" at this spacious store, which specializes in biker gear and unusually patterned clothes, primarily from the 1960s–1980s, for him, her and baby; East Village vintage lovers also note that "every item is in excellent condition" – naturally, since most have never been worn.

Rug Company, The S   – | – | – | VE
88 Wooster St. (bet. Broome & Spring Sts.), C/E to Spring St.; 212-274-0444; www.therugcompany.info
The British have landed at this new SoHo offshoot of a five-year-old London-based firm featuring an extensive collection of carpets – from hand-knotted Nepalese ones to classic wovens and a designer collection from well-known English names like Marni, Paul Smith and Nina Campbell; but whatever you want you're covered, since the rugs can be made to any size.

Sacco ●SC   21 | 18 | 18 | M
324 Columbus Ave. (75th St.), 1/2/3/B/C to 72nd St., 212-799-5229
14 E. 17th St. (5th Ave.), 4/5/6/L/N/Q/R/W to 14th St./Union Sq., 212-243-2070
94 Seventh Ave. (bet. 15th & 16th Sts.), 1/9 to 18th St., 212-675-5180
111 Thompson St. (Prince St.), N/R to Prince St., 212-925-8010
www.saccoshoes.com
■ Offering a "fashionable" "comfort line" that's one of the "best" for "pounding the pavement" "in style" "without making you look like a school nurse", this chainlet stalwart also stocks an "extensive range" of "sensibly creative" high heels, "beautifully crafted" in Italy; prices are "reasonable", and take heed: insiders confide "they have very good sales."

Safavieh Carpets SC   ▽ 24 | 20 | 22 | E
902 Broadway (bet. 20th & 21st Sts.), N/R to 23rd St., 212-477-1234; 866-422-9070; www.safavieh.com
■ This "destination for Oriental rugs" in the Flatiron devotes 25,000 sq. ft. to carpeting "from regions" all over the world, ranging from India to Turkey and China; while the antique-oriented have plenty to choose from, the Hampton and SoHo collections are colorful experiences for contemporary types.

Saint Laurie Merchant Tailors   – | – | – | E
22 W. 32nd St., 5th fl. (bet. 5th & 6th Aves.), B/D/F/N/Q/R/V/W to 34th St./Herald Sq., 212-643-1916; www.saintlaurie.com
A broad selection of fabrics and "excellent craftsmanship" characterizes the experience at this menswear manufacturer where the made-to-measure goods are "worth the longer wait", since the "tailors clothe your mediocre midsection magnificently"; finance types swear by all the saints that this is the "best buy on quality suits", even though they regret a recent "move to a far less convenient spot" in the Garment District.

SAKS FIFTH AVENUE S   26 | 24 | 20 | E
611 Fifth Ave. (bet. 49th & 50th Sts.), B/D/F/V to 47-50th Sts./ Rockefeller Ctr., 212-753-4000; www.saks.com
■ The "old-world elegance" and "open, airy" atmosphere of this Midtown "landmark" make it a "pleasure to shop" its "top-drawer" women's collections (including "fabulous" petites and plus sizes),

vote at zagat.com

"ultra-civilized" menswear and "a nice mix" of "serious and stylish shoes" for both ("sales are to run for"); "eager makeup artists abound" among the "varied" cosmetics counters, and "kudos" also go to bridal-salon trunk shows, "lovely leather goods" and "lust-inducing" accessories, especially the lingerie department ("best bra-fitting in town"); a "splendid" restaurant, an "A+ return policy" and a staff that's "happy to find merchandise at another location" help "uphold its reputation" for service; and at year's end, "you can feel the holiday spirit the minute" you walk in.

Salon Moderne — | — | — | E
281 Lafayette St. (bet. Houston & Prince Sts.), N/R to Prince St., 212-219-3439

This SoHo home-furnishings store's Italian imports include plush modern sofas, mirrors, luscious pillows, throws and a few well-chosen vintage pieces; the showroom also offers custom-work.

Salvation Army 13 | 6 | 8 | I
536 W. 46th St. (bet. 10th & 11th Aves.), A/C/E to 42nd St./Port Authority, 212-757-2311; www.salvationarmy.org
Additional locations throughout the NY area

■ "If you've time to sort through the mayhem, then dive on in" to "the old standby of second-hand shops", which "carries everything donate-able" at low "prices, regardless of brand or era"; among the army of branches, the "Grand Kahuna" on 46th Street is "interesting for clothing and cheap furniture"; the staff, however, needs to do some KP.

Sam & Seb 🅢🅒 — | — | — | M
208 Bedford Ave. (bet. N. 5th & 6th Sts.), Brooklyn, L to Bedford Ave., 718-486-8300; www.samandseb.com

Done up in bright pink and orange, this hard-to-miss Williamsburg boutique offers an arty selection that's keyed into neighborhood demands; the cool collections include plenty of items from local Brooklyn designers, bright Oink! baby apparel and whimsical rain boots, plus Black Sabbath, Bob Marley and Beastie Boys T-shirts and Blondie and Billy Idol onesies for budding superstars who just want to rock on, at least through the night.

Sam Ash 🅢🅒 24 | 18 | 18 | M
160 W. 48th St. (bet. 6th & 7th Aves.), N/R/W to 49th St., 212-719-2299; 800-472-6274; www.samashmusic.com

■ An "excellent selection of guitars and amps", "great brass and woodwinds", an "orgasmic drum shop", "hard-to-find sheet music", plus "nightclub-oriented" soundboards and decks and a burgeoning software department, are bursting 48th Street's seams at this music "mecca" sprawling "chaotically" down the block; if you "know your merchandise before you come" and are game to brave the "cheesy setting" and "aggressive salespeople", you can score at "lower prices than at other stores."

Sam Flax 23 | 20 | 16 | E
425 Park Ave. (55th St.), 4/5/6/N/R/W to 59th St./Lexington Ave., 212-935-5353
12 W. 20th St. (5th Ave.), F/V to 23rd St., 212-620-3038 🅢
800-628-9512; www.samflax.com

■ "Buy something to treat yourself" at this "overstuffed" Flatironist where "everything is quality" and "to the point in style and function", from "beautiful" Aeron chairs to "writing implements

228 subscribe to zagat.com

you never knew you needed"; budding Picassos say it's "really a high-end office supply" place, so "skip the art materials, since you can find a better, cheaper selection elsewhere", and "go straight to the gifts and the furniture."

Sam Goody 14 | 13 | 10 | M
230 E. 42nd St. (bet. 2nd & 3rd Aves.), 4/5/6/7/S to 42nd St./ Grand Central, 212-490-0568
19 Fulton St. (Pearl St.), 2/3/4/5/A/C/J/M/Z to Fulton St./B'way/Nassau, 212-571-9706
Manhattan Mall, 901 Sixth Ave. (34th St.), B/D/F/N/Q/R/V/W to 34th St./Herald Sq., 212-947-9650
390 Sixth Ave. (8th St.), A/C/E/F/V to W. 4th St., 212-674-7131 ● S
5100-47 Kings Plaza (bet. Flatbush Ave. & Ave. U), Brooklyn, 718-253-6701
107-18 Continental Ave. (Austin St.), Queens, 718-263-1140
66-26 Metropolitan Ave., Queens, 718-456-0085
90-15 Queens Blvd., Queens, G/R/V to Woodhaven Blvd./Queens Blvd., 718-592-2268
2655 Richmond Ave., Staten Island, 718-698-7070
www.samgoody.com

☛ "Need Britney at full retail?" – this "not-so-Goody" of a veteran chain with branches all over has "got it"; it sure is convenient, and the staff is up on "current hits" and "hip-hop, but good luck finding anyone who knows anything about another genre", and though the "excellent loyalty program" can pay off in long-term savings, the everyday "ridiculous prices" have even the "teenybopper crowd" grumbling "this is why they invented Napster."

Samuel Jackson Design Company ● S | _ | _ | _ | E
31 Crosby St. (bet. Broome & Grand Sts.), N/R to Prince St., 646-613-9379; www.samueljacksondesigns.com

It may be hard to spot from the street, but this moody basement SoHo shop with exposed-brick walls and abstract paintings is filled with lushly knit accessories, slouchy leather and suede bags in funky and whimsical shapes and swinging, '70s-style knitwear that make it worth seeking out; you may not run into Samuel L. behind the counter – the actor has nothin' to do with these groovy goods – but more than a few rockers have been known to bop by.

S&W S C 21 | 9 | 11 | M
165 W. 26th St. (7th Ave.), 1/9 to 28th St., 718-431-2800
4217 13th Ave. (bet. 42nd & 43rd Sts.), Brooklyn, M/W to Fort Hamilton Pkwy., 718-431-2800

☛ You must "go early in the season" for "best buys" on "top-quality" "designer coats, shoes and bags" at this "little place for the odd treasure" that's been in Chelsea and Brooklyn "for eons"; "their purses are their strong suit", but cheapsters with a "memory of the past" say "their clothing selection has suffered in recent years" while the saleswomen are as "high pressure" as ever, but not on Friday evening or Saturday, "since they are Shomer Shabbat."

Sanrio (aka Hello Kitty Store) ● S C | _ | _ | _ | M
233 W. 42nd St. (bet. 7th & 8th Aves.), 1/2/3/7/9/N/Q/R/S/W to 42nd St./ Times Sq., 212-840-6011; www.sanrio.com

Blaring pop music, tween tourists and a whole lotta that cartoon icon, Hello Kitty, come together in the mystical blend of "fun Japanese pop" adorableness that only Sanrio can bring to NY; for a company seemingly poised to conquer the world with cuteness,

vote at zagat.com

| M | P | S | C |

this Time Square shop furthers the agenda with branding on items big and small, so say *konnichi wa* to the über-"girlie" feline, plus "bad-boy penguin" Badtz-Maru and all her other friends on pencil cases, bubble gum, waffle irons and pink TVs.

Sansha ⓈⒸ | – | – | – | M |
1717 Broadway, 2nd fl. (bet. 54th & 55th Sts.), N/Q/R/W to 57th St., 212-246-6212; 800-398-9562; www.sansha.com
Twinkle-toed customers of all ages and sexes hotfoot it up the steps to this Midtown dancer's delight for stage-worthy footwear, such as handcrafted "good-quality" split-sole ballet slippers and *pointe*, jazz, flamenco, tap and character shoes; the *grande* selection of leotards and legwear, ranging from unitards to *All That Jazz*-esque fishnets, is enough to make any trouper *jeté* for joy.

Satellite Records ⓄⓈ | – | – | – | M |
259 Bowery (bet. Houston & Prince Sts.), F/V to 2nd Ave., 212-995-1744; www.satellite-records.com
The place to beat for dance music, with numerous CD and vinyl listening stations, this "true club-life superstore" in a "new, much better" Bowery space (with branches in Atlanta and Boston) has one of "the best selections for trance, house", jungle, hip-hop and drum 'n' bass; the "help is pretty knowledgeable and responsive", and they definitely can tell you where the party is – check out the rack of invites near the album cases up front.

Scandinavian Ski & Sport Shop Ⓢ | 23 | 18 | 16 | VE |
40 W. 57th St. (bet. 5th & 6th Aves.), F to 57th St., 212-757-8524; www.skishop.com
◪ Steep yourself in "top-of-the-line" skis, ski boots, snowboards and some of the "best Norwegian sweaters in New York", plus mountain bikes, sporting goods and apparel at this retail chalet, a Midtown fixture since 1948; still, some bad sports scoff the selection is "limited", adding "how do you say overpriced in Swedish?"

Schneider's Ⓒ | ▽ 22 | 11 | 15 | M |
20 Ave. A (2nd St.), F/V to 2nd Ave., 212-228-3540
■ It may be a "schlep to get to" this Alphabet City children's supply store, "but where else are you going to buy your Maclaren stroller in the East Village?" – this is "the place for all baby needs", from furniture to gifts and toys.

School Products Co. Ⓒ | 21 | 14 | 20 | M |
1201 Broadway, 3rd fl. (bet. 28th & 29th Sts.), N/R to 28th St., 212-679-3516; 800-847-4127; www.schoolproducts.com
■ A "bargain-basement atmosphere" reigns at this 55-year-old on the fringes of the Flatiron District, and that's why it's a "favorite", with oceans of "yarns on cones – a delight for machine knitters" and weavers – and "terrific buys on cashmere and upscale yarns" for hand-knitters; it's "truly a place for those who love their craft", and it's all finished off with a "really helpful, low-key staff."

Schweitzer Linen Ⓒ | 26 | 14 | 14 | E |
457 Columbus Ave. (bet. 81st & 82nd Sts.), B/C to 81st St., 212-799-9642
1053 Lexington Ave. (bet. 74th & 75th Sts.), 6 to 77th St., 212-570-0236
1132 Madison Ave. (bet. 84th & 85th Sts.), 4/5/6 to 86th St., 212-249-8361
800-554-6367; www.schweitzerlinen.com
■ "Gorgeous", "sophisticated" European-style linens at "great prices" and scallop-edged Egyptian-cotton towels that are

Porthault look-alikes for less are the draws at this trio of specialty shops; they have a "terrific" mail-order catalog that offers other bed-and-bath-oriented items like tapestry pillows and will also produce fully customized bedding from customers' color schemes and design ideas.

Sco S — | — | — | E

230 Mulberry St. (bet. Prince & Spring Sts.), 6 to Spring St., 212-966-3011; 866-966-7268; www.scocare.com

The name of this "great, little" relative newcomer to the NoLita scene stands for Skin Care Options, and flexible, "custom-made products" are just what they offer: customers choose from the line of existing cleansers, toners, creams and scrubs, then elect to have them infused with natural ingredients (ranging from papaya to parsley) based on the specific needs of their skin; converts leave with containers labeled with their name, the product's expiration date – and a little less money in the bank.

SCOOP ●SC 23 | 21 | 13 | VE

532 Broadway (bet. Prince & Spring Sts.), N/R to Prince St., 212-925-2886
1275 & 1277 Third Ave. (bet. 73rd & 74th Sts.), 6 to 77th St., 212-535-5577
873 Washington St. (bet. 13th & 14th Sts.), A/C/E/L to 14th St./8th Ave., 212-929-1244
www.scoopnyc.com

☑ It's like a "trip around the Downtown boutiques all in one place" exclaim enthusiasts of these "high-energy" spots pulsating with the "hottest" "high-end brands" – a "great selection of shoes, separates and going-out clothes" – familiar to "fashion-forward", "small-sized" "It girls"; the thrifty sniff it's "expensive considering it's all trendy stuff", but if you can "splurge, go for it" and overlook the "self-congratulatory" salespeople (who tend to "ignore" you too); N.B. Washington Street also has menswear.

Scoop Men's ●SC — | — | — | VE

1273 Third Ave. (bet. 73rd & 74th Sts.), 6 to 77th St., 212-535-5577; www.scoopnyc.com

Adjacent to the bustling women's boutique, this new East 70s adjunct lets guys scoop up a cool collection of clothes, shoes and accessories; such designer goodies as John Varvatos shearlings, Etro knits and Paul Smith yarn-dyed shirts complement a wide offering of slacks and jeans, including distressed Levi's Gold Rush 501s; all is conveniently organized for easy coordination within a creamy-walled, brushed-metal–accented space.

Scott Jordan Furniture S 25 | 22 | 26 | E

137 Varick St. (Spring St.), 1/9 to Canal St.; C/E to Spring St., 212-620-4682; www.scottjordan.com

■ "If you like solid cherry furniture, start here first" profess proponents of this SoHo warehouse space selling "supremely beautiful", "handcrafted" "heirloom-quality" Mission-style chairs, tables, sofas and beds, which are produced in the former Brooklyn Navy Yard; "reasonable prices" for the quality and a "very patient" staff make shopping here a pleasure.

Screaming Mimi's ●S 21 | 20 | 17 | M

382 Lafayette St. (E. 4th St.), 6 to Astor Pl.; N/R to 8th St., 212-677-6464; www.screamingmimis.com

☑ "Funkadelic possibilities" abound at this NoHo store "catering to the kids from NYU and neighboring high schools" with its "large

| M | P | S | C |

selection of '60s and '70s clothes", "crazy shoes" and costume jewelry; but while groupies groove on the "glitzy decor", skeptics scream the scene is strictly "for browsing rather than buying", since the "merchandise is expensive for what it is."

Scuba Network ●◐ | – | – | – | M |
124 E. 57th St. (bet. Lexington & Park Aves.), 4/5/6/F/N/R/W to 59th St./ Lexington Ave., 212-750-9160 ◼
655 Sixth Ave. (bet. 20th & 21st Sts.), F/V to 23rd St., 212-243-2988 ◼
290 Atlantic Ave. (Smith St.), Brooklyn, F to Bergen St., 718-802-0700
800-688-3483; www.scubanetwork.com
Divers go off the deep end for the "good scuba stuff" at these Manhattan and Brooklyn offshoots of the 20-year-old chain; "the knowledgeable staff" really "knows how to swim" and how to outfit water sports enthusiasts of all ages with equipment that "fits you correctly", while instructors also help you "get certified" and plan your next excursion below sea level.

Scully & Scully ◐ | 27 | 25 | 21 | VE |
504 Park Ave. (59th St.), 4/5/6/N/R/W to 59th St./Lexington Ave., 212-755-2590; 800-223-3717; www.scullyandscully.com
■ Since 1934, this "aristocratic" Park Avenue home-furnishings grande dame has been catering to collectors of Herend china, repro Chippendale- and Sheraton-style chairs, animal figurines and velvet bed steps; if your tastes tend toward the "traditional" (some say "stuffy"), it's an "ideal", albeit very expensive, place for adding "final touches to a room or for house presents."

Seaman Schepps ◐ | – | – | – | VE |
485 Park Ave. (bet. 58th & 59th Sts.), 4/5/6 /N/R/W to 59th St./ Lexington Ave., 212-753-9520
Since the early '20s, the "rich and elite" of New York, Palm Beach and Nantucket have supported this Park Avenue jeweler; as the founder's name implies, the house specialty is diamond-studded, coral pieces designed in the shape of shells, starfish or other creatures of the sea (opal, chalcedony and other cabochon stones are "fabulous" too); each creation is signed and numbered – an exclusive, artistic touch that alleviates the heavy price points.

Sean ◐ | ▽ 22 | 19 | 16 | M |
224 Columbus Ave. (bet. 70th & 71st Sts.), 1/2/B/C to 72nd St., 212-769-1489 ●◼
132 Thompson St. (bet. Houston & Prince Sts.), C/E to Spring St., 212-598-5980
www.seanstore.com
■ Known for its "great selection of cotton shirts in a myriad of colors" by French designer Emile Lafaurie, this brown-and-orange-hued West 70s and SoHo duo also offers European-made "good-quality coats, shirts and pullovers without being *très cher*"; styles manage to be "mod" *sans* changing drastically from year to year.

Searle ●◼ | 24 | 22 | 19 | E |
156 Fifth Ave. (bet. 20th & 21st Sts.), N/R to 23rd St., 212-924-4330
1124 Madison Ave. (84th St.), 4/5/6 to 86th St., 212-988-7318
1035 Madison Ave. (79th St.), 6 to 77th St., 212-717-4022
805 Madison Ave. (68th St.), 6 to 68th St., 212-628-6665
609 Madison Ave. (E. 58th St.), 4/5/6/N/R/W to 59th St./Lexington Ave., 212-753-9021
1296 Third Ave. (bet. 73rd & 74th Sts.), 6 to 77th St., 212-717-5200

subscribe to zagat.com

M | P | S | C

(continued)
Searle
1051 Third Ave. (62nd St.), 4/5/6/N/R/W to 59th St./Lexington Ave., 212-838-5990
www.searlenyc.com
◪ Though known for its own line of "good-investment" raincoats and "legendary shearlings", there's "a lot more than coats" at this mini-chain nowadays – specifically, "a mix of classic and trendy" womenswear, including some "sexy tops and dresses that make men look twice"; however, even those who "love the clothes, hate the price tags", while a "personable" staff that "does not leave you alone" is a plus for some, a minus for others.

Seize Sur Vingt 🆂🄲 ▽ 25 | 20 | 22 | E
243 Elizabeth St. (bet. Houston & Prince Sts.), N/R to Prince St., 212-343-0476; www.16sur20.com
■ Owners James and Gwendolyn Jumey are "some of the nicest neighbors on the block", with a "spacious, lovely" NoLita shop specializing in "elegant hip", "hand-tailored" shirts with a "fabulous fit" for men and women in "exquisite" Egyptian cotton that's "far beyond one's imagination"; the "good-looking" button-downs, bolstered by a small selection of suits, coats and boxer shorts, can be made to measure at the rear of the shop or bought "off-the-rack" (rolling racks, that is) for a little less.

Selia Yang 🆂🄲 – | – | – | E
328 E. Ninth St. (bet. 1st & 2nd Aves.), 6 to Astor Pl.; N/R to 8th St., 212-254-9073; www.seliayang.com
No blushing brides at this clean, white-walled East Village shop – just hip and happening gals who adore the custom-made wedding gowns and formalwear from an "incredible" designer who "understands how to cut clothes for real women" with body-flattering appeal; the "nice" saleswomen amiably soothe pre-big-day jitters.

SELIMA OPTIQUE 🆂 28 | 25 | 23 | E
84 E. Seventh St. (bet. 1st & 2nd Aves.), F/V to 2nd Ave., 212-260-2495
899 Madison Ave. (bet. 72nd & 73rd Sts.), 6 to 77th St., 212-988-6690
59 Wooster St. (Broome St.), C/E to Spring St., 212-343-9490
www.selimaoptique.com
■ "Fantastic, funky, flirty", "wonderfully made" and "boldly" hued eyeglasses as well as "gorgeous shades" that "you won't see on every Joe on the street" attract admirers to Selima Salaun's mini-chain of boutiques that originated in Paris; service "varies by location" ("excellent" to "friendly" to "unhelpful"), but regardless of the staff, the "cool merchandise" means "addicts" have "difficulty walking out without" making a purchase or two.

Selvedge 🆂 ▽ 22 | 24 | 21 | E
250 Mulberry St. (Prince St.), N/R to Prince St.; 6 to Spring St., 212-219-0994
◪ A "hot space" for a "cool collection", this NoLita boutique displays "high-end" Levi's (they "carry a lot of the Red collection"), "not your basic stuff", on rugged wall pegs and small shelves, with photos of hipsters and Native Americans standing watch; individualists indulge in the "one-of-a-kind" collectibles, including jeans with arty renderings; "too many wanna-bes" wail a few, fearful they'll detract from this "great store."

| M | P | S | C |

SEPHORA ●S   26 | 24 | 18 | M
2103 Broadway (bet. 73rd & 74th Sts.), 1/2/3/9 to 72nd St., 212-362-1500
1500 Broadway (bet. 43rd & 44th Sts.), 1/2/3/7/9/N/Q/R/S/W to 42nd St./Times Sq., 212-944-6789
555 Broadway (bet. Prince & Spring Sts.), N/R to Prince St., 212-625-1309
119 Fifth Ave. (19th St.), 4/5/6/L/N/Q/R/W to 14th St./Union Sq., 212-674-3570
1129 Third Ave. (67th St.), 6 to 68th St., 212-452-3336
130 W. 34th St. (bet. 7th & 8th Aves.), 1/2/3/9 to 34th St./Penn Station, 212-629-9135
www.sephora.com

■ "Great one-stop-shopping" "beauty supermarkets", with almost "every brand" of cosmetics, body products and fragrance "under the sun", that have changed the lives of "makeup junkies", who love the "freedom" to "smudge, dab and spritz" with testers "without encountering the dreaded overeager department-store help"; "if you know what you want", it's "the ultimate candy shop for every lip-gloss-loving girl."

SERGIO ROSSI C   27 | 23 | 21 | VE
772 Madison Ave. (66th St.), 6 to 68th St., 212-327-4288;
www.sergiorossi.com

■ "Hot, hot, hot" chorus stylesetters who sizzle in the "drop-dead gorgeous Italian" "shoes of the gods" (think "rhinestone evening sandals and "sexy" stiletto boots) they scoop up at this "chic" Madison Avenue shop; men get a foot up on fashion here too with "beautiful", "impeccably made" footwear that's also indulgently "expensive"; while enthusiasts exult in the "exceptional" staff, the put-off pout about "snobby salespeople" who don't "seem interested in selling" their wares.

Seven New York SC   24 | 22 | 19 | E
180 Orchard St. (bet. Houston & Stanton Sts.), F/V to 2nd Ave., 646-654-0156; www.sevennewyork.com

■ "A bit out of the way", and locked within a steel-door-and-cement exterior, this Lower Eastsider measures its cool in "established and emerging avant-garde designers" (Bernhard Wilhem, Benjamin Cho), plus accessories from the likes of As Four, "for the hipster who doesn't want to look like every other" trendoid in NYC; the "service-oriented" staff provides almost "too much information" on the inventory.

17 at 17 Thrift Shop   19 | 16 | 15 | M
17 W. 17th St. (5th Ave.), 4/5/6/L/N/Q/R/W to 14th St./Union Sq., 212-727-7516; www.ujafedny.org

■ "If you catch them at the right time", there are "great high-quality bargains to be had" at this Flatiron "treasure hunt" of a thrift store, "especially on furniture" (including a steady supply of pianos) and a "surprising amount of designer clothes", "particularly when they get the society donations"; best of all, "you feel good buying" here, as proceeds go to owner UJA-Federation of NY and Gilda's Club.

Sew Brooklyn S   ▽ 18 | 21 | 19 | M
228 Seventh Ave. (bet. 3rd & 4th Sts.), Brooklyn, F to 7th Ave., 718-499-7383; www.sewbrooklyn.com

☑ "Very neat, organized" and "cozy" with a "helpful staff", this Park Slope shop offers a "nice selection of cottons and basic sewing supplies" that are particularly "good for quilters or people making

| M | P | S | C |

kids' clothes", but bummed Brooklynites retort there's "not a great selection"; N.B. a wide variety of quilting classes is offered.

S Feldman Housewares S | 24 | 16 | 22 | E |
1304 Madison Ave. (92nd St.), 6 to 96th St., 212-289-3961; 800-359-8558; www.wares2u.com

■ "From tacks to espresso machines", you'll find "anything you need in the way of housewares" and "gadgetries" at this nearly 75-year-old store on the Upper East Side; locals who shop here for Miele vacuums, Oxo utensils and the colorful "selection of Alessi products" "pay full price" but get a "great choice" of unusual, often trendy, merchandise and "excellent service."

Shabby Chic S C | 21 | 24 | 16 | E |
83 Wooster St. (bet. Broome & Spring Sts.), N/R to Prince St., 212-274-9842; www.shabbychic.com

■ Those who "love the cozy, comfy, country" style evoked by oversized, slipcovered chairs, ottomans and sofas in faded florals flock to this SoHo fabric and home-furnishings shop inspired by designer Rachel Ashwell; while a few fume that her "original" "pricey" flea-market look has been "knocked off by all" and is getting a "bit worn", most maintain it remains among the "prettiest stuff in the world."

Shanghai Tang S | 22 | 24 | 18 | E |
714 Madison Ave. (bet. 63rd & 64th Sts.), N/R/W to 5th Ave., 212-888-0111; 888-252-8264; www.shanghaitang.com

◪ "Stimulating" "jolts of color" give shoppers the sense of traveling "in the Orient" "without the jet lag" when they visit the Upper East Side outpost of this Chinese conglomerate; "vibrant", "authentic" Asian clothing for adults and kids in "fabulous fabrics" (especially the "exquisite silk pajamas") and "unique gifts" help create an atmosphere of "feng shui at its finest" for fans; but critics carp it'd be "cheaper to go to Hong Kong" – not to mention NY's Chinatown.

Sharper Image | 21 | 22 | 18 | E |
900 Madison Ave. (bet. 72nd & 73rd Sts.), 6 to 68th St., 212-794-4974 S
Pier 17, South Street Seaport, 2/3/4/5/A/C/J/M/Z to Fulton/B'way/ Nassau, 212-693-0477 ◐ S
50 Rockefeller Plaza (bet. 5th & 6th Aves.), B/D/F/V to 47-50th Sts./ Rockefeller Ctr., 646-557-0861 ◐ S
4 W. 57th St. (bet. 5th & 6th Aves.), F to 57th St., 212-265-2550 800-344-4444; www.sharperimage.com

◪ The multiple locations of this "whimsical", "high-tech" "FAO Schwarz for adults" represent a "slicker-than-slick" "gadgeteer's heaven" full of things you "don't really need, but can't resist", like "massage chairs they may have to evict you from"; sober shoppers say "justifying these prices" for "shine-over-substance", "battery-operated things" like a toy Beetle/CD alarm clock or the world's smallest hand-held color TV "requires some fuzzy logic."

Sherle Wagner International, Inc. | – | – | – | VE |
60 E. 57th St. (Park Ave.), 4/5/6/F/N/R/W to 5th Ave./59th St., 212-758-3300; www.sherlewagner.com

Offering a "bit of Palm Beach" decadence in "the heart of Gotham", this East 50s bathroom shrine caters to the Park Avenue set and Sun King wanna-bes seeking gold-plated swan-head fixtures, hand-painted basins and tiles and taps encrusted with semiprecious stones; it also purveys lighting accessories, linens and wallpaper.

vote at zagat.com

| | | | M | P | S | C |

Shirt Store, The   – | – | – | E
51 E. 44th St. (Vanderbilt Ave.), 4/5/6/7/S to 42nd St./Grand Central, 212-557-8040; 800-289-2744; www.shirtstore.com
Suit-and-tie guys swear this small, unassuming store outside Grand Central is "the only place for shirts", whether custom- or ready-made; the fine stitching, "excellent selection of fabrics" and "wide range of colors and styles" (from 14/32 to 18.5/37) ensures there's "something for everyone" here, and the "service is top-notch" too.

Shiseido ⓈⒸ   – | – | – | E
298 Fifth Ave. (31st St.), N/R to 28th St., 212-629-9090
This over-a-century-old Japanese cosmetics giant is far less well known in America, but its small, understated and relatively new Fifth Avenue outpost offers the opportunity to try its sleekly packaged makeup and skincare products, particularly creams designed to counter signs of sun damage and age spots.

Shoe Biz ●ⓈⒸ   19 | 10 | 13 | M
2315 Broadway (84th St.), 1/9 to 86th St., 212-799-4221
■ "Upper West Side moms and girlie-girls alike flock to this addictive emporium" owned by shoe mogul Steve Madden "for bowling"-style kicks, "kitten heels and glammed-up thongs to wear tomorrow and forget next year"; the "varied selection of current trends", represented by lines like Puma and David Aaron, leads most mavens to conclude you "usually find what you're looking for"; N.B. there's also a small selection of trendy men's footwear.

Shoofly ⓈⒸ   26 | 23 | 16 | E
465 Amsterdam Ave. (bet. 82nd & 83rd Sts.), 1/9 to 86th St., 212-580-4390
42 Hudson St. (bet. Duane & Thomas Sts.), 1/2/3/9 to Chambers St., 212-406-3270
www.shooflynyc.com
■ "If you have a daughter who is an arty version of Imelda Marcos" and/or a style-savvy son, head to these "*très* adorable" shops Uptown and Down; what's in-store: "cute European shoes" "from the funkiest casualwear to gorgeous galoshes" from labels like Aster, Babybotte, Mod 8 and Minibel, plus some of the "best hats around", all "imaginatively presented" in a cabin-like setting in TriBeCa and a treehouse-like branch on the Upper West Side.

Shop ⓈⒸ   ∇ 26 | 24 | 22 | E
105 Stanton St. (Ludlow St.), F/V to 2nd Ave., 212-375-0304
■ "Favorite shopping hideaway" for those in-the-know that focuses on the "feminine" – a point of view that's rather "unexpected" for the Lower East Side; "whimsical" pink painted-tile floors and cream walls lend "adorable" atmosphere to the "cute clothes", even "cuter" patrons and the "nice salespeople", creating an "awesome experience."

Shop Noir ●ⓈⒸ   21 | 22 | 18 | E
248 Mott St. (bet. Houston & Prince Sts.), N/R to Prince St., 212-966-6868
■ "Sparkly sweet", this NoLita shop "bedazzles your world" with "up-to-the-minute" accessories; the "sexy-with-a-street-vibe" jewelry, belts and "funky doodads" are "different by every stretch of the imagination", with some items displayed on a shiny crystal countertop; P.S. the "great salespeople are "quite inventive – they know what will make an outfit look fantastic."

M | P | S | C

Shu Uemura Beauty Boutique S   24 | 23 | 20 | E
121 Greene St. (bet. Houston & Prince Sts.), N/R to Prince St., 212-979-5500; 888-540-8181

■ A "beautiful, sparse" SoHo space is a suitably Zen setting for this line of "high-end" Japanese cosmetics, featuring "unique colors", "the best brushes on the market" and of course its award-winning eyelash curler; "superb service" and the surprising absence of NY crowds enhance the experience.

Sid's S   ▽ 21 | 16 | 19 | M
345 Jay St. (Willoughby St.), Brooklyn, A/C/F to Jay St./Borough Hall, 718-875-2259

■ "There's no one in Brooklyn Heights who hasn't walked the aisles" of this "essential" "classic", with "endless rooms" full of hardware, lumber and paint in a "labyrinthine building" that its "brethren" believe is "absolute paradise"; penny-pinchers profess there are "no bargains" and the service can be "quirky" but admit that "most times you can find what you need."

Sigerson Morrison S C   27 | 23 | 18 | VE
28 Prince St. (Mott St.), 6 to Spring St., 212-219-3893

■ "Always an outfit maker" chorus "chic career girls" and stylish night owls who flock to this "hip" NoLita destination for an "amazing array" of "happy little shoes" in a "rainbow of colors" ranging from "detailed and feminine" "strappy sandals and winter heels" to "pointy shapes" "with a bit more edge"; "granted", these "little masterpieces" "for the well heeled" are "not cheap, but good footwear never is"; as for service – "they know they don't have to sell you."

Sigerson Morrison Bags S C   – | – | – | E
242 Mott St. (bet. Houston & Prince Sts.), 6 to Spring St., 212-941-5404

Small and sparsely appointed, this NoLita hot spot stocks handbags, totes and wallets in an array of snappy shades with the clean and clever styling that designers Kari Sigerson and Miranda Morrison have made their own; if the tall prices aren't a problem, their sister shoe store – formerly housed in this space and now located in larger digs just around the corner – is worth stepping into.

Simon Pearce Glass S C   26 | 25 | 23 | E
500 Park Ave. (59th St.), 4/5/6/N/R/W to 59th St./Lexington Ave., 212-421-8801
120 Wooster St. (bet. Prince & Spring Sts.), N/R to Prince St., 212-334-2393
www.simonpearceglass.com

■ "Once you start, you can't stop" buying some of the "beautiful" "handcrafted" "classic glass" stemware, bowls, vases and lamps at these "addictive" Midtown and SoHo stores that also purvey pottery and customized etched or inscribed items; while prices are "surprisingly low for what you get", the "real value is the seconds merchandise", which is offered "at a discount", making it a "great place to get a wedding present" or register for one.

Simon's Hardware & Bath   26 | 20 | 17 | E
421 Third Ave. (bet. 29th & 30th Sts.), 6 to 28th St., 212-532-9220; 888-274-6667; www.simons-hardware.com

☑ "For knobs, hinges and hardware", this Gramercy Park shop "has the best selection in the city", offering a "vast", "eye-popping"

vote at zagat.com   **237**

assortment ("nice knockers!"); sadder-but-wiser types sigh the "gold-mine" goods come at "gold-mine prices" and add the service can be "aggravating", but most agree that it's all "worth it" for the "fantastic" and otherwise "hard-to-find" fixtures and plumbing on offer.

Sisley ●S | 20 | 19 | 15 | M

2308 Broadway (bet. 83rd & 84th Sts.), 1/9 to 86th St., 212-769-0121
469 W. Broadway (bet. Houston & Prince Sts.), C/E to Spring St., 212-375-0538
www.sisley.com

■ "Why aren't they more crowded?" ask buyers who believe these Upper West Side and SoHo fashion chain stores "have a very cosmopolitan European feel"; this "Benetton brethren" "lives up to its benefactor's" reputation with "sophisticated", "adorable" "clothes that fit true to size and last" at a "decent" price; "buy something for you and your boyfriend" and "you both will not be disappointed", if you can get past the staff's "attitude problem."

Skechers ●S | 18 | 18 | 16 | M

2169 Broadway (76th St.), 1/9 to 79th St., 212-712-0539
530 Broadway (Spring St.), C/E to Spring St.; N/R to Prince St., 212-431-8803
150 Fifth Ave. (W. 20th St.), N/R to 23rd St., 212-627-9420
55 W. Eighth St. (bet. 5th & 6th Aves.), A/C/E/F/S/V to W. 4th St., 212-253-5810
140 W. 34th St. (bet. 6th & 7th Aves.), B/D/F/N/Q/R/V/W to 34th St./ Herald Sq., 646-473-0490
800-561-9486; www.skechers.com

■ "Really cool shoes at affordable prices" that "promise to get you noticed with their high heels and fun looks", plus "comfy sneaks" that "hold up to heavy wear", draw guys and girls of all ages to this chain with "lots of energy"; but a smattering of sophisticates swipes it's "fun if you're 12" and like "hitting the mall and talking on your pink cell phone all day."

Smiley's ⌀ | 22 | 16 | 20 | I

92-06 Jamaica Ave. (bet. 92nd St. & Woodhaven Blvd.), Queens, J/Z to Woodhaven Blvd., 718-849-9873; www.smileysyarns.com

■ Though "nothing exotic or high fashion" awaits at this wool-filled Woodhaven shop, it's "worth the subway ride" to enthusiasts, who rejoice in the "bags and bags of the most wonderful yarns" at "bargain-basement prices" and "very helpful" service; some products are sold online, plus every fall this "avid knitter's" haven hosts a "once-a-year sale" featuring bulk skeins in select hotels in the New York area.

Smith & Hawken ●SC | 24 | 24 | 21 | E

394 W. Broadway (bet. Broome & Spring Sts.), C/E to Spring St., 212-925-0687; 800-940-1170; www.smithandhawken.com

■ "The place for English gardening tools" is this SoHo showroom that's also hailed for its "great teak furniture", "healthy plants" and "equipment from around the world"; its "pretty", "well-maintained" setting makes it a "fun place to hang out", and the "salespeople seem to love what they do"; despite quibbles that it's "a bit pricey", the "quality", "sensible" merchandise supplies "good value" for green thumbs.

| M | P | S | C |

SMYTHSON OF BOND STREET C 27 | 27 | 22 | VE
4 W. 57th St. (5th Ave.), F to 57th St., 212-265-4573; 877-769-8476; www.smythson.com

■ "If it's good enough for the Queen, it's good enough for me" say loyal subjects of this "darling" British import on West 57th Street, with its "addictive", "luxurious" selection of "classic, elegant" stationery and "little leather notebooks and diaries in eye-popping colors" that "are a pleasure to use"; though a few yell "yikes" over the prices, most insist it's "truly worth it" for the "high quality."

Soccer Sport Supply C – | – | – | M
1745 First Ave. (bet. 90th & 91st Sts.), 4/5/6 to 86th St., 212-427-6050; 800-223-1010; www.homeofsoccer.com

Drenched in history, as evidenced by the display of memorabilia dating back to the early 1900s, this Upper East Side sporting-goods store has been kicking it since 1933; players score everything for soccer here, from Diadora balls, Adidas shoes, Puma King Pro shin guards and Reusch goalkeeper apparel to Official International Club Team wear (i.e. Nike Barcelona home jerseys *and* away jerseys) and Official World Cup Replica clothing.

Sol Moscot S – | – | – | I
118 Orchard St. (Delancey St.), F/V to Delancey St., 212-477-3796
69 W. 14th St. (6th Ave.), F/L/V to 14th St./6th Ave., 212-647-1550
107-20 Continental Ave. (bet. Austin St. & Queens Blvd.), Queens, E/F/G/R/V to Forest Hills, 718-544-2200
www.solmoscotopticians.com

Envision the past from one of the original seats in the octogenarian Orchard Street branch of this venerable, family-run optician with Flatiron and Queens stores as well; old-timey discounts and customer service meet newfangled frames from Calvin, Giorgio, Christian, Alain (Mikli) and the rest of the designer gang for a formula with staying power.

Sonia Rykiel C – | – | – | E
849 Madison Ave. (bet. 70th & 71st Sts.), 6 to 68th St., 212-396-3060; www.soniarykiel.com

This East 70s boutique reflects French chic at its best, from a veteran Parisian designer known for her knitwear – "always nice" sweaters and "uniquely designed" dresses; while "expensive", the clothes are "never dated", so it's possible to "wear them again and again for years."

Sonic Groove ◐C – | – | – | M
41 Carmine St. (bet. Bedford & Bleecker Sts.), A/C/E/F/S/V to W. 4th St., 212-675-5284; www.sonicgroove.com

When you crave rave, "the godfathers of the techno scene are chilling it out and playing records behind the counter" in the Village at this "legendary shop" with a house label co-owned by mega-DJs Frankie Bones, Adam X and Heather Heart; it opens at 1 PM, just in time for the kids to stumble out of the clubs and score that new "hard house" hit or electro classic they just finished dancing to.

Sony Style S 22 | 23 | 15 | E
550 Madison Ave. (bet. 55th & 56th Sts.), E/V to 5th Ave./53rd St., 212-833-8800; www.sonystyle.com

◪ If you're one of those "tech-happy people" who's infatuated with Sony WEGA TVs and DVD Dream Systems, this East 50s store,

vote at zagat.com

connected to the "museum-like", interactive Wonder Technology Lab, is "a great place to look at products" and "keep abreast of tech developments"; though the staff "truly knows" its stuff, gearheads argue that their "fine mass-market merchandise" is "more fun to play with than buy" at "prices that are beatable" by others.

Sorelle Firenze C | – | – | – | E |
139½ Reade St. (bet. Greenwich & Hudson Sts.), 1/2/3/9 to Chambers St., 212-528-7816; www.sorellefirenze.com
"Feel like a princess" at this inviting, recently expanded TriBeCa boutique where the super-feminine chic of Florentine co-owners Monica and Barbara Abbatemaggio comes across in a cozy little world filled with Italian fashions (some made by the sisters' mama), accessories, sexy lingerie and adorably detailed childrenswear.

Sound and Fury ◐ S C | – | – | – | I |
192 Orchard St. (bet. Houston & Stanton Sts.), F/V to 2nd Ave., 212-598-4300; www.soundandfury.com
On the Lower East Side, this idiosyncratic CD/LP shop may be small, but it packs a wallop for indie and local rock, punk and hip-hop, with some classic headbangers like Black Flag thrown in; nod along to the occasional in-store entertainment, check out tunes at the listening station, leaf through the cheap used section, or peruse the message board for your shot at that vacant drummer spot in a neighborhood thrasher band.

SOUND BY SINGER S | 28 | 21 | 15 | VE |
18 E. 16th St. (bet. 5th Ave. & Union Sq. W.), 4/5/6/L/N/Q/R to 14th St./Union Sq., 212-924-8600
■ "Hard-core audio nerds" will feel at home in this Union Square boutique where the extensively, expensively adorned demo rooms allow buyers to evaluate the "mega-buck systems"; "if it's worth owning, they have it", admirers attest, but sensitive shoppers shudder the "extreme attitude" that permeates the place reflects a staff that has "egos to match" the prices.

Sound City | – | – | – | M |
58 W. 45th St. (bet. 5th & 6th Aves.), B/D/F/V to 47-50th Sts./Rockefeller Ctr., 212-575-0210; 800-326-1677
Whether you are looking for a new FireWire to download your digital pictures or just need to upgrade to a better-integrated amplifier for your stereo, this West 40s retailer "will get you what you want"; serving the community since 1978, they can guide you through the audio bells and whistles as well as the computer basics.

Space Kiddets C ▽ | 25 | 13 | 15 | E |
46 E. 21st St. (bet. B'way & Park Ave.), 6/N/R to 23rd St., 212-420-9878
■ "Trendy" parents and their offspring are over the moon about this "tiny", brightly colored Gramercy Park destination packed with "a great selection of unusual, fun, urban fashions", "party stuff" and "European clothing lines" from newborn sizes to pre-teen; sure, "your breath will be taken away by the exorbitant prices", but remember, "the sales are great."

Speedo Authentic Fitness ◐ C | 18 | 13 | 15 | M |
150 Columbus Ave. (bet. 66th & 67th Sts.), 1/9 to 66th St., 212-501-8140 S
500 Fifth Ave. (42nd St.), 4/5/6/7/S to Grand Central, 212-768-7737 S

M | P | S | C

(continued)
Speedo Authentic Fitness
90 Park Ave. (39th St.), 4/5/6/7/S to Grand Central, 212-682-3830
www.speedo.com

▸ "If you swim for fitness, these are the stores" for "good, basic bathing suits" that have a "bit of pizzazz", as well as "great gym bags", all kept afloat by a "helpful" staff; workout wear, however, draws a split decision: "fun and functional" vs. "hit-or-miss", but the "reasonable prices" for "professional"-grade gear make a big splash.

Spence-Chapin Thrift Shops S   17 | 14 | 15 | M
1850 Second Ave. (bet. 95th & 96th Sts.), 6 to 96th St., 212-426-7643
1473 Third Ave. (bet. 83rd & 84th Sts.), 4/5/6 to 86th St., 212-737-8448 ●
www.spence-chapin.org

▸ "Many well-heeled New Yorkers seem to bless" these Upper East Side thrift shops "with their designer clothes", "vintage sweaters" and "excellent secondhand furniture"; the merchandise is "well organized", and though some sniff prices are "inflated", "it's worth it when one scores" at this adoption services charity.

Spoiled Brats ●SC   – | – | – | M
340 W. 49th St. (bet. 8th & 9th Aves.), C to 50th St., 212-459-1615;
www.spoiledbratsnyc.com

The "friendly" owners and staff are "true animal lovers" at this "Hell's Kitchen favorite" that's "one of the few places you can get raw organic meat and other healthy things" for your dog or cat at "reasonable prices"; it also offers a "great supply of toys" as well as gifts that extend to odor-masking candles.

Sports Authority ●S   18 | 13 | 10 | M
636 Sixth Ave. (19th St.), 1/9 to 18th St.; F to 23rd St., 212-929-8971
845 Third Ave. (51st St.), 6 to 51st St.; E/V to 53rd St./Lexington Ave., 212-355-9725
57 W. 57th St. (6th Ave.), F to 57th St., 212-355-6430
www.thesportsauthority.com

▸ Fans fawn that these three branches of a national chain are "one-stop-shopping" headquarters for sports galore, including fishing, basketball and yoga apparel and gear, but the less impressed pummel the "middle-of-the-road selection" – it's "not the best place for specialty gear" – and sound off about "no visible help."

Stacia ●SC   – | – | – | E
267 Smith St. (DeGraw St.), Brooklyn, F to Carroll St., 718-237-0078;
www.staciany.com

Young designer Stacy Johnson (a Cynthia Rowley vet) invites basics-weary, color-starved fashionistas to her cozy Carroll Gardens boutique, which has a vintage feel with its pale turquoise walls, chandeliers and wrought-iron accents; her whimsically named collections (Film Noir, Antiquity) are heavy on va-va-voom dresses, suits and separates in lush tweeds and silks; knitwear, lingerie and the best-selling duffel bags round out the inventory.

Stackhouse ●SC   – | – | – | E
276 Lafayette St. (bet. Houston & Prince Sts.), N/R to Prince St.; F/R/6 to B'way/Lafayette, 212-925-6931

Snowboard and skate rats and just plain cool kids air down to this Lafayette Street destination for edgy, urban-cool sweaters, hoodies, trainers, hats and accessories from labels like Blue Marlin,

vote at zagat.com

| | | | | M | P | S | C |

Staples
<u>19</u> <u>14</u> <u>11</u> M
1065 Sixth Ave. (40th St.), 1/2/3/7/9/N/Q/R/S/W to 42nd St./Times Sq., 212-997-4446; 800-378-2753; www.staples.com
Additional locations throughout the NY area
◼ With the "convenience" of more branches than you can shake a scanner at, this "office supply" "supermarket" chain is perfect "for a quick work-related emergency", as "you can slip in and pick up" "peripherals and accessories" from PDAs to printers, toners to telephone cables; true, the "messy" presentation and sales associates who play "hard-to-get" might have you crying "bring back the mom-and-pop stationery store" – until you get a load of the "efficient online shopping" and "wonderful delivery policy."

Star Magic ●SC
<u>22</u> <u>19</u> <u>16</u> M
745 Broadway (bet. 8th St. & Waverly Pl.), N/R to 8th St., 212-228-7770
1256 Lexington Ave. (bet. 84th & 85th Sts.), 4/5/6 to 86th St., 212-988-0300
www.starmagic.com
◼ Welcome to "gift city" – these "truly trippy" Greenwich Village and Upper East Side soul mates are chockablock with "glittery toys", magic tricks, novelties and "new-age tchotchkes; they're "great for astronomy nuts", so "bring a kid who's into science and space" to "browse through the interesting" otherworldly selection; P.S. it's also "full of the kind of stuff college freshman go crazy for", from lava lamps to disco balls.

Starting Line, The ●SC
– – – E
180 Eighth Ave. (bet. 19th & 20th Sts.), A/C/E to 14th St.; 1/9 to 18th St., 212-691-4729; www.thestartinglinenyc.com
. . . And they're off, to this busy Chelsea boutique with lime-green walls and aisles filled with a "hot potluck" of casual clothes, including Puma work-out wear and sport shoes as well as après-gym garb from NYBased and Itsus T-shirts; goal-oriented guys appreciate the "no-frills" atmosphere and "helpful staff."

Steinlauf & Stoller
▽ <u>24</u> <u>13</u> <u>16</u> M
239 W. 39th St. (bet. 7th & 8th Aves.), A/C/E to 42nd St./Port Authority; 1/2/3/7/N/Q/R/S/W to 42nd St./Times Sq., 212-869-0321; 877-869-0321; www.steinlaufandstoller.com
◼ From shears and steel pins to cording, braiding and ribbon, all the "wonderful things that used to be in Woolworth's can still be found" at this 55-year-old Garment Center sewing notions stalwart; "if you want it, it's probably there, but you may have to ask for help" as you "dodge stray elbows" and "mix with designers and dressmakers matching swatches."

Steinway and Sons
▽ <u>28</u> <u>26</u> <u>24</u> VE
109 W. 57th St. (bet. 6th & 7th Aves.), N/R/Q/W to 57th St., 212-246-1100; www.steinway.com
◼ "Even non-players want a piano, just walking into this store" filled with "concert grands galore" inside a West 57th Street landmark building where the "beautiful rooms", "trick"-receded front window and "rotunda alone are worth a visit"; the staff at "Carnegie Hall's neighbor" "knows how to pamper their artists" who, despite the "museum"-like setting, are free to tickle the ivories on the "Rolls-Royces" of instruments.

| M | P | S | C |

Stella 🆂🅲 — | — | — | VE
138 W. Broadway (bet. Duane & Thomas Sts.), 1/2/3/9 to Chambers St., 212-233-9610; www.stellastore.com

Lust-worthy must-haves for the bedroom, bathroom and beyond beckon browsers to this TriBeCa haven, owned by two decorating pros; set against mustard-colored walls, the displays are as inviting as the merchandise, with custom drapes hanging from the high ceiling, antique beds (yes, they're for sale) boasting handmade coverlets and towering cabinets crammed with luxurious imported linens; for those who'd rather stay between the sheets, there's even a rack of silk robes.

Stella Dallas ⬤🆂 ▽ 21 | 16 | 19 | M
218 Thompson St. (bet. Bleecker & W. 3rd Sts.), A/C/E/F/V/S to W. 4th St., 212-674-0447

■ "A nice selection of '40s, '50s and '60s dresses" co-exists with a collection of mid-century sweaters, "skinny ties" and even kids' clothes at this veteran Village vintage shop; it's a "massive amount for such a small space", but given that everything's "in good condition", "in decent sizes and at uninflated prices", most love to dally here.

Stella McCartney 🆂 — | — | — | VE
429 W. 14th St. (bet. 9th Ave. & Washington St.), A/C/E/L to 14th St./8th Ave., 212-255-1556; www.stellamccartney.com

Having made her name at Chloé, this young Brit (daughter of musician Paul) opens her first stand-alone store in the rapidly gentrifying Meatpacking District; inside, the pink silk walls and mannequins walking on water in a reflecting pool suggest the tongue-in-cheek sensibility of the designer's womenswear, which features chain-trimmed chiffons, transparent-colored shoes and hand-knit cashmere sweaters; however, as her dad once warbled, you'll need money to shop in this place.

Stephane Kélian 🅲 25 | 25 | 21 | VE
717 Madison Ave. (bet. 63rd & 64th Sts.), N/R to 5th Ave./59th St., 212-980-1919
158 Mercer St. (bet. Houston & Prince Sts.), N/R to Prince St., 212-925-3077 🆂
www.kelian.fr

■ Using the "best woven leathers and comfortable lasts", this "innovative" designer, "a master at staying true to his heart", handcrafts "fabulous French footwear" with a "twist of the latest trend built in"; the "professional" service at his Madison Avenue and SoHo boutiques caters to men and "women who really have style", a clientele that realizes that "when these shoes are good, they're very, very good", and though they're "pricey, they're worth every penny"; N.B. the Madison Avenue store is open only on Sundays during wintertime.

Stephen Russell 🅲 — | — | — | VE
962 Madison Ave. (bet. 75th & 76th Sts.), 6 to 77th St., 212-570-6900; www.stephenrusselljewelry.com

"If you need a 19th-century diamond tiara, this is the place to go" attest antique-jewelry acolytes of this petite Upper East Side boutique, which prides itself on museum-quality merchandise; the wares include new pieces as well, but whatever the date of origin, the goods are "high class."

	M	P	S	C

Stereo Exchange ●🅂🄲   23 | 14 | 17 | E
627 Broadway (bet. Bleecker & Houston Sts.), N/R to Prince St., 212-505-1111
■ With all those audiovisual animals "drooling" over an inventory that includes "everything under the sun in higher-end merch", this "superior" NoHo store "can be a zoo"; the "knowledgeable staff" is, thankfully, more concerned with "guiding you to the right" plasma TV or performing a multi-room, multi-source installation than giving the "hard sell", and while "most of what they carry isn't cheap", the "value is always excellent."

STEUBEN 🄲   29 | 28 | 23 | VE
667 Madison Ave. (61st St.), N/R to 5th Ave./59th St., 212-752-1441; 800-424-4240; www.steuben.com
■ A "glass-lover's paradise" where "stunning merchandise" – voted Tops in our Home/Garden category – is "beautifully showcased" in a soaring, three-story Madison Avenue space that serves as the flagship of this 100-year-old "premier" American company; crystal animals, apples, bowls, sculptures and engraved and etched objects are offered at shattering prices, but it's "worth every penny" for a "gift to show appreciation" or seal the deal.

Steve Madden 🅂   16 | 16 | 14 | M
540 Broadway (Spring St.), N/R to Prince St., 212-343-1800 ●
105 E. 86th St. (bet. Lexington & 3rd Aves.), 4/5/6 to 86th St., 212-426-0538
41 W. 34th St., B/D/F/N/Q/R/V/W to 34th St./Herald Sq., 212-736-3283
5380 King's Plaza (Farragut Rd.), Brooklyn, 718-677-3985
2655 Richmond Ave. (bet. Platinum Ave. & Ring Rd.), Staten Island, 718-494-6459
888-275-3633; www.stevemadden.com
■ From "platform sandals to Frankenstein-esque boots", every "modern man" and "trendy" "girl has to have a pair" of this "omnipresent" chain's "funky", "reasonably priced shoes" that are "easier to walk in than they look"; but the less impressed aren't mad for the "clunky look – so late '90s" – and find it "truly an uncomfortable experience, from snotty sales clerks" "too hip to help" to footwear that's "not top-quality" and that you "get to wear for only one season."

Steven Alan 🅂🄲   22 | – | 18 | E
103 Franklin St. (bet. Church St. & W. B'way), 1/9 to Canal St., 212-343-0692
60 Wooster St. (bet. Broome & Spring Sts.), C/E to Spring St.; N/R to Prince St., 212-334-6354
www.stevenalan.com
■ For the "younger, fashion-savvy set" whose taste runs "left of center", this "edgy" men's and women's boutique, which opened its spacious TriBeCa digs post-*Survey*, showcases "small designer lines from NY, LA and Tokyo" with "price points that aren't too bad" for "cool labels"; still, "this ain't H&M", so bring the bucks for basics that "can't be found" elsewhere; N.B. the original SoHo location currently spotlights Vanessa Bruno's collection.

Steven Stolman 🄲   – | – | – | E
22 E. 72nd St., 4th fl. (bet. 5th & Madison Aves.), 6 to 68th St., 212-249-5050; www.stevenstolman.com
Located on the fourth floor of an Upper East Side townhouse, this toile-de-Jouy–accented shop offers wares by the designer dubbed "the new Lilly Pulitzer" by the Palm Beach and Hamptons set;

| M | P | S | C |

his "wonderful print skirts and pants" (the latter for gentlemen too) call out in all their preppy splendor: "when you wear a Stolman, everyone knows it."

Stickley, Audi & Co. 🆂🅲 — | — | — | E

160 Fifth Ave., 4th fl. (bet. 20th & 21st Sts.), N/R to 23rd St., 212-337-0700; www.stickley.com

Named in part after Gustave and Leopold Stickley, who were synonymous with the American Arts & Crafts movement, this three-floor Flatiron District furniture showroom features reissues of their Mission Style sofas, chairs, cabinets, beds and tables; each piece is made to order, handcrafted and bears the company seal.

Stitches East 🅲 22 | 20 | 14 | E

Park Avenue Plaza, 55 E. 52nd St. (bet. Madison & Park Aves.), E/V to 5th Ave./53rd St.; 6 to 51st St., 212-201-0112

◪ "If you're looking for" "intriguing", "high-end yarns, needlepoint canvases and supplies", head to this "refined environment", "tucked into the lobby of a Midtown office building"; but put-out patrons point to a "snooty" "sales staff that barely registers customers' presence", adding "dilettantes, beware."

ST. JOHN 🆂 26 | 26 | 24 | VE

665 Fifth Ave. (bet. 52nd & 53rd Sts.), E/V to 5th Ave./53rd St., 212-755-5252; www.stjohnknits.com

◼ When the need arises to "dress like the wife of a Congressman", this East 50s boutique beckons with Marie St. John's "ladies-who-lunch" suits ("unbelievable what they can do with knits") and "glitzy" evening confections, "as well as matching accessories"; the "gracious" service and "environment befit a queen", a "senior investment banker" or any "discerning" customer who doesn't mind the "very pricey" tags.

St. Marks Sounds 🌒🆂≠ ▽ 25 | 15 | 15 | I

16 St. Marks Pl. (bet. 2nd & 3rd Aves.), 6 to Astor Pl., 212-677-2727
20 St. Marks Pl. (bet. 2nd & 3rd Aves.), 6 to Astor Pl., 212-677-3444

◼ "Maybe the best used sections in the whole world" are found a couple of doors down from each other on the East Village's most honky-tonk block; the street-level store also "has fair prices" on "breaking bands" and other "new stuff", "but if you're bargain hunting, go to the upstairs location", where the goods are mostly previously played CDs and "promos in great condition."

Straight from the Crate 🅲 14 | 6 | 13 | I

1251 Lexington Ave. (bet. 84th & 85th Sts.), 4/5/6 to 86th St., 212-717-4227 🌒🆂
261 Madison Ave. (38th St.), 4/5/6/7/S to 42nd St./Grand Central, 212-867-4050 🌒🆂
464 Park Ave. S. (bet. 31st & 32nd Sts.), 6 to 33rd St., 212-725-5383 🆂
161 W. 72nd St. (B'way), 1/2/3/9 to 72nd St., 212-579-6494 🆂
344 W. 57th St. (bet. 8th & 9th Aves.), 1/9/A/B/C/D to 59th St./ Columbus Circle, 212-541-4350
www.straightfromthecrate.com

◪ These "cramped" furniture stores are more akin to "storage rooms" than "showrooms", but for "twentysomething" "dorm"-dwellers or those furnishing a "first apartment", that's a "small price to pay" for affordable desks, dressers, bookcases and shelving units; but snobs sniff the stuff "looks like it was made from a crate rather than taken out of one" and shrug "you get what you pay for."

vote at zagat.com

M | P | S | C

Strawberry ●🅢🅒   9 | 9 | 8 | I
129 E. 42nd St. (Lexington Ave.), 4/5/6/7/S to 42nd St./Grand Central, 212-986-7030; www.strawberrystores.com
Additional locations throughout the NY area
◪ "Stylish" "teenyboppers" "who aren't millionaires" "keep up with short-lived trends" in "cheeky" "club gear", "costume jewelry", "fun shoes" and other "flashy" "throwaways" at this "fad"-meister; like Velveeta is to cheese, this chain is to designer boutiques, churning out "knockoffs galore" for "dirt cheap"; still, some sniff "stay away unless" you're "at work, get a horrible stain" on your outfit and "need something to change into."

Strider Records   - | - | - | E
22 Jones St. (bet. Bleecker & W. 4th Sts.), 1/9 to Christopher St.; A/C/E/F/V/S to W. 4th St., 212-675-3040; www.striderrecords.com
Connie Francis cohabitates with Jimi Hendrix at this Village veteran stocking thousands upon thousands of 45s, LPs and even 78s of tunes from the '40s to the '70s; these oldies experts buy collections and have been known to broker heady deals, such as the consignment sale of the rarest rock album ever: a version of Bob Dylan's 1963 *Freewheelin'* – including four tracks deleted shortly after release.

String Yarns 🅢🅒   - | - | - | E
1015 Madison Ave. (bet 78th & 79th Sts.), 6 to 77th St., 212-288-9276; www.stringyarns.com
This brand-new Upper Eastsider offers luxury and hand-painted yarns, hand-knit apparel and scads of supplies, along with a big helping of sophisticated advice to customers who want to try new ideas and sample some of the owner's own designs.

STUART MOORE 🅢   28 | 26 | 21 | VE
128 Prince St. (Wooster St.), N/R to Prince St., 212-941-1023
◪ A "cool vibe" emanates from this SoHo "emporium of gems that excites the heart" with its "unique styles and extremely creative use of metals" from European designers; it's best known for its own namesake "modern" line of engagement and wedding rings, so "amazing" they'll "make you want to get married"; P.S. "they'll even do custom designs."

Stuart Weitzman 🅢   24 | 22 | 21 | E
625 Madison Ave. (bet. 58th & 59th Sts.), N/R/W to 5th Ave./59th St., 212-750-2555; www.stuartweitzman.com
■ "Luxury meets comfort and sophistication meets sass" at this "attractive" Madison Avenue "source" that tempts would-be Cinderellas with "creative and daring window displays"; the "lovely" staff helps "event-going ladies" select "some of the most beautiful and comfortable" footwear, ranging from "perfect choices" for "dressy" "occasions" "you can walk and dance in all night" to "practical and funky styles" that last "season after season" to "great wedding shoes" ("a must for brides"); P.S. check out the "fantastic scarves and accessories too."

Stubbs & Wootton 🅒   - | - | - | E
22 E. 72nd St. (bet. 5th & Madison Aves.), 6 to 68th St., 212-249-5200; 877-478-8227; www.stubbsandwootton.com
"Super-preppy" needlepoint, velvet and suede slippers in whimsical and classic patterns for day or night bedeck this

| M | P | S | C |

elegant East 70s boutique on the second floor of a cozy townhouse; traditionalists of all stripes also swoop down on this oh-so-Palm-Beach mainstay for mules, slides, grosgrain-trimmed shoes with storybook themes for junior and a monogramming service.

Studio Museum of Harlem Gift Shop S — | — | — | M
144 W. 125th St. (bet. Lenox & 7th Aves.), 2/3/A/B/C/D to 125th St., 212-864-0014; www.studiomuseum.org
Take the A train, and you'll get to this Harlem museum showcasing artists of African and African-American descent; a separate street-side entrance leads to an ample, airy shop with a wide, well-displayed selection of literature, posters, postcards, jewelry, T-shirts and classy gift items; the "children's books are a highlight", as is the tantalizing half-price table, and the "wonderful customer service" makes for a pleasing vibe, enhanced by the likes of Dinah Washington over the sound system.

Stussy NYC S C   20 | 19 | 15 | M
140 Wooster St. (bet. Houston & Prince Sts.), N/R to Prince St., 212-995-8787; www.stussy.com
☑ "Awesome for 20 years" swear supporters of this "stylin'" surfer-dude label, who slide into the skylit SoHo shop to update their casual wardrobes with a new "T-shirt or hat or key chain" ("nice bags" of nylon from Head Porter too); but cynics say it's "losing ground to newer brands" – or "maybe there's just not a lot there for us thirtysomethings anymore."

Suarez S   — | — | — | E
450 Park Ave. (57th St.), 4/5/6/F/N/R/W to 59th St./Lexington Ave., 212-753-3758
"New York bag ladies feel like they've died and gone to heaven" at this venerable, third-generation Park Avenue boutique filled with one of "the most complete selections" of fine-quality handbags in town, plus "well-designed accessories" and shoes; though made by the same Italian "craftsmen" who create the status purses many of these styles resemble, these leather lovelies come without the designer "brand sticker shock"; always evolving, this luxury line is diverse enough to delight a hipster "teenager and her professional mother and her wealthy grandmother" alike.

Subterranean Records ● S   — | — | — | I
5 Cornelia St. (W. 4th St.), A/C/E/F/V/S to W. 4th St., 212-463-8900; www.recordsnyc.com
'Underground' has both connotations at this Village basement music shop "filled with dusty charm" where "veteran NYC rockers like Patti Smith or Bob Quine may drop in to chat" and browse through the "amazing variety of '60s rock", "'70s punk" on "hard-to-find vinyl" and CDs; presentation's scruffy, so "be prepared to dig."

Sude S C   ∇ 20 | 18 | 26 | M
829 Ninth Ave. (bet. 54th & 55th Sts.), 1/9/A/C to 59th St./Columbus Circle, 212-397-2347
■ In an area not known for super-femme boutiques, this "much-needed addition" is the "perfect place to stop when you need that little something for a first date" – or to get tempted by one of the "trendy, reasonably priced items" like cool vintage belt buckles; the "amazingly helpful", eponymous owner "writes a description on each tag" with styling suggestions, a heavenly approach in this Hell's Kitchen hideaway.

vote at zagat.com

				M	P	S	C

Suncoast Motion Picture Co. C   16 | 14 | 12 | M
Manhattan Mall, 901 Sixth Ave. (bet. 32nd & 33rd Sts.), B/D/F/N/Q/R/W to 34th St./Herald Sq., 212-268-2171 ●S
5402 Kings Plaza (Ralph Ave.), Brooklyn, 718-951-0076
www.suncoast.com

■ "Different from other chain video stores", these Manhattan and Queens branches of a Best Buy subsidiary offer "corporate movie" posters and novelty items on the bill as well; despite mediocre marks, vocal critics applaud the "decent" price and selection.

Super Runners Shop S C   25 | 18 | 25 | M
360 Amsterdam Ave. (77th St.), 1/9 to 79th St., 212-787-7665
Grand Central, 4/5/6/7/S to 42nd St./Grand Central, 646-487-1120
1337 Lexington Ave. (89th St.), 4/5/6 to 86th St., 212-369-6010
1246 Third Ave. (72nd St.), 6 to 68th St., 212-249-2133
www.superrunnersshop.com

■ "Geared toward active people", this "must-see" outfit will "keep you running back again and again for their fine prices" and "excellent selection of sneakers, apparel and gadgets" from big-name brands like New Balance, Brooks, Adidas, Hind and Saucony; the "extremely knowledgeable staff of avid" athletes is full of "insight and enthusiasm" and will not only "hand you" the "proper shoe" that "your gait requires", but offer "marathon advice you can bank on."

Surprise, Surprise S   16 | 9 | 10 | I
91 Third Ave. (12th St.), L to 3rd Ave., 212-777-0990;
www.surprisesurprise.com

◪ "Very crowded" East Village home-furnishings store that's "stuffed to the gills" with a "hodgepodge" of "good" "inexpensive" stuff, from small appliances to "folding furniture", shelving systems, "knickknacks" and "trendy" "decor items" by Umbra; with "prices like this, the dollar-store presentation is no surprise", but the attitude sure might be.

Suzanne Couture Millinery   – | – | – | E
27 E. 61st St. (bet. Madison & Park Aves.), 4/5/6/F/N/R/W to 59th St./Lexington Ave., 212-593-3232; www.suzannemillinery.com

"Expensive" couture toppers and bridal headpieces engage single sophisticates and the betrothed alike at this milliner's Upper East Side boutique, set in the parlor floor of a brownstone; elegant veils are festooned with brightly colored silk roses or floppy satin bows, while tiaras are encrusted with flourishes like pretty pearls; ladies who lunch and celebs of all stripes make a beeline for the close-up-worthy cocktail hats, fedoras and newsboy caps.

Swarovski S   21 | 25 | 20 | E
625 Madison Ave. (bet. 58th & 59th Sts.), N/R/W to 5th Ave./59th St., 212-308-1710; www.swarovski.com

■ Once known mainly for its little faceted figurines, this Austrian crystal palace has recently started to shine as the fashion crowd's favorite supplier of sparkly tattoos and high-quality costume jewelry; with its honey-colored wood floors and terra cotta walls, the Midtown store features such "sparkling treasures", plus a "fine selection of small gifts" and tabletop accessories "for every taste and budget."

	M	P	S	C

Swatch ◐ S
19 | 21 | 19 | I

640 Broadway (Bleecker St.), 6 to Bleecker St., 212-777-1002
5 E. 57th St. (5th Ave.), N/R/W to 5th Ave./59th St., 212-317-1100
100 W. 72nd St. (Columbus Ave.), 1/2/3/9 to 72nd St., 212-595-9640
438 W. Broadway (Prince St.), N/R to Prince St., 646-613-0160
888-800-1021; www.swatch.com

☑ "You can always find new designs at these now-classic" watch "candy shops" whose "cheap", "casual", plastic timepieces "truly do last"; but while the "staff's super" (especially the "'doctor' at the 57th Street main store") and the styles are still "fun for Swatch addicts" and "the younger generation", foes find the appeal's all "a little '80s"; N.B. there's now also a jewelry collection made from "cool" materials like silicon, resin and stainless steel.

SYMS ◐ S C
16 | 10 | 11 | I

400 Park Ave. (54th St.), 6/E/V 53rd St./Lexington Ave., 212-317-8200
42 Trinity Pl. (Rector St.), N/R/W to Rector St., 212-797-1199
www.syms.com

☑ Browsing "here is like going on a safari" – you practically have to "bring your machete to sort through" the hordes of "stock on hand", "but the finds can be rather spectacular at low prices" boast "bargain hunters" who love to "save money" at this popular discounter in the East 50s and the Financial District; "gambling shoppers" "play the waiting game", since "prices go down as time goes by", while "educated consumers" "stick to menswear", as it's "more classic" than the "out-of-date, gaudy" women's collection.

Tag Heuer S C
26 | 23 | 21 | VE

422 W. Broadway (bet. Prince & Spring Sts.), C to Spring St.; N/R to Prince St., 212-965-5304; 800-321-4832; www.tagheuer.com

■ Sporting an entire wall carved from an old maple tree, this SoHo store is the U.S.'s sole company-owned source for the stainless steel, high-performance, multi-functional watches that have sports fanatics salivating; these "top-of-the-line timepieces with top-of-the-line prices" "last forever" and work "for every occasion", since they now come in a variety of styles.

Tahari, Ltd.
24 | 20 | 18 | E

520 Fifth Ave. (bet. 43rd & 44th Sts.), 7/B/D/F/V to 42nd St./5th Ave., 212-398-2622; www.tahari.com

■ Situated right up the block from the NY Public Library, this "well-stocked" "secret" appropriately carries "smart clothes for smart people" – specifically Elie Tahari's "last-forever", "worth-every-cent" sportswear, but all at 30 percent off retail; whether you seek suits that are "well tailored" for "the working girl" or "ultra-feminine", out-on-the-town dresses, "the salespeople are helpful, but not overbearing."

Tah Poozie ◐ C
19 | 18 | 17 | I

50 Greenwich Ave. (bet. 6th & 7th Aves.), 1/9 to Christopher St., 212-647-0668 S
78A Seventh Ave. (15th St.), 1/2/3/9 to 14th St., 646-638-0750

■ These "fun", "funky" Downtown holes-in-the-wall are crammed with "low-priced" "gag gifts", toys, tchotchkes, trinkets and postcards – just the sort of "cool", "cute" stuff that "never fails to delight" "kids or kid-like adults"; the "salesperson will inform you" the name means 'orange-y' in Hebrew (and will also let you "try before you buy").

vote at zagat.com   **249**

| | | | M | P | S | C |

TAKASHIMAYA 🅢🅒   25 | 28 | 22 | VE
693 Fifth Ave. (bet. 54th & 55th Sts.), E/V to 5th Ave./53rd St., 212-350-0100; 800-753-2038

■ A "good example of less is more", this "feel-the-Zen" "hybrid department store/boutique" from Japan is a "serene" "culture trip" in Midtown; the "spare-but-inviting" environs are punctuated by "haunting displays" that encourage enthusiasts to "just stop by to see the [Christian Tortu arrangements of] flowers" or finger the "elegant" clothing for adults and kids, "rare cosmetics brands", "exquisite" linens, "design museum"–quality housewares or "gifts for a finicky friend"; it may be "a tad overpriced", but fans "buy anything just to get it wrapped" in the distinctive triangular box; P.S. "no visit is complete" without a trip to its tearoom.

Talbots 🅒   19 | 19 | 20 | M
2289-2291 Broadway (bet. 82nd & 83rd Sts.), 1/9 to 79th St., 212-875-8753
525 Madison Ave. (bet. 53rd & 54th Sts.), E/V to 5th Ave./53rd St., 212-838-8811 🅢
South Street Seaport, 189 Front St., 2/3/4/5/A/C/J/M/Z to Fulton St./B'way/Nassau, 212-425-0166
1251-1255 Third Ave. (72nd St.), 6 to 68th St., 212-988-8585
800-825-2687; www.talbots.com

■ Shoppers "know what to expect" at this fashion chain "where tradition reigns" in "classic" "career" and "casual" wear that "epitomizes American taste" for "conservative young business women", "mature" "suburbanite" "moms" and all shapes and sizes of "wanna-be Wasps"; "this is not the store to go to if you want to look hot", but if you need to dress "like a lady" "to fool the future in-laws", you can do it here "at an affordable price."

Talbots Kids and Babies 🅢🅒   22 | 21 | 22 | M
1523 Second Ave. (79th St.), 6 to 77th St., 212-570-1630; 800-992-9010; www.talbots.com

■ For "classic" clothes that are "more preppy/traditional than trendy", make tracks to this Upper East Side chain offshoot; it's "good" for "well-made" "basics like shorts, cardigans, blouses and T-shirts" and prices are "reasonable"; still, a few taunters tut that the togs are "a little too luxe for everyday", quipping it's "very Connecticut – pass my daughter her pearls", please.

Tano ●🅢🅒   19 | 14 | 14 | M
2286 Broadway (bet. 82nd & 83rd Sts.), 1/9 to 79th St., 212-362-5070

■ "Go in for one pair and come out with enough shoes for a centipede" at this Upper Westsider whose "wide variety" of "hip, funky" styles, "good basics" and "trendy" "copies of designer faves" "are too cute to resist"; sure, this "little" sliver of a shop is a "neighborhood convenience", but boosters believe it's "not to be overlooked when you can't find the right footwear elsewhere" – plus they have a "great bag and wallet selection."

T. Anthony 🅒   26 | 25 | 25 | VE
445 Park Ave. (56th St.), 4/5/6/F/N/R/W to 59th St./Lexington Ave., 212-750-9797; www.tanthony.com

■ "Guaranteed to turn heads at the airport", the "movie-star-quality luggage" (owned by Marilyn Monroe) at this "very upper-class", "very Madison Avenue" boutique conveys "understated wealth"; the "wide variety" of wares, including handbags and

| M | P | S | C |

leather goods, comes in "classic lines and stand-out colors that never fail to please"; once tried, "you cannot return to anything else" – and why would you, when it's such a "pleasure to shop" here, though you may "feel like you need to get dressed up" first.

Target ●S — | — | — | I
519 Gateway Dr. (Erskine St.), Brooklyn, 718-235-6032
8801 Queens Blvd. (55th Ave.), Queens, G/R/V to Grand Ave., 718-760-5656
13505-20th Ave. (Whitestone Expwy.), Queens, 718-661-4346
www.target.com
Savvy skinflints seeking "stylish stuff" "love Tar-jay", a "wonderful alternative for inexpensive shopping" that offers "everything – clothing, appliances, cosmetics, books, CDs and automotive supplies", as well as the bonus of exclusive, limited-edition tie-ins with housewares and apparel designers like Michael Graves, Todd Oldham and Liz Lange – all under one "mega-store" roof; it's "fun" to tour the "well-organized" branches, and "there are plenty of cashiers to get you out in a hurry."

TARTINE ET CHOCOLAT S C 27 | 27 | 23 | VE
1047 Madison Ave. (80th St.), 6 to 77th St., 212-717-2112
475 Park Ave. (bet. 57th & 58th Sts.), 4/5/6/N/R/W to 59th St./Lexington Ave., 212-508-0090
www.tartine-et-chocolat.com
■ "*Vive la France* for beautiful clothing" exclaim enthusiasts of the "exquisite", "classical" "designs for little ones" and "beautiful layette" items "for the cultured baby" at these "*très* chic" boutiques staffed with "lovely help"; *mais, oui*, "the clothing is adorable, but awfully expensive" and "not for everyday wear" claim euro-counters, who quip that "TC stands for *très cher*."

Tarzian True Value S C ▽ 20 | 14 | 22 | M
193 Seventh Ave. (bet. 2nd & 3rd Sts.), Brooklyn, F to 9th St., 718-788-4120; www.tarzianhardware.com
■ This "Park Slope gem" satisfies "all your hardware desires" with a "good selection" ranging from "esoteric accessories to everyday glasses"; regulars rave about the "knowledgeable", "friendly", "first-rate" staff and "not-bad-at-all prices" that "differentiate" this store, but deplore the "crammed"-in goods set in a "rabbit-warren layout" that's "difficult" to maneuver.

Tarzian West For Housewares S C ▽ 21 | 15 | 17 | M
194 Seventh Ave. (2nd St.), Brooklyn, F to 7th Ave., 718-788-4213
■ "Cramped" "little store" that's been selling what locals "need for the kitchen and bath" in the Park Slope neighborhood for two generations, long before the status-stroller set moved in; the stock includes everything from "spoon rests and bath mats" to gadgets and cookware, making it "Brooklyn's answer to Gracious Home."

Tatiana — | — | — | M
767 Lexington Ave. (bet. 60th & 61st.), 4/5/6/F/N/R/W to 59th St./Lexington Ave., 212-755-7744; www.tatianas.com
In a corner space of an East 60s office building resides this women's consignment shop that's a "great place for designer duds" – "a little bit of everything from Chanel to Laundry", with "party-style goods" especially well represented, as well as an array of shoes and handbags; the staff wins praise for being "not too pushy", and "prices are among the most reasonable around."

vote at zagat.com 251

| M | P | S | C |

Ted Baker 🆂🅲   24 | 21 | 19 | E
107 Grand St. (Mercer St.), N/R to Canal St., 212-343-8989
■ You too "can now look like a Brit" – and a "hip" one at that – at this "cool SoHo store" for men decorated with rough-hewn wooden display tables, murals and a mechanical dog; comprised of "nifty patterns" and "the best materials", the "modern stylings" are "edgy enough to be interesting, but conservative enough for the office" – especially the "versatile" micro-fiber shirts that "always look crisp, without ironing"; N.B. there's also a smattering of womenswear.

Ted Muehling 🅲   ▽ 29 | 28 | 27 | E
27 Howard St. (bet. B'way & Lafayette St.), 6/J/M/N/Q/R/W/Z to Canal St., 212-431-3825
■ Some say NYC "can be divided into those who wear Ted Muehling earrings and those who don't"; indeed, when it comes to "perfectly simple", "original and ethereal" work, this artisan "reigns" (and "don't miss the ceramics he's now making" too); the earthy atmosphere of his SoHo shop, which also carries Gabriella Kiss' line, offers an "amazing respite from the ordinary shopping experience", so in between that, the "gorgeous jewelry and the impeccable service, what more could you want?"

Tekserve   25 | 22 | 26 | M
119 W. 23rd St. (bet. 6th & 7th Sts.), F/V to 23rd St., 212-929-3645; www.tekserve.com
■ In a "new, bigger" space featuring an "interesting waiting area with a 10-cent Coke machine", this "Mac paradise" in Chelsea is "very in among the cognoscenti" for all things Apple, as well as repairs, upgrades and custom video and audio configurations; the "extremely knowledgeable" and "caring" staff will "almost bring tears to your eyes", despite the odd "long wait" and "retail" prices.

TENDER BUTTONS 🅲   28 | 22 | 20 | E
143 E. 62nd St. (bet. Lexington & 3rd Aves.), 4/5/6/N/R/W to 59th St./ Lexington Ave., 212-758-7004
■ An "Upper East Side must", this "charming" "little paradise" "raises button selection to an art form" – "who knew there were so many on the planet, let alone in one store?"; the "glorious selection" of "unique adornments" ranging from the "wild and wacky" to "everyday replacements" to antique cuff links offers fasten-ating "fun" for all – little wonder you "bump into everyone from fashion designers to teenagers" here.

Ten Thousand Things 🅲   – | – | – | VE
137 W. 19th St. (bet. 6th & 7th Aves.), 1/9 to 18th St., 212-352-1333
Converts claim this Chelsea temple is "the place to go for super-delicate, wispy-looking" "Zen jewelry" (the store name comes from a Tao quote) made of oxidized silver and "unique stones", as well as more precious substances; "prices can be high, but often you're paying for the design, as opposed to the materials."

Tents and Trails 🆂   27 | 7 | 20 | M
21 Park Pl. (bet. B'way & Church St.), 1/2/3/9/A/C to Chambers St., 212-227-1760; 800-237-1760
☑ Camping is the only game at this "beloved hideaway" in the Financial District that stocks a "wide variety at various price levels" of "anything you could want for the outdoors" from tents, stoves and backpacks to Patagonia and North Face apparel; expect an

| | | | M | P | S | C |

"extremely knowledgeable and personable staff", though take heed: bread crumbs and "patience may be needed to hack through the jungle of merchandise."

Terence Conran Shop, The ◐🅢🅒   24 | 25 | 17 | E
407 E. 59th St. (1st Ave.), 4/5/6/N/R/W to 59th St./Lexington Ave., 212-755-9079; www.conran.com
■ Located in a "must-see", albeit "out-of-the-way", location under the Queensboro Bridge is this "modern, clean" home-furnishings emporium named after its knighted English owner; two floors of "slightly edgy" furniture by hot, young designers like Christophe Pillet and the Bourellec brothers, along with "unusual" accessories for the tabletop, kitchen and bath are part of a "limited" "tasteful selection" that's "beautifully presented."

TG-170 ◐🅢🅒   22 | 17 | 20 | E
170 Ludlow St. (bet. Houston & Stanton Sts.), F to 2nd Ave., 212-995-8660; www.tg170.com
■ The pop feel of this Lower East Side boutique, "one of the first" to bring style to the area, underscores the "Downtown hip" goodies you find courtesy of owner Terri Gillis, whose "slightly alternative yet womanly personality" shows in her "nice cross-section" of "cool li'l finds" from small lines of clothes (Birgit, Lauren Moffitt) and accessories, including the best-selling Freitag bags.

Theatre Circle ◐🅢🅒   – | – | – | M
268 W. 44th St. (bet. B'way & 8th Ave.), 1/2/3/7/9/N/Q/R/S/W to 42nd St./Times Sq., 212-391-7075; www.broadwaynewyork.com
Play out your Fanny Brice fantasies beneath the faux stage lights covering the ceiling of this wood-paneled shop in the Theater District; sister to One Shubert Alley and Broadway New York, the larger store is an extravaganza of kitsch covering the Great White Way, past and present; the back room holds quite a selection of scripts, sheet music and books for aspiring Andrew Lloyd Webbers.

30th Street Guitars   – | – | – | E
236 W. 30th St. (bet. 7th & 8th Aves.), 1/9 to 28th St., 212-868-2660; www.30thstreetguitars.com
"Lots of choice vintage and used" fretted instruments line the soaring walls of this music store with a "knowledgeable staff", a "great repair shop" and its own fledgling line of NYC axes; on a Madison Square Garden–area block that has blossomed into a mecca for rehearsal studios, this "guitarist's paradise" will make you "wish upon a rock star."

37=1 🅢🅒   – | – | – | E
37 Crosby St. (bet. Broome & Grand Sts.), N/R to Prince St., 212-226-0067
Long, narrow and gallery-like, with wispy little nothings hanging from wall pegs like delicate pieces of art, Jean Wu's peachy sliver of a store in SoHo caters to coquettes who prefer garter belts and sultry stockings (of the never-worn vintage variety) to pantyhose, and dresses and luxurious lingerie on the silky side; for fashionistas who like their fit just so, she also makes made-to-measure undies.

Thomas Moser Cabinetmakers 🅢   – | – | – | VE
699 Madison Ave., 2nd fl. (bet. 62nd & 63rd Sts.), F to 63rd St./ Lexington Ave., 212-753-7005; 800-708-9016; www.thosmoser.com
Each "glorious" piece of furniture is handcrafted, signed and dated in the company's workshop in Maine then shipped to this Madison

vote at zagat.com

M | P | S | C

Avenue showroom; enthusiasts exclaim that the clean-lined, black-cherry chairs, cabinets and tables are "absolutely to die for" and worthy of "passing down to your grandchildren."

Thomas Pink   25 | 24 | 21 | VE
*520 Madison Ave. (53rd St.), E/V to 5th Ave./53rd St., 212-838-1928;
888-336-1192* S
*1155 Sixth Ave. (45th St.), 1/2/3/7/9/N/Q/R/S/W to 42nd St./Times Sq.,
212-840-9663*
www.thomaspink.co.uk

▫ "Every banker worth a bonus" gets bewitched by these British stores in Midtown, with their "fabulous presentation" of "top-of-the-line shirts" and "great office blouses" in "fantastic colors" and "superb fabrics" ("nice cuff links" and ties too); negatives natter "no way these [goods] are worth these prices", but the scores side with those who say for the "ultimate in Jermyn Street" style, "think Pink."

Thomasville S   23 | 22 | 20 | E
*91 Seventh Ave. (16th St.), 1/2/3/9 to 14th St., 212-924-7862
217-04 Northern Blvd. (217th St.), Queens, 7 to Main St., 718-224-2715
800-225-0265; www.thomasville.com*

▫ For nearly 100 years, this manufacturer of "beautiful furniture" has crafted "high-quality" "traditional styles" for the living room, bedroom and dining room, and its Chelsea showroom carries a selection ranging from rococo to Mission styles; but whether you feel helped or "hounded" by the sales staff will have to be your call.

TIFFANY & CO. S C   27 | 27 | 21 | VE
*727 Fifth Ave. (57th St.), N/R/W to 5th Ave./59th St., 212-755-8000;
800-843-3269; www.tiffany.com*

▫ Fifth Avenue's "quintessential NYC landmark", this "mammoth emporium" is a multi-floored "sight to behold", carrying all things of "classic" luxury that "make you feel so glam" – "breathtaking" diamond solitaires, "silver baby rattles", "beautiful china and crystal" and "designer jewelry from Elsa Peretti and Paloma Picasso"; on weekends, when you need to "duck around" the "fanny-pack–clad tourists", the "well-trained staff" that "treats Trumps and tramps" alike can be "hard to get to", and critics carp that with "mass-marketing" "the institution is becoming a factory", but most will still gladly "buy something here – if only to get that famous robin's egg–blue box."

Timberland S C   21 | 18 | 16 | M
*707 Madison Ave. (63rd St.), F to 63rd St./Lexington Ave., 212-754-0436;
888-802-9947; www.timberland.com*

▫ Urban rangers find a "nice presentation" of "excellent rugged clothing and shoes", including the signature waterproof leather boot, at this "ubiquitous chain's" "woodsy Madison Avenue" outpost; while a few skeptics sniff the stuff's strictly "for taking the SUV out of the city", most praise the "great return policy" (they take back "defective articles *sans* question").

Tip-Top Shoes S C   22 | 14 | 21 | M
*155 W. 72nd St. (bet. B'way & Columbus Ave.), 1/2/3/9 to 72nd St.,
212-787-4960; 800-925-5464; www.tiptopshoes.com*

■ A "classic family", "service-oriented" footwear store "with actual" "experienced salespeople" who "unhurriedly" "help you find the right size and style" "like in the old days", this Upper

West Side stalwart is "a shoe-lover's dream"; the "amazing variety" of "excellent", "high-quality brand names" like Clarks, Ecco, Frye, Merrell and Rockport are the "comfiest" – "my feet really thanked me."

T.J. MAXX S C   16 | 9 | 7 | I
620 Sixth Ave. (bet. 18th & 19th Sts.), 1/9 to 18th St., 212-229-0875
1509 Forest Ave. (Marianne St.), Staten Island, 718-876-1995
2530 Hylan Blvd. (New Dorp Ln.), Staten Island, 718-980-4150
800-926-6299; www.tjmaxx.com

■ "Decorate your whole apartment in Ralph Lauren" and the like for "dirt cheap", and "no one will ever believe you got it" all at this discount "chain store" with Chelsea and borough branches that are also "wonderful" for "plus sizes" and "children's clothes and toys"; still, "digging's required" to "strike it lucky" amid "last season's name brands" that are "jammed together" by a "surly staff."

TKNY ● S C   – | – | – | M
21 Ave. B (bet. 2nd & 3rd Sts.), F/V to 2nd Ave., 212-677-0500;
www.tkny.com

Hip new idea lab in the East Village where the digerati convene to check out the latest Japanese gadgets, like a device that can turn any surface into a speaker, a truly compact compact disc player and a key-chain accessory that recharges cell phones; you can network with like-minded hipsters and expats from Tokyo at the lounge in back, which serves Onigiri rice snacks and sake.

TLA Video ● S   27 | 19 | 23 | I
52 W. Eighth St. (bet. 5th & 6th Aves.), A/C/E/F/S/V to W. 4th St.,
212-228-8282; www.tlavideo.com

■ "Believe it or not, we have Philadelphia to thank for this fine movie store" sans "attitude" in Greenwich Village; the "excellent, eclectic", "large selection" of "foreign and alternative" titles, including a "not-quite-Disney" kiddie section, is perhaps the "best in NYC", if not "in the world"; "films organized by actor or theme" "make for pleasant browsing and interesting discoveries of what stars would prefer to keep the lesser-knowns of their oeuvre."

Today's Man ● S C   16 | 15 | 16 | M
529 Fifth Ave. (44th St.), 4/5/6/7/S to 42nd St./Grand Central, 212-557-3111
625 Sixth Ave. (19th St.), 1/9 to 18th St., 212-924-0200
www.todaysman.com

■ "Two shirts, two ties and out the door in less than 10 minutes" laud "lunch hour" shoppers who find that even for the "fashion-challenged", it's not mission impossible at this menswear chain in Midtown and Chelsea thanks to "salespeople who help you put your look together" with a variety of merchandise from "socks to underwear to tuxedos" in "sizes from short/portly to tall/large"; as your financial planner will tell you, "high quality + low prices = great value", even if your wardrobe consultant deems the stuff fit only for "yesterday's man."

Todd Hase   – | – | – | VE
261 Spring St. (bet. Hudson & Varick Sts.), C/E to Spring St., 212-334-3568;
www.toddhase.com

Sophisticated SoHo furniture store specializing in the eponymous interior designer/owner's handcrafted, pared-down contemporary pieces with classic lines made the old-world way – eight-way hand-tied springs support upholstered mohair or silk seating, and hand-

M | P | S | C

fitted marquetry patterns top some of the tables; "great lamps" made of leather and wood are apt accents for the chic sofas, settees and chairs that have a celebrity and fashion following.

Tod's S   26 | 25 | 20 | VE
650 Madison Ave. (60th St.), N/R/W to 5th Ave./59th St., 212-644-5945; www.tods.com

■ "Once you wear a pair" of these "preppy", "princely slippers" "there's no turning back" confides a "certain Upper East Side set"; the "ultimate in loafers" and "well-made casualwear", these "unbelievably comfortable and practical" "instant classics are in a class by themselves" – "don't buy the driving moccasins unless you drive a Mercedes"; "bright, airy and perfectly minimalist", "everything about this shop shines, from the shoes to the clerks' smiles to the entertaining doormen", though a handful feels the "salespeople could use some fine-tuning."

Toga Bikes S C   24 | 19 | 21 | E
110 West End Ave. (64th St.), 1/9 to 66th St., 212-799-9625; www.togabikes.com

■ "They have everything, know everything" and "will get you on the bike that's right for you" exclaim enthusiasts of this "clean, well-organized" "ultimate high-end" Upper Westsider that's "almost a bicycle boutique"; as at Gotham, its sibling Downtown, the "friendly", "helpful" staff takes "tremendous time" with customers, offering "fantastic" services like free lifetime tune-ups with major purchases and appointments for time-pressed cyclists.

Tokio 7 ●S   22 | 14 | 14 | M
64 E. Seventh St. (bet. 1st & 2nd Aves.), 6 to Astor Pl., 212-353-8443; www.tokio7.com

■ "At this East Village consignment shop", an ever-changing, "reasonably priced" "hodgepodge" of "vintage and off-season designer wear" ("from no-names to big names") keeps the low-ceilinged setting hopping with "young NYU students", entry-level executives and "hip fashionistas on a budget"; there's "not much to speak of service-wise – but the merchandise is why we're here, so who cares?"

Tokyo Joe   22 | 12 | 16 | M
334 E. 11th St. (bet. 1st & 2nd Aves.), L to 1st Ave., 212-473-0724 ●S
240 E. 28th St. (bet. 2nd & 3rd Aves.), 6 to 28th St., 212-532-3605

■ This East Village and Gramercy Park used-clothing duo is a "closet of wonders" (even if both are scarcely bigger than a walk-in) say the Joes and Janes who "pop in to check out" the "high-profile designer brands" – "anything from Marc Jacobs skirts to Coach straw-and-leather totes" – at "perfect prices" and in "very decent condition"; "just don't expect ambiance, as there is none."

Tommy Hilfiger S C   17 | 18 | 16 | E
372 W. Broadway (Broome St.), C/E to Spring St., 917-237-0983; www.tommyhilfiger.com

■ A neon American flag presides over this multi-level SoHo store, chock-full of the designer's "faux-prep" classics for both sexes, as well as all of his rah-rah accoutrement – belts, hats, ties, watches and fragrances – for this born-in-the-USA brand; however, cynics sneer you "look like a walking ad" in the logo-laden clothes.

256   subscribe to zagat.com

M | P | S | C

Totem Design Group C — | — | — | VE
71 Franklin St. (bet. B'way & Church St.), 1/9 to Franklin St., 212-925-5506; www.totemdesign.com

"Cutting-edge" TriBeCa furniture store and hot spot showcasing the work of over 30 American and European designers; the "colorful merchandise" with a high style quotient includes chairs and desk accessories from Karim Rashid, colorful rugs by Verner Panton and glass products from London-based Marc Newson.

Tourneau C — 26 | 22 | 19 | E
12 E. 57th St. (Madison Ave.), N/R/W to 5th Ave./59th St., 212-758-7300 S
500 Madison Ave. (52nd St.), E/V to 5th Ave./53rd St., 212-758-6098
200 W. 34th St. (7th Ave.), 1/2/3/9 to 34th St., 212-563-6880 S
www.tourneau.com

☑ "If it ticks they have it" at this timepiece chain, "arguably the most complete watch store in NYC", which also offers "terrific" (if "overpriced") repair service; while the "well-organized" "vast displays" are "great for browsing", some shoppers compare the "knowledgeable staff" to "used-car salesmen", meaning "be prepared to bargain."

TOWER RECORDS/VIDEO ●SC — 24 | 19 | 14 | M
1961 Broadway (66th St.), 1/9 to 66th St./Lincoln Ctr., 212-799-2500
692 Broadway (E. 4th St.), 6 to Astor Pl., 212-505-1500
20 E. 4th St. (Lafayette St.), F/S/V to B'way/Lafayette; 6 to Astor Pl., 212-505-1500
383 Lafayette St. (bet. E. 4th & Great Jones Sts.), 6 to Astor Pl., 212-505-1166
Trump Tower, 725 Fifth Ave. (57th St.), N/R/W to 5th Ave./59th St., 212-838-8110
www.towerrecords.com

■ It can be "overwhelming", but this "sprawling", "stacked to the gills" "big-box chain" "always has what you want if you can figure out where it is"; don't expect much help from the "aloof" staff, but do know that the DVD/video store faces the world music/record annex on Lafayette, Lincoln Center is the "last bastion of broad classical selections" and the NoHo flagship has some of "the best jazz and Broadway" offerings around with an "'80s disco interior."

Town Shop ●S — 24 | 10 | 20 | M
2273 Broadway (bet. 81st & 82nd Sts.), 1/9 to 79th St., 212-787-2762

■ "An Upper West Side institution" done up in pink retro-style decor, this "real neighborhood store" not only stocks "all of the basic and some higher-end lingerie labels", it's also one of the "best places to get truly fitted for a bra" or a bathing suit; "it might be crowded at times, but that's because everyone knows" that owner "Mrs. K and her staff have the magic touch" – indeed, Townies toast "Mrs. Koch is a national treasure"; "everyone should go once."

Toys in Babeland ●S — 26 | 24 | 28 | M
94 Rivington St. (bet. Ludlow & Orchard Sts.), F to Delancey St., 212-375-1701; 800-658-9119; www.babeland.com

■ The staff at this "woman-centered", "super sex" store on the Lower East Side makes everyone "feel totally comfortable" – gals "can shop here without feeling leered at, and couples can get frank

vote at zagat.com

| M | P | S | C |

advice on the relative merits of battery versus plug-in" stuff; with "help books" and "classes to teach you how to get the most out of" "the superb selection" of "tools", "a potentially embarrassing trip" becomes an "extremely pleasurable" "education."

Toys R Us ⓞⓢ
23 | 19 | 13 | M

1514 Broadway (44th St.), 1/2/3/7/9/N/Q/R/S/W to 42nd St./Times Sq., 800-869-7787
24-32 Union Sq. E. (15th St.), 4/5/6/N/Q/R/W/L to 14th St./Union Sq., 212-674-8697
Albee Square Mall, 1 DeKalb Ave. (Fulton St.), Brooklyn, 3/4 to Nevins St., 718-858-8697
66-26 Metropolitan Ave. (69th & Mt. Oliver Sts.), Queens, M to Metropolitan Ave., 718-326-2038
35-00 48th St. (Northern Blvd.), Queens, G/R/V to Northern Blvd., 718-937-8697
Highland Shopping Plaza, 105 Mill Rd. (Highland Blvd.), Staten Island, 718-979-8697
2845 Richmond Ave. (Yukon St.), Staten Island, 718-698-8821
www.toysrus.com

■ Bound to leave "any kid in total awe" (including "your husband – aka kid for a day"), this "must-stop" Times Square flagship, the "big boy in discount toys", is like a "mini-amusement park"; while mavens are over the moon about the "massive selection" and "huge" Barbie Dream house larger than many NYC apartments, it's the "delightful" "Ferris wheel that takes the cake"; but killjoys growl that it's "all glitz for tourists – I can find the same merchandise without the chaos", "pushy parents and wailing children."

Toy Tokyo ⓢⓒ
▽ 25 | 18 | 17 | M

121 Second Ave. (bet. 7th & 8th Sts.), N/R to 8th St.; 6 to Astor Pl., 212-673-5424; ww.toytokyo.com

■ "If Anime and robots are your bag, check out this second-floor" East Village shop stuffed with modern-day and decades-past "eclectic, eccentric collectibles from A to Z", "imported from Japan" and "all over the world"; the "He-Man, My Little Pony and Smurf" stuff may "bring you back to your youth", and if you have a yen for wind-ups, Transformers, Star Wars and Star Trek action figures, grab a "big kid" and jet on over.

Tracy Feith ⓢⓒ
▽ 21 | 25 | 20 | E

209 Mulberry St. (bet. Kenmare & Spring Sts.), 6 to Spring St., 212-334-3097

■ "It's dangerous, but so much fun" to dip into this small shop, where the onetime surfer-dude designer offers up his "rich-girl garb" alongside actual surfboards; the vibe is as "relaxed and beachy" as you get in NoLita, affording ample time to play among the "decadently beautiful" dresses, "sparkly shoes" and "fab handbags" with a "one-of-a-kind feel."

Transit ⓞⓢ
20 | 18 | 12 | M

665 Broadway (bet. Bleecker & Bond Sts.), 6 to Bleecker St.; F/V/S to B'way/Lafayette, 212-358-8726; www.transitnyc.com

◪ "Old-school to new-school" urbanites get on track at this multi-level mass-transit-themed NoHo store, where "trendy, sporty streetwear" and kicks from labels like Adidas, Nike, ENYCE and Sean Jean are "well presented" (the sneaker wall resembles a makeshift train); while fans are down with the "phat threads", most

| | | | **M** | **P** | **S** | **C** |

Trash & Vaudeville ◐ S C   21 | 19 | 17 | M
4 St. Marks Pl. (bet. 2nd & 3rd Aves.), N/R to 8th St.; 6 to Astor Pl., 212-982-3590
■ The name "says it all" – the "rock 'n' roll gear" and "punk, goth" and "just bad taste" clothing make this "famous" East Village legend "super-wonderful" to teens and twentysomethings, who can't wait to "upset mom at the next family dinner"; fans fall for the "excellent selection of British shoes (Doc Martens, etc.)", "tons" of "huge platforms" and yes, even "fetish wear" ("bondage pants", anyone?); at times the staff may be "too cool to help you."

Treasure Chest, The S C   – | – | – | M
171 Seventh Ave. (1st St.), Brooklyn, F to 7th Ave., 718-768-6292
Crammed with cases full of fun jewelry, unusual picture frames and tchotchkes, this wee, "wonderful" Park Slope standby lives up to its name and then some; the helpful staff happily shows you whatever takes your fancy, from Skagan watches with colorful leather bands to unique novelty necklaces and earrings to art deco rings; N.B. it's owned by the same folks who run Facets.

Treillage C   – | – | – | VE
418 E. 75th St. (bet. 1st & York Aves.), 6 to 77th St., 212-535-2288; www.treillageonline.com
Interior design luminaries Bunny Williams and John Rosselli showcase their "beautiful" garden-related vintage finds – Parisian benches, faux-bois tables, stone sculptures and such – at this picturesque Upper East Side store; alas, it's "very expensive", so wags suggest heading here for inspiration, "then travelling to France to buy."

Tribal Soundz ◐ S   – | – | – | E
340 E. Sixth St. (bet. 1st & 2nd Aves.), N/R to 8th St.; 6 to Astor Pl., 212-673-5992; www.tribalsoundz.com
If you're in the mood to tap the tablas after a Little India meal, you can get yourself a pair, along with other "worldbeat" wonders at this "source for musical exotica" in the East Village; you can even take a class to learn to play your new digeridoo, but not in the AM – it's open only 3–11:30 PM weekdays and 12–12 AM weekends.

Triple Five Soul ◐ S C   – | – | – | M
290 Lafayette St. (bet. Prince & Houston Sts.), N/R to Prince St.; F/S/V to B'way/Lafayette, 212-431-2404; www.triple5soul.com
Even if you're not down with Lafayette's decidedly skateboarder vibe, you may fall for this cleanly furnished SoHo gallery shop filled with "hip-hop fashions for the rest of us"; denim, twill and cord pants, super-cool T-shirts and heavy-duty wool sweaters sit alongside nifty accessories that include "fetish-worthy bags with more zippers than you could ever need", rolling DJ cases (with pouches for headphones and records) and the duffle roller – rounded out with wheels, of course.

Troy S C   – | – | – | VE
138 Greene St. (bet. Houston & Prince Sts.), N/R to Prince St., 212-941-4777; www.troysoho.com
Since Troy Halterman opened his SoHo store eight years ago, the soaring space has been home to "tony furniture" and accessories

vote at zagat.com

found on his travels to South America and Europe; unique vintage pieces sit alongside spare contemporary designs by Living Devani, e15 and other hip manufacturers; equally stylish jewelry, art and tabletop items are displayed in the back cases and at the register.

TSE Cashmere
24 | 22 | 18 | VE

827 Madison Ave. (bet 68th & 69th Sts.), 6 to 68th St., 212-472-7790
■ This East 60s store is a "great place to lust after" luxurious, "softer-than-your-kitty" knitwear for men, women and children; "treat yourself at least once" to the "simple, modern" styles in "gorgeous" colors, all the while remembering that "cashmere doesn't have C-A-S-H in its name for nothing."

Tucker Robbins C
– | – | – | E

33-02 Skillman Ave. (33rd St.), Queens, 7 to 33rd St., 718-764-0222; 888-880-6442; www.tuckerrobbins.com
MoMA QNS isn't the only new stop in Long Island City – designer Tucker Robbins transplanted himself here from Chelsea and brought his signature Asian and African finds, which range from Philippine Capiz-shell screens to Yoruba ladders, with him; there's also a line of contemporary furniture made primarily with recycled wood that exudes a similar exotic sensibility.

Tumi S C
27 | 21 | 22 | VE

520 Madison Ave. (54th St.), E/V to 5th Ave./53rd St., 212-813-0545
Rockefeller Ctr., 53 W. 49th St. (bet. 5th & 6th Aves.), B/D/F/V to 47-50th Sts./Rockefeller Ctr., 212-245-7460
Grand Central, Lexington Passage (42nd St.), 4/5/6/7/S to 42nd St./Grand Central, 212-973-0015
www.tumi.com
■ "If you actually use your luggage", "save your money" for these "top-of-the-line" travel bags and leather goods that "endure all that wear and tear"; the staff offers "superior service" and "stands by the warranty"; sure, the suitcases may be "hard to pick out on airport carousels", but just the sight of one may "speed your check-in at hotels."

TURNBULL & ASSER C
29 | 28 | 28 | VE

42 E. 57th St. (bet. Madison & Park Aves.), 4/5/6/N/R/W to 59th St./Lexington Ave., 212-752-5700; 877-887-6285; www.turnbullandasser.com
■ Pray, sir, step into the "old-gentlemen's-club" atmosphere of this East 57th Street "prestige" British haberdasher, outfitter of "important male dressers from Prince Charles" to James Bond; aided by "wonderful service" (voted the *Survey*'s No. 1), you can "always please a guy by buying him a silk tie" or a "stylishly colored", "custom-made shirt" in fine Egyptian or Sea Island cotton from here (women get this royal treatment too).

Uncle's Stereo
▽ 19 | 6 | 15 | M

216 W. 72nd St. (bet. B'way & West End Ave.), 1/2/3/9 to 72nd St., 212-721-7500; www.unclestereo.com
▨ Look past the "shabby" ambiance and fulfill your top-shelf stereo desires "without having to travel to Midtown" at this "local store" in the West 70s offering "great selection and service" on DTS receivers, DLP projectors, subwoofers and more at what some Uptowners say are the "best prices anywhere", particularly if you "try bargaining."

| M | P | S | C |

Union 🆂🅲
▽ 23 | 20 | 19 | E

172 Spring St. (bet. Thompson St. & W. B'way), C/E to Spring St., 212-226-8493

🗹 Supporters say this SoHo shoebox seems a streetwise "staple of true NYC/British style", from the eccentric aesthetic of designer Oliver Spenser to Cooperstown Authentic re-issued baseball jerseys to "their own original-logo T-shirt that'll be on display at MoMA one day"; but skeptics sniff "skate on" – the menswear here is too "pricey."

Unisa 🆂🅲
19 | 18 | 17 | M

701 Madison Ave. (bet. 62nd & 63rd Sts.), 4/5/6/N/R/W to 59th St./Lexington Ave., 212-753-7474; www.unisa.com

■ "Cute", "delicately shaped shoes that knock off designer looks convincingly" at "reasonable" prices draw stylish bargain-hunters to this minimally designed Madison Avenue standby; it's "a good source for footwear" "you need after you've spent your spending money on the outfit" and "great for trendy shoes that can be worn only one season."

Untitled ●🆂🅲
– | – | – | VE

26 W. Eighth St. (bet. 5th & 6th Aves.), A/C/E/F/V/S to W. 4th St., 212-505-9725

"In a little nook on Eighth Street", this two-floor boutique has "been around serving up high-fashion before anyone else" (well, since the mid-'80s, anyway); the friendly, relaxed atmosphere features "fun, helpful" clerks who ease male and female customers – many of them in the drama and music biz – into "very trendy" threads and jeans for Big Apple nights.

Upland Trading 🅲
– | – | – | M

236 E. 13th St. (bet. 2nd & 3rd Aves.), 4/5/6/L/N/Q/R/W to 14th St./Union Sq., 212-673-4994

Tucked away on East 13th Street is this pocket-sized, woodsy shop chock-full of quality outerwear, handcrafted Italian bags, Irish scarves by Inis Meàin and "a great collection of the safari/rugged look" for male and female cosmopolites; owner/manager Armando Nagron is such "a truly elegant, laid-back kind of guy" that you "can't go into the store and not buy anything."

Uproar Home 🆂🅲
– | – | – | E

121 Greene St. (bet. Houston & Prince Sts.), N/R to Prince St., 212-614-8580; www.uproarhome.com

Expansive upholstered sofas (available as sleepers) and chairs and sturdy, handmade wooden cabinets are the focus of this SoHo store housed in a cast-iron building with beautiful interior columns; smaller-scale home accessories include throws, trays, mirrors and handblown glass lamps.

Urban Angler 🅲
– | – | – | VE

118 E. 25th St., 3rd fl. (bet. Lexington & Park Aves.), 6 to 23rd St., 212-979-7600; 800-255-5488; www.urbanangler.com

If you want to find one of "the greatest fishing stores in the world", just look for the gargoyle outside the Luxene Building near Madison Square Park and wend your way up to this sign-less, third-floor 4,000-sq.-ft. loft; the spirit of adventure is evident from the boats hanging from the ceiling to the wide array of rods, reels, lines, tackle, vises, technical clothing and luggage; while you're docked,

vote at zagat.com

| M | P | S | C |

you may also want to catch some casting lessons, seminars, demonstrations and book signings.

Urban Archaeology C   27 | 25 | 21 | VE
143 Franklin St. (bet. Hudson & Varick Sts.), 1/9 to Franklin St., 212-431-4646
239 E. 58th St. (bet. 2nd & 3rd. Aves.), 4/5/6/N/R/W to 59th St./ Lexington Ave., 212-371-4646
www.urbanarchaeology.com

■ "A must if you're renovating a home", these "amazing stores" in TriBeCa and the East 50s provide a "one-of-a-kind shopping" experience with a "grand selection" of "unique" fixtures and fittings salvaged from "old buildings", "absolutely gorgeous tiles" and reproductions of "antique" plumbing and lighting; the "pleasant staff" is "knowledgeable", but the "prices are outrageous" for anyone who's not a "millionaire."

Urban Monster S C   – | – | – | M
396 Atlantic Ave. (bet. Bond & Hoyt Sts.), Brooklyn, F/G to Bergen St.; A/C/E to Hoyt-Schermerhorn, 718-855-6400; www.urbanmonster.com

Vibrant and kid-friendly, with Jolly Roger apple-green and grape-soda-colored floors, this Boerum Hill newcomer addresses the needs of babies, moms and moms-to-be with a retail emporium and romper room for classes galore, from Mommy & Me to pilates; the merchandise goes the gamut from hip children's clothing from labels like Oink! Baby and Celeste to baby essentials like Avent bottles, Combi Activity Rockers and Maclaren strollers to maternity apparel, nursing gear and bras, diaper bags and bath toys.

Urban Optical S   – | – | – | E
152 Bedford Ave. (bet. 8th & 9th Sts.), Brooklyn, L to Bedford Ave., 718-388-5078
330 Seventh Ave. (9th St.), Brooklyn, F to 7th Ave., 718-832-3513

"A nice selection of fashionable frames" from hot properties like Alain Mikli, Oliver Peoples, Chanel and Ralph Lauren pack the windows and vitrines of these two small yet appealing Williamsburg and Park Slope siblings; owner "Dr. Adam Friedland is the best" believe boosters – "he is so accommodating and has great taste too", plus his staff is "knowledgeable and friendly"; little wonder these eyewear havens usually brim with browsers and buyers.

Urban Outfitters ●S C   18 | 18 | 11 | M
2081 Broadway (72nd St.), 1/2/3/9 to 72nd St., 212-579-3912
628 Broadway (Bleecker St.), F/V to B'way/Lafayette; 6 to Bleecker St., 212-475-0009
162 Second Ave. (bet. 10th & 11th Sts.), 6 to Astor Pl.; L to 3rd Ave., 212-375-1277
526 Sixth Ave. (14th St.), F/L/V to 14th St./6th Ave., 646-638-1646
374 Sixth Ave. (bet. Washington & Waverly Pls.), A/C/E/F/S/V to W. 4th St., 212-677-9350
800-282-2200; www.urbn.com

❷ "Downtown" goes "all around town" with this "poseur-cool" chain of "duds" for "dudes and chicks"; "funky-punky" clothes for the "fast and furious" sit alongside "wacky", "kitschy" knickknacks and "heading-off-to-college" dorm-room decor, making it "a fun place to wander" ("where else can you get a cool scarf and penis pasta" at the same time?), despite the

subscribe to zagat.com

M | P | S | C

"overly inflated" price tags and "intimidating", "multi-pierced" "alterna-teen" staff.

Utrecht | 22 | 17 | 17 | M |
111 Fourth Ave. (bet. 11th & 12th Sts.), 4/5/6/L/N/R/W to 14th St./ Union Sq., 212-777-5353

◪ "A clean, serene, art-selling machine", this East Village "all-purpose" "artists paradise" offers a "good selection" of paint, easels, brushes, canvas and graphic arts supplies for painters with promise and professionals too; prices are "reasonable", especially on the "house brand's" acrylics and oils, and the staff is "student-friendly"; but the less-impressed paint another picture, pouting that the choices "are not as wide" as some competitors.

Valentino C | 26 | 25 | 25 | VE |
747 Madison Ave. (bet. 64th & 65th Sts.), 6 to 68th St.; F to 63rd St./ Lexington Ave., 212-772-6969; www.valentino.it

■ "High-end" refinement meets "friendly and knowledgeable" service at this limestone-floored East 60s boutique – a "beautiful space to shop in" – "catering to wealthy Upper Eastsiders" and bi-coastal celebrities (e.g. Julia Roberts, Ashley Judd), who love the legendary Italian designer's "classic" "stunning eveningwear, shoes and accessories"; P.S. gents, "great clothes of the most European style" await you too.

VAN CLEEF & ARPELS S | 29 | 28 | 27 | VE |
744 Fifth Ave. (bet. 57th & 58th Sts.), N/R/W to 5th Ave./59th St., 212-644-9500; www.vancleef.com

■ Located next to Bergdorf Goodman, this venerable French house is the "friendliest of the big-name jewelers" profess fans of the "incredible designs" – especially the familiar clover and other exquisitely updated art nouveau fauna and flora creations – executed with invisibly set gems; though there's lots of "nice ice", it's the "surprisingly warm" staff that makes it "a dream to shop" in the intimate lime-green-and-lavender environs.

Varda S | 24 | 21 | 18 | E |
786 Madison Ave. (67th St.), 6 to 68th St., 212-472-7552
2080 Broadway (71st St.), 1/2/3/9 to 72nd St., 212-873-6910 ●
149 Spring St. (Wooster St.), C/E to Spring St., 212-941-4990
118 Spring St. (bet. Greene & Mercer Sts.), 6 to Spring St., 212-343-9575

■ A "dream come true" proclaim those taken by the "timeless", "beautifully crafted", "quality leather shoes and boots" and "good service" at this "classic" quartet; while the "comfortable, conservative" styles may "not be for the hipster, trendy crowd, they're dependable when you need a break from dancing all night in *Sex and The City* heels."

Variazioni ●SC | 20 | 18 | 15 | E |
309 Columbus Ave. (bet. 74th & 75th Sts.), 1/2/3/9 to 72nd St., 212-874-7474
104 Fifth Ave. (bet. 15th & 16th Sts.), 4/5/6/L/N/Q/R/W to 14th St./ Union Sq., 212-627-4444
1376 Third Ave. (bet. 78th & 79th Sts.), 6 to 77th St., 212-744-9200

◪ For a good *variazioni* of "out-of-the-ordinary" options in "breezy" separates and "great eveningwear", everyone from "the struggling actress to the Wall Street banker" would do well to "check out the sale racks" at this mini-chain; however, critics claim the clothes "walk the walk, but can't talk the talk" (quality control is "not the

vote at zagat.com

greatest") and warn the "pushy salespeople" "won't let you leave empty-handed."

Ventilo 🆂🅲   – | – | – | E

69 Greene St. (bet. Broome & Spring & Sts.), N/R to Prince St., 212-625-3660
810 Madison Ave. (68th St.), 6 to 68th St., 212-535-9362
www.ventilo.fr

The old world charm of these inviting boutiques caters to rich SoHo gypsies and Madison Avenue acolytes who "always want one of everything" produced by this French firm – embroidered satin suits, hand-painted floral purses, fringed silk shawls or poetically named perfumes; sweet salespeople encourage visitors to look around and get in tune with the beaded, bohemian vibe.

Venture Stationers 🆂   24 | 16 | 16 | E

1156 Madison Ave. (bet. 85th & 86th Sts.), 4/5/6 to 86th St., 212-288-7235; 888-388-2727

■ Upper Eastsiders have ventured to this "great neighborhood place" for over 30 years for "lovely and varied merchandise" from engraved stationery and "pens galore" to Longchamp bags to "cute little notebooks" and "colored paper clips" (it's an "office supply hoarder's paradise"); in fact, it's so "well stocked", it's "easy to spend money here whether you plan to or not."

Vera Wang Bridal Salon   26 | 25 | 20 | VE

991 Madison Ave. (77th St.), 6 to 77th St., 212-628-3400
980 Madison Ave., 3rd fl. (bet. 76th & 77th Sts.), 6 to 77th St., 212-628-9898
www.verawang.com

◪ "The place to call the minute you get engaged" rhapsodize romantics who love "the queen of bridal gowns'" "always tasteful" designs at this Upper East Side by-appointment-only destination; the "lovely staff" proffers "the royal treatment", presenting the "superlative" "dreams on a hanger, inviting you to be a star" for a day; while the less-rapturous retort "if attitude is your thing, it's here, along with the cost", even they rationalize that "it's simply a rite of passage"; N.B. Wang's Maids Salon at 980 Madison specializes in bridesmaid and flower girl dresses.

Vercesi Hardware 🆂   23 | 14 | 25 | I

152 E. 23rd St. (bet. Lexington & 3rd Aves.), 6 to 23rd St., 212-475-1883

■ "The service is key" at this "great, old-fashioned" Gramercy Park hardware store, where the "excellent", "funny", "no-attitude" staff provides a "deep repository of advice on all home fix-it projects" and can help you identify "any widget you need"; the shop stocks a "large variety" of goods at "reasonable prices", and even though it's a "madhouse on Saturdays", its devotees deem it "worth the wait."

Verdura 🅲   – | – | – | VE

745 Fifth Ave., Ste. 1205 (bet. 57th & 58th Sts.), N/R/W to 5th Ave./ 59th St., 212-758-3388; www.verdura.com

"For the best in jewelry" with an idiosyncratic flair, "it doesn't get better than Verdura" declare the cult-like cognoscenti who patronize this showroom high above 57th Street; using the original, oft-imitated designs of its legendary namesake (whose signature Maltese-cross cuff bracelets adorned the wrists of Chanel and Diana Vreeland), the firm turns out witty, glamorous pieces that sparkle with precious and semiprecious stones alike.

M P S C

Veronique ⓈⒸ ▽ 20 | 20 | 20 | VE
1321 Madison Ave. (93rd St.), 6 to 96th St., 212-831-7800; 888-265-5848; www.veroniqued.com

■ "The answer for the sexy pregnant woman", this sleek, newly renovated Upper East Side boutique offers "unique merchandise" from Italy, France and America; it's "expensive, but worth it for the flattering clothes" and "friendly", "knowledgeable staff" (including personal shoppers) "who help find what will be the gems of your maternity wardrobe", including "womanly bathing suits."

Versace Ⓒ 23 | 25 | 21 | VE
647 Fifth Ave. (bet. 51st & 52nd Sts.), E/V to 5th Ave./53rd St.; 6 to 51st St., 212-317-0224
815 Madison Ave. (68th St.), 6 to 68th St., 212-744-6868
www.versace.com

☑ "You gotta say wow" as you glide through the "imposing" entry of the Fifth Avenue flagship or the "modern" Madison Avenue branch of the late Italian maestro, whose "big-budget" womens- and menswear is now designed by sister Donatella; the "staff can seem standoffish at first, but they warm up" and become "extremely helpful", especially with the "wonderful selection of accessories"; but while fans find "fun" in the "fashion-first" clothes, the "bold looks" are deemed "too bizarre" for others.

Vertigo ⓈⒸ 20 | 20 | 17 | E
755 Madison Ave. (bet. 65th & 66th Sts.), F to 63rd St./Lexington Ave.; 6 to 68th St., 212-439-9626; 888-783-7844; www.vertigo2000.com

■ Since 1985, this Madison Avenue women's boutique, the flagship for the familiar "trans-seasonal" label, has specialized in "sharp looks in separates and suits" with a "sexy, European feel" (lots of "lean Lycra"); the "versatility" of its "defined, recognizable style" overcomes any dizziness induced by the high-altitude prices.

Verve ◐ⓈⒸ – | – | – | E
282 Columbus Ave. (bet. 73rd & 74th Sts.), 1/2/3/9 to 72nd St.; B/C to 72nd St., 212-580-7150
353 Bleecker St. (bet. Charles & W. 10th Sts.), 1/9 to Christopher St., 212-691-6516
105 Christopher St. (bet. Bleecker & Hudson Sts.), 1/9 to Christopher St., 646-336-1147

"Can't walk by without lightening my wallet" – it's one of my "favorite traps" fawn fashionistas who surrender all willpower when faced with this trio's "unique selection" of accessories from up-and-coming designers; "love the shoes" and purses at the Christopher Street site sigh the smitten, who also fall hard for the "cutest bags, hats, scarves and jewelry" at the Bleecker Street and vintage-mirror-appointed Upper West Side shops; P.S. the "friendly staff helps you find" pieces "specific to your style."

Vespa Ⓒ – | – | – | VE
13 Crosby St. (bet. Grand & Howard Sts.), 6/J/M/N/Q/R/W to Canal St., 212-226-4410 ◐Ⓢ
40-34 Crescent St. (bet. 40th & 41st Ave.), Queens, 7/N/W to Queensboro Plaza, 718-786-9739
www.vespausa.com

Trend-seekers searching for a new way to rev their engines (or recreate the European élan of Jean-Paul Belmondo) zip into these new offshoots of Piaggio USA's revitalized Tuscany, Italy-based

vote at zagat.com

chain in SoHo and Long Island City and onto this updated classic motor scooter, available in vibrant va-va-vroom colors; drivers create their own hip on-the-road look with hot-hued helmets, customized suede seats and a battery of accessories including T-shirts and watches, all displayed in minimalist spaces that feel like the coolest garages ever; the staffs also assist would-be riders with the licensing process.

Via Spiga S C — 23 | 21 | 20 | E
765 Madison Ave. (bet. 65th & 66th Sts.), 6 to 68th St., 212-988-4877
390 W. Broadway (bet. Broome & Spring Sts.), N/R to Prince St., 212-431-7007
800-557-0250; www.viaspiga.com
■ "They usually hit fashion right on the head" at these SoHo and Madison Avenue "meccas" maintain mavens, who take a shine to the "friendly, reliable service" as well as the "wonderfully styled shoes" that not only "stand out", but "also withstand wear and tear and are – gasp – comfortable"; fence-straddlers feel it "bounces between a little too out there and a little too boring, but when they find the middle ground – yum"; N.B. they also carry outerwear, cashmere sweaters, accessories and men's footwear.

Victoria's Secret ● S — 17 | – | 17 | M
1328 Broadway (34th St.), B/D/F/N/Q/R/V/W to 34th St./Herald Sq., 212-356-8383; www.victoriassecret.com
For additional locations, see Top Chain Store index
☒ It's "like walking into a silky pink boudoir" breathe brevity-boosters – "once you shop" at this "wonderland of intimate apparel" "you're hooked"; "the formula works" thanks to a "great presentation" of "perpetually sexy stuff", from "trendy little nighties" to "everyday undies", but patrons put off by the "cloying salespeople" and "so-so quality" pout "her secret is that these undergarments belong in the mall, not Midtown"; N.B. the 34th Street flagship, replete with Moulin Rouge-esque mannequins and arty photos of model Giselle Bundchen, opened post-*Survey*.

Vilebrequin — 25 | 24 | 21 | VE
1070 Madison Ave. (81st St.), 6 to 77th St., 212-650-0353; 888-458-0051; www.Vilebrequin.com S
436 W. Broadway (Prince St.), C/E to Spring St., 212-431-0673
■ The search for "wonderful, creative bathing suits for men and adorable ones for little boys" terminates at these Upper East Side and SoHo boutiques where the spirit of Saint-Tropez reigns; the "unique" "European styling", executed in colorful prints and stretch fabrics, offers a "very flattering fit"; "granted, the prices are prohibitive, but one can get a lot of mileage out of swimming trunks."

Villeroy & Boch S — 24 | 25 | 23 | E
901 Broadway (20th St.), N/R to 23rd St., 212-505-1090; 800-845-5376; www.villeroy-boch.com
■ Flatiron purveyor of the 1748 Luxembourg-based company's "classy" dinnerware and serving pieces that are a "perennial hit at housewarmings" and "great for wedding gifts"; there are "lots of lovely" "classic" patterns, but an "attentive" and "helpful" staff can guide the china-challenged when it comes to creating more contemporary "mix-and-match" looks; N.B. in addition, the space also serves as a showroom for the company's tiles, bathroom fixtures and ceramic kitchen sinks.

	M	P	S	C

V.I.M. ◐ S C   14 | 8 | 8 | I
16 W. 14th St. (6th Ave.), F/L/V to 14th St./6th Ave., 212-255-2262; 800-800-3742; www.vim.com
Additional locations throughout the NY area
☑ "More jeans than you will ever know what to do with" reside at this convenient mega-chain of "good-for-hanging-out" labels like Fubu, Phat Farm and Mudd, plus "lots of cheap basics", from urban streetwear and must-have activewear to sneakers galore by Adidas, Puma and Skechers; while "prices are decent", the less-impressed opine there are "better alternatives" to be found.

Vinylmania ◐   – | – | – | M
60 Carmine St. (bet. Bedford St. & 7th Ave. S), 1/9 to Houston St., 212-924-7223; www.vinylmania.com
"For vinyl junkies", this Carmine Street ol' reliable is "the place to get your" dance music; wax enthusiasts groove to the wide selection of popular and hard-to-find acid jazz, progressive house, trance and Eurodance LPs that includes everyone from Ashanti to the Thievery Corp; "breakbeats, imports and CDs are on the menu" too, and so are DJ accessories; P.S. the "staff knows what they're talking about", plus "special orders don't upset 'em."

VIRGIN MEGASTORE   25 | 22 | 14 | M
1540 Broadway (bet. 45th & 46th Sts.), 1/2/3/7/9/N/Q/R/S/W to 42nd St./Times Sq., 212-921-1020; www.virginmega.com ◐ S
52 E. 14th St. (5th Ave.), 4/5/6/L/N/Q/R/W to 14th St./Union Sq., 212-598-4666
■ These "big, scary" Times Square and Union Square "FAO Schwarzes for music fans" "saturate the senses", boasting a "huge selection of imports and other genres" "you can spend all day listening to on headphones" "before you buy"; "like New York City itself, it offers the extreme of everything" – in fact, you might join the chorus of shoppers "over 14 years old" who plead "turn down the volume" on the piped-in tunes.

Vitra S C   – | – | – | VE
29 Ninth Ave. (bet. 13th & 14th Sts.), A/C/E/L to 14th St./8th Ave., 212-929-3626; www.vitra.com
Hot new Meatpacking District showroom for the Swiss furniture maker designed by buzz-generating young architect Lindy Roy; a molded walnut staircase connects the two-storied space, which features conveyer-belt-like displays of iconic pieces from 20th-century masters like Jean Prouvé, Verner Panton and Frank Gehry.

Vivienne Tam S C   24 | 23 | 17 | E
99 Greene St. (bet. Prince & Spring Sts.), N/R to Prince St., 212-966-2398; www.viviennetam.com
■ There's a whole lotta "daring" going on at this SoHo boutique, and it's not just the red walls with a painted dragon; the vibe also lies in the "unique Asian-inspired" womenswear; "although it can be an ego-kicker" for those not sleek enough for "skin-tight T-shirts and skirts", "you won't see yourself coming and going in these outfits."

Vivienne Westwood S C   25 | 25 | 19 | VE
71 Greene St. (bet. Broome & Spring Sts.), C/E to Spring St.; N/R to Prince St., 212-334-5200; www.viviennewestwood.com
■ She goes back over 30 years, but SoHo's "imaginative" British "style guru" is still "ahead of the pack", with her "fun, figure-

vote at zagat.com

hugging" "punk takes on suits and evening gowns", "asymmetrical sweaters" and, of course, those corset-inspired tops, all of them guaranteed to "cause double-takes"; just "don't take the sizing personally" (try going one notch larger than usual instead).

Walter Steiger   23 | 22 | 18 | VE
417 Park Ave. (55th St.), E/V to 53rd St./Lexington Ave.; 6 to 51st St., 212-826-7171; www.walter-steiger.com

■ "Comfortable and luxurious at the same time – who knew you could get that in a high-end, high-heeled shoe?" crow customers who flock to this Park Avenue designer boutique; the footwear "with flair", ranging from stiletto boots to fashionable flats, and the "beautiful bags" are made from unusual and über-soft leathers – little wonder that Walter-ites whine "expensive."

Warren Edwards   ▽ 24 | 19 | 18 | VE
107 E. 60th St. (Park Ave.), 4/5/6/N/R/W to 59th St./Lexington Ave., 212-223-4374; www.warrenedwards.com

■ Two fox terriers set the tone at this pricey East 60s shop that caters to cab-riding women and nattily dressed men (like Luther Vandross) with "true couture" footwear that can be "customized to your exact details" or bought off the shelf; twice a year this "living legend" designer – half of the famed 1980s Susan Bennis Warren Edwards label – rolls out ultra-femme collections of sexy heels, sling-backs and mules spiced with a little leopard print or the like and fabulous footwear for guys made from all kinds of skins.

Watch World 🆂   ▽ 17 | 15 | 16 | M
649 Broadway (Bleecker St.), 6 to Bleecker St., 212-475-6090; www.sunglasshut.com
Additional locations throughout the NY area

■ Owned by the Sunglass Hut chain, with several "convenient locations" around town, this well-equipped NoHo outpost offers what fans find are the "best prices" on "basic watches" (plus new batteries); it's the sort of place where you can "get a great deal on a Swiss Army watch."

WATERWORKS   28 | 28 | 19 | VE
475 Broome St. (Greene St.), N/R to Prince St., 212-274-8800 🆂
225 E. 57th St. (bet. 2nd & 3rd Aves.), 4/5/6/F/N/R/W to 59th St./Lexington Ave., 212-371-9266
www.waterworks.com

◪ "Wish I had more bathrooms" sigh friends of these "beautiful" SoHo and East 50s stores selling "wonderful fixtures", the "chicest supplies" and an "amazing array of decorative tiles"; though they're "not large", it's a "pleasure to walk around the showrooms", and the "helpful staff" "doesn't hound you", but bashers bemoan the "ridiculous prices" that make it all too easy to "get soaked."

Wedding Library ●🅲   ▽ 17 | 19 | 16 | E
50 E. 81st St. (bet. Madison & Park Aves.), 6 to 77th St.; 4/5/6 to 86th St., 212-327-0100; www.weddinglibrary.net

◪ An "information gathering spot" for brides that's "extremely helpful in resourcing reception venues, photographers, musicians", DJs and invitations, this Upper East Side townhouse is also the "place to come" for "gorgeous headpieces", accessories and bridesmaid shoes, dresses and favors; but naysayers file the research-end under "unimaginative", opining "if you've read even one magazine, chances are you know as much as the 'librarians.'"

| M | P | S | C |

Wempe C 27 | 24 | 23 | VE
700 Fifth Ave. (55th St.), E/V to 5th Ave./53rd St., 212-397-9000; 800-513-1131; www.wempe.com
■ Although this Midtown "looks like nothing from the outside" (IWC, Patek Philippe, Rolex, etc.), the interior is a treasure trove for timepieces of a "high-end" nature; the staff's "butler-like service" makes shopping here "a real joy", and while a "my-watch-cost-more-than-your-car ambiance" fills the air, regulars report that "price cuts come with the asking."

Westside Kids S C 22 | 17 | 19 | M
498 Amsterdam Ave. (84th St.), 1/9 to 86th St., 212-496-7282
■ You "can always find a rainy-day game that's engaging", "good educational" and "handcrafted toys", "inexpensive stocking stuffers" and Zutano clothing at this "cramped" Upper West Side staple where the "staff is very knowledgeable" and will help you "through any birthday" gift dilemma.

Wet Seal C 13 | 15 | 12 | I
670 Broadway (Bond St.), 6 to Bleecker St., 212-253-2470 ● S
65 E. Eighth St. (B'way), N/R to 8th St., 212-228-6188
901 Sixth Ave. (32nd St.), B/D/F/N/Q/R/W to 34th St./Herald Sq., 212-216-0622
www.wetseal.com
✘ "Tanned Britney wanna-bes" "stuff themselves into sparkly T-shirts", "lacy dresses, peasant tops" and other "post-Contempo Casuals" at this "juniors'" fashion chain for "prom queens" still wet behind the ears; the service is less than sterling, but the "one-season" "girlie" wear is so "cheap", you won't have to blow all your "babysitting money" at once.

What Comes Around Goes Around ● S 25 | 21 | 18 | E
351 W. Broadway (bet. Grand & Broome Sts.), A/C/E to Canal St., 212-343-9303; www.nyvintage.com
✘ "Western wear never went out" at this SoHo store, whose dude-ranch decor makes for dang-good displays of plaid shirts, fringed skirts and a "world-class collection of collectible denim"; the "knowledgeable staff" helps navigate among the "great vintage" items and the store's own line of reconstructed pieces; however, those unwilling to spend bucks on buckskin banter the place "should be named What Comes Around Goes Up In Price."

Whitney Museum Store S 18 | 15 | 15 | M
945 Madison Ave. (75th St.), 6 to 77th St., 212-570-3614; www.whitney.org
✘ "Richard Avedon waited for me to buy his books and signed them: what more do you want?" – well, how about "geometric-patterned mini-umbrellas, giant-hand salad scoopers" and other "unique", "modern" "Americana" "at moderate prices" from this Upper East Side museum shop; unfortunately, being banished to the basement "between the staircase and the bathroom", it's "more of a counter than a full-fledged store."

Wicker Garden ▽ 26 | 22 | 21 | VE
1327 Madison Ave. (bet. 93rd & 94th Sts.), 6 to 96th St., 212-410-7001; www.wickergarden.com
■ "Eloise probably shopped here" quip fans who head to this Victorian-style Upper East Side spot to pore over the "storybook children's clothes"; there's also a "large selection" of "unique

vote at zagat.com 269

baby" items to choose from, including "beautiful" wicker furniture designed by the owner, bassinets and layette essentials; sure, it can be "over-the-top in price", but hey, browsing never hurt anyone.

William Barthman ☉　　　24 | 21 | 22 | E
174 Broadway (Maiden Ln.), 4/5/6 to Fulton St., 212-732-0890 ☒
1118 Kings Hwy. (Coney Island Ave.), Brooklyn, N to Kings Hwy., 718-375-1818
800-727-97825; www.williambarthman.com

■ Like the "old-time jeweler back home", this "historical place" (founded in 1884) is a "great spot to drop a wad of cash" on "good, classic watches and jewelry" (from Aaron Bascha to David Yurman) and pens; the "repair service is stellar", as are the "appraisers on-site", all of which makes this vet a "favorite in the Financial District" and Gravesend too.

Williams-Sonoma ●☒☉　　　25 | 24 | 20 | E
1175 Madison Ave. (86th St.), 4/5/6 to 86th St., 212-289-6832
121 E. 59th St. (Lexington Ave.), 4/5/6/N/R/W to 59th St./Lexington Ave., 917-369-1131
110 Seventh Ave. (bet. 16th & 17th Sts.), 1/9 to 18th St., 212-633-2203
800-541-2233; www.williams-sonoma.com

■ This chain has "the best of everything" – from All-Clad cookware and German knives to always-cool KitchenAid mixers – a status-loving cook or bride-to-be could want; there are "no bargains, but it's a pleasure shopping here" because the "helpful" staff and "well-organized", "beautifully presented" merchandise "make you want to buy."

William Wayne ☉　　　– | – | – | M
40 University Pl. (9th St.), N/R to 8th St.; 6 to Astor Pl., 212-533-4711
846-850 Lexington Ave. (bet. 64th & 65th Sts.), 6 to 68th St., 212-737-8934
800-318-3435; www.william-wayne.com

Could there possibly be "too many wonderful items" in these "fun" home-furnishings stores in Greenwich Village and in the East 60s, where ceramic garden seats, cachepots and bumblebee-topped honey jars share space with mother-of-pearl-handled servers, tinware and "monkey-themed things"?; the owners have "really got an eye", so "it's a great place" "to find an unusual gift, even if it's for yourself."

Willoughby's ☒　　　19 | 15 | 14 | M
136 W. 32nd St. (bet. 6th & 7th Aves.), 1/2/3/9 to 34th St./Penn Station, 212-564-1600; 800-378-1898; www.willoughbys.com

◪ Beyond the cell phones, wristwatches and blood-pressure machines lurk "cameras, cameras, cameras", new and old, at this centenarian "granddaddy" in the Garment District; with a "good selection" of "prices as low as you can get without really shopping around", it remains a "safe place to buy", though shutter snobs dis the "once-proud" place for employing "staffers who are ignorant of even the most basic rules of photography."

Wiz, The ●☒　　　17 | 13 | 9 | M
2577 Broadway (bet. 96th & 97th Sts.), 1/2/3 to 96th St., 212-663-8000
212 E. 57th St. (bet. 2nd & 3rd Aves.), 4/5/6 to 59th St./Lexington Ave., 212-754-1600
555 Fifth Ave. (46th St.), B/D/F/V to 47-50th Sts./Rockefeller Ctr., 212-557-7770

| M | P | S | C |

(continued)
Wiz, The
1534-1536 Third Ave. (86th St.), 4/5/6 to 86th St., 212-876-4400
17 Union Sq. W. (15th St.), 4/5/6/L/Q/N/R to 14th St./Union Sq., 212-741-9500
www.thewiz.com

◪ On the positive side, these electronic outlets offer a "decent selection" and "good prices on specials", "their return policy is pretty fair" and a recent redo might rectify the atmosphere's "lack of charm"; however, opponents assert the "lackadaisical" "salespeople think reading the box to you is being informative", adding "now that they don't match the competition's prices", the standard jingle is "everybody beats The Wiz."

Wolford C | 26 | 21 | 21 | VE |
122 Greene St. (Prince St.), N/R to Prince St., 212-343-0808 ●S
619 Madison Ave. (bet. 58th & 59th Sts.), 4/5/6/N/R/W to 59th St./ Lexington Ave., 212-688-4850
996 Madison Ave. (bet. 77th & 78th Sts.), 6 to 77th St., 212-327-1000
800-965-3673; www.wolford.com

■ "Steep prices indeed, but these are no ordinary undies" assert enthusiasts who consider this Austrian "luxe lingerie" "the gold standard"; "nothing looks sleeker under a jacket than their [string] bodysuits", the "fishnets, stay-up stockings and everyday hose", available in "patterns, textures" and "every color in the spectrum", are "sublime", plus "the salespeople, from SoHo to Madison, are happy to help find your size and style"; P.S. Vivienne Westwood collaborated with Wolford on a small collection that's a "little wild."

Wool Gathering S C | 21 | 18 | 15 | E |
318 E. 84th St. (bet. 1st & 2nd Aves.), 4/5/6 to 86th St., 212-734-4747

◪ "Beautiful buttons and wools" abound in this "charming little" Yorkville shop where the needle-and-canvas set find a "good range of yarn" and supplies, including skeins that are "excellent for children's" wear; one catch: knit-pickers pout that you may "get a chilly reception from the staff"; N.B. beginner knitting classes are held on Sundays and Wednesdays.

Workbench S | 18 | 18 | 18 | M |
161 Sixth Ave. (bet. Prince & Spring Sts.), C/E to Spring St., 212-675-7775
470 Park Ave. S. (32nd St.), 6 to 33rd St., 212-481-5454
336 E. 86th St. (bet. 1st & 2nd Aves.), 4/5/6 to 86th St., 212-794-4418
2091 Broadway (72nd St.), 1/2/3/9 to 72nd St., 212-724-3670
130 Clinton St. (Joralemon St.), Brooklyn, 2/3/4/5/M/N/R/W to Court St./Borough Hall, 718-625-1616
800-736-0030; www.workbenchfurniture.com

■ Long-standing furniture chain that stocks solid "modern-looking but not eccentric" basics like shelving (the Nimbus Wall System is a standout), bedroom sets and sofas "at reasonable prices"; the "attentive" staff is "courteous and helpful."

World, The ●S C | – | – | – | M |
1501 Broadway (43rd St.), N/Q/R/S/W/1/2/3/7/9 to 42nd St./Times Sq., 212-398-2563; www.theworldny.com

Fronting the WWE's Times Square restaurant, this store reflects professional wrestling in all its lowbrow glamour, with its black-and-corrugated-steel interior and a giant screen that plays fluffy biopics of masters of the mat; it all eggs fans into purchasing caricature

vote at zagat.com 271

sippy cups, tight T-shirts, butch leather wallets and Hulkamania stuffed bears sporting Hogan's signature handlebar whiskers.

World of Golf, The 🄲 | 25 | 15 | 23 | E |

189 Broadway (Dey St.), 4/5/6 to Fulton St.; N/R to Cortlandt St., 212-385-1246
147 E. 47th St. (bet. Lexington & 3rd Aves.), 6 to 51st St., 212-775-9398 🅂
800-499-7491; www.theworldofgolf.com

◪ "The name says it all" – these huge "candy stores for avid golfers" in Midtown and the Financial District showcase "all the fine brands" of equipment, from Callaway to Odyssey, including one of the "best putter selections in the city" and athletic apparel, plus they do custom club fitting; fans find the "staff knowledgeable and helpful", but critics wonder whether "anything ever goes on sale" here; N.B. at the Broadway branch's studio, professionals use analysis technology to diagnose your swing.

X-Large 🅂🄲 | – | – | – | M |

267 Lafayette St. (bet. Prince & Spring Sts.), N/R to Prince St., 212-334-4480; www.xlarge.com

Don't let the "misleading store name" keep you from crossing the threshold of this urban NoLita shop, founded over 10 years ago by Beastie Boy Mike D and recently renovated with a super-slick new look; the ramped-up jackets, hoodies, jeans, beanies, accessories and "cool" graphic tees appeal to grown-up skateboarder types, and tweens and teens won't be left behind, as there's plenty to turn them on.

Xukuma ⬤🅂🄲 | – | – | – | M |

183 Lenox Ave. (119th St.), 2/3 to 116th St., 212-222-0490;
www.xukuma.com

On the parlor floor of a Harlem rowhouse, this hip, new lifestyles store brings a little of everything that's Downtown to Uptown, from chandeliers to bath products; Sia candles, frames and vases, Wonderfully Delicious gourmet edibles and Torre and Tajus clocks are perfect fillers for the shop's unique twist on the gift basket.

Yankee Clubhouse Shop ⬤🅂 | 22 | 19 | 16 | M |

110 E. 59th St. (bet. Lexington & Park Aves.), 4/5/6/N/R/W to 59th St./Lexington Ave., 212-758-7844
245 W. 42nd St. (bet. 7th & 8th Aves.), 1/2/3/7/9/N/Q/R/S/W to 42nd St./Times Sq., 212-768-9555
393 Fifth Ave. (bet. 35th & 36th Sts.), B/D/F/N/Q/R/V/W to 34th St./6th Ave., 212-685-4693
www.sportsavenue.com

◪ This is "by far the best store in New York" – "if you're a Yankees nut", that is; "everything that you could possibly dream of" related to the Bronx Bombers is here, from "the latest styles" of "hats and T-shirts" to "hard-to-find items" like bobbing-head collectible dolls and Babe Ruth rubber duckies, plus "you can buy tickets" to the games at this "one-stop shop"; the service can be "world-champ arrogant" and the merchandise is "overpriced, but if you're a fan, it won't matter."

Yarn Co., The 🄲 | 25 | 18 | 14 | E |

2274 Broadway, 2nd fl. (bet. 81st & 82nd Sts.), 1/9 to 79th St., 212-787-7878; 888-927-6261; www.theyarnco.com

◪ "It's all here, including top-shelf knitters to remedy beginner blues" and stacks of high-end and "novelty yarns", chorus the

| M | P | S | C |

crafty who congregate on the second-floor of this Upper Westsider; but critics are in a snit, saying "being a friend of the house gets you good service, otherwise expect to be ignored."

Yarn Connection C   22 | 14 | 22 | M

218 Madison Ave. (bet. 36th & 37th Sts.), 6 to 33rd St., 212-684-5099
■ "About the size of a small closet", this Murray Hill knitting and needlework shop "feels like a hidden jewel", offering "a great selection of smashing yarn", "good patterns and books"; the "absolute angel" of an owner and her staff "embody the knitting grandmother" most "never had" and make you feel "welcome", "even if you're not known or not planning to spend a bundle."

Yellow Door S C   – | – | – | M

1308 Ave. M (bet. 13th & 14th Sts.), Brooklyn, Q to Ave. M, 718-998-7382; www.theyellowdoor.com
"Madison Avenue in Midwood" describes this "savvy shoppers' mecca", which carries a "wide range of gifts, fashion-forward jewelry and home-design" items at "prices you can only find in Brooklyn"; as you peruse the MacKenzie-Childs crockery, SeidenGang rings or Versace trays, the "nicest people help you find just what you need."

Yohji Yamamoto S C   27 | 24 | 22 | VE

103 Grand St. (Mercer St.), N/R to Prince St., 212-966-9066
■ Away from the madding SoHo crowd, this boutique – "more a museum than a store" – is a quiet "treasure" for "true aficionados" (male and female) of this "creative, thoughtful" Japanese designer; the "surprisingly low-pressure" staff lets shoppers browse the predominantly black collection and "innovative" denim goods, or just gaze at the "interesting artwork."

Yumi Katsura   26 | 25 | 21 | VE

907 Madison Ave. (bet. 72nd & 73rd Sts.), 6 to 77th St., 212-772-3760; www.yumikatsura.com
◪ If you "want to live out every girl's fantasy, get a dreamy" "gown with a twist of originality" at this "calm" Upper East Side bridal boutique – "you'll spend a lot of money, but you get a top-quality dress with personality", plus "personalized service" from designer Erisa Katsura, Yumi's niece, and her "very helpful", "attentive" consultants; but a few underwhelmed customers "expected a little more glamour" to "justify such high prices."

Yves St. Laurent Rive Gauche   26 | 25 | 24 | VE

855 Madison Ave. (bet. 70th & 71st Sts.), 6 to 68th Sts., 212-988-3821; www.ysl.com
■ "Brilliant, classic, forever" fawn fashionistas over this legendary Left Bank house, transplanted to the coolly sophisticated, "stylish environment" of his-and-hers boutiques on the Upper East Side; the highly acclaimed collections, now designed by Tom Ford, create a buying frenzy among aficionados, from the must-have Mombasa bag to the slim-cut suits to the curvy, elegant eveningwear.

ZABAR'S ◐ S C   26 | 16 | 15 | M

2245 Broadway (80th St.), 1/9 to 79th St., 212-787-2000; 800-697-6301; www.zabars.com
■ "Look here before you buy housewares anywhere else" because the "quality and prices" at this "densely stocked" West Side "institution", which was voted the No. 1 Major Gourmet Store in our

vote at zagat.com

NYC Marketplace Survey, are "hard to beat" and the "eclectic" cookware and appliances, plus "every imaginable gadget", will "make you want to refurnish your kitchen every time you visit"; be prepared for "crowds and chaos" on the weekends, but take comfort in the fact that "you can pick up dinner while you're here."

Zales Jewelers 14 | 16 | 15 | M

535 Broadway (bet. Prince & Spring Sts.), N/R to Prince St., 212-625-0998 ●S
170 Fifth Ave. (22nd St.), N/R to 23rd St., 917-606-1406 S
1187 Third Ave. (69th St.), 6 to 68th St., 212-717-7871
Queens Center Mall, 90-15 Queens Blvd. (Woodhaven), Queens, G/R/V to Woodhaven Blvd., 718-760-3702
Staten Island Mall, 2655 Richmond Ave. (Ring Rd.), Staten Island, 718-982-6562 ●S
800-311-5393; www.zales.com

■ This nationally known retailer is ok for "high-school, first-love type of gifts" like "affordable" diamond rings, pendants and bracelets; Manhattanites may mutter it's all "mall jewelry", but hey, "it's a chain, for God's sake."

Zany Brainy ●S ▽ 21 | 18 | 14 | M

2407 Broadway (bet. 88th & 89th Sts.), B/C to 86th St., 917-441-2066
112 E. 86th St. (bet. Lexington & Park Aves.), 4/5/6 to 86th St., 212-427-6611
2530 Hylan Blvd. (New Dorp Ln.), Staten Island, 718-980-4282
www.zanybrainy.com

■ "Educational toys can be fun too" when you shop at these wacky-colored chain branches that offer an exclusive line of products including art sets and puppets, a "decent selection" of brands like Hasbro, Crayola and Mattel and "an excellent book department"; boosters boast it's a "good place to find basics" "with prices to match"; still, foes find the "poor layout" a bit of a brain drain.

Zara ●S 19 | 19 | 13 | M

580 Broadway (bet. Prince & Spring Sts.), N/R to Prince St., 212-343-1725
101 Fifth Ave. (bet 17th & 18th Sts.), 4/5/6/L/N/Q/R/W to 14th St./Union Sq., 212-741-0555
750 Lexington Ave. (59th St.), 4/5/6/N/R/W to 59th St./Lexington Ave., 212-754-1120
39 W. 34th St. (bet. 5th & 6th Aves.), B/D/F/N/Q/R/W to 34th St./Herald Sq., 212-868-6551
www.zara.com

■ No need to "pawn the TiVo" to "inject verve" into your wardrobe – this "hot label" from Spain dishes out "shockingly affordable" "runway-inspired" looks for men and women; on the "pulse" of "what's new", the chain's "sexy" stylings give "great bang for the buck", though "sizing can be a bit tricky" since the garments are "European cut."

Z. Baby Company ●S C 24 | 18 | 17 | VE

100 W. 72nd St. (Columbus Ave.), 1/2/3/9/B/C to 72nd St., 212-579-2229
996 Lexington Ave. (72nd St.), 6 to 68th St., 212-472-2229
www.zbabycompany.com

■ "For a special outfit" for the kids or a "unique baby gift", zip over to these "crazy-expensive" but "chic, upscale" bookend stores on the Upper East and Upper West Sides; while devotees declare the selection of "trendy, fashionable" childrenswear is "unbeatable" and "even the boys' clothes are cute", conservatives archly counter "shop here" "if you want your kid to dress like Britney Spears."

Zeller Tuxedo 17 | 13 | 16 | M
459 Lexington Ave. (45th St.), 4/5/6/7/S to 42nd St./Grand Central, 212-286-9786; 800-464-0462; www.zellertuxedo.com
Additional locations throughout the NY area
▐ Fans find this formalwear chain, with an East 40s flagship, the "first and only stop to pick up tuxedos" (either to buy or rent) given a collection that ranges from Joseph Abboud to Hugo Boss to Versace; but dissenters deem the digs "dingy" and warn "don't expect white-glove service at this black-tie event", especially during the month of June.

Zero – | – | – | E
225 Mott St. (bet. Prince & Spring Sts.), 6 to Spring St., 212-925-3849
If you're one of those who likes to display your art on your back instead of your wall, this NoLita "half-boutique, half-gallery" is an "ultra-esoteric" rite of passage; the "original, well-crafted" women's garments are created behind the "frosted-glass wall in the back", so meet the artists before the contents of your wallet become less than zero.

Zitomer Pharmacy ●S 24 | 17 | 17 | VE
969 Madison Ave. (bet. 75th & 76th Sts.), 6 to 77th St., 212-737-4480; 888-219-2888; www.zitomer.com
▐ "You can buy a tube of toothpaste or a $300 party dress for a little girl" at this "if-you-need-it-they-got-it" Upper East Side drugstore and "beauty mecca" "packed" with high-end cosmetics, skincare and toiletries, "every hair accessory you can imagine", an assortment of "odds and ends" like hosiery, plus an entire toy floor called Zittles; of course, such "convenience comes at a price" (somebody's got to pay for that "friendly doorman").

Z Spot ●S C ▽ 28 | 24 | 19 | VE
965 Madison Ave. (bet. 75th & 76th Sts.), 6 to 77th St., 212-472-4960; 888-219-2888; www.zitomer.com
■ "I wish shopping for myself was this much fun" affirm fervent fans of this "incomparable" East 70s pet emporium attached to the venerable Zitomer apothecary; the "fabulous" merchandise includes Burberry leashes, mosaic feed stations and outfits by Pucchi, and even though "mommy" has to "pay a high price" for it all, it's "worth it" for this "ultimate" experience.

vote at zagat.com

Indexes

STORE TYPE
LOCATIONS
MAPS
MERCHANDISE
SPECIAL FEATURES

Indexes list the best of many within each category.

Store Type Index

AUCTION HOUSES

If you are looking for a truly interactive shopping experience, try any of the Manhattan auction houses listed here.

Christie's
Rockefeller Ctr., 20 Rockefeller Plaza, 212-636-2000; www.christies.com

Doyle New York
175 E. 87th St., 212-427-2730; www.doylenewyork.com

Guernsey's
108 E. 73rd St., 212-794-2280; www.guernseys.com

Phillips, de Pury & Luxembourg
3 W. 57th St., 212-940-1200; www.phillips-dpl.com

Sotheby's
1334 York Ave., 212-606-7000; www.sothebys.com 9-5 72 New Yor Av.

Swann Auction Galleries
104 E. 25th St., 212-254-4710; www.swanngalleries.com

Tepper Galleries
110 E. 25th St., 212-677-5300; www.teppergalleries.com

Store Type Index

CHAIN STORES

This list represents stores with 10 or more locations in the NYC area; we've included the flagship address for each chain with its review. See Branches for Top Chains on page 280 for the NYC addresses for the 10 top-rated chains.

- Abercrombie & Fitch
- Aerosoles
- American Eagle
- Ann Taylor
- Ann Taylor Loft
- Athlete's Foot
- Bally
- Banana Republic
- Banana Republic Men's
- Bebe
- Benetton
- Blockbuster Video
- Body Shop, The
- Bolton's
- Brooks Brothers
- Children's Place
- Club Monaco
- Cohen's Fashion Optical
- Eddie Bauer
- Eileen Fisher
- Express
- Express Men (fka Structure)
- Foot Locker
- French Connection
- Gap
- Gothic Cabinet Craft
- H&M
- Hollywood Video
- Home Depot
- Janovic Plaza
- J.Crew
- Jennifer Convertibles
- Joyce Leslie
- Liz Claiborne
- Men's Wearhouse
- Modell's
- Motherhood Maternity
- Nautica
- Nine West
- Old Navy
- Payless Shoe Source
- P.C. Richard & Son
- Perfumania
- Petland Discounts
- Radio Shack
- Rochester Big & Tall
- Salvation Army
- Sisley
- Staples
- Strawberry
- Talbots
- Today's Man
- Urban Outfitters
- V.I.M.
- Victoria's Secret
- Wet Seal
- Zara
- Zeller Tuxedo

vote at zagat.com

Store Type Index

BRANCHES FOR TOP CHAINS

The following are the NYC branch locations for the 10 top-rated chains.

Aerosoles
107-22 Continental Ave., 718-263-4469
1155 Second Ave., 212-751-6372
Chrysler Building, 137 E. 42nd St., 212-370-0094
18 John St., 212-577-9298
206 Front St., 212-608-4980
2649 Broadway, 212-865-4934
2913A Broadway, 212-665-5353
30-29 Steinway St., 718-267-6332
709 Lexington Ave., 212-755-0683
310 Columbus Ave., 212-579-8659
36 W. 34th St., 212-563-0610
63 E. Eighth St., 212-358-7855

Ann Taylor
1055 Madison Ave., 212-988-8930
1166 Sixth Ave., 212-642-4340
1320 Third Ave., 212-861-3392
149 Fifth Ave., 212-253-1445
2 World Financial Ctr., 225 Liberty St., 212-945-1991
2015-17 Broadway, 212-873-7344
2380 Broadway, 212-721-3130
330 Madison Ave., 212-949-0008
575 Fifth Ave., 212-922-3621
645 Madison Ave., 212-832-9114
850 Third Ave., 212-308-5333
South Street Seaport, 4 Fulton St., 212-480-4100
Staten Island Mall, 2655 Richmond Ave., 718-983-7744

Ann Taylor Loft
1155 Third Ave., 212-772-9952
1290 Sixth Ave., 212-399-1078
1492 Third Ave., 212-472-7281
150 E. 42nd St., 212-883-8766
2 Broadway, 212-809-1435
2344 Bell Blvd., 718-423-2755
35 W. 34th St., 212-244-8926
488 Madison Ave., 212-308-1129
5325 Kings Plaza Shopping Ctr., 718-758-0795
560 Broadway, 212-625-0427
70-31 Austin St., 718-275-6873
770 Broadway, 646-602-1582

Banana Republic
111 Eighth Ave., 212-645-1032
1110 Third Ave., 212-288-4279
1136 Madison Ave., 212-570-2465
114 Fifth Ave., 212-366-4691
130 E. 59th St., 212-751-5570
133-35 Montague St., 718-852-8742
1529 Third Ave., 212-360-1296
17-19 W. 34th St., 212-244-3060
205 Bleecker St., 212-473-9570
215 Columbus Ave., 212-873-9048
2360 Broadway, 212-787-2064
528 Broadway, 212-334-3034
Kings Plaza, 5375 Flatbush Ave., 718-338-7834
Staten Island Mall, 2655 Richmond Ave., 718-982-8286
554-556 Broadway, 212-925-0308
626 Fifth Ave., 212-974-2350
71-18 Austin St., 718-268-4714
89 Fifth Ave., 212-366-4630
Grand Central, 107 E. 42nd St., 212-490-3127

Body Shop
125th St., 212-348-4900
1145 Madison Ave., 212-794-3046
135 Fifth Ave., 212-254-0145
142 W. 57th St., 212-582-8494
2159 Broadway, 212-721-2947
479 Fifth Ave., 212-661-1992
509 Madison Ave., 212-829-8603
5100 Kings Plaza, 718-338-7834
714 Lexington Ave., 212-755-7851
Staten Island Mall, 2655 Richmond Ave., 718-983-1677

280   subscribe to zagat.com

Store Type Index

71-03 Austin St., 718-983-7422
747 Broadway, 212-979-2944
Manhattan Mall, 901 Sixth Ave., 212-268-7424
Rockefeller Ctr., 1270 Sixth Ave., 212-397-3007
South Street Seaport, 16 Fulton St., 212-480-9876

Children's Place

1164 Third Ave., 212-717-7187
1319 Kings Hwy., 718-336-3317
22 W. 34th St., 212-904-1190
1420 Metropolitan Ave., 718-824-8430
1937 Turnbull Ave., 718-862-0929
211-17 26th Ave., 718-281-1028
61-32 190th St., 718-454-9220
142 Delancey St., 212-979-5071
1460 Broadway, 212-398-4416
173 E. 86th St., 212-831-5100
2039 Broadway, 917-441-2374
211-17 26th Ave., 718-281-1028
2187 Broadway, 917-441-9807
248 W. 125th St., 212-866-9616
2501-2511 Grand Concourse, 718-563-5591
2655 Richmond Ave., 718-494-7480
31-53 Steinway St., 718-956-1999
36 E. 16th St., 212-529-2201
37-16 82nd St., 718-533-0800
417-419 86th St., 718-491-2711
471-485 Fulton St., 718-243-1150
5344 Kings Plaza, 718-253-9721
57-37 Myrtle Ave., 718-381-4205
600 W. 181st St., 212-923-7244
650 Sixth Ave., 917-305-1348
70-34 Austin St., 718-263-0241
90-15 Queens Blvd., 718-760-8384
Manhattan Mall, 901 Sixth Ave., 212-268-7696

Gap

1 Astor Pl., 212-253-0145
11 Fulton St., 212-374-1051
1131-49 Third Ave., 212-472-4555
1212 Sixth Ave., 212-730-1087
125 Montague St., 718-797-3542
136-39 Roosevelt Ave., 718-961-4707
1511 Third Ave., 212-794-5781
122 Fifth Ave., 917-408-5580
1466 Broadway, 212-382-4500
31-48 Steinway St., 718-721-9895
335 Columbus Ave., 212-873-9270
60 W. 34th St, 212-760-1268
680 Fifth Ave., 212-977-7023
734 Lexington Ave., 212-751-1543
900 Third Ave., 212-754-2290
159-10 Jamaica Ave., 718-291-1228
Cross Bay Plaza, 160-20 Cross Bay Blvd., 718-323-4795
1988 Broadway, 212-721-5304
2101-2109 86th St., 718-372-3170
211-14 26th Ave., 718-631-4941
2373 Broadway, 212-873-1244
250 W. 57th St., 212-315-2250
2530 Hylan Blvd., 718-980-4863
Staten Island Mall, 2655 Richmond Ave., 718-370-0014
271-85 E. Fordham Rd., 718-733-8550
277 W. 23rd St., 646-336-0802
345 Sixth Ave., 212-727-2210
423 86th St., 718-833-6621
5100 Kings Plaza, 718-253-1125
657-59 Third Ave., 212-697-3590
6939 Austin St., 718-544-3588
734 Lexington Ave, 212-751-1543
750 Broadway, 212-674-1877
90-15 Queens Blvd., 718-592-5900

Gap/BabyGap

1037 Lexington Ave., 212-327-2614
1131-49 Third Ave., 212-472-4555
122 Fifth Ave., 917-408-5580
1466 Broadway, 212-382-4500
341 Columbus Ave., 212-875-9196
11 Fulton St., 212-374-1051
Staten Island Mall, 2655 Richmond Ave., 718-370-0645
6939 Austin St., 718-544-3588
90-15 Queens Blvd., 718-760-5909
60 W. 34th St., 212-760-1268
680 Fifth Ave., 212-977-7023
Kings Plaza, 5100 Kings Plaza Shopping Ctr., 718-253-1125

Store Type Index

GapKids
South Street Seaport, 11 Fulton St., 212-374-1051
1212 Sixth Ave., 212-730-1037
122 Fifth Ave., 917-408-5580
1466 Broadway, 212-382-4500
1535 Third Ave., 212-423-0033
159-10 Jamaica Ave., 718-291-1228
250 W. 57th St., 212-315-2250
1988 Broadway, 212-721-5304
2300 Broadway, 212-873-2044
271 E. Fordham Rd., 718-733-8550
354 Sixth Ave., 212-777-2420
545 Madison Ave., 212-980-2570
657 Third Ave., 212-697-3590
2655 Richmond Ave., 718-370-0645
60 W. 34th St., 212-760-1268
680 Fifth Ave., 212-977-7023
Queens Ct., 90-15 Queens Blvd., 718-760-5909

Home Depot
124-04 31st Ave., 718-661-4608
131-35 Avery Ave., 718-358-9600
132-20 Merrick Blvd., 718-977-2081
1806 E. Gunhill Rd., 718-862-9800
2501 Forest Ave., 718-273-5069
2970 Cropsey Ave., 718-333-9850
50-10 Northern Blvd., 718-278-9031
550 Hamilton Ave., 718-832-8553
112-20 Rockaway Blvd., 718-641-5500
545 Targee St., 718-818-9334
75-09 Woodhaven Blvd., 718-830-3323
King's Plaza, King's Plaza, 5700 Ave. U, 718-692-7296

Nine West
115 Fifth Ave., 212-777-1752
134 Montague St., 718-797-4451
1419 Kings Hwy., 718-376-0286
179 Broadway, 212-346-0903
184 E. 86th St., 212-987-9004
2 Broadway, 212-968-1521
Loehman's Plaza, 2027 Emmons Ave., 718-616-1614
2125 Ralph Ave., 718-444-7206
2305 Broadway, 212-799-7610
Staten Island Mall, 2655 Richmond Ave., 718-698-1813
341 Madison Ave., 212-370-9107
420 86th St., 718-748-4250
425 Lexington Ave., 212-949-0037
Kings Plaza, 5145 Kings Plaza, 718-951-1316
577 Broadway, 212-941-1597
675 Fifth Ave., 212-319-6893
750 Lexington Ave., 212-486-8094
757-A Third Ave., 212-371-4597
A & S Plaza, 901 Sixth Ave., 212-564-0063
Queens Center, 90-15 Queens Blvd., 718-760-2228
Rockefeller Ctr., 1230 Sixth Ave., 212-397-0710

Victoria's Secret
10 W. 57th St., 212-758-5592
115 Fifth Ave., 212-477-4118
1240 Third Ave., 212-717-7035
1328 Broadway, 212-356-8383
165 E. 86th St., 646-672-9183
South Street Seaport, 19 Fulton St., 212-962-8133
1981 Broadway, 646-505-2280
Bay Terrace Shopping Center, 213-25 26th Ave., 718-281-2481
2333 Broadway, 212-595-7861
Staten Island Mall, 2655 Richmond Ave., 718-982-9311
3135 Steinway St., 718-932-3924
34 E. 57th St., 212-758-5592
Kings Plaza Mall, 5100 Flatbush Ave., 1st fl., 718-758-1502
565 Broadway, 212-274-9519
70-36 Austin St., 718-261-9512
901 Sixth Ave., 646-473-0950
Queens Center Mall, 90-15 Queens Blvd., 718-592-1244

Store Type Index

Department/Large Specialty Stores
ABC Carpet & Home
Barneys Co-op
Barneys New York
Bed, Bath & Beyond
Bergdorf Goodman
Bergdorf Men's
Bloomingdale's
Gracious Home
Henri Bendel
Kmart
Lord & Taylor
Macy's
Pearl River Mart
Saks Fifth Avenue
Takashimaya
Target

Discounters/Outlets
Aaron's
Bolton's
Burlington Coat Factory
Century 21
Costco Wholesale
Daffy's
Enzo Angiolini
Filene's Basement
Find Outlet
Forman's
Loehmann's
Luxury Brand Outlet
Marshall's
National Wholesale Liquidators
Nice Price
Prato Fine Men's Wear
S&W
Syms
Tahari, Ltd.
T.J. Maxx

Museum Shops
American Craft Museum Shop
American Folk Art Museum
American Museum/Nat. History
AsiaStore/Asia Society
Brooklyn Museum Shop
Cloisters, The
Cooper-Hewitt Shop
El Museo Del Barrio
Frick Collection
Guggenheim Museum Stores
International Ctr. Photography
Intrepid Sea-Air-Space
Jewish Museum
Met. Museum of Art Shop
MoMA Design Store
Morgan Library Shop
Museum/City of New York
Neue Galerie
New Museum Store
New York Public Library Shop
New York Transit Museum
Studio Museum/Harlem
Whitney Museum Store

Theme Stores
Disney
ESPN Zone
Hard Rock Cafe
Harley Davidson of NY
Mets Clubhouse Shop
MTV Store
NBA Store
NBC Experience
New York Firefighter's Friend
New York 911
One Shubert Alley
Pop Shop
Sanrio (aka Hello Kitty Store)
Theatre Circle
World, The
Yankee Clubhouse Shop

Location Index

LOCATIONS

Where necessary, we've noted merchandise type.

MANHATTAN

Chelsea
(30th to 24th Sts., west of 5th Ave., and 24th to 14th Sts., west of 6th Ave.)
AF Supply Corp., *Bath Fixtures*
Angel Street Thrift Shop
Barking Zoo, *Pet*
Barneys Co-op, *Dept. Store*
Bed, Bath & Beyond, *Home*
Benetton, *Fashion Chain*
Best Buy, *Electronics*
Blades Board and Skate
Bowery Kitchen Supplies
Burlington Coat Factory, *Discount*
buybuy Baby, *Children's*
Camouflage, *Men's Clothing*
Capitol Fishing Tackle Co.
Carlyle Convertibles, *Home*
Chelsea Second Hand Guitars
Chelsea Wholesale Flower Market, *Garden*
City Quilter, *Fabrics/Notions*
Comme des Garçons, *Designer*
DeMask, *Sex Shops*
Desiron, *Home*
Details, *Home*
Door Store, *Home*
Family Jewels, *Vintage*
Find Outlet, *Discount*
Fisch for the Hip, *Consignment*
Gerry's Menswear
Giraudon, *Shoes*
Here Comes the Bridesmaid
Hold Everything, *Home*
Housing Works Thrift Shop
Innovation Luggage
In the Market, *Garden*
Janovic Plaza, *Hardware*
Jazz Record Center
Jensen-Lewis, *Home*
Jim Smiley, *Vintage*
La Cafetière, *Home*
Lightforms
Loehmann's, *Discount*
Men's Wearhouse, *Fashion Chain*
Metro Bicycles
Midnight Records
Myoptics, *Eyewear*
New York Golf Center
Noose, The, *Sex Shops*
Olde Good Things, *Home*
Parke & Ronen, *Men's & Women's Clothing*
Portico, *Home*
Purple Passion/DV8, *Sex Shops*
Reminiscence, *Vintage*
Sacco, *Shoes*
S&W, *Discount*
Scuba Network
Sports Authority
Starting Line, *Men's Clothing*
Tah Poozie, *Gifts/Novelties*
Tekserve, *Computers*
Ten Thousand Things, *Jewelry*
Thomasville, *Home*
T.J. Maxx, *Discount*
Today's Man, *Fashion Chain*
Urban Outfitters, *Fashion Chain*
V.I.M., *Jeans*
Williams-Sonoma, *Cookware*

Chinatown
(South of Hester St. & north of Pearl St., bet. Bowery & B'way)
Canal Hi-Fi Inc, *Electronics*
Kam Man, *Home*
Pearl Paint, *Art Supplies*
Pearl River Mart, *Dept. Store*

East Village
(14th to Houston Sts., east of B'way)
Academy Records & CDs
a.cheng, *Women's Clothing*

284 subscribe to zagat.com

Location Index

Alan Moss, *Home*
Alpana Bawa, *Men's & Women's Clothing*
Alphabets, *Gifts/Novelties*
Amarcord Vintage Fashion
Amy Downs Hats
Angela's Vintage Boutique
Arche, *Shoes*
Bag House, *Luggage*
Barbara Feinman Millinery
Blue, *Women's Clothing*
Body Shop
Crunch, *Activewear*
Demeter, *Cosmetics/Toiletries*
Dö Kham, *Accessories*
Downtown Yarns, *Knitting*
Eight Ball Records
Eileen Fisher, *Fashion Chain*
Enelra, *Hosiery/Lingerie*
Eugenia Kim, *Accessories*
Fab 208 NYC, *Women's Clothing*
Filth Mart, *Thrift*
Finyl Vinyl, *Record*
Footlight Records
Gown Company, *Bridal*
Gringer & Sons, *Appliances*
Jammyland, *CD/Record*
Jam Paper & Envelope
Joe's CDs
John Derian, *Home*
Kiehl's, *Cosmetics/Toiletries*
Kim's Mediapolis, *CD/DVD/Video*
Love Saves the Day, *Vintage*
Magry Knits
Martin, *Women's Clothing*
Meg, *Women's Clothing*
Metro Bicycles
Myoptics, *Eyewear*
New York Central Art Supply
1950, *Home*
99X, *Clothing*
Norman's Sound & Vision, *CD/DVD/Record/Video*
Religious Sex, *Hosiery/Lingerie*
Rue St. Denis, *Vintage*
Schneider's, *Children's*
Selia Yang, *Designer*
Selima Optique, *Eyewear*
St. Marks Sounds, *CD/Record*
Surprise, Surprise, *Home*
TKNY, *Gadgets*
Tokio 7, *Consignment*
Tokyo Joe, *Consignment*
Toy Tokyo, *Toys*
Trash & Vaudeville, *Men's & Women's Clothing*
Tribal Soundz, *Musical Instruments*
Upland Trading, *Men's Clothing*
Urban Outfitters, *Fashion Chain*
Utrecht, *Art Supplies*

East 40s

Adriana's Caravan, *Gifts/Novelties*
Allen Edmonds, *Shoes*
Ann Taylor Loft, *Fashion Chain*
Arnold Tobacco Shop
Art of Shaving, *Cosmetics/Toiletries*
Barami Studio, *Women's Clothing*
Barclay-Rex, *Cigar/Smoke*
Benetton, *Fashion Chain*
Biscuits & Baths Doggy Village
Bloom, *Jewelry*
Botticelli, *Shoes*
Brooks Brothers, *Fashion Chain*
Caswell-Massey, *Cosmetics/Toiletries*
CCS Counter Spy Shop, *Gadgets*
Cellini, *Jewelry/Watches*
Charles Tyrwhitt, *Men's & Women's Clothing*
Children's General Store, *Toys*
Coach, *Handbags*
Crabtree & Evelyn, *Cosmetics/Toiletries*
Crouch & Fitzgerald, *Luggage*
Daffy's, *Discount*
Eddie Bauer, *Fashion Chain*
Enzo Angiolini, *Shoes*
Equinox Energy Wear
For Eyes, *Eyewear*
Forman's, *Discount*
Fossil, *Watches*
Grand Central Racquet

vote at zagat.com

Location Index

HMV, *CD/DVD/Video*
Innovation Luggage
International Cutlery, *Cookware*
J.Crew, *Fashion Chain*
Johnston & Murphy, *Shoes*
Joon, *Stationery*
Jos A. Bank, *Men's Clothing*
Joseph Edwards, *Watches*
J. Press, *Men's Clothing*
JR Cigar
Kavanagh's, *Consignment*
Kenneth Cole, *Designer*
Legs Beautiful Hosiery
Links of London, *Jewelry*
L'Occitane, *Cosmetics/ Toiletries*
Men's Wearhouse, *Fashion Chain*
Michael C. Fina, *Home*
Michael Eigen, *Jewelry*
Nat Sherman, *Cigar/Smoke*
New York Look, *Women's Clothing*
New York Public Library Shop
New York Transit Museum
Origins, *Cosmetics/Toiletries*
Orvis Company, *Sporting Goods*
OshKosh B'Gosh, *Children's*
Paul Stuart, *Men's Clothing*
Pink Slip, *Hosiery/Lingerie*
Radio Shack, *Electronics*
Richard Metz Golf
Ricky's, *Cosmetics/Toiletries*
Robert Marc, *Eyewear*
Saks Fifth Avenue, *Dept. Store*
Sam Goody, *CD/DVD/Video*
Shirt Store, *Men's Clothing*
Speedo Authentic Fitness
Strawberry, *Fashion Chain*
Super Runners Shop
Tahari, Ltd., *Designer*
Today's Man, *Fashion Chain*
Tumi, *Luggage*
Wiz, The, *Electronics*
World of Golf
Zeller Tuxedo

East 50s
Agatha, *Jewelry*
A La Vieille Russie, *Jewelry*
Alkit Pro Camera
Allen Edmonds, *Shoes*
Amsale, *Bridal*
Anne Fontaine, *Designer*
Ann Sacks Tile & Stone
Artistic Tile
Asprey, *Jewelry/Watches*
A. Testoni, *Shoes*
Avon Salon and Spa, *Cosmetics/Toiletries*
A/X Armani Exchange, *Designer*
Baccarat, *Home*
Bally, *Fashion Chain*
Banana Republic, *Fashion Chain*
B&B Italia, *Home*
Barami Studio, *Women's Clothing*
Barclay-Rex, *Cigar/Smoke*
Bebe, *Fashion Chain*
Belgian Shoes, *Shoes*
Bergdorf Goodman, *Dept. Store*
Bergdorf Men's, *Dept. Store*
Bernardaud, *Home*
bliss, *Cosmetics/Toiletries*
Bloomingdale's, *Dept. Store*
Bottega Veneta, *Handbags*
Botticelli, *Shoes*
Brass Center, *Bath Fixtures*
Bridal Atelier by Mark Ingram
Bridge Kitchenware
Brioni, *Men's Clothing*
British American House, *Men's Clothing*
Brooks Brothers, *Fashion Chain*
Bruno Magli, *Shoes*
Buccellati, *Jewelry/Watches*
Bulgari, *Jewelry/Watches*
Bumble and bumble, *Cosmetics/Toiletries*
Burberry, *Designer*
Camera Land
Cartier, *Jewelry/Watches*
Cassina USA, *Home*
Cellini, *Jewelry/Watches*
Chanel, *Designer*
Christian Dior, *Designer*
Christian Dior Joaillerie, *Jewelry/Watches*

Location Index

City Sports
Claire's Accessories, *Jewelry*
Club Monaco, *Fashion Chain*
Coach, *Handbags*
Cole Haan, *Shoes*
Crabtree & Evelyn, *Cosmetics/Toiletries*
Crate & Barrel, *Home*
Daffy's, *Discount*
Dana Buchman, *Designer*
Davidoff of Geneva, *Cigar/Smoke*
David Saity Jewelry
David Webb, *Jewelry/Watches*
Davis & Warshow, Inc., *Bathroom Fixtures*
Dempsey & Carroll, *Stationery*
Disney, *Theme*
Door Store, *Home*
Dunhill, *Cigar/Smoke*
Eileen Fisher, *Fashion Chain*
Einstein-Moomjy, *Home*
Elizabeth Arden, *Cosmetics/Toiletries*
Emporio Armani, *Designer*
Enzo Angiolini, *Shoes*
Equinox Energy Wear
Eres, *Hosiery/Lingerie*
Ermenegildo Zegna, *Designer*
Erwin Pearl, *Jewelry*
Escada, *Designer*
Façonnable, *Men's & Women's Clothing*
FAO Schwarz, *Toys*
Felissimo, *Home*
Fendi, *Designer*
Ferragamo, Salvatore, *Designer*
Florsheim Shoe Shops
Fogal, *Hosiery/Lingerie*
Fortunoff, *Home*
Fratelli Rossetti, *Shoes*
Frédéric Fekkai, *Cosmetics/Toiletries*
Furry Paws
Fye, *CD/DVD/Video*
Gant, *Men's Clothing*
Georgette Klinger, *Cosmetics/Toiletries*
Ghurka, *Luggage*
Gucci, *Designer*
Gym Source
Hammacher Schlemmer & Co., *Gadgets*
H&M, *Fashion Chain*
Harley Davidson of NY, *Theme*
Harry Winston, *Jewelry*
Helene Arpels, *Shoes*
Helen Woodhull, *Jewelry*
Henri Bendel, *Dept. Store*
H. Herzfeld, *Men's Clothing*
Hickey Freeman, *Men's Clothing*
H.L. Purdy, *Eyewear*
Holland & Holland, *Men's & Women's Clothing*
H. Stern, *Jewelry/Watches*
Hugo Boss, *Designer*
Ideal Tile
Innovation Luggage
Innovative Audio, *Electronics*
James Robinson, *Home*
James II Galleries Ltd., *Jewelry*
Janet Sartin, *Cosmetics/Toiletries*
Jil Sander, *Designer*
Jimmy Choo, *Shoes*
Jobson's Luggage
Johnston & Murphy, *Shoes*
Joon, *Stationery*
Ken Hansen Photographic
Kentshire Galleries, *Jewelry*
Kreiss Collection, *Home*
Lacoste, *Designer*
Legs Beautiful Hosiery
Lighting Center
Linda Dresner, *Women's Clothing*
Links of London, *Jewelry*
Liz Claiborne, *Fashion Chain*
L'Occitane, *Cosmetics/Toiletries*
Louis Vuitton, *Designer*
Lowell/Edwards, *Stereos/HiFi*
Maraolo, *Shoes*
Mario Badescu Skin Care, *Cosmetics/Toiletries*
Mason's Tennis Mart
Maurice Villency, *Home*
Mets Clubhouse Shop, *Theme*

Location Index

Michel Perry, *Shoes*
Mikimoto, *Jewelry*
Montblanc, *Stationery*
NBA Store, *Activewear*
New Balance, *Activewear*
Niketown, *Activewear*
Nine West, *Shoes*
Original Levi's Store, *Jeans*
Origins, *Cosmetics/Toiletries*
Otto Tootsi Plohound, *Shoes*
Oxxford Clothes, *Men's Clothing*
Palazzetti, *Home*
Piaget, *Jewelry/Watches*
Pierre Deux, *Home*
Pottery Barn, *Home*
Prada, *Designer*
RCS Computer Experience
Reaction by Kenneth Cole, *Designer*
Rebecca Moss Ltd., *Stationery*
Repêchage: Spa de Beauté, *Cosmetics/Toiletries*
Robert Marc, *Eyewear*
Sam Flax, *Art Supplies*
Scuba Network
Scully & Scully, *Home*
Seaman Schepps, *Jewelry*
Searle, *Women's Clothing*
Sherle Wagner, *Bathroom Fixtures & Tiles*
Simon Pearce Glass, *Home*
Sony Style, *Electronics*
Sports Authority
Stitches East, *Knitting/Needlepoint*
St. John, *Designer*
Stuart Weitzman, *Shoes*
Suarez, *Handbags*
Swarovski, *Jewelry*
Swatch, *Watches*
Syms, *Discount*
Takashimaya, *Dept. Store*
Talbots, *Fashion Chain*
T. Anthony, *Luggage*
Tartine et Chocolat, *Children's*
Terence Conran Shop, *Home*
Thomas Pink, *Men's Clothing*
Tiffany & Co., *Jewelry/Watches*
Tourneau, *Jewelry/Watches*
Tower Records/Video
Tumi, *Luggage*
Turnbull & Asser, *Men's Clothing*
Urban Archaeology, *Bathroom Fixtures & Tiles*
Van Cleef & Arpels, *Jewelry*
Verdura, *Jewelry*
Versace, *Designer*
Walter Steiger, *Shoes*
Waterworks, *Bathroom Fixtures*
Wempe, *Watches*
Williams-Sonoma, *Cookware*
Wiz, The, *Electronics*
Wolford, *Hosiery/Lingerie*
Yankee Clubhouse Shop, *Theme*
Zara, *Fashion Chain*

East 60s

Aaron Basha, *Jewelry*
American Kennels
Anne Fontaine, *Designer*
Ann Taylor, *Fashion Chain*
Anya Hindmarch, *Handbags*
Arche, *Shoes*
Art of Shaving, *Cosmetics/Toiletries*
Aveda, *Cosmetics/Toiletries*
Barneys New York, *Dept. Store*
BCBG by Max Azria, *Designer*
Bear's Place, A, *Toys*
Bebe, *Fashion Chain*
Bed, Bath & Beyond, *Home*
Bellini, *Children's*
Betsey Johnson, *Designer*
Billy Martin's Western Wear, *Men's & Women's Clothing*
Bombay Company, *Home*
Bonpoint, *Children's*
Boyd's Madison Avenue, *Drugstores*
Bulgari, *Jewelry/Watches*
Calvin Klein, *Designer*
Capezio, *Activewear*
Carlyle Convertibles, *Home*
Caron Boutique, *Cosmetics/Toiletries*
Celine, *Designer*
Cerruti, *Designer*

Location Index

Cesare Paciotti, *Shoes*
Champagne Video
Chanel Fine Jewelry
Chopard, *Jewelry/Watches*
Christofle, *Home*
Chrome Hearts, *Jewelry*
Chuckies, *Shoes*
Club Monaco, *Fashion Chain*
Cohen's Fashion Optical
Cole Haan, *Shoes*
Creed, *Cosmetics/Toiletries*
Crush, *Women's Clothing*
Daum, *Home*
Davide Cenci, *Men's Clothing*
David Yurman, *Jewelry*
Diesel Superstore, *Jeans*
DKNY, *Designer*
Dolce & Gabbana, *Designer*
Domain, *Home*
Donna Karan, *Designer*
Dooney & Bourke, *Luggage*
Dylan's Candy Bar, *Gifts/Novelties*
E. Braun & Co., *Home*
Eddie Bauer, *Fashion Chain*
Elgot, *Cabinetry*
Emanuel Ungaro, *Designer*
Emilio Pucci, *Designer*
Equinox Energy Wear
Erica Wilson Needle Works
Erwin Pearl, *Jewelry*
Ethan Allen, *Home*
Etro, *Designer*
FACE Stockholm, *Cosmetics/Toiletries*
Floris of London, *Cosmetics/Toiletries*
Fred Leighton, *Watches*
Frette, *Home*
Furla, *Handbags*
Gallery of Wearable Art, *Bridal*
Gallery Orrefors, *Home*
Georg Jensen, *Home*
Giorgio Armani, *Designer*
Givenchy, *Designer*
Graff, *Jewelry*
Gucci, *Designer*
Gymboree, *Children's*
Hermès, *Designer*

Hold Everything, *Home*
H20 Plus, *Cosmetics/Toiletries*
Il Makiage, *Cosmetics/Toiletries*
Jacadi, *Children's*
Jaeger, *Designer*
Janovic Plaza, *Hardware*
Jean Paul Gaultier, *Designer*
J. Mendel, *Furs*
J.M. Weston, *Shoes*
John Lobb, *Shoes*
Joon, *Stationery*
Joseph, *Designer*
Judith Ripka, *Jewelry/Watches*
Kraft, *Bathroom Fixtures*
Krizia, *Designer*
La Brea, *Gifts/Novelties*
Lalaounis, *Jewelry*
Lalique, *Home*
Lana Marks, *Handbags*
La Perla, *Hosiery/Lingerie*
La Petite Etoile, *Children's*
Le Chien Pet Salon
Legs Beautiful Hosiery
Léron, *Home*
Les Copains, *Women's Clothing*
Ligne Roset, *Home*
Lingerie on Lex
Liz O'Brien, *Home*
L'Occitane, *Cosmetics/Toiletries*
Longchamp, *Handbags*
Loro Piana, *Designer*
Luca Luca, *Women's Clothing*
Lucky Brand Dungarees
MacKenzie-Childs, *Home*
Malo, *Designer*
Manfredi, *Watches*
Max Mara, *Designer*
Michael Dawkins, *Jewelry*
Mimi Maternity
Miu Miu, *Designer*
Morgane Le Fay, *Designer*
Morgenthal Fredericks, *Eyewear*
Moschino, *Designer*
Mrs. John L. Strong, *Stationery*
Munder-Skiles, *Garden*
New York Doll Hospital, *Toys*
Nicole Farhi, *Designer*
Nicole Miller, *Designer*

vote at zagat.com

Location Index

Oliver Peoples, *Eyewear*
Oriental Lamp Shade Co.
Paron Fabrics
Paul & Shark, *Men's Clothing*
Pilar Rossi, *Bridal*
Porthault, *Home*
Pratesi, *Home*
Ricky's, *Cosmetics/Toiletries*
Robert Clergerie, *Shoes*
Robert Marc, *Eyewear*
Roberto Cavalli, *Designer*
Robert Talbott, *Men's Clothing*
Searle, *Women's Clothing*
Sephora, *Cosmetics/Toiletries*
Sergio Rossi, *Shoes*
Shanghai Tang, *Men's & Women's Clothing*
Stephane Kélian, *Shoes*
Steuben, *Home*
Suzanne Couture Millinery, *Bridal*
Tatiana, *Consignment*
Tender Buttons, *Fabrics/Notions*
Thomas Moser Cabinet, *Home*
Timberland, *Men's Clothing*
Tod's, *Shoes*
TSE Cashmere, *Designer*
Unisa, *Shoes*
Valentino, *Designer*
Varda, *Shoes*
Ventilo, *Designer*
Versace, *Designer*
Vertigo, *Women's Clothing*
Via Spiga, *Shoes*
Warren Edwards, *Shoes*
William Wayne, *Home*
Zales Jewelers

East 70s

ABH Design, *Home*
Adrien Linford, *Home*
Alain Mikli, *Eyewear*
Anik, *Women's Clothing*
Antiquarium, *Jewelry*
A Pea in the Pod, *Maternity*
Arche, *Shoes*
A Second Chance, *Consignment*
AsiaStore/Asia Society
Ballantyne Cashmere, *Men's & Women's Clothing*
Bang & Olufsen, *Electronics*
Barami Studio, *Women's Clothing*
Bardith, *Home*
Barkley, *Pet*
Bebe, *Fashion Chain*
Ben's for Kids
Betsey Bunky Nini, *Designer*
Big Drop, *Women's Clothing*
Bra Smyth, *Hosiery/Lingerie*
Calling All Pets
Calypso, *Women's Clothing*
Carlyle Convertibles, *Home*
Carolina Herrera, *Designer*
Chloé, *Designer*
Christian Louboutin, *Shoes*
Clea Colet, *Bridal*
Clyde's, *Drugstores*
Creed, *Cosmetics/Toiletries*
Edith Weber & Assoc., *Jewelry*
Eileen Fisher, *Fashion Chain*
Elizabeth Locke, *Jewelry*
Eric, *Shoes*
Forréal, *Women's Clothing*
French Sole, *Shoes*
Frick Collection, *Museum Shops*
Gianfranco Ferré, *Designer*
Gracious Home, *Home*
Gymboree, *Children's*
H.L. Purdy, *Eyewear*
Homer, *Home*
Housing Works Thrift Shop
Il Papiro, *Stationery*
Ina, *Consignment*
Intermix, *Jewelry*
Issey Miyake, *Designer*
Jacadi, *Children's*
Jamie Ostrow, *Stationery*
Jay Kos, *Men's Clothing*
Jennifer Tyler, *Designer*
J. Mavec & Company, *Jewelry*
J. McLaughlin, *Men's & Women's Clothing*
Judith Leiber, *Jewelry/Watches*
Kate's Paperie, *Stationery*

Location Index

Knits Incredible
Knitting 321
La Boutique Resale, *Consignment/Thrift/Vintage*
Lady Foot Locker
Le Décor Français, *Home*
Leonard Poll, *Eyewear*
Lexington Gardens
Liliblue, *Jewelry*
Little Eric, *Children's*
Liz Lange Maternity
L'Occitane, *Cosmetics/Toiletries*
Luca Luca, *Women's Clothing*
Luxury Brand Outlet, *Discount*
Maraolo, *Shoes*
Mariko, *Jewelry*
Marimekko, *Home*
Mary Arnold Toys
Mecox Gardens, *Home*
Michael Ashton, *Jewelry*
Michael Kors, *Designer*
Michael's, *Consignment*
Mish, *Jewelry*
Missoni, *Designer*
Morgenthal Frederics, *Eyewear*
Oilily, *Children's*
Penhaligon's, *Cosmetics/Toiletries*
Peters Necessities for Pets
Pookie & Sebastian, *Women's Clothing*
Prada, *Designer*
Ralph Lauren, *Designer*
Reinstein Ross, *Jewelry*
Rita's Needlepoint
Robert Marc, *Eyewear*
Schweitzer Linen, *Home*
Scoop, *Women's Clothing*
Scoop Men's, *Men's Clothing*
Searle, *Women's Clothing*
Selima Optique, *Eyewear*
Sharper Image, *Gadgets*
Sonia Rykiel, *Designer*
Stephen Russell, *Jewelry*
Steven Stolman, *Women's Clothing*
String Yarns, *Knitting*
Stubbs & Wootton, *Shoes*
Super Runners Shop
Talbots, *Fashion Chain*
Talbots Kids and Babies
Treillage, *Garden*
Variazioni, *Women's Clothing*
Vera Wang Bridal Salon, *Bridal*
Whitney Museum Store
Wolford, *Hosiery/Lingerie*
Yumi Katsura, *Bridal*
Yves St. Laurent Rive Gauche, *Designer*
Z. Baby Company, *Children's*
Zitomer Pharmacy, *Drugstores*
Z Spot, *Pet*

East 80s

Agnès B., *Designer*
Anik, *Women's Clothing*
Art and Tapisserie, *Toys*
Artbag, *Handbags*
Au Chat Botte, *Children's*
Bebe Thompson, *Children's*
Betsey Johnson, *Designer*
Biscuits & Baths Doggy Village
Bis Designer Resale, *Consignment*
Blacker & Kooby, *Stationery*
Blades Board and Skate
California Closets, *Home*
Calling All Pets
Cécile et Jeanne, *Jewelry*
Champagne Video
Circuit City, *Electronics*
Cose Bella, *Bridal*
Cosmophonic Sound, *Electronics*
Council Thrift Shop
Dempsey & Carroll, *Stationery*
Designer Resale, *Consignment*
E.A.T. Gifts
Encore, *Consignment*
Equinox Energy Wear
Eric, *Shoes*
Forréal, *Women's Clothing*
Fresh, *Cosmetics/Toiletries*
Gateway Country, *Electronics*
Great Feet, *Children's*
Greenstones, *Children's*
Guggenheim Museum Stores

Location Index

Gymboree, *Children's*
H.L. Purdy, *Eyewear*
Infinity, *Children's*
Jaded, *Jewelry*
Jane Wilson-Marquis, *Bridal*
Janovic Plaza, *Hardware*
Karen's for People and Pets, *Pet*
Kimara Ahnert, *Cosmetics/ Toiletries*
La Brea, *Gifts/Novelties*
Laytner's Linen & Home
LeSportsac, *Handbags*
Lester's, *Children's*
Little Eric, *Children's*
Livi's Lingerie
Lyric Hi-Fi, *Electronics*
Magic Windows, *Children's*
Marsha D.D., *Children's*
Memorial Sloan-Kettering Shop, *Thrift*
Metro Bicycles
Met. Museum of Art Shop
Michael Eigen, *Jewelry*
Mimi Maternity
Montmartre, *Women's Clothing*
Motherhood Maternity
Nancy & Co., *Women's Clothing*
Neue Galerie, *Museum Shops*
Olive and Bette's, *Women's Clothing*
Original Leather Store, *Men's & Women's Clothing*
Out of the Closet Thrift Shop
Petco
Peter Elliot, *Men's Clothing*
Petit Bateau, *Children's*
Pier 1 Imports, *Home*
Planet Kids
Schweitzer Linen, *Home*
Searle, *Women's Clothing*
Spence-Chapin Thrift Shops
Star Magic, *Gifts & Novelties*
Steve Madden, *Shoes*
Straight from the Crate, *Home*
Super Runners Shop
Tartine et Chocolat, *Children's*
Venture Stationers
Vilebrequin, *Men's Clothing*
Wedding Library

Williams-Sonoma, *Cookware*
Wiz, The, *Electronics*
Wool Gathering, *Knitting/ Needlepoint*
Workbench, *Home*
Zany Brainy, *Toys*

East 90s & Up

Adrien Linford, *Home*
Annie & Company Needlepoint
Bonpoint, *Children's*
Capezio, *Activewear*
Catimini, *Children's*
Cooper-Hewitt Shop, *Museum Shops*
Crabtree & Evelyn, *Cosmetics/ Toiletries*
Dimitri Nurseries, *Garden*
East Side Kids
El Museo Del Barrio, *Museum Shops*
Furry Paws
Jacadi, *Children's*
Jewish Museum
J. McLaughlin, *Men's & Women's Clothing*
Kid's Supply Co.
Koos & Co., *Designer*
Lion & the Lamb, *Knitting/ Needlepoint*
L'Occitane, *Cosmetics/ Toiletries*
Museum/City of New York
New York Replacement, *Bath Fixtures*
Paterson Silks, *Fabrics/Notions*
Penny Whistle, *Toys*
Roberta's Lingerie
Robert Marc, *Eyewear*
S Feldman Housewares
Soccer Sport Supply
Spence-Chapin Thrift Shops
Veronique, *Maternity*
Wicker Garden, *Children's*

Financial District

(South of Chambers St.)
Barclay-Rex, *Cigar/Smoke*
Century 21, *Discount*
Equinox Energy Wear

Location Index

Forman's, *Discount*
Fountain Pen Hospital, *Stationery*
Fourteen Wall Street Jewelers
Fragments, *Jewelry*
J&R Computer World
J&R Music World
Joon, *Stationery*
Legs Beautiful Hosiery
Men's Wearhouse, *Fashion Chain*
Mimi Maternity
Montmartre, *Women's Clothing*
Prato Fine Men's Wear
Record Explosion
Sam Goody, *CD/DVD/Video*
Syms, *Discount*
Tents and Trails, *Sporting Goods*
William Barthman, *Jewelry*
World of Golf

Flatiron District
(Bounded by 24th & 14th Sts., bet. 6th Ave. & Park Ave. S., excluding Union Sq.)

ABC Carpet & Home
ABC Carpet (Carpets/Rugs)
Abracadabra, *Toys*
Academy Records & CDs
Adorama Camera
A.I. Friedman, *Art Supplies*
Alkit Pro Camera
Anthropologie, *Fashion Chain*
Apartment 48, *Home*
Artistic Tile
Aveda, *Cosmetics/Toiletries*
Banana Republic Men's, *Fashion Chain*
Bang & Olufsen, *Electronics*
Bath & Body Works
Beads of Paradise, *Jewelry*
Bebe, *Fashion Chain*
Beckenstein Fabrics/Int.
Birnbaum & Bullock, *Bridal*
Bombay Company, *Home*
Carapan Urban Spa & Store, *Cosmetics/Toiletries*
Charles P. Rogers Bed, *Home*
Classic Sofa, *Home*
Club Monaco, *Fashion Chain*
Coach, *Handbags*
Country Home & Comfort, *Home*
Daffy's, *Discount*
Dave's Army Navy, *Discount*
David Z., *Shoes*
Domain, *Home*
Drexel Heritage, *Home*
Eileen Fisher, *Fashion Chain*
Emporio Armani, *Designer*
Equinox Energy Wear
Filene's Basement, *Discount*
Fishs Eddy, *Home*
Fossil, *Watches*
Hastings Bath & Tile
Illuminations, *Home*
Intermix, *Jewelry*
Jam Paper & Envelope
J.Crew, *Fashion Chain*
Jennifer Convertibles, *Home*
Jo Malone, *Cosmetics/Toiletries*
Just Bulbs
Kenneth Cole, *Designer*
Kidding Around, *Toys*
Krups Kitchens & Bath
Ligne Roset, *Home*
Lucky Brand Dungarees
M.A.C. Cosmetics
Medici, *Shoes*
Nemo Tile Company
Noir et Blanc...Bis, *Women's Clothing*
Origins, *Cosmetics/Toiletries*
Otto Tootsi Plohound, *Shoes*
Paper Access, *Stationery*
Paul Smith, *Designer*
Petco
Pier 1 Imports, *Home*
Portico, *Home*
Princeton Ski Shop
Print Icon, *Stationery*
Restoration Hardware, *Home*
Sacco, *Shoes*
Safavieh Carpets, *Home*
Sam Flax, *Art Supplies*
School Products Co., *Knitting/Needlepoint*
Searle, *Women's Clothing*

Location Index

Sephora, *Cosmetics/Toiletries*
17 at 17 Thrift Shop
Skechers, *Shoes*
Sol Moscot, *Eyewear*
Space Kiddets, *Children's*
Stickley, Audi & Co., *Home*
Variazioni, *Women's Clothing*
Villeroy & Boch, *Home*
Zales Jewelers
Zara, *Fashion Chain*

Garment District
(40th to 30th Sts., west of 5th Ave.)
Aldo, *Shoes*
Athlete's Foot
BabyGap, *Children's*
B&H Photo-Video Pro Audio
B&J Fabrics
Barami Studio, *Women's Clothing*
Beckenstein, *Fabrics*
Ben Kahn Furs
Champs, *Sporting Goods*
Children's Place, The
Claire's Accessories, *Jewelry*
CompUSA
Daffy's, *Discount*
Downstairs Records
Dr. Jays, *Activewear*
Enzo Angiolini, *Shoes*
Express Men, *Fashion Chain*
Fenaroli by Regalia, *Bridal*
Florsheim Shoe Shops
Foot Locker, *Sneakers*
Gap, *Fashion Chain*
GapKids, *Children's*
Gerry Cosby & Co., *Sporting Goods*
Goldin-Feldman, *Furs*
H&M, *Fashion Chain*
Hyman Hendler and Sons, *Fabrics/Notions*
J.J. Hat Center, *Accessories*
KB Toys
Kmart, *Discount Stores*
LaDuca Shoes

Lady Foot Locker
Macy's, *Dept. Store*
M&J Trimming/Buttons
Met. Museum of Art Shop
Modell's, *Sporting Goods*
Mood Fabrics Inc.
Motherhood Maternity
New York Golf Center
Olden Camera
Old Navy, *Fashion Chain*
Payless Shoe Source
Perfumania, *Cosmetics/Toiletries*
Prato Fine Men's Wear
R.A.G., *Men's Clothing*
Record Explosion
RK Bridal, *Bridal*
Rogue Music, *Instruments*
Rosen & Chaddick Textiles
Saint Laurie Merchant Tailors, *Men's Clothing*
Sam Goody, *CD/DVD/Video*
Sephora, *Cosmetics/Toiletries*
Skechers, *Shoes*
Steinlauf & Stoller, *Fabrics/Notions*
Steve Madden, *Shoes*
Suncoast Motion Picture Co., *DVD/Video*
30th Street Guitars
Tourneau, *Jewelry/Watches*
Victoria's Secret, *Hosiery/Lingerie*
Wet Seal, *Fashion Chain*
Willoughby's, *Cameras/Video*
Zara, *Fashion Chain*

Gramercy Park
(30th to 24th Sts., east of 5th Ave., and 24th to 14th Sts., east of Park Ave. S.)
Angelo & Maxies, *Cigar/Smoke*
Bridal Garden
Casual Male Big & Tall, *Men's Clothing*
City Opera Thrift Shop
DataVision, *Electronics*

294 subscribe to zagat.com

Location Index

Door Store, *Home*
Furry Paws
Goodwill Industries, *Thrift*
Housing Works Thrift Shop
Janovic Plaza, *Hardware*
OM Boutique, *Men's & Women's Clothing*
Park Avenue Audio, *Electronics*
Pearl Paint, *Art Supplies*
Petland Discounts
Simon's Hardware & Bath
Tokyo Joe, *Consignment*
Urban Angler, *Sporting Goods*
Vercesi Hardware

Greenwich Village
(14th to Houston Sts., bet. B'way & 7th Ave. S., excluding NoHo)

Aedes De Venustas, *Cosmetics/Toiletries*
Alphabets, *Gifts/Novelties*
Beasty Feast, *Pet*
Benetton, *Fashion Chain*
Bleecker Bob's Golden Oldies
Bleecker Street Records
Bombalulus, *Children's*
Carmine Street Guitars
Claire's Accessories, *Jewelry*
C.O. Bigelow Chemists, *Drugstores*
David Z., *Shoes*
Disc-O-Rama Music World
Dö Kham, *Accessories*
Estella, *Children's*
Fat Beats, *CD/Record*
Fetch, *Pet*
Fye, *CD/DVD/Video*
Generation Records
Geppetto's Toy Box
Girl Props, *Jewelry/Watches*
Gotta Knit
Howard Kaplan Bath Shop
Ibiza, *Women's Clothing*
Janovic Plaza, *Hardware*
Joyce Leslie, *Fashion Chain*
Kate's Paperie, *Stationery*
Kentshire Galleries, *Jewelry*
Kim's Mediapolis, *Video*
Kmart, *Discount Stores*
Laina Jane, *Hosiery/Lingerie*
La Petite Coquette, *Hosiery/Lingerie*
Le Fanion, *Home*
L'Occitane, *Cosmetics/Toiletries*
M.A.C. Cosmetics
Matt Umanov Guitars
Music Inn, *Instruments*
Olde Good Things, *Home*
OM Yoga, *Activewear*
Original Leather Store, *Men's & Women's Clothing*
Pink Pussycat, *Sex Shops*
Purdy Girl, *Women's Clothing*
Ricky's, *Cosmetics/Toiletries*
Sam Goody, *CD/DVD/Video*
Skechers, *Shoes*
Sonic Groove, *CD/Record*
Star Magic, *Gifts & Novelties*
Stella Dallas, *Vintage*
Strider Records, *Record*
Subterranean Records
Tah Poozie, *Gifts/Novelties*
TLA Video
Untitled, *Women's Clothing*
Urban Outfitters, *Fashion Chain*
Wet Seal, *Fashion Chain*
William Wayne, *Home*

Harlem
(North of W. 110th St. & south of W. 157th St.; east of Morningside Ave./St. Nicholas Ave. & west of 5th Ave.)

Demolition Depot, *Home*
Disney, *Theme*
Goodwill Industries, *Thrift*
H&M, *Fashion Chain*
HMV, *CD/DVD/Video*
New York Public Library Shop
Studio Museum/Harlem
Xukuma, *Home*

Location Index

Lower East Side
(Houston to Canal Sts., east of Bowery)
Alife Rivington Club, *Sneakers*
Altman Luggage
A.W. Kaufman, *Hosiery/Lingerie*
Bowery Lighting
DDC Lab, *Men's & Women's Clothing*
Design Source/Dave Sanders, *Bathroom Fixtures*
Foley & Corinna, *Women's Clothing*
Forman's, *Discount*
Harris Levy, *Home*
Jelena Behrend, *Jewelry*
Jimmy Jazz, *Men's Clothing*
Joe's Fabric Warehouse
Jutta Neumann, *Shoes*
Lighting by Gregory
Mary Adams, The Dress, *Bridal*
Mendel Goldberg Fabrics
O'Lampia Studio, *Lighting*
Orchard Corset, *Hosiery/Lingerie*
Seven New York, *Women's Clothing*
Shop, *Women's Clothing*
Sol Moscot, *Eyewear*
Sound and Fury, *CD/Record*
TG-170, *Women's Clothing*
Toys In Babeland, *Sex Shops*

Meatpacking District
(Gansevoort to W. 15th Sts., west of 9th Ave.)
Alexander McQueen, *Designer*
auto, *Home*
Bodum, *Home*
Boucher, *Jewelry*
Dernier Cri, *Women's Clothing*
Destination, *Accessories*
Diane von Furstenberg, *Designer*
Jeffrey, *Dept. Store*
Karkula, *Home*
Noose, The, *Sex Shops*
Rubin Chapelle, *Designer*
Scoop, *Men's & Women's Clothing*
Stella McCartney, *Designer*
Vitra, *Home*

Murray Hill
(40th to 30th Sts., east of 5th Ave.)
Aerosoles, *Shoes*
Barton-Sharpe, *Home*
David Z., *Shoes*
ddc domus design collections, *Home*
Doggie-Do & Pussycats Too
Ethan Allen, *Home*
42nd Street Photo
Furry Paws
LaCrasia, *Accessories*
Lord & Taylor, *Dept. Store*
Morgan Library Shop
On Stage Dance Shop
Petco
Pier 1 Imports, *Home*
Quark Spy, *Gadgets*
Roche Bobois, *Home*
Shiseido, *Cosmetics/Toiletries*
Speedo Authentic Fitness
Straight from the Crate, *Home*
Workbench, *Home*
Yankee Clubhouse Shop, *Theme*
Yarn Connection, *Knitting*

NoHo
(Bet. 4th & Houston Sts., bet. Bowery and W. B'way)
Andy's Chee-Pees, *Thrift*
Avirex, *Activewear*
Blades Board and Skate
Bond 07 by Selima, *Women's Clothing*
Capezio, *Activewear*
Crate & Barrel, *Home*
Creed, *Cosmetics/Toiletries*
Eye Candy, *Jewelry*
French Connection, *Fashion Chain*
Ghost, *Designer*

Location Index

Katayone Adeli, *Designer*
KD Dance & Sport
National Wholesale Liquidators, *Discount*
1 on G, *Men's & Women's Clothing*
Other Music
Paul & Joe, *Designer*
Rafe, *Handbags*
Screaming Mimi's, *Vintage*
Stereo Exchange, *Electronics*
Swatch, *Watches*
Tower Records/Video
Transit, *Clothing*
Wet Seal, *Fashion Chain*

NoLita
(South of Houston St. & north of Delancey St.; bet. Bowery & Lafayette St.)
Amy Chan, *Handbags*
Blue Bag, *Accessories*
Built by Wendy, *Designer*
Cadeau, *Maternity*
Calypso, *Women's Clothing*
Dö Kham, *Accessories*
Edmundo Castillo, *Shoes*
e. Harcourt's, *Cosmetics/Toiletries*
Erica Tanov, *Women's Clothing*
Eva, *Women's Clothing*
Find Outlet, *Discount*
Fresh, *Cosmetics/Toiletries*
Gas Bijoux, *Jewelry*
Geraldine, *Shoes*
Hable Construction, *Home*
Hedra Prue, *Women's Clothing*
Henry Lehr, *Designer*
Hollywould, *Shoes*
Illuminations, *Home*
Ina, *Consignment*
Janet Russo, *Designer*
John Fluevog, *Shoes*
Just Shades, *Lighting*
Kar'ikter, *Home*
Kelly Christy, *Accessories*
Kremer Pigments, *Art Supplies*
Language, *Women's Clothing*
Lisa Shaub, *Accessories*
Lunettes et Chocolat, *Eyewear*
Malia Mills Swimwear, *Designer*
Mayle, *Designer*
Me & Ro, *Jewelry*
Michael Anchin Glass Co., *Home*
Miss Sixty, *Women's Clothing*
Mixona, *Hosiery/Lingerie*
Mommy Chic, *Maternity*
Nancy Koltes at Home, *Home*
New York 911, *Theme Stores*
Nisa, *Hosiery/Lingerie*
Only Hearts, *Hosiery/Lingerie*
Papivore, *Stationery*
Paul Frank Store, *Clothing*
Pearldaddy, *Jewelry*
Pearl River Mart, *Dept. Store*
Push, *Jewelry*
Ralph Lauren, *Designer*
Resurrection, *Vintage*
SCO, *Cosmetics/Toiletries*
Seize Sur Vingt, *Men's & Women's Clothing*
Selvedge, *Jeans*
Shop Noir, *Accessories*
Sigerson Morrison, *Shoes*
Sigerson Morrison Bags
Tracy Feith, *Designer*
X-Large, *Men's & Women's Clothing*
Zero, *Women's Clothing*

SoHo
(South of Houston St. & north of Canal St.; west of Lafayette St.)
A. Atelier, *Women's Clothing*
Active Wearhouse, *Activewear*
Add, *Accessories*
Adidas, *Activewear*
Aero, *Home*
Agent Provocateur, *Hosiery/Lingerie*
Agnès B., *Designer*

vote at zagat.com

Location Index

Agnès B. Homme, *Designer*
Alexia Crawford, *Accessories*
Alice Underground, *Vintage*
Alpana Bawa, *Men's & Women's Clothing*
American Eagle Outfitters, *Fashion Chain*
Anna Sui, *Designer*
Anne Fontaine, *Designer*
Anne Klein, *Designer*
Anthropologie, *Fashion Chain*
Anya Hindmarch, *Handbags*
Apartment, The, *Home*
A.P.C., *Men's & Women's Clothing*
Apple Store SoHo, *Electronics*
Arche, *Shoes*
Armani Casa, *Home*
Artemide, *Lighting*
A-Uno, *Women's Clothing*
A/X Armani Exchange, *Designer*
Bagutta, *Men's & Women's Clothing*
Banana Republic Men's, *Fashion Chain*
Barbara Bui, *Designer*
Barneys Co-op, *Dept. Store*
BCBG by Max Azria, *Designer*
BDDW, *Home*
Beau Brummel, *Men's Clothing*
Betsey Johnson, *Designer*
Bicycle Habitat
Big Drop, *Women's Clothing*
Bisou-Bisou, *Women's Clothing*
bliss, *Cosmetics/Toiletries*
Bodyhints, *Hosiery/Lingerie*
Boffi SoHo, *Cabinetry*
Borealis, *Jewelry*
Broadway Panhandler, *Cookware*
Burberry, *Designer*
Calypso, *Women's Clothing*
Calypso Bijoux, *Women's Clothing*
Calypso Enfant & Bebe
Calypso Homme, *Men's Clothing*
Camper, *Shoes*

Cappellini Modern Age, *Home*
Cap Sud, *Home*
Catherine Malandrino, *Designer*
Cécile et Jeanne, *Jewelry*
Ceramica, *Home*
Chanel, *Designer*
Charles Jourdan, *Shoes*
Chuckies, *Shoes*
C.I.T.E. Design, *Home*
Clio, *Home*
Club Monaco, *Fashion Chain*
Coach, *Handbags*
Coconut Company, *Home*
Costume National, *Designer*
Craft Caravan, *Home*
Cynthia Rowley, *Designer*
Daffy's, *Discount*
D & G, *Designer*
David Aaron, *Shoes*
David Z., *Shoes*
Dean & Deluca, *Appliances*
Deco Jewels
Desiron, *Home*
Dialogica, *Home*
Diesel Denim Gallery, *Jeans*
Diesel Style Lab, *Men's & Women's Clothing*
DKNY, *Designer*
Dosa, *Designer*
Earl Jean
Eddie Bauer, *Fashion Chain*
Eileen Fisher, *Fashion Chain*
Emporio Armani, *Designer*
EMS, *Sporting Goods*
Enchanted Forest, *Toys*
Erbe, *Grooming/Toiletries*
Eres, *Hosiery/Lingerie*
Express, *Fashion Chain*
FACE Stockholm, *Cosmetics/Toiletries*
Facial Index, *Eyewear*
Ferragamo, Salvatore, *Designer*
Flou, *Home*
Fossil, *Watches*
Fragments, *Jewelry*
French Connection, *Fashion Chain*

298   subscribe to zagat.com

Location Index

French Corner, *Women's Clothing*
Furla, *Handbags*
Gant, *Men's Clothing*
George Smith, *Home*
Girl Props, *Jewelry/Watches*
Global Table, *Home*
Guess?, *Jeans*
H&M, *Fashion Chain*
Harriet Love, *Women's Clothing*
Hat Shop
Helena Rubenstein, *Cosmetics/Toiletries*
Helmut Lang, *Designer*
Helmut Lang Parfums, *Cosmetics/Toiletries*
Hogan, *Shoes*
Hotel Venus by Patricia Field, *Women's Clothing*
House of Oldies, *Record*
H20 Plus, *Cosmetics/Toiletries*
Hunting World, *Luggage*
IF, *Women's Clothing*
Il Bisonte, *Handbags*
Ina, *Consignment*
Industrial Plastic Supply, *Art Supplies*
Ingo Maurer Making Light
IS: Industries Stationery
Jack Spade, *Luggage*
Jamson Whyte, *Home*
Jane Wilson-Marquis, *Bridal*
Janovic Plaza, *Hardware*
J.Crew, *Fashion Chain*
Jill Stuart, *Designer*
J. Lindeberg Stockholm, *Men's Clothing*
Joan Michlin Gallery, *Jewelry*
Joël Name Optique de Paris
John Varvatos, *Men's Clothing*
Jonathan Adler, *Home*
Joovay, *Hosiery/Lingerie*
Joseph, *Designer*
Julian and Sara, *Children's*
Juno, *Shoes*
Just for Tykes
Kartell, *Home*
Kate Spade, *Accessories*
Kate Spade Travel, *Luggage*
Kate's Paperie, *Stationery*
Keiko, *Activewear*
Kenneth Cole, *Designer*
Kenzo, *Designer*
Kerquelen, *Shoes*
Kirna Zabête, *Women's Clothing*
Knoll, *Home*
Kors Michael Kors, *Designer*
La Perla, *Hosiery/Lingerie*
La Petite Princesse, *Jewelry*
Laundry by Shelli Segal, *Designer*
Le Corset by Selima, *Hosiery/Lingerie*
LeSportsac, *Handbags*
Ligne Roset, *Home*
Lilliput, *Children's*
L'Occitane, *Cosmetics/Toiletries*
Louis Vuitton, *Designer*
Lucky Brand Dungarees
M.A.C. Cosmetics
Madina Milano, *Cosmetics/Toiletries*
Make Up For Ever, *Cosmetics/Toiletries*
Malo, *Designer*
Marc Jacobs, *Designer*
Mare, *Shoes*
Marni, *Designer*
Mavi Jean
Max Mara, *Designer*
Max Studio, *Designer*
Metropolitan Lumber
Met. Museum of Art Shop
Miss Sixty, *Women's Clothing*
Miu Miu, *Designer*
Modernica, *Home*
Modern Stone Age, *Home*
MoMA Design Store, *Museum Shops*
Montblanc, *Stationery*
Mood Indigo, *Home*
Morgane Le Fay, *Designer*
Morgenthal Frederics, *Eyewear*

vote at zagat.com 299

Location Index

Moss, *Home*
Movado, *Watches*
Myoptics, *Eyewear*
Nancy Geist, *Shoes*
Nanette Lepore, *Designer*
New Museum Store
New York Firefighter's Friend, *Theme*
New York Look, *Women's Clothing*
Nicole Miller, *Designer*
North Beach Leather, *Men's & Women's Clothing*
OK Cigars
Olive and Bette's, *Women's Clothing*
Oliver Peoples, *Eyewear*
Original Leather Store, *Men's & Women's Clothing*
Original Levi's Store, *Jeans*
Origins, *Cosmetics/Toiletries*
Otto Tootsi Plohound, *Shoes*
Patagonia, *Activewear*
Patina, *Vintage*
Perlier Kelemata, *Cosmetics/Toiletries*
Peter Fox Shoes
Peter Hermann, *Luggage/Leather Goods*
Phat Farm, *Men's & Women's Clothing*
Philosophy di Alberta Ferretti, *Designer*
Pleats Please, *Designer*
Plein Sud, *Designer*
Pop Shop, *Theme*
Portico, *Home*
Pottery Barn, *Home*
Prada, *Designer*
Puma, *Activewear*
Pumpkin Maternity
Purl, *Knitting/Needlepoint*
Quiksilver, *Men's & Women's Clothing*
Ralph Lauren, *Designer*
Rampage, *Women's Clothing*
Reinstein Ross, *Jewelry*
Repertoire, *Home*
Replay Store, *Men's Clothing*
Reva Mivasagar, *Bridal*
Ricky's, *Cosmetics/Toiletries*
Robert Lee Morris, *Jewelry*
Rocks in your Head, *CD/DVD/Record*
Rooms & Gardens, *Home*
Rug Company, *Home*
Sacco, *Shoes*
Salon Moderne, *Home*
Samuel Jackson Design, *Handbags*
Satellite Records
Scoop, *Women's Clothing*
Scott Jordan Furniture, *Home*
Sean, *Men's Clothing*
Selima Optique, *Eyewear*
Sephora, *Cosmetics/Toiletries*
Shabby Chic, *Home*
Shu Uemura Beauty Boutique, *Cosmetics/Toiletries*
Simon Pearce Glass, *Home*
Sisley, *Fashion Chain*
Skechers, *Shoes*
Smith & Hawken, *Garden*
Stackhouse, *Activewear*
Stephane Kélian, *Shoes*
Steve Madden, *Shoes*
Steven Alan, *Men's & Women's Clothing*
Stuart Moore, *Jewelry*
Stussy NYC, *Men's Clothing*
Swatch, *Watches*
Tag Heuer, *Watches*
Ted Baker, *Men's & Women's Clothing*
Ted Muehling, *Jewelry*
37=1, *Hosiery/Lingerie*
Todd Hase, *Home*
Tommy Hilfiger, *Designer*
Triple Five Soul, *Luggage*
Troy, *Home*
Union, *Men's Clothing*
Uproar Home, *Home*
Varda, *Shoes*
Ventilo, *Designer*

Location Index

Vespa, *Sporting Goods*
Via Spiga, *Shoes*
Vilebrequin, *Men's Clothing*
Vinylmania, *CDs/DVDs/Records/Videos*
Vivienne Tam, *Designer*
Vivienne Westwood, *Designer*
Watch World
Waterworks, *Bathroom Fixtures*
What Comes/Goes Around, *Vintage*
Wolford, *Hosiery/Lingerie*
Workbench, *Home*
Yohji Yamamoto, *Designer*
Zales Jewelers
Zara, *Fashion Chain*

South Street Seaport
Abercrombie & Fitch, *Fashion Chain*
American Eagle Outfitters, *Fashion Chain*
Benetton, *Fashion Chain*
Brookstone, *Gadgets*
Champs, *Sporting Goods*
Coach, *Handbags*
Express Men, *Fashion Chain*
Guess?, *Jeans*
J.Crew, *Fashion Chain*
Sharper Image, *Gadgets*
Talbots, *Fashion Chain*

TriBeCa
(South of Canal St. & north of Chambers St.; west of B'way)
Assets London, *Women's Clothing*
A-Uno, *Women's Clothing*
Baker, *Home*
Bu & the Duck, *Children's*
Donzella, *Home*
Dune, *Home*
Gotham Bikes
Hattitude, *Accessories*
Intérieurs, *Home*
Issey Miyake, *Designer*
Janovic Plaza, *Hardware*
Lafco, *Home*
Les Migrateurs, *Home*
Little Folk Art, *Children's/Home Furnishings*
Metro Bicycles
Mika Inatome, *Bridal*
P&S Fabrics
Pompanoosuc Mills, *Home*
Room, *Home*
Shoofly, *Children's*
Sorelle Firenze, *Women's Clothing*
Stella, *Home*
Steven Alan, *Men's & Women's Clothing*
Totem Design Group, *Home*
Urban Archaeology, *Bathroom Fixtures & Tiles*

Union Square
(Bounded by 17th & 14th Sts., bet. Union Sq. E. & Union Sq. W.)
Agnès B., *Designer*
Ann Sacks Tile & Stone
Cheap Jack's, *Thrift*
Circuit City, *Electronics*
Country Floors, *Bathroom Fixtures & Tiles*
Desiron, *Home*
Diesel Superstore, *Jeans*
Disc-O-Rama Music World
Gateway Country, *Electronics*
Paragon Sporting Goods
P.C. Richard & Son, *Electronics*
Poggenpohl U.S. Inc., *Cabinetry*
Rothman's, *Men's Clothing*
Sound by Singer, *Electronics*
Toys R Us
Virgin Megastore, *CD/DVD/Video*
Wiz, The, *Electronics*

Washington Hts. & Up
(North of W. 157th St.)
Cloisters, The, *Museum Shops*
Goodwill Industries, *Thrift*
KB Toys

vote at zagat.com 301

Location Index

West Village
(14th to Houston Sts., west of 7th Ave. S., excluding Meatpacking District)
An American Craftsman, *Home*
Beasty Feast, *Pet*
Betwixt, *Children's*
Beyul, *Home*
Chelsea Garden Center Home
Cherry, *Vintage*
Constança Basto, *Shoes*
Details, *Home*
Equinox Energy Wear
Flight 001, *Luggage*
Four Paws Club, The, *Pet*
Fresh, *Cosmetics/Toiletries*
Galileo, *Home*
Gerry's Menswear
Jamson Whyte, *Home*
Joe's CDs
Leather Man, The, *Sex Shops*
Lucy Barnes, *Designer*
Lulu Guinness, *Handbags*
L'Uomo, *Men's Clothing*
Marc by Marc Jacobs, *Designer*
Marc Jacobs Accessories, *Designer*
Mxyplyzyk, *Home*
Myoptics, *Eyewear*
Patch NYC, *Accessories*
Peanutbutter & Jane, *Children's*
P.E. Guerin, *Bathroom Fixtures*
Pleasure Chest, *Sex Shops*
Rags-A-Go-Go, *Thrift*
Rebel Rebel, *CD/DVD/Record/Video*
Verve, *Handbags*

West 40s
Arthur Brown & Brothers, *Stationery*
Colony Music, *CD/Record*
Crane & Co., Paper Makers
Disney, *Theme*
ESPN Zone, *Theme*
48th Street Custom Guitars
Gothic Cabinet Craft, *Home*
Harvey Electronics
International Ctr. Photography, *Museum Shops*
Intrepid Sea-Air-Space, *Museum Shops*
Manny's Music, *Instruments*
Metro Bicycles
Metropolitan Lumber
Met. Museum of Art Shop
Mets Clubhouse Shop, *Theme*
Movado, *Watches*
MTV Store, *Theme*
NBC Experience, *Theme*
New Balance, *Activewear*
New York Elegant Fabric
New York Look, *Women's Clothing*
One Shubert Alley, *Theme*
Pan Aqua Diving
Paron Fabrics
P.J. Huntsman, *Men's Clothing*
Poli Fabrics
R.A.G., *Men's Clothing*
Ray Beauty Supply, *Cosmetics/Toiletries*
Rudy's Music Shop, *Instruments*
Salvation Army, *Thrift*
Sam Ash, *Musical Instruments*
Sanrio (aka Hello Kitty Store), *Theme*
Sephora, *Cosmetics/Toiletries*
Sharper Image, *Gadgets*
Sound City, *Electronics*
Spoiled Brats, *Pet*
Staples, *Electronics*
Theatre Circle, *Theme*
Thomas Pink, *Men's Clothing*
Toys R Us
Tumi, *Luggage*
Virgin Megastore, *CD/DVD/Video*
World, The, *Theme*
Yankee Clubhouse Shop, *Theme*

West 50s
Aaron Faber Gallery, *Jewelry*
Addison on Madison, *Men's Clothing*
Alkit Pro Camera

Location Index

American Craft Museum Shop
American Folk Art Museum
An American Craftsman, *Home*
Angelo & Maxies, *Cigar/Smoke*
Arche, *Shoes*
Ascot Chang, *Men's Clothing*
Aveda, *Cosmetics/Toiletries*
Blockbuster Video
Bolton's, *Discount*
Brookstone, *Gadgets*
Capezio, *Activewear*
Carnegie Cards & Gifts
Champs, *Sporting Goods*
Claire's Accessories, *Jewelry*
CompUSA, *Electronics*
Daffy's, *Discount*
De La Concha Tobacconist
Equinox Energy Wear
Erwin Pearl, *Jewelry*
Eve's Garden, *Sex Shops*
Frank Stella Ltd., *Men's Clothing*
French Connection, *Fashion Chain*
Fye, *CD/DVD/Video*
Garden Shop/Hort. Soc.
Gateway Country, *Electronics*
Hard Rock Cafe, *Theme*
Illuminations, *Home*
Innovation Luggage
Janovic Plaza, *Hardware*
J.Crew, *Fashion Chain*
Joseph Patelson Music House
Kenjo, *Watches*
Laura Biagiotti, *Designer*
Lee's Art Shop
Lee's Studio, *Home*
Leonard Poll, *Eyewear*
Louis Féraud, *Designer*
Manolo Blahnik, *Shoes*
Maternity Works
Michelle Roth, *Bridal*
MoMA Design Store, *Museum Shops*
Nautica, *Fashion Chain*
N. Peal, *Men's & Women's Clothing*
OMO Norma Kamali, *Designer*
Paron Fabrics
Peck & Goodie Skates, *Sporting Goods*
Ricky's, *Cosmetics/Toiletries*
Ritz Furs, *Consignment*
Rochester Big & Tall, *Fashion Chain*
Sansha, *Activewear*
Scandinavian Ski & Sport Shop
Sharper Image, *Gadgets*
Smythson of Bond Street, *Stationery*
Sports Authority
Steinway and Sons, *Musical Instruments*
Straight from the Crate, *Home*
Sude, *Women's Clothing*

West 60s

Agatha, *Jewelry*
American Folk Art Museum
Bonne Nuit, *Hosiery/Lingerie*
Danskin, *Activewear*
Details, *Home*
Disney, *Theme*
Domain, *Home*
Eddie Bauer, *Fashion Chain*
EMS, *Sporting Goods*
Ethan Allen, *Home*
Furry Paws
Gracious Home, *Home*
Gymboree, *Children's*
Innovation Luggage
Juilliard Bookstore, *Sheet Music*
Lincoln Stationers
L'Occitane, *Cosmetics/Toiletries*
Mimi Maternity
New York Look, *Women's Clothing*
Paper Access, *Stationery*
Pottery Barn, *Home*
Reebok Store, *Activewear*
Robert Marc, *Eyewear*
Speedo Authentic Fitness
Toga Bikes
Tower Records/Video

vote at zagat.com

Location Index

West 70s
American Museum/Nat. History
At the Gryphon, *Record*
Bang & Olufsen, *Electronics*
Berkley Girl, *Children's*
Betsey Johnson, *Designer*
Blades Board and Skate
Bombalulus, *Children's*
Brief Encounters, *Hosiery/Lingerie*
Champagne Video
Eileen Fisher, *Fashion Chain*
Equinox Energy Wear
FACE Stockholm, *Cosmetics/Toiletries*
Filene's Basement, *Discount*
Fishs Eddy, *Home*
French Connection, *Fashion Chain*
Goodwill Industries, *Thrift*
Granny-Made, *Children's*
Housing Works Thrift Shop
Intermix, *Jewelry*
Janovic Plaza, *Hardware*
Kenneth Cole, *Designer*
La Belle Epoque, *Home*
La Brea, *Gifts/Novelties*
Laura Ashley, *Designer*
Lucky Brand Dungarees
Montmartre, *Women's Clothing*
Olive and Bette's, *Women's Clothing*
Only Hearts, *Hosiery/Lingerie*
Oriental Lamp Shade Co.
Original Leather Store, *Men's & Women's Clothing*
Paterson Silks, *Fabrics/Notions*
Really Great Things, *Women's Clothing*
Ricky's, *Cosmetics/Toiletries*
Roslyn, *Accessories*
Sacco, *Shoes*
Sean, *Men's Clothing*
Sephora, *Cosmetics/Toiletries*
Skechers, *Shoes*
Straight from the Crate, *Home*
Super Runners Shop
Swatch, *Watches*
Tip-Top Shoes
Uncle's Stereo
Urban Outfitters, *Fashion Chain*
Varda, *Shoes*
Variazioni, *Women's Clothing*
Verve, *Handbags*
Workbench, *Home*
Z. Baby Company, *Children's*

West 80s
Allan & Suzi, *Consignment/Vintage*
Alphabets, *Gifts/Novelties*
April Cornell, *Designer*
Assets London, *Women's Clothing*
Avventura, *Home*
Bath Island, *Cosmetics/Toiletries*
Bicycle Renaissance
Bombay Company, *Home*
Bruce Frank Beads, *Jewelry*
Circuit City, *Electronics*
Club Monaco, *Fashion Chain*
Darryl's, *Women's Clothing*
Door Store, *Home*
Eye Man, *Eyewear*
Frank Stella Ltd., *Men's Clothing*
Greenstones, *Children's*
Gymboree, *Children's*
Harry's Shoes
Hollywood Video
KB Toys
Laina Jane, *Hosiery/Lingerie*
Laytner's Linen & Home
Lightforms
L'Occitane, *Cosmetics/Toiletries*
Maxilla & Mandible, *Toys*
Medici, *Shoes*
Morris Brothers, *Children's*
Nice Price, *Discount*
NYCD, *CD/DVD*
Origins, *Cosmetics/Toiletries*
Patagonia, *Activewear*
Penny Whistle, *Toys*
Pet Stop
Pondicherri, *Home*
Portico, *Home*
Schweitzer Linen, *Home*

subscribe to zagat.com

Location Index

Shoe Biz
Shoofly, *Children's*
Sisley, *Fashion Chain*
Talbots, *Fashion Chain*
Tano, *Shoes*
Town Shop, *Hosiery/Lingerie*
Westside Kids, *Toys*
Yarn Co., The, *Knitting*
Zabar's, *Appliances*
Zany Brainy, *Toys*

West 90s
Albee Baby Carriage Co.
Children's General Store, *Toys*

Equinox Energy Wear
Janovic Plaza, *Hardware*
La Brea, *Gifts/Novelties*
Luxury Brand Outlet, *Discount*
Metro Bicycles
Wiz, The, *Electronics*

West 100s
(West of Morningside Ave.)
Jimmy Jazz, *Men's Clothing*
Kim's Mediapolis, *CD/DVD/Video*
Marshall's, *Discount*
Planet Kids

BRONX

ABC Carpet & Home Warehse.
Casa Amadeo
Casual Male Big & Tall, *Men's Clothing*
Fye, *CD/DVD/Video*
Goodwill Industries, *Thrift*

Kmart, *Discount Stores*
Loehmann's, *Discount*
Men's Wearhouse, *Fashion Chain*
National Wholesale Liquidators, *Discount*

BROOKLYN

Bay Ridge
Century 21, *Discount*
Claire's Accessories, *Jewelry*
Joyce Leslie, *Fashion Chain*
Kleinfeld & Son, *Bridal*

Bensonhurst
Claire's Accessories, *Jewelry*
Kids R Us
Kmart, *Discount Stores*
National Wholesale Liquidators, *Discount*

Boerum Hill
Bark, *Home*
Breukelen, *Home*
Butter, *Women's Clothing*
Foundation, *Home*
Gumbo, *Children's*
Jelly, *Shoes*
Kimera, *Women's Clothing*
Knitting Hands
Layla, *Home*
Little Eric, *Children's*
Olde Good Things, *Home*
Rico, *Home*

Scuba Network
Urban Monster, *Children's*

Borough Park
Jacadi, *Children's*
National Wholesale Liquidators, *Discount*
S&W, *Discount*

Brooklyn Heights
Heights Kids
Innovative Audio, *Electronics*
Sid's, *Hardware*
Workbench, *Home*

Canarsie
Casual Male Big & Tall, *Men's Clothing*
Target, *Dept. Store*

Carroll Gardens
df, *Home*
Flirt, *Women's Clothing*
Frida's Closet, *Women's Clothing*
Oculus 20/20, *Eyewear*
Stacia, *Women's Clothing*

vote at zagat.com

Location Index

Clinton Hill
Circuit City, *Electronics*

Cobble Hill
Brooklyn Public Couture, *Vintage*
Green Onion, *Children's*

Coney Island
Drimmers, *Appliances*
Loehmann's, *Discount*

Crown Heights
AF Supply Corp., *Bath Fixtures*

Downtown
Domsey's, *Thrift*
Goodwill Industries, *Thrift*
Marshall's, *Discount*
Toys R Us

Dumbo
ABC Carpet & Home

Dyker Heights
Casual Male Big & Tall, *Men's Clothing*
David's Bridal
Prato Fine Men's Wear

Flatbush
Boss, The, *Men's Clothing*
Canal Jean Company

Fort Greene
Hot Toddie, *Children's*

Gravesend
Jimmy's, *Women's Clothing*
Lester's, *Children's*
William Barthman, *Jewelry*

Greenpoint
Domsey's Express, *Thrift*

Kings Plaza
Disney, *Theme*
Express Men, *Fashion Chain*
Guess?, *Jeans*
H&M, *Fashion Chain*
Joyce Leslie, *Fashion Chain*
Lady Foot Locker
Sam Goody, *CD/DVD/Video*
Steve Madden, *Shoes*
Suncoast Motion Picture Co., *DVD/Video*

Midwood
Yellow Door, *Jewelry*

Mill Basin
Casual Male Big & Tall, *Men's Clothing*
Joyce Leslie, *Fashion Chain*

Park Slope
Aaron's, *Discount*
Baby Bird, *Children's*
Beacon's Closet, *Consignment/Thrift*
Bird, *Women's Clothing*
Clay Pot, *Jewelry*
Eidolon, *Women's Clothing*
Facets, *Jewelry*
Holy Cow, *CD/Record*
Hooti Couture, *Vintage*
Kimera, *Women's Clothing*
Kiwi Design, *Women's Clothing*
Loom, *Accessories*
Nest, *Home*
Pink Pussycat, *Sex Shops*
Pintchik, *Hardware*
Sew Brooklyn, *Fabrics/Notions*
Tarzian True Value, *Hardware*
Tarzian West For Housewares
Treasure Chest, *Jewelry*
Urban Optical, *Eyewear*

Prospect Heights
Brooklyn Museum Shop
Castor & Pollux, *Women's Clothing*
Pieces, *Men's & Women's Clothing*

Red Hook
Costco Wholesale, *Discount*

Sunset Park
Lady Foot Locker

Williamsburg
Beacon's Closet, *Consignment/Thrift*
Mini Mini Market, *Accessories*

Location Index

Moon River Chattel, *Home*
Oculus 20/20, *Eyewear*
Sam & Seb, *Children's*
Urban Optical, *Eyewear*

QUEENS

Astoria
Goodwill Industries, *Thrift*
Metropolitan Lumber
Prato Fine Men's Wear

Bayside
Claire's Accessories, *Jewelry*
Paterson Silks, *Fabrics/Notions*
Thomasville

Bellerose
Toys R Us

College Point
Target, *Dept. Store*

Corona
London Jewelers
Metropolitan Lumber

Elmhurst
Daffy's, *Discount*
H&M, *Fashion Chain*
Lady Foot Locker
Target, *Dept. Store*
Zales Jewelers

Flushing
Best Buy, *Electronics*
Brookstone, *Gadgets*
Circuit City, *Electronics*
Filene's Basement, *Discount*
Joyce Leslie, *Fashion Chain*
National Wholesale
   Liquidators, *Discount*

Forest Hills
Claire's Accessories, *Jewelry*
Eddie Bauer, *Fashion Chain*
Ethan Allen, *Home*
Sol Moscot, *Eyewear*

Forest Meadows
Kmart, *Discount Stores*
Sam Goody, *CD/DVD/Video*

Howard Beach
Petco
Sam Goody, *CD/DVD/Video*

Jamaica
Brookstone, *Gadgets*
Metropolitan Lumber
Nemo Tile Company

Long Island City
Costco Wholesale, *Discount*
Home Depot, *Hardware*
Marshall's, *Discount*
Tucker Robbins, *Home*
Vespa, *Sporting Goods*

Middle Village
Kmart, *Discount Stores*

Rego Park
Bed, Bath & Beyond, *Home*
Circuit City, *Electronics*
CompUSA, *Electronics*
Metro Bicycles

Ridgewood
Joyce Leslie, *Fashion Chain*

Rockaway Beach
Sam Goody, *CD/DVD/Video*
Toys R Us

Woodhaven
Smiley's, *Knitting/Needlepoint*

Woodside
Kids R Us

STATEN ISLAND

Abercrombie & Fitch, *Fashion Chain*
American Eagle Outfitters, *Fashion Chain*
Best Buy, *Electronics*
Bombay Company, *Home*
Casual Male Big & Tall, *Men's Clothing*

vote at zagat.com

Location Index

Champs, *Sporting Goods*
Circuit City, *Electronics*
Costco Wholesale, *Discount*
Ethan Allen, *Home*
Guess?, *Jeans*
Gymboree, *Children's*
Joyce Leslie, *Fashion Chain*
Kids R Us
Kmart, *Discount Stores*
Mandolin Brothers, *Musical Instruments*
Men's Wearhouse, *Fashion Chain*
Mimi Maternity
On Your Toes Dancewear
Petco
Sam Goody, *CD/DVD/Video*
Steve Madden, *Shoes*
T.J. Maxx, *Discount*
Toys R Us
Zales Jewelers
Zany Brainy, *Toys*

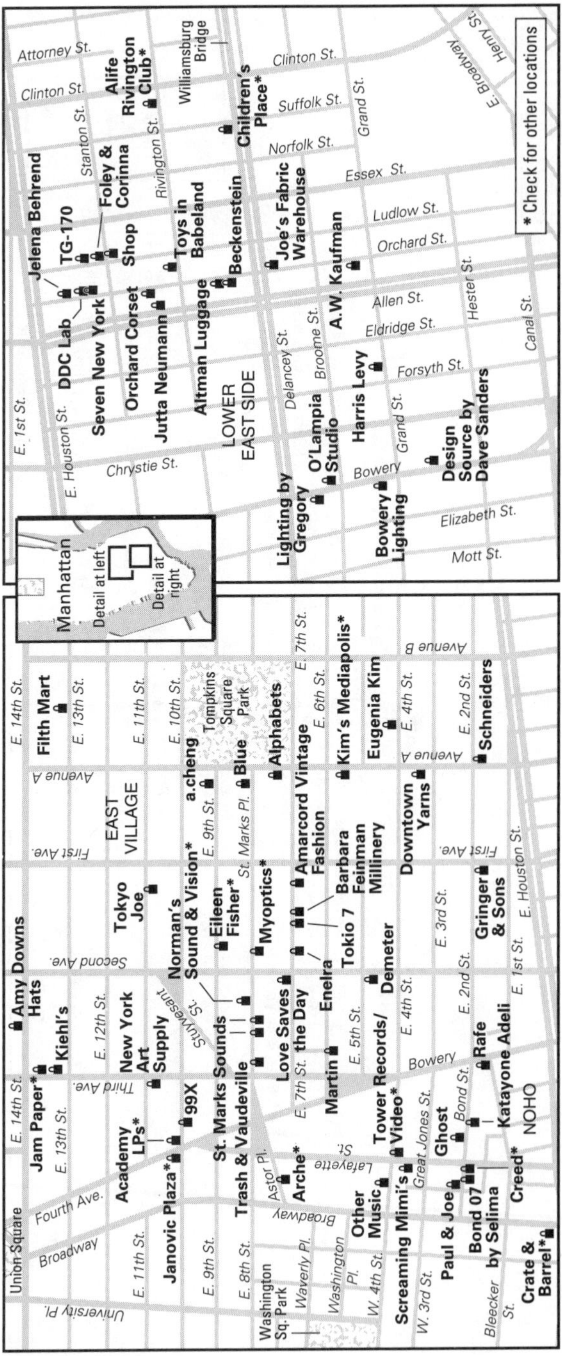

East Village/Lower East Side/NoHo

*Check for other locations

vote at zagat.com

Flatiron/Union Square

Midtown

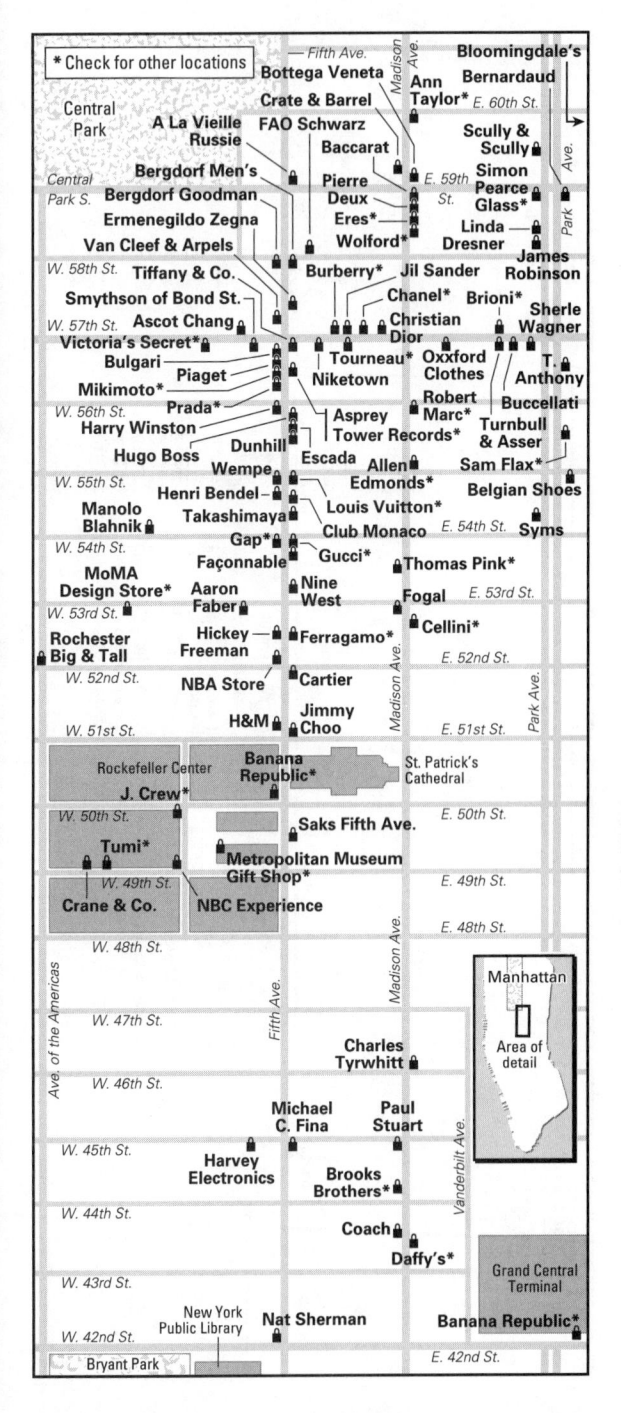

* Check for other locations

Map of Midtown Manhattan shopping locations, bounded approximately by Central Park to the north and Bryant Park / Grand Central Terminal to the south, Avenue of the Americas to the west and Park Ave. to the east.

Locations shown (north to south, roughly):

- Bloomingdale's
- Bernardaud
- Bottega Veneta
- Ann Taylor*
- Crate & Barrel
- FAO Schwarz
- A La Vieille Russie
- Baccarat
- Scully & Scully
- Bergdorf Men's
- Pierre Deux
- Simon Pearce Glass*
- Bergdorf Goodman
- Eres*
- Ermenegildo Zegna
- Wolford*
- Linda Dresner
- Van Cleef & Arpels
- James Robinson
- Tiffany & Co.
- Burberry*
- Jil Sander
- Smythson of Bond St.
- Chanel*
- Brioni
- Ascot Chang
- Christian Dior
- Sherle Wagner
- Victoria's Secret*
- Tourneau*
- Oxxford Clothes
- T. Anthony
- Bulgari
- Niketown
- Robert Marc*
- Buccellati
- Piaget
- Turnbull & Asser
- Mikimoto*
- Asprey
- Prada*
- Tower Records*
- Sam Flax*
- Harry Winston
- Dunhill
- Escada
- Allen Edmonds*
- Belgian Shoes
- Hugo Boss
- Wempe
- Louis Vuitton*
- Henri Bendel
- Takashimaya
- Syms
- Manolo Blahnik
- Club Monaco
- Gap*
- Façonnable
- Gucci*
- Thomas Pink*
- MoMA Design Store*
- Aaron Faber
- Nine West
- Fogal
- Cellini*
- Rochester Big & Tall
- Hickey Freeman
- Ferragamo*
- NBA Store
- Cartier
- H&M
- Jimmy Choo
- Rockefeller Center
- J. Crew*
- Banana Republic*
- St. Patrick's Cathedral
- Tumi*
- Saks Fifth Ave.
- Crane & Co.
- Metropolitan Museum Gift Shop*
- NBC Experience
- Charles Tyrwhitt
- Michael C. Fina
- Paul Stuart
- Harvey Electronics
- Brooks Brothers*
- Coach
- Daffy's*
- Grand Central Terminal
- New York Public Library
- Nat Sherman
- Banana Republic*
- Bryant Park

Streets: Fifth Ave., Madison Ave., Park Ave., Ave. of the Americas, Vanderbilt Ave., Central Park S., W./E. 42nd St. through E. 60th St.

Inset: Manhattan — Area of detail.

vote at zagat.com   311

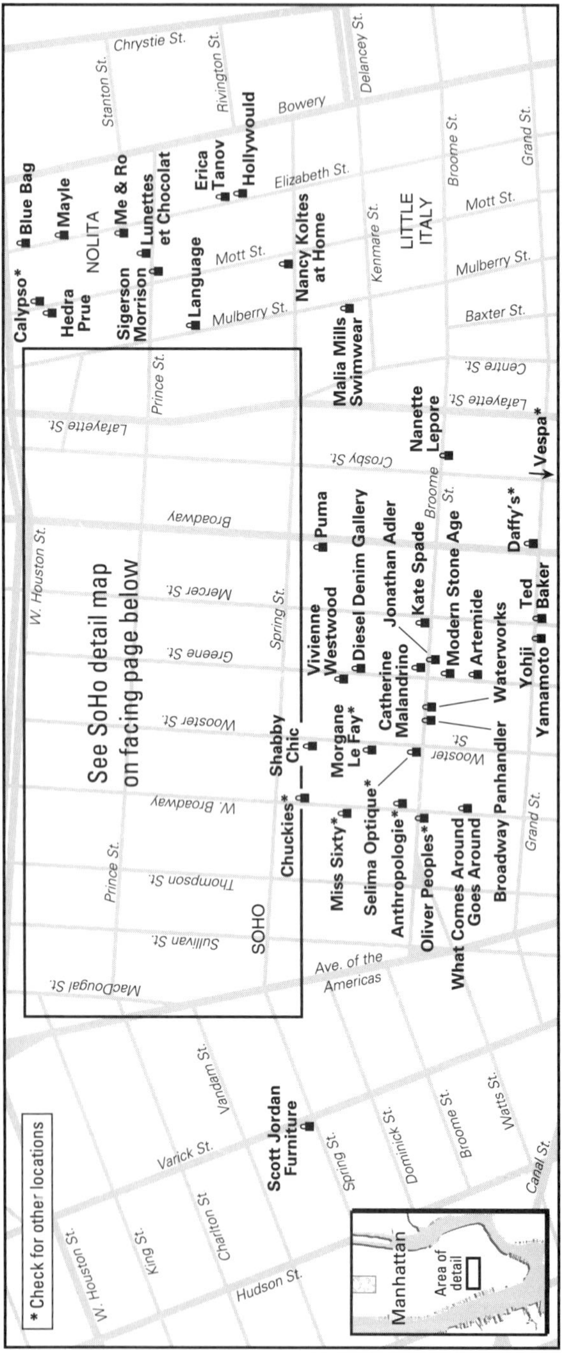

SoHo/NoLita

Map content:

NoLita area:
- Blue Bag*
- Mayle
- Me & Ro
- Lunettes et Chocolat
- Erica Tanov
- Hollywould
- Calypso*
- Hedra Prue
- Sigerson Morrison
- Language
- Nancy Koltes at Home
- Malia Mills Swimwear
- Nanette Lepore
- Vespa*
- Daffy's*

SoHo area:
- Puma
- Diesel Denim Gallery
- Jonathan Adler
- Kate Spade
- Modern Stone Age
- Artemide
- Ted Baker
- Vivienne Westwood
- Catherine Malandrino
- Waterworks
- Yohji Yamamoto
- Shabby Chic
- Morgane Le Fay*
- Broadway Panhandler
- Chuckies*
- Miss Sixty*
- Selima Optique*
- Anthropologie*
- Oliver Peoples*
- What Comes Around Goes Around
- Scott Jordan Furniture

Streets shown: Chrystie St., Stanton St., Rivington St., Delancey St., Bowery, Elizabeth St., Mott St., Mulberry St., Kenmare St., Broome St., Grand St., Baxter St., Centre St., Lafayette St., Crosby St., Broadway, Mercer St., Greene St., Wooster St., W. Broadway, Thompson St., Sullivan St., MacDougal St., Prince St., W. Houston St., Spring St., Ave. of the Americas, Vandam St., Varick St., Charlton St., King St., W. Houston St., Hudson St., Dominick St., Broome St., Watts St., Canal St.

LITTLE ITALY

See SoHo detail map on facing page below

*Check for other locations

Manhattan — Area of detail

312   subscribe to zagat.com

SoHo/NoLita

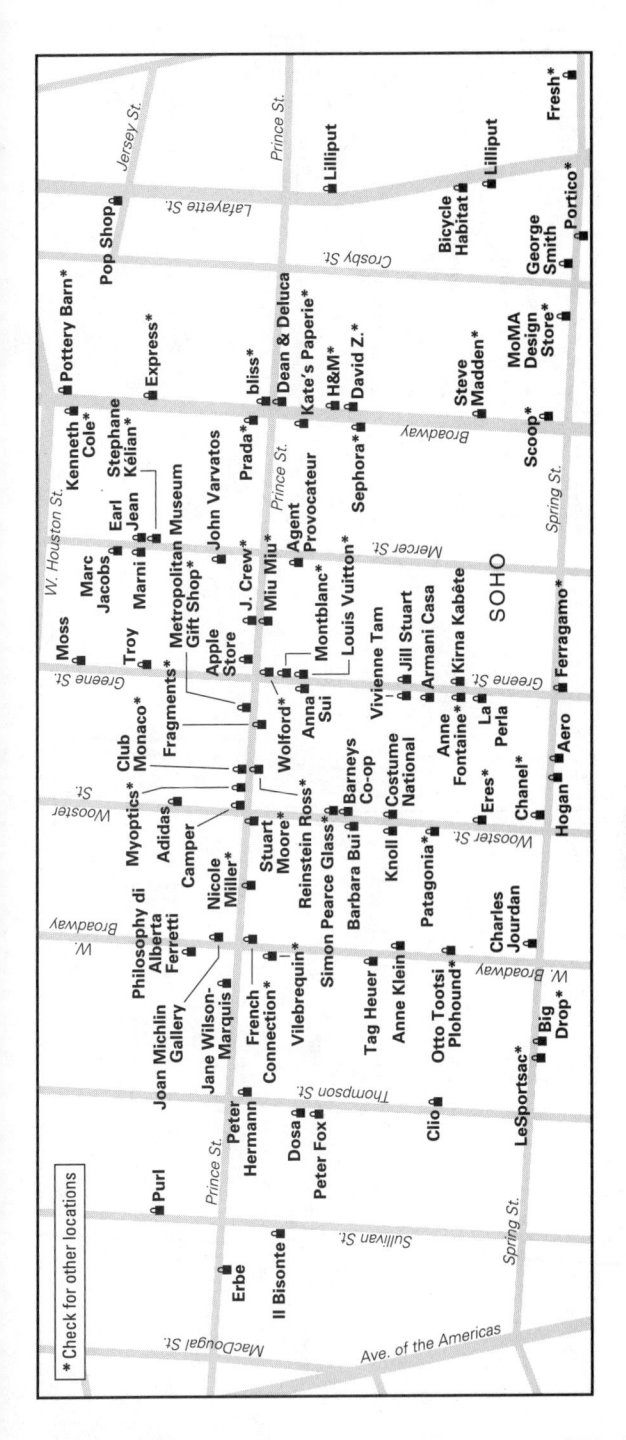

TriBeCa/Financial Dist./Seaport

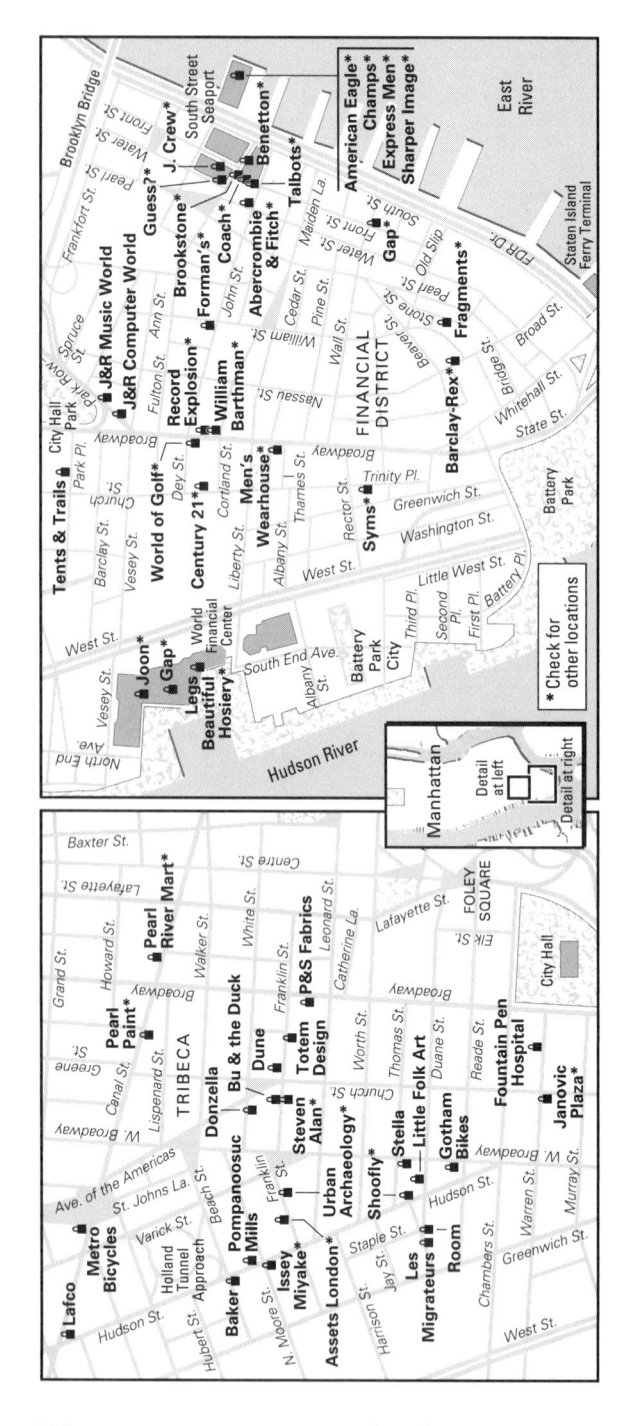

Upper East Side

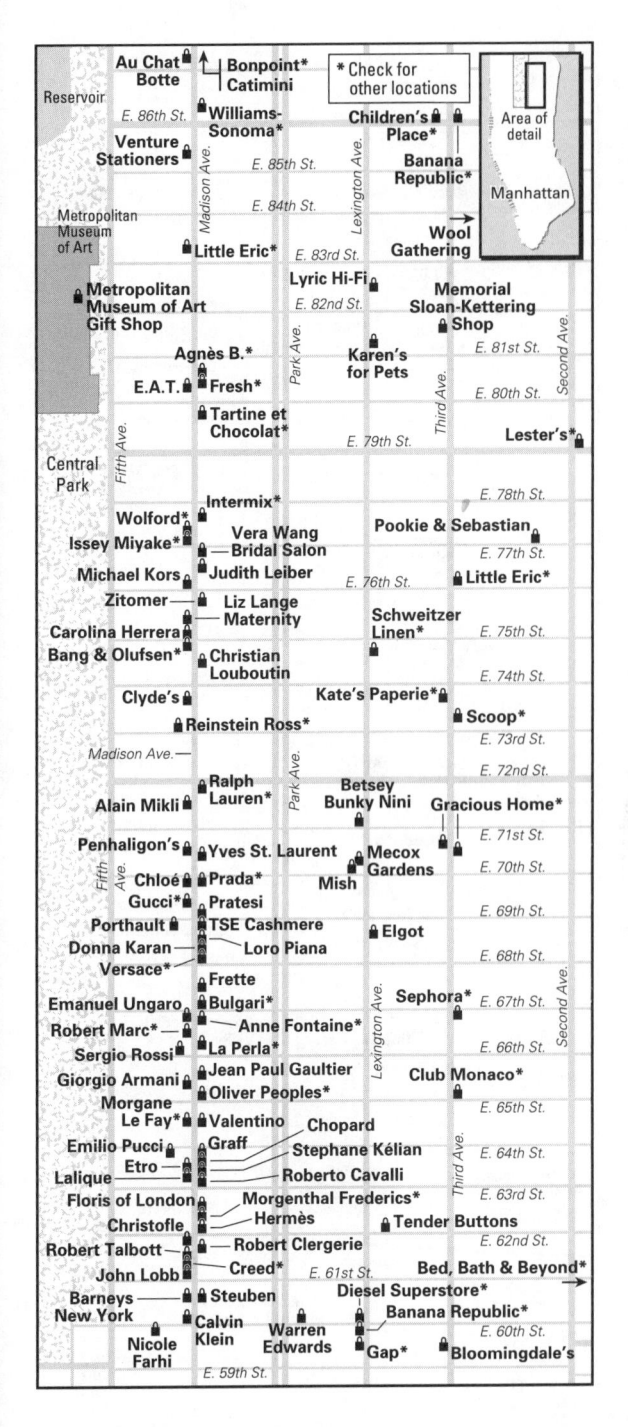

*Check for other locations

Area of detail — Manhattan

- Au Chat Botte
- Bonpoint*
- Catimini
- Williams-Sonoma*
- Venture Stationers
- Children's Place*
- Banana Republic*
- Metropolitan Museum of Art
- Little Eric*
- Lyric Hi-Fi
- Metropolitan Museum of Art Gift Shop
- Memorial Sloan-Kettering Shop
- Wool Gathering
- Agnès B.*
- Karen's for Pets
- E.A.T.
- Fresh*
- Tartine et Chocolat
- Lester's*
- Intermix*
- Wolford*
- Vera Wang Bridal Salon
- Pookie & Sebastian
- Issey Miyake*
- Judith Leiber
- Little Eric*
- Michael Kors
- Zitomer
- Liz Lange Maternity
- Schweitzer Linen
- Carolina Herrera
- Bang & Olufsen*
- Christian Louboutin
- Clyde's
- Kate's Paperie*
- Scoop*
- Reinstein Ross*
- Ralph Lauren*
- Betsey Bunky Nini
- Gracious Home*
- Alain Mikli
- Penhaligon's
- Yves St. Laurent
- Mecox Gardens
- Chloé
- Prada*
- Mish
- Gucci*
- Pratesi
- Porthault
- TSE Cashmere
- Elgot
- Donna Karan
- Loro Piana
- Versace*
- Frette
- Emanuel Ungaro
- Bulgari*
- Sephora*
- Robert Marc*
- Anne Fontaine*
- Sergio Rossi
- La Perla*
- Giorgio Armani
- Jean Paul Gaultier
- Club Monaco*
- Morgane Le Fay*
- Oliver Peoples*
- Valentino
- Chopard
- Emilio Pucci
- Graff
- Stephane Kélian
- Etro
- Roberto Cavalli
- Lalique
- Floris of London
- Morgenthal Fredericks*
- Christofle
- Hermès
- Tender Buttons
- Robert Talbott
- Robert Clergerie
- John Lobb
- Creed*
- Bed, Bath & Beyond*
- Barneys New York
- Steuben
- Diesel Superstore*
- Banana Republic*
- Calvin Klein
- Warren Edwards
- Gap*
- Bloomingdale's
- Nicole Farhi

vote at zagat.com

315

Upper West Side

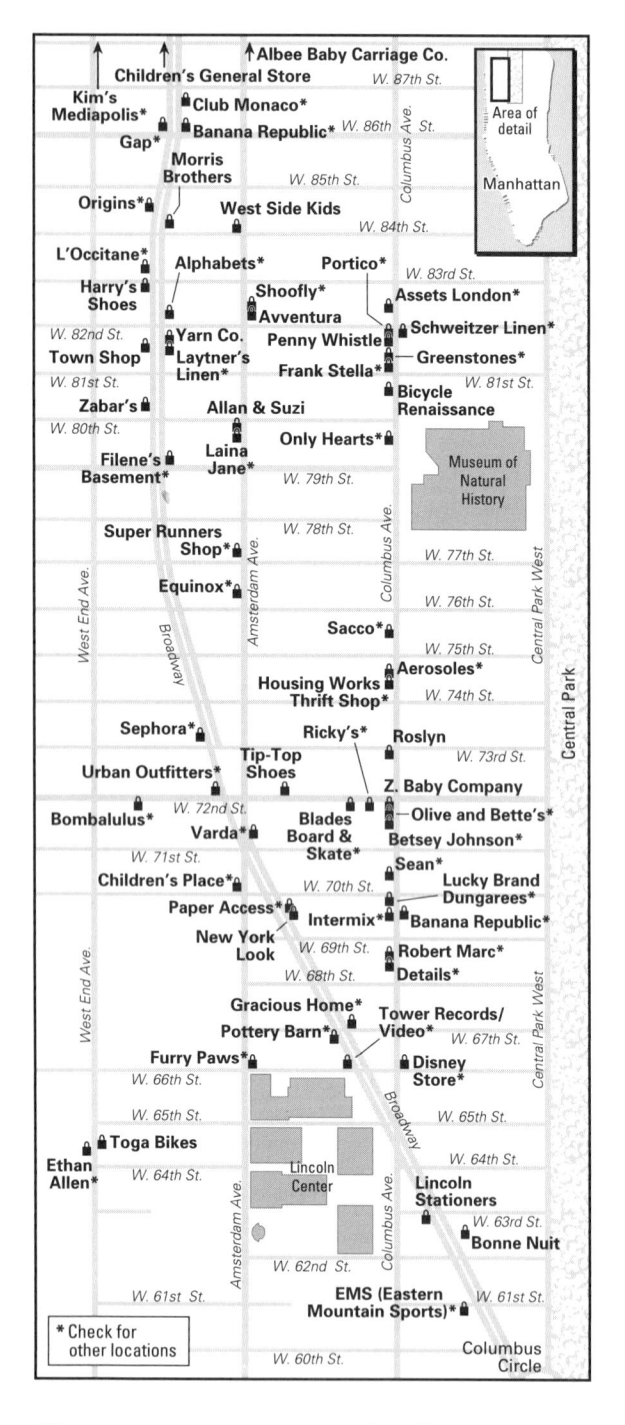

↑ Albee Baby Carriage Co.
↑ Children's General Store
W. 87th St.
Kim's Mediapolis*
Club Monaco*
Gap* Banana Republic* W. 86th St.
Morris Brothers
W. 85th St.
Origins* West Side Kids
W. 84th St.
L'Occitane* Alphabets* Portico* W. 83rd St.
Harry's Shoes Shoofly* Assets London*
Avventura Schweitzer Linen*
W. 82nd St. Yarn Co. Penny Whistle
Town Shop Laytner's Linen Frank Stella* Greenstones*
W. 81st St. Bicycle Renaissance
Zabar's Allan & Suzi
W. 80th St. Museum of Natural History
Filene's Basement* Laina Jane Only Hearts*
W. 79th St.
Super Runners Shop* W. 78th St.
W. 77th St.
Equinox*
W. 76th St.
Sacco*
W. 75th St.
Housing Works Thrift Shop* Aerosoles*
W. 74th St.
Sephora* Ricky's Roslyn
W. 73rd St.
Urban Outfitters* Tip-Top Shoes Z. Baby Company
Bombalulus* W. 72nd St.
Varda* Blades Board & Skate* Olive and Bette's*
W. 71st St. Betsey Johnson*
Children's Place* Sean*
W. 70th St. Lucky Brand Dungarees*
Paper Access* Intermix* Banana Republic*
New York Look W. 69th St.
W. 68th St. Robert Marc*
Details*
Gracious Home* Tower Records/Video*
Pottery Barn* W. 67th St.
Furry Paws* Disney Store*
W. 66th St.
W. 65th St. W. 65th St.
Toga Bikes W. 64th St.
Ethan Allen* Lincoln Center Lincoln Stationers
W. 63rd St.
Bonne Nuit
W. 62nd St.
W. 61st St.
EMS (Eastern Mountain Sports)* W. 61st St.
* Check for other locations
W. 60th St. Columbus Circle

316 subscribe to zagat.com

West Vlg./Greenwich Vlg./Meatpacking District

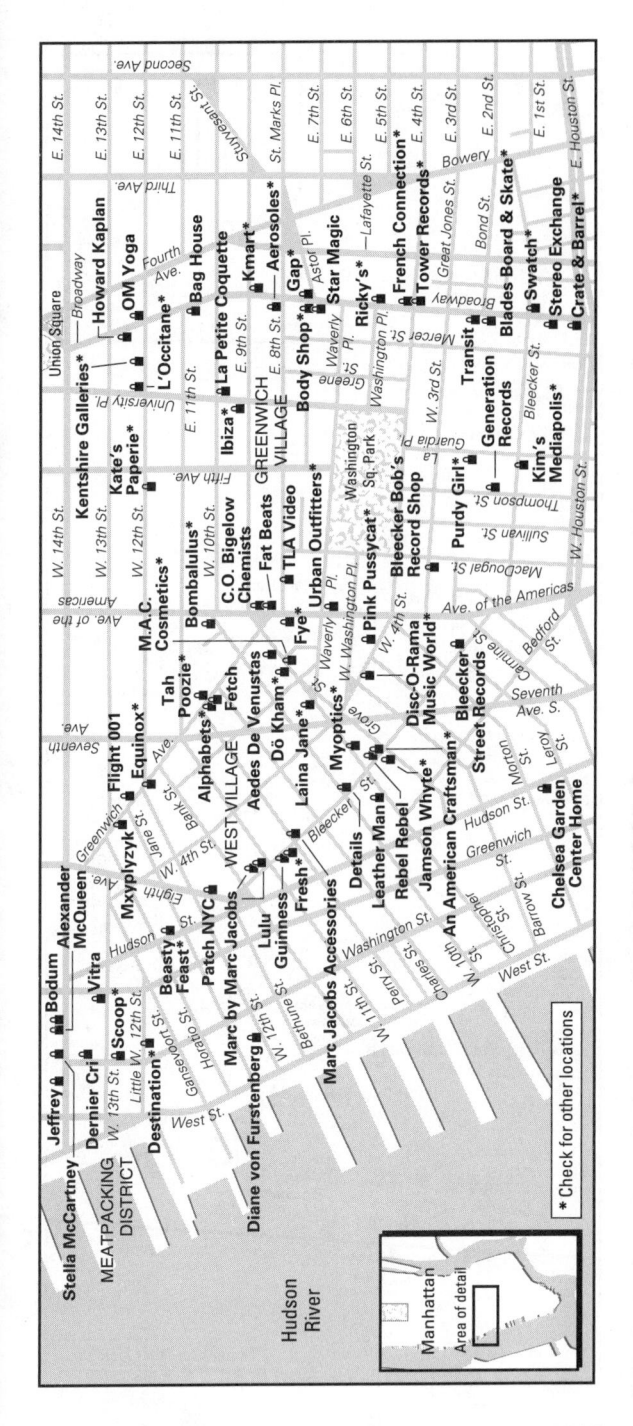

vote at zagat.com

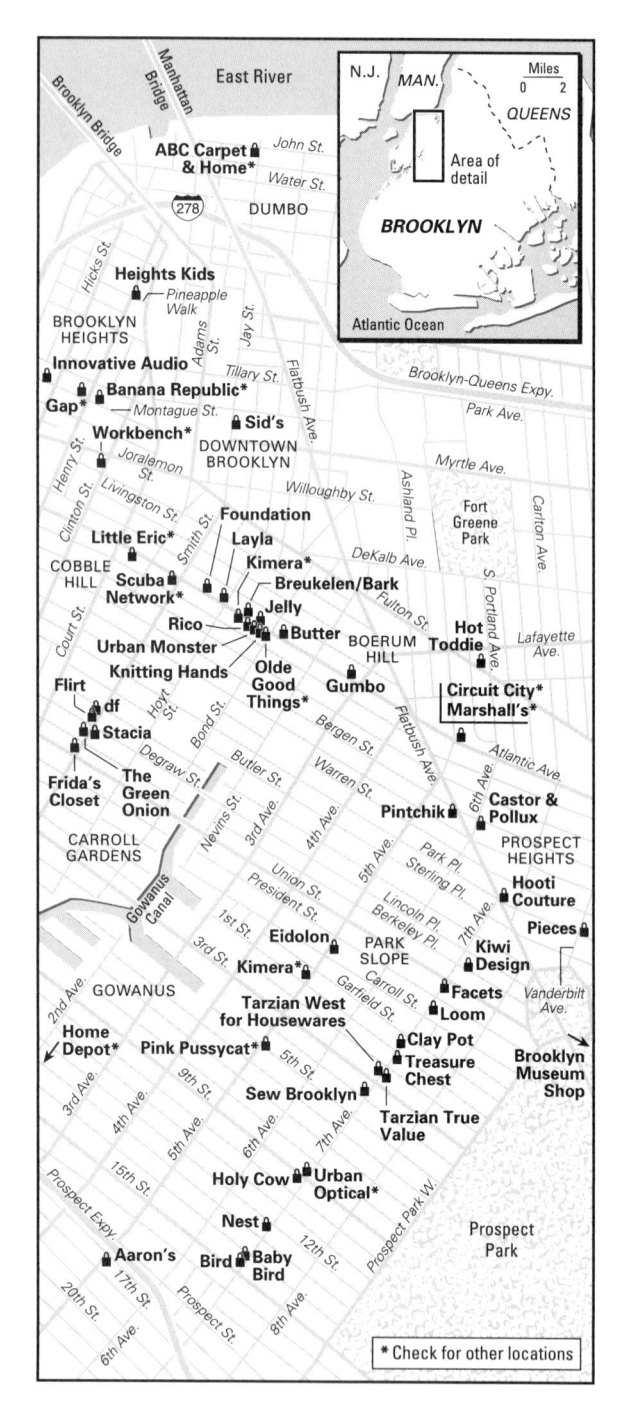

Brooklyn

Merchandise Index

MERCHANDISE

FASHION/BEAUTY

Accessories
Add
Alexia Crawford
Amy Downs Hats
Asprey
Barbara Feinman Millinery
Barneys Co-op
Barneys New York
Bergdorf Goodman
Bergdorf Men's
Bloomingdale's
Blue Bag
Bond 07 by Selima
Claire's Accessories
Destination
Eugenia Kim
Ferragamo, Salvatore
Girl Props
Hat Shop
Hattitude
Henri Bendel
Hermès
Intermix
Jack Spade
Jeffrey
J.J. Hat Center
Kate Spade
Kelly Christy
LaCrasia
Liliblue
Lisa Shaub
Loom
Lord & Taylor
Macy's
Marc Jacobs Accessories
Marsha D.D.
Mini Mini Market
Patch NYC
Paul Frank Store
Pearl River Mart
Roslyn
Saks Fifth Avenue
Shop Noir
Takashimaya
Urban Outfitters
Verve

Activewear
Active Wearhouse
Adidas
Avirex
Capezio
Champs
Crunch
Danskin
Dr. Jays
Equinox Energy Wear
KD Dance & Sport
Keiko
Lacoste
Malia Mills Swimwear
NBA Store
New Balance
Niketown
OM Yoga
On Stage Dance Shop
On Your Toes Dancewear
Paragon Sporting Goods
Patagonia
Princeton Ski Shop
Puma
Quiksilver
Reebok Store
Sansha
Scandinavian Ski & Sport Shop
Speedo Authentic Fitness
Sports Authority
Stackhouse
Starting Line
Super Runners Shop

Bridal
Amsale
Barneys New York
Bergdorf Goodman
Birnbaum & Bullock
Blue
Bridal Atelier by Mark Ingram
Bridal Garden
Clea Colet
Cose Bella
David's Bridal

vote at zagat.com 319

Merchandise Index

Fenaroli by Regalia
Gallery of Wearable Art
Gown Company
Here Comes the Bridesmaid
Jane Wilson-Marquis
Kleinfeld & Son
Macy's
Manolo Blahnik
Mary Adams, The Dress
Michelle Roth
Mika Inatome
Pilar Rossi
Reva Mivasagar
RK Bridal
Saks Fifth Avenue
Selia Yang
Stuart Weitzman
Suzanne Couture Millinery
Vera Wang Bridal Salon
Wedding Library
Yumi Katsura

Clothing: Designer
Agnès B.
Agnès B. Homme
Alexander McQueen
Anna Sui
Anne Fontaine
Anne Klein
April Cornell
A/X Armani Exchange
Barbara Bui
BCBG by Max Azria
Betsey Bunky Nini
Betsey Johnson
Built by Wendy
Burberry
Calvin Klein
Carolina Herrera
Catherine Malandrino
Celine
Cerruti
Chanel
Chloé
Christian Dior
Comme des Garçons
Costume National
Cynthia Rowley
Dana Buchman

D & G
Diane von Furstenberg
DKNY
Dolce & Gabbana
Donna Karan
Dosa
Emanuel Ungaro
Emilio Pucci
Emporio Armani
Ermenegildo Zegna
Escada
Etro
Fendi
Ferragamo, Salvatore
Ghost
Gianfranco Ferré
Giorgio Armani
Givenchy
Gucci
Helmut Lang
Henry Lehr
Hermès
Hugo Boss
Issey Miyake
Jaeger
Janet Russo
Jean Paul Gaultier
Jennifer Tyler
Jill Stuart
Jil Sander
John Varvatos
Joseph
Katayone Adeli
Kenneth Cole
Kenzo
Koos & Co.
Kors Michael Kors
Krizia
Lacoste
Laundry by Shelli Segal
Laura Ashley
Laura Biagiotti
Loro Piana
Louis Féraud
Louis Vuitton
Lucy Barnes
Malia Mills Swimwear
Malo
Marc by Marc Jacobs

Merchandise Index

Marc Jacobs
Marni
Max Mara
Max Studio
Mayle
Michael Kors
Missoni
Miu Miu
Morgane Le Fay
Moschino
Nanette Lepore
Nicole Farhi
Nicole Miller
OMO Norma Kamali
Paul & Joe
Paul Smith
Philosophy di Alberta Ferretti
Pleats Please
Plein Sud
Prada
Ralph Lauren
Reaction by Kenneth Cole
Roberto Cavalli
Rubin Chapelle
Sonia Rykiel
Stella McCartney
St. John
Tahari, Ltd.
Tommy Hilfiger
Tracy Feith
TSE Cashmere
Valentino
Ventilo
Versace
Vivienne Tam
Vivienne Westwood
Yohji Yamamoto
Yves St. Laurent Rive Gauche

Clothing: Men's

Abercrombie & Fitch
Active Wearhouse
Addison on Madison
Agnès B. Homme
Alice Underground
Alpana Bawa
American Eagle Outfitters
Andy's Chee-Pees
A.P.C.
Ascot Chang
A/X Armani Exchange
Banana Republic
Banana Republic Men's
Barneys Co-op
Barneys New York
Beacon's Closet
Beau Brummel
Benetton
Bergdorf Men's
Billy Martin's Western Wear
Bloomingdale's
Boss, The
Brioni
British American House
Brooklyn Public Couture
Brooks Brothers
Burberry
Burlington Coat Factory
Calvin Klein
Calypso Homme
Camouflage
Canal Jean Company
Casual Male Big & Tall
Century 21
Cerruti
Cherry
Club Monaco
Comme des Garçons
Costume National
Daffy's
D & G
Dave's Army Navy
Davide Cenci
DDC Lab
Designer Resale
Diesel Denim Gallery
Diesel Superstore
DKNY
Dolce & Gabbana
Domsey's
Donna Karan
Dr. Jays
Earl Jean
Eddie Bauer
Emporio Armani
Encore
Ermenegildo Zegna
Etro

Merchandise Index

Express Men
Façonnable
Family Jewels
Ferragamo, Salvatore
Filene's Basement
Fisch for the Hip
Frank Stella Ltd.
French Connection
Gant
Gap
Gerry's Menswear
Gianfranco Ferré
Giorgio Armani
Gucci
Guess?
H&M
Helmut Lang
Henry Lehr
Hermès
H. Herzfeld
Hickey Freeman
Hugo Boss
Ina
Issey Miyake
Jay Kos
J.Crew
Jean Paul Gaultier
Jeffrey
Jil Sander
Jimmy Jazz
J. Lindeberg Stockholm
J. McLaughlin
Jos A. Bank
J. Press
Kenneth Cole
Kenzo
Kmart
Krizia
Lacoste
Loehmann's
Lord & Taylor
Loro Piana
Louis Vuitton
Lucky Brand Dungarees
L'Uomo
Macy's
Malo
Marc by Marc Jacobs
Marc Jacobs

Marni
Marshall's
Men's Wearhouse
Nautica
Nicole Farhi
99X
North Beach Leather
Old Navy
Original Leather Store
Original Levi's Store
Oxxford Clothes
Parke & Ronen
Paul & Joe
Paul & Shark
Paul Smith
Paul Stuart
Peter Elliot
Phat Farm
P.J. Huntsman
Prada
Prato Fine Men's Wear
Quiksilver
R.A.G.
Rags-A-Go-Go
Ralph Lauren
Reaction by Kenneth Cole
Reminiscence
Replay Store
Roberto Cavalli
Robert Talbott
Rochester Big & Tall
Rothman's
Rubin Chapelle
Rue St. Denis
Saint Laurie Merchant Tailors
Saks Fifth Avenue
Scoop Men's
Sean
Seize Sur Vingt
Selvedge
Shirt Store
Sisley
Starting Line
Steven Alan
Stussy NYC
Takashimaya
Target
Ted Baker
Thomas Pink

Merchandise Index

Timberland
T.J. Maxx
Today's Man
Tokio 7
Tommy Hilfiger
Transit
Trash & Vaudeville
Turnbull & Asser
Union
Upland Trading
Urban Outfitters
Valentino
Versace
Vilebrequin
V.I.M.
What Comes/Goes Around
X-Large
Yohji Yamamoto
Yves St. Laurent Rive Gauche
Zara
Zeller Tuxedo

Clothing: Men's/Women's
(Stores carrying both)
Abercrombie & Fitch
Active Wearhouse
Alice Underground
Alpana Bawa
American Eagle Outfitters
Andy's Chee-Pees
A.P.C.
A/X Armani Exchange
Bagutta
Ballantyne Cashmere
Banana Republic
Barneys Co-op
Barneys New York
Beacon's Closet
Benetton
Billy Martin's Western Wear
Bloomingdale's
Brooklyn Public Couture
Brooks Brothers
Burberry
Burlington Coat Factory
Calvin Klein
Canal Jean Company
Century 21

Cerruti
Charles Tyrwhitt
Cherry
Club Monaco
Comme des Garçons
Costume National
Daffy's
D & G
DDC Lab
Designer Resale
Diesel Denim Gallery
Diesel Style Lab
Diesel Superstore
DKNY
Dö Kham
Dolce & Gabbana
Domsey's
Donna Karan
Earl Jean
Eddie Bauer
Emporio Armani
Encore
Ermenegildo Zegna
Etro
Façonnable
Family Jewels
Ferragamo, Salvatore
Filene's Basement
Fisch for the Hip
French Connection
Gant
Gap
Gianfranco Ferré
Giorgio Armani
Gucci
Guess?
H&M
Helmut Lang
Henry Lehr
Hermès
Holland & Holland
Hugo Boss
Ina
Issey Miyake
J.Crew
Jean Paul Gaultier
Jeffrey
Jil Sander
J. McLaughlin

Merchandise Index

Kenneth Cole
Kenzo
Kmart
Krizia
Lacoste
Loehmann's
Lord & Taylor
Loro Piana
Louis Vuitton
Lucky Brand Dungarees
Macy's
Malo
Marc by Marc Jacobs
Marc Jacobs
Marni
Marshall's
Nautica
Nicole Farhi
99X
North Beach Leather
N. Peal
Old Navy
OM Boutique
1 on G
Original Leather Store
Original Levi's Store
Parke & Ronen
Paul & Joe
Paul Frank Store
Paul Stuart
Phat Farm
Pieces
Prada
Quiksilver
Rags-A-Go-Go
Ralph Lauren
Reaction by Kenneth Cole
Reminiscence
Roberto Cavalli
Rubin Chapelle
Rue St. Denis
Saks Fifth Avenue
Seize Sur Vingt
Selvedge
Shanghai Tang
Sisley
Takashimaya
Target
Thomas Pink
T.J. Maxx
Tokio 7
Tommy Hilfiger
Transit
Trash & Vaudeville
Treasure Chest
Turnbull & Asser
Urban Outfitters
Valentino
Versace
V.I.M.
What Comes/Goes Around
X-Large
Yohji Yamamoto
Yves St. Laurent Rive Gauche
Zara

Clothing: Women's

A. Atelier
Abercrombie & Fitch
a.cheng
Active Wearhouse
Agnès B.
Alexander McQueen
Alice Underground
Alpana Bawa
American Eagle Outfitters
Andy's Chee-Pees
Anik
Anna Sui
Anne Fontaine
Anne Klein
Anthropologie
A.P.C.
April Cornell
Assets London
A-Uno
A/X Armani Exchange
Ballantyne Cashmere
Banana Republic
Barami Studio
Barbara Bui
Barneys Co-op
Barneys New York
BCBG by Max Azria
Beacon's Closet
Benetton
Bergdorf Goodman
Betsey Bunky Nini

Merchandise Index

Betsey Johnson
Big Drop
Billy Martin's Western Wear
Bird
Bisou-Bisou
Bloomingdale's
Blue
Bond 07 by Selima
Brooklyn Public Couture
Brooks Brothers
Built by Wendy
Burberry
Burlington Coat Factory
Butter
Calvin Klein
Calypso
Canal Jean Company
Carolina Herrera
Castor & Pollux
Catherine Malandrino
Celine
Century 21
Cerruti
Chanel
Cherry
Chloé
Christian Dior
Club Monaco
Comme des Garçons
Costume National
Crush
Cynthia Rowley
Daffy's
Dana Buchman
D & G
Darryl's
DDC Lab
Dernier Cri
Designer Resale
Diane von Furstenberg
Diesel Denim Gallery
Diesel Superstore
DKNY
Dolce & Gabbana
Domsey's
Donna Karan
Dosa
Earl Jean
Eddie Bauer
Eidolon
Emanuel Ungaro
Emilio Pucci
Emporio Armani
Encore
Erica Tanov
Ermenegildo Zegna
Escada
Etro
Eva
Express
Fab 208 NYC
Façonnable
Family Jewels
Fendi
Ferragamo, Salvatore
Filene's Basement
Fisch for the Hip
Flirt
Foley & Corinna
French Connection
French Corner
Frida's Closet
Gant
Gap
Ghost
Gianfranco Ferré
Giorgio Armani
Givenchy
Gucci
Guess?
H&M
Harriet Love
Hedra Prue
Helmut Lang
Henri Bendel
Henry Lehr
Hermès
Hotel Venus by Patricia Field
Hugo Boss
Ibiza
IF
Ina
Intermix
Issey Miyake
Jaeger
Janet Russo
J.Crew
Jean Paul Gaultier

vote at zagat.com 325

Merchandise Index

Jeffrey
Jill Stuart
Jil Sander
Jimmy's
J. McLaughlin
Joseph
Katayone Adeli
Keiko
Kenneth Cole
Kenzo
Kimera
Kirna Zabête
Kiwi Design
Kmart
Koos & Co.
Kors Michael Kors
Krizia
Lacoste
Language
Laundry by Shelli Segal
Laura Ashley
Laura Biagiotti
Les Copains
Linda Dresner
Loehmann's
Lord & Taylor
Loro Piana
Louis Vuitton
Luca Luca
Lucky Brand Dungarees
Lucy Barnes
Macy's
Malia Mills Swimwear
Malo
Marc by Marc Jacobs
Marc Jacobs
Marni
Marshall's
Martin
Max Mara
Meg
Michael Kors
Missoni
Miss Sixty
Miu Miu
Montmartre
Morgane Le Fay
Moschino
Nancy & Co.

Nanette Lepore
Nautica
New York Look
Nicole Farhi
Nicole Miller
Noir et Blanc...Bis
North Beach Leather
N. Peal
Old Navy
Olive and Bette's
OMO Norma Kamali
Original Leather Store
Original Levi's Store
Parke & Ronen
Paul & Joe
Paul Stuart
Pearl River Mart
Phat Farm
Philosophy di Alberta Ferretti
Pieces
Pleats Please
Plein Sud
Pookie & Sebastian
Prada
Purdy Girl
Rags-A-Go-Go
Ralph Lauren
Rampage
Reaction by Kenneth Cole
Really Great Things
Reminiscence
Roberto Cavalli
Rubin Chapelle
Rue St. Denis
Saks Fifth Avenue
Scoop
Searle
Seize Sur Vingt
Selia Yang
Selvedge
Seven New York
Shanghai Tang
Shop
Sisley
Sonia Rykiel
Sorelle Firenze
Stacia
Stella McCartney
Steven Alan

Merchandise Index

Steven Stolman
St. John
Sude
Tahari, Ltd.
Takashimaya
Target
TG-170
Thomas Pink
T.J. Maxx
Tokio 7
Tommy Hilfiger
Tracy Feith
Trash & Vaudeville
TSE Cashmere
Turnbull & Asser
Untitled
Urban Outfitters
Valentino
Variazioni
Versace
Vertigo
V.I.M.
Vivienne Tam
Vivienne Westwood
What Comes/Goes Around
Yohji Yamamoto
Yves St. Laurent Rive Gauche
Zara
Zero

Clothing/Shoes: Children's

April Cornell
Au Chat Botte
Baby Bird
BabyGap
Barneys New York
Bebe Thompson
Ben's for Kids
Bergdorf Goodman
Berkley Girl
Betwixt
Bloomingdale's
Bombalulus
Bonpoint
Bu & the Duck
buybuy Baby
Calypso Enfant & Bebe
Catimini
Century 21
Children's Place, The
Daffy's
East Side Kids
Erica Tanov
Estella
Filene's Basement
GapKids
Granny-Made
Great Feet
Green Onion
Greenstones
Gumbo
Gymboree
Harry's Shoes
Hot Toddie
Infinity
Jacadi
Julian and Sara
Just for Tykes
Kids R Us
Kmart
La Petite Etoile
Laura Ashley
Lester's
Lilliput
Little Eric
Lord & Taylor
Macy's
Magic Windows
Marsha D.D.
Marshall's
Morris Brothers
Oilily
OshKosh B'Gosh
Peanutbutter & Jane
Pearl River Mart
Petit Bateau
Planet Kids
Saks Fifth Avenue
Sam & Seb
Shoofly
Space Kiddets
Talbots Kids and Babies
Target
Tartine et Chocolat
Tip-Top Shoes
Urban Monster
Z. Baby Company

vote at zagat.com

Merchandise Index

Clothing/Shoes: Tween/Teen
Abercrombie & Fitch
Active Wearhouse
Adidas
Aldo
American Eagle Outfitters
Anthropologie
Avirex
Bebe
Berkley Girl
Betsey Johnson
Betwixt
Big Drop
Bloomingdale's
Brooks Brothers
Camper
Century 21
Champs
Claire's Accessories
Daffy's
Domsey's
Dr. Jays
Earl Jean
Express
French Connection
Gap
H&M
Infinity
J.Crew
Joyce Leslie
Kmart
Lester's
Lucky Brand Dungarees
Macy's
Magic Windows
Marsha D.D.
Morris Brothers
Old Navy
Patagonia
Paul & Shark
Paul Frank Store
Petit Bateau
Phat Farm
Planet Kids
Pop Shop
Puma
Purdy Girl
Quiksilver
Ralph Lauren
Reaction by Kenneth Cole
Reebok Store
Replay Store
Rothman's
Saks Fifth Avenue
Skechers
Stackhouse
Steve Madden
Strawberry
Timberland
Triple Five Soul
Urban Outfitters
Vertigo
V.I.M.
Wet Seal
What Comes/Goes Around
X-Large
Zara

Consignment/Thrift/Vintage
Alice Underground
Allan & Suzi
Amarcord Vintage Fashion
Andy's Chee-Pees
Angela's Vintage Boutique
Angel Street Thrift Shop
A Second Chance
Beacon's Closet
Bis Designer Resale
Brooklyn Public Couture
Cheap Jack's
Cherry
City Opera Thrift Shop
Council Thrift Shop
Designer Resale
Domsey's
Encore
Family Jewels
Filth Mart
Fisch for the Hip
Goodwill Industries
Hooti Couture
Housing Works Thrift Shop
Ina
Jim Smiley
Kavanagh's
La Boutique Resale

Merchandise Index

Love Saves the Day
Memorial Sloan-Kettering Shop
Michael's
Out of the Closet Thrift Shop
Patina
Rags-A-Go-Go
Reminiscence
Resurrection
Ritz Furs
Rue St. Denis
Salvation Army
Screaming Mimi's
17 at 17 Thrift Shop
Spence-Chapin Thrift Shops
Stella Dallas
Tatiana
Tokio 7
Tokyo Joe
What Comes/Goes Around

Cosmetics/Toiletries

Aedes De Venustas
Anna Sui
Art of Shaving
Aveda
Avon Salon and Spa
Barneys Co-op
Barneys New York
Bath & Body Works
Bath Island
Bergdorf Goodman
Bergdorf Men's
bliss
Bloomingdale's
Body Shop
Boyd's Madison Avenue
Bumble and bumble
Calvin Klein
Carapan Urban Spa & Store
Caron Boutique
Caswell-Massey
Chanel
Clyde's
C.O. Bigelow Chemists
Crabtree & Evelyn
Creed
Demeter
e. Harcourt's
Elizabeth Arden
Erbe
FACE Stockholm
Floris of London
Frédéric Fekkai
Fresh
Georgette Klinger
Giorgio Armani
Helena Rubenstein
Helmut Lang Parfums
Henri Bendel
H20 Plus
Il Makiage
Janet Sartin
Jo Malone
Kiehl's
Kimara Ahnert
L'Occitane
Lord & Taylor
M.A.C. Cosmetics
Macy's
Madina Milano
Make Up For Ever
Mario Badescu Skin Care
Origins
Penhaligon's
Perfumania
Perlier Kelemata
Prada
Ray Beauty Supply
Repêchage: Spa de Beauté
Ricky's
Saks Fifth Avenue
SCO
Sephora
Shiseido
Shu Uemura Beauty Boutique
Takashimaya
Yves St. Laurent Rive Gauche
Zitomer Pharmacy

Eyewear

Alain Mikli
Cohen's Fashion Optical
Eye Man
Facial Index
For Eyes
H.L. Purdy
Joël Name Optique de Paris
Leonard Poll

Merchandise Index

Lunettes et Chocolat
Morgenthal Frederics
Myoptics
Oculus 20/20
Oliver Peoples
Robert Marc
Selima Optique
Sol Moscot
Urban Optical

Furs
Ben Kahn Furs
Bergdorf Goodman
Bloomingdale's
Fendi
Goldin-Feldman
J. Mendel
Ritz Furs
Saks Fifth Avenue

Handbags
Add
Anya Hindmarch
Artbag
Bally
Barneys Co-op
Barneys New York
Bergdorf Goodman
Bloomingdale's
Blue Bag
Bottega Veneta
Botticelli
Celine
Chanel
Charles Jourdan
Christian Dior
Coach
Cole Haan
Crouch & Fitzgerald
D & G
Deco Jewels
Destination
Dolce & Gabbana
Dooney & Bourke
Express
Fendi
Ferragamo, Salvatore
Fratelli Rossetti
Furla
Ghurka
Gianfranco Ferré
Gucci
Henri Bendel
Hermès
Hogan
Holland & Holland
Il Bisonte
Jeffrey
Judith Leiber
Jutta Neumann
Kate Spade
Lana Marks
LeSportsac
Longchamp
Loom
Lord & Taylor
Louis Vuitton
Lulu Guinness
Macy's
Marc Jacobs Accessories
Missoni
Miu Miu
Nine West
Patch NYC
Peter Hermann
Prada
Rafe
Robert Clergerie
Saks Fifth Avenue
Samuel Jackson Design
Sergio Rossi
Sigerson Morrison Bags
Steve Madden
Suarez
T. Anthony
Triple Five Soul
Verve
Via Spiga
Walter Steiger
Yves St. Laurent Rive Gauche

Hosiery/Lingerie
ABH Design
Agent Provocateur
Anthropologie
A.W. Kaufman
Barneys New York
Bergdorf Goodman
Bloomingdale's

Merchandise Index

Bodyhints
Bonne Nuit
Bra Smyth
Brief Encounters
Burlington Coat Factory
Century 21
Daffy's
Enelra
Eres
Filene's Basement
Fogal
H&M
Henri Bendel
Joovay
Laina Jane
La Perla
La Petite Coquette
Le Corset by Selima
Legs Beautiful Hosiery
Lingerie on Lex
Livi's Lingerie
Loehmann's
Lord & Taylor
Macy's
Marshall's
Mixona
Nisa
Only Hearts
Orchard Corset
Pink Pussycat
Pink Slip
Religious Sex
Roberta's Lingerie
Saks Fifth Avenue
Takashimaya
Target
37=1
T.J. Maxx
Town Shop
Urban Outfitters
Victoria's Secret
Wolford

Jeans
Active Wearhouse
Barneys Co-op
Barneys New York
Bergdorf Goodman
Bloomingdale's
Canal Jean Company
Diesel Denim Gallery
Diesel Superstore
Dr. Jays
Earl Jean
Forréal
Gap
Guess?
Henri Bendel
Jill Stuart
Lucky Brand Dungarees
Macy's
Mavi Jean
Miss Sixty
Original Levi's Store
Pookie & Sebastian
Selvedge
Transit
V.I.M.
What Comes/Goes Around

Jewelry
Costume/Semiprecious
Add
Agatha
Alexia Crawford
Anna Sui
Beads of Paradise
Boucher
Calypso Bijoux
City Opera Thrift Shop
Claire's Accessories
Cooper-Hewitt Shop
Dö Kham
Encore
Erwin Pearl
Family Jewels
Filene's Basement
Fragments
Gas Bijoux
Henri Bendel
Intermix
Jaded
Jelena Behrend
Kmart
Layla
Loom
Lord & Taylor
Macy's

vote at zagat.com 331

Merchandise Index

Mariko
Marsha D.D.
Met. Museum of Art Shop
Michael's
New York Look
OM Boutique
1 on G
Roslyn
Saks Fifth Avenue
Screaming Mimi's
17 at 17 Thrift Shop
Shop Noir
Spence-Chapin Thrift Shops
Steven Alan
Steven Stolman
Tatiana
Tokio 7
Verve
Yellow Door

Fine
Aaron Basha
Aaron Faber Gallery
ABC Carpet & Home
Anne Klein
Asprey
Barneys New York
Bergdorf Goodman
Bloom
Borealis
Buccellati
Bulgari
Cartier
Castor & Pollux
Cécile et Jeanne
Cellini
Chanel Fine Jewelry
Chloé
Chopard
Christian Dior Joaillerie
Chrome Hearts
Clay Pot
David Saity Jewelry
David Webb
David Yurman
Destination
Elizabeth Locke
Facets
Fenaroli by Regalia
Filene's Basement
Fortunoff
Fourteen Wall Street Jewelers
Fragments
Georg Jensen
Graff
Harry Winston
Helen Woodhull
H. Stern
Jeffrey
J. Mavec & Company
Joan Michlin Gallery
Lalaounis
Lalique
Language
La Petite Princesse
Liliblue
Links of London
London Jewelers
Lord & Taylor
Macy's
Me & Ro
Met. Museum of Art Shop
Michael C. Fina
Michael Dawkins
Michael Eigen
Mikimoto
Mish
MoMA Design Store
Pearldaddy
Piaget
Push
Really Great Things
Reinstein Ross
Robert Lee Morris
Roslyn
Saks Fifth Avenue
Seaman Schepps
Stephen Russell
Stuart Moore
Swarovski
Takashimaya
Ted Muehling
Tiffany & Co.
Tourneau
Van Cleef & Arpels
Verdura
William Barthman
Yellow Door
Zales Jewelers

Merchandise Index

Vintage
Aaron Faber Gallery
ABC Carpet & Home
A La Vieille Russie
Alice Underground
Angela's Vintage Boutique
Antiquarium
Barneys New York
Deco Jewels
Destination
Edith Weber & Assoc.
Eye Candy
Family Jewels
Fred Leighton
James Robinson
James II Galleries Ltd.
Jim Smiley
J. Mavec & Company
Kentshire Galleries
Michael Ashton
Ralph Lauren
Rue St. Denis
Saks Fifth Avenue
Screaming Mimi's
Stella Dallas
Stephen Russell
Tender Buttons
What Comes/Goes Around

Maternity
A Pea in the Pod
Bloomingdale's
Cadeau
H&M
Kmart
Liz Lange Maternity
Macy's
Maternity Works
Mimi Maternity
Mommy Chic
Motherhood Maternity
Pumpkin Maternity
Target
Veronique

Shoes: Men's/Women's
Aerosoles
Aldo
Allen Edmonds
Arche
A. Testoni
Bally
Barneys Co-op
Barneys New York
Belgian Shoes
Bergdorf Goodman
Bergdorf Men's
Bloomingdale's
Botticelli
Bruno Magli
Burberry
Camper
Century 21
Cesare Paciotti
Chanel
Charles Jourdan
Christian Louboutin
Chuckies
Cole Haan
Constança Basto
Daffy's
David Aaron
David Z.
Edmundo Castillo
Enzo Angiolini
Eric
Ferragamo, Salvatore
Filene's Basement
Florsheim Shoe Shops
Fratelli Rossetti
French Sole
Geraldine
Giorgio Armani
Giraudon
Gucci
Harry's Shoes
Helene Arpels
Hogan
Hollywould
Jeffrey
Jelly
Jimmy Choo
J.M. Weston
John Fluevog
John Lobb
Johnston & Murphy
Juno
Jutta Neumann
Kenneth Cole

vote at zagat.com 333

Merchandise Index

Kerquelen
Kmart
LaDuca Shoes
Loehmann's
Lord & Taylor
Macy's
Manolo Blahnik
Maraolo
Mare
Marshall's
Medici
Michel Perry
Nancy Geist
New York Look
Nine West
Otto Tootsi Plohound
Payless Shoe Source
Peter Fox Shoes
Prada
Ralph Lauren
Reaction by Kenneth Cole
Robert Clergerie
Sacco
Saks Fifth Avenue
Sergio Rossi
Shoe Biz
Sigerson Morrison
Skechers
Stephane Kélian
Steve Madden
Stuart Weitzman
Stubbs & Wootton
Syms
Tano
Target
Timberland
Tip-Top Shoes
T.J. Maxx
Tod's
Unisa
Varda
Verve
Via Spiga
Walter Steiger
Warren Edwards

Sneakers
Active Wearhouse
Adidas
Alife Rivington Club
Athlete's Foot
Blades Board and Skate
Champs
City Sports
Dr. Jays
EMS
Foot Locker
Grand Central Racquet
Harry's Shoes
Kmart
Lady Foot Locker
Lester's
Lord & Taylor
Macy's
Mason's Tennis Mart
Modell's
NBA Store
New Balance
Niketown
99X
Paragon Sporting Goods
Paul Frank Store
Payless Shoe Source
Puma
Scandinavian Ski & Sport Shop
Soccer Sport Supply
Sports Authority
Starting Line
Super Runners Shop
Target
Tip-Top Shoes
Transit
V.I.M.

Watches
Asprey
Barneys New York
Bloom
Buccellati
Bulgari
Cartier
Cellini
Chanel Fine Jewelry
Chopard
Christian Dior Joaillerie
David Webb
David Yurman
Dunhill

Merchandise Index

Flight 001
Fortunoff
Fossil
Fourteen Wall Street Jewelers
Fred Leighton
Gucci
Harry Winston
H. Stern
Joan Michlin Gallery
Joseph Edwards
Kenjo
Kmart
London Jewelers
Lord & Taylor
Macy's
Manfredi
Michael Ashton
Michael Eigen
MoMA Design Store

Movado
Niketown
Paragon Sporting Goods
Paul Frank Store
Piaget
Really Great Things
Robert Lee Morris
Saks Fifth Avenue
Stuart Moore
Swatch
Tag Heuer
Tiffany & Co.
Tourneau
Treasure Chest
Van Cleef & Arpels
Via Spiga
Wempe
William Barthman
Zales Jewelers

HOME/GARDEN

Bathroom Fixtures/Tiles
AF Supply Corp.
Ann Sacks Tile & Stone
Artistic Tile
Bed, Bath & Beyond
Brass Center
Country Floors
Davis & Warshow, Inc.
Design Source/Dave Sanders
Gracious Home
Hastings Bath & Tile
Howard Kaplan Bath Shop
Ideal Tile
Kraft
Nemo Tile Company
New York Replacement
P.E. Guerin
Restoration Hardware
Sherle Wagner
Simon's Hardware & Bath
Urban Archaeology
Villeroy & Boch
Waterworks

Bed/Bath
ABC Carpet & Home
ABC Carpet & Home Warehse.
Apartment, The

Apartment 48
April Cornell
Armani Casa
auto
Baker
Bark
Bed, Bath & Beyond
Bergdorf Goodman
Bloomingdale's
Calvin Klein
Charles P. Rogers Bed
Crate & Barrel
Details
Dö Kham
Drexel Heritage
E. Braun & Co.
Ethan Allen
Filene's Basement
Flou
Frette
Gracious Home
Hammacher Schlemmer & Co.
Harris Levy
Howard Kaplan Bath Shop
Jennifer Convertibles
Jensen-Lewis
John Derian
Kmart

vote at zagat.com

Merchandise Index

Kreiss Collection
La Cafetière
Laura Ashley
Layla
Laytner's Linen & Home
Léron
Ligne Roset
Macy's
Marshall's
Maurice Villency
Nancy Koltes at Home
Nest
OM Boutique
Palazzetti
Pearl River Mart
Pier 1 Imports
Pondicherri
Porthault
Portico
Pottery Barn
Pratesi
Ralph Lauren
Restoration Hardware
Schweitzer Linen
Shabby Chic
Stella
Takashimaya
Target
Tarzian West For Housewares
Terence Conran Shop
Thomasville
Waterworks

Cabinetry
Boffi SoHo
Elgot
Home Depot
Krups Kitchens & Bath
Poggenpohl U.S. Inc.

Children's Bedding/Layette
Au Chat Botte
Baby Bird
Bellini
buybuy Baby
Erica Tanov
Heights Kids
Jacadi
Just for Tykes
Kid's Supply Co.
La Petite Etoile
Macy's
Saks Fifth Avenue
Wicker Garden

Cookware
Bed, Bath & Beyond
Bloomingdale's
Bodum
Bowery Kitchen Supplies
Bridge Kitchenware
Broadway Panhandler
Crate & Barrel
Dean & Deluca
Gracious Home
International Cutlery
Kam Man
Kmart
Macy's
Moss
Pearl River Mart
S Feldman Housewares
Tarzian West For Housewares
Williams-Sonoma
Zabar's

Fine China/Crystal
Avventura
Baccarat
Bardith
Barneys New York
Bergdorf Goodman
Bernardaud
Bloomingdale's
Christofle
Daum
Fortunoff
Gallery Orrefors
Georg Jensen
James Robinson
Lalique
Macy's
Michael C. Fina
Moss
Saks Fifth Avenue
Simon Pearce Glass
Steuben
Swarovski
Takashimaya

subscribe to zagat.com

Merchandise Index

Tiffany & Co.
Villeroy & Boch

Furniture/Home Furnishings
Babies'/Children's
ABC Carpet & Home
Albee Baby Carriage Co.
Apartment, The
Au Chat Botte
Bear's Place, A
Bellini
Ben's for Kids
Bombay Company
buybuy Baby
Ethan Allen
Gracious Home
Just for Tykes
Kid's Supply Co.
Little Folk Art
Planet Kids
Schneider's
Wicker Garden

General
ABC Carpet & Home
ABC Carpet (Carpets/Rugs)
ABC Carpet & Home Warehse.
ABH Design
Adrien Linford
Aero
Alan Moss
American Folk Art Museum
An American Craftsman
Anthropologie
Apartment, The
Apartment 48
April Cornell
Armani Casa
AsiaStore/Asia Society
auto
Baker
Banana Republic
B&B Italia
Bark
Barneys New York
Barton-Sharpe
BDDW
Bed, Bath & Beyond
Bergdorf Goodman

Beyul
Bloomingdale's
Bodum
Bombay Company
Breukelen
Brooklyn Museum Shop
Brookstone
California Closets
Calvin Klein
Cappellini Modern Age
Cap Sud
Carlyle Convertibles
Cassina USA
Ceramica
Charles P. Rogers Bed
C.I.T.E. Design
Classic Sofa
Clio
Coconut Company
Cooper-Hewitt Shop
Country Home & Comfort
Craft Caravan
Crate & Barrel
ddc domus design collections
Demolition Depot
Desiron
Details
Dialogica
Domain
Donna Karan
Donzella
Door Store
Drexel Heritage
Dune
Einstein-Moomjy
Ethan Allen
Fishs Eddy
Flou
Fortunoff
Foundation
Galileo
George Smith
Global Table
Goodwill Industries
Gothic Cabinet Craft
Gracious Home
Hable Construction
Hammacher Schlemmer & Co.
Hold Everything

vote at zagat.com

Merchandise Index

Homer
Housing Works Thrift Shop
Illuminations
Intérieurs
Jamson Whyte
Jennifer Convertibles
Jensen-Lewis
John Derian
Jonathan Adler
Kam Man
Kar'ikter
Karkula
Kartell
Kentshire Galleries
Kimera
Kmart
Knoll
Kraft
Kreiss Collection
La Belle Epoque
La Cafetière
Lafco
Laytner's Linen & Home
Le Décor Français
Lee's Studio
Le Fanion
Les Migrateurs
Ligne Roset
Liz O'Brien
MacKenzie-Childs
Macy's
Marimekko
Marshall's
Maurice Villency
Mecox Gardens
Memorial Sloan-Kettering Shop
Met. Museum of Art Shop
Michael Anchin Glass Co.
Michael C. Fina
Modernica
Modern Stone Age
MoMA Design Store
Mood Indigo
Moon River Chattel
Moss
Mxyplyzyk
Nest
Neue Galerie
Nicole Farhi
1950
Olde Good Things
Palazzetti
Patina
Pearl River Mart
Pier 1 Imports
Pierre Deux
Pompanoosuc Mills
Pondicherri
Pottery Barn
Ralph Lauren
Repertoire
Restoration Hardware
Rico
Roche Bobois
Room
Rooms & Gardens
Rug Company
Safavieh Carpets
Saks Fifth Avenue
Salon Moderne
Salvation Army
Scott Jordan Furniture
Scully & Scully
17 at 17 Thrift Shop
S Feldman Housewares
Shabby Chic
Shanghai Tang
Spence-Chapin Thrift Shops
Stickley, Audi & Co.
Straight from the Crate
Surprise, Surprise
Takashimaya
Tarzian West For Housewares
Terence Conran Shop
Thomas Moser Cabinet
Thomasville
Todd Hase
Totem Design Group
Troy
Tucker Robbins
Uproar Home
Villeroy & Boch
Vitra
Wicker Garden
William Wayne
Workbench
Xukuma
Yellow Door

Garden
Bed, Bath & Beyond
Chelsea Garden Center Home
Garden Shop/Hort. Soc.

Merchandise Index

In the Market
Kmart
Lexington Gardens
Mecox Gardens
Munder-Skiles
Smith & Hawken
Takashimaya
Treillage

Hardware
Gracious Home
Home Depot
Janovic Plaza
Kmart
Metropolitan Lumber
Pintchik
Sid's
Simon's Hardware & Bath
Target
Tarzian True Value
Vercesi Hardware

Lighting
Artemide
Bowery Lighting
Cap Sud
Gracious Home
Ingo Maurer Making Light
Just Bulbs
Just Shades
Kid's Supply Co.
Lee's Studio
Les Migrateurs
Lightforms
Lighting by Gregory
Lighting Center
Michael Anchin Glass Co.
O'Lampia Studio
Oriental Lamp Shade Co.
Rico

Art Supplies
A.I. Friedman
Industrial Plastic Supply
Kremer Pigments
Lee's Art Shop
New York Central Art Supply

Major Appliances
Bed, Bath & Beyond
Bloomingdale's
Bowery Kitchen Supplies
Brookstone
Costco Wholesale
Drimmers
Elgot
Gracious Home
Gringer & Sons
Home Depot
Kmart
Krups Kitchens & Bath
Macy's
P.C. Richard & Son
Poggenpohl U.S. Inc.
S Feldman Housewares
Target
Tarzian West For Housewares
Williams-Sonoma
Zabar's

Silver
A La Vieille Russie
Asprey
Barneys New York
Bergdorf Goodman
Bloomingdale's
Buccellati
Cartier
Christofle
Fortunoff
Georg Jensen
James Robinson
James II Galleries Ltd.
Macy's
Michael C. Fina
Moss
Saks Fifth Avenue
Scully & Scully
Tiffany & Co.

LIFESTYLE

Pearl Paint
Sam Flax
Utrecht

Baby Gear
Albee Baby Carriage Co.
Bellini

vote at zagat.com 339

Merchandise Index

Ben's for Kids
Bloomingdale's
buybuy Baby
Heights Kids
Just for Tykes
Kmart
Macy's
Planet Kids
Schneider's
Target
Urban Monster

Cameras/Video Equipment
Adorama Camera
Alkit Pro Camera
B&H Photo-Video Pro Audio
Camera Land
Circuit City
42nd Street Photo
Ken Hansen Photographic
Olden Camera
Sony Style
Willoughby's

CDs/Videos/Records/DVDs
Academy Records & CDs
At the Gryphon
Bleecker Bob's Golden Oldies
Bleecker Street Records
Blockbuster Video
Casa Amadeo
Champagne Video
Colony Music
Disc-O-Rama Music World
Downstairs Records
Eight Ball Records
Fat Beats
Finyl Vinyl
Footlight Records
Fye
Generation Records
HMV
Hollywood Video
Holy Cow
House of Oldies
Jammyland
J&R Music World
Jazz Record Center
Joe's CDs
Kim's Mediapolis
Midnight Records
Norman's Sound & Vision
NYCD
Other Music
Rebel Rebel
Record Explosion
Rocks in your Head
Sam Goody
Satellite Records
Sonic Groove
Sound and Fury
St. Marks Sounds
Strider Records
Subterranean Records
Suncoast Motion Picture Co.
TLA Video
Tower Records/Video
Vinylmania
Virgin Megastore

Cigar/Smoke Shops
Angelo & Maxies
Arnold Tobacco Shop
Barclay-Rex
Davidoff of Geneva
De La Concha Tobacconist
Dunhill
JR Cigar
Nat Sherman
OK Cigars

Drugstores (Specialty)
Boyd's Madison Avenue
Clyde's
C.O. Bigelow Chemists
Zitomer Pharmacy

Electronics
Apple Store SoHo
Bang & Olufsen
Best Buy
Canal Hi-Fi Inc
Circuit City
CompUSA
Cosmophonic Sound
DataVision
Gateway Country
Harvey Electronics
Innovative Audio
J&R Computer World

Merchandise Index

Lyric Hi-Fi
Park Avenue Audio
P.C. Richard & Son
Radio Shack
RCS Computer Experience
Sony Style
Sound by Singer
Sound City
Staples
Stereo Exchange
Tekserve
Uncle's Stereo
Wiz, The

Fabrics/Notions
ABH Design
B&J Fabrics
Beckenstein
Beckenstein Fabrics/Int.
City Quilter
Hyman Hendler and Sons
Il Bisonte
Joe's Fabric Warehouse
Le Décor Français
M&J Trimming/Buttons
Marimekko
Mendel Goldberg Fabrics
Mood Fabrics Inc.
New York Elegant Fabric
P&S Fabrics
Paron Fabrics
Paterson Silks
Pierre Deux
Poli Fabrics
Rosen & Chaddick Textiles
Sew Brooklyn
Steinlauf & Stoller
Tender Buttons

Gadgets
Brookstone
CCS Counter Spy Shop
Hammacher Schlemmer & Co.
Quark Spy
Sharper Image
TKNY

Gifts/Novelties
Adriana's Caravan
Alphabets

American Craft Museum Shop
American Folk Art Museum
American Museum/Nat. History
AsiaStore/Asia Society
Brooklyn Museum Shop
Carnegie Cards & Gifts
Cloisters, The
Cooper-Hewitt Shop
Disney
Dylan's Candy Bar
E.A.T. Gifts
El Museo Del Barrio
ESPN Zone
Frick Collection
Guggenheim Museum Stores
Hard Rock Cafe
Harley Davidson of NY
Illuminations
International Ctr. Photography
Intrepid Sea-Air-Space
Jewish Museum
La Brea
Met. Museum of Art Shop
Mets Clubhouse Shop
MoMA Design Store
Morgan Library Shop
MTV Store
Museum/City of New York
NBC Experience
Neue Galerie
New Museum Store
New York Firefighter's Friend
New York 911
New York Public Library Shop
New York Transit Museum
One Shubert Alley
Pop Shop
Sanrio (aka Hello Kitty Store)
Studio Museum/Harlem
Tah Poozie
Theatre Circle
Whitney Museum Store
World, The
Yankee Clubhouse Shop

Instruments/Sheet Music
Carmine Street Guitars
Chelsea Second Hand Guitars
Colony Music

vote at zagat.com

Merchandise Index

48th Street Custom Guitars
Joseph Patelson Music House
Juilliard Bookstore
Mandolin Brothers
Manny's Music
Matt Umanov Guitars
Music Inn
Rogue Music
Rudy's Music Shop
Sam Ash
Steinway and Sons
30th Street Guitars
Tribal Soundz

Knitting/Needlepoint
Annie & Company Needlepoint
Downtown Yarns
Erica Wilson Needle Works
Gotta Knit
Knits Incredible
Knitting Hands
Knitting 321
Lion & the Lamb
Magry Knits
Purl
Rita's Needlepoint
School Products Co.
Smiley's
Stitches East
String Yarns
Wool Gathering
Yarn Co., The
Yarn Connection

Luggage
Altman Luggage
Bag House
Bloomingdale's
Bottega Veneta
Crouch & Fitzgerald
EMS
Flight 001
Ghurka
Gucci
Holland & Holland
Hunting World
Innovation Luggage
Jack Spade
Jobson's Luggage
Kate Spade Travel
Kmart
LeSportsac
Longchamp
Lord & Taylor
Louis Vuitton
Macy's
Paragon Sporting Goods
Patagonia
Peter Hermann
Rafe
Robert Clergerie
Saks Fifth Avenue
T. Anthony
Target
Triple Five Soul
Tumi

Pet Supplies
American Kennels
Barking Zoo
Barkley
Beasty Feast
Biscuits & Baths Doggy Village
Calling All Pets
Doggie-Do & Pussycats Too
Fetch
Four Paws Club, The
Furry Paws
Karen's for People and Pets
Le Chien Pet Salon
Petco
Peters Necessities for Pets
Petland Discounts
Pet Stop
Spoiled Brats
Z Spot

Sex Shops
DeMask
Eve's Garden
Leather Man, The
Noose, The
Pink Pussycat
Pleasure Chest
Purple Passion/DV8
Toys In Babeland

Sporting Goods
Blades Board and Skate
Capitol Fishing Tackle Co.

Merchandise Index

Champs
City Sports
EMS
Gerry Cosby & Co.
Grand Central Racquet
Gym Source
Kmart
Mason's Tennis Mart
Modell's
New York Golf Center
Orvis Company
Pan Aqua Diving
Paragon Sporting Goods
Peck & Goodie Skates
Princeton Ski Shop
Richard Metz Golf
Scandinavian Ski & Sport Shop
Scuba Network
Soccer Sport Supply
Sports Authority
Target
Tents and Trails
Urban Angler
Vespa
World of Golf

Stationery

Arthur Brown & Brothers
Blacker & Kooby
Cartier
Crane & Co., Paper Makers
Dempsey & Carroll
Fountain Pen Hospital
Il Papiro
IS: Industries Stationery
Jamie Ostrow
Jam Paper & Envelope
Joon
Kate's Paperie
La Brea
Lincoln Stationers
Montblanc
Mrs. John L. Strong
Paper Access
Papivore
Print Icon
Rebecca Moss Ltd.
Smythson of Bond Street
Tiffany & Co.
Venture Stationers

Toys

Abracadabra
Art and Tapisserie
Bear's Place, A
Children's General Store
E.A.T. Gifts
Enchanted Forest
FAO Schwarz
Geppetto's Toy Box
KB Toys
Kidding Around
Kmart
Macy's
Mary Arnold Toys
Maxilla & Mandible
New York Doll Hospital
Penny Whistle
Star Magic
Target
Toys R Us
Toy Tokyo
Westside Kids
Zany Brainy

Special Feature Index

SPECIAL FEATURES

Avant-Garde
Agent Provocateur
Alain Mikli
Alexander McQueen
Amy Downs Hats
Anna Sui
auto
Barneys Co-op
Barneys New York
Bird
Bond 07 by Selima
Borealis
Castor & Pollux
Chrome Hearts
Comme des Garçons
Costume National
Dernier Cri
Destination
Dolce & Gabbana
Fragments
Hedra Prue
Helmut Lang
Hotel Venus by Patricia Field
IF
Ingo Maurer Making Light
Issey Miyake
Jean Paul Gaultier
Jeffrey
J. Lindeberg Stockholm
Joan Michlin Gallery
John Fluevog
Karkula
Kenzo
Kirna Zabête
La Petite Princesse
Liliblue
Lulu Guinness
Mary Adams, The Dress
MoMA Design Store
Moschino
New Museum Store
Noose, The
1 on G
Other Music
Pleats Please
Prada
Roberto Cavalli
Samuel Jackson Design
Seven New York
Shop Noir
Steven Alan
Takashimaya
Ted Baker
Tekserve
Vivienne Westwood
Yellow Door
Yohji Yamamoto

Browsing Appeal
Aaron Faber Gallery
ABC Carpet & Home
Abracadabra
Academy Records & CDs
Adidas
Aedes De Venustas
A La Vieille Russie
Alphabets
American Folk Art Museum
American Museum/Nat. History
Angela's Vintage Boutique
Angel Street Thrift Shop
Apartment 48
Apple Store SoHo
Art of Shaving
AsiaStore/Asia Society
Asprey
At the Gryphon
Avventura
B&H Photo-Video Pro Audio
Barneys Co-op
Barneys New York
Bergdorf Goodman
Bergdorf Men's
Betwixt
Beyul
Bis Designer Resale
Bleecker Bob's Golden Oldies
Bleecker Street Records
Broadway Panhandler
Brooklyn Museum Shop
Brookstone
Bruce Frank Beads
Burberry

344   subscribe to zagat.com

Special Feature Index

Cartier
Catimini
Clay Pot
Colony Music
Cooper-Hewitt Shop
Craft Caravan
Davidoff of Geneva
David Saity Jewelry
Designer Resale
Diesel Superstore
Dolce & Gabbana
Dunhill
E.A.T. Gifts
El Museo Del Barrio
Enchanted Forest
FACE Stockholm
Family Jewels
FAO Schwarz
Finyl Vinyl
Footlight Records
Fragments
Fresh
Frick Collection
Fye
Galileo
Gallery Orrefors
Global Table
Gracious Home
Graff
Greenstones
Guggenheim Museum Stores
Hammacher Schlemmer & Co.
Hastings Bath & Tile
Hat Shop
Hedra Prue
Henri Bendel
HMV
H. Stern
Ibiza
Issey Miyake
Jack Spade
Jay Kos
Jeffrey
Jim Smiley
John Derian
Just for Tykes
Kam Man
Kate's Paperie
Kiehl's
Kirna Zabête
La Cafetière
Language
La Petite Coquette
La Petite Princesse
Lee's Art Shop
Le Fanion
Lexington Gardens
Liliblue
Loom
Lulu Guinness
M.A.C. Cosmetics
MacKenzie-Childs
Madina Milano
Make Up For Ever
M&J Trimming/Buttons
Manny's Music
Met. Museum of Art Shop
Michael's
Mikimoto
MoMA Design Store
Mommy Chic
Movado
Nancy Koltes at Home
NBA Store
NBC Experience
New Museum Store
New York Public Library Shop
Norman's Sound & Vision
Oilily
One Shubert Alley
Other Music
Patch NYC
Pierre Deux
Prada
Puma
Ralph Lauren
Restoration Hardware
Resurrection
Robert Lee Morris
Rocks in your Head
Roslyn
Rue St. Denis
Saks Fifth Avenue
Sam Ash
Screaming Mimi's
Sephora
Sharper Image
Shoofly

vote at zagat.com   **345**

Special Feature Index

Shu Uemura Beauty Boutique
Sony Style
Spoiled Brats
Star Magic
Stuart Moore
Studio Museum/Harlem
Swarovski
Swatch
Tah Poozie
Takashimaya
Tender Buttons
Theatre Circle
Tourneau
Toys In Babeland
Urban Archaeology
Virgin Megastore
What Comes/Goes Around
Williams-Sonoma
William Wayne
Yellow Door

Celebrity Clientele
Aaron Basha
ABC Carpet & Home
Alain Mikli
Alexander McQueen
Barneys New York
BDDW
Bergdorf Goodman
Bergdorf Men's
Billy Martin's Western Wear
bliss
Bumble and bumble
Burberry
Calvin Klein
Calypso
Carolina Herrera
Catherine Malandrino
Chanel
Chloé
Christian Dior
Christian Louboutin
Chrome Hearts
Creed
Dernier Cri
Dolce & Gabbana
Donna Karan
Dylan's Candy Bar
Emilio Pucci

Fat Beats
Fendi
Filth Mart
Fragments
Frédéric Fekkai
Fred Leighton
Fresh
Giorgio Armani
Gucci
Hermès
Hogan
Issey Miyake
Janet Sartin
Jeffrey
Jimmy Choo
Jonathan Adler
Joseph
Joseph Patelson Music House
Judith Leiber
Katayone Adeli
Kimara Ahnert
LaDuca Shoes
Lana Marks
La Petite Princesse
Louis Vuitton
Lulu Guinness
Manolo Blahnik
Marc Jacobs
Mario Badescu Skin Care
Marni
Martin
Mayle
Michael Kors
Mish
Miu Miu
Moss
North Beach Leather
Oliver Peoples
Prada
Rafe
Ralph Lauren
Robert Marc
Roberto Cavalli
Room
Rooms & Gardens
Steinway and Sons
Stella McCartney
Todd Hase
Tod's

Special Feature Index

Urban Archaeology
Valentino
Versace
Yohji Yamamoto

Comfortable Loos
ABC Carpet & Home
Apartment, The
Apple Store SoHo
Barneys New York
Bergdorf Goodman
Chanel Fine Jewelry
Lord & Taylor
Moschino
Saks Fifth Avenue
Takashimaya

Custom-Made Goods
Aaron Basha
Aaron Faber Gallery
ABC Carpet (Carpets/Rugs)
ABH Design
Aero
Alexia Crawford
Amy Downs Hats
An American Craftsman
Ann Sacks Tile & Stone
Armani Casa
Artbag
Artistic Tile
Ascot Chang
Asprey
Baker
Barbara Feinman Millinery
BDDW
Bernardaud
Birnbaum & Bullock
Blue
Borealis
Brass Center
Brioni
Buccellati
California Closets
Carlyle Convertibles
Carmine Street Guitars
Cellini
Charles P. Rogers Bed
Chrome Hearts
C.I.T.E. Design
Classic Sofa

Clay Pot
Clea Colet
Creed
Davide Cenci
Davidoff of Geneva
ddc domus design collections
De La Concha Tobacconist
Desiron
Dö Kham
Dune
E. Braun & Co.
Einstein-Moomjy
Elgot
Elizabeth Locke
Ermenegildo Zegna
Eugenia Kim
Facial Index
Flirt
Flou
Frette
Gallery of Wearable Art
George Smith
Gown Company
Granny-Made
Harris Levy
Harry Winston
Hat Shop
Hickey Freeman
IF
Il Makiage
Il Papiro
Jamson Whyte
Jane Wilson-Marquis
Jay Kos
Jelena Behrend
Jennifer Convertibles
J.J. Hat Center
J. Mavec & Company
J.M. Weston
Joan Michlin Gallery
John Derian
Judith Leiber
Just Shades
Jutta Neumann
Kelly Christy
Kid's Supply Co.
Kimara Ahnert
Kimera
Kiwi Design

vote at zagat.com 347

Special Feature Index

Koos & Co.
Kraft
Kreiss Collection
Krups Kitchens & Bath
LaDuca Shoes
Leather Man, The
Le Corset by Selima
Le Décor Français
Lee's Art Shop
Léron
Lighting by Gregory
Lisa Shaub
Lucy Barnes
Magry Knits
Marimekko
Mary Adams, The Dress
Maurice Villency
Mecox Gardens
Michael Anchin Glass Co.
Michael Eigen
Michelle Roth
Mika Inatome
Mish
Mixona
Modern Stone Age
Moss
Munder-Skiles
Nemo Tile Company
1950
Oculus 20/20
O'Lampia Studio
OMO Norma Kamali
Oriental Lamp Shade Co.
Oxxford Clothes
Palazzetti
Parke & Ronen
P.E. Guerin
Pierre Deux
Pilar Rossi
Porthault
Pratesi
Push
Reinstein Ross
Reva Mivasagar
Robert Lee Morris
Roche Bobois
Room
Roslyn
Rug Company

Safavieh Carpets
Saint Laurie Merchant Tailors
Salon Moderne
Samuel Jackson Design
Schweitzer Linen
SCO
Seize Sur Vingt
Selia Yang
Shabby Chic
Sherle Wagner
Shirt Store
Shop Noir
Simon Pearce Glass
Stella
Steuben
Steven Stolman
Stickley, Audi & Co.
Stuart Moore
Stubbs & Wootton
Suzanne Couture Millinery
Ted Muehling
37=1
Thomas Moser Cabinet
Thomasville
Tiffany & Co.
Todd Hase
Treillage
Troy
Tucker Robbins
Turnbull & Asser
Uproar Home
Valentino
Van Cleef & Arpels
Vera Wang Bridal Salon
Vivienne Westwood
Warren Edwards
Yumi Katsura

Final Sale
(No-returns is standard policy)
ABC Carpet & Home Warehse.
Add
Alice Underground
Allan & Suzi
Amarcord Vintage Fashion
Andy's Chee-Pees
Angela's Vintage Boutique
Angel Street Thrift Shop

Special Feature Index

Anik
Ann Sacks Tile & Stone
A Second Chance
Baker
B&B Italia
B&J Fabrics
Barclay-Rex
Beacon's Closet
Beckenstein Fabrics/Int.
Ben Kahn Furs
Birnbaum & Bullock
Bis Designer Resale
Blue
Bridal Atelier by Mark Ingram
Bridal Garden
California Closets
Cappellini Modern Age
Carlyle Convertibles
Cheap Jack's
Cherry
City Opera Thrift Shop
Classic Sofa
Clea Colet
Coconut Company
Cosmophonic Sound
Council Thrift Shop
Creed
David's Bridal
Davis & Warshow, Inc.
ddc domus design collections
Demolition Depot
Designer Resale
Dialogica
Domsey's
Donzella
Door Store
Drexel Heritage
Edith Weber & Assoc.
Elgot
Encore
Ethan Allen
Eugenia Kim
Eve's Garden
Facial Index
Family Jewels
Fat Beats
Filth Mart
Find Outlet
Foundation

Fred Leighton
Furry Paws
Gallery of Wearable Art
Generation Records
George Smith
Gown Company
Hastings Bath & Tile
Here Comes the Bridesmaid
Holy Cow
Homer
Hooti Couture
Housing Works Thrift Shop
Ina
In the Market
James Robinson
Jane Wilson-Marquis
Jean Paul Gaultier
Jennifer Convertibles
Jim Smiley
Joe's CDs
Joseph Patelson Music House
Kavanagh's
Kreiss Collection
Kremer Pigments
La Belle Epoque
La Boutique Resale
Lana Marks
Ligne Roset
Livi's Lingerie
Love Saves the Day
Mandolin Brothers
Mary Adams, The Dress
Maurice Villency
Memorial Sloan-Kettering Shop
Metropolitan Lumber
Michael's
Midnight Records
Mika Inatome
Mish
Morgenthal Frederics
MTV Store
Munder-Skiles
New York Elegant Fabric
1950
Nisa
Oculus 20/20
Out of the Closet Thrift Shop
Patina
P.E. Guerin

vote at zagat.com

Special Feature Index

Pilar Rossi
Pink Slip
Pleasure Chest
Poggenpohl U.S. Inc.
Poli Fabrics
Pompanoosuc Mills
Quark Spy
Repêchage: Spa de Beauté
Resurrection
Reva Mivasagar
Ricky's
Ritz Furs
RK Bridal
Robert Marc
Rooms & Gardens
Rue St. Denis
Salon Moderne
Salvation Army
Satellite Records
Screaming Mimi's
17 at 17 Thrift Shop
Sol Moscot
Spence-Chapin Thrift Shops
Stella Dallas
St. Marks Sounds
Strider Records
Suzanne Couture Millinery
Tahari, Ltd.
30th Street Guitars
Thomasville
Tod's
Tokio 7
Tokyo Joe
Toys In Babeland
Tribal Soundz
Urban Optical
Vera Wang Bridal Salon
Vinylmania
Walter Steiger
What Comes/Goes Around
Yumi Katsura

Frequent-Buyer Programs
Alkit Pro Camera
Altman Luggage
A/X Armani Exchange
Banana Republic
Banana Republic Men's
Barami Studio

Barneys New York
Bergdorf Goodman
Bergdorf Men's
bliss
British American House
Crouch & Fitzgerald
Dana Buchman
DeMask
Disney
Eileen Fisher
Hard Rock Cafe
Harry's Shoes
HMV
Intermix
Johnston & Murphy
Legs Beautiful Hosiery
Little Eric
Luxury Brand Outlet
Meg
MoMA Design Store
On Your Toes Dancewear
Petco
Prato Fine Men's Wear
Purdy Girl
Quiksilver
Saks Fifth Avenue
Sam Goody
Sanrio (aka Hello Kitty Store)
Sean
Sharper Image
Smith & Hawken
Sound and Fury
Subterranean Records
TLA Video
Tourneau
Toys R Us
V.I.M.
Westside Kids

High-Design
Adidas
Aero
Alain Mikli
Alexander McQueen
Apple Store SoHo
Artemide
AsiaStore/Asia Society
B&B Italia
Barbara Bui

Special Feature Index

Barneys New York
Boffi SoHo
Borealis
Boucher
Bulgari
Cappellini Modern Age
Cartier
Cassina USA
Chanel Fine Jewelry
Chopard
Christian Dior Joaillerie
Christian Louboutin
Comme des Garçons
Cooper-Hewitt Shop
Costume National
Desiron
Donna Karan
Dune
Gucci
Helmut Lang Parfums
Henri Bendel
Hugo Boss
Ingo Maurer Making Light
Issey Miyake
Jaded
Jean Paul Gaultier
Jil Sander
Joan Michlin Gallery
John Varvatos
Karkula
Kartell
Kenzo
Knoll
Les Migrateurs
Ligne Roset
Linda Dresner
Lowell/Edwards
Me & Ro
Michael Dawkins
Modernica
MoMA Design Store
Morgane Le Fay
Moss
O'Lampia Studio
Philosophy di Alberta Ferretti
Prada
Push
Repertoire
Robert Lee Morris
Robert Marc
Roberto Cavalli
Rubin Chapelle
Sony Style
Stella McCartney
Tag Heuer
Takashimaya
Ted Muehling
Ten Thousand Things
Terence Conran Shop
Todd Hase
Totem Design Group
Van Cleef & Arpels
Vitra

Hip/Hot Places

a.cheng
Adidas
Agent Provocateur
Alain Mikli
Alexander McQueen
Amy Chan
Anna Sui
Apple Store SoHo
Armani Casa
Baby Bird
Bark
Barneys Co-op
Barneys New York
BCBG by Max Azria
Betwixt
Big Drop
Bird
Blades Board and Skate
bliss
Bond 07 by Selima
Bottega Veneta
Breukelen
Burberry
Calypso
Calypso Enfant & Bebe
Camper
Catherine Malandrino
Cécile et Jeanne
Cherry
Chloé
Christian Dior
Christian Louboutin
Chrome Hearts

vote at zagat.com 351

Special Feature Index

Chuckies
Club Monaco
Costume National
Creed
Crush
D & G
DeMask
Dernier Cri
Destination
df
Diane von Furstenberg
Diesel Denim Gallery
Diesel Superstore
Dolce & Gabbana
Dune
Dylan's Candy Bar
Earl Jean
Eidolon
Erica Tanov
Eugenia Kim
Eye Candy
Fab 208 NYC
Fat Beats
Fetch
Flight 001
Foley & Corinna
Fossil
Foundation
Four Paws Club, The
Fragments
Fresh
Ghost
Gucci
H&M
Hedra Prue
Helmut Lang
Henry Lehr
Hollywould
Homer
Hot Toddie
Infinity
Intermix
Jack Spade
Jeffrey
Jill Stuart
Jimmy Choo
J. Lindeberg Stockholm
John Varvatos
Jonathan Adler

Jutta Neumann
Katayone Adeli
Kate Spade
Kirna Zabête
Knitting Hands
Language
LeSportsac
Lilliput
Lucy Barnes
Lulu Guinness
Lunettes et Chocolat
Manolo Blahnik
Marc Jacobs
Marni
Marsha D.D.
Martin
Mavi Jean
Mayle
Me & Ro
Michael Kors
Miss Sixty
Miu Miu
MoMA Design Store
Moschino
Moss
99X
Only Hearts
Other Music
Otto Tootsi Plohound
Patch NYC
Paul & Joe
Paul Frank Store
Paul Smith
Petit Bateau
Phat Farm
Pieces
Plein Sud
Pookie & Sebastian
Prada
Puma
Pumpkin Maternity
Quiksilver
Rafe
Reaction by Kenneth Cole
Resurrection
Robert Marc
Roberto Cavalli
Roslyn
Sam & Seb

Special Feature Index

Satellite Records
Scoop
Seize Sur Vingt
Selima Optique
Selvedge
Seven New York
Shop
Sigerson Morrison
Sonic Groove
Space Kiddets
Stella McCartney
Steven Alan
Swarovski
Tekserve
Terence Conran Shop
TG-170
TKNY
Tokio 7
Totem Design Group
Tracy Feith
Tribal Soundz
Triple Five Soul
Troy
Urban Outfitters
Vespa
Vitra
Vivienne Tam
Vivienne Westwood

House Charge

Ann Taylor
Ann Taylor Loft
BabyGap
Banana Republic
Barami Studio
Barneys Co-op
Barneys New York
Bergdorf Goodman
Bergdorf Men's
Bloomingdale's
Bombay Company
British American House
Brooks Brothers
Burberry
Circuit City
CompUSA
Costco Wholesale
Crate & Barrel
Disney

Domain
Ethan Allen
Express Men
Façonnable
Gap
GapKids
Gracious Home
Harvey Electronics
Henri Bendel
Home Depot
J&R Music World
Jeffrey
Liz Claiborne
Loehmann's
Lord & Taylor
Macy's
Men's Wearhouse
Old Navy
Petit Bateau
Pier 1 Imports
Ralph Lauren
Rochester Big & Tall
Saks Fifth Avenue
Sam Ash
Stickley, Audi & Co.
Syms
Talbots
Talbots Kids and Babies
Today's Man
Tourneau
Tower Records/Video
Toys R Us
Urban Outfitters
Wiz, The
Zales Jewelers

Insider Secrets

Alife Rivington Club
Alpana Bawa
Amarcord Vintage Fashion
Bis Designer Resale
Blue
Bowery Kitchen Supplies
Built by Wendy
Butter
Chelsea Second Hand Guitars
Constança Basto
Darryl's
DDC Lab

Special Feature Index

Dö Kham
Domsey's
Dosa
Edmundo Castillo
Eva
Family Jewels
Find Outlet
Finyl Vinyl
Footlight Records
Frida's Closet
Gallery of Wearable Art
Geraldine
Goldin-Feldman
IF
Jammyland
Jay Kos
Jazz Record Center
Jelly
John Derian
Joseph Patelson Music House
Just Shades
Kavanagh's
KD Dance & Sport
Kimara Ahnert
Kremer Pigments
La Petite Princesse
Layla
Lowell/Edwards
Magry Knits
Mandolin Brothers
Manny's Music
Mariko
Mary Adams, The Dress
Matt Umanov Guitars
Mika Inatome
Mini Mini Market
Mood Indigo
Morgan Library Shop
Neue Galerie
New York Replacement
OM Boutique
Oriental Lamp Shade Co.
Pearldaddy
P.E. Guerin
Peter Hermann
Purl
Purple Passion/DV8
Push
Quark Spy
Ray Beauty Supply
Rebel Rebel
Religious Sex
Repêchage: Spa de Beauté
Rico
Rogue Music
Rudy's Music Shop
Samuel Jackson Design
Sean
Sorelle Firenze
Stackhouse
Stella
Stephen Russell
Tatiana
Ted Baker
30th Street Guitars
Untitled
Urban Angler
Urban Archaeology
Yellow Door

Legendary
(Date company founded)
1730 Floris of London
1748 Villeroy & Boch
1752 Caswell-Massey
1760 Creed
1781 Asprey
1818 Brooks Brothers
1826 Lord & Taylor
1831 Takashimaya
1835 Holland & Holland
1837 Tiffany & Co.
1838 C.O. Bigelow Chemists
1839 Crouch & Fitzgerald
1847 Cartier
1851 A La Vieille Russie
1857 P.E. Guerin
1860 Chopard
1860 Frette
1863 Bernardaud
1870 Penhaligon's
1872 Bloomingdale's
1872 Shiseido
1878 Daum
1878 Dempsey & Carroll
1878 Salvation Army
1885 Turnbull & Asser
1887 Smythson of Bond Street

Special Feature Index

1891 J.M. Weston
1893 Mikimoto
1895 Swarovski
1896 Henri Bendel
1897 ABC Carpet (Carpets/Rugs)
1898 Gallery Orrefors
1899 Bergdorf Goodman
1900 Tourneau
1902 Dunhill
1902 J. Press
1902 Macy's
1904 Seaman Schepps
1906 Montblanc
1906 Van Cleef & Arpels
1908 Paragon Sporting Goods
1910 Léron
1912 James Robinson
1914 Chanel
1919 Buccellati
1920 Ben Kahn Furs
1921 Gucci
1924 Zales Jewelers
1925 Fendi
1927 Davide Cenci
1932 Artbag
1933 N. Peal
1935 Fred Leighton
1938 Knoll
1939 Verdura
1940 Boyd's Madison Avenue
1940 Coach
1941 Georgette Klinger
1941 Kleinfeld & Son
1946 Christian Dior
1946 T. Anthony
1948 David Webb
1950 Morris Brothers
1950 Sergio Rossi
1950 Wolford
1950 Zitomer Pharmacy

New Age/Health-Oriented

Aveda
Bath Island
Body Shop
Carapan Urban Spa & Store
Fresh
Illuminations
Origins
SCO
Star Magic

Noteworthy Newcomers

ABH Design
Adidas
Agent Provocateur
Alexander McQueen
Anne Klein
Annie & Company Needlepoint
Apple Store SoHo
Baby Bird
Baker
Berkley Girl
Bodyhints
buybuy Baby
Cadeau
Calypso Bijoux
Calypso Homme
Chanel Fine Jewelry
Charles Tyrwhitt
Clio
Constança Basto
Dernier Cri
df
Edmundo Castillo
Estella
Flou
Gas Bijoux
Hable Construction
Hickey Freeman
Hollywould
Hot Toddie
In the Market
Jean Paul Gaultier
Jelly
Jil Sander
Jim Smiley
Kiwi Design
Knitting Hands
Knitting 321
Loom
Marni
Miss Sixty
Nest
Neue Galerie
Pearldaddy
Petit Bateau

Special Feature Index

Purl
Rubin Chapelle
Rug Company
Sam & Seb
Scoop Men's
Sigerson Morrison Bags
Stella McCartney
Tag Heuer
37=1
TKNY
Tribal Soundz
Vespa
Vitra
Xukuma

Offbeat
Alphabets
Apartment, The
Beads of Paradise
Bruce Frank Beads
CCS Counter Spy Shop
Craft Caravan
DeMask
Demeter
Dylan's Candy Bar
Flight 001
Footlight Records
Generation Records
Industrial Plastic Supply
Layla
Maxilla & Mandible
Midnight Records
Moon River Chattel
Music Inn
Mxyplyzyk
Norman's Sound & Vision
NYCD
Olden Camera
Papivore
Rebel Rebel
Rocks in your Head
Sound and Fury
Spoiled Brats
Subterranean Records
Toy Tokyo
Tracy Feith

Only in New York
Academy Records & CDs
At the Gryphon
B&H Photo-Video Pro Audio
Betwixt
Capitol Fishing Tackle Co.
Colony Music
Demolition Depot
E.A.T. Gifts
ESPN Zone
Footlight Records
Hyman Hendler and Sons
Intrepid Sea-Air-Space
Kleinfeld & Son
Lunettes et Chocolat
Maxilla & Mandible
Mets Clubhouse Shop
MoMA Design Store
MTV Store
Museum/City of New York
NBC Experience
New York Firefighter's Friend
New York 911
New York Public Library Shop
New York Transit Museum
One Shubert Alley
Pop Shop
Ray Beauty Supply
Ricky's
Tender Buttons
Theatre Circle
TKNY
Zabar's

Registry: Baby
Au Chat Botte
Baby Bird
Bear's Place, A
Ben's for Kids
Bu & the Duck
buybuy Baby
Calypso Enfant & Bebe
Estella
FAO Schwarz
Green Onion
Ibiza
Julian and Sara
Just for Tykes
Kidding Around
Little Folk Art
Mommy Chic
Planet Kids

Special Feature Index

Sam & Seb
Space Kiddets
Tartine et Chocolat
Tiffany & Co.
Urban Monster
Westside Kids
Z. Baby Company

Registry: Bridal/Gift

Aaron Faber Gallery
ABC Carpet & Home
Adrien Linford
Aero
Agent Provocateur
An American Craftsman
Armani Casa
Avventura
Baccarat
Bark
Barneys New York
Bed, Bath & Beyond
Bergdorf Goodman
Bloomingdale's
Bodyhints
Bonne Nuit
Borealis
Boucher
Breukelen
Bridge Kitchenware
Broadway Panhandler
Bulgari
Calvin Klein
Charles P. Rogers Bed
Chelsea Garden Center Home
Clay Pot
Clio
Crate & Barrel
Daum
E. Braun & Co.
e. Harcourt's
Ethan Allen
Fortunoff
Frette
Galileo
Gallery Orrefors
Georg Jensen
Global Table
Gracious Home
Hable Construction
Harris Levy
Helen Woodhull
Hermès
Il Makiage
James II Galleries Ltd.
Jensen-Lewis
Jewish Museum
John Derian
Kar'ikter
Karkula
Kentshire Galleries
La Cafetière
Laina Jane
Lalique
La Perla
La Petite Coquette
Laytner's Linen & Home
Léron
MacKenzie-Childs
Macy's
Mario Badescu Skin Care
Met. Museum of Art Shop
Michael C. Fina
Moss
Nancy Koltes at Home
Nicole Farhi
Papivore
Peanutbutter & Jane
Pier 1 Imports
Pierre Deux
Porthault
Pottery Barn
Pratesi
Rebecca Moss Ltd.
Religious Sex
Repêchage: Spa de Beauté
Restoration Hardware
Saks Fifth Avenue
Scully & Scully
Sherle Wagner
Simon Pearce Glass
Steinway and Sons
Steuben
Takashimaya
Terence Conran Shop
37=1
Tiffany & Co.
Uproar Home
Via Spiga

vote at zagat.com

Special Feature Index

Victoria's Secret
Villeroy & Boch
Williams-Sonoma
William Wayne
Yellow Door
Zabar's

Repairs/Alterations on Premises

Aaron Basha
A. Atelier
Addison on Madison
Agatha
Agnès B. Homme
Alain Mikli
Albee Baby Carriage Co.
Alexia Crawford
Allen Edmonds
Amsale
Annie & Company Needlepoint
Anya Hindmarch
Artbag
Asprey
A. Testoni
A/X Armani Exchange
Bagutta
Banana Republic
Banana Republic Men's
Barneys Co-op
Barneys New York
Beads of Paradise
Beau Brummel
Belgian Shoes
Ben Kahn Furs
Ben's for Kids
Bergdorf Goodman
Bergdorf Men's
Bicycle Habitat
Bicycle Renaissance
Birnbaum & Bullock
Bisou-Bisou
Blades Board and Skate
Bloomingdale's
Bombalulus
Borealis
Boss, The
Bottega Veneta
Bra Smyth
Bridal Atelier by Mark Ingram
Bridal Garden
Brioni
British American House
Bruno Magli
Bu & the Duck
Bulgari
Burberry
Cadeau
Calypso Bijoux
Calypso Homme
Camper
Carmine Street Guitars
Carolina Herrera
Celine
Cerruti
Cesare Paciotti
Chanel
Chanel Fine Jewelry
Charles P. Rogers Bed
Charles Tyrwhitt
Cheap Jack's
Chelsea Second Hand Guitars
Chloé
Christian Dior
Christian Dior Joaillerie
Christian Louboutin
Chrome Hearts
Clea Colet
Club Monaco
Coach
Cohen's Fashion Optical
Cole Haan
CompUSA
Costume National
Dana Buchman
D & G
David Aaron
David Saity Jewelry
David's Bridal
David Yurman
Deco Jewels
Desiron
Doggie-Do & Pussycats Too
Dolce & Gabbana
Dooney & Bourke
Dune
Eidolon
Elizabeth Locke
Emanuel Ungaro

Special Feature Index

Enchanted Forest
Erica Wilson Needle Works
Ermenegildo Zegna
Erwin Pearl
Escada
Ethan Allen
Etro
Eugenia Kim
Façonnable
FAO Schwarz
Flight 001
Flirt
For Eyes
48th Street Custom Guitars
Fossil
Fountain Pen Hospital
Fourteen Wall Street Jewelers
Fragments
Frank Stella Ltd.
Fratelli Rossetti
French Corner
Frette
Georg Jensen
Geraldine
Ghurka
Giorgio Armani
Givenchy
Goldin-Feldman
Gotham Bikes
Gown Company
Gracious Home
Graff
Grand Central Racquet
Gucci
Hat Shop
Helmut Lang
Henri Bendel
Here Comes the Bridesmaid
Hermès
H.L. Purdy
Hogan
Holland & Holland
H. Stern
Hugo Boss
Issey Miyake
Jaded
James II Galleries Ltd.
Jane Wilson-Marquis
J.Crew
Jean Paul Gaultier
Jeffrey
Jennifer Convertibles
Jensen-Lewis
Jimmy Choo
J. Mendel
J.M. Weston
Joan Michlin Gallery
Jobson's Luggage
Joël Name Optique de Paris
John Varvatos
Joon
Joseph
J. Press
Judith Leiber
Judith Ripka
Jutta Neumann
Karen's for People and Pets
Kate Spade
Kenjo
Kimera
Kirna Zabête
Kleinfeld & Son
Krizia
Lacoste
LaDuca Shoes
Lalaounis
La Perla
La Petite Coquette
Laura Biagiotti
Le Chien Pet Salon
Leonard Poll
Léron
Les Copains
Lightforms
Ligne Roset
Liliblue
Linda Dresner
Links of London
Lisa Shaub
London Jewelers
Longchamp
Lord & Taylor
Loro Piana
Louis Vuitton
Lowell/Edwards
Luca Luca
Lunettes et Chocolat
L'Uomo

vote at zagat.com   359

Special Feature Index

Macy's
Magry Knits
Mandolin Brothers
Marc Jacobs
Mare
Marni
Matt Umanov Guitars
Maurice Villency
Mavi Jean
Max Mara
Medici
Meg
Men's Wearhouse
Metro Bicycles
Michael Eigen
Michelle Roth
Mika Inatome
Mikimoto
Missoni
Mixona
Montblanc
Moon River Chattel
Morgane Le Fay
Morgenthal Frederics
Movado
Music Inn
Myoptics
Nancy Geist
New York Doll Hospital
New York Look
Noir et Blanc...Bis
North Beach Leather
Oculus 20/20
Oliver Peoples
OM Boutique
Orchard Corset
Oriental Lamp Shade Co.
Otto Tootsi Plohound
Oxxford Clothes
Park Avenue Audio
Parke & Ronen
Patagonia
Paul & Shark
Paul Smith
Paul Stuart
Pearldaddy
Peck & Goodie Skates
Peter Elliot
Peter Hermann
Piaget
Pierre Deux
Pilar Rossi
Pop Shop
Prato Fine Men's Wear
Princeton Ski Shop
Push
Rafe
Reaction by Kenneth Cole
Rebecca Moss Ltd.
Reinstein Ross
Reva Mivasagar
Ritz Furs
RK Bridal
Robert Clergerie
Robert Lee Morris
Rogue Music
Roslyn
Rothman's
Rudy's Music Shop
Sacco
Safavieh Carpets
Saks Fifth Avenue
Sam Ash
Samuel Jackson Design
S&W
Scoop
Scoop Men's
Sean
Searle
Selia Yang
Selima Optique
Sergio Rossi
Seven New York
Shanghai Tang
Shoe Biz
Sigerson Morrison
Sigerson Morrison Bags
Simon's Hardware & Bath
Sol Moscot
Sonia Rykiel
Sorelle Firenze
Stereo Exchange
Steuben
Stickley, Audi & Co.
St. John
Stuart Moore
Suarez
Suzanne Couture Millinery

Special Feature Index

Swatch
Tag Heuer
Tahari, Ltd.
Takashimaya
T. Anthony
Ted Muehling
Tekserve
30th Street Guitars
37=1
Tiffany & Co.
Today's Man
Tod's
Toga Bikes
Tommy Hilfiger
Tourneau
Treasure Chest
Tribal Soundz
TSE Cashmere
Tucker Robbins
Tumi
Turnbull & Asser
Untitled
Urban Angler
Urban Optical
Valentino
Van Cleef & Arpels
Varda
Variazioni
Vercesi Hardware
Verdura
Vespa
Wempe
William Barthman
Workbench
Yellow Door
Yumi Katsura
Yves St. Laurent Rive Gauche

Special Delivery Services

(F=free, S=same day)
Adrien Linford (F)
Alain Mikli (S)
Apple Store SoHo (F, S)
Arthur Brown & Brothers (S)
Assets London (F, S)
Barneys New York (S)
Bear's Place, A (S)
Bed, Bath & Beyond (S)
Ben's for Kids (F, S)
Bodum (S)
Boucher (S)
Bowery Kitchen Supplies (S)
Bridge Kitchenware (S)
Bulgari (S)
Burberry (S)
buybuy Baby (S)
Camper (S)
Chanel Fine Jewelry (F)
Clio (S)
C.O. Bigelow Chemists (F, S)
Costume National (S)
Dana Buchman (F, S)
Disc-O-Rama Music World (F)
Disney (F)
Dylan's Candy Bar (S)
East Side Kids (F, S)
E.A.T. Gifts (S)
Einstein-Moomjy (S)
Elizabeth Locke (S)
Eric (F)
Eugenia Kim (S)
FAO Schwarz (S)
Gracious Home (F)
Guess? (S)
Holland & Holland (S)
Home Depot (F, S)
Il Makiage (S)
Infinity (S)
Jam Paper & Envelope (S)
J&R Computer World (S)
J. Lindeberg Stockholm (S)
J. Mendel (F)
Jo Malone (S)
Judith Leiber (S)
Krups Kitchens & Bath (S)
La Brea (S)
Lee's Art Shop (S)
Little Eric (S)
Louis Vuitton (S)
Luca Luca (F, S)
Malia Mills Swimwear (S)
Manny's Music (F)
Manolo Blahnik (S)
Mary Arnold Toys (S)
Meg (F)
Modern Stone Age (S)
New York Central Art Supply (S)
New York Golf Center (S)

vote at zagat.com 361

Special Feature Index

Paper Access (F)
Patagonia (S)
Paterson Silks (F, S)
Pet Stop (F)
Planet Kids (F)
Rochester Big & Tall (S)
Saks Fifth Avenue (S)
Sam Ash (S)
Satellite Records (S)
Scuba Network (S)
S Feldman Housewares (F)
Sigerson Morrison (S)
Sigerson Morrison Bags (S)
Simon's Hardware & Bath (S)
Space Kiddets (S)
Spoiled Brats (F)
Steinway and Sons (F)
Stickley, Audi & Co. (F)
St. John (S)
Suarez (S)
Super Runners Shop (F)
Takashimaya (S)
Urban Outfitters (S)
Ventilo (S)
Veronique (S)
Westside Kids (S)
Williams-Sonoma (S)
Z. Baby Company (S)

Status Goods

Aaron Basha
Aedes De Venustas
Alan Moss
A La Vieille Russie
Alexander McQueen
Allen Edmonds
Amsale
Ann Sacks Tile & Stone
Antiquarium
Armani Casa
Artistic Tile
Asprey
A. Testoni
Au Chat Botte
Baccarat
Bagutta
B&B Italia
Bang & Olufsen
Barneys New York
Barton-Sharpe
Belgian Shoes
Bellini
Bergdorf Goodman
Bernardaud
bliss
Boffi SoHo
Bonpoint
Borealis
Bottega Veneta
Botticelli
Brioni
Buccellati
Bulgari
Burberry
Calvin Klein
Carolina Herrera
Caron Boutique
Cartier
Cassina USA
Catimini
Celine
Cellini
Cerruti
Cesare Paciotti
Chanel
Chloé
Chopard
Christian Dior
Christian Louboutin
Christofle
Clea Colet
Country Floors
Creed
Daum
Davide Cenci
Davidoff of Geneva
David Saity Jewelry
David Webb
David Yurman
Dean & Deluca
Dempsey & Carroll
Destination
Dolce & Gabbana
Donna Karan
Donzella
Dunhill
Elizabeth Locke
Emanuel Ungaro

Special Feature Index

Emilio Pucci
Ermenegildo Zegna
Escada
Etro
Ferragamo, Salvatore
Fratelli Rossetti
Frédéric Fekkai
Fred Leighton
Fresh
Frette
George Smith
Georg Jensen
Ghurka
Gianfranco Ferré
Givenchy
Graff
Gucci
Harry Winston
Helene Arpels
Helen Woodhull
Henri Bendel
Hermès
Hickey Freeman
Hogan
Howard Kaplan Bath Shop
Hugo Boss
Ingo Maurer Making Light
Issey Miyake
Jacadi
Jaeger
Jean Paul Gaultier
Jil Sander
Jimmy Choo
J. Mavec & Company
J. Mendel
J.M. Weston
Joan Michlin Gallery
Joël Name Optique de Paris
John Lobb
Johnston & Murphy
John Varvatos
Joon
Judith Leiber
Judith Ripka
Kavanagh's
Kleinfeld & Son
Krizia
Lacoste
Lalique
Lana Marks
Laura Biagiotti
Le Décor Français
Léron
Lexington Gardens
Linda Dresner
Liz O'Brien
Loro Piana
Louis Vuitton
Lowell/Edwards
Lyric Hi-Fi
Malo
Manfredi
Manolo Blahnik
Marc Jacobs
Marni
Michael Ashton
Michael Dawkins
Michael Kors
Mika Inatome
Mikimoto
Mish
Missoni
Miu Miu
Morgenthal Frederics
Moschino
Movado
Mrs. John L. Strong
Oliver Peoples
Oxxford Clothes
Paul & Shark
P.E. Guerin
Penhaligon's
Piaget
Pierre Deux
Pilar Rossi
Plein Sud
Porthault
Prada
Pratesi
Ralph Lauren
Rebecca Moss Ltd.
Reinstein Ross
Reva Mivasagar
Robert Lee Morris
Robert Marc
Roberto Cavalli
Robert Talbott
Seaman Schepps

vote at zagat.com

Special Feature Index

Sergio Rossi
Sherle Wagner
Sigerson Morrison
Smythson of Bond Street
Sonia Rykiel
Sound by Singer
Steinway and Sons
Stella
Stella McCartney
Stephane Kélian
Stereo Exchange
Steuben
Suarez
Tag Heuer
Takashimaya
T. Anthony
Tartine et Chocolat
Ted Muehling
Tekserve
Thomas Moser Cabinet
Thomas Pink
Tiffany & Co.
Tod's
Tracy Feith
TSE Cashmere
Turnbull & Asser
Valentino
Van Cleef & Arpels
Verdura
Vitra
Walter Steiger
Waterworks
Wempe
Yohji Yamamoto
Yumi Katsura
Yves St. Laurent Rive Gauche

Tween/Teen Appeal
Abracadabra
Adidas
Alphabets
Andy's Chee-Pees

Apple Store SoHo
Barneys Co-op
Blades Board and Skate
Body Shop
Capezio
Claire's Accessories
Crunch
Daffy's
David Z.
Demeter
Dylan's Candy Bar
EMS
ESPN Zone
Fossil
Fye
Girl Props
Hard Rock Cafe
HMV
Hooti Couture
M.A.C. Cosmetics
Maxilla & Mandible
Metro Bicycles
Mets Clubhouse Shop
MTV Store
NBC Experience
Niketown
Perfumania
Pop Shop
Puma
Rags-A-Go-Go
Sanrio (aka Hello Kitty Store)
Screaming Mimi's
Sephora
Sony Style
Star Magic
Tah Poozie
Tokio 7
Tower Records/Video
Virgin Megastore
Yankee Clubhouse Shop

Look before you watch.

ZAGATSURVEY®

MOVIE GUIDE

Watch it on

E!

Enjoy the Show.

After 24+ years of helping choose the right restaurant, Zagat Survey is now helping you with the rest of the evening's entertainment by introducing the Zagat Survey Movie Guide, covering the top 1,000 films of all time. Ratings and reviews are by avid moviegoers, i.e. people like you.

Available wherever books are sold, at zagat.com
or by calling 888-371-5440.